HIJACKING A RIVER

A POLITICAL HISTORY
OF THE COLORADO RIVER
IN THE GRAND CANYON

JEFF INGRAM

Cover design and layout assistance by Ron Short.
Map design by Tom Martin

Cover photograph © 1965 Margaret Eiseman
Helicopter boat portage at Hance Rapid during a Goldwater family charter trip.

Vishnu Temple Press, LLC
P O Box 30821
Flagstaff AZ 86003-0821
www.vishnutemplepress.com

Dedicated to
DAVID BROWER
For the word, for the spirit

Table of Contents

INTRODUCTION

Orientation and Prejudices

The sun is hot. The river, swimmable, cools. It is alternately serene and tempestuous. During our nineteen-day trip, we see few people other than ourselves. It is September 1966, and we are among the last of the 1100 people that year to boat down the Colorado River, its entire length in the Grand Canyon, 277 miles from Lees Ferry to the Grand Wash Cliffs.

That was my first trip. On my latest, much was the same. We saw even fewer people not on our trip. The sun, as always in the American Southwest, could be strong, hot. The river kept its stretches of serenity, of drifting, its episodes of play, the rapids. As before, we did much hiking. This trip, ten days longer and fifty miles shorter, did have the uncertainties and discomforts of some wintry weather. The beaches, in 1966 too often fouled by charcoal, trash, toilet paper and worse, were, in January 2001, shrunken, yet always cleaner. We were the first of what would be 20,000 or so people, the current usual number, to ride the river.

This, however, is not a book about a man in Nature. It is about humans and their nature, that part of our behavior we call politics; in particular the politics of land and who controls it and its use; environmental politics, bureaucratic politics, electoral politics, the politics of civility and of abuse, of truth and its lack, of some bravery, some weakness, a lot of business as usual; a lot of business, period. Specifically, this book is about the politics of managing boating on the Colorado River in the Grand Canyon, given its wild character, its status in a National Park, people's desire to travel through the Canyon on the river, and a few people's desire to control and profit from those travelers.

An Englishman, J. B. Priestley, caught the inspirational aspect of the enterprise, when he wrote in his 1937 *Midnight on the Desert*:[1]

> "It is useless to try to describe the Grand Canyon. Those who have not seen it will not believe any possible description; and those who have seen it know that it cannot be painted in either pigments or words.
>
> I have heard rumors of visitors who were disappointed. The same people will be disappointed at the Day of Judgment. In fact, the

Grand Canyon is a sort of landscape Day of Judgment. It is not a show place, a beauty spot, but a revelation. The Colorado River, which is powerful, turbulent, and so thick with silt that it is like a saw, made it with the help of the erosive forces of rain, frost, and wind…It is the largest of the eighteen canyons of the Colorado… it is the world's supreme example of erosion.

But this is not what it really is. It is, I repeat, a revelation. The Colorado River made it, but you feel when you are there that God gave the Colorado River its instructions. Even to remember that it is still there lifts up the heart.

If I were an American, I should make my remembrance of it the final test of men, art, and policies. I should ask myself: Is this good enough to exist in the same country as the Canyon? How would I feel about this man, this kind of art, these political measures, if I were near that Rim? Every member or officer of the federal government ought to remind himself, with triumphant pride, that he is on the staff of the Grand Canyon."

Another Englishman, George Orwell, nailed the underside:

"It is ridiculous to get angry, but there is a stupid malignity in these things which does try one's patience."

 For much of the period I write about, I was ridiculous, kept angry by the recurrent attacks of stupid malignity by that "staff", federal and otherwise, making decisions about the Canyon. (Chapter 1 has a summary of my early Canyon years. Dates of my involvements are in the Reader's Guide Part A. The Reader's Guide, by the way, collects names, dates, and other information to help the reader keep straight the who, what, and when. If you have not already, please look through its several parts. Reader's Guide Part A tries to include all people, organizations, abbreviations and other items that are major and/or recurring.) To be accurate, this book contains two sets of anger. First, there is the historical ire; what I felt, spoke, and wrote about at the time. Recording it here is legitimate reportage, if sometimes painful, depressing, and even embarrassing. Second, there is today's re-ignited anger, perhaps less justifiable, since I suppose at this point, I should be mature, forgiving, and passionless. I am not, and much of what I have to tell you does make me steam all over again, sometimes in terms that may sound excessive. My apologies.

As the author of this book, I have a definite point of view, shaped over almost 20 years in the 1960s and '70s fighting to protect the Grand Canyon and to enhance people's ability to enjoy it in ways that do not damage the place and allow us to enjoy it on its terms. The fighting was necessary, is still necessary, will continue to be necessary, because others see the Canyon very differently. This book is therefore a history and a memoir of fights past, and a platform for helping the reader understand why the fighting continues. I would like it to be more than a battle book; I hope to present rounded stories that recount the events. I am not, of course, entirely fair. I do yield to the pressure to comment on, as well as paraphrase, others' words. I am free with interpretation, and though I hope to avoid being ridiculous, there is a measure of the scorn that arises when trying to comprehend how others can be so wrong-headed.

The politics of the Grand Canyon in the 1960s and '70s were determined by three large controversies. Though separable as narratives, they did intertwine and react on each other. In brief, the period opened with a full-fledged effort to obtain congressional approval for the construction of two hydroelectric dams, one in the lead-in, Marble Gorge, section of the Grand Canyon; the other in the western Canyon, just above the high-water mark for Hoover Dam's Lake Mead. Out of this battle, essentially decided in 1966-7, grew a determination to expand the Grand Canyon National Park (GCNP) to include, so as to protect and present, as much of the topographic Canyon as was feasible. The legislative effort to draw more adequate Park boundaries peaked in 1973-4, and was carried on inseparably with the effort to establish an expanded Havasupai Indian Reservation out of Park and adjacent Kaibab National Forest lands. (The Reader's Guide Part D contains maps that will help with these locations.)

Due in part to the dam fight, recreational trips on the Colorado through the Canyon underwent a stupefying, unregulated rise, going from about 500 people in 1965 to over 16,000 in 1972. Concurrent with this inflation in almost wholly commercial activity was the effort to settle on acceptable boundaries for Wilderness within the Grand Canyon National Park, as mandated by the 1964 Wilderness Act. However, commercial river trip operators had chosen overwhelmingly to offer only motor-driven trips, for a variety of what turned out to be unjustified or inappropriate reasons. Since Wilderness status for the Canyon and its river would have meant the end of motor use, the main river controversy through 1981 became driven by defenders of motorized river travel. And yet this was, as I hope this book shows, not what it really was. As one pro-motor excuse after another was deflated, I came to see that motors were symbiotic with commercial dominance over Canyon river travel. To lose motors was to lose power, to cede control to the Park Service and wilderness advocates over concessionaires' freedom to do business as they saw fit.

In writing this book, I was faced again and again with the question of why the motor-boaters reacted so quickly, virulently, and uncompromisingly to proposals for change. We were not dealing, after all, with downtown Chicago. The American people, speaking through their elected representatives, set up Grand Canyon National Park within the National Park System to protect and present its unique natural character, and established a National Wilderness System in which the Grand Canyon obviously belongs. Brandishing their motors, the commercial river operators defied, and defy, it all. Their defiance paid off in 1980, but the price to the public has been high. A pivotal national election gave them the chance to cement in their ascendancy, and the ensuing status quo regime has been one that in its lack of equity, innovation, outreach, and environmental progress, has cheated the public of the rich opportunities offered by river travel in the Grand Canyon.

It must always be a pleasure for history writers to be able to claim continuing currency for their subject. Here are my claims for Relevance. The efforts to create appropriate National Park boundaries, to legislate an appropriate Wilderness within

the Park, and to establish public control over Colorado river travel, all came to a
seemingly permanent halt in late 1980 with the accession of the Reagan-Watt-
Marks administration. (Please see the Reader's Guide Part A for identifications of
people.) The surprise has been that this Grand Canyon Dark Age started to lift in
the mid-1990s and the issues now show renewed vigor. The 1980s' lid that had
been clamped on public involvement matters has blown off, leading to revived
contention. And rightly, for the rigid status quo system run by the commercial
operators with the support of their political allies is broken; it fails too much of the
public, and falls much too far short of the legitimate purposes of Grand Canyon
National Park. In our dynamic, forward-looking society, the cramped inflexible
status quo of the motor-boaters is an anomaly; a monument to retrograde fears and
controls. It is time—not just for change; it is time for renewal.

Renewal is also overdue to reverse the ongoing ecological decline of the
Canyon's river environment as a result of Glen Canyon Dam. For the 1970s, the
dam's impact was a given. Yet, a sensitivity to, as well as a model, and base for
research on the dam's effect, emerged in the 1980s from running impact studies
done earlier. Research continues to detail the silent and slow, but still lethal, effects
of the dam on the Canyon from, for example, lowered water temperature, loss of silt
and nutrients, and the unnatural flow regime. We still need a forceful response by
federal officials (remember Priestley) to this quiet disaster.

But my task is the past. There is a main narrative through 1973. Chapters 1-4
present it. Matters then splinter, and several topics have their own chapters. In
particular, National Park boundary legislation in Chapter 5, the mid-seventies
research program in Chapters 8 and 12, Wilderness recommendations in Chapter
10, summary of the 1977-80 Colorado River Management Plan in Chapters 16 and
18. Chapters 6 and 9 deal mostly with self-guided, or private, river-runners. Chapter
14 is an out-of-the-horses'-mouths picture of the commercial operators. Chapters 7,
11, 13, and 15 try to give a feel for the raveled multi-strand nature of the main mid-
seventies narrative. Chapters 17, and 19 through 22 tell of the final battles into
1981. The epilogue chapters summarize in a necessarily sketchy way the status quo's
reign through the 1980s and into the present.

Publication in this area has been sparse, and I therefore felt an obligation to seek
out relevant primary sources, including interviews. For my own files, this is a source
book. The other major sources of material are publicly available archives of agencies,
public officials, and others that have donated papers. They are described in the
Reader's Guide Part E on Sources. Sadly, some papers and participants have
disappeared or were not available to me. I wish it was not true, but conversations
dissipate and memories deteriorate. Consequently, my contribution is that of an
informed participant reconstructing with the aid of archival prompts how the stories
went, what events were decisive, and even what went right and wrong. Participants
who were generous with their recollections and opinions are listed in the Reader's
Guide Part E on Sources. Unsurprisingly in a fight involving private parties, their
papers were usually not available to me except insofar as they had found their way to
agencies and other public venues. So I cannot claim any kind of completeness for
this book. Although I have tried to get in all the story I know, there is much that

remains hidden; indeed not all those I asked agreed to be interviewed. More surprisingly, there are public archives that are missing or thin. Sadly there must be errors I did not catch. I apologize to you for them. For all these information gaps, please excuse me. Perhaps this book, with its biases, will prompt others not yet extinct, with differing views and experiences, to burrow into their own files; an exploiters' view of Canyon controversies would be entertaining, as well as ridiculous in its own right.

When in 1981 I withdrew from the battlefield, defeated and weary (see Chapter 22), I did so in part because I was convinced that if the Grand Canyon carries the level of social, cultural, and political meaning I believe it does, then there would always be new champions. They would come, fresh with ideas, concerns, and energy, to defend the Canyon. Twenty years later, I can assert the truth of that belief. This book will have succeeded if it provides today's champions with material so they can know what a long, frustrating battle they are now a part of, and what a long, honorable tradition they are continuing. Though it cannot provide them with a forecast of what is to come, that's all right, for it is their drive, commitment, and imagination that will combine to end the Darkness and staleness of today's status quo, bringing in a future of openness and excitement for the public and its Grand Canyon.

CHAPTER 1

1966-69: The Grand Canyon's Political Frames

The Primordial Setting

The Grand Canyon, the place, is always there—inescapably present THERE. It is the major character in any story about it. For humans, it has always been there, and in spite of our clawing and prancing, will be long after. So is it ignorance, our arrogance, a sort of stupid fearfulness, that so much of what we say and do about the Canyon happens, not just off-stage, but in another theater entirely? As if our behavior could not be carried on in its presence, was not up to the standard pointed out by J. B. Priestley, of us all being "on the staff of the Grand Canyon".

In August 1966, the theater was Washington, D.C.—sweaty outside, fevered inside—as proponents and opponents of a scheme to construct dams in the Grand Canyon rushed about the House of Representatives, trying to determine an answer to the question: Would a majority of representatives, knowing little of the complex and obscure issues, commit themselves to support a piece of pro-dam legislation called the Colorado River Basin Project Act (CRBP)? Would that commitment extend to repelling every single attempt to amend the legislation? Such a broad commitment was necessary to the legislation's sponsors because there would certainly be a strong attempt to remove authorization of any Grand Canyon dams, and the compromises in the bill were so interlocked that if any piece were altered or removed, many of its sponsors would abandon it. So only if there were a solid majority committed not to amend, would the legislation move to the House floor for a vote; if not, then the bill would not be considered in that Congress. Master legislative choreographers were at work; the rhetorical leaps were stunning; the final scenes both satisfying and contentious.

At 29, I was one of the young, fresh (in every sense) participants in that congressional dance. The story of how the powers-that-were got beaten when they tried to build dams in the Grand Canyon is itself grand. However, it is, unless the world goes mad, a completed story; the idea that the Colorado can or should have any more dams imposed on it, a stomach-wrenching stinker when proposed, is now so decayed it is redolent only of historians' dust. The story this book tells is, on the other hand, a long time from completion. So the effort to block the dams—to Save the Grand Canyon, in our slogan of the time—receives brief attention here only as the necessary scene-setter for all that follows. And to introduce myself.

Four years earlier, my family and I (another transplanting Easterner) were searching the American West for a place to live. We mixed inspection and inspiration, and one of the places we casually stopped by was that little piece of the Canyon called the South Rim, Grand Canyon Village. Now, you won't get a lot of description from me; my basic belief is that when asked about the Canyon, the most appropriate reply is to point and say, "Go there." Nevertheless, this size and scope thing has to be dealt with, for it has been as much a political concept as a topographic one. Standing on that rim or buzzing along the bit of paved road checking out the viewpoints, visitors are often really, really impressed with how big the Canyon is, how deep, how far across, how way down the river seems. Yet those most-visited points, with a view of less than a fifth of the Canyon, that make our eyes water and cameras click, are a tease, an invitation. A day trip to the rim is like seeing the awakening of Adam scene at the Sistine Chapel, and then going home; well really, it is like your sweetie giving you a great big kiss, then not inviting you in. Casual visitors may be impressed by the Canyon; but they do not get to "see" it. It is a place we have to go to, here, and here, and over there, from above, down inside, across and again across, and along it; putting it together in our bodies and heads. And it took a century for us Americans to get that place altogether in our collective mind through the process of exploration, definition, more exploration, protection, and legislation, and then more legislation.

The Grand Canyon National Park still does not include all of the Grand Canyon. Nor will it ever, though should we humans ever reach such enlightenment, we might someday all get together to celebrate, create, and protect a Grand Canyon Global Park. Still, imperfect as it is, the existing National Park does run from the Canyon's beginning at Lees Ferry, where the Paria River joins the Colorado, down through the Marble Gorge, past the Little Colorado junction, out into that big space most visitors see, and then on down the river through more big spaces to the Canyon's end at the Grand Wash Cliffs, 277 miles in all. (The maps in the Reader's Guide Part D may serve as orientation.) A fair amount of the north side of the Canyon, including its rims, plateaus and side canyons, is included in the Park. Some—one of our little political jokes—is labeled a National Forest, and some a National Monument. The south side, except for that rim bit most of us visit, is private, land of the Navajo, Havasupai, and Hualapai.

In the 1960s, constricted minds were insisting that the Canyon be diminished to fit inside a then more restrictively defined National Park. (See map A in the Reader's Guide Part D.) From early in the twentieth century, dam-builders had luxuriated in their fantasies of capturing the Colorado River in a stair-step of electricity generators. By 1962, when I wandered onto the scene, Grand Canyon dams were such an article of Western faith that road maps showed the sites where they would be built. And so, at the same time that I first saw the Canyon (organ music, please), I was also aware that some people wanted to do a stupid thing there (Bronx cheers, please). I have never recovered; to me the Canyon is ineffable, a place of the mind, and a place for the body to be. It is also a target of minds darkened by greed and exploitation. Therefore, all at once a place to be celebrated and to be protected.

The effort to secure congressional authorization of dams in the Grand Canyon was decades old, but in 1964, it was re-launched in earnest. Part of the dam-builders' propaganda effort tried, as I said, to shrink the Canyon, lopping off its upper 50 and its lower 150 miles, pretending that the then-Park defined the Canyon. They also resisted the idea that their dams and reservoirs would flood the Canyon, as if ten feet of water in a city's streets were not a flood—a disaster only if all the skyscrapers were covered. There was much other nonsense, such as pretending the dams were essential for bringing water to Arizona cities, and that the Colorado had so much water, it did not matter that a desert city's-worth would be evaporated each year from the new reservoirs.

In 1964, as well, I became aware that other people wanted to Save the Grand Canyon. I heard of the Sierra Club, and attended a November conference it held in Santa Fe, where we were living. There I met, talked to, and lunched with the Club's David Brower (The Reader's Guide Part A briefly describes persons and abbreviations that are important and/or appear often. This listing is intended to be of great help to the reader in keeping straight both the people and my sometimes idiosyncratic usages.) I heard him speak, and was swept up by his rhetoric and truth telling about the Canyon and its defense. Brower was a hero both for his mountaineering exploits and for his work in helping defeat the authorization of a dam in Dinosaur National Monument a decade before. Excited by the idea that there were many people who, like me, wanted to stop the dam building, I started pestering government agencies, trying to understand just what the dams were for. Becoming knowledgeable about how they were to be used, I cut through the guff as I found all the stuff about costs and benefits was just so much hand-waving necessitated by one or another particular scheme for financing projects to move water around. Since the dam scheme aimed at using governmental power to tax all the people in order to pay for helping some of the people, the schemers' problem was to get the support of the representatives of most of the people. The political calculations were far more important than the economic ones, though they did feed off each other.

A year later, at the second Santa Fe conference, Brower asked me if I would be interested in showing my commitment by becoming the first Southwest Representative, a staff position, for the Club. Would I! And in January 1966, I started working full-time, almost all of it fighting the dams. Perhaps that pivotal period seems so intense now because it was all crammed into eight months; actually, it was intense. Those who were putting together the legislation that included authorizing the dams, that Colorado River Basin Storage Project, were trying to include a lot of mutually suspicious, often-conflicting interests, while at the same time trying to pacify or ignore the interests they could not satisfy. First of the latter, they had real, though behind-the-scenes, political trouble because part of their scheming depended on the pipe-dream of diverting water from the Columbia River, an idea scorned by well-placed Northwest senators. Second, they had real and very public political trouble because they wanted to dam up the Grand Canyon for no good reason, and truly to generate electricity dollars to help pay for a pipeline from the Columbia. The Grand Canyon! Are you kidding?!

I have liked to think that my special contribution was, in early 1966, advancing the idea that we needed a positive proposal to highlight the Grand Canyon, not just opposition to the dams. In March, Martin Litton and I, ... Well, let me tell you about Martin, for he appears much in the pages ahead. Litton was a long-time travel editor at *Sunset* magazine, a boater of the Colorado in the old style, and a friend of Brower's, who encouraged him to run for the Sierra Club Board of Directors. There, at a crucial moment, Brower told me, Litton gave a passionate speech about the Grand Canyon and the need to defend all of it, not just the part that happened to be in the Park. This led to the Club's all-out effort to Save the Grand Canyon, not just protect the legal entities. In March, Litton and I sat down and worked up a wild-eyed legislative proposal for a Grand Canyon National Park that would include all of the Grand Canyon. A fine old friend of conservation, John Saylor, Republican Representative from Pennsylvania, introduced this impossibility, much to the derision of proper Arizonans. Who cared? We had made our point and the proposal was on the table, waiting for its moment (1974; see Chapter 5).

All this political theater was wonderful, with confrontations at the Canyon and debates with famous figures (one of whom, Barry Goldwater, is a major player in the story this book tells; at this point, he was just another, though nationally known, dammer-wannabe), newspaper ads, including a comparison of the Canyon to the Sistine Chapel, followed by attacks from shocked, shocked congressmen. So shocked that the IRS set off to investigate whether the Sierra Club, given its tax status, was illegally lobbying. Journalists and editorial writers across the US needed nothing more. Who cared about the fine points of tax law? IRS RAIDS SIERRA CLUB!!! What a feast; the over-bearing government trying to shut up those plucky few defending that great American icon, the Grand Canyon, by sending in the taxman. Some of the legislative choreographers had taken a pratfall.

Meanwhile, we—including many, many volunteers and staff, from all across the country—spent much time in Washington lobbying, going around to congressional offices, meeting with each other in hotels and restaurants, walking and taxiing, testifying before mostly hostile representatives—I remember a mean little Californian badgering a witness who stuttered. They did not even want us to be near their cozy little dining room, much less trying to keep them from wolfing down the goodies.

Weighing up the impacts of the obstacles to the dams is a job for another book. The critical point came because the tensions within the pro-CRBP forces had to reach a balance such that everyone agreed that their agreements would attract overall support that could withstand any opposition attempts to alter any of the arrangements. In part because that point came in August 1966, too near that congress's end, our noisiness and the Northwest's strategic placement upended the balance. The events that followed not only led to a CRBP in 1968 without any Grand Canyon dams, but to a dam ban and a Presidential proclamation protecting the upper stretch of the Canyon within a National Monument. I stayed on into 1969 as the Southwest Representative, spending somewhat more time on matters aside from the Canyon, but as you will see, still cherishing my role as one of its protectors.

It is a National Park; It is Wilderness; It is the Grand Canyon, After All

The importance of that August 1966 watershed for this book is that, with the dam-builders thwarted, Grand Canyon politicking came face to face with the question of how people—and how many of us—would enjoy river trips in an unspoiled wilderness. Well, not entirely unspoiled.

Upstream from the Grand Canyon squats Glen Canyon Dam, at one and the same time a gigantic destroyer of wild, extraordinary lands and a major incentive to protectors of the Grand Canyon to prevent any such destruction downstream. In a further irony, that dam's operation changed the river's flow such that the downstream natural riparian zone—the river, the beaches, the wildlife, the plants—began to change in significant and unfortunate ways, yet river-running could now be a year-round operation.

Something to have in mind should you take a Grand Canyon river trip is that the existing dam's effects are minor compared to what would have happened had the two Grand Canyon dams been built. (See locator map in the Reader's Guide Part D.) One would have been at about mile 40 in Marble Gorge, some 340 feet high, with its reservoir running back 53 miles to Glen Canyon Dam, past the Canyon's beginning. The second, called Bridge Canyon or Hualapai, was even more of a monster, 660 feet up and 93 miles back, from mile 237 to Kanab Creek. Since both dams were for generating electricity in a profit-maximizing way, they would have been operated with even more radical fluctuations than Glen Canyon Dam. Added to that destruction would have been all the stuff that goes with such construction and electric generation and flat-water zoom-zoom recreation. What a mess. By the way, Lake Mead, the reservoir behind Hoover Dam, ends just downstream from the Bridge Canyon site, a 40-mile intrusion into the Grand Canyon. And once upon a time, the more extreme engineering romantics nightmared up a tunnel to carry the river from the dam in Marble to generators in Kanab Creek. Why did these destructionists call themselves an agency of Reclamation?

In 1966, however, what seemed most clear to a few people who knew about river-running was that the dam's regulated release of water in the summer would make it possible to transport more and more of the people who had heard about river trips, in part because of publicity generated during the Grand Canyon dams fight. This recreation-benefiting flow change shows up in a comparison of 1960 and 1966. In the earlier year, the average monthly flow, as measured in cubic feet passing by each second (cfs), ranged from under 4000 cfs in late summer up to 38,000 in the spring. In the dam-regulated 1966 flow, the water went at a nearly steady 10,500 cfs to 16,500 during the warm months. And although not even 400 people in a year had traveled the river before the dam was completed, travel went to over 550 in 1965, over 1000 in 1966, doubling again to 2100 in 1967. And ever more river-runners meant more people who cared about a regular waterflow. Indeed, having counted their one big blessing, they began to complain that on smaller time scales like a day or week, the flow still fluctuated inconveniently, since water was released to optimize electricity generation. Kept to the level of grumbling for years and years, questions about waterflow grew into a major controversy in the 1980s.

August 1966 was a pivotal month for another reason. In response to the Wilderness Act of 1964, NPS Director Hartzog issued a wilderness policy, writing, (all my emphasis) "Boating **except with motorboats** and airboats is an acceptable use of park wilderness." [1] The policy then allowed that if the use of motors had become established by custom prior to inclusion, the use **may** continue subject to restrictions to protect wilderness. Applied to the Grand Canyon right at the beginning of mass recreation on the Colorado, this August 1966 NPS Wilderness statement could have ended motor use before some became accustomed to it. Instead it set up the major political debate over the river. Absolute in its intention, qualified in its application, the statement made irreconcilable points of view equally valid to their holders.

To lessen burdening our story with repetition, I am bringing in debaters for the two sides to help put the reader in control of their rhetoric. Here is how the arguing went, and still goes, between **Wil**, the earnest advocate for wilderness, and **Mo**, the noisy pro-motor.

Wil: The intent and foundation of the Wilderness Act is clear: no motors in wilderness; therefore, there should be no motorboats on the very obviously wilderness Colorado River in the prime wilderness of the Grand Canyon.

Mo: The Wilderness Act has been interpreted to allow motors that had already been in use in wilderness to continue. Motors have been on the Colorado, including on commercial trips, since the 1950s, so they may continue.

Wil: Their use was very recent and minor, not traditional. Traditionally, trips were taken in boats with oars, and this recent use is not protected since the 1964 Wilderness Act altered basic assumptions about motor use in Wilderness before commercial motor use started growing in 1965.

Mo: Congress has not designated a Wilderness in the Grand Canyon yet, so we are free to establish motors as a dominant use.

Wil: Studies have been done and recommendations made. When Congress does designate a Grand Canyon Wilderness, it will want to consider the river for its wild quality and its location through the heart of the Canyon. Since the only non-wilderness use is the recent addition of motorboats, their use should not be allowed to override the higher priority of wilderness and the experience of it.

Mo: If and when Congress does designate such a Wilderness, it will decide whether motors are an established use, and can accept that they are. So until Congress does act, the motors may stay on.

Wil: That argument would allow any wilderness-degrading use to be allowed, and thus nullify the purpose of studying lands for their designation as Wilderness. If the land is wilderness, then it should be protected and managed as such until Congress acts so that congressional choice will not be pre-empted.

Mo: Motorboat impact is transient. The boats just pass on through; they do not make any difference in the wilderness environment. Furthermore, the effects of Glen Canyon Dam are much more damaging, and make the riparian zone non-wilderness.

Wil: Management to protect wilderness must not wait on temporary effects like those of Glen Canyon Dam. If we allow all wild areas impacted by any external human activity to be kept out of Wilderness, then there won't be any. Look at how widespread the effects of air pollution can be.

Mo: If we can put up with the dam's impacts, we can put up with motor impacts.

Wil: Motorboats create air, noise, and water pollution in their locality, and if there are lots of them, the pollution can be nearly continuous. Motors encourage larger trips that impact river camps and attraction sites more heavily.

Mo: These effects have been shown not to be significant permanent impacts on the Canyon if properly managed. So whenever Congress gets around to it, it could order motors off if it wishes and the pollution will go away.

Wil: Grand Canyon river trips have a wilderness character, which motors impact in a very personal way for visitors, changing a wilderness trip into a rush-em-through amusement park ride. So while we are waiting for Congress, thousands of current visitors get short-changed.

Mo: Yet they say they like these rides.

Wil: Of course; they are in the Grand Canyon. And they deserve (especially given the cost of commercial trips) to have the best trip the Grand Canyon provides, a river-powered rowing trip in which the essential wilderness qualities of the Grand Canyon and the river running through its heart are not rushed through and degraded.

So whom do these debaters stand for in this dialectic that never reaches a synthesis? Before we get to that, we need to face the fact that there are not many people involved. Even if we look at all those who take a river trip, reaching toward 20,000 a year, there have been about half a million or so since the dams idea was junked almost four decades ago. This is not mass entertainment. Not only that, but sociologically speaking, river-runners are not a diverse group. There is some age distribution, with the usual gender discrimination. Ethnically, we mostly look far more the same than like a cross section of America. Income is a little more interesting; about 40% of commercial passengers are in the upper 10% of the American income bracket.

However, even were *those who get to go* an accurate representation from the American population (and the Grand Canyon attracts visitors from around the world), the sociological and statistical truth is that anyone who gets to travel on the Colorado is part of an elite, as a rough calculation shows. The population of the U.S. is about 270 million. So 20,000 river trippers per year means about 1 out of 10,000 Americans take a Grand Canyon river trip, many a very truncated one. Let us be generous, and extrapolate that to approximately 3 million in a century. That is one, 1, percent. In a century. In your lifetime, you have one chance out of a hundred to go once. In reality, because these numbers include repeaters, it is maybe half that, but the point is that *those who get to go* are an elite.

Moreover, the selection process is not random. The statistical elite is distorted by two real sub-elites: one of opportunity, knowledge, and connection; the other of wealth. And as is the privilege of elites, there are many repeaters: those who operate the commercial trips, researchers, Park Service staff. Anyone who can pay can go on commercial trips over and over. As well, opportunities for repeat trips exist for those with connections and/or knowledge of how to take advantage of the opportunities.

But, elite or not, it is well to keep in mind that most of this elite take no part in the controversies this book is about. Certainly, there is nothing new in the notion that American politics is about struggles between the committed few trying to sound like the blessed majority. The group with the fewest members of all, yet a very deep commitment, and who deserve to be mentioned first since there would be no story if they had not contested regulation, are the owners and operators of the commercial trips (call them comm ops). Throughout the 1970s, there were 21 river companies. Most ran motor trips; a few rowed, or offered both. A core motorized group early formed a lobbying group. It would be convenient to say that this group was activated by its desire to protect its economic interests; they sometimes do say that. They say other things, too, as in the debate above. However, my interpretation of their fundamental motive for resisting a motor ban is the desire by the comm ops to control management of river traffic.

Then sometimes I wonder. Is there something deeper? Do some people have a , conviction that wilderness is not a quality of the world to be enjoyed, explored, understood? Instead wilderness is to be dominated, conquered, kept at bay. Do some wilderness opponents find wilderness offensive to their sense of well-being? This may be fanciful, yet those of us who celebrate wilderness may need to see an emotional, spiritual chasm here. Just as we are spurred on by the joy and excitement of wilderness, others may deeply feel wilderness as something to be pushed back, the very antithesis of an ordered existence. Well, back to work.

Another grouping, though little heard from in an organized way in the 1970s, was the comm ops' employees, called variously guides, boatmen, commercial staff. It was an occasion when they spoke against the comm ops' interests.

Those who favor and work to achieve Wilderness include large-scale organizations with wide-ranging claims on their attention, like the Sierra Club and The Wilderness Society; ad hoc or permanent groups for a particular interest, issue or locality; and interested individuals who know and care for the place. The question of whether they (ahem, I), too, were at bottom concerned only with power and control is again one for the reader to ponder.

Those who have the experience and desire to run their own trips might, it would seem, not have a separate boat to row in this race about wilderness. However, individually and in organizations, they have often promoted the importance of wilderness. As well, the core determination of the commercial operators to control river-running, or at least set the ground rules, has often made enemies of those who promote the interests of people running their own trips. I use the term "self-guided" for such river users. However, the word "private" was the usual term starting from the 1960s. Another offering was "non-commercial". Disliking the negative sound, and to make a fundamental point, some describe these as "public" users, in contrast to commercial passengers who get on the river simply by paying fares to the privately owned comm op businesses. Whatever the label, the critical difference for the self-guided group is that each trip has to receive a permit from the Park, and the wait for such permits, right now in 2003, may be twenty years.

We circle back to that large segment of our elite, the have-been and want-to river trippers, and to those who support wilderness and environmental health. Though only occasionally active, these publics may hear appeals for support from the more intensely involved. Usually, clients and organization members are the recipients. Such appeals can lead to a few, up to a few hundred, responses when an effort is made, through meetings, websites, e-mail, and letters. The question here is, by asking people what they want and/or by urging them to express their desires, are the activists trying to involve them in influencing decisions, or is it less than that, only our need to demonstrate strength through numbers, rather than strength of argument and conviction? What does it really mean in American political life to have public participation in decision-making? More particularly, what does it mean in the politics of the Grand Canyon?

In the pages ahead, tracing groups' interactions and attempts to influence, some individuals will stand out, described as I see them. In some sense, they become, by virtue of speaking out and being recorded, representative of all those who maintain a position. This is not entirely fair or accurate; there is much subterranean activity, and those with the megaphones may not be planted as deeply as they sound. Nevertheless they become the voices, they constitute the record. These voices will become distinct as we proceed.

Finally, there is the National Park Service, an institution, an ever present, shifting set of actors. Internally, it is divided in many ways. Externally, it has multiple political bosses. There is a hierarchy. There are worker bees and saboteurs. There are persons with authority, of greater and less competence, and varying degrees of political sensitivity and backbone. In our story, there were heroes, even if, like all of us, sometimes with clay feet. There were probably no real villains; Orwell is my guide.

It is of some importance that there is an organic law governing NPS activity. Here is the fundamental statement of American law on the purpose of our National Park System (my emphases):

> "to conserve the scenery and the natural and historic
> objects and the wild life therein
> AND
> to provide for the enjoyment of the same
> IN SUCH MANNER AND BY SUCH MEANS
> as will leave them unimpaired for the
> enjoyment of future generations."[2]

The view is put forward by those interested in profiting from the parks that this charge has two equal parts: to conserve AND to provide for enjoyment. Some NPS employees like to wring their hands over how they have these two equal mandates, so often conflicting.

For those, like me, who take off from why there is a Park System at all, the plain reading, which I have emphasized, is that there is a primary purpose, to conserve, and a secondary, to provide for enjoyment, which is qualified by the primary. Indeed, the qualification is an even stronger amplification of the primary statement. In the first instance, the purpose is to conserve objects and wild life; in the second, to "leave them unimpaired". Moreover, more subtly, and even more pertinently, the mandate inhibiting the means of providing enjoyment is itself doubled. The objects conserved are to be left unimpaired, oh yes, and as well *the enjoyment is to be unimpaired* by the means of providing it. What else could it mean? Can we leave the objects unimpaired while allowing an impaired enjoyment? Does the Act say that it is enough that the scenery is safe, but that it is all right to impair the people's enjoyment of that scenery? If we keep a river undammed, is it sensible to then provide access to the river in ways that impair the enjoyment of it? A dam is ruled out because it would impair the river and canyon to be conserved, and because it would impair the enjoyment provided by running the river. Motors on the river in Park Wilderness are ruled out if their pollution impairs the riverine environment, and/or if their noise and hurry-up mode impair the enjoyment and Park experience river-running is to provide.

This exegesis does have a point. We, call us Friends of the Canyon, believe it is mandated, proper, and wonderful to preserve and also present this place for the enjoyment, in the deepest sense, of millions. We worry when we see the Canyon victimized by the careless, sloppy thinking that allows the exploitation of the Canyon and the public for commercial purposes. Were the Park Service able to carry out its mission clearly and consistently, that is, to conserve the place, with both the place and the enjoyment unimpaired, NPS staff could make decisions grounded in its Organic Act. As it is, the conceptual confusion, including within the organization itself, bouncing back and forth between conserving and providing enjoyment as if they were equals, entails more trouble and expenditure of time and energy than the exploiters themselves cause. Specific to this book, the decision to allow motors on the river is a decision to impair the enjoyment of the river for all generations having to experience the anti-wilderness effects of those motors. How did decision-making about the river get so far off the track?

Early Political Life on the River

1966. In August, the threat of Grand Canyon dams passed; the Park Service published its Wilderness management policy. In September, I spent nineteen days floating with, among others, Brower and the photographer Ernie Braun (a book came out of that), being rowed by, among others, Litton and Francois Leydet (a book had already come from their previous trips), through the Canyon. We were among the last of that year's 1100 visitors, and at the beginning of the inflation in river travel.

In November, Theodore Thompson, Chief Park Ranger, wrote seven pages on "Colorado River Boating", a document of the moment worth paraphrasing at length for its scrupulous snaring of the new age.[3] He presented, almost naively, issues soon to be too contentious for candor. He wanted to report to GCNP Superintendent Stricklin because that "could be valuable in developing uniform regulations". "There is no doubt publicity concerning the proposed construction of two dams" stimulated the interest increase, and the nine commercial operators took advantage to make a record number, a doubling, of traverses, made possible because the "relatively consistent" waterflow now extended the season from 2-3 months to all but the winter, when, since "keeping dry is impossible, ... damp or wet clothes combined with the low temperatures would produce a very uncomfortable condition." "Now widely publicized", the experience was participated in by people from "all walks of life." The full trip, down into Lake Mead, was 310 miles, taking an average of two weeks at an average cost of $300, sounding high but "not excessive from the operator's point of view", due to the complicated logistics and "usually excellent" food. All river outfitters (comm ops, in my usage here) used pontoon rafts with motors or oars. When motors are used extensively, the time can be cut to 7-9 days. A few trips went out the very primitive road in Diamond Creek. Several requests were made to take equipment out by helicopter at Phantom Ranch, and though these were dropped when our regulations were explained, there is still pressure to airlift passengers within the Park. Georgie White did have people airlifted from outside the Park. "There will be more of this in the future." Permits were issued for each trip; a revised method to issue a single yearly permit for the comm ops would reduce paperwork for them and us. "There are no plans to relax any of the qualifications or requirements whatsoever." Relationships between NPS and comm ops have been "excellent"; we have received their full cooperation on all matters. Several Park employees accompanied boat parties as guests or working members, giving them "a better understanding of the many problems". The number of commercial trips increased from 19 in 1965 to 39 this year. One record was set by a trip of 15 pontoon rafts with 150 mostly high school students. "An ideal situation is 3 boats with no more than 20 passengers", though the average party was 20-40 people. Safety remains the main concern. Upsets occasionally occurred even with improved boats and more experience, but there were no boating injuries these two years. "A serious sanitation problem has developed" due to increased use and the regulated flow. With no more high flows flushing beaches clean, what is left behind accumulates. Toilet facilities were improvised. Tin cans and other waste need to be disposed of. This "real" problem must be resolved "quickly", and comm ops and NPS are studying it. "An economical solution does not appear to be possible." The dwindling supply of driftwood is a problem; in a few years little will be left. We will discuss this at the Western River Guides Association (WRGA) meeting we plan to attend in February to strengthen relationships. Many neophytes, about 50 parties, unaware of the many hazards involved, wrote for permits to use kayaks, one and two man rafts, inner-tubes, canoes, etc. They lost their enthusiasm after qualifications, requirements and hazards were explained. We sent a list of comm ops to these "adventurous people". The number of "private" parties dropped from four last year to three.

Thompson left the Park then, succeeded by George von der Lippe, who in 1967 had the historic Bass cable across the river cut down because it threatened helicopters.[4] Late that year, von der Lippe went to the WRGA meeting to announce that there would soon be five-year concession permits for commercial river operators, now numbering ten. They were somewhat concerned, but von der Lippe noted that the earlier change of instituting a permit with a fee had brought no comment. Again the number of commercial trips had doubled, up to 79; the number of passengers to 2000. Self-guided trips also increased, to ten. Park staff worried about congestion at the launching point, Lees Ferry. The problem then, as now, is that the launch days that most conveniently tie into vacations are around the weekend. This congestion then translates downstream, so that the largest clumps of people hit the popular attraction spots, like Redwall Cavern, Elves Chasm, Deer Creek, Havasu Canyon, and Tapeats Creek, about the same time, or get rushed along downriver to be clear of the crowds.

Safety could have been a concern, for in March 1967 a boatman on a commercial motor raft had drowned when his pontoon rig turned over, his lifejacket tangled in the motor. Indeed, in November 1967, the Regional Director wrote the Director that "we must control river-running on the Colorado River. [It is] a rough stream and contains extremely dangerous rapids."[5] He seemed particularly concerned that letting inexperienced people on the river would be to sign their "death warrant". This fear-filled language sounded like the dam-builders mantra: Few come, thousands drown.

Another incident that summer, though with no death, had greater reverberations. As part of the campaign to gain congressional approval for building dams in the Grand Canyon, the pro-dam forces would run river trips for what they hoped were influential people. Their idea was that the flacks on the trip could hype the idea that the Canyon was obviously so big, the dams could not fill it up, so no problem. One mouthpiece, a Bureau of Reclamation staffer, wrote to the Superintendent thanking him for help in getting two men airlifted out. He also noted that river-running is not as simple as the Sierra Club would have us believe, as witness Oren Beaty's accident. This cryptic reference was unraveled when Congressman Wyatt of Oregon wrote a Sunday magazine piece for *The Oregonian*. He told of his adventures on a VIP trip organized by Congressman Morris Udall, the heavy lifter for the Arizona House delegation on the CRBP. Ten representatives in all went, and along with them Mr. Beaty. He worked for Morris Udall's brother, Stewart, then Secretary of the Interior, who, hardly coincidentally, had run a family trip in June. Congressman Wyatt was suitably impressed (and in any case never had to commit himself since opposition to the dams was strong enough that the matter was never put to a vote). He wrote about his "chastening thought when one realizes that he has taken part in a trek few men have been privileged to witness, has seen a spectacle that is without parallel on this planet *for the purpose of challenging this overwhelming nature with man-made structures designed to help him face this very environment.*" Those are my italics; this purple prose hardly needs them, but it is too sad that his thoughts did not lead more to defend the unparalleled spectacle. But then he was on a river trip set up by the Bureau of Reclamation, run by a commercial operator, one of the majority of comm ops using the Canyon while others fought to protect it. Wyatt wrote of the rapids, their "thrills and fears", "raging maelstrom(s)", recording that each boat broke a motor, and that spares were lost. For them, a helicopter was available to bring replacements, but that wasn't the end. In Deubendorff Rapid, Beaty was "bounced so hard that his grip on the line was broken. He was thrown over the back of the raft head first, striking his head on the outboard motor. This blow knocked him unconscious. Luckily the helicopter was hovering overhead at the time ... Beaty suffered some very bad facial cuts and a dislocated nose, and was immediately flown to the hospital". This made such an impression on Wyatt that his article included a photo of Beaty being loaded into the helicopter.

The incident impressed another congressman on the trip, Rogers C. B. Morton, a Maryland Republican, whom we shall meet in the 1970s as Secretary of the Interior under President Nixon. It seems reasonable that someone witnessing such an incident on such a trip might wonder whether motors were a hazard. As we will see, reason does not always prevail over political connections.

With that experience as focus, let's go back to June when Secretary Udall, family and friends, rode the river[6]. He wrote, "I had anticipated an oar-guided float trip and was disappointed to find that each raft was powered by a small outboard motor." But the comm op on this trip, Jack Currey claimed that motors were needed on such rafts in order to position the boat properly, and, of course, to move it quickly down river, since "a true float would mean an extra week on the river". Strange, since Udall's trip, "nearly two weeks", was the standard length of a float trip using oars. Fortunately, there were no motor-caused accidents.

(Dee Holladay, now a river trip operator in Dinosaur National Monument et al., then a Currey employee, says that in the early 1960s, Currey did not trust motors and wanted to stay with rowing.[7] However, Dee and another boatman, Art Gallenson, talked Currey into adopting motors so that they could use larger rafts to carry more people at once. Currey then became a devotee, according to Holladay. Georgie White had set the example of large motorized trips; two other comm ops, Hatch and Cross, always used motors.)

The Secretary was "officially anxious to see those sections of [the Canyon] involved in the bitter dams and parks controversy". He describes the rapids in language from a boxing match, leaving him "limp". "But the Colorado contains much more than rapids." He speaks of side canyons, wildlife, Indian ruins. It all "taught me once again that the Secretary of the Interior should never make armchair judgments on national conservation issues", now thinking the burden of proof was on the dam builders. Perhaps, but the burden of educating this Secretary and almost all other officials on the value of the Grand Canyon and the dams' destructive effects had been up to the public. He and his family were thrilled by a trip that would have been made impossible had his "armchair judgment" of a few years previous not been blocked by public opinion able to express itself through the legislative process.

Although Secretary Udall spoke of "this pristine country", later that year he is reported to have ordered the Park Service to clean up this "foul canyon". As noted, in November 1966 the Chief Park Ranger had expressed his concern about campsite sanitation, saying no economical solution appeared possible. A few months later, NPS staff told the February WRGA meeting that they had decided to install pit toilets. A river survey in April 1967, loaded with officialdom, identified and photographed 17 suitable "sandbars", plus several other possibilities, on which to locate the toilets, described as a perforated 55-gallon drum sunk in the sand, topped by a seat surrounded by camouflaging plastic.[8] Four campsites were given priority. The report did suggest that until the toilets were installed, boats carry chemical disposal units, but it emphasized the determination to construct, "whether or not they are visible from the river", a string of facilities that river-runners would be required to use. Reflecting further the attitudes of this period, still not fully cognizant of the river as a closed, deteriorating environment in which people had to be intensively managed, the report also settled for hauling unburnable trash in provided burlap bags while completely burning wet garbage. Fire pits were to become semi-permanent to minimize their number, and fires drowned, not buried. The writer opined that when the dwindling supply of driftwood became a shortage, boating permits would have to require carrying in a supply of firewood, since otherwise living trees, already being maimed, would be further threatened.

At the December 1967 WRGA meeting, the chief ranger had heard no objection to the privy installation, though the audience wanted them inconspicuous and no other facilities. Still, in May 1968, the Superintendent wrote they were not sure about privies, having in mind something more primitive and unobtrusive to enclose the sunken oil drum; "we are not committed to any particular facility as yet". Nevertheless, a Park ranger reported in September 1968 that the four privies had been installed, scattered along the river at Nankoweap (with two), Tuckup Canyon, and 204 mile. They were, he averred, enthusiastically received, and everybody liked them at the November 1968 WRGA meeting.

This harmony became discordant starting in April 1968, when the Sierra Club, I as Southwest Representative and John Ricker as Chapter Chairman, wrote the Superintendent.[9] Ricker did not want hikers to have to encounter permanent structures in wilderness. I generalized this concern, calling the toilets the first and easiest step in a long road using the construction approach in caring for river traffic, rather than the regulation approach. We opposed man-made objects "privies, picnic tables, garbage pits, helispots, boat docks, signs, corrals, and what-not." I urged considering other means including portable chemical toilets, and "generally working toward rules which would lead to self-contained trips", noting that the patrol boat they were inaugurating could be used for experimenting. After seeing the new proposed rules, I went on to worry that any continued dependence on wood in the Canyon would lead to people going after trees, and urged that all cooking be done on stoves, and that campfires be given up. The Park also heard from those who did not want to be regulated, who wanted to be able to hike and boat, and take the consequences. NPS, however, said it could not shrug off public safety, and uncontrolled boating should never be allowed.[10] They had a special concern since 1969 is the centennial of John Wesley Powell's first trip, and "the river will be full of boaters".

Our comments led to Ken Sleight, as WRGA President, arranging a meeting at the Park in June where the matter was discussed by him, me and Superintendent Stricklin accompanied by his top ranger, maintenance, and naturalist staff.[11] The strongest memory I have of this meeting is the laughter provoked when I urged that human waste, along with other trash, be carried out of the Canyon. (It takes until Chapter 13 to get the last, best laugh on this issue.) Ambivalent, the Park staff said that if the toilets to be installed were not successful, then either more would be put in or that method would be discarded for something else. NPS planners seemed more concerned with the esthetics of well-engineered privies than with those of soiled beaches, and concluded that the best course would be for them to be ugly, inadequate, and fill quickly, so that the issue would have to be faced. Chemical toilets, a new development at the time, were thought by the comm ops to be too small to be practical, and Sleight made a strong plea for a cooperation-not-control approach by NPS toward river problems. The comm ops would work to solve them. They would coordinate scheduling to avoid congestion and competing at the start and campsites, they would clean up recent and old trash, they would police members who leave dirty sites. Most fires, he said, were social; there might be several at any site, and Sleight preferred that there be pressure to clean up ashes instead of going to one fire-pit. He did not want any Smokey the Bear type on river trips outshining company employees. I asked the Park Service to document conditions before and after the installation, using the new once-a-month river patrol.

In writing about this meeting, I ended by ruminating about NPS's stand-back attitude. Again and again NPS staff present pointed out that they do not push themselves on the visitor. There are services; visitors have to ask about them. They did not like the idea of NPS naturalists on commercial trips. I came away thinking that a good nickname might be "the reticent service", so different from agencies who actively promoted multiple use and resource development. Would a more aggressive Park Service be better able to protect the Park System, instead of leaving that task to citizen organizations like the Sierra Club? What the following decades showed me more clearly was a Service split over its Organic Act; some all too ready to emphasize providing enjoyment at the expense of wilderness, a view that fit right in with the increasing rise in commercial river use pressure.

This split became apparent because we were moving onto new ground. Park Service planning and development decisions had always been internal matters. Now, in part because the Wilderness Act called for a public meeting process, changes were occurring. The Sierra Club was urging public meetings on Park master plans, which had only been held at Yosemite and Yellowstone. Now we wanted them for Grand Canyon. We first proposed a pre-plan meeting in January 1968, to help focus our own activity.

The old habits persisted, making it much harder for even a very interested citizen to keep track of agency work. One item that would have been of great importance to us, and of which we remained ignorant, was that on March 15, 1968, Superintendent Stricklin sent the Regional Director a proposal for Wilderness in the Park.[12] It was very much in the old style, mostly a real estate description. In this quickly neglected document, the Colorado River had no special mention though it was included where it was not the Park boundary. The accompanying text did no more than mention river-running. Nevertheless, how we would have loved to have had that view on the river publicized and encouraged. Yet apparently no one, even inside NPS, paid any attention to this first attempt at GCNP wilderness planning.

Other actions we too often did not know about were more development-oriented: a new two-story motel was put on the rim; a church was being completed near the visitor center; planning was underway for a huge new interpretive site, to be blasted into the rim so it would not stick up too high; there was heavy construction to build a water pipeline down in the Canyon. Decisions were being made and formed into concrete that would shape the visitor perceptions of the Canyon for decades to come. We wanted to be heard before these decisions were made; we wanted public involvement. No one reminded me, "Be careful what you wish for, you may get it."

The promise of public meetings to deal with wilderness proposals in the context of a Park master plan was one reason for us to focus. Another was that, as a citizen volunteer organization, we needed to discover, through discussion, what our organization wanted. If a group of people with a common interest can express that interest, relate it to proposed agency decisions, then, the theory goes, the group is able to act, and its actions may translate into the ability to influence those decisions. With discussion, and resolution of individual ideas, some sort of commitment is generated, some sort of validation permeates the expressions of the interest, and some sort, often an overwhelming sort, of passion drives the desire to present views in a convincing way.

Too easily, the idea of a citizen volunteer organization can be mimicked as if it were simply based on membership, as if numbers equaled influence. In fact, public involvement is the gathering and winnowing of views together so that commitment and energy come out, propelling people into conviction and the willingness to state and push for those views in what too often is a series of numbing reiterations. We have not solved the democratic problem of what constitutes public opinion, how to express it effectively over time, and how not to corrupt its validity.

Nevertheless, the public involvement process as it worked out through the 1970s was a giant step, and it truly began when, founded on mandates like those in the Wilderness Act, people got together as they did in Phoenix on September 23 1968.[13] Members and guests of the Grand Canyon (Arizona) chapter of the Sierra Club discussed a GCNP master plan proposal, focusing on river use, rim development, trail use, and what areas should be classified as Wilderness areas. This general discussion did show a consensus that land below the rim except for Phantom Ranch and Indian Garden deserved wilderness protection, as did some above-rim lands. The increasing river use was seen as posing practical problems in sanitation, wood supply, and what sort of limits there should be.

A month later, a follow-up meeting on river and rim use brought forward two points of view.[14] First, some argued that river trips were not wilderness experiences because of the motors, manmade structures, and alterations due to the upstream dam. Also, more people can be accommodated if management is for recreation not wilderness. This point of view still involved setting some limit; otherwise the river would be ruined for recreation. The other, wilderness, view saw the river as the heart of the wilderness the Park was set up to protect. Leaving it unimpaired meant a smaller number of visitors, and solving problems without development. The discussion indicated no great passion for grappling with the overall problem, but many suggestions for how to handle visitors, several of which were non-wilderness in nature.

We developed our ideas over the next several months into a firm statement against any facilities along the river except at Lees Ferry, Phantom Ranch, and Diamond Creek.[15] The desirable total of river-runners was 4000. (As we worked away on our position, the actual number jumped from 3600 in 1968 to 6000 in 1969, with not a peep from the Park Service.) If motors were to be used, we wanted them to be small outboards, but the ideal was a float trip using oars only. A few months later, we resolved this equivocation in favor of managing the river as wilderness, not as a mass recreation area, yet still added that "if raft motors must be used, they should be limited to 25 hp." In this same vein, aircraft were to be restricted to 10,000 feet above sea level within five miles of the Canyon. The Club's master plan proposals also objected to over-restrictive regulations, imposed on self-guided trips, that made it almost impossible for people to run the river except on commercial trips.

Our recommendations aimed at leaving the natural scene as such, without any constructed, man-made items, especially calling for toilets carried on the boats. We also wanted open fires only for warmth, not cooking. We urged a launch limit at Lees Ferry of one trip per day with no more than 30 people, a total of 5000 visitors over the six month season. We called for a study "by the Park Service in cooperation with independent ecologists and conservationists to determine the amount of traffic the riparian area can stand without upsetting the natural balance", a long-winded way of calling for the determination of the river physical carrying capacity. We emphasized the need for the Park Service to actively engage with visitors.

The Sierra Club Board of Directors approved our proposals as official policy in mid-1969, in time for the first public meeting on Canyon affairs, announced by the Park Service on July 8. Park staff would listen to the public's comments on August 6 as to what should be in the GCNP Master Plan. Were we just naive, that we did not know it was already too late for such measured responses? I was not to realize this for a while, since I spent the next three years with my family in the East, deluded into thinking that income trumped interest, until we realized, as some wise head put it, that we had sandstone in our blood, and returned to the Southwest.

CHAPTER 2

1969-71: Weaving the Web - Tangled, Sticky, Durable

Motor is a Curse Word

The years 1969-71 appeared like a gold-rush frenzy, as commercial outfits by the twos and threes got permits from the Park and launched; a jump from 11 operators in 1968 to 20 in 1971. This doubling of operators helped make possible, but was overshadowed by, the tripling in trips, going from 108 to 387, and people, from 3500 to 10,500. This increase was heavily driven by the largest, oldest comm ops. (See Reader's Guide Part C for comm op information.) These were the years of the superintendency of Robert Lovegren, years that turned what had been a situation with serious problems of impact and regulation into runaway exploitation. The key to this excess was the outboard motor, pushing large rafts that carried parties of over 40 people down the river on faster, shorter trips. And when, in 1972, people concerned about the quality of trips, about impact on the river environment, and about wilderness, were able to check this wild increase, those 21 (one more was added in 1972) comm ops saw themselves as entitled. As with all newcomers, they claimed they had a fundamental right to be there.

Doubts and suspicions of motors probably started with their first commercial use in the 1950s. Their inappropriateness was indicated in Secretary Udall's comment about his disappointment. The use of big "baloney" boats—large pontoon rafts, sometimes lashed together to carry even larger groups—had been generating contempt particularly from those who traveled in smaller, quiet, more maneuverable boats with oars. These smaller boats give visitors far more of a feel of the river, both when in the river's rapids and on its flat water, where it moves serenely and massively. Since the use of motors is the inescapable factor in this story of the struggle for power over how to run the river, this is a good place to contrast the arguments by which the comm ops justify using motors with views in favor of a more natural canyon-oriented experience. I will bring back Wil and Mo for this debate, taking off from the Udall-Currey, exchange, since it captured many of the differences.

Mo: "A true float", as Udall paraphrased Currey, "would mean an extra week on the river. Later Currey demonstrated that the safe passage of a large raft rests on the pilot's ability to 'position' it at the head of each rapids and maneuver in mid-passage in order to 'cheat' around the most dangerous boulders and holes."[1]

Wil: The statement that it takes longer to make a trip without a motor is at the heart of the National Park System ethic. You come to a National Park to have an experience that, as much as possible, is unimpaired by the means of providing it, that comes as close as possible to meeting the place, the wilderness Grand Canyon in this case, on its own terms. If motors are used to mechanize and rigidify a schedule just in order to get done quickly, the visitor is having less of a Park-defined, and more of a concessionaire-defined, experience; the visitor is being cheated of a National Park wilderness experience.

Mo: Currey talked about "safe" passage, too; large rafts require motors in order to maneuver. Therefore, motor trips are safer.

Wil: Of course, this logic is false. Indeed, of all the arguments the comm ops make, the "motors are safer" slogan is the most scandalous because it is totally untrue. Stated as Udall originally did, rafts large enough to carry 20-40 people jammed together—rafts too big to be rowed—do require motors. That does not make them safe where rowing trips are not, as the two 1969 accidents recounted above bear witness. The correct course is to use rafts that are the right size for rowing a wilderness river, carrying six people or so, gaining the benefit of optimizing the Park experience while maintaining safety.

Mo: Motors are safer. Motors are safer. Motors are safer…

Wil: Repeating this canard remained standard in the pro-motor arsenal. Yet serious attempts to study safety produced numbers that showed that the trips were equally safe. Even though a river trip has its thrills and tense moments, the chances of a river accident are very, very small as compared to hurting yourself on shore (most reported accidents take place off the boats). The primary reason is that as experience in running the river accumulated, people learned what to do to be safe.

Mo: Motors are safer. Motors are safer…

Wil: Why some comm ops and their allies tried to make motors look necessary for safety may be obvious, but all the argument really does is belie the expertise of the industry. River trips are safe adventures, regardless whether propulsion is by the river or by a motor.

Mo: Nevertheless, studies have shown that people planning on taking a river trip think motor trips are safer.

Wil: This does seem to be true. According to surveys done over the years, some inexperienced people traveling on motor trips have the prejudice that the big motor rafts they are on are safer. So let's go back to our statistics, and remember that it is an elite of an elite that ever gets to run the Colorado River. The population forming that elite is largely self-defined. Many others define themselves out of the commercial-passenger elite by making other choices. For instance, those who do not want to camp out, do not go. People who believe that they will be beset by snakes and scorpions, do not go. People who most enjoy racing or water skiing on large flat-water reservoirs, do not go. People who prefer urban vacations, do not go. People who prefer to ski in Switzerland, do not go. People who want a cruise on a large ocean liner, do not go. Yet the absence of those who have such preferences does not de-populate the river. However, it would be a queer, as well as an anti-Park anti-Wilderness, notion to install hotels, clear out poisonous creatures, build reservoirs and cities, and widen the Canyon to carry large ships, just in order to attract those who opt out. Likewise, if motors were not used in the Grand Canyon then people, who mistakenly thought that motors were needed for safety, would join the ranks of those that exercise other preferences and do something at which they thought themselves safe. Of course, if they really did want to go, and had explained to them the facts about river-running being a safe adventure, and still wanted to go only with a motor for false comfort, they would surely form an elite of an elite of an elite. Surely, since these are Parks for the public, such a tiny elite should not be allowed to impose their choice on the rest of the public.

Mo: But we who run motor trips claim that this group of motor-lovers is the public.

Wil: Anybody who gets to go on the river, whether using their wealth or their perseverance, is an elite. Visitor surveys—discussed in later chapters—revealed just how much of an elite. Right now, we just point out that people who think motor trips are necessary for safety are not only a minority elite, but an unnecessarily deluded group crowding out others who want to go.

Mo: Yes, but visitors on rowing trips really are an elite. As the December 2001 website of one of the most established comm ops, Grand Canyon Expeditions, said: motors "make the canyon accessible to people who could never otherwise take a trip ... because they are too young or too old to make the steep, sweltering hike down into the Canyon. Motorized rafts are roomier and more stable than rowed boats, so children, the elderly, the handicapped, and people simply not in great physical condition can enjoy the trip."[2]

Wil: First of all, did you notice the "more stable"? Even now, when everyone knows better, the pro-motor crowd will try to sneak in the motors-are-safer fiction. For the truth, go back to Secretary Udall's story, as he grips the ropes along the sides of his motor-driven pontoon raft, barreling down the rapid into a "maelstrom of churning froth". The first wave "tosses the front end skyward; the raft shudders, ... then dips downward as twisting cross-waves drench everything aboard. The pontoons are now a plaything of explosive water: the bronco action accelerates as the river pummels each raft with a left jab, a right cross". Etc. You get the idea. Stable! Who goes on the Colorado River for a stable ride? Being tossed around is half the fun. Once again, in the eagerness to slyly stick in the safety stiletto, the motor-boaters distort the point that in part people come for the excitement. The point of it being a National Park experience is that it is not a smoothed-out commute; it is a wild ride.

Mo: GC Expeditions is only trying to point out that motor trips make it possible for children, the elderly, the handicapped, and the physically-unconditioned to go, since without motors they could not go.

Wil: Of course, that is false, as well. People of all ages and physical abilities can and do go on all sorts of river trips. Like the motors-are-safer untruth, the young-and-fit untruth only exists because motorizers keep repeating it over and over. Moreover, if motors disappeared, there would be all kinds of innovative thinking about how to broaden access.

Mo: There must be some truth in it, since motor-boaters do have overwhelmingly the largest share of the river-running market.

Wil: People do not have an open and equal choice. They have the "choice" offered them by the comm ops, who for 30 years have concentrated their use (three-fourths of commercial use) on motor trips.

Mo: That is what people want. As GC Expeditions says, "Many - perhaps most - people cannot afford to devote so much time to a vacation ... [row trips] take twice as long". Motor trips take "eight days, while row trips take fourteen".

Wil: Right, 2 times 8 is 14. Typical motor-boater "fuzzy math". More suspect however, is the lack of change in comm op behavior over the past three decades. In how many aspects of American life has the status quo prevailed since 1966?

Mo: You can dodge and dodge; it takes longer for a rowboat to make the trip. People do not have that kind of time.

Wil: More misstatements. Looking at all the comm op offerings, a visitor can spend as little as two nights (a day and parts of two others), all the way up to 21 days. The spread of choice is greater on rowing trips, all the way from the shortest to the longest. Motorboats only cover more miles per day; there are more choices of length on rowing trips. The motor-boaters concentrate theirs on fast, big trips taking less than a week, pretending these are full-Canyon trips, and then imply only their trips are short.

Mo: To repeat, we offer what people will buy, a trip that fits within a week's vacation.

Wil: We are talking about the trip of a lifetime. If any trip is worth saving up vacation days for, a float trip down the Colorado certainly is. A three-day motor trip in a little bit of the Canyon costs over a thousand dollars. Maybe people who can afford that sort of fee do not want to take a full Grand Canyon trip, but it is more likely that they take what the comm ops want to offer. The comm ops offer way more motor trips; in 2002, GC Expeditions offered 4 rowing trips and 63 motor trips.

Mo: And why not? That is what people want.

Wil: That is what the comm ops want. And GC Expeditions tells you why when they say row trips "require many more crew members". Motor trips carry more passengers in their bigger rafts and push them through in fewer days; they need fewer crew and supplies. What is then surprising is that motor trips actually cost the visitor more per day. The numbers vary from company to company, but currently motor-boater customers pay $100/day more than rowing trips. Which, for a business, is a good reason to push the product.

Mo: Excuse me, you are avoiding the fact that rowing trips cost more, much more, as much as $1-2000 more!

Wil: Which is a sly way of avoiding the fact that a comm op can run two super-short 6-day motor trips charging $2000 per person while a 14-day float trip charges $3000 per. That is, the comm op is getting $4000 from each seat in a two-week period if motors are used, instead of $3000. Put that together with motor-driven rafts being bigger and using fewer crew, so overhead costs are lower, and voila! You have the reason for motor trip dominance—lots more off the top for the motor-boater.

Mo: While you are trying to make us look like greedy exploiters, 99.99% of our passengers are ecstatic about the trip. They tell us that, and they tell polltakers that.

Wil: Well, duh, it is the Grand Canyon! Who wouldn't be impressed? And there are better and worse ways, the Park way and the motorizer way, of enjoying it.

Mo: If the motor experience is so inferior, how come people keep coming back and sending their friends to us?

Wil: What choice do they have, given the great imbalance comm ops maintain for motor trips? The "choice" is go motor or stay at home.

Mo: But all comm ops support keeping motors.

Wil: Of course. The rowing businesses are able to protect themselves from competition by joining the motor comm ops to form an inflexible status-quo oligopoly that is just the opposite of an open, innovative, free market where consumers have a wide range of choices.

Mo: So you say; I claim we serve the public the way it wants to be served.

Wil: Even were that true, it comes at the sacrifice of Park and wilderness values, which is what the American people, through their elected representatives, have said Grand Canyon National Park is about. Yet, if the comm ops would let those values have their full play, they would still be able to provide enjoyment, unimpaired, and make money.

As we trace the battle over motors on the Colorado, and why the comm ops fought so fiercely, all this verbiage spilled about safety, choice, variety, time, etc., will be endlessly repeated. True, perspective is gained by remembering the superficial economics; running motor rafts seems more profitable than rowing. More fares (people) can be run through faster, in a shorter time, at less cost. Yet economics, too, only gives us a partial understanding of why the comm ops fought so hard. In politics, economics, like other arguments, is often only the outer show masking a more naked truth about the contestants. This would become glaringly obvious in 1977 when an economic study of each comm op showed that a healthy, profitable river industry could exist if motors disappeared.

In 1969, only the comm ops were adding one and one, then two plus three and even more, as river traffic grew toward overpopulation. Conservation staff in the Southwest was new and distracted by other issues. The pressure by commercial river-runners pushed on a new superintendent, Robert Lovegren. Though fortunately short, Lovegren's time at the Park was long enough to give the comm ops the conviction that their desires were paramount.

This kowtowing was not necessary. A strong Superintendent, intent on carrying out Park and Wilderness mandates, would have had agency support. In March 1969, an NPS Committee on River Over-Use had called for carrying capacities, consistent regulations, and control through permits. Nevertheless, in November, GCNP was still debating whether, in the face of accelerating use and conservationist warnings, there should even be a limit on the number of commercial permits.

The one accomplishment of the 1969 season is that everyone recognized that the privy installations were not the answer; they filled quickly, and then attracted flies, stunk, and ended up not being used. Since no alternative was in sight, there could be no satisfaction in "winning" this argument; the problem was not to be able to say, "we told you so", but to get people's imaginations working on a real solution.

Lovegren's superintendency was a time for problems, not solutions, however.

The Park Service Yields Control

Now we are ready for the 1970s.[3] This brings us, I am sorry to say, to user-days, introduced in 1970 by the Park Service as a way to quantify river use. It would be more comfortable if we could talk about people: visitors, crew, Park staff, etc. NPS was not comfortable with that, however, and once it began to categorize people, the user-day was convenient to hide the discriminatory classifications, and to cloak in obscurity arguments over how to cut up the river traffic pie. At one point, the attempt was made to substitute the count of visitors launched (actually, this was a count of boat "seats" or spaces), and it will be a measure of the conservative nature of river traffic management that this effort failed.

The user-day concept has not brought consistency; the comm ops often brag about the 20,000 people they bring down the river each year, even though 75% of these get only partial trips, over 25% of all commercial passengers getting just two to four days. Such quickie trips might sound like a wonderful opportunity. The comm ops might crow: See the Grand Canyon over a weekend! Fits the vacation of any harried wealthy executive! Well, they are not so explicit, but that is the message, and it blatantly contradicts the opposite claim: Grand Canyon: The Emperor of River Trips! The Sistine Chapel of White Water Thrill Rides! Which is true, but as I say, only an elite of the elite of the elite commercial passengers are allowed to see the whole ceiling; most have to be content with a few panels.

Back to the subject of user-days, it is the fact of different trip lengths that helps give the user-day (u-d) idea its hold. Sometimes the difference is travel speed; rowing trips go at the river's speed; motors travel up to twice as fast. Time off-river can vary even more, doubling or more the trip length. As well, the full Grand Canyon trip of 277 miles has been broken into segments. Some people go all the way, taking from 8-30 days. Some people go on one segment. Lees Ferry to Phantom is offered as a two-night trip—by motors. People-friendly trips on the same stretch can take up to nine days. Rushing, Lees to Whitmore can be done on a five-night trip. Whitmore Wash to Lake Mead takes from three days up, or not at all for those who get jerked out by helicopter. Given all the variations in length and quality, the Park Service wanted a way to count all the flavors of trip as apples, so GCNP staff came up with the user-day: one person on the river all or part of one day. Superficially, the concept may seem to be a convenient way to parcel out use, but it is as much worms as apple.

As pointed out above, there are different costs and income per day depending on what is offered on the trip. Since motor trips rush through the Canyon faster, for instance, to give them the same user-days as rowing trips would mean that rowers could take fewer fares. What really caused the kink in the problem, however, was that when the idea was introduced, the Park was not trying to limit or apportion use. Before 1972, each comm op would request some number of user-days, and the Park would grant it. So the number was only each company's idea of how much business there would be, and the numbers were larger than could be used. There was no NPS allocation or ceiling on use. The numbers of user-days had no relation to any idea of carrying capacity or what constituted a Park-worthy trip; there was no meaningful input from the Park Service. Each year, the number requested and the number used reflected only the comm ops' business calculations. That these were not predictors of much is illustrated by the ceilings going up every year, even though actual user-days declined from 1970 to 1971.[4]

At some point, to make the problems more binding, the user-day became an indicator of impact. Seemingly, more user-days mean more impact. But again, impact from a day spent doing what? Going down the river, lolling on the camping beaches, clambering around crowded attraction sites, hiking over-used trails or unexplored routes? Moreover, the quality of the impact could be, and is, a contentious issue. Were some visitors more careful than others, more sensitive to the environment, more obedient to regulation? Had the Park Service been in control of its duties, the difficulties might have been worked out. However, this would have required a steady hand offering education and orientation on the one hand, and chastisement for transgressors on the other. Instead, NPS talked about the need for control, but allowed the comm ops to develop their practices so that they could claim their concerns should be paramount, if not exclusive. A particularly offensive result was the comm ops slander of other river-runners and backpackers, and their puffing up of themselves as voluntary keepers of the Canyon.

The user-day measure, favoring some over others, became a straitjacket. Here is an example to give a sense of the discomfort: one person on a motor trip counts for 8 user-days, say, and on a rowing trip, 14 user-days. Now suppose the Park Service limits river use because it fears damage to the Canyon, or impairment of the experience. Each comm op will then have a maximum use counted in user-days. Suppose each runs 10 trips, with 20 passengers each. The motor-boater then has a limit (or allocation, as it came to be called) of 1600 u-d; the rower of 2800 u-d. Now suppose, wilderness advocates come and pound the table about getting rid of motors. Whoops! The motor-boater complains his 1600 will now be divided by 14 instead of 8, and he would be reduced to about 115 people on 6 trips. So what looked like a qualitative policy change to a more person-oriented wilderness experience becomes a quantitative question of a comm op's income. Can you hear the screams? And if NPS tried to add user-days to make up for the change, the yelling would come from those worried about unjustifiably increasing impacts.

Another example affected trips taken by people who wished to go on their own, what I am calling the self-guided groups. There was this difference between commercial and self-guided trips; the former work by setting up their own gate and charging a tariff for people going through the gate for a fixed trip, the aim being to fill up the seats of each boat launched. With such predictable goals, having a fixed number of user-days each year suits them just fine. The self-guided groups are far more often family and friends or friends of friends. Their concerns are for smaller trips and spending more time in the Canyon, to hike and explore. User-days are of no use to them, their planning is for one trip, of a congenial group, launching with a more or less detailed plan of where and when they will stop. As we will see, these differences set up a very bad situation due to the fact that commercial travel grew without let, while self-guided use numbers stayed relatively small. Indeed, as events turned out, it was all much worse than these simple examples convey.

In this initial period of unchecked commercial increases, motors were not always loved by all comm ops. In 1970, a long-established comm op, Grand Canyon Expeditions, owned by Ron Smith, was circulating a petition calling for the elimination of motors because they detracted from the wilderness experience. (Yes, this is the same comm op that 30 years later, and in other hands, devotes part of its website to the pro-motor fabrications.) Another reason cited by petition supporters was that the great increase in river traffic was in fact a great increase in motor-driven river traffic and comm ops who used motors. So, if motors were not allowed, there would be fewer trips and even fewer operators, thus less adverse impact on the river environment and on the river traveler. Smith stated that by the end of the season he had turned in 75 pages of signatures.[5] GCNP staff wrote to Smith in March that they proposed consideration be given to excluding motors at an in-house master plan review and were thinking about limiting the number of comm ops, not allowing "many more" than the 12 in 1969.[6] NPS noted that the Sierra Club, and self-guided users, were also calling for motor elimination, suggesting that the former had originated the idea. Smith's effort was, however, an independent one, and he asked the Club to help, since several large commercial outfitters were set against the idea.[7] Smith thought the Park Service "friendly" to the idea. (Dee Holladay recalls that NPS "stiffed" Smith and his initiative.) Barry Goldwater, then Senator from Arizona, joined in, "I am completely opposed to motors of any kind on the River." Goldwater, who had first traveled the river long enough ago (1940) that he considered himself a pioneer, insisted there would have to be an absolute limitation on the number of river trippers, to be determined by a scientific approach. He doubted the efficacy of chemical toilets.[8] GCNP thought 19 operators might be enough now, and there might have to be a maximum use. Pete Cowgill, a Tucson outdoor writer, reported that NPS Director Hartzog wanted a study soon of carrying capacity, noting that Goldwater and Representative Udall were in favor of limits.[9]

On the other hand, one rowing operator, Mexican Hat, re-invented itself as Canyoneers with some of the largest motor rafts on the river. The owner, Staveley, then attacked the Smith initiative, saying Smith had a company that was selling smaller rowing rafts and thus had "a rather pecuniary ulterior motive".[10] (This is an example of the kind of comm op rhetoric I mentioned above; Staveley was one of the more public practitioners.) He also engaged in some fuzzy math to express his fear that using just rowing craft would lead to a cut in the number of visitors, claiming that there are not enough "competent oarsmen available, nor would there ever be". As so often, the debate seemed to bring out the reckless side of the motor-boater; the world will come to an end unless you keep us around to save it.

The report that Georgie White, the first to run the big motorized trips, signed the Smith petition might have seemed a contrary straw. But any breeze against motors was countered by the strong wind set up by eight motorized comm ops who decided to organize. Six of these—Western, Cross, Hatch, Sanderson, Tour West, WhiteWater—are important to the story since they have remained as Grand Canyon comm ops. (See Reader's Guide Part C for these groupings.) Determined to keep motors, they formed the Colorado River Outfitters Association in September 1970, meeting at the home of Jack Currey, comm op for Secretary Udall's trip.

They wanted a group focussed on protecting motor use and on the Grand Canyon. CROA goals included maintaining the use of motors, a goal that has never changed, even as the group name and composition have. They also wanted to keep the same number of comm ops and solve the sanitation problem. They even tacked on the idea of preserving the Canyon in a pristine condition. Lovegren met with the group in October. He had expressed his satisfaction with the group's formation, since it dealt just with the Grand Canyon, although he wished all comm ops were members.[11] The next month, NPS announced it would now measure use by counting "people-days". It asked each comm op how many user-days (to use the name that was finally settled on) were needed as the company's economic minimum, and what number each wanted to grow to.[12]

Another limit being contemplated was that no permit or concession contract would be issued for operations that used helicopters. This was an NPS flanking action; GCNP could not directly ban helicopter use since what the comm ops plotted was to have the helicopters come down on Navajo or Hualapai land, not in the Park. (For a few years, one comm op, Fort Lee Company, ran 62-mile trips to Navajo land at the Little Colorado and then used helicopters to exit.) Lovegren then heard from and talked with a lawyer who was retained by both a helicopter operator and Currey's outfit. Government lawyers also came out against the Park's maneuver, due to its questionable legality, and because the comm ops had "extensive economic commitments". Also, helicopters make the Park more accessible, as Secretary of the Interior Walter Hickel wanted. So the Park Service was left to hope that exits using mules at Whitmore Wash or vehicles up Diamond Creek would be attractive enough to end use of helicopters with their noise and mechanized ending to a wilderness trip.

As the prime marker of "a clean beach", regulation of fecal waste disposal was sorely vexed by the failure of the privies at Nankoweap. One NPS staff suggested a pit filled with lime and sand, topped by a seat. This would be a temporary measure; using portable toilets was better. The eventual goal was to find a way to containerize fecal waste so that it could, along with other human leaving, be taken out of the Canyon. In May 1970, the Coconino County Health Department supported this goal in a report that said that the beaches were not suitable for privies and burying had reached its limit. The best course would be to remove fecal waste from the Canyon, perhaps using plastic bags in containers. (Prescient, but too soon.) This approach was reinforced by a federal opinion from the Health, Education and Welfare Department that burying was not the best way, and although it might be tried, if it fails, the waste should be carried out. NPS may have agreed in principle, but it stayed with chemical porta-potty "experiments", noting that a brush fire had ended the career of the Nankoweap privies. The inability of the GCNP staff to take county and federal health officials' advice meant that for several more years, boat trips would keep trying chemical toilets, dumping the contents in holes, and leaving blue-chemical stains as markers of waste on the beach. More NPS staff needed the exposure made vivid in a visitor's detailing of trash left behind, piles of garbage, visual and nasal effects of human excrement, a film of campfire smoke every morning, and destruction of archeological artifacts.[13]

The motor-boater effort paid off when, in November 1970, even as the debate was still growing and before any formal process was started to hear the public, Lovegren was blown the comm ops way. He wrote, and it is worth quoting in full for its sheer effrontery:

> "We are having a real difficult time with this motor, no-motor controversy. Originally my thinking was to come out with a strong no-motor position in the Master Plan. However, I feel that basically it is not honest. I would have a very difficult time pushing for a strictly no-motor approach. I have not been down the river in other than a motor powerboat. I really do not know how dangerous it is to row only. I feel that many of the people advocating no-motors really are concerned with carrying capacity, size of craft, etc. These matters can be handled with other management means."[14]

Here is a supposedly responsible official, confessing his ignorance, yet flabby-mindedly reaching policy conclusions only on the basis of personal thinking. There were no studies, no data, no paying attention to the range of opinion being voiced, no attempt to consult experts, no desire to cure his ignorance by taking a rowing trip. Worse, he took two motor trips with Arizona River Runners owned by Fred Burke. Burke was a former Republican state legislator with political connections he would use, and use on behalf of the motorizers in the years ahead.[15] So crucial a decision, made by so unprepared a person, was in violation of any sound idea of governmental process. With CROA's formation and Lovegren's immediate welcoming of it, is it unreasonable to see his tilt, not just as an indicator of the motor-boaters' determination to yield no ground, but of an NPS pre-disposition to give it to them? It is scarcely surprising that with this foundation, environmental advocates shortly felt justified in going around and over the Park Service.

I want to pause to discuss a preposterous notion. Why did the management of river traffic become so vexed a matter, so contentious so instantaneously in 1970, so troublesome even today, thirty-three years later, and counting? Let me turn this rock over and ask, in a puzzled way, why did the motor-boaters feel they had to fight so hard to preserve one particular way of going down the river—the fast, large, short trip? Throughout the debate, it was assumed and stated explicitly that should there be a change to a motor-free river, the comm ops would have time to make the transition in an economically favorable way. Why did the motor-boaters never accept the notion that they could have had decent businesses and profits running rowing trips? And that they could have reached this goal of a stable industry without ten years of controversy, and without their continuing fear that sometime the pro-wilderness forces would gain the upper hand? What made argument and controversy so much more attractive?

The other side can certainly accuse those of us arguing for wilderness and the elimination of motors of being readier to fight than compromise. Our answer was, and still is, that our position only has one element: a motor-free Grand Canyon Wilderness including the Colorado River. Within that parameter, the comm ops were welcome and even encouraged to provide their services and make a profit, since they would be providing a worthwhile Park experience, "enjoyment unimpaired" by the noise and anti-wilderness effects of motors.

Yes, I can understand that some might believe more profit is to be made from shorter, faster, bigger motor trips (although even that turned out not to be the case). I can understand that some might think there is more economic value in motor-based enterprises. I can understand that the rowing comm ops would have wanted to keep motors, since if everyone ran oar trips, the competition would have been tougher. Yet I still cannot understand, and so the reader is warned that I am more scornful than I might otherwise be, why this "extra" profit and these economic values should have produced such bitter argument by the comm ops when they could have had a good business under a wilderness rubric without the years, the decades, of battle. What made them so fierce? Why were they, are they, so incapable of envisioning a stable future in a wilderness environment? Why are they so determined to maintain a position that forces them to repeat their phony cover arguments about safety, convenience, elitism, cost, etc.?

It seems a controversy that need never have happened. Suppose right from 1966, the Park Service at Grand Canyon had acted on their governing principles of the Wilderness Act and the National Park Act, consistently making the decision for a motor-free wilderness. Suppose the comm ops had agreed, and worked with NPS to adjust their businesses to these principles over a reasonable time. Remember how quickly they went from 9 to 21 comm ops and 4,000 to 11,000 passengers—just three years. Yet they could not, would not, translate that business expansion experience into building a prosperous, non-contentious future. What they had at a particular moment was good enough; so never mind rosy visions of doing good business in a wilderness.

Again, did we cause the trouble by agitating for wilderness and motor elimination? Yet there is no law mandating motors (to the contrary), and there are laws setting forth our, America's, vision for places like the Grand Canyon, its National Park, and the wilderness there. And these laws, and that place, do create in the minds of many a priority, a vision, a goal worth fighting for. That was true in 1970; it remains true.

But in 1970, the comm ops were feeling no discomfort; business was booming. And according to the comm ops, "The canyon is in good condition, and is being cared for."[16] There seemed to be agreement, even from the Sierra Club, that the beaches were relatively clean; chemical toilets were surely helping to solve the human waste problem. Another potential problem dissolved when the Coast Guard, seeing the Colorado being navigated, wondered if it had jurisdiction, but then decided not to rock that boat. As 1971 went on, the Park Service was inching toward regularizing business through multi-year concession contracts, and now some Park staff thought that larger boats with motors and carefully monitored increases in use marked the right path.

Running the river was a trendy tourist item, and some researchers were getting stirred up. The Grand Canyon Natural History Association (GCNHA) was funding a couple of studies of visitors, who they were, and what they got out of the trips. Geologists had always studied the Canyon, but how Glen Canyon Dam affected the river and the shore was a new topic, and included interest in its biological diversity and how it was changing.

Once the idea of user-days was in place, the wriggling began to keep or gain advantage. The regularization of the permits stirred the smaller comm ops to agitate for more trips, or in the new jargon, a larger allocation of passenger- (or visitor- or user-) days.[17] Lawyers were busy writing letters, complaining that their clients did not have enough; others have more. In a clever side-step, the Park Service decided to exclude guides and other trip employees from the count of user-days, thus providing a bonus of about 15%, though actual use was not close to the new allocations, still based on comm op wishing. Of course, tracking use would be even more confusing. Commercial trips would now seem to have less impact than they actually did. Moreover, another class of user was created, one that ended up further stigmatizing self-guided river-runners, since they were not allowed to have guides. In September, the Superintendent moved more obviously to meet the comm ops wishes. He proposed a modest increase in their allocations for 1972, claiming it might go as high as 15%. He then let it rise to 33%.

In this quiet, the Sierra Club Board of Directors reaffirmed its opposition to motors, looking toward an effort to designate a Grand Canyon Wilderness. There had been a moment when the Park Service joined in this effort, basing its decisions on its laws. That moment was briefly grasped at in August 1970. The Park's Preliminary Wilderness Study said:

> "The desired river experience is felt to be the slow float trip in small
> parties without power. Management direction is to eliminate the
> motor from the river trip in a phased program prior to
> recommending to Congress the placement of the Colorado River in
> a wilderness."[18]

It was a shining moment, but one that did not become public, and it was only a moment. As related above, Lovegren put his personal biases first. The 1970 study was superseded by the Park's January 1971 Preliminary Wilderness Study that said:

> "The desired river experience is felt to be the slow float trip in
> small parties. Management direction is to control motorboat use on
> the river. However, the plan for continued use of motors precludes
> wilderness classification for the river itself."[19]

Buried at its end, the document recalled NPS policy, "Boating, except with motorboats and airboats, is an acceptable use of park wilderness." Faced with a clear choice, the Park Service at Grand Canyon had chosen motorboats instead of wilderness, fast recreation instead of Park-level quality. As so often, the lower-quality use drove out the higher-quality. This course was not stumbled into. The Park's own staff knew the no-motor wilderness choice was the one that accorded with policy, and had proposed it. That choice, though not then controversial, had been endorsed by the previous Superintendent in March 1968 (see Chapter 1). But all this weighed too little on Lovegren compared with the pressures exerted by the motor boaters with whom he said he exclusively cavorted.

A third way was available because the Wilderness Act of 1964 incorporated a loophole saying that while the Act generally prohibited motorboat use, it could continue where it had already become established, subject to any restrictions determined to be desirable. The Act applied this provision specifically to the Secretary of Agriculture. To gain the same discretionary authority, Interior Department legislation to establish wilderness areas includes this loophole and indeed, any others that apply to the Secretary of Agriculture. So the 1971 recommendation could have included the river, but subject to this loophole. What would have happened had this course been adopted stirs the joys of speculation. The action would have shifted first to Congress, where there would have been a big fight. If Congress waffled and left final action to the Secretary, then it would have come back to the Park Service, but years later. Possibly Lovegren did not appreciate the value of this loophole, or perhaps he really did think the river should be the site of motorized recreation.

The Park Service's position was not clarified in its GCNP Master Plan.[20] This skimpy document suggested: uncontrolled use will end wilderness; sanitation problems were appearing; people's interest will lead to congestion; motor noise will reach undesirable levels. And so on, as if these conditions might come about in some future time. It wound up its fantasy by praising the experience it planned to degrade by continuing motors:

"The most desirable river experience is felt by some persons to be the slow, 10-to-15-day float trip, in small parties, without power— a true wilderness experience."

Those "some persons" did not include the Superintendent. In a letter justifying motor use, Lovegren skipped past the fundamental issue, ignoring the law-abiding language of the 1970 wilderness study.[21] He admitted that his staff had thought the motor ban would be a good solution because it would limit passengers and cut the sanitation problem. However, Lovegren said, he wanted to attack each "problem" head on. He parroted the motor-boater line on safety and cost, even swallowing the claims about motor noise coming and going in a moment. He took up one part of the anti-motor argument, that it would limit the number of visitors, pretending he was going to do that anyway. He was unworried about motor noise and boasted there would be a maximum horsepower. And, in a burst of braggadocio, he said if conditions were not satisfactory by January 1974, motors would be banned. (Actually, the new concession contracts he was working on would lock everything in for years beyond that.) The views in this letter were presented as interim guidelines in the Master Plan, and by and large were immediately violated, e.g., limit on number of outfitters, number of user-days, reduction of motor noise and emissions, and helicopter takeouts.

The public, however, knew what the fundamental issue was, and when the hearings mandated by the Wilderness Act were held on May 15, 1971, the Park Service was told that its rationale of safer, more available trips was an anti-Park and anti-Wilderness smokescreen. Preliminary work had been done by the Sierra Club when, on March 25, it resolved in favor of a ban on motors, which it had not done two years earlier in approving its master plan. Now the Club felt that motors must be prohibited to maintain the wilderness qualities of the Colorado River in the Grand Canyon, a position it knew a few of the trip operators favored. This resolution was passed even though the Club had been chartering motorized trips in the Canyon, a practice it would soon end.

Twelve local and national organizations supported The Wilderness Society's Grand Canyon Wilderness proposal. It called for including the river and a total of 850,000 acres compared to the Park Service proposal of 505,000.[22] Even so, their leaflet picked up on the Wilderness Act loophole, noting that the law provided for keeping established motorboat use, and so claiming that wilderness designation for the river ought not to be dependent on eliminating motorboats. This have-it-both-ways position melted away when the fight got hot. Two stalwarts of the position that there should be a rowing-only wilderness were starting to publicize their views: Arizona Senator Barry Goldwater and his friend, Fred Eiseman, a self-guided river-runner who had taken his first trip in 1954, and who volunteered time and effort to GCNP support organizations. Their views were echoed by Ben Avery, outdoors columnist for the largest Phoenix newspaper. As Ben said, "Only a leisurely trip with oars can give such a trip its full meaning, and it is the exploration and enjoyment of the many side canyons that reveal the full beauty and historic significance of the Canyon."[23] These Arizonan views, the gold standard in coming years, were not listened to yet by the Park Service, which also ignored almost everybody else.

Thirty people went to the Phoenix hearings to make various statements; many more wrote. Those who attended heard a soon-to-be-superseded Regional Director use safety and convenience to justify motors. Park ideals prevailed over convenience for most, however, and in the final tally, 700 people urged that a GCNP wilderness include the river. The Park Service plan had 13 supporters.[24]

But the Park Service had made its bed, and preferred to stay under its covers. The August 1971 recommendation stayed the same, the final recommendation in November insisting that the river could not be included because motor use was to be continued. NPS indifference to its own policies and to the public response was capped by the letter of transmittal sent by the Secretary of the Interior to the President asserting that the majority of comments were favorable to wilderness.[25] To the Park Service, the covers seemed all smooth, the corners tucked in. The Park Service had prepared what it thought would be permanent rest for the idea of a motor-free Wilderness in the Grand Canyon.

CHAPTER 3

1972: Damming the Flood

Meeting the Folks

For me, 1972 was a good year; after three years (the same period Lovegren was superintendent) living elsewhere, I returned to the Southwest in late August of 1972. No doubt as a consequence of being personally present, I see that year as the hinge on which the struggle over river policy caused a move from one set of basic assumptions to another. This is no attempt to lay claim to any personal impact, only a warning that my participation and the records I could now collect do color my sense of 1972's importance.

My reappearance was not the only difference in personnel.[1] Chief among the actors who showed up at this time was the new Superintendent, Merle Stitt, Lovegren having faded away in this crucial year of dealing with his mess. Also relatively new was the post of river manager, occupied by Bob Yearout, a specialist in dealing with the businesses having concessions at the Park. Stitt's immediate boss was also new, for the Park had been shifted, administratively, from the Southwest to the Western Region. The Regional Director, Howard Chapman, and Stitt were tried hard throughout the 1970s; Merle so much that he died of a heart attack right after retiring—those books about Grand Canyon deaths should include his name. A moment of silence here for a gentle man riding a chip in a maelstrom. Howard rode the storm as well, from San Francisco to D.C., up to the heights and then down into the ignominious 1980s. Angry as I would too often get at them in years to come, I do believe they tried.

Others already present, especially Fred Eiseman, Senator Goldwater, and Sierra Club Southwest Representative John McComb, ratcheted up their involvement.

Activity was focussed in this year by the addition of a new arena, an advisory group to the Park on river matters, composed of people with varying views who could offer and react to ideas on river management.[2] Membership included comm ops (four motor boaters), conservationists (Eiseman, McComb, plus Bill Winter from the National Wildlife Federation) and two researchers (Brickler and Taylor). Several had organized and run their own trips. Such advisory groups encourage people of differing views to come together and confront each other's distortions. They are a fine antidote to the ascendancy of any one interest, which is why this one lapsed after a short life, doomed by the rush of events and antagonism.

The number of comm ops had doubled in my absence, reaching 21. The motor-boaters had their CROA, the Colorado River Outfitters Association, and connections to congressional stalwarts like Senator Moss (D-Utah) and Congressman Steiger (R-Arizona). The 21 were a mix of "old" Colorado hands, like White, Hatch, Staveley, and Currey, and newcomers jumping on the gravy train. Certainly noteworthy was that Martin Litton, stalwart against the dams (which most comm ops had not been), had moved into the commercial ranks, launching as a business the running of trips using the wooden dories that so many of us believe give the best trip of all.

Fred Burke is worth mentioning, both as one of the chief pro-motor lobbyists and for leaving some of his papers to Northern Arizona University for all to consult. By and large, though, this bunch is not a sight for me to detail; they must have admirers who can fill out river history with an account of the river traffic business. To help orient the reader, in the Reader's Guide Part C, I have attempted to trace comm op lineages and bring together other information on this near-closed group.

In place of lurid details about joy among the motor-boaters, here are a few thoughts about the joys of political conflict. Controversy is a riotous stew of intellect and emotion, so bound up in each other that when combatants state what they claim is a fact on their side, they get a glow from it. The declamation of arguments, sober and otherwise, engenders a sense of well-being, even power. Contestants listen to themselves and their allies and feel *right*, justified, healthy. To hear an enemy twisting the truth brings a surge of righteous anger. These are not universal human traits. For people not involved, or who are repelled by conflict, the tendency is to stand back, even decry unnecessary (verbal) violence, speak up for the middle ground, compromise. This is irrelevant to the strugglers; the hunt is on, the wind is up, so charge, blowing horns, lances lowered! What thrills! To be right! To be telling the truth to power and to your enemies! The mixture is the headier because it has nothing to do with the content of the argument; it has to do with the sense of being true, of having something worthwhile to defend and/or advance, of needing to win in order that decay and death be staved off.

Nor is argument to be discounted; history is full of passionate outsiders whose views later become orthodoxy in spite of obdurate opposition from accepted wisdom. Americans have a guarantee of free speech, we have a *right* to speak freely, although that is not the same as a right to what we speak freely about. There is no constitutional right to use motors or to enjoy wilderness; there is a right to argue about these activities. Somehow this all comes together in our minds as conviction: I *believe* my arguments for a motor-free wilderness and the Park are right. Motor boaters *believe* they provide a necessary, appropriate, non-harmful public service. The comm ops *believe* in profit as a justification for their actions. I *believe* every person who wants to go on the river should have an equal chance in any year, without regard to economics and wealth. This emotional-intellectual activity of believing, and then acting to project those beliefs into policy, is too often dismissed as subjective or biased. I think rather that it is a legitimate, valid human way of grappling with our differences. Even the only valid way, if the alternative is imposed decisions. Yet sometimes arguments seem to go on forever. Colorado River-running policy is still a battleground after thirty-five years (and Colorado River Basin policy in all its manifestations for far longer; on the other hand, there was a final decision on the dams). Is there ever to be a resolution? The range of answers, good and bad, has to include that some conflicts do not get resolved. Administrative declarations, legislative acts, compromise and suppression, jousting in courts, exhaustion and death; all have been tried on river matters. The fight for our beliefs goes on, even as the "we" changes.

Anyway. There are lots of people I have not introduced here; we will meet them in a more chronologically proper place. There are also those you can only wonder about at the time; who else was playing a quieter, more shadowy role we did not know about? After the fact, we may get to identify them. It could also be that there are some we will never know. Certainly, some we are not rid of yet.

Smooth Running for the Concessionaires

The winter is a quiet time on the river; a time for meetings and consideration of what comes next. The beginning of 1972 was not revolutionary; the concessionaires were in charge. In response to the Park Service's September 1971 prospectus for concession contracts, Lovegren reported, 21 had applied for and as of 1972 were protected by five-year contracts.[3] This was the same number as had been issued single-year permits in 1970-1, with one dropping out, and another, using dories, added. No significant new competitors had applied. Nine wannabes, Lovegren sniffed, offered nothing new. He went on, in a defense that was closer to a swan song, that the "cosmetic" problem of trash on the beaches was "licked", thanks to the comm ops. Motors would become less of a problem; they would be improved, cutting noise, air, and water pollution. CROA was so pleased with its cleanup plans that it told Lovegren they did not want any system of monitoring beach use.[4] It also complained about the impact of self-guided river parties, and comm ops passed on to the Park Service anecdotes of behavior they did not like. Chemical toilets, Lovegren continued, were helping. We are limiting summer use. Research is needed, he said, but since the beaches are better and use is being spread out, increasing use is justified.

During his three years, use had already increased, by two-and-one-half times. As an aide to Congressman Sam Steiger—a good friend of the comm ops—noted, Lovegren had a remarkable ability to see through red tape to the real point of the problem.[5] By "real point", the aide no doubt meant Lovegren's help for the comm ops. On the other hand, in mid-1972, Lovegren was off to a new job.

Another support for the Lovegren "Let the good times roll" policy, came from a Master's thesis based on questionnaires to a sample of those commercial passengers who had run the river in previous years.[6] Major findings included the high-income status of half the passengers (though somehow, this never got translated by the comm ops into an admission that they were catering to an elite), and that everybody really, really enjoyed the trip. Overwhelmingly, visitors had enough vacation time for a full rowing trip (only 10% had less than two full weeks—another finding that the comm ops ignored; indeed, they have always claimed their truncated motor trips were necessary because Americans do not have enough vacation). However, what the author, M. A. Boster, emphasized, in a preview presentation at the Park in February, was that the visitors did not perceive the Canyon as crowded, and therefore "the Colorado River is capable of carrying many more people on more trips with little or no contact with other expeditions on the River." This was helpful to Lovegren as well in his meeting with concessionaires that month, where he agreed that it was important to get them a sound economic base. This had become a more weighty matter, because the comm ops were now operating under those five-year concession contracts. What the Park Service had contracted for, was to provide each comm op with an allocation of a certain number of user-days each year. So each concessionaire, pushing for a larger allocation of more user-days and thus potentially more business, was only trying to reach that goal of a sound economic base. This was fine with Lovegren; he announced he would meet with each comm op to discuss their needs. What would he hear?

Fred Burke, founder of Arizona River Runners, did leave us a picture of his good points, as he argued in 1972 for a 1973 allocation of 3000 user-days, leading someday to 6000 user-days.[7] He cited his investment in land and facilities nearby, and what he had spent on equipment. He had done "extensive" advertising allowing him to fill his 1972 quota, and even though he had a loss in 1971, he never cut his price "in order to push people down the Canyon and build up our allotment". "We are honest and aboveboard". He was retired from the army, and so could work at a reduced rate. He believed in limits, he said, on maximum passengers per trip and on overall use.

Of course, what all this pleading would come down to was that each comm op could make an excellent case for increasing its allocation, which meant that the overall so-called limit would keep increasing. Sometimes the increase was direct, and sometimes it was done through re-definitions such as not counting employees (and there were worries that some employees were really customers) or changing the season dates or adding on "educational" supplements. This flimflam was necessary as long as the Park Service chose to speak with a forked tongue, helping its now-contractual concessionaires increase their economic base while pretending it was setting an overall limit in order to conserve the riverine environment and the visitor experience. In fact, as mentioned before, that overall limit was more or less a sum of comm op dreams each year. From the point of view of the Park Service mission, the number was, and remains, arbitrary and irrelevant, having no basis in information gathered to help conserve the Park and provide an unimpaired enjoyment.

Here are some accounting footnotes to make the above concrete:[8]

Commercial Allotments and Actual Use 1970-1972

	1970	1971	1972
Allotment, in u-d			
Visitors	N/A	*80,000	105,000
Total (includes crew)	N/A	91,400	*120,000
Actual Use, in u-d			
Visitors	62,800	66,000	88,100
Total (includes crew)	72,000	66,000	104,900
Total people	9,500	10,500	15,900
Days per person (average length)	7.6	6.3/7.2	6.6
Trips	307	387	548

(The allotment numbers without * are from NPS. The two numbers with * are my estimates, based on the conservative assumption there was one crew member for every seven passengers.)

No, I don't believe those 1971 numbers either, though there was a pause in increases due to the overall economy and individual company matters. The reason 66,000 appears in two contradictory places is that different NPS documents use different labels. Nevertheless, the increases in allotment and use from 1970 to 1972 are obvious. Just for fun, I put in the calculation for average trip length, figuring 1971 two ways. The 7.2 average trip length would be the result if the total of crew and visitors were 76,000. This makes some sense, since shortening of trips is a long-term trend. However, that 1.3-day drop for 1971 looks too drastic. From 1971 to 1972, NPS made tracking the numbers harder by changing the allotment accounting so the number did not include crew. Numbers were important because Lovegren was claiming there was a "modest increase", about "15 per cent".[9] Using my estimates, Lovegren's modest increase was twice what he claimed, over 30%. He also did a bit of a shell game by citing a total use that included self-guided users, while writing about the increase as if it were just commercial use.

As it turned out, from 1971 to 1972, the increase in the number of trips was over 40%, in the number of people, 50%, as the comm ops worked to make sure the 1971 slow-down was only temporary. It does seem to be true that the total including crew of actual user-days in 1972 equaled the allotment for visitors only. Yet, since the "limit" of 105,000 passenger-days was not reached, there was room for another jump in actual use, of up to 20%, in 1973. The comm ops, as we will see, were not content with that prospect. They had come to expect a steep growth path since 1965; here is a summary (the figures are rounded, and are of people including crew):

Year	1965	1966	1967	1968	1969	1970	1971	1972
People	550	1100	2000	3500	5800	9500	10,500	15,900

Not unexpectedly, the nine comm ops operating in 1966 dominated that growth. In 1972, they had three-fourths of the use; the twelve add-ons shared the other quarter. Six of the early birds accounted for two-thirds of the use. And although there have been shifts in comm op personnel, as well as agglomerations that have reduced the comm ops from 21 to 15 in 2003, the comm ops descending from those six still control two-thirds of the use. (See Reader's Guide Part C.) This is more than one of those interesting facts; it is a marker for the conservatism—some might say stability, others rigidity—of Grand Canyon river-running. It is, I will try to show, conservatism based on a so far unshakeable institutionalized political status quo.

The above numbers have not come easily. The Park Service, over the decades, has committed a great disservice by not annually publishing consistent records including the numbers, allotted and actual, of people and of user-days, broken down by visitors and crew, for all the different categories of use and user. There have been a few periods, such as parts of the 1970s and early 1990s, when the information effort was creditable. The lack of a full record not only makes history-writing more difficult, it raises suspicions.

River management, a management of unsatisfied demand for a fragile resource, is controversial, yes. Even if it were not, non-disclosure would be a vexed matter because the comm ops are privileged users of the public's lands. Their claim, and NPS support of it, that making some data public might reveal trade secrets heightens the sense that the regulators and the regulated might be, behind closed doors, cooking up nefarious schemes to exploit public resources while keeping the public out in the dark. The need for public confidence in NPS policy-making is surely far greater than any danger of commercial espionage (or embarrassment).

If NPS figures are credible—and the point is that they were used in setting policy, they became policy, and thus provoked endless squabbling—then the average days a person spent in the Canyon on a commercial trip dropped from 7.6 in 1970 to 6.6 in 1972, which stands as another measure of the pressure exerted by the user-day concept to trim trip length and/or of the increasing predominance of the short-fast-big motorized trips. After all, if you have a fixed overall allocation, and you can shorten the time each passenger spends, you can run more trips and sell more seats. To some degree, these are rubbery numbers, since endpoints for trips varied—there were four main ones, and visitors could take partial trips. As well, the days/trip figure varied from one comm op to another, all the way from the rush-em-through trips taking less than 5 days, to the rowing companies, averaging 12 days and above. The five largest companies, some of whom offered rowing trips, took average times of from 5.5 to 7 days per trip.

Numbers do not count, the sage said, only counters count. And while the comm ops could count 1972 to be a triumph as they moved almost 14,000 people on their trips, they did not count on how upsetting this huge increase would sound when publicized in the context of Lovegren's statements that use was being limited and that environmental and social research was needed. His credibility was further undermined by his suggestion that special consideration should be given to small rowing trips to preserve variety, followed by his awarding the massive increases requested by the largest comm ops for motor trips. Had these increases come out of a real NPS policy of basing use and limits on resource impacts while enhancing choice, he would have followed through by assigning any increases to the small rowing comm ops. Taking such actions, however, is part of what a strong Superintendent does.

Grand Canyon's Friends Counterattack

Even early in 1972, there were signals of concern. Fred Eiseman wrote to both Sierra Club staffer McComb and Senator Goldwater.[10] Eiseman knew Goldwater from a trip the latter took on which the former was a boatman. However, Eiseman's interest in the Canyon was more extensive; he was involved in NPS-related advisory and support groups. Goldwater's interest went back even further; to a 1940 trip when it really was a near-pioneering adventure every time. That adventure translated to legislative interests; his first attempt to enlarge the Park was in the 1950s, and he was dedicated to the idea. However, like most public Arizonans, he was tainted by his support for the Grand Canyon dams, and, reciprocally, did not trust conservation groups who always wanted more. McComb was more land-based; he was a backpacker of wide and deep experience. More importantly, he had been a fighter for Canyon protection since the 1960s' dam fight. As Southwest Representative after I left in 1969, he was the point man for the Club advocacy of the concept I had introduced in early 1966 of a "complete" Grand Canyon National Park. In short, all three had extensive and intensive concern for, in support of, (forget the dam, forget the dam) Grand Canyon and its National Park status.

Eiseman worried to Goldwater about the seemingly uncontrolled growth in river traffic. Goldwater replied that he was drafting legislation to impose strict controls, keeping the river trip a wilderness experience. Goldwater also wrote about his great difficulty in getting a Park expansion bill started because the conservation groups opposed him with a different approach. (His proposals had been pretty minimal.) So Eiseman suggested to McComb a meeting of these "intelligent and sensitive individuals" to reconcile what he hoped were only minor differences of opinion. He continued to push this idea as the year went on.

Meanwhile, McComb queried Lovegren about the increases, doubtful about a policy that only depended on visitors not objecting, and suspicious that some comm ops would try to count visitors as boat crew to get more on a trip.[11] The lack of Park Service concern was evidenced at the July 17 meeting of the new river advisory committee, at which a further increase was proposed. The 1973 allotments were to be held to the 105 KUD (KUD = thousand user-days) 1972 total for visitors. However, 10 KUD more would be available for anyone who needed extra at the end of the season. This meeting was attended by four motorized comm ops and a number of other people, not all fully aware of the concerns, including the new GCNP Superintendent, Merle Stitt. Neither Eiseman nor McComb were present.[12] The Park Service stated there was unanimity for this increase, though this was later denied. Whatever the status of the group's agreement, that was the end of quiet on the Colorado.

On July 27, Eiseman, having returned from a river trip, fulminated to Goldwater and others about the additional 10 KUD, as well as the over-100 encounters he had had with mostly commercial parties on his six-week trip.[13] He again proposed a meeting to hash out differences. Goldwater replied that he was in complete agreement on meeting, since he had heard from many this year who feared the river and its banks were already wrecked. He also wrote to Secretary of the Interior Rogers Morton (remember him from Chapter 1, one of the congressmen from that ill-fated 1967 motor trip) that something had to be done about the increase in river traffic. He noted that in 1940 he had been the 70th person ever to run the river. Now there were 12,000 people each year, and there was no way the river or the banks or the tributaries could handle this many people. The Canyon bottom was going to be completely desecrated and extremely unhealthy, with a dangerous problem in sanitation. He went on to complain that the Park Service had just handed the decision along, hoping something would happen. (As I was to learn, Goldwater's style often relied on inflated statements, passionately stated. Given his position, and his aversion to personal confrontation, he nevertheless could be effective. His intervention at this point must have made a difference. And if he had not…?)

Eiseman attacked again on August 16, writing to Morton, Goldwater, the Sierra Club, Superintendent Stitt, and others, saying that the problem was "simple".[14] We do not have the research done to determine carrying capacity, and over the several years the research will take, it is sensible to limit traffic severely. NPS, on the contrary, keeps increasing the use. There should be strict controls on user-days immediately, lest damage be done before we know what the carrying capacity of the riverine environment is. If there were a wilderness designation and a motorboat ban, this would automatically limit the number who would and could make the trip. (Lovegren had already manipulated this argument to scuttle having to face up to a wilderness recommendation.) Fred concluded by urging a meeting to discuss river travel, wilderness, and the master plan. All concerned can then discuss, compromise, and present a common front ("all", but no comm ops were invited).

Innocent, I returned to the Southwest in August, and visited the new Superintendent. Just imagine; I had taken a little hike down the Hermit Trail with my three kids, and then waltzed up to Stitt's office, where he welcomed me in and we talked for half an hour – those were different times. On September 1, I summarized to him what I had heard him say, after discussing my visit with John McComb.[15] Stitt had talked about visitor use of 90 KUD in 1972, and the limit being the same for 1973 plus 10 KUD to be allocated at his discretion. However, the numbers I came up with, including crew (those, too, are real impacts, after all), showed that the use could reach 130 KUD, i.e., 105 KUD for passengers + 15 KUD for crew + 10 KUD for season-end additions. Yet the master plan set a 70 KUD limit. We are alarmed, Mr. Stitt; please explain.

Sidelight: on August 8, Currey's Western River Expeditions, one of the largest Grand Canyon comm ops, which also ran other rivers, sent out a letter to clients who had signed up to run in the Dinosaur National Monument.[16] The day before, the Park Service had announced that the maximum number of river visitors had been reached in Dinosaur, and trips would have to go to another place. So Western told its customers, even though they had signed up for Dinosaur, it was switching Dinosaur trips to the Desolation Canyon on the Green River. Just like that. Keep the contrast with Dinosaur in mind as we deal with the fuss, muss, and congressional outcry downstream. It seems curious that the comm ops did not follow the Dinosaur example in the Grand Canyon, but then, it is a special place, for better, and for the worst it brings out in some.

By early September, Eiseman had set up an October 25 meeting, which Goldwater said he would attend, at the Museum of Northern Arizona (MNA) in Flagstaff, to discuss river traffic and research, and wilderness designation in the Park.[17] As well, he wanted to discuss the reviving project to expand the boundaries of Grand Canyon National Park.

At the same time, the Park advised the comm ops that the 10 KUD addition would not be just a discretionary add-on, but an educational supplement, to make it more possible to run cheaper trips out of the high season for school-organized groups.[18] There could be no promises of additional user-days in 1973. However, if an allotment was under 3 KUD, a comm op could ask for more. (This applied to half the comm ops, and what do you know, if they were all brought up to 3 KUD, the total additional use would be 10 KUD. By the way, all the user-day numbers here refer to passengers, unless I specify "total" to include crew.) Stitt also called on the advisory committee to attend a September 25 meeting to discuss the issues raised in the letters Goldwater and Eiseman had written to the Secretary. And at this busy time, the Park Service acknowledged there had been a number of accidents at House Rock Rapid this year, including one drowning when a motor rig tipped over.

One member of the advisory committee, Vern Taylor of Prescott College, sent members a pre-meeting report on his August river trip. He recorded a number of rude actions on the part of comm ops including the no-no of camping in Redwall Cavern, blocking the course of his boats, defecating and leaving trash on beaches, even near Taylor's camp, overcrowding at Hance Rapid, racing for camps, etc. He concluded that boat employees needed to be educated and licensed. The chemical toilets had to be more available, and he was worried about the chemicals being buried on the beaches. He criticized beach clean-up of waste water, wet garbage, and fire pits. Several were so smelly and dirty they needed to be closed. At the end, he commended a few comm ops.

Comm op Staveley tried to deal with the blasts from Goldwater by writing directly to Secretary Morton.[19] He claimed there was no dangerous sanitation problem on the river, just as the news was breaking of a dysentery epidemic there (see below). He defended the Park Service, saying Goldwater was too hard. NPS had asked the comm ops to observe limits, and they were. (He did not point out that the so-called limits were comm op blue-sky requests, were way above use, and were raised each year.) He asserted "user-day consumption has been held at virtually the same level at which it was frozen in 1971". (However, as the numbers above show, the ceiling had been raised from 91.4 KUD in 1971 to 105 KUD in 1972, while use went from 66 KUD to 105 KUD including crew, a number not broken out in 1971). He claimed the comm ops were blamed for litter from hikers, self-guided river trips, and the Navajo Reservation; there was practically no trash along the river. He implied use was being spread out, relieving congestion. (In fact, spreading out use over each week and through the season remains a perennial problem.) Staveley then claimed that the river experience derives from the canyon and the river, not from the means of conveyance. (The greatest ally the motor-boaters have is that the Grand Canyon is so magnificent a place that trivial matters like dirty beaches, sunburn, crowding, motor noise and stink, snakebite, dysentery, and raft-flipping do not stop visitors from being enchanted and overwhelmed. As someone said, you could go in a battle cruiser and still have the greatest time of your life. A small battle cruiser.)

The September 25 advisory meeting centered on the argument over quotas. Since McComb obtained permission for me to attend, the comm ops also added a couple of allies. Eiseman attacked, calling for a limit of 70 KUD.[20] The comm ops pushed their line of business survival, then in a conciliatory mood offered to put up $3000 for designing the research study that the Park Service thought might cost $350,000. The CROA commentary on this meeting focussed on Eiseman's attacks, crowing that once CROA had proposed funding the research proposal, everybody was on its side and Eiseman didn't have a leg to stand on. My notes from this first encounter with the comm ops included references to them such as "the ol' compromiser" and "unctuously offensive".

Nevertheless, a September 27 meeting confirmed even more trouble for the comm ops. On September 7, a meeting of health officials in Flagstaff revealed a dysentery-type epidemic on the river. The consensus was that boating employees needed health cards, and the 27th was set as a meeting to take action. For the meeting, a federal report was prepared. Through much of the summer, people on a number of river trips had come down with shigellosis, a thoroughly unpleasant intestinal disease likely spread by the failure of boating employees to use and encourage proper sanitation procedures, including hand-washing. The report said "the scope of the epidemic was large", "as many as 50 percent of river travelers in June and July may have been ill."[21] At least seven boat companies were involved. At the September 27th meeting, attended by county, state, and federal health officials, as well as comm ops, the Park Service, Eiseman, and me, there was a strong effort by the comm ops to continue pretending that they could police themselves. A research proposal countered this, noting that the US Public Health Service had approved chemical toilets on certain conditions, which had not been satisfied.[22] The evidence was that the comm ops were not training their crews well or were not making sure the rules were obeyed, resulting in an estimated one in ten river passengers getting sick that summer. The first result of this meeting was a draft of rules by county health officials; I called it "atrociously weak".

Eiseman fired another September salvo, asking the Park Service for an environmental impact statement (EIS) on the 10 KUD educational increase.[23] Let's pause here to introduce our friend, NEPA and its child, the Environmental Impact Statement (EIS). Protection of the environment, as a full-fledged governmental charge, was codified at the beginning of 1970 by the National Environmental Policy Act (NEPA). That Act directed the preparation of statements on the environmental impact of major actions recommended by federal agencies. All federal agencies were to be in compliance with NEPA's provisions by July 1, 1971. Theoretically, then, this evaluative tool was available to GCNP, when it moved from yearly permits to five-year contracts for the comm ops, when it stopped counting crew against the comm op allotments (an average of 20% of the passenger level), and when it raised the passenger use limit to 105 KUD for 1972. GCNP knew that the actual total use in 1970 and 1971 hovered around 70 KUD. And it knew that if the so-called limit for 1972 were reached, comm ops' impact would have increased to about 125,000 total user-days. There were therefore (looked at in light of what is common practice today) plenty of grounds for an EIS on river management in the last half of 1971. That there was no call for an EIS in 1971 or early 1972 represents the newness of the idea, I hope, rather than a failure of vigilance on the part of the Canyon's guardians, governmental or not.

Now Eiseman was using our new friend, NEPA. In his letter, he also claimed to be working on an injunction, the first whisper of the coming deep involvement by the third branch of government. He scoffed at the comm ops' claim of a right for economic survival, saying that economic considerations should not have one iota of importance in allotment decisions.

McComb joined in, regretting his previous neglect of GCNP, dismayed that the financial well-being of some small businesses could dominate the management of the river in the Grand Canyon.[24] The claim by comm ops that they were dependent on good river conditions is not convincing; some things may be beneficial to their passengers and still inappropriate in a national park. McComb asked that GCNP prepare an EIS, thus informing the public and requiring the Park Service to carefully think out its actions. An EIS prior to previous increases would have prevented present controversy, so please seek the best course from here, instead of merely justifying the past.

At the same time, eddying in a backwater of its own, the Washington directorate of the Park Service published its Grand Canyon National Park Wilderness Recommendation.[25] Changed only at the margins from the proposals we had denounced as completely inadequate, that Recommendation continued the line that "the Colorado River does not qualify because of the use of motors on the river". Unlike the river management changes for 1972, there was an EIS for this Recommendation. The EIS language about the river was curiously different from the proposal itself, "The Colorado River is excluded, due to present usage of motors on float trips." Yet the draft wilderness legislation gave the Secretary the power to continue that present usage, if desirable, even within the designated wilderness. So why exclude the river?

To confound matters even more, the Recommendation called for certain lands, not including the river, that had "temporary" encumbrances—grazing, private lands, too much forest fire fuel—to be classified as "potential wilderness", which meant that once the encumbrance was lifted, the Secretary could make it a full-fledged wilderness. Used many times since, "potential wilderness" apparently was an innovation, since the five occurrences of the phrase are pasted in over the phrase "wilderness reserve"—yet a shrinking violet by any other name still cannot hold its head up. If potential worked for grazed lands, why not even more so for motored waters? Anyway, the real issue is that the river should have been included in a motor-free Wilderness. Period.

In the section on adverse effects, the environmental statement failed to note that there would be an adverse effect on wilderness lands if motorboats were allowed right through, as Canyon friends called it, the "heart" of the Canyon, the park, the wilderness. The report duly recorded in its summary of responses that the public favored more wilderness, and inclusion of the river, by 7 to 1. Too small almost by half, and soon to be totally irrelevant, this proposal can stand as a monument to bureaucratic fuzzy-mindedness and inertia, a marker for the Lovegren era.

The culmination of the efforts of Eiseman and Goldwater occurred out of the limelight. In early October the Assistant Secretary of the Interior responsible for Parks, Nathaniel Reed, chose to set the 1973 allotment at 1972 actual use. That is, instead of 105 KUD for passengers, maximum use would be 89 KUD. (Use stayed at this level through the 1970s; nobody went out of business.) Reed later took full credit for this decision. Relevant Park Service staff may not even have known about the change beforehand. They were all on the river checking the place out from October 2 through 8: the river manager, deputy superintendent, superintendent, regional director, Lake Mead superintendent, science advisor, and others. One could see this as a time when they bonded, girding up for the tough fight ahead. Or at least got a real appreciation of the place they were charged with protecting. I wonder if it was a rowing or a motor trip.

Hard at work, however, though still ignorant of the Reed decision, I wrote Stitt that the comm op line that their boat staff, once on the river, were free of surveillance, was no reason not to adopt sound health rules and then enforce them.[26] And enforcement would happen, if the Park Service insisted on it happening. I also followed Eiseman in suggesting that, if we put our heads together, we could come up with plans for a motor-free river and for how to manage river use in the future. I joined in the call for an EIS on river-running. In the course of research for this book, I found my letter in the Park Service archives. It had hand-written notes on it by Deputy Superintendent Bruce Shaw:[27]

> "I don't agree, as a park manager, with the No motors bit for the River—Is the mechanical bit the test for Wilderness? possibly manufactured ... boats are also an intrusion. Being a bit facetious, perhaps only 'bull boats' should be allowed in a Wilderness Waterway—Also perhaps a motor-free optimum number of people on the river would be less than the river could carry. I do think Mr. Ingram has expressed some of the feelings that many of us are concerned over—the control or lack of, by NPS over its concessionaires. This, I know, you are aware, is because of many factors, not the least of which is Manpower and Funds for us to carry out properly our mission. Bruce."

Mr. Shaw remained in his position throughout the 1970s. Unlike us, Sisyphus knew of the boulder he had to keep rolling uphill.

CROA met on October 16, and worked as if they knew they had a problem. Each member was assessed to raise the $3000 for the research proposal.[28] They acknowledged that the wilderness proposal protected motor use, though that could change with "little" effort. They worked out rules to ease congestion at five often-crowded places. They called racing for camps unethical and frowned on switching loads out of one boat to lighten it so it could motor ahead and grab a camp. Still, they thought a clean camp allowed leaving liquid waste and ashes. At the end, they urged support for a comm op who was running for the Arizona Senate. Apart from this last, they sent on their ideas to the Park.[29]

Eiseman, meanwhile and still not knowing about Reed's decision, was setting up the October 25 agenda, including a 1973 quota, a research program to determine carrying capacity, and a wilderness proposal that included the river.[30] His background material made the case for a severe limit on river-running based on the need to hold some line until the impacts on the ecosystem and the river experience were studied. He used his experience to describe the bad conditions: smell of gas, quiet pools full of people, races for campsites. He noted there had been no EIS, and that the wilderness proposal was inconsistent on the river. He scorned the safety argument, claiming the motor rigs were more at risk, and that smaller boats would be best.

Shortly after his mailing, Eiseman received a letter from Interior saying staff had been working on the matter, and we have now directed the Superintendent to set a limit on user-days for 1973 equal to that actually used in 1972. The limit would be in force until scientific and management information was available to determine carrying capacity—a function of the environment, desired experience, and level of development. We expect to involve you as we work to resolve this issue. How gratifying! Government is responsive!

Eiseman followed up with his proposal for an even lower "interim" quota, calculated by allowing one trip per day for the six-month season, no more than 30 people on board. This gave a limit of 5400 people, the 1969 level, as compared to almost 16,000 in 1972. He thought that one trip per day was good because encounters with other groups detract greatly from a wilderness experience, and he wanted to eliminate that. (Perhaps an absolute no-sighting rule suits some; it does not hold for all of us. Meeting another group now and then for a bit does not necessarily degrade the wilderness experience; it can be fun to exchange stories about hikes and rapids and such. On the other hand, if the encounters are a more or less continuous stream of motorized boat-buses, or if they are as nasty as those described by Vern Taylor, then yes, that's bad. The correct point between those two situations is yet to be found.

Eiseman also sent out a list of possible participants for his meeting: Park Service, legislators, conservationists and researchers. He wanted a constructive discussion, so he insisted on invitees only. Goldwater reaffirmed his stand just before the meeting in reply to a member of a prominent Phoenix family that had just bought a controlling interest in one of the comm ops, writing that the river-shore condition "sickens me". Travel has to be reduced; "that's all there is to it."[31]

In this fraught period, the Superintendent and his Deputy were not always available to sign the bad news letters, and that duty fell to one Pedro Suazo. In August, Mr. Suazo, delivering a piece of edgy news to the comm ops, added "Don't panic!" His Oct 19 missive to the same group should have been headed Panic![32] He noted the two-months-old news of an educational supplement and additional user-days. "But, going on, we have had discussions with our superiors. We feel we should advise you further. There will be no supplement for 1973. There will be no increases in allotments through 1975. You should plan for your 1972 allotment to be the maximum." (In fact, Reed's office had written that actual use would be the limit. There would be no room for increases at all). The annual comm op meeting with Park staff was set for November 17-18.

As if to add to the comm ops' woes, *The New York Times* of October 10 carried the story about those "who shot the Colorado River rapids on rafts [and] were victims of an epidemic of dysentery".[33] The "epidemic" lasted ten weeks and affected nine companies. No one died, but four were evacuated by helicopter. Investigation made it likely that the bacterium was acquired at a common eating place where the young raft pilots congregated between trips, and then, becoming ill, spread the infection on a person-to-person basis and by contaminating food and water. In the future, boat crews were to be taught better water, food and waste handling procedures.

In responding on that date to the draft on river sanitation rules, I urged the following: the full Rules and Regulations of the Coconino Country Board of Health be followed. All comm ops should correct their operations so they could receive a health permit, even if day-to-day monitoring cannot be done. And if a company cannot comply, then deny them use of the river. Instruction of boat staff was too vague. The hand-washing rules were inadequate. Finally, human waste needs to be taken out in storage tanks, and health officials could help this come about by insisting on their regulations being followed.

The Balloon Goes Up

October 25 arrived dim and snow-filled in Flagstaff, the designated meeting site. Due to road conditions, the meeting was held at Eiseman's home in rural Scottsdale. Senator Goldwater did not make it. Jim Ruch, an aide to Reed, flew in from Washington—the bearer, after all, of good news. The Park Service was well represented from the Park and by Regional Director Chapman. It was ill-served by the appearance of Lovegren, kicked upstairs to some sort of state coordinator job, who made, I wrote in my journal, an ass of himself by defending the comm ops, saying he had tried to get some to the meeting. His old ground trodden over, he then subsided—and, some days later, told McComb he was bowing out.

Just how out-of-place his views were was made clear as Ruch announced Reed's October 3 decision to revise the use ceiling down from 105 KUD to the 1972 actual use of 89 KUD. This startlingly good news was followed by a discussion of the need for research; a number of researchers were also present to give some perspective on what was estimated to be a $350,000 (in 1972 dollars) program. There was much discussion about motors, leaving Eiseman, McComb, and me hopeful that the current pro-motor policy would be reversed.

We quickly followed up this excellent news. Eiseman offered the anti-motor arguments at length to Ruch and to his mailing list, urging the latter to write letters, supporting quota reduction and a motor ban.[34] On November 7, he saw Goldwater, who embodied their discussion in a letter to Secretary Reed supporting a quota of 5000 people per year and a motor ban, "I think I made the first trip ... where an outboard motor was used, and we silenced it after the first hour." He went on: I am having a meeting on December 4 at my house to confirm the river situation and to discuss GCNP boundary changes. Goldwater also told Fred he thought the Sierra Club was overbearing on these matters. In a letter a few days later, he went further with respect to a personality matter: Lovegren "is a man that, frankly, we can do without in this state. Nothing against him of a personal nature, just that he didn't do a good job at the Grand Canyon."

Since GCNP was in Representative Sam Steiger's district, Eiseman wrote to him saying Goldwater wanted him at the December 4 meeting. Steiger said he couldn't make it, and decided on comm op Fred Burke to represent him.

McComb and I collaborated on an alert sent to Arizona and New Mexico conservationists asking for letters to Reed of thanks and support for reduced river use and motor ban. The previous increases were done without adequate knowledge, we said, and conditions are crowded, filthy, with too many boats, and trampling of vegetation. Our recommendation was for 5000 people per year. McComb requested that the Club's Grand Canyon chapter make the Grand Canyon its first priority, noting that many of us were lulled by the Park Service's master plan, but now the alarm has been sounded, and there is work to be done on the river, wilderness, and other Canyon matters.[35]

We also fired away at the EIS for the wilderness recommendation.[36] Eiseman snorted at the illogicality of excluding the river, saying that the EIS was the place to consider alternatives, including an alternative for putting the river in. He followed with a salvo of over twenty "corrections". McComb and I also made the case for banning motorboats, and added a call to restrict airplanes. We again made the point that interpretive services needed to be expanded "to promote active appreciation of the Grand Canyon Wilderness by all visitors".

During that first week in November, the Park Service, GCNP and Region, were rushing a briefing statement on the river.[37] Arrangements were made for a river advisory meeting on November 11; Ruch was to be present, and as well, some boatmen who had been complaining about river conditions had been asked to speak—and no doubt grilled, since the comm ops would be present.

The scientists, too, were busy. On November 2, the Ecological Studies Lab at the Park finished its first draft of the research proposal for the river, with an estimated cost over three years of $386,000.[38] The authors covered a range of points. Several endemic species were being endangered. Some ecosystems have yielded to stress. We must know how visitors perceive wilderness and what they would like to do. The river is not a simple resource; there must be the best possible input from political, biological, sociological, and management sectors. They said their objectives were to find out about ecosystems and about people's experience; how to have minimum impact on biota with maximum impact on visitor. Data were needed to evaluate economic and political pressures on park resources. There would be teams for administration, and for riparian, limnological, and sociological research. Some detail was provided of how these teams would work. This document was not the research design; that would require CROA's $3000, and about four months. At the optimum funding level, there should be significant results for management by the end of the third year (which might be read, optimistically, as saying they would affect the 1976 season.)

Since the advisory meeting was set for November 11, the group working on health guidelines scheduled November 10 to discuss its draft "guidelines for good sanitary practices" on the river. These meetings were to be followed a week later by the annual comm op meeting with the Park Service at the Park, and two weeks later, the Goldwater gathering. Those were just the announced get-togethers. Powered by delight or outrage, and the certain knowledge that decisions were being made, changes were coming, Canyon life would never be tidy again. All those concerned, Park Service, Canyon friends, comm ops, scientists, were honing arguments, plotting and speculating, calculating advantage and seeking allies.

The interlocking nature was shown in the topics the Park Service set for the advisory meeting: discussion of river use, so final decision on allowed use could be made a few days later; congestion at the launching place at Lees Ferry; sanitation standards; the research proposal. After setting forth this agenda, NPS reminded invitees that they were not supposed to be acting as organization representatives, but as interested, experienced persons; the park had responsibility for all management decisions.[39] (Dream on.)

The health meeting discussed a second draft of guidelines; I found it to be a great improvement.[40] It emphasized that visitors depend on the behavior of the boat employees; a monkey see, monkey do situation. If staff practices proper sanitation, it will be practiced by all. The river-specific guidelines were a supplement to existing regulations for food establishments, which the river trips are. Details included preventing staff from taking a trip if illness was diagnosed; more rigorous hand-washing procedures including strategically located, chlorinated, frequently changed water supplies; sanitizing all kitchen items; more rigorous standards for food handling and refrigerating containers; disinfecting drinking water, which could come from the Colorado if properly treated. There would be inspections before and after trips, with Park Service help. These guidelines were formalized for the 1973 season, with the hope that they would "prevent the spread of disease among travelers on the Colorado River". In spite of foot-dragging and bleats about self-regulation and unique situations from the comm ops, another level up had been reached in the effort to make river-running truly safe.

With one success scored for sound river practice, we moved to the next day's meeting in the den of the beast, labeled in my notes as comm op Sanderson's "palace" in Page. We were very apprehensive, suspicious of the Park Service, knowing that this was the comm ops' chance to shake the decision on quotas. Seven comm ops attended, as well as Park Service staff, and Jim Ruch from Reed's office in Washington. The meeting started quietly with mentions of the search for a research person and $20,000 in funds. Then Stitt stated the 1973 allotment would not exceed 1972 actual use. Two comm ops immediately asked why the change. Stitt's answer that it was concern about the Canyon brought comm op Burke's reply: It's political pressure. Furthermore, he said, the Canyon is in better shape than years ago. Ruch answered that the concern was voiced in letters from conservationists, boat staff, and later by Senator Goldwater. Burke replied the comm ops had letters, too. Stitt insisted that maximum allotments had to be set, which brought out a division between large and small comm ops. One of the biggest,

Currey, claimed he thought the 1970 level was a proposal and that more people could go through. A small comm op complained Lovegren had failed them. When asked to hold the big companies steady, and let the smaller ones rise to 4 KUD a year, Lovegren had told them to cut down, and that he would push for an economic base—but then the big ones grew anyway. This comm op added that the motors fight led to CROA and a comm op split, so he wanted motors dropped and stable allotments given. When asked if motors were an economic issue, Currey said no; it was just safety—and the best trip; anyway, banning motors would not change the numbers going. When challenged by a Park scientist who argued that motors were just to push trips through quickly, Currey replied that there were more upsets in the Grand Canyon, so bigger boats were needed. Then Joe Tonsmeire, a brave soul, boatman for one of the other largest comm ops, spoke up and said motors were not for safety, but for speed. Currey's reply was simple: Keep the numbers high, since we put up the money and we keep the Canyon clean. The debate then switched to launch schedules and consequent crowding from too many trips launched around the weekend. Eiseman's claim of campsites being jammed was denied by CROA.

Then it was the turn of the boatmen. Tonsmeire spoke of the petition he and others had been circulating among employees that summer. Twenty-five had signed. They had wanted to give it to the comm ops first, but could not get to their meeting in Salt Lake. Addressed to the Park Service, as the "appointed protector" of the Canyon, the petition opened with soaring rhetoric about the loss of a wilderness experience, went on to a page of specific occurrences of problems, and closed with seven recommendations. The problems were "extremely heavy use by the outfitters", traffic jams at some places such as House Rock Rapid and Elves Chasm, launching crowds at Lees Ferry. There was improper and unauthorized camping, too many fire-pits at campsites, trash and garbage left on beaches, special attraction sites with toilet paper and fire-pits. "Many outfitters" were not using toilets. The boatmen's recommendations called for reducing the number of trips launching on the same day, not increasing use, ending the use of attraction sites for camping, doing a better job of qualifying boat crew on health and campsite care, and stricter enforcement, including fining violators in user days. Joe ended by stating that boat staff had their own point of view, not just an echo of employers. Breaking for lunch cut off discussion, and when the meeting resumed, it ran down. I wrote in my journal that it was a GOOD MEETING. The comm ops did badly; we were business-like. Two for two, and we were getting giddy—just as the comm ops had been only a few months earlier.

The reaction of the comm ops can be gauged from a letter from Burke's wife, written two days later to Goldwater, in which she accused Eiseman and him of bias, saying he had not been down in seven years, and the Canyon was not a disaster area.[41] She ended by offering that they would like to work things out. (The Burkes could have hopes here; he was a long-time Republican activist and had been in the Arizona legislature.) Less violently, Grand Canyon Expeditions wrote to Congressman Steiger about the way the comm ops had been treated.[42] In the summer, he complained, GCNP had told the comm ops they would have an increase; then in the fall, no increase; on November 11, a surprise announcement of a possible reduction. He continued, we do not think the river is really congested; a study has shown that increases would be O.K. (he was referring to the Boster thesis). We are dealing with sanitation problems. We are opposed to motors; those trips are shorter, noisier, and less intimate; the longer trip is a better trip.

We were further buoyed when Eiseman told us that Ruch had quizzed a former GCNP employee; as a friend of Eiseman, he had already been prepped. Letters continued to come into Reed's office in favor of wilderness and banning motors, Ruch told me, including from Grand Canyon Expeditions—yes, the same comm op complaining above, but also the same who had passed around the no-motors petitions two years earlier (and the same whose website in 2003 defends motor use). We too were receiving letters from Canyon friends who had been on the river, providing evidence of leavings from trips, strengthening our sense that there was a problem, even if we were not personally down there witnessing it.

A November 14 Park Service briefing paper stressed the need for research in dealing with the several river issues: use limits, health guidelines, safety, improved toilets, pollution standards, rules for self-guided trips.[43] That same day, Chapman called Stitt to report on a Park Service-Interior staff meeting with Reed. There was no decision on motors yet, but use levels for 1973-5 were needed, and Stitt should check out the 1970 master plan numbers. Reed had said that past decisions were tilted toward comm op concerns, not toward protecting the resource, and it was necessary to justify any use figure and to find a number for self-guided trips. He suggested a phase-out of motors to be complete at the end of 1975. Other initiatives were needed, to schedule launches, set trip limits, and cut campsite crowding. The Solicitor thought an EIS was needed (a little late). There would be a decision on allotments soon, so Reed directed GCNP to send a registered letter to the comm ops that NPS was doing an EIS, and that the evaluation might result in a maximum of the current use or might be reduced, and motors might be phased out. Chapman ended by telling Stitt: Get an EIS done in two weeks.

Ruch's report to me the next day was that there was no decision on motors yet, and that there was to be a meeting with him, Steiger, and two comm ops, Sanderson and Burke, on the 16th. He then said his personal views were for a motor phase-out and a cutback from 1972 over two years. Either Reed or he would be coming to the December 4 meeting at Goldwater's.

With barely a pause, the comm ops gathered at the Park on November 17 to meet with the Park Service; I was there as an observer, and so obtained (and recorded in my journal) a vivid sense of the tensions. An evening session on health standards was disappointing, as the speaker hedged and qualified what should have been strong statements. The next day, Superintendent Stitt presented the Interior-NPS position of having a ceiling of 89,000 visitor days (the amount of actual 1972 use), and a number of other limits: trip size, maximum people at Lees Ferry and at any campsite. He spoke of a three-year motor phase-out, saying they wanted to try an oars-only period. The current contracts ran out in 1975, so the new regime would be completely in place in 1976. The individual allotments had not been decided, so the meeting would recess so the comm ops could meet to try to figure out what to do. After an hour-and-a-half deliberation, the comm ops announced they had been able to reduce the 105 KUD of the 1972 ceiling down to 104 KUD, not too close to the 89 KUD target. Burke later claimed he had tried to get comm ops to divide up the 89 KUD, but Currey refused to budge, "He is always a pain and needs to be taught a lesson."[44] If he had come down, others would have.

My notes support this; in open session, Currey said he had already filled his allotment with passengers for 1973, so he could not come down. (Please contrast Currey's truculence here to that letter he had written three months before to his signed-up clients about the cut-off in Dinosaur National Monument.) Stitt replied then he would decide, and released his division of the allotments, even though they were supposed to be confidential. (Later, Ruch told me Stitt had forgotten the verbal advice from the Solicitor about an EIS.)

The discussion now turned to motors and was a rare opportunity to hear views from these people, with their range of experience on the river. The largest rowing company thought a third of the people went on rowing trips. An old-time comm op thought people just liked the motor operations, but in any case, told Stitt to make a decision and stick to it. One of the largest comm ops called for a further study of safety, and argued that comm ops should be able to run the kind of trip *they* want, within reason. A rowing comm op retorted that his rowers were highly professional and his trips were safe. Someone tried to cut off the discussion by saying we have said it all. Burke reported that his Washington visit was not a discouraging time. Notwithstanding the discussion at Page a week earlier, he claimed the economic impact would be considerable, and urged that everyone send stuff to Washington people. A summary of pro and con indicated there were 10 of the 21 who did or would do rowing, although the largest rowing comm op made clear in a letter after the meeting that he was not opposed to motors; after all, as he told me, his competition would increase if everybody rowed.[45]

The boatmen who had spoken at Page now spoke again, and the pressures brought on them were obvious, as they started by claiming the views they had presented the previous week had been distorted. The comm ops jumped on them, wanting to know why they went public before talking to their bosses. The back and forth was vigorous, with even the mild-mannered Yearout putting Burke down once. The comm ops rejected the criticisms by and large; when one said he could go along with some of the suggestions, he was ignored. Some of the small rowing comm ops offered support, but were countered by other comm ops who claimed their boat crews were to blame for any problems, not the employers. The comm ops scoffed at these "personal views", and their reception of these criticisms from knowledgeable people can be judged by the two petition presenters moving shortly thereafter to the Northwest—"You'll never work in this town again."

The fierceness of the attack was surely a measure of the comm ops' sensitivity to this criticism; it went to the heart of the case they had been making for themselves as self-policing, caring guardians of the river environment. It may also be a measure of how beleaguered they felt already from publicity about the epidemic, and from the change in Interior and Park Service leadership leading to a reversal of their dominance of GCNP river decisions. Currey's insistence that they, the comm ops, were the ones who put up the money, who took the people through, who kept the Canyon clean, rang out as only an especially direct form of what, in their self-justifying hermetic world, they all thought. And after all, if you are going to keep on fighting when you are losing on all fronts, being direct with no time for criticism may be your greatest asset. Having money to spend on trips to Washington helped, too.

Needing some reassurance after witnessing this onslaught, I talked to Ruch on the 21st, and he supported Stitt as being on the right track with his decisions. No surprise there; they were what Reed had said he wanted in his meeting with Chapman, who had then relayed them by phone to Stitt. In fact, Stitt had reported to Ruch the day before about what he had presented to the comm ops, and had received full support. They also agreed the Park needed more people on river patrols, so Stitt called Chapman to push for filling positions. Ruch told me he, not Reed, would be at Goldwater's, and maybe there would be a decision on motors. Meanwhile, a temporizing letter was being sent, saying that research was underway, but for now subjective reasoning is being used in a study of the use problem, with a decision soon.[46] Ruch then summarized the meeting with Burke, who complained about unfairness and about there being too many comm ops. Burke wanted allotments based on performance, though he offered no criteria.

Reporting on the same meeting from the other side, Burke wrote on the 24th to Steiger that he wanted a harder look taken at the motor vs. oars thing. The comm ops were to meet on the 29th in Las Vegas to muster their forces to fight for motors. Burke followed this up with a phone call on the 28th.

A tremor of things to come: Burke wrote to the Superintendent, explaining away his coming "unglued" at Joe Munroe—a non-commercial river runner we will hear more from later—by saying that the latter's petition about his type of use was only going to muddy the waters with Eiseman.[47] River-running by people who organized and ran their own trips, with their own boats—they were often called non-commercial or private trips; I prefer self-guided—seemed at this time to be a minor matter; although increasing, self-guided use was dwarfed by paid trips, 15 to 1. However, self-guided trips are the "real thing", posing an ideological if not an economic threat to comm ops' claims of being the only ones who make it possible for the public to see the Canyon from the river. The report by Vern Taylor of his August experiences running a self-guided trip, and being harassed by a number of comm op crew, was an indication of conflicts to come as self-guided demand began to increase, running up against comm op resistance and new Park Service restrictions. The self-guided position will get fuller treatment starting in Chapter 6; at this point, it was just another, and small, cloud in the stormy skies pouring rain on the comm ops' parade.

The action was now with the Park Service, as staff raced to draft a river management plan. On November 22, Chapman told Stitt the plan had to be in the Regional office by the 27th; it was faxed on that date. Chapman called right away, saying that they should have used the 1970 use figure of 72 KUD. Also there had to be definite numbers on other limits. He was going to fax this to Washington. Two days later, Stitt talked with Washington NPS. Then Chapman called him to say that his staff had agreed to recommend Stitt's figures to the Director. He called again after checking with Washington; the plan was O.K. except that Ruch wanted GCNP to tell the comm ops—at the right time!—that NPS planned to cut down how many there would be when the new contracts were issued in 1976. By the 30th, Chapman could report that the river management plan had been approved by everybody up to Reed. No doubt this was all helped along by a letter from Goldwater to Chapman on the 27th, in anticipation of the December 4 get-together at the former's house, that a large number of people were concerned now about the decision.[48] It has to be made, Goldwater asserted, maybe at once. Goldwater continued: I hope legislation is not needed; the Park Service can do this. You, as Regional Director, can make these decisions quickly, and then see to it that the Park Service backs up these decisions that political heat has brought. In my humble opinion, one trip each day is enough, and motors must be prohibited. "I don't think that nature ever intended the loud reverberating noise of putt-putts to be heard in these Canyon reaches."

Against this opinion from on high, what did comm op Burke's claim weigh that the trip was not a wilderness experience, but an outdoors experience?[49] Still, he was game and asked Stitt not to ban motors. Other comm op statements were to follow. However, on the 24th Stitt sent the comm ops a summary of his positions at the November 18 meeting about the use ceiling and the likely motor phase-out, preferably over the contract life. During this period, as well, our pro-wilderness efforts were showing up in letters to Reed's office, numerous enough to cause a variety of form replies to be generated, and numerous enough, I may suppose, to offer support for Reed's decisions.[50]

The culmination came on December 4. Senator Goldwater's call to meet at his home was a broad-based attempt. The attendees included the congressional delegation or their representatives, most importantly Congressman John Rhodes, a member of the Appropriations Committee. Eiseman, and Interior-NPS representatives Ruch, Chapman, and Stitt did come on behalf of the river controversy. Still, the only comm op at the meeting was Fred Burke, and as he explained, he was there to represent Steiger, not the river industry. The rest of us had a more or less strong involvement in the GCNP boundary legislation Goldwater was determined to bring about in 1973: McComb and me; two hunter representatives along with outdoors columnist and Goldwater friend Ben Avery; Goldwater staffer (with a bias against the Sierra Club) Terry Emerson; and Ned Danson, Goldwater friend and Museum of Northern Arizona director.

Chapman presented the new river management plan. (Simultaneously, the Park was calling the comm ops about the plan, and on the 6th a news release followed.) There was no debate at this meeting about the major river issues; Burke, in his usual style, put in that some of the comm ops were trying to work with the Park Service. For many attendees, the river was a marginal matter. The divided jurisdiction over the river was brought up, with Goldwater saying he wanted to change that, bringing the upper river under the Park, and Eiseman urging that the lower end be included. The problem caused by fluctuating water releases from Glen Canyon Dam upstream was mentioned, and Rhodes offered to help. His value showed most when the subject of money for research came up. On being told by Ruch that a research proposal could be ready before June, Rhodes thought he could fit it into the appropriations bill.

And so, in this uncharacteristically conciliatory setting, the great reversal in river traffic management, four months in the making and two months after Reed's major decision, was sanctified. Chapman reported to Washington that general agreement was reached after discussion, and was told that Reed wanted a press release quickly. Surely, for us, it was a time to celebrate. With Arizona's congressional delegation and the Interior Department lined up, where could the weak points be?

The comm ops, however, were not interested in the new dispensation; they had been getting fat and happy with a tame Park Service. They wanted their own back, and so, scorning a great opportunity, they launched their counter-revolution. If any moment in this controversy deserves the name of tragedy, it is this one when, blinded by passion for their position and powered on by grievance, they could not find a way to align their ostensible aim of offering a public service at a profit with the goals embodied in the National Park System and the Wilderness Act; goals finally being enunciated by the Park Service and its bosses, with the somewhat unlikely blessing of much of Arizona's political power. What a difference for the contestants and the public, had the comm ops determined to make the new situation work for them. Instead, they went down a darker track, one they are still on, fending off all other claimants, determined to maintain their grasp on power over river traffic management, yet fearing that they can never rest secure. Fearing that if they weaken, those who believe in the river as a truly public resource and the Grand Canyon as a true wilderness, will carry the day. A fear soundly based in reality.

CHAPTER 4

1973: How Do We Get This Thing In Reverse?

From out of the comm ops corner, indeed the very day of Goldwater's meeting, came the thud of CROA's statement, a quasi-brief from its lawyer.[1] Several other comm ops were voicing their views too. Two days later, December 6, 1972, the Park Service released its river and backcountry use plans.[2]

In between these weighty events, Ben Avery got the news out; his version read: U.S. Restricts Canyon Travel![3] He led with the phase-out of motors, wilderness status for the river, and a reduction in "people impact", asserting that the announcement was "approved" by representatives of the Arizona and National Wildlife Federations and the Sierra Club. He had Burke representing the comm ops, a status the latter correctly denied. He wrote that Burke agreed with most of the restrictions, except for the reduction in visitors and Avery reported this Burke-Chapman exchange: The former brought up the comm ops' commitment to research, and hoped that river use would be held steady while the studies were done. Chapman "promised" the situation would be looked at annually.

The Park Service press release was sent from the Regional Office, having been developed with Washington. Eiseman told me it was spurred by the Avery article and by Reed's desire to get Interior's version out.[4] What I find strange about this document as I look it over today is that it reads like a guideline memo for deeply interested parties, not a statement for the general public. It consists mostly of detailed, even arcane, prescriptions for river-running. There is almost no stirring rhetoric. It does not set forth the history and the justification for bringing these matters to public attention. The drama of the grand reversal is missing. Somehow, the chance for rousing a wider public was missed. This was the more strange given the pace of events over the previous four months, which left us jubilant. Yet, there were no supportive releases from us either; nor any declaration of victory from Senator Goldwater. In retrospect, the chance was not taken up to secure internal agency commitment by making it, loudly, a public policy. *The New York Times* might carry a story about an epidemic on the river, but this revolutionary change putting the Park Service on the side of the environment, wilderness, and a true Park experience never got beyond a local story. What was the matter with us? Today as I look back, I am mystified that none of us grabbed this opportunity.

The NPS release started off by offering "a potential answer, and a beginning" for the question of how to protect the "relatively unspoiled" river from the impact of thousands of river users. Of first importance, use would be cut over five years by almost 40%. Visitor numbers would drop from 14,000 to 10,000. Ecological and sociological studies would be expanded and used to monitor for degradation.

Of second importance, motors would be eliminated over the same period by setting up a schedule for a mandatory phase-in of rowing use. The river would be promoted to a "potential wilderness", and join the top-rank as Wilderness when motors were gone in 1977. (I have much more to say about this upside-down logic in Chapter 10.) Several other regulations were set forth: on behavior (no soap in tributaries); on trip size (passengers per party limited to 40, per boat to 20); on speed (40 miles per day).

Then, something odd appeared. Limits would now be set on trips undertaken by people who chose to do their own provisioning and guiding, the so-called private or self-guided users. Such a limit might seem only fair, though there was no provision for reviewing and revising it, as there was for commercial use. The limit was to be one such party a day, with a maximum of 30 people. This really did not make sense as a limit, since it would allow even up to 5000 persons each year on self-guided trips, ten times greater than use. (A technical note: while only passengers are counted against the commercial allocation, all persons on a self-guided trip count. Ethically, this was bizarre, since commercial crews impact the river themselves, and more important, by example and instruction, massively affect, and effect, their passengers' impact. Numerically, this exclusion made the commercial ceiling off, by about 15-20%, in ringing up user-days. And too, it was a loophole if an outfitter wanted to count a passenger as crew. Remembering that this was a Lovegren innovation helps to explain it, but it is an offensive archaism in keeping track of river traffic and its impacts.) Meaningless at first, the idea of a self-guided limit shortly became a strait-jacket the Park Service strapped itself into, binding, pinching, and griping their policy and its victims in an acceleratingly intense way with the boom in do-it-yourself recreation (much more on this starting in Chapter 6).

The comm ops' reactions were all over the place. Litton, who rowed elegant wooden boats and scorned what he called large, motor-driven "baloney boats", nevertheless had thought motors might help keep adverse use down. However, for him the crucial straw was the exclusion of the river from the September wilderness plan. That meant motors are hurting the Canyon, he said, and the only reasons for having them are to speed trips and make more money. He was willing to face the competition if all started rowing. The largest rowing outfit, ARTA, was not willing, and so did not oppose motor use (they did run motor trips, too). The other large pro-rowing comm op, Grand Canyon Expeditions—which ran motor trips mostly—still supported the superiority of rowing trips and wilderness, but was more concerned about the use reduction, which, it claimed, was not justified by actual conditions, and which penalized longer trips like theirs as well as rowed trips. At the other extreme, the short-trip motor comm op, Tour West, countered that motors have nothing to do with the quality of the trip, pushing the standard pro-motor distortions.

CROA's attorney Brown concentrated on the use ceilings in the December 4 missile he launched at the Secretary of the Interior, loaded with "meaningful and factual information". The copy I have of that letter contains several sharp handwritten notes by "B.W.", Bill Winter of the National Wildlife Federation (NWF), a member of the Park's river advisory committee. The NWF was sometimes an opponent, sometimes an ally, of the Sierra Club. The notes are valuable, therefore, in providing a different non-comm op viewpoint. So, when Brown stated that the committee had made a "unanimous" recommendation for a use increase, Winter countered with, "This is not true", and noted that he made the Park Service admit at the November river meeting that it was not true, undercutting the comm ops' groaning about the suddenness of the use ceiling cut. Brown's complaint continued that the comm ops had been booking 1973 trips for two months, from August until they were notified of the reduction to the 1972 level, though no documentation was offered in the seven attachments; Winter wrote, "I doubt this." Brown attacked Eiseman, "too extreme even for the Park Service", claiming his opposition was due only to the lack of studies. Brown stated the studies would show the Canyon was just fine and could handle even more people. He really went after the "anonymous" boatmen who presented the petition of concern about increased quotas and increased congestion. They had, Brown implied, backed down. Anyway, the comm ops were more knowledgeable than anyone else, and had been suggesting solutions before any of the critics. To that, I can say, using Winter's words, not true. Winter commented that the scheduling problems were not solved, with 400-500 people leaving Lees Ferry in one day. He also did not recall the boatmen retracting their concerns. (Which they did not, telling me that they were ready to back up their statements, even testify in court.) Brown strangely suggested that the major fear of those in favor of limits was contaminated campsites, about which Winter notes, correctly, "This is not true." Brown used that false characterization to brag about the comm ops' efforts to clean up the messes they leave each season. He marred his boasting by pretending the comm ops proposed chemical toilets and the Park Service resisted their use (again, the opposite of the facts). He moved on to the 1972 Boster survey, saying it concluded that the current limits were too low, and many more people could go with little contact with other parties. Winter says, "I doubt this"; he had already noted the failure to solve the scheduling problem, which is the key to much of the congestion. (Scheduling was key as well to Boster's idea of more people with little contact. Brown also ignored Boster's conclusion that with their high family income, the comm ops customers were a "unique group seldom found in other recreation areas".)

Brown wound up trying to align Park Service goals with those of the comm ops, by turning the former on their head: Parks are to provide access to the maximum number of people consistent with the resources' ability to provide access. (Missing was the word "unimpaired".) He found the comm ops' interest in a profit "entirely harmonious" with their interest in a clean Canyon. Finally, noting the "hundreds" unnecessarily turned away in 1972, he decried the lack of facts to support any reduction or other limitations. In all its seven pages, Brown's letter never mentioned the word "motors".

Brown called the Superintendent a few days after he sent off his cannonade, wanting to know what the new individual allotments would be. Stitt recorded, "Of course" Brown wants us to set them at the actual use, since his client, Western, would benefit, but I said to expect a 16% reduction from his 12 KUD allotment. The same day, the 8th, Reed was informed of the numbers. The Park Service hedged a little in view of the comm ops already having accepted reservations, settling on the 1972 actual use. On December 11, the new individual allotments were set and sent to the comm ops.[5] 1972's actual use by passengers was 89 KUD, 16% down from 1972's total ceiling, so each company was given a 1973 allotment of 16% less than its 1972 allotment. No company was penalized for not using its full 1972 allotment, and some user-days left over were given to the smaller companies. An effort was made to help the smallest reach 2 KUD. These allotments stayed the same throughout the push and pull, stresses and strains, of the next 8 years.

Still pushing hard, the GCNP had its "River Use Plan" ready, also on December 11.[6] Unlike the press release, this was intended as a rulebook, a guide to river operation. It insisted on management's need for flexibility in the face of changing conditions and review. The first year, 1973, would allow for existing commercial commitments, followed by three years of the real thing, a permanent plan. The document started off with a tendentious history that missed the opportunity to state the need for Grand Canyon's protectors to take control of a runaway situation. It implied that GCNP had cut comm ops 1972 requests by 10%, not mentioning that same amount was approved for the next year. And it skipped the chance to pinpoint what outraged people by not saying that this request was 42 KUD more than they used in 1972 and 65 KUD more than they used in 1971, i.e., the comm ops had wanted to nearly double use in two years. The document noted it had to balance the Concessions Policy Act, calling for "a reasonable opportunity ... to realize a profit", with the need to protect the Canyon and the visitor experience. "It is felt", NPS said, 89 KUD will do this, admitting that "we also suffer for lack of information". What is a little strange is that all these new people—Reed, Chapman, Stitt—did not just come out and say there was no justification for the policy of increase; their predecessors had violated NEPA, and something had to be done to get legal. Such bureaucratic cover had a faint echo a little later when Chapman assured us that "the idea of reducing the number of comm ops was not abandoned, and would be "executed" at the time of the prospectus for new contracts in 1976.[7] Although clearly there was a dramatic change from Lovegren's day, the language was such that we (and the comm ops, too) could never quite rest with what NPS said.

The river management document then went over the detailed limits mentioned in the press release. Self-guided parties, it added, would be limited to one trip per year, a limit not imposed on passengers or crew of commercial trips, introducing another inequity. Now, more than a year late, *after* the concession contracts had been granted, there was to be a "profile" of each company as a business proposition. (This matter of the comm ops furnishing required information kept being an embarrassment, as we shall see.) Another gem is this, "The park has found that boatmen often are unaware of information that they should have at their disposal." What, one wonders, were their bosses doing—aside from rushing as many people as they could every summer down the river, and counting their money? And what was the Park doing by not insisting that they become "aware"?

The section on motors was most strange; it started off as if written by a motor comm op. "Motorized craft have been preferred by most companies for reasons of safety." "A 10-day motorized trip ... can also be a very rewarding trip." "Thousands of satisfied visitors" used motor rafts. Referring to cost, "Oars-only may well exclude some from a full trip." Nevertheless, we believe motor trips should be phased out, "based on some preliminary sociological study results" (not cited), plus "value-judgements". There was no mention of Park System *values*, no discussion of Wilderness *values*, no indication of how short-fast-big motor trips degraded the *values* of a river trip, no countering of the misleading safety distortion, no memory of the Boster study's finding that most of the people on commercial river trips were from a moneyed elite. Possibly, lame language like this becomes a little more understandable if we remember Deputy Superintendent Shaw's expressing, in notes to his boss, motor bias and his lack of understanding of what wilderness is about. Such opinions stand as an indicator that the Park Service was, is, itself split internally in its attitudes and opinions about Park and wilderness values. We were to see over and over the lesson of 1972, that policy reversals may only bring lip service from some, not conversion. There are always those quiet behind-the-scenes struggles waged by those burrowing away until the time is ripe for a re-reversal.

A week later, the comm ops' heavyweight swung into action. Senator Moss, a Democratic senator from Utah was, one can suppose, appealed to by comm op Currey and his attorney Brown (Salt Lakers all). Moss wrote to the Secretary that he had "serious" reservations about the limit on use and the elimination of motors.[8] He claimed that since hundreds were already being turned away, there would be even less opportunity to take a river trip under the December 5 plan. He insisted that rafts needed motors for guidance, so eliminating them would cut trips even more. He supported Brown's call for a face-to-face meeting with the Secretary, or at least with his representatives.

On the other hand, what were we doing? Celebrating the good news, in our quiet way, innocents all. I wrote to the Canyon's friends, "We seem to be enjoying a time when the people involved are both right-headed and trustworthy."[9] And I suggested, quietly, that people might send thanks to Chapman and Stitt. Perhaps I would have been less sanguine had I been able to read Senator Moss's letter. Or if I had seen some of the letters, exasperated and angry, written to Senator Goldwater by the comm ops.[10] Perhaps I was a little bothered by a talk with Stitt when he said that the river policy was solid, though there would probably be some court action over reducing the number of comm ops and the allotments. Yet, I doubt it; in a battle as fast and furious as this one had been, to see what seemed such a complete change for the better provided too much good cheer. I am of the school that says celebrate your victories when you get them; don't wait for the final Big One. I did think what I wrote to the Canyon's friends, "The New Year May Really be a Happy One!"

It certainly was a busy one. Explosively so, due to Senator Goldwater's determined push for legislation to expand the boundaries of Grand Canyon National Park. I have confined that two-year blood bath to Chapter 5. A taste of the monster is given by this January 5 remark Goldwater wrote to Eiseman, "I will abide by any decision you reach relative to the Sierra Club just so their demands will not once again prevent us from accomplishing what we want."[11] And we thought we were on the same side.

The major impact the boundary legislation might have had on river policy was deleted early. At the December 4 Goldwater meeting, his aide Terry Emerson had included a draft provision for river regulation, directing the Secretary to issue rules to prevent overuse, including limiting launches to "one watercraft of any form each day", setting a lid on total use of 6000 a year, and banning motors. The language embodied the ideas that Eiseman and Goldwater had been pushing, and was the concrete form of the threat the senator had made that if the administration did not act, he would. Now the administration had acted. All who spoke up at the meeting agreed that Assistant Secretary Reed's action and the subsequent implementing decisions by the Park Service had made legislation unnecessary, so the provision was eliminated. The Park Service was relieved, though Eiseman fretted, as did we all, about "the transient nature of personnel" and decisions being reversed.[12] Still, Goldwater had gotten his way. As you read through the events of the following years, you may wonder, legitimately, how he lost it.

The Park Service moved along the path set for it, the Park and Regional Office managing to produce a draft EIS on the use limits on February 13 with a negative finding as to environmental impact.[13] The document looked straightforward. The limits will improve the quality of the trip and lessen the amount of impact on the river environment. The number of visitors might be reduced, and there might be adverse financial impact on some smaller companies. That would be offset by a drop in diluted, fast, thrill trips. Environmental insults from noise, congestion, air and water pollution would be lessened. The discussion of alternatives noted that a no-limits policy was untenable, and keeping the status quo would just postpone a day of reckoning until comm ops were even more over-committed to large groups and fast trips, with consequent irreversible degradation. Now is the best time to hold steady over the three years of study to determine a true carrying capacity.[14]

Then, in that irritating bureaucratic mode in which current actions are made hostage to past failure and ignorance, the use level was held acceptable since "no irreversible damage seems to have occurred". Of course, there had been no studies in the early 1960s to set pre-dam baselines, and no studies before use took off in 1966 to set baselines for the conditions resulting from the dam plus river use. And the "evidence" from 1966 through 1973 was anecdotal, episodic, biased, and contested; seat-of-the-pants vs. smell-of-the-beach. The real problem had nothing to do with research; it was that the Park Service said in the master plan it intended to hold the line at 1970 commercial use, and it did not, use increasing by 50% in 1972. If use had been held at the 1970 level, the 1972 explosion might well have been avoided. The conclusion is inescapable that the comm ops and their ally Lovegren brought these troubles on, but no NPS document attached blame.

Blameless or not, the comm ops were fighting for their ill-gotten gains. The archives available from the period indicate the comm ops were using their mailing lists to stir up letters to the government and to Congress. Congressman Steiger received about 300 pro-motor letters; GCNP's stack amounted to several inches; the crew of motor operators, some on their employers' letterheads, wrote using the "safety" issue; Senator Goldwater commented that the comm ops were even threatening to stop his park bill.[15] The protest letters were spread throughout the year from former and current customers, rising and falling in number, as people were pulsed by different comm ops. The latter were also direct, sending the usual bundle of distortions about safety, choice being restricted, and cost. One comm op, Sanderson, had a good time attacking "radical, so-called ecology groups" and "radical nature groups", claiming their massive letter-writing campaign was one-sided.[16] This missive posited that people's attitudes about scenery cannot be changed, and that each citizen should have an equal opportunity to go on the river. (The first statement has been disproved by the history of our regard for the Canyon, and the second is a sour joke in the mouth of a comm op.) Staveley chimed in, calling for the retention of "choice" between motors and oars. On a personal trip through the Canyon, *he* would row; but motors are "the best way to deliver a safe trip for hire, on a *predetermined schedule*." (My emphases, and though both claims are hooey in their comparisons, the second comes close to admitting the real purpose for motors.) He claimed small rowing-only companies favored having motorboats on the river. After all, the large companies could convert easily, and thus dominate the market. (Yet they already dominated the market, and they were the ones fighting the motor ban the hardest.) He then attacked self-guided trips: they "inflict" 2-5 times as much use as a comm op trip. (Given the disparity in numbers, this at its worst meant the comm ops did four times as much damage in absolute terms. Of course, the claim was just more snide pot-shooting.)

The political uses of research were emphasized when University of Arizona professor R. Gum, who had supervised the Boster thesis, told me that the comm ops were using that study in their efforts with the Utah delegation. Another UofA researcher, Stan Brickler, also engaged in studying visitors, said GCNP had distributed the Boster report, but that Park officials were not disturbed, being ready to discredit it in any legal action the comm ops might bring.[17] (And what about any public relations action?)

Although the comm ops' intense effort seemed aimed at getting the Reed decision reversed, they were implicitly accepting the change for the immediate future. They did prevent a phase-down of use from 89 KUD to 55 KUD and any phase-out of motors, both of which were supposed to be in place for the 1977 season and the new contracts that would become effective then. Since the end result of all the back and forth was that the use level for passengers stayed at 89 KUD through the 1970s, it would seem that both sides could claim victory. Those worried about increasing use obtained a ceiling, though higher than they thought desirable. The comm ops avoided having to cut back their use below their historic maximum, and may even have gained from having a stable use level for the next several years. This interpretation sounds to me like a watered drink at a best friend's funeral.

The result of the comm op outcry was a Washington conference on January 26, attended by Ruch, the Park Service, CROA reps, and congressional staff from the Arizona and Utah delegations. The comm ops had met the day before with Senator Moss, who was taking the lead in raising questions on the new policy and had set up the next day's face-off. On the 26th, the main argument from the comm ops was that there were no studies to justify eliminating motors and reducing use. (Of course, there were no studies done when use was permitted to double, nor when motors were being used to shorten trips, nor when five-year contracts were entered into.)

We had a couple of reports on the meetings.[18] Congressman Udall had sent one of his aides, Terry Bracey. Politically cautious and unfamiliar with the issues, Bracey sought the safe line. He had been impressed with some of the comm op arguments, but finally accepted the position that a use ceiling made sense while studies were done. The other report was from Ruch, who much more colorfully described the bombing and shelling the comm ops indulged in, which the Park Service withstood. He noted that the safety ploy had been undermined when Staveley inadvertently admitted that the insurance rates for motor and rowing trips were the same. The comm ops had said nothing new, and failed to explain why motors should not be excluded. He called on us to generate letters to the Utah and Arizona delegations. A couple of weeks later, Ruch was feeling better about that, telling McComb that the opposition, which had been running 10-to-1 against the Park Service, was "tapering off". He may also have felt better on receiving a follow-up from Currey, of CROA, accepting the ceiling set at the 1972 actual commercial passenger use of 89 KUD, even as he pushed continued motor use.[19]

In order to put this acceptance in its context, let me go over the numbers again. Had there been no change of policy, and if actual use had reached 105 KUD for passengers, there would have been the additional impact from the estimated 20 KUD for crew. If we add in the 10 KUD "educational" supplement, with another 2 KUD for crew, the total rises to 137 KUD. Then there were the smaller comm ops, clamoring for a few hundred more user-days to "stabilize" their operations. The Park Service pattern of the 1969-72 period would have been to give in, and we are easily at 150 KUD. Had there been no outcry about congestion and environmental impact, the comm ops would have continued pushing and pushing. With the floor at 150 KUD, how easy to keep adding trips to get total commercial use of 200, 250 KUD; you choose what it might have reached in 1980. Instead, the ceiling of 105 KUD total use held throughout the rest of the 1970s, while the question of whether to reduce use was not even raised until the research was done.

A month later, Park Service personnel were feeling less pressured, thinking the comm ops had "settled down" for the upcoming season. Policy had also jelled further, in Reed's reactions to the comm ops' pressures. He wrote to one comm op leader that he was glad to meet and learn about your concerns first-hand.[20] However, Reed continued, motors must go if a quality experience is to be provided for visitors. We gave you a four-year phase-out so you could amortize, and because the contracts expire then. We froze the use in order to allow a chance to collect data. The level of 105 KUD plus a 10 KUD educational supplement was just not acceptable given the data we now have. If the information shows more use is all right, we will reconsider the cut to 55 KUD, although likewise, a further cut might be needed based on data. We will try, he promised, to get you the figures for each year by September 15, since we cannot tell what the data will show yet.

Reed sent a fuller reply March 2 to CROA's lawyer Brown, using language that provides a baseline to check future government statements against.[21] Reed started with the assurance that the limitations decision on motors and use was not taken hastily, and did take the interests of "those who use the river as a source of income" into account. He asserted: This decision was made in the Washington office of the Park Service, and approved by me. (This face-saving for NPS serves history poorly, since we had already been told that Reed had become interested early because of his personal interest in boating and that he had been glad to take full credit for the decision on October 3.) On use limits, the Assistant Secretary cited the draft master plan that called for a limit of 76,350 user-days including passengers and crew. (Not quite; the January 1971 draft set a commercial limit at about 72 KUD, the 1970 actual use. So Reed could have added that in 1971, commercial use went down to 66 KUD, well and good. Then Lovegren let 1972 total commercial use balloon to 105 KUD, and the fan started spraying.) Detailed research data not being available to set the limit, he went on, we have used the best judgment of our people who have worked most intimately with the resource. We think the public will appreciate our effort to protect the resource. Anyway, the great increase in use took place over such a short span that we cannot adequately assess effects now, so this limit allows the time to do the research. Further, there may be too many comm ops for all to profit, so we may drop some when current contracts expire. (You got yourselves into this mess, and watch out, or I will throw you babies out with the dirty bathwater.) Reed's reply then moves on to motors, and makes the unequivocal statement, "Motors are antithetical to the quality of a wilderness experience that is, and should be, available in the Grand Canyon." There may be some pollution, but that is not the point. This unique escape from civilization should not be impaired by modern technology in the form of motors "with all that they connote". Whether designated as Wilderness or not, "this canyon sanctuary [from the pressure of modern life] deserves to be preserved and perpetuated." "None [of our wild canyons] is more important to the human experience than the Grand Canyon." (Finally, Reed is going directly back to the founding principles of the Park System: Motors impair the enjoyment, and enjoyment is supposed to be provided in a Park in an unimpaired way.) He dismisses the safety argument, suggesting motor use has more to do with "convenience", which is not compelling in the context of wilderness travel. Partial trips are available for those who do not want to spend the time, money, or stamina for a 12-day trip. He wound up hoping that the comm ops could be utilized to provide the unique experience so as to preserve the Canyon for posterity, and so as to provide a viable economic operation. At the same time as the letter was sent to Brown, the Park Service put out the bulk of it as a policy statement, and as you read about the vicissitudes of the coming years, it is worth holding this thought: the above policy, here receiving its finest expression, remained the stated policy for eight years—though weakened in application, it was only overturned by a radical shift in the American electorate.

Even as the numbers issue seemed to ease, the comm ops pressed on their central concern, keeping motors. In mid-March, the Park Service heard that CROA would file suit in federal court, based on the lack of an EIS. Early in April, Burke wrote "dear Barry" that Goldwater was not being objective in taking motors off the river.[22] You, Burke told the senator, have a preference for hard rowboats. You refuse to take a motor trip. You refused to meet informally with the comm ops, even though Staveley and Sanderson asked. You never consulted the four comm ops located in Arizona. What is the point of getting money for research when an arbitrary decision has already been made? How about allowing motors with strict limits, like making motor trips the same length as rowing, ten to twelve days?

What this question may suggest to the reader is that there were chances for negotiation. Burke frequently would throw out some idea or other as if he were a reasonable person, as when he assured people, "I realize there must be a limit on people going down the river. In my opinion, the 1972 quota was just about the limit."[23] Such words can be measured against the futile attempt back in November, when the comm ops had a chance to offer use alternatives, and could not agree among themselves. This failure was an indicator of a general hard-headedness. No one, *no one*, ever did the hard work that would have been necessary for compromise to be discussed. We all felt justified in choosing to fight, though our styles may have differed; as Congressman Steiger said to his friend: Fred, "you are as moderate and soft-spoken a bomb thrower as I've seen", or as one congressional aide said of me, "Ingram is really a bit abrasive." Of course, the idea of compromise was hard to sell to people all pumped up and hopeful. In the letter just quoted, Steiger encouraged Burke, saying he must not despair, things were happening, and he would let him know shortly.[24] Whatever he let him know, Burke kept the letters happening, from his customers, and from himself to Steiger, Reed, Moss, Ruch—preaching the gospel of motors, while complaining he was being ill-treated.[25]

At this time, we suffered a real loss. Fred Eiseman had gone down the river many times; rowing trips of several weeks' duration with friends were a standard vacation. The Park Service, in some sort of crazed attempt at even-handedness, decided in its 1973 rules to regulate those few hundred self-guided river travelers just as hard as they did the comm ops. Yet comparing the two, in 1972, comm ops sent down 30 times as many people consuming 14 times as many user-days. NPS, claiming that requests for self-guided trips had jumped four times over the previous year, was worried about how to respond to this demand just as they were limiting comm op use. One of their efforts was a new rule limiting trip length to three weeks. This was much shorter than Fred was used to, and so in February, he quit, really quit, resigning from his four Park advisory committees and from the Grand Canyon Natural History Association board, refusing to provide any more help on the river, and changing his will.[26] Later he wrote me saying that he had not been told about the new rules, and they made him pretty mad since he had done all the preparation for his usual six-week trip. He blamed the Park Service for not upsetting the comm ops' plans and for not treating self-guided river-runners on an equal basis. Whatever Fred meant by this, this complaint appears in my files as the first reaction to the continuing inequity in river access between the self-guided and the commercial trip. Fred admitted that he had been active to preserve the area both as a worthy cause and also out of selfishness. Later, he softened a bit, writing to Reed full of praise for his eloquence, though noting he, Eiseman, was no longer in the fray. Fred claimed he only cared about the length of his trip, and could accept other restrictions such as when or how often or even whether he could go.[27]

Goldwater was sympathetic, saying he was "very shook up" at Fred's decision, and that he was sure there would have been no problem "getting you permission to take as long a trip as you want ... I would stake my bottom dollar on that."[28] He hoped Fred would reconsider "because all of us owe this beautiful work of God more than it owes us." What Goldwater's letter says to me is that, in the effort to preserve the gains brought by the Reed decision, a vital link between the Canyon's strongest congressional friend and us, the citizen friends of the Canyon, was broken when Eiseman no longer provided an active mediating role. A response by Goldwater earlier in the month to McComb is another measure of that loss, as he noted "an unusual amount of pressure here in Washington" to get Interior to change its river plan.[29] "You might alert your members that we may need their help", he wrote. With Fred around, this tone might possibly have been preserved on river matters, even as the Park enlargement fight heated up (next chapter). But maybe not; we were awfully strident for Goldwater's taste. In any case, Fred's return to his tent meant the loss of a champion for the Canyon.

Comm op activity quickened. Park Service and Congressman Steiger's archives give some indication of the volume of letters. Utah, seemingly the ideological center of anti-Park sentiment, got in some more local cheerleading, when the state legislature considered a resolution, complete with over-blown rhetoric about clean trips and economic deprivation, calling for an end to restrictions.[30] A Utah congressman backed up by comm op Hatch tried to press safety, but they undercut themselves by saying there were too few rowing trips to judge the dangers.[31]

Senator Moss, through the chairman of the Senate Parks Subcommittee, made the Park Service provide answers to what he hoped would be embarrassing questions about the arbitrariness of the decision on the new policy. At first, the Park Service worried about answering, given the possibility of being sued. After discussion with the Solicitor's Office, they prepared a draft, dancing through the minefield, denying the comm ops' contentions about an arbitrary, secretive decision, the advantages of big boats, safety, etc. NPS asserted they were protecting the resource, that generalizations from the Boster report were invalid, and conceding only that any reductions would only happen if needed. Research has to be done, and we had to stop the increase because so little was known. The letter reaffirmed that motors were antithetical to quality wilderness experience. So far, so good.[32]

With no yielding indicated by the Park Service, CROA was working on its court suit. The Park Service had a visit from an attorney who went through the files. There were consultations with the Solicitor's office, and the latter wanted another memorandum on the basis of the decision. Also, officials were told to prepare a chronological record of Park Service actions.[33] The shoe finally dropped on April 18, when a complaint was filed in federal District Court by the CROA companies against the Secretary and Park Service officials.[34] They sought an injunction against restrictions on river travel in GCNP, since their January request for relief was denied. Their first charge was that no EIS had been done as required by NEPA (they did not offer to rescind their previous increases and contracts, which had also been done without an EIS). Great harm would be done if reservations had to be canceled, and "large numbers of the public as a whole will be deprived of the unique experience" of a river trip. Then the complaint undercuts its EIS charge by saying that the Park Service had announced an increase for 1973 (though the complaint failed to note that no EIS had been prepared for that).

The motor decision was attacked as representing a "personal" preference of the Park Service and "private conservation groups", claiming there existed no statutory authority for such a decision (although they had accepted such regulatory authority when they entered into their concession contracts). The self-righteous conclusion the lawyers drew was that the action was due to "improper deference to pressures and threatened legal actions" from private conservation groups. (It is a terrible thing to try to gore another ox, and look down to see the blood dripping from your belly. Politics hath no fury like an interest group scorned.) They asked for an injunction against the imposition of arbitrary and capricious restrictions until proper considerations could be formulated. In doing so, they revealed a truly fundamental misreading of the Park Service's "fundamental statutory responsibility to preserve the resource for the widest possible use and enjoyment and to maintain diversity and variety of individual choice." Of course, this is exactly *not* NPS's fundamental statutory responsibility.

The Park Service did get ready to be grilled; on May 3, Chapman called Stitt to join him in Salt Lake to give evidence on the 11th. A little later that day, Chapman called again, saying the deposition was called off. We, too, did a little preparation, drafting a document to support a request to intervene on behalf of the Park Service, stressing our agreement with its current course of a multi-year plan to assess visitor impact. The Interior lawyers prepped their Justice colleagues, saying that the use level of 55 KUD *might* be reached based on research, but there was no decision yet.[35] The concession contracts gave NPS the right to limit use. An EIS was not required, since NPS had concluded that the action was not major. Finally, there was no improper deference to political pressure; this was all part of public consultation.

CROA comm ops, like Currey and Hatch, continued to solicit letters to legislators and Interior to retain motors (their euphemism was "choice", which translated into motor boaters keeping 80% of all use) and the 1972 allotment of 125 KUD total use.[36] They continued to charge that the Park Service was arbitrary in setting its number (ignoring how arbitrary NPS had been when it did their bidding). They claimed nothing had been done on the study, which they said was "vitally needed", noting that until an EIS was completed, visitation would be controlled by guesswork. There was the scare language, "locking everyone out" and rowboats are "more vulnerable to upset".

On June 4, Judge Willis Ritter dismissed the complaint.[37] Noting that oral and documentary evidence had been presented, he wrote that none of the evidence CROA presented warranted an injunction and that the officials "acted within their statutory authority and upon a reasonable and rational basis". The UPI quoted the judge as orally asking why he should stick his oar into the management of a National Park, then slyly brought up that the same judge had ordered the filling of Lake Powell stopped earlier in the year, to keep water out of Rainbow Bridge National Monument. The Judge went on that Glen Canyon Dam had destroyed enough, and we had to be careful about what was downstream. On July 9, CROA filed notice that it would appeal Ritter's dismissal.

Ironically, Judge Ritter had been over-ruled on the Lake Powell filling in May, which meant that flow from Glen Canyon Dam was drastically cut, causing the Park Service to complain that their patrol boat had been hung up, and more advance notice was needed.[38] They wanted twice as much water released during the summer, from 6,000 to 12,000 cubic feet per second (cfs). That number was interesting, since the comm ops with big boats wanted at least 12,000 cfs, too. However, it was three small rowing companies that filed suit this time, trying in July to force larger releases, since otherwise river-running was hazardous. They also claimed there should have been an EIS before such a cutback. Again, a district judge ruled against them, in August giving the Bureau of Reclamation a free hand in operating the dam. This ruling was upheld by the appeals court a year later. The appeals court declined to rule on whether there was an obligation to supply enough water for float trips; that issue would be taken up many years later.

The comm ops, on hold in the courts, concentrated on bringing pressure to bear on the executive branch, using their legislative contacts. Since they charged in their court suit that political pressure improperly brought about a policy they did not like, you might think that, souls of integrity that they were, they would not have sunk to such means. In any case, Senator Moss made his trail clear, by bragging in the *Congressional Record* about all he had done to get the Park Service to justify its actions.[39] He brought about the meeting in January with comm ops and Interior and NPS officials. Then, at a hearing before the Senate's Parks subcommittee on June 21, he attacked the NPS Director, calling the use ceiling a "rash action". He further complained NPS was ignoring the comm ops' expertise on motors. He boasted that he had received hundreds of letters from across the United States. He cited the Utah legislature's call for ending the limits. (This call was reduced to a squeak by anti-motor river-runners whose own clamor forced the bottling up of the resolution.[40]) Throughout, however, Moss maintained he only wanted to keep the status quo while research was being done. What upset him was that the Park Service wanted to "turn the numbers down" and phase out motors without evidence from studies. He went on and on, retailing the usual distortions.

Burke, adopting Moss's position in favor of keeping the status quo, charged that Interior was not doing this.[41] He complained to Ruch that the Park Service was still making reductions; Interior was speaking with a forked tongue. He spoke of "numerous tip-overs of small boats". Fortunately motor rafts were there to help, otherwise there would have been a tragedy. (He did not mention that the only Grand Canyon drowning in the three seasons 1971-3 had been in 1972—from a motorized raft).

Burke was active in other ways. He got Congressman Rhodes on one of his August trips. Later, Rhodes wrote to the Secretary of the Interior, passing on a standard complaint, that allotments for each comm op were arbitrary, and should be on the basis of quality. Rhodes offered as an example that he observed "crowded boats" of some outfitters, and that some "refused to pause ... to allow passengers to enjoy and absorb the beauty of the Canyon".[42] Burke was also writing Steiger that the Park Service was just stalling until Congress had cooled off, when they would insist on mandatory reductions in motor use. Though he worried because of the "uncertainty" as to what equipment to buy, the only uncertainty arose because of the comm ops' determination to upset the policy. Burke would not change this tune, no matter how many times the Park Service restated its position, and he would keep on for years trying to create the uncertainty he could then complain about.

Revealing windows are opened here: the congressman's trip, Burke's criticism of other comm ops and his claim to be a compromiser—unlike CROA, of which he was not a member and whose suit he did not join (another comm op said it was because of the cost).[43] It was rare that at the time, we had much sense of the strategies of, and differences among, our opponents.

From Senator Moss, the lead passed to Representative Steiger. Early in 1973, he was replying to those who sent him letters that the rules are in effect, and we can only study.[44] In March, he was still saying that Interior has the right and responsibility to regulate use, but he had not heard an effective argument for banning motors. His case for motors grew stronger, saying he thought small motors were consistent with Park mandates. (One admirable quality: Sam answered letters whether they came from his district or not, and this in the days of carbon copies.) In May, he had yet to hear a "really cogent" argument for a ban, and he was hearing lots against one. Staveley, with a mid-sized allotment, thought motors could be kept if everybody would be like him—satisfied with a couple of boats a week and carrying out all waste. Burke talked about rowboat drownings he had heard about, saying the Park Service would not discuss them (they did not happen, after all). He listed a bunch of incidents where motor rafts had rescued rowers, and cried out: If motors are gone, who will help these guys? Burke's advice to Steiger: Do not talk to Reed, get Morton to reconsider. In June, Steiger was writing that the motor ban was unwise. There was no EIS, and he was doing all he could on the issue. The campaign also stirred up the lesser senators from Arizona and Utah, who wrote to Morton asking for a review of the policy. Steiger replied to a particularly heavy pile of letters in July and August, an indication of a renewed pulse of letters from passengers, and also of the mail going to other legislators and Interior.

The form replies from the Park Service also shifted. In June, removing motors was "essential to a quality experience".[45] The phase-out was to help the comm ops amortize the cost and to coincide with contract expiration. Two months later, the safety issue led off, with the Park Service insisting that neither rowing nor motors had a margin of safety over the other. The wilderness experience was stressed, and the need to ban motors in order to have a designated wilderness. "Visitors are entitled to a true wilderness experience."

The impact of this mail was not evident to the Superintendent, who was talking in August about clean beaches.[46] Next year, he assured me, the use would be the same, while each operator would have no more than 75% motor trips. At this time, Reed wrote to Burke: I really do give a damn about your opinions. The Park Service is working on a full evaluation of the river problem. (I think it is important to keep in mind that Reed, Steiger, Morton, Goldwater and most of the other politicians were all Republicans in a time—until 1977—of Republican administrations. Moss and Congressman Udall were exceptions, and clearly indicate that the river issue cut across party lines.)

Secretary Morton gave even more of a damn.[47] On September 5, he met with Steiger about the use level and motor ban, after an NPS briefing the day before. Based on these encounters, the Secretary decided, in a memo to NPS Director Walker, "to have a study conducted on the use of motors on the river—the parameters of such a study to be agreed upon by the NPS and the boat concessionaires". The feasibility of eliminating use of all motors more powerful than 20-25 horsepower should be determined "immediately or in the near future". The next day, a memo went to Reed (and Ruch) from a Special Assistant, Richard Curry, reaffirming that Steiger had urged Morton to study the issue prior to action, and Morton agreed to that and also dropping the more powerful motors. The next day Reed's office wrote the Solicitor that Morton had requested a study of motor use. But this memo brought in a new element by saying, "In view of the public expressions in opposition to this decision, we are presently reevaluating the requirement for a reduction beginning in 1974." Where had this reduction re-evaluation come from? What had happened to a discussion of the "parameters" for the study? And who deep-sixed the decision to move toward a ban of bigger motors? In none of the memos is safety mentioned or even hinted at. Even more weird is that NPS, surely working overtime, immediately drafted a response to public inquiries that stated the phasing out of motors was postponed because of public concern.[48] There would be a definitive study on which future decisions would be based.

In a conversation with me a week later, Ruch lamented the "decision", but claimed that the change was not set in concrete. He had "shot his wad" at the Morton-Steiger meeting, and all he had achieved was agreement that if study supported the ban, then it would hold. He stressed that the action was with Morton. However, it was he, Ruch, who had suggested to the Park Service that it prepare a memo on safety. Some weeks later, following telephoned instructions, Reed confirmed to Chapman that "the Secretary and I agree that (the 25% reduction) should not be made operative pending further study".[49] In addition to "other aspects", please carefully assess the issue of safety and motor use.

But what had Morton decided? On the one hand, Steiger gloated in late October to McComb about his river "victory", saying Morton was convinced motors were safer. His letters at that time thanked Morton for following through on the motor ban issue by agreeing not to implement a ban without a detailed EIS showing it is really needed.[50] Currey too, was bragging about his victory to the other comm ops, and his lawyer was emboldened enough to argue that the concession contracts gave some rights, so we want the educational user-day supplement, allotments based on customer applications, and an overall increase.[51] Reed, and the Park Service following his lead, certainly softened up by the heavy anti-phaseout mail, seemed to think there had been a decision. Senator Fannin (R-Arizona) wrote Morton he supported the decision to do a "one-year" study. A California senator, John Tunney, said he favored the phase-out, and asked Morton why he had changed to a study.[52] On the other hand, Ruch was still telling McComb he was optimistic that Morton could be changed, and he would work to get Reed involved. In early December, I talked with one witness, Richard Curry (the Interior official, not Currey the motor boater), who recounted that at the Steiger meeting, Morton had only told "a story" (which we know from Chapter 1) to show he knew about safety, but, Curry insisted, had not made any decision. It was his "subordinates in the Secretariat" who then immediately conveyed to the Park Service the notion that there had been a decision. Curry even claimed that Morton was surprised when he heard there would be a delay in the phase-out. Yet, when Eiseman—active again—

tried in September to get Curry to repeat his account in writing, he received the reply that the Secretary's concern was safety due to his 1967 experience when a motor helped rescue Oren Beaty (who had, you will remember, hit his head on a motor). Further than that, Fred could not get him to go.[53] Eiseman, in distress, had written Goldwater as well, only to get confirmation that Steiger, along with senators and congressmen from the Colorado River states, did "put the pressure on Morton", and "my lone plea fell on deaf ears".[54] Goldwater understood there would have to be a study; "Lord knows when that might come about", but he would keep pushing for a wilderness declaration, which is what Fred had said was the most important part of the river plan.

Yet if, as Curry suggested, some subordinates "created" a policy change for Morton, who were they? Paranoia can always supply answers. In this period, Richard Marks was working in the NPS directorate on river matters. This would be relevant when Marks became GCNP Superintendent in 1980, overseeing through the following decade the change from a dynamic wilderness river policy to a pro-motor status quo. Could his management in the 1980s have been a reflection of opinions developed in 1973-5? In this same 1973 period, one John Kyl was Assistant Secretary for Congressional and Legislative Liaison and involved, with Marks, in dealing with the response to the river policy. Kyl was a former Republican congressman from Iowa, and had been Morton's colleague on the House Interior Committee. His son, Jon, is at this writing a staunchly conservative Arizona senator who has been actively championing the comm op cause since 1980.

How wonderful coincidence is. Some mysterious "subordinates" work to subvert the Reed policy, just a little, but enough to give the comm ops a taste of blood and victory, enough to spur them in their intransigence. Then we can trace possible, even ephemeral, connections to later support for the comm ops. This is speculation, not connection, not to mention guilt by scant association. But what fun would politics be without a few conspiracy theories to titillate us?

Whatever the machinations, the fact is that on September 12, just one week after the Morton-Steiger meeting, GCNP sent letters to all the comm ops about the 1974 season.[55] Each was given an allocation equal to the 1973 amount, the total of which added up to the 89 KUD for passengers that was the amount they had actually used in 1972, as per the Reed decision. Then came the announcement that the requirement for a 25% reduction in motor use was dropped, though there was no mention of any study parameters. NPS was "suggesting" that each comm op "voluntarily" use a minimum of 25% of their allocation in rowing trips, "as we continue our research and study".

Well, reader, what do you think? Reaction to "public concern"? Real change? Hand-waving? Victory for the comm ops and defeat for friends of the Canyon's wilderness experience? Was Eiseman right that "the first step has been taken to reverse the plan"? Sometimes, you can only decide whether you've had a good or bad day when you get ready for bed and discover someone swiped your sheets hours before.

The Park Service continued losing no time in getting the changed message out. The form reply from the Western Region three weeks after the Morton-Steiger meeting asserted the necessity of the freeze at 89 KUD for commercial passengers.[56]

The goal for 1977 was still 55 KUD, but research would evaluate the impacts, and use could be set anywhere between 55 and 89 KUD. We cannot set a figure for each year now. We are deferring the motor phase-out, and asking comm ops to voluntarily row on 25% of their trips, pending that definitive study on which to base future decisions. In mid-October, the GCNP River Manager wrote up a briefing: The "dramatic escalation" of river use was checked; 1973 use was slightly lower than 1972 and the 1974 limit was set at the 1973 limit.[57] He noted the voluntary 25% for rowing would be followed by a "mandatory 50% industry-wide use of oars" in 1975. Accidents continue to be scattered, and "do not support the contention that oar-powered boats are a greater safety hazard". He called it "significant" that the limit on the number of persons who started trips at Lees Ferry would drop from 200 in one day to 150. The change was further cemented by a Western Region news release at the end of October.[58] "The mandatory phase-out of motor-powered rafts ... has been deferred pending further study." There was not adequate information on the impact of these rafts. "Through a vigorous program of research", NPS hoped to determine the impact of motors and the "maximum optimum" use of the River. A face was briefly put on this position when Chapman appeared before the House Parks Subcommittee on November 12. I watched as he answered all questions about the phase-out and the relation of motors to the need for large rafts by saying they were questions that would be answered by the studies.

Research, ah yes; where was that vigorous program of research? The draft research plan done the previous November had been slightly re-cast in May 1973 to refine the dollars needed—about $600,000 for the first three years.[59] Stitt then got a prod from his boss in mid-year: We need to get moving on the research.[60] We said we needed three years, Chapman reminded him; are we one-third through? As if in answer, by September contracts had been signed with the Museum of Northern Arizona research center for some of the biological work. At the same time, the Park Service took away one of the comm ops' bragging rights, returning the $3000 they had put up the year before for a research design. There was nothing yet on the social survey work, one goal of which would be exactly to look at the impacts motors had on visitors. One researcher actually doing work in the field had been discouraged in his search for funds, in part because it appeared NPS was looking for someone it thought more reputable.

GCNP got rid of still another irritation when it was able to announce, "with a great deal of regret", that the river advisory committee was dead, done in by a new law and Secretarial policy.[61]

And the lion was bearded: in November, an "acting" Secretary of the Interior wrote Goldwater that "after considerable public comment against annual reduction amounts" in motor use, the mandatory cut for 1974 was made voluntary, and we will expect "the best effort" by each comm op to provide an "optimum wild river experience". Next year, there would be a definitive study on safety and motor use on the river, though these studies will "in no way" alter the goal of recommending wilderness designation for the river in 1977, which is conditional on a motor ban.[62] Stitt interpreted this letter for me, saying he thought that the plan was modified and still in force. Whatever that meant, Chapman was manifestly more honest when he wrote Eiseman, "We want some time." We do not want to make any final statements or have a firm position until the study results can be "objectively" evaluated. If we make a final decision now, we will be faced with another situation where we might be reversed. "That is where we found ourselves recently and I don't want to repeat it." "I ask you for patience and understanding".

Well, time he would get. But life had gotten a bit too complicated to expect tea and sympathy.

CHAPTER 5

1972-75: So who was that Park Fight I saw you with Last Night?

This is no place to elaborate at length the intense, tortuous, tortured, torturing, cliffhanging—that is to say, normal—legislative history of Public Law 93-620, the Grand Canyon National Park Enlargement Act. Instead, in order to give the reader interested in the history of river policy some idea of what was absorbing so much of our attention from December 1972 through January 1975, I have relied on my journal to summarize how we spent our time, a distracted time. The coming and going of other Grand Canyon issues did not help our concentration; each seemed to exist in its separate compartment. It is typical that events following Reed's 1972 river decision dealt with matters substantively different from those in the Park enlargement battles.

There were two changes the Park enlargement legislation could bring about that we wanted for their effect on river policy: settling the boundary between the Hualapai Reservation and the National Park, and ordering a new Wilderness study for the enlarged Park. They were two of the ingredients needed to make a uniform policy for the river under a single, public ownership.

In the first place, we believed that the enlargement legislation was the place to remove any ambiguity about the Park boundary along the Colorado River; a need indicated by the Superintendent calling the river in the western Canyon a "no man's land"[1] and by the river discussion at Goldwater's house on December 4. The obvious solution was to resolve any ambiguity in favor of public ownership of the river surface. The other linkage we wanted was between a new Wilderness study and implementation of the Reed motor phase-out. We knew the linkage had to be strong, since the only way to absolutely ensure a ban on motors would be to have a congressionally designated Wilderness including the river and a time-certain motor ban. Therefore our goal was to mandate an NPS recommendation for Wilderness in the enlarged GCNP that would include the river. We wanted this recommendation to appear at the same time as the research was done and as the comm ops' contracts expired—the end of 1976—all feeding into the formulation of the new river management policy. A good strategy. We came close.

Before we start the story, a word about the subtext of public affairs. Underneath all the public statements and actions, what were the people really like, what did they really think and say, what were their real attitudes toward each other? Whether we like it or not, the unremitting hostility of Goldwater aide Emerson created almost by itself a barrier to our being able to deal openly with Goldwater. Though certainly, the senator's own love of the big picture and sweeping gesture was no help when it came to our wanting to explain in detail our approach to Park enlargement. A possible link frayed and disappeared as Fred Eiseman, Goldwater's friend, moved out and in and finally out of active participation. The end result is that we were "disrespected" as the enlargement legislation moved through the Senate, and Goldwater concluded we double-crossed him, when truly, we were fighting for what we had told him and announced to all that we were going to fight for. The impact on river policy of these feelings and attitudes would reverberate, most dramatically in late 1980.

Baffled in our attempts to work with Goldwater, we turned to a truer environmental ally, Morris Udall, the congressman from southern Arizona (where McComb and I lived). As a senior member of the House Interior and Insular Affairs Committee, he was perfectly located to hear our pleas for adequate Park legislation. And after a slow start, Udall committed himself and, most helpfully, one of his staff, to our dreams. That this was not enough is why there is a story. Which I will tell using only my journal—a vehicle tendentious, not complete, sometimes indecipherable, occasionally erroneous, yet to this re-reader always sobering—to chronicle our ride through those yesteryears of the 92nd Congress.

For background, Senator Goldwater had wanted to enlarge the Park, though in a minimal way, starting in the 1950s. The prospect of dam building got that initiative shelved. Then during the height of the war over the Grand Canyon dams, in early 1966, one of my bright ideas was that the Sierra Club should take a positive stand in favor of a "complete" Grand Canyon National Park, as well as being against the dams. In an intense session, under Brower's aegis, Martin Litton and I decided on what such a Park would include. Our fundamental axiom was that the Park should encompass the Grand Canyon and its "immediate drainage", that is, the entire 277 miles of the river from Lees Ferry to the Grand Wash Cliffs, the main canyon back to the rims, and the significant parts of its side canyons and the plateaus the Canyon was cut into. We drafted legislation, and it was introduced in Congress by Senator Case (R-New Jersey; he was an original; blessed be his memory) to the hoots and howls of Arizonans and other dam supporters. Well, it was a weird sort of craft, and certainly unflyable. Nevertheless, we had stated our principle: a Grand Canyon National Park that included the **entire** Grand Canyon. This is the principle we were now ready to promote in the 92nd Congress. Though it put us at odds with Goldwater and others, we did not intend that, nor did the story start out that way.

1972

November
Some interested parties first met, you will recall, at Goldwater's house, on December 4, 1972. John McComb and I, colleagues from the 1960s, were there as the Park

enlargement extremists. However, without abandoning our belief in that basic principle, we had been innovating. We visited with interested people to talk about enlargement from the direction of trying to find middle ground; not compromises, exactly, but different approaches toward the goals of protecting and celebrating the Canyon. Could exploiters, users, and preservationists deal with each other constructively, and avoid a big fight as Goldwater wished? We had primed ourselves for December 4 by our travels up and down, and down and up, the state from Tucson (115 miles to Phoenix, 261 to Flagstaff, 350 to the Canyon) in either his VW bug or my VW bus (all right, all right; but I did not wear birkenstocks). Some of the meetings dealt with the river, but we were also aiming at people we thought would be influential on various aspects of a bigger Park, e.g., people who worked with the Navajo, with Arizona's water resources, with hunting. And Fred Eiseman was always good for the gossip: Goldwater was "fired up"; he had been given the green light by the Senate Interior Committee chairman, Henry Jackson, if he could get agreement and avoid a big fight. Our goal too. We knew that the hunters would be less than enthusiastic about any Park expansion. The Havasupai would push to expand their tiny reservation to a more legitimate area that included plateau lands they had long used—lands unfortunately inside the Park System and the adjoining Kaibab National Forest. Steiger and Goldwater supported the expansion, but Eiseman reported the latter saying that if the Indians objected to his ideas, "damn 'em!" But that was Goldwater, who also grumbled to Fred about the Sierra Club being overbearing.

So in that river-busy November, we also checked with potential park expansion road-blockers, and came away feeling pretty good. Our proposal was that instead of just plumping for the Big Park, we would accommodate the water and grazing and hunting and tribal interests with appropriate face-saving language and what we were calling a Conservation Zone. The latter would take in the areas around the Park that were part of the Grand Canyon, but Park status for which would generate opposition. The Grand Canyon Conservation Zone would be an area for recreation, some roads, and would allow grazing and hunting, but not mining or logging. It would preserve the Grand Canyon, presenting it to the world within a jurisdiction wrapped around the Park itself. We also wanted our wilderness study, and would argue for the boundary of the Park to include all the Colorado River (all of its water surface, that is) from Lees Ferry to the Grand Wash Cliffs.

December

On the 4th, Goldwater led off by mentioning his worries: Navajo development on the East Rim, the Hualapai pushing for their dam, the Havasupai's inadequate land base. Goldwater aide Emerson reviewed the bill he had drafted for his boss. After discussion on that, I presented our views. My summary note was, "no good, result is negative." A meeting was scheduled for January 29 to see whether there was any better chance of agreement.

Over the next week, I drafted a bill and drew boundary maps—a rewarding fantasy activity, and more tedious work without today's reproduction capabilities. Then we wound up our VWs and went calling again on the wise men, hunters, congressmen, future governors, etc. One pleasant item: Emerson irritated everybody, a condition he did not help by giving out a premature press release before Christmas. Meanwhile, we consulted our own congressman, Morris Udall, "former son-of-a-bitch, now great friend" (it was funny when Mo said it), and he agreed to consider our approach if Goldwater brushed us off. Later he offered to have our bill drafted through his office. We also had Washington sources, and they told us the Park Service was casting around trying to find something to support, since they were not going to like any approach that moved land from the Park to the Havasupai.

1973

January
Meetings continued as we sought common ground. We had to accept the change that any Conservation Zone lands would continue under the jurisdiction of their current administrators. (There is a surprise kicker here; see this chapter's postscript.) So we shifted, the new aim being to get the Park Service into the Conservation Zone lands to do interpretation. This was easy compared to convincing everyone that the work we were doing was to bring about a bill that all parties could accept. At this point, our goal and, we assumed, Goldwater's was agreement. But that did not mean that any interest groups gave up their long-held views. For instance, the Sierra Club would still be on record for the complete National Park described above, even though it could accept a bill with some enlargement plus a zone that was a non-development buffer area. No wonder it was easy to accuse us of being two-faced, zipping around trying to get everyone to accept one approach when we believed in something much more extreme. Maybe we should just have sat there instead of trying to compromise the uncompromisable, or with the uncompromising. And maybe that is me. On river management, in a few years I was once again trying to push what I thought was reasonable, instead of sticking out for untarnished principle. I can only admire Brower's integrity, not emulate it; I am just too excited by the thought of being involved in getting something good done. Is practical innovation therefore the enemy of principled imagination? Are cakes only for eating, and should the other half loaf be left to mold?

McComb went to Washington, and heard good reactions. I met with the Park Service, and we seemed in good shape with them. The hunters gave us various answers; they wanted to sit quiet while Goldwater introduced a bill, then they would decide what to aim at. The Forest Service was, we learned, gearing up to be sure it maintained its jurisdiction and discretion; both the Havasupai and we wanted some of their land. As the month went on, it was clear there were a lot more players and they were mostly going to watch and wait. The January 29 meeting at Goldwater's was much more crowded: more bureaucrats, lots of hunters, congressmen, cattlemen, many Hualapai and Havasupai, and us too. What a joke: we wanted a real Park, Goldwater wanted some Park, and we were talking to about 20 people who would rather not have any more Park, thank you very much. In a sign of what was to come, the biggest discussion was about the Havasupai desire for a decent land base. The Hualapai dam dream was brought up and Goldwater emphatically said it would never be built. Those two items were the lead in media reports that followed the meeting. My most vivid memory is of Emerson, when we went up to him after the meeting, refusing to discuss the boundary with us even though Goldwater had publicly agreed with our idea of taking the boundary to the western end of the Canyon.

February - March 9
So much for seeking cooperation and agreement. It had been a long shot anyway; there were too many other conservation groups who would oppose taking any land out of a Park for economic purposes, including for the Havasupai. Our incentive was further diminished when McComb got a frosty reception from Emerson in his early-February Washington visit. Emerson re-drafted the bill on his own with more for the Havasupai and for the Park, and then went about collecting other senators' endorsements; he had twenty co-sponsors in early March.

March
A new voice was heard on behalf of the Havasupai, as their publicists distributed material attacking environmentalists. Our two-month effort at compromise seemed more and more quaint as we analyzed the Goldwater bill, realizing the distance it was from our hopes, and the emphasis it put on the Havasupai land. Worse, some land was to be deleted from the Grand Canyon National Monument for the ranchers and hunters. We tried to slow endorsements of the Goldwater bill, but Udall joined up, his staff saying we would get our chance in the House. The bill was introduced on March 20, having absorbed much of our attention for four months— a crucial four months in the viability of the Reed river decision.

May - July 10
The next four months were quiet—for me. I did other things, including travel to Baja California, coming back to go to the hospital with a kidney stone. Meanwhile, Goldwater was pressing for action on his bill. Efforts were being made by the Havasupai, including pressuring the Sierra Club chapter in Arizona. Goldwater was rewarded with Senate hearings on June 20, at exactly the time I was hospitalized. McComb spent ten days in Washington and, as his reward, received a personal letter from Goldwater, who was hurt, shocked and flabbergasted that McComb had testified against Goldwater's bill. So he really gave us the back of his hand. On July 10, we saw his "refined" version. It dropped anything like a conservation or buffer zone, kept the Monument deletions, and deleted the river, with the Havasupai getting only one more study.

July 15 - 25
I went to Washington, in full-dress lobbying mode for the first time in five years, re-establishing old contacts and trying to map out how the ground lay. I did see Emerson and received another blow: he would not include any wilderness provision. With all this bad in the bill, we focussed on what seemed the most pressing evil to us: how to keep lands from being deleted from the National Monument for hunting and grazing. In practice, an effort of this kind involves round after round of visits to

aides in the offices of senators who were likely to oppose the deletion on principle—the lands themselves were too remote and unknown. We searched out people who could talk to people. Walking and taxiing in Washington in the suit-and-tie uniform in July! No wonder lobbyists demand enough money to afford limousines.

At first it seemed the effort went wrong. We had not dramatized the issue and so we had to be negative, opposing the bill. We had no qualms about that part since, although the boundary of the Park was re-drawn, the lands included were mostly already under Park jurisdiction. We did not see it as adding much protection or recognition to the Canyon. Then, after pushing the line against the deletions for a week, I got in to see one key Park System supporter, Senator Metcalf of Montana. He agreed to stand fast on the principle of no deletions from the Park System. He was also pushing another matter that would delay Parks Subcommittee action, giving us time for more lobbying. We were able to obtain active help from another senator. Another plus was that Goldwater was not on the Interior Committee, so his influence as the sponsor and home state senator was at one remove.

August
Back in Arizona in August (dry heat, no suit), the Superintendent told me about being interviewed on the Havasupai matter for the television program *60 Minutes* during a trip to Supai village. "Stacked", Stitt told me about the interviewing. And he thought it important that the Park Service had recently learned of a "big ruin" being found in the lands to be deleted.

Turning up the heat, Goldwater put in the *Congressional Record* a long attack on the Sierra Club and its activities on his bill, and summed it up in a letter to the Arizona Republic on August 4. Could we have earned his enmity any more thoroughly had we, from the beginning, just stated our principled position for an enlarged Park, and let him, the politician, work on getting agreement? Non-combatants often wonder and whine: Well, why can't you just compromise? The best answer I can come up with is that advocates push their views, and it is the job of politicians to weigh the competing pressures and do the compromising. We worked too hard at carrying Goldwater's water, and he left the dirty work to his underling. Two wrongs made a disaster.

September 5 - 13
After recess, the fight picked up again, with Emerson on the offensive about the lands to be deleted not being Park-worthy, and the Sierra Club being isolated. The Park Service's position had become confused, so we had to bounce between senatorial staff, a conservation lobbyist in Washington, the Park Service, and Reed's aide Curry, to get a Departmental letter of position against the deletions. (And this was being done at exactly the time, to the day, of the Morton meeting with Steiger, and with this same Curry, at which the motor phase-out policy was changed.)

A few days later I was back in Washington. (Later on, I estimated that from July 1973 to the end of 1974, I spent about 20% of my time in D.C.) The Senate Interior Committee staff called a meeting to explore the issues, getting NPS and Emerson together with conservationists. This was a lovely moment. Emerson told Chapman it was time to let the deletions go. Chapman said no. Emerson retorted, "we will see about that" and dashed out of the meeting. Curry said the letter we had gotten generated was the official position, and I chimed in that we would fight every step of the way. Emerson came back; he stated the arguments for hunting and grazing, and said there would be a new position, "I guarantee". Chapman piped up and said he had heard about an understanding between Morton and Goldwater, but nothing in writing. Committee Staff Director Verkler: The committee will want to know exactly what the position is. Emerson, "You will know!!" Verkler, referring to the appearance on national TV of the Havasupai campaign, asked if the bill had become so controversial it would have to go on the backburner. Another tiff broke out between Emerson and Stitt, so Verkler asked if the deletions were taken out of the bill, would Goldwater oppose the entire bill? Yes, said Emerson.

After the meeting, Curry talked with Morton, who (does this sound familiar?) had no recollection of a conversation about the deletions with Goldwater. Curry intercepted Goldwater's call, full of senatorial pique. The next day, Verkler was telling us he had had a "mad" call from Goldwater the evening before. And just at that moment, Goldwater called again, apologetic, saying he only wanted to get the bill out. Verkler suggested a study of the deletions, but Goldwater said "no need for any study b.s."; get the bill out; I want to protect the Canyon. Then Reed returned Verkler's call, saying that Morton saw Goldwater at a reception last night, and there was no trouble, thanks to Reed's aides. After that, Verkler gave us the job of drafting changes on the deletions. (Equal time: "we" here included George Alderson, who then worked for The Wilderness Society; a good man.)

This was all such fun. We scurry about the halls, from office to office, pushing this, getting in on that. Oh, there's the Great Man himself. Please sir, a minute. No, no; I'm too busy, send me a memo. Or: Stop your lobbying; we're on the same side; just relax. Meanwhile in private, the Great Ones carry on in the Great Manner. What a fizz.

The major hunting group, the National Federation of Wildlife, got testy, and said it would not support the bill anymore. It had heard from its Arizona hunting affiliate, which was really, really upset. The next day or so was very tense, a round of concern and reassurance, as we worked toward the Subcommittee meeting to vote on the bill. I took the time to visit Udall, and told the juicy story of Emerson's reversal. As our key hope in the House, Udall said he might be willing to do something about adding more land, but the problem was Taylor, the chairman of the Parks Subcommittee, who did not like controversy. (These guys! What do they get elected for?) He agreed to spend some time on the matter, with the idea that there could be House hearings in early 1974.

On the day of the vote, September 13, the suspense was over whether there would be a quorum. My notes record senators wandering in and out, complaining and joking. The chairman was there at 10 a.m. One friendly senator said he understood the deletions were deleted. Another noted objections of conservation groups had been met. Verkler said, "Everybody's happy." We needed 8 for the vote to be formalized; one senator went out, another came in, the other guy came back; we were at 7. Then, at 10:35, Metcalf came in for number 8, and it was done. I thanked Metcalf, Verkler, and another senator who had been helpful at a crucial moment. I had other thank yous to make, but as far as the Senate action was concerned, Verkler assured me it would be moved along without problems. I took myself out to an excellent dinner; as I said, it is important to celebrate victories when they happen.

September 20 - 24

And indeed, a week later, back home, I learned from Verkler that Goldwater had changed his mind once again, at the behest of the hunters and their friends, and now wanted that "b.s." study as to whether the lands that had been kept were actually worthy of their Park status. McComb and I drafted some language to retain the lands and have them studied for their Park values. We checked the provision with allies, and sent it to Verkler who saw that it was, as he put it, "added to the bill in the stilly waters of the night". So, on September 24, the Senate, quietly, approved a Grand Canyon bill, much maimed but with the deletion lands still in the Park. So quietly that Goldwater did not even know of the event and was angry about it, Verkler said. The Senate had worked its will—for the moment.

September 28 - October 31

We had already been making contacts and having conversations in the House of Representatives, particularly with Udall. He was certainly the most likely person to be of some help in getting the bill changed to add the provisions important to us: 225,000 more acres of river, canyon, and rim lands; a wilderness study within two years; GCNP jurisdiction over the entire river; a few other odds and ends. After taking our lumps and giving a few in the Senate, we were even more fervent about fighting for a Park closer to our basic principles.

A few days after Senate passage, McComb talked to Udall but heard discouraging words. The latter did not want to take any lead or even a visible part, and thought that there might be hearings in 1973, but no chance of passage. It seemed as if he was not going to be helpful. Meanwhile, on the opposition side, Steiger—perhaps juiced up by his river victory a few weeks previous, but in any case always feisty and ready for a brawl, though I also swear, always courteous and never remote to us—was going to fight for the Havasupai, for the Hualapai and their dam, and for the hunters. However, when McComb talked to him, he was not yet ready to cause trouble, since Goldwater had recently had him to lunch and pressed him hard. McComb told him what we wanted to accomplish; Steiger was wary about the impact on grazing.

A pause now to recognize a friend lost. After a period of heart trouble, John P. Saylor, a long-time Republican Representative from Pennsylvania, died in October 1973. One of the strongest voices for Wilderness, the big voice of big John had been heard since he introduced a Wilderness bill in 1956. An easterner on the westerners' preserve, the Interior and Insular Affairs Committee, he was full of seniority. From this seat, he had been a formidable threat to the development coalition, roaring against the Grand Canyon dams. Those horrors done in, he turned to legislating a National Park that would keep dams out for good. He had introduced his latest Park bill in early January 1973, but his death occurred a couple of weeks before House action actually started. His absence changed the complexion of Republican response to the bill on the Interior Committee, giving Steiger full scope to dominate that side. Another what-if to mull over.

November 5 - 14

All of a sudden, on November 5, we heard that hearings had been set before the House Parks Subcommittee, and in only one week's time. Shock and disorder. Udall's staffer, Bracey, told us he had not had any forewarning. Udall might not even be there, but the Havasupai would come in full force to argue their case for a substantial reservation made up from National Forest and Park lands. So off we went to Washington again, accompanied by several others who could give testimony at the hearings and visit congressional offices. These are the best kind of spokespeople: folks from back home, volunteers for their beliefs. Perhaps I should mention at this point that I was a citizen activist in these years and unpaid, though reimbursed for many expenses like travel.

We checked with various Park Service officials; hoping to avoid trouble for our ideas on additions, since the first thing a Committee will do is ask the relevant bureaucracy for its opinion, and we had not had the chance we needed to convince Stitt and Chapman of the need for our additions. I tried to talk to the Subcommittee chairman with not much effect, and worked with its staff on questions that could be asked during the hearing to bolster our case, or at least not hurt it. We consulted the usual allies, and found some support, once again from an easterner, John Seiberling of Ohio.

When we visited Udall, he said he was glad to see action; he had been the one to push for it because he did not want it to cause delay on some "bigger" issues that he was working on. His idea was that this Grand Canyon thing would not be an overly controversial, time-absorbing item. We worked the Subcommittee members, sometimes the congressmen, more often a staffer, and got various reactions: suspicion, readiness, ignorance, awareness. Checking with the Park Service after Stitt's arrival in Washington to testify gave me some hope they would not mess things up for us.

The hearing itself dropped the flag on the battle to come, as Steiger declared that he had been fighting for the Havasupai for years, and was ready to work to get them the land they wanted. Any more study (which the Senate-passed bill called for) was a cop-out. Goldwater had given up too easily, and the only real opposition was from the Forest Service and the conservationists; there were no significant cattle interests. The last was important to Sam, since as later events proved, white cattle-growers were higher on his value hierarchy than the Havasupai.

The Park Service testimony was conservative: We want to do some more study. The Committee Chairman floated a distorted version of a buffer zone, and the Park Service promptly sank it as unnecessary. The chairman and another member then asked what NPS thought of the lands we wanted to add. Stitt said they were Park quality, but he was not fully informed about other uses on those lands, so NPS was not changing its position. Our concerns about the river were addressed, but little light was shed, in part because the witness accompanying Stitt was ignorant and insisted on answering; shortly thereafter he went to another agency.

The Havasupai were next up, their new (white) spokesman detailing the tribe's long history of trying to get a decent land base. The Hualapai and an Arizona state agency then asked for permission to build their dam.

Our delegation from home, talking with Udall after the hearing, complained that the aide he had assigned to this bill was too political. Udall agreed, calling him "over-protective". He told us to provide him various options so he could decide what he would do. He could ask allies on the Committee to help. He opined that Goldwater might quit (he did not), and that Sam was erratic. But when we visited Steiger, he proved just the opposite, pushing the Havasupai moral and human claim. He said we would lose politically by opposing a reservation enlargement. He and Goldwater were driving a train that would run down any opposition, ensuring that Park and Reservation changes would move together. The next day we made the rounds, talking to over ten of the committee members. Our reception was friendly, but we knew other parties were doing the same.

November 19 - December 12
Udall finally gave us an opening, assigning Dale Pontius as his staff person on the bill. In conversation, McComb found him responsive when shown our map and he could see how our boundary appeared logical. In early December, Mo met with Pontius and his more political aide, and agreed to go with an amendment to add land to the Park along the lines we were asking for. In pondering Goldwater's reaction, we argued that he just wanted some kind of Grand Canyon bill. Another break was that some personnel changes at Interior gave us a friendlier ear on our additions. So I talked to Stitt, assuring him that he could ignore the Interior testimony at the hearings and listen to us since Udall seemed willing to help.

December
McComb had a meeting with the Havasupai. They were angry, and wanted to know why the Sierra Club could not help them get their land out of the National Park and Forest. Moreover, they were pushing to get all or part of the Arizona Sierra Club chapter to back them.

These are vexing matters, and deserve some discussion here even though their bearing on river issues is not direct:

1. The question of restoring land and other rights to various tribes was not peculiar to the Grand Canyon. There had been, and would be, fierce battles in various parts of the country on the question. For some people, there was no problem; they just opposed transferring land to any tribes, period, and particularly if their own interests would be hurt. For others, this was a classic cross-pressuring issue. We believed in the essential goodness and worthiness of the National Park idea, and we defended it and the Park System against attacks (like putting dams or their reservoirs in Parks). In particular, we worried that taking land out of a Park for an economic purpose, say to log trees, was bad on its face (the trees belonged in the Park) and as precedent (take lands from one Park, and soon no Park will be safe). On the other hand, many, including some of us same do-gooders, worried about centuries of maltreatment and worse of the first Americans. These people were sympathetic to claims for help by disadvantaged tribes, including enlarging their reservations or paying money for lands taken.

So here was where not a few Sierra Club members stood: We revere the Grand

Canyon and want to protect the National Park. We understand and sympathize with the Havasupai, whose reservation was grossly inadequate when it was set up— more grossly than usual. We support their desire to have sovereignty over the lands necessary for them to live well according to their own ideas. Some of these lands are in the National Park System. Crash! Whether or not some formula could have been devised to accommodate these two incompatibles, the facts are that no one really tried. Had Goldwater or his staff had the right temperaments, maybe something could have been worked out, since the former certainly had the clout and position to have insisted had he wished to. Udall was a more likely candidate for working toward a compromise solution. However, no one did step forward and the old battle lines were maintained. The Sierra Club and its allies, including me, became the most visible leaders in the fight to keep lands in the Park.

2.   So what about those cross-pressured people? They had to make a choice. There were pro-Havasupai organizations they could work with, or they could help maintain the Sierra Club principles, one primary value of which had to do with the Canyon and its protection and presentation in a Park. What they ought not to have done, what I thought improper and unethical to do, was to confuse the two goals by pursuing them under the same organizational umbrella. There were two quite clearly defined groups: the Havasupai and their allies, who pursued the Reservation's expansion, at whatever cost; and the Sierra Club and their pro-Grand Canyon allies, who defended the Park's integrity, at whatever cost. Unmuddied presentation of these two views was a benefit to the public process of decision-making.

Understand, as lobbyists and advocates, we are all petitioners; it is the folks with votes, the representatives and senators, who are paid to make the actual decision. They were the ones to be squeezed, to be made to feel the cross-pressures, to figure out how to balance them, and then vote accordingly. Of course, they often tried to squeeze the petitioners, to get off the hook. But, as I say, they sought the job, and they are paid to get squeezed. Our job, we and the Havasupai, was to present our petitions adequately and strongly. For instance, for over a year, the Havasupai had no effective lobbyist. They had an effective campaign to awaken public sympathy, but no person to carry the battle in and through the congressional process. In March 1974, they remedied that problem. We, on the other hand, had members who sympathized so strongly with the Havasupai that they thought the Sierra Club should drop its pro-Park principles and support the Havasupai, thus leaving the Canyon without, arguably, its most effective spokes-group. Had this effort succeeded, and the Club retired from the battle, or worse, had come out in favor of dismembering the Park, that too would have left one side inadequately represented. Instead, both sides argued through 1974 at strength, the positions put fully before first the Committee, then the entire House of Representatives. At the end, everyone could say that they had had the chance to make their case. And the final decision, no untrammeled victory for either, has held. Enough pontificating; back to the story.

1974

January

Part of the January story concerned local Sierra Club members learning about and sympathizing with the Havasupai. The Flagstaff group supported moving Park land to the Reservation, and urged the state chapter to follow suit. The chapter executive committee considered the matter in early January following a trip to Havasu Canyon by some members. Lovegren came as NPS representative and a former GCNP Superintendent. The meeting was contentious; people were upset; apology letters were written; some resigned; a pro-Havasupai resolution was voted down; the Havasupai mistakenly thought the opposite; a split in the Havasupai surfaced; another meeting was set.

A five-member Havasupai delegation, three of whom were white, came to Tucson for a chat. The meeting was somewhat raucous with everyone, except the Havasupai tribal members, chipping in great wisdom about the doom of civilization should this or that happen. The end result was more friction. McComb, who had not been at the meeting, became adamant about not changing the status quo on the Havasupai, and told the chapter officers not to involve him, since the Club had a position and he was employed to move it. This was disingenuous, since he believed in keeping the lands in the Park. The result was that, though no longer even a member of the Club, I spent a chunk of time in January trying to prevent the chapter from dive-bombing itself.

When the Executive Committee did do its work, it was quite orderly, and the resolution was a compromise that started in favor of the Havasupai, but put transfer of Park land on the bottom of its list of alternatives. McComb told me that the Club headquarters planned to kill the chapter's resolution bureaucratically, but that did not stop the Havasupai supporters from saying the Club had approved a land transfer, and using that mis-statement to pressure other groups.

January 16 - 31

Having resolved his previous ambivalence, Udall reassured McComb he was ready to go. Dale Pontius had been working with us on crafting a bill moving in the direction of significant Park enlargement and protection. We were also fortunate that Clay Peters, on the Republican staff of the Interior Committee, understood what we wanted to achieve, and planned to talk to Park Service officials to obtain their approval or at least neutrality on adding more lands. A new map embodying our ideas was being prepared by the Park Service. (Boundaries were not described in the bill using words since legal lines were often not surveyed; of course, being drawn on maps left a real chance for future misunderstandings and arguments.)

In January, armed with the facts and figures I was working up on acres and uses, McComb went on a lobbying trip to Washington. Part of this effort was to search out other land, some privately-owned, that could go into a Havasupai reservation, leaving the Park alone, since Udall said he wanted to consider alternatives beyond more studies. I should stress that this kind of talk—a stream of checking status, probing for agreement, searching for the route most likely to be successful, weighing political strengths and weaknesses, prognosticating (most often wrongly) the future—is a constant, with a heavy larding of sheer gossip. I think of it all as legislation by conversation, with an occasional vote to relieve the tension.

McComb's trip produced more of this talk. Udall, hoping to avoid an open fight with Steiger, had talked with him; the result was uncertain. Richard Curry, in charge of legislative liaison for the Park Service, was uncertain about our additions, preferring to leave it to the Superintendent's discretion. A Havasupai ally on the Committee staff tried to talk a Democratic representative into supporting a transfer. His answer was no; although he was uncertain what the best course was, a simple confirmation of existing rights was not enough. Speculation was current that Steiger's support was uncertain; he might just offer an amendment, and accept being voted down. McComb, uncertain if we could prevail, suggested a fallback of Wilderness status, and brought up the zone of influence, but to a lukewarm, not to say uncertain, response. At this point, everybody just wanted something to happen. That much was certain.

Also certain were distractions on top of distractions. The tourist development just south of the Park, Tusayan, was started and maintained on water hauled from fifty miles away. The developers wanted to use water from inside the Park, which had a source that NPS stored a few miles away. The only reason to bring this up, aside from its being another distraction, was that some of the developers had connections to the Senate Interior Committee chairman, Jackson of Washington, and they had been lobbying his office and committee staff. The Park Service was taking a stiff line against using a Park resource for private uses outside the Park. We agreed, but it was touchy, since we did not really want to alienate the senate people whom, a few months earlier on the Park deletions, we had worked so hard to cultivate.

February 1 - 21

Udall, Steiger and Goldwater talked; they seemed, in the way of such conversations, to be in a sort of agreement on the Havasupai; perhaps because the latter had not been active in Washington since November. Also, no fuss was made when Udall brought up the additions. Pontius came to see the land, and on February 2, we went up to the Canyon, where the Superintendent had arranged a fly-over. Once seen, the arguments go away as far as Park-worthiness goes, and the only substantive alteration as a result of the flight was to take the Park boundary to the geologically more sound point of the mouth of the Paria River, rather than the short distance further upstream to the boat launch point of Lees Ferry. Udall was pleased with Pontius's report, and they worked to set the date for the Parks Subcommittee to discuss the bill and mark it up, i.e., vote on amending it. March 4 was named.

For the next month I tried to be persuasive about details. It is one thing to argue for the big sweeping measure; then having won the point, there are the ambiguities to confront, and we had to determine how far to push and how hard. Since some of the side canyon and rim country we wanted to add was in Kaibab National Forest, questions were raised by the Forest Service. Fortunately the Forest Supervisor had been on the plane trip, and we agreed about the Havasupai. Others were concerned about proceeding without the full process of bureaucratic, professional vetting. Doubts were raised about the western stretch of the river surface, since about 40 miles of it were part of Lake Mead, backed up and fluctuating, no longer its true self. Our feelings about "completeness" and our stand for having a single administration for the river remained stronger than our doubts about adding the reservoir's tail to the Park.

Then the Havasupai issue pole-vaulted past us. *60 Minutes* ran its presentation, and it set all political antennae to vibrating. There were more efforts to beef up what the tribe was being offered without actually transferring any federal lands. Interestingly, Steiger seemed willing to go along. However, he dug in his heels against a wilderness study.

With Mo, we refined our additions' boundaries. The Hualapai, with Arizona supporters, went around trying to stir up the dam issue; they wanted something that would recognize their claim, their right to have a dam, and the oil crisis of that period gave them a ready argument: clean, home-grown energy.

February 22 - March 3

In the last week before the mark-up session, in Washington, we reached agreement on boundary details, first with Udall's staff, then receiving his blessing. The Parks chairman decided to handle the contentious issues in the Subcommittee, instead of sending them to full committee. Emerson pushed Udall's staff to give something to the Havasupai. We checked with Steiger, and again he had no feeling about our boundary additions, and would go along with Udall. He mentioned a complaint from the state game officials, but waved it off.

I must explain that while we did not think of ourselves as working behind anyone's back, we were not consulting any of those whom, a year or more before, we had tried to line up behind a Goldwater lets-all-get-together bill. That time was over. We had tried and been stiffed. Goldwater had publicly attacked us. The Senate fight over the deletions was public. If anyone, hunters and ranchers in particular, wanted to make a show in the House, that was their look-out. We wanted House action that would move toward our vision, and tried to keep up the contacts that would ease passage of what we wanted. There was even talk at that point that the Senate might just accept the House version and thus avoid the need for a Senate-House conference to work out differences. There is always talk.

Steiger was determined to push pro-dam language into the bill. We had to build a backfire against that, drafting letters for Udall to send to colleagues, asking them for their votes or, if they were absent, their proxies. Congressman Meeds, who had been asked by Udall to offer the latter's changes in the Subcommittee, was all set. However, a couple of days before the mark-up, affected by the Havasupai publicity and pro-Havasupai staff arguments, Meeds parted with Udall on that issue, deciding to offer his own amendment.

March 4

The mark-up was a bit odd. Meeds was offering most of Udall's changes, but Mo was there, and offering corrections, trying to keep him following the order. We started off well, getting approval of a definition of the entire Grand Canyon, "from the mouth of the Paria River to the Grand Wash Cliffs, including tributary side canyons and surrounding plateaus". This would be a congressional declaration, an American declaration, of what constituted the Grand Canyon and was worthy of protection and presentation, regardless of land ownership. The Udall-sponsored boundary map, including the entire river surface, was approved without a murmur. So was the Wilderness study, a survey to be done of all the lands in the enlarged Park, including the river, within two years of the Act's passage. Then, having disposed of the Park enlargement as if it were a yawn, the fights started, first over the Havasupai, then the dam. Was it logical, giving birth, and then arguing over whether to dismember or drown the infant? No, but it was politics. The dam language and the Havasupai transfer had no chance as legislation on their own; so the proponents tried to turn our bill (and Goldwater's, yes) into their anti-Park weapon.

Once upon a time, mark-ups were closed. Now we could all come and watch. It is a terrible thing to sit there, immobilized, unable to correct mistakes, forbidden to reply to specious arguments, seeing your lovely handiwork teetering on the brink of collapse. I told my journal: I do not know how I can hold back. Yet this is what we pay our Representatives for, to argue with and try to persuade each other, and eventually, sometimes, to make a decision. In this case, decisions were made. The dam provision was defeated. The Havasupai were to be allowed to select 100,000 acres, but not out of GCNP. And we got more Park including the entire river, a Wilderness study, and our odds and ends.

We were elated by the results, calling supporters and thanking congressmen before returning home. It seemed that the issues were out in the open and dealt with. We had made significant strides in Park designation and, as a by-product, on river protection. We considered we had worked hard, had good contacts, and a real chance at prevailing. As I said, celebrate when you win. Tomorrow . . .

March 11 - April 4

Tomorrow was consideration and reporting out by the full Committee. First there was talk about that in early April. Now that we had come out ahead, all we could see were troubles: from hunters, ranchers, the Forest Service, the Havasupai, the dam supporters. All wanted to do something to take away part of what we had won. In the event, the full Committee met in early August, and in between, the Grand Canyon National Park Enlargement bill became the Havasupai Reservation Enlargement bill.

The impact of the *60 Minutes* show was evident in the greater sympathy I encountered during a conversation with Senate Interior Committee staff in mid-March. The real news, however, came from McComb who encountered a Havasupai delegation in late March that included a new lobbyist, Joe Sparks, who, true to his name, was giving a fresh, high level of energy and sophistication to their campaign. The commitment was backed up by money from other tribes so that the Havasupai group could stay and lobby right through the Committee action. In the conversation, Sparks assured McComb he would lobby like hell to get title to the land, pushing for a big land transfer. Other Indian support organizations also became active at this time, doing what we had been doing for the past several months. Goldwater became active for the moment, sending letters to key

Representatives not to delay his bill, and that he would help the Havasupai later; indeed he is reported to have told the Havasupai to stay out of things until next year. Pontius told McComb that Udall was O.K. and was just looking to make some changes. Sparks told us we had Udall solid, leading me to wonder if he was trying to lull us.

April 5 - May 4

In early April, both sides were going strong, working the offices of those Representatives on the Committee. Rumors were flung or snuck back and forth, providing excellent excuses to check and see if any positions were being changed. The Havasupai were reported to have been to see everybody, including Udall in early April. We heard that Udall was moving to support a transfer, but Pontius said not so, and the language was still fluid. On another front, a Forest Service biggie had called Udall about the trophy deer down in the bottom of Kanab Canyon. Later in the month, Sparks was using Park Service actions against the Havasupai to manufacture sympathy for a transfer. The Interior Department appeared as a player, with the BIA pushing hard for a transfer. And on April 25, Pontius warned us, "I cannot rule out trust at this moment", code words for Udall getting ready to support an enlarged reservation, with lands held in trust. Udall himself was meeting with Goldwater, and Sparks was to meet with Udall shortly. Pontius had also heard from Arizona opponents of additional Park lands. In a conversation, Udall told me he had heard we were coming around, and I said no we were not; we still wanted an alternative to transferring land in trust to the Havasupai. Sparks was seeing him the next day, and Udall thought there might be a confrontation if we could not compose our differences. He had not decided what side to come down on.

Conversations with the Park Service indicated they did not know of any change as far as Interior was concerned. I talked with Bureau of Indian Affairs people, but they were not part of the land transfer fight, and had mixed ideas about what the tribe wanted. I even spoke to Emerson. He assured me that Goldwater was fighting for the study, but that if Sparks can get the land, more power to him. He accused us of having put forth all of Udall's ideas, and ended by stressing Goldwater's desire for a bill.

Suddenly, Chapman reported to Stitt from Washington that Interior was giving up on opposition to the Havasupai land transfer. My despairing journal item from April 26: We cannot reach anybody. The next day, though, Chapman confirmed the bad news, that the administration position had changed, and a proposal was being forwarded to the President to transfer National Forest and Park lands to the Havasupai. And indeed, when President Nixon, with four months to go, came to Phoenix on May 2, he announced his support for that vital Republican principle of returning land to the Indians. (Although we did not know it at the time, years later I found out that it was Sparks' contacts and effective lobbying at the White House that created this new Presidential stand. It surely helped that Goldwater's support was absolutely crucial to Nixon, then in extremis.)

May 5 - 31

Shocked and alarmed now at the possibility that other tribes would follow the

Havasupai's lead, the Sierra Club reaffirmed its position in favor of keeping the Park intact. And back we went to Washington. Udall, for all that he was letting us down gently, was now firmly on the other side. On May 7, McComb and I tried to argue, especially about sensitive areas like the Great Thumb, a plateau that the Canyon takes a big curve around, and an all too likely place for tourist development if not protected. No go; there was no percentage for him to be the anti-Indian now. We talked to other Committee members, but with few exceptions, ended up with sympathy here and there, but only vague hopes. For instance, when I talked with the Parks Subcommittee chairman, he assured me that the Committee would go with Udall's position. So, I groaned to myself, who will defend the Parks? One person who was willing to help was John Seiberling of Ohio, and he did talk to Udall about the Great Thumb, and about the bad precedent of settling land claims by cutting up Parks.

Don't give up; get beat, that is what you do. So we pushed the possibility of private land, and Udall agreed to fly Sparks and McComb over a big private ranch up for sale south of the Canyon, although Sparks made it clear it was not the answer. And, anyway, we were told, the lobbyists for the Havasupai were already convinced they had the committee sewed up. I could not disagree. The May 26 flight was a failure; as Sparks and McComb fought, Udall stayed silent. Worse, as May closed, Pontius assured us that Udall was thinking of going down over the rim into the main Canyon for even more Havasupai land.

June 1 - 17

I found an antidote for this depressing situation. Since, in early June, I could see no relief from the above situation without an effort to generate mail to the Committee members, I went off for a two-week camping trip with my daughters. It helps to have fond memories. They had a price: McComb was mad at me for going off, so we did not deal for a while. He was probably right; as events turned out, we could have benefited from a near-continuous presence in Washington that summer.

June 17 - July 16

Meanwhile, the Sierra Club had stirred itself some more, and McComb went back to Washington in late June. He found that Udall and committee chairman Taylor—the one who told me it was all over—had talked over the latter's worries about the problems raised by the transfer. He was quite likely prompted in this by Committee staff, which was adamantly opposed to and appalled by the idea. Whatever the influences, on June 27, Udall had moved some more, and Pontius had to tell Sparks that Udall was working with Taylor.

One story McComb heard from Udall was that he thought the Indian guilt trip had gone too far, and he was irritated that the Grand Canyon stuff was taking up time he wanted to spend on his land use legislation. He had a three-inch stack of mail, split evenly for and against the transfer. He mentioned his thoughts about running for President in 1976. So he was thinking about dividing up the lands under discussion, leaving some in the Park as an area the Havasupai could use in traditional ways, and the rest being transferred. The former area would be set back from the rim to avoid detrimental development. McComb heard from the committee staff that it was determined to minimize the transfer and add restrictions so severe no tribe would want to try it again. The Sierra Club chief Washington lobbyist, thinking McComb too pessimistic, had started pushing hard in mid-June. The end result, they thought, was a committee split between pro-Park but not anti-Havasupai on one side, and on the other, pro-Havasupai who were more pro-Udall or pro-Steiger.

The Havasupai lobbyists stayed even more active, calling every office every week. Nevertheless, early in July, McComb had heard from committee staff that we were gaining ground. Following the placement of an ad in *The New York Times* by Friends of the Earth, Brower talked to me about his visits in Washington to see Udall and others, so the battle would not just be by the Sierra Club. He thought Congressman Burton (from San Francisco, the Club's home) would help out, even perhaps take the lead in protecting the Park. I thought his most worthwhile point was that the Senate Interior Committee chairman and staff were against any transfer. Other conservation organizations did get involved, and the mail turned more pro-Park. Sparks was reported to be resigned to the land transfer being fewer acres than he had hoped. The activity got hotter as the summer did, with full committee action expected each week, then being postponed.

Not surprisingly, this gave the hunters time to bestir themselves, and they came to Washington to complain about the additions. When I talked to Steiger though, he still was not voicing opposition. He also told me that he was going along with Udall on his new approach of a larger reservation plus some "use lands" inside the Park, except for one piece where a rancher was objecting to part of his grazing area being taken into the Reservation, and Steiger was supporting him. Then I talked with Udall; he thought he could hold the line on the additions, though there was this fuss, and much more would kill the whole bill. He pressed me on whether there was hunting in the canyons, and I said there was not. I was pretty sure; there is little easily accessible (much less drive-able) land below the rims we wanted the boundary on.

July 16 - 31
We also followed up on the Senate side, but only heard again that Jackson was against any transfer, but would do nothing. For the last two weeks in July, we tried various approaches, hoping we might find some support, but what was really happening was just waiting and waiting, postponement after postponement. Letters did start showing up from Arizona hunters. When the Committee meeting was set for July 31, there was a final flurry of contacts, drawing on the talents of a number of conservationist lobbyists. The work was done, but as I can attest from the calls I made, the vote would have as much to do with following the lead of Udall or Steiger (it was their state, after all) as with the substance of pro-Park or pro-Havasupai. The debate was spirited enough, but the truth was in the 24-11 vote in favor of transferring land to the Havasupai.

August 1 - September 9
Immediately following that vote, I spent time checking with allies as to what might be done, perhaps killing the bill in the Rules Committee, stalling it altogether, or

fighting when it came to the full House. In part, of course, the strategy for those with the long view was to make any victory as costly as possible to avoid any repetition. Stalling always seems like a possibility; after all, it took over four months from the Subcommittee to the full Committee. Even then, there was delay in recording a final vote, and more time for the formal report to be written; the bill was finally reported on September 25, exactly one year after it had been referred to the Committee. And this was legislation about which everyone said, again and again, they did not want to argue; they just wanted to move it along. For a bill with so many people wishing to avoid controversy, there was an awful lot of blood, or ink and hot air spilled along the way.

September 10 - October 11

After the recess was over, a press conference was held on September 10 by pro-Park and anti-Indian figures, congressmen and organization spokespeople. I was not there. Indeed since the committee action, I made few or no journal entries, recording here and there something passed on from one source or another. It seemed that after a hectic year, the battle had moved on to another place with other armies. This was not helped by a run-in with Pontius, and then McComb, about the status of private land within our additions; even firm allies can have snits. There was a real battle, though, at the press conference, to which pro-Havasupai speakers came and started a debate, allowing all the ill will to spray out.

Perhaps all this delay and wordy action was having an effect, or perhaps it was just another time for people to speculate and wait. Udall talked about moving the boundary farther back from the rim. Maybe if the bill was good enough, a conference could be avoided. But the Senate Committee staff remained adamant: If a transfer is in the bill, there will be a conference to try to get it out. Some maneuvering occurred as the Rules Committee was lobbied, and a thin hope was extended of having the bill referred to another committee. More blather; the usual procedure was followed, and the bill set for debate on the House floor on October 11. No grand effort was set up by the anti-Havasupai forces.

The bill came through unscathed by the cut-and-thrust of debate either by those who opposed the transfer or those who wanted to take our additions out. The vote on the Havasupai matter was not lopsided; 180 to 147. Post-mortems followed the line of being surprised at how close it was, and whether a greater effort might have defeated the Havasupai transfer. Again, I had not been called in, and given what I heard of the nastiness that went on, it may have been a good time to go hiking, which I did, into the Grand Canyon, where on the day after the vote, I was bitten by a rattlesnake. I only mention this for the chance to tell a couple of relevant stories about human nature. First, generosity. When I next returned to Washington, I attended a large committee meeting at which, among many others, Sam Steiger was present. I came in, and with many of the other spectators, sat down against the wall. Sam, seeing me, got up and came over, and squatting in front of me, said he had heard about the bite. He asked me how I was doing, and commiserated. Second, not so generous. The white folk who were putting out a Havasupai newsletter, taking note of my having been bitten, opined that it was the spirit of the Canyon getting its own back on a Havasupai enemy. An issue a few months later reported that at their village in the Canyon, a Havasupai boy had been bitten by a coral snake, rarer and potentially far more dangerous. As with me, the spirits and a helicopter were on his side; our timely evacuations avoided any serious effects.

October 20 - December 12

So we come to the last act. The Senate and the House had passed different versions of the bill. There would be a conference of involved members from both sides to decide how to resolve the differences. After months of being marginalized, I was called from my tent to go back to Washington. I spent almost an entire month seeing what could be done about keeping our additions and removing the Havasupai transfer. The main problem for the former was that Udall might be the only Conference member in favor; other House members and the senators were likely to oppose the additions. The problem on the Havasupai was to find if there was anyone at all likely to oppose the transfer. As always, the strategy was to state the goal, and work toward it as if it could be reached, even if in all likelihood, it is unattainable. So under this unpromising rubric, I spent from November 18 to December 12 (including the two-year anniversary of that Goldwater meeting) wandering the corridors of Congress, looking for a magic combination to an impossible lock.

The key was likely to be Verkler, head of the senate staff. He thought Metcalf would be a fighter against the transfer, something Verkler did want to stop. He was not too happy about the additions, telling me we had already crapped on the hunters once. I offered the notion of adding the lands with a study. He repeated that he thought the best course was to let the bill die; there were too many bad things in it from his point of view.

One of the early conversations I had was with Joe Sparks, who suggested that together we agree to get the key senators to just accept the House bill as passed, giving us our additions, and the Havasupai their transfer. I do not really know if such a plea could have succeeded. I could not imagine other conservation groups accepting such a course, nor could I imagine even asking them. So, though the temptation was great, I said no. Was that the better course? I still debate the point.

One prong of the effort was to encourage friendly members to be on the conference. To that end, I approached Seiberling; he said he would ask. Udall was not cheery about the Havasupai changes, "This isn't the way I wanted to go." Verkler tried to line up some willing senators, and keep pro-Havasupai members off. We talked through the idea of letting the bill die without a conference, but the worry there was having it come back the next year. One ally was lost when Metcalf was convinced by the Havasupai arguments. I tried various approaches, but it was too late.

Goldwater made life harder when he wrote to Jackson and argued against the additions, blustering he did not want them, that tens of thousands of hunters would be excluded, that the Park Service could not handle such a Park, and that many, many people would be unhappy, including him. Another senator asserted Jackson was on the Havasupai side. Jackson denied it, having said only that he wanted to help, not transfer land.

Another voice was heard from when a Phelps-Dodge subsidiary made a case that there was a fair amount of uranium near the edges of one of our additions. My feeling changed to thinking that it was time to cut losses; after a week there were no real hopes for good compromise. The question became: Can we defend any of our gains? Or from Verkler's point of view, what can be done to make sure the Havasupai restrictions are tight? I drafted a couple of alternatives for him to consider, including a congressional permit to the land. I also talked to Metcalf for one last plea, which was futile. He had an open mind, he said, but he was not on the conference after all.

Seeking punishment, I talked with Steiger. As always he was friendly as he told me there was no hope for anything I wanted. I gave Verkler the material on a permit so he could discuss it with his boss. He did, and the conference members were chosen. I tried to persuade him on the additions, but he was not interested in crossing any more swords with the Arizona senators, allies of the hunters and stockmen.

On the House side, I worked with Pontius and McComb long distance, as we tried to counter the hunters' exaggerations. We knew exactly which people to talk to. Of course, so did everyone else, and it was another dreary-go-round of treading on each other's heels. The Havasupai permit idea, which had a bit of breath, got strangled when Sparks heard of it. Our Wilderness study seemed to be in the clear. Of course, Emerson was adamant against us on everything, I was told. This did not matter in the end. Senator Bible, leading the Senate conferees, talked with Goldwater, and Bible backed Verkler. One late afternoon in the Senate Committee room, one of the Havasupai's lobbyists came across me and started yelling at me to come outside and fight like a man. I wondered what they were worried about.

There was talk that if the conference were not held soon, Bible would leave and that would be the end of it. Verkler made a last try with "his" senators, but no luck on the Havasupai transfer. I wrote that the Senate side of the conference was a disaster. Our only hope was that Udall could pull something off. The conference was held December 12, with Bible in the chair. Many Havasupai and their supporters were there. So was I. Sparks and another spoke to me of the future when conservationists and Indians could work together on something. I hope I was gracious.

The members discussed tightening up the restrictions on the transfer, its supporters fighting all the way. They worked for an hour, then recessed to get the language right. One ally told me it was delicate, since our opponents did have the votes. I suggested some things to Verkler. The conference went into executive session to make the changes final. Some additional restrictions were put on what the Havasupai could do on the transferred lands.

Udall then tried to get something from the senators on our additions. He battled, retreating step by step. Keep the additions? No. How about keeping them, with a study such that they can be dropped by a congressional veto? No. O.K., let's take out just the most-complained-about area; leave the rest? No. Then how about a study in the bill? No. At this point, Steiger prevailed on his allies, and Udall's House support evaporated. His reward for tenacity was that the conference report would be written to contain language directing the Secretary of the Interior to study the lands for Park-worthiness and report his recommendations to Congress. At which point the conference ended, and when Udall came out, he came over and commiserated with me about how little he had been able to keep. Later Pontius told me how hard Mo had pushed.

So we had lost on our big efforts. Failed. But, although I have barely mentioned them, we got all our river-related goals: at every point, Congress rebuffed the effort to promote a dam. The new Park did include "the entire Colorado River from the Paria River to the Grand Wash Cliffs", and the entire river surface was under GCNP administration. We had our two-year wilderness study, "including the entire river from the mouth of the Paria to the headwaters of Lake Mead". The wounds gaped too wide for celebration, but as the fight over the river re-heated, we did have some new useful tools.

A postscript: That study in the conference report of our additions' Park-worthiness was done. Completed in the Reagan administration, it said the lands were of Park quality, but that their status should not be changed. The Kanab Canyon section (administered by the Forest Service and the Bureau of Land Management) was later designated a Wilderness by Congress. Then, in the mid-'90s, one story goes, the study was brought to the attention of President Clinton's Secretary of the Interior, Bruce Babbitt. Whatever the source, in 1998 Babbitt launched a proposal for a National Monument covering land west of Kanab and north of GCNP, much of which had been in our 1972 Park and Conservation Zone proposals. After some hullabaloo, the Grand Canyon-Parashant National Monument was proclaimed by President Clinton in January 2000. Another piece of the Canyon had been accorded recognition. Since hunting and grazing could continue but not mining, it sounded much like our Conservation Zone. So maybe that face-saving gesture to Udall on that grim December day had a useful outcome, and it only took 25 years.

1975

January - June
The story was not quite done. Many anti-Indians were still incensed, and an effort was mounted after the Senate and House approved the Conference report on December 18 to have President Ford veto the bill. He signed it into law on January 3, 1975.

Shortly after, in reading my copy of what was now Public Law 93-620, I discovered a curious thing; instead of 12 sections, there were only 11. The wilderness study provision was gone. A few calls and some checking uncovered the problem. On being sent to be officially printed, that section had been left out, so the President had signed an "incomplete" bill. Back to Orwell-land again: it was ridiculous to get angry, but one's patience was tried. The only remedy was to pass a little bill amending 93-620 by reinstating its section 11. That was done, and on June 10, 1975, the legislative history of the Grand Canyon National Park *Enlargement* (my italics) Act whimpered to an end.

CHAPTER 6

1973: Faster, Are Motors Always First?

Rowing With Half An Oar

So if Morton's was such a flimsy, unjustifiable, willfully misinterpreted non-decision, how was it that we could not prevent its solidification? The comm ops were trying every trick in the activist's book we conservationists had made work over the past decade, tricks with some of our innovations—mass letter writing appeals to constituents, legal action and court suits, acting as outsiders picked on by Big Government. Where were we while our opponents were deploying their resources across the full range of American government? Yes, from early in 1973, we were still around. We were just not doing much more than trying to keep track of efforts to weaken the Reed decision. Chapter 5 explained some of our distraction, a distraction that in retrospect looks more like a pattern.

Ruch had mentioned to us in January 1973 that Goldwater and Reed had talked about a mechanism for putting the Colorado River in the GCNP Wilderness. Whatever their conclusion, Goldwater did not include Wilderness in his Park legislation, perhaps with an understanding that the administration would make some recommendation. We nudged the wilderness idea in March, asking Congressman Udall at least to help set up hearings on a Grand Canyon Wilderness; that front remained quiet, too.[1] This may have bothered us less since in those early days some congressional aides were telling us the Park enlargement legislation was not going anywhere.

Occasional news reports seemed to get some things right, and kept river issues bubbling, which we assumed would do us good in the long run.[2] And did it really matter that *Newsweek* reported, a week after Judge Ritter dismissed the case, that arguments had just begun? And that some motor trips took 350 people on 18 rafts lashed together? And that a 60-year-old was swept to his death off a motorless raft in Cataract Canyon, 150 miles upstream of the Grand Canyon? Of course, not all the errors were the writers' fault; the interviewees contributed disinformation of their own, e.g., they claimed that a new management plan had been cooked up in a private meeting at Goldwater's; that the Canyon was being locked up for a few hardy conservationists; that without motorboats, there were going to be fatalities. Was anybody really paying any attention?

The replies we were getting from comm op allies were not combative. Steiger at first seemed open-minded. In April, Senator Moss wrote to the Utah Sierra Club chapter that, if allocations remained at the 1972 use level and if "the <u>choice</u> of motors or oars" was retained pending availability of evidence developed by the ecological studies, it seemed reasonable to him to hold things steady.[3] No fire-breathing here. Like the comm ops, we were in danger of being confused by forked tongues, from the Park Service and our elected representatives.

In mid-May, after a two-month lapse, I gave my journal an overall assessment that we were in a weak, defensive stance on the river issue. We were expending almost no energy compared to the outfitters, who were using their suit and Moss as weapons to intimidate the Park Service, with the goal of scoring an indefinite postponement of cutbacks and wilderness. No doubt, I gloomed, this will be seen as a critical period.

We had hopeful news from some rowing comm ops. Five had formed Grand Canyon Rowing Outfitters (GCRO) in September 1972, to advance rowing trips as a safe and esthetically desirable alternative to motors, and to advocate wilderness. They met at the Sierra Club in April 1973 determined to address the issue of river management by trying to obtain the understanding of all, instead of just locking horns with the motorizers. I was pleased and urged them to speak out, partly because we had reports that the Park Service was not able to defend its decisions well, and partly because the rowing outfitters were the most knowledgeable voice on rowing and its advantages.[4] They could, we thought, effectively refute the motor comm ops' slanders about elitism and safety. I told them I thought CROA's assault would be sustained and nasty (I was right), and they needed to defend themselves pretty vigorously to keep the Park Service leaning their way (I was wrong). I urged them to send information to their client lists. Even though we had different sets of interests, there would be great benefit for both of us in breaking the grip of the large, motorized outfits.

When GCRO distributed its proposals on September 4, it was clear why the motor comm ops would disdain them.[5] They started with the causes of congestion: too many people launching together; too many at major attractions; noise from boat and helicopter motors; constant passing due to the rapid pace of motor trips; beach overuse. Spreading out launches, slowing trip pace, and reducing party size could reduce congestion.

GCRO went after the safety issue with the same abandon that the motor comm ops used. Since motor rafts carry many more people, when one does flip, there was greater danger with three tons of rubber and steel crashing down. Motor boatmen "often" complained of "motor drown-out and propeller break-down" as "common" events, during which the raft spun out of control, a known cause of injury and even death. Rowing trips can steer around dangerous rapids, "an option motor guides rarely elect". In a saner tone, GCRO argued that their smaller ratio of guide to passenger (1 to 6 vs. 1 to 15 for motors) meant that a rower could more quickly notice someone who fell off. Then more hyperventilation: motor passengers "frequently" fall overboard without notice until "sheared" by the propeller or lost upstream. Single-boat motor trips did not have the safety margin of multi-boat rowing parades. Anyway, statistics show rafting of any kind is safer than driving a car. I guess that last comment was intended as a comfort. GCRO's rhetoric could hardly be more convincing than the motor-boater hyperbole about the dangers of rowing. The biggest problem in evaluating accident frequency was that if the hurt person were not evacuated the guides did not report trouble to GCNP. The Park Service ended up only evaluating accidents where an evacuation took place, and one can suppose there were many unreported incidents, scary maybe, or exciting, but with too little injury to lead to a report. Yes, river-running in the Grand Canyon was safe, and the truth about safety was a mystery, guarded by all involved.

GCRO's next step was to figure out the consequences of the NPS "temporary" remedy of an 89 KUD passenger lid and motor reductions of 25% each year. They calculated that the number of people on motor trips would have to drop about 10% in 1974, because motor passengers were 90% of the total, and more user-days were consumed on a rowing trip of 12 days than on a motor trip of 7 days. With motors all gone in 1977, GCRO projected the motorized comm ops would lose the equivalent of one-third of their full-trip customers, leaving them running a number somewhere near the 1969-70 amount. Thus far, so good, since the reduction could have been applauded by us, even if jeered at by other comm ops.

However, GCRO then complained that the user-day concept penalized rowing comm ops, especially the small ones. With rowing now the approved NPS mode, there was a "moral obligation" to these small operators, since they were proving oar trips could work in spite of economic hardship—though ARTA had told me no one was going out of business. The remedy was to add some user-days for the small guys, then add more to make up for the user-day "penalty" on the longer rowing trips, giving an overall passenger use increase of 30% to 116 KUD in 1977. (Just about the level, remember, that the comm ops claimed they had been promised for 1973.) This was twice as much as the Reed/NPS "goal" of 55 KUD.

So far, the GCRO recipe contained a handful of self-serving smacks at motorizers, sugar for some comm ops, face-saving for the reducers among us, and for the comm ops used to wild growth, the old refrain that a loss in business could ruin some.

The ARTA aide who wrote this document described the choice issue as one of trying to assure mass appeal by adding convenience and comfort: tour packages, open bars, generators, cushioned seats, sleeping cots. These comforts were supposed to increase accessibility. I questioned this, since such extras reduce choice by boosting the cost per day for such Cleopatra-barge luxury trips, restricting them even more to the monied elite. That was why there could be no surprise that almost half the commercial passengers come from the top annual income brackets (as measured by the social surveys of 1972 and 1998).[6]

The GCRO centerpiece undercut hope it might help our case. They pled for mitigation of the effects on rowing comm ops of the user-day measure, which encourages maximizing the number of paying customers by minimizing time spent on the trip. In doing their poor-mouth routine, they offered comfort to anti-rowers by claiming that rowing trips use 42% more user-days for each person on a trip, and they are more costly, require more crew, earn 25% less per day, and pay more in insurance (contradicting the earlier motor-boater admission). The Park Service must consider such factors in these wilderness-friendly trips, and assign more user-days to make up for traveling at the river's pace. Motor operations would convert to rowing only if given more user-days to avoid a possible 40% revenue cut. GCRO forecast a set of horrors as comm ops pushed their crew to move more people faster on rowing trips, producing long hours on the river, infrequent stops, cramped camp time, crew fatigue and carelessness, and to top it all, large fare increases. Increasing the number of user-days, especially for small comm ops, educational group trips, and extra-long trips could alleviate these problems. The overall impact would not be greater, since rowing trips were smaller, and "fewer people spending more time on the river is no worse than many people spending little time". (Why then not continue to argue for dropping the user-day idea, counting instead people and trips launched?)

So, in the end, GCRO offered a picture of commercial rowing trips with more passengers, and receiving special consideration because they would be the ones to make the new policy work.

A moment's overview: The Park Service implemented—on paper—Reed's strong October 1972 decision over the next few months. The motor comm ops, led by the Utah contingent through CROA, counterattacked throughout 1973 using mailings to customers, congressional contacts, and the courts to score an ambiguous over-ruling of Reed by Morton in September. The backdown was solidified in the next few months, wistfully marked by Chapman's December plea for patience. Against that background, there can be no surprise that GCNP wrote GCRO that some of their ideas were used, some were considered, and some have to be looked at more closely.[7] This vague brush-off was clear enough that there would be no flexibility for rowers as the good guys, just because they were doing what NPS was supposed to achieve.

The Park and GCRO did agree that there was research to be done. The latter specifically wanted the Park Service to analyze visitor impact on water quality, vegetation, soil stability, geologic features, and archeological sites. The research should monitor the "by-products" of visitation: effluent, garbage, littering, damage from fires and firepits, noise, trail rutting, crowding. GCRO's ideas were fine as far as they went. However, as wilderness advocates, we wanted research that aimed at impacts from motorized trips. Motors could have a direct impact on water quality and noise, but on the rest of the GCRO's items, the impact would be indirect and had to be connected by reasoning. Something like this: motor trips rush a big group of people through; there is less time to orient this larger bunch to the fragility of the environment; motor passengers therefore are less likely to know how to avoid damage than rowing passengers. Such reasoning is highly challengeable. With 21 different operations and guides of varying quality, motorizers might get away with saying that bad impacts were done by bad individuals, denying any tie with motor trips as a type of operation. This would change the question. Where harm is done, are motor-trip people (crew and passengers) responsible for disproportionately more than rowing-trip people? The difference would have to be marked, since while the research was going on, surely all comm ops would push their people to be on their best behavior. If all people are obeying the rules and being really, really careful, was it conceivable that damage could be pinned conclusively on people from motorboats, that researchers could measure blatant messing by the crude motorists, while the delicate rowers floated above the landscape?

So GCRO's explicit statement about research sharpened our concern about the relevance of research to a motor ban. It reinforced the view that the decision to do a hold on the motor phase-out pending research might only be a ploy to get the Park Service on the defensive. Instead of relying on Park and Wilderness values, NPS would look for some "scientific" conclusion that motors were evil. It would be diverted from the central strong argument as Reed stated it, "Motors are antithetical to the quality of a wilderness experience that is, and should be, available in the Grand Canyon."

Encouragement for the GCRO initiative came from other quarters, but with a qualification. One group praised GCRO and the motor phase-out, warning it was not ready to endorse a compensatory increase in user-days for rowing comm ops.[8] Another supportive letter spent most of its time attacking the "inequitable" allocation for self-guided trips of less than 10% of use.[9] It should be 50-50, since, "While there is not a present demand for 45,000 private user days on the river, the demand will come, and must be accommodated." (Prescient on the first point; whistling in the dark on the second.) At least, for now, add 16% to the self-guided allocation.

I urged GCRO to send mailings to their customers and make a visit to Washington. Curiously, GCRO was not interested in reaching out to other comm ops. McComb, for the Sierra Club, endorsed the GCRO proposal, except for the 30% user-day increase.[10] David Kay, apparently GCRO's spokesperson as well as an ARTA staffer, pled for conservation community support and cooperation as GCRO prepared to combat CROA on the political level, noting their plans to mail out to a list of 55,000 people in a nationwide campaign. Further, he was trying to put together a group for a Washington visit to Morton, and wanted Club participation.

Eiseman had now "un-resigned" because the Park Service had dropped the trip limit rule, and "was back in the thick of things."[11] He enthusiastically supported the GCRO effort with some reservations. He called it an "excellent proposal" with "careful, incisive thinking and accurate analysis". He took the opportunity to ride his own hobby-horse of longer trips, but ended noting that GCRO was on the Park Service's side and oar people were "essentially and fundamentally different" from motor people. Pay attention, he said, to these people; they are operating right now in the manner we want all to perform in come 1977.[12] More contact between Eiseman, Kay, and McComb generated the idea that Eiseman or a good friend could join in a Washington foray.[13] Eiseman was bothered because he was getting no response from Goldwater, the Park Service, or anybody. As the potential allies discussed GCRO's user-day increase, they saw it as a possible rock in the river, so they sheared off, talking of finding a new way to measure use. We were still rooted in the belief that use was already too high, and could not see GCRO's approach as compensation for conversion. Instead, it generated suspicion.

A GCNP River Report in September eked out some good news: launch crowding would be reduced when a limit of 150 people per day was set.[14] However, the survey of sanitation measures found toilets not being used during the day, passengers not being oriented to hygiene needs, and various infractions of rules for food and water preparation. The report's announcement that there would be daily NPS surveillance plane flights incensed Eiseman, as did the idea of counting user-nights instead of user-days.[15] This would mean that a five-day trip would count for four, and a twelve-day for eleven. Although the report said allotments would be adjusted, Fred asked, "Isn't the Park Service violating every point of the management plan announced last December?" I was not much more polite in writing to Morton, suggesting he had taken a viable, sane policy and reversed it so that the overwhelming majority would have no choice but a fast-trip-for-a-fast-buck.[16] Why no more than ineffectual letters? Surely the combination of Goldwater, prompted by Eiseman, with some rowing comm ops and us in tow, could have gotten a hearing at Morton's desk as easily as Steiger and friends. We seem never to have tried. Was that one of the after-effects of the nasty fight over the Park legislation?

Not that the Park Service seemed interested in our support.[17] The Superintendent for Dinosaur National Monument, noting the Sierra Club's boycott of motor comm ops, warned that other outfitters might not be able to handle Club trips. McComb tartly replied that "you should feel absolutely no obligation to make any special concessions to the Club". At the same time, the Solicitor's office sent a memo to the Park Service Director that "your idea to treat Sierra Club trips as business because of fees is not good since they are a non-profit organization".

I was disconcerted by a conversation in November with Ron Smith, a large comm op who had previously lobbied for rowing. He was tired of NPS changes, and wary of GCRO or any other organization. He was ready to do rowing trips, but not to go broke, so he would not change unless all were forced to "take their medicine". He speculated about whom he could talk to, what other comm ops might go along; but in the end, like the GCRO effort, no sustained effort was made and an opportunity dribbled away. Could we have been trying to be placatory, as Chapman wished?

The dispiriting period continued with a stiff exchange between Eiseman and Congressman Rhodes. Eiseman thought the latter had lobbied for an allocation increase for comm op Burke, so he wrote, charging Rhodes with a lack of river experience and of requesting a business favor without any evaluation of the real situation.[18] Rhodes shot back, "I do not know your source of information but you should get a new one." He asked Eiseman why he opposed allocations based on merit, "Does it put you at a disadvantage?", and enclosed the letter he had written to Morton. Since Fred had been given the false information originally by Stitt, he immediately wrote and apologized, since Rhodes was quite right in chewing him out. A year before, this senior Arizona Republican congressman was helping us all out at Goldwater's. Whether it was the Burke touch, or Eiseman's slap, he would not be asked for help now.

Eiseman was not doing much better with Interior, trying to get a clear statement of the relationship between motors and safety.[19] He hooted with disdain at the story Morton had told about his experience, cast doubt on the validity of some data GCNP had collected on recent river accidents, and sneered at the idea that the comm ops would report all their accidents, as the Park Service hoped they would do in 1974. Interior was backing a motor phase-out that it had suspended, and was asking for a determinative safety study, which could not be done. He pleaded for a clear policy.

The safety data given to Fred was a compilation of helicopter evacuations for 1971-3, prepared by GCNP.[20] Fred indicated it "signified absolutely nothing". From my point of view, however, what it did not say was important, that is, there was nothing to support the idea that motor trips were safer. The report took the small number of incidents (41 total in three years), and separated out those on shore from on boats. Of the latter, there were 2 on rowing trips and 17 on motor trips. Therefore rowing, with 12% of the user-days, accounted for 11% of the trouble. The only drowning was from a motor raft. Yes, the numbers are too small to be meaningful—if what you want to do is discriminate between rowing and motors. But that is not the most important point; the meaning here is that the numbers are so small. These are safe trips. All right, safe adventures. Taking all 41 accidents, this is about 1 accident requiring evacuation for 1000 people each year. Data are insufficient to tell which kind of trip is safer because both kinds are really, really safe.

Stitt told me he thought this conclusion clear enough that he hoped for definitive Secretarial action, and if asked would recommend going back to the position of December 1972. The report went to Washington, in response to a personal request from Reed in November.[21] Strangely, although NPS could have drawn the same conclusion I had, its memo to Reed pretended that it could not distinguish between beach and boat accidents, even though the report is very clear about the two groups. Perhaps this was just dim, although as always it is worthwhile entertaining the thought that NPS simply did not want to be seen as saying anything definitive at all. In keeping with this murkiness, we kept hearing baseless rumors that Morton was "soon" to review the decision he may never have made. Again, this was a missed moment when, if united and undistracted, we might have made a strong presentation to Interior.

Where Eiseman was correct, cutting to the crux, was that a decision about ending motor use and going to all rowing, was a decision based on values. Go back to how Assistant Secretary Reed put it, "Motors are antithetical to the quality of a wilderness experience that is, and should be, available in the Grand Canyon." This unique escape from civilization should not be impaired by modern technology in the form of motors "with all that they connote". Whether designated as Wilderness or not, "this canyon sanctuary deserves to be preserved and perpetuated". "None [of our wild canyons] is more important to the human experience than the Grand Canyon." Reed is stating National Park and Wilderness *values*. Indeed, they are American values, for they have been embodied through legislation in the laws that were the foundation of NPS policy on the river. The Grand Canyon is a wilderness that is part of what is conserved within the National Park; enjoyment provided in that Park is not to impair resources or anyone's enjoyment, or be impaired by the enjoyment of others.

Is the question—Do motors impair?—a researchable question? True though it is that people can have opinions about whether motors impair wilderness and the experience thereof, it is not necessary to study the question, for the fundamental law has already answered it. Back in 1967, when Secretary of the Interior Udall said he was surprised he was to travel in a motorboat, he expressed the value, and he got the comm op answer: Big boats can take more people faster, and big boats need motors. Five years later, Reed got the chance to give the comeback: Well, then, since motors are antithetical to the unimpaired Park experience, there can be no motors, and no big boats. Business convenience is not a fundamental National Park value.

So what happened when the Park Service, seemingly in a matter of hours, "agreed to", or "was ordered to follow", or "invented", the policy of switching from a mandatory to a voluntary phase-out, and the idea that the final phase-out would depend on research? Simply put, NPS gave up its unassailable position based on fundamental American values. These values were orders from the American people, acting through their elected representatives, embodied in the Acts setting up and strengthening the National Parks, the Wilderness System, and Grand Canyon National Park itself. Instead, NPS pretended that some research could rule its decision, even if that meant over-ruling the fundamentals that give the agency its reason to exist.

Some in the Park Service seemed to agree. A September 24 draft of items to be covered by the research noted that the surveys would help set quotas, but the authors did not believe that preference surveys could help managers make the motors decision; the data can never decide.[22] But that was September 24; as the record shows, the higher up the official, the colder the feet, and a policy froze into place of delaying action, pending research. One can only fantasize about what would have happened had we mounted an effort, and the safety data had been used as a basis to reinstate the phase-out.

And for the record, in November, another version of the GCNP master plan came out, even mealier-mouthed and shorter than before. On the cover was, "This planning publication has neither been approved nor disapproved ... and it may undergo considerable revision." What metaphor could beat that for characterizing the situation?

Paddling Hard, A New Voice

Eiseman's reappearance was not a solo. Other people who ran the river on their own were beginning to voice their needs. These complainants drew their strength and their grievances from two linked changes: more and more people wanted to run their own trips and the Park Service regulations were rigid and discriminatory. Variously called private or non-commercial or self-guided (my preference) river runners, they joined the commercial, environmental, and wilderness interests in clamoring for NPS attention. The general introduction that follows weaves together quantitative and qualitative material, contemporary as well as past items. The self-guided point-of-view was one I often sympathized with, but was not at the heart of my personal Grand Canyon efforts.

In 1972, self-guided river-runners in the Canyon seemed numerically negligible. There were 12 times more commercial than self-guided trips, carrying almost 30 times as many people. One of the benefits of self-guided trips is that they can be more leisurely, so the user-day disparity was only 14 times. In raw numbers, in

1972, commercial crew plus passengers totaled almost 16,000 people, using 105,000 user-days on 520 trips, while there were 550 self-guided river trippers using 7700 user-days on 44 trips. If you took the total self-guided use, and compared it to each comm op, self-guided would rank after the six largest of the latter. There is added edge to the overall picture of increase: from 1967 to 1972, self-guided use went up 5-1/2 times, while commercial use increased 8 times, from its much larger base.

The qualitative differences are the ones that really provide the edge to the argument that self-guided river-runners are discriminated against compared to commercial passengers. The major difference arises because commercial passengers just pay-and-go; the Park Service has no say in how often those persons go or how many days they spend in the Canyon each year, a fact even more true for commercial employees. In contrast, each self-guided trip has to receive a permit directly from the Park Service, allowing GCNP great control and impact on those who wish to run their own trips. With this discretion comes the temptation for the Park Service to make changes more often in the self-guided rules. One of the most vexatious, variously applied over the years, tries to limit how often a person may take a self-guided trip. Mislabeled a "no-repeat" rule, it clearly creates two classes of citizens, those who are forbidden to go on their own trips because of their previous experience, in contrast to those who take as many trips as they wish on commercial boats.

The overall limit on self-guided use causes the greatest trouble. For the would-be commercial traveler, it is simply a matter of shopping around, looking for the kind of comm op they wish to travel with, and then making a reservation, usually a few to several months ahead of time. Now since the comm ops use almost all their allocations every year, it might be thought that every year, many are turned away. What seems more likely is that those who wait until the last minute may not be able to get exactly the reservation they want, and end up taking another date.

This pay-and-go mode is in stark contrast to the Park Service insisting that self-guided applicants join a waiting list. Constantly growing over the past 30 years, demand so exceeds supply that the wait in 2002 is about 20 years. So, not only is there discrimination in favor of the easy access commercial passengers have, there is also a stratified discrimination among self-guided applicants based on when they got on the list. This internal discrimination of who gets to go when is compounded because the waiting list is a list of trips or trip leaders, not a list of all those who are likely to be on those trips when a permit is granted. Thus there is no assurance that someone who wishes to take a trip in any usual frame of time, say a year or two, can do so unless that person knows one or more trip leaders who are likely to be selected. This factor complicates the picture of a very, very long waiting line, since there is a fluctuating population of people knowing people who know people, and who seek different ways to make themselves available when a trip they might join receives a permit. More complications are added because of the looseness of the commercial trips, so that people who might wish to take their own trip end up, out of frustration or opportunity, going on commercial trips as passengers, guests, or even employees. Indeed, many in the last category also do self-guided trips.

Another discriminatory aspect arises because the workings of commercial operations are largely invisible to the public, while everyone, and most especially comm ops, feels self-guided trips and their environment are open targets. I have mentioned already the silly attempt to blame self-guided trips for dirty beaches, and cited the experience of the 1972 Taylor trip. It was all too easy going through the record or listening to conversations to pick up the bad feelings aimed by comm ops and their employees toward self-guided trips, and often reciprocated. The comm ops, behind their fortifications, feel no compunction about offering gratuitous advice on how to make life more complicated for those who wish to run their own trips.

The comm ops are a compact group; 21 in 1972, 15 thirty years later. They have had high continuity in personnel and outlook. Over the years they have concentrated themselves, through business consolidation, familial ties, and by joining in various lobbying groups. They have direct, intimate access to the Park Service which, instead of maintaining a proper distance between regulators and regulated, believes that the comm ops have a special claim on their attention and even protection from open policy debate. Although there has not been complete uniformity of opinion among comm ops on many matters of river policy, the initiative has usually been with the dedicated motorizers, tightening the focus to their linked goals of keeping large, fast motor trips and maintaining the overall use allocations. Added together, they have a mailing list of tens, perhaps hundreds, of thousands of customers. With a beamed call for preserving choice or some other distortion, it is relatively easy to generate a high percentage response of several hundred messages from concerned citizens. The numbers were smaller in the 1970s, but these factors remain the same today.

In comparison, the population was small of those who wished to run their own trips and who organized themselves to advance their views. I can attest that they were not easily reachable, rarely focussed and coordinated, and did not, indeed could not in the nature of things, generate the continuity of institutions and personnel exercised by the big-and-fast motor comm ops. The comm ops mailing list is organized and ready for use; there was no such registry for self-guided organizers. The local and national organizations that are concerned with and for self-guided boaters often deal with many rivers and many different issues. The comm ops' goals are intrinsic to their existence; no self-guided boaters' organization has existed or could exist with the same intentness of purpose; there are too many cooks with too many recipes in a kitchen with too few utensils, and no stove.

Furthermore, the way the Park Service handled regulations for self-guided trips resulted in minimum input from, and maximum frustration for, users. In an ideal system, a group of persons would apply for a permit, just as commercial passengers make a reservation, and depending on demand, be able to run the river that season or the next. Instead, the growing demand was strait-jacketed within the 1972 allocation and subjected to changing rules that those who saw themselves as victims had little organized way of impacting. Whether the self-guided can ever be organized in the same way as the comm ops remains open to question. After all, the comm ops have for so long themselves been so focussed and had such easy access to the Park Service, that they can thwart and confound the efforts of self-guided boaters to influence policy. At the same time, the Park Service helps protect the comm ops' deliberations from similar transparency. Part of this sad picture is

GCNP's complete disinterest in being creative and working to develop the same sort of continuing, organized relationship with self-guided boaters that it has with the monied operations. From the political point of view, I cannot stress this enough: With the comm ops, the regulators have bent over backward to maintain strong, mutually supportive ties—in spite of disagreements. With self-guided users, the regulators have been bent on maintaining them as an unorganized, unrecognized, even anonymous, mass of individuals held at arm's—two arms—length.

Central to the comm ops is the goal of maintaining their allocations. Any suggestion that has the slightest odor of hinting that commercial numbers could be lowered to accommodate self-guided demand is cause for harsh rhetoric and war.[23] Instead, since the total amount of river traffic is not of prime importance to them, they have been willing at times to accept enlarging the overall pie to give the self-guided boaters more trips. Of course, they are also ready to argue, if anybody peeps about motors being banned, that their user-day allocation would have to be adjusted upward so they can keep the same number of customers for the longer trips. This is quite similar to the position that the rowing comm ops got into: if motors were banned, the big motor companies would convert to large rowing companies, and eat up more user-days. The motor comm ops can similarly argue that if motors were banned, they would suck up a whole bunch of user-days that could otherwise go to self-guided trips. The result is that river management preferentially protects motor users over rowers' trips, and commercial users (especially employees) over public, self-guided applicants.

In summary, the self-guided user has been heavily discriminated against, from the direct regulation by the Park Service, through the barriers to being well-organized and tightly focussed, to having the comm op interest so positioned that self-guided boaters have had to choose between being clamoring outsiders or cringing supplicants at the comm ops' table.

Another development that has intensified self-guided demand is how self-guided trips are outfitted and conducted. This difference in trip methodology intensifies the class difference. At the start and for many years, those who went on a self-guided trip would own their boats, and take care of all planning and supplies. Indeed, NPS rules developed in the early 1970s required that all trip preparation and conduct had to be shared by members of the group, and not done through an outfitter. It was forbidden to rent commercial craft to use on a self-guided trip. The experience necessary to run the Grand Canyon would come from having been on someone else's trips, self-guided or perhaps as crew for a comm op. Such on-the-water experience could come to some degree from running other rivers. There was (and still is) no training program comparable to anything offered commercial employees.

Although self-guided trips are still cooperative and cost-sharing, the range of experience has widened and deepened in recent decades; many are still first-timers, but the number has grown greatly of the addicted who have taken multiple trips, whether on commercial or self-guided trips. The rules forbid hiring a guide to take you down the river (though it is all right for a group to charter or buy out an entire commercial trip), but it is quite legal for a group of Canyon novices to go with someone who has much experience. It is now also within the rules to contract with an outfitter who will do all the supply work, from providing boats to complete menus; though hiring an experienced chef for your trip is not permitted. Using such outfitting companies, it is quite possible for a group to obtain a permit, and then turn all preparations over to the outfitter, needing only to arrive at the trip start point with personal gear. Such services have made river-running ever more open and in demand. The dollar costs are spectacularly lower than a comm op trip, and it is no longer necessary to belong to that elite—mythical anyway—of boat-owners.

Of course, this is an interface of commerce and private activity, just as it is when river-runners do not grow their own food or fell trees from the Lees Ferry forest to make dug-outs. The question of money for services can still be vexed. If a chef cannot be hired, can one be taken who plans menus in exchange for going on the ride? How much of the common tasks does a person have to do who does not row a boat? Is it necessary for all trip members to row? Since experienced river-runners cannot be hired as guides, can one go along who gets free food in exchange for advice on how to run the rapids and where to camp? Is it legal to pay someone to help you plan campsites and timing, if that person does not go on the trip? Can a geologist go whose only task is to provide a stream of information about the Canyon throughout the trip?

Much of this sort of hair-splitting is moot. Participants in self-guided trips are eager to be on their own rather than being led by the nose, and quite willing to share the lower cost in exchange for joining in the common work, quite willing to share their expertise without extra compensation. That is, regardless of how the outfitting is done, the attitude of those on self-guided trips is 180 degrees from the commercial passenger. The former look forward to participating in every way as an integral part of the trip's enjoyment. The latter looks forward to being provided for, with no requirement to know or do anything in order to enjoy the trip.

To this source of difference in how trips operate, there is the experience of river encounters, of which there can be several—3,4,5, even more, a day. Most river travelers therefore see enough of other kinds of trips that they can easily form or reinforce opinions, disdain included. Here are some NPS numbers to ponder, keeping in mind anything you know about rowing being the most pleasant, most richly rewarding, highest quality, experience on the wilderness Colorado[24]. On a self-guided trip, you travel with, on average, 12 companions; on a commercial, there may be 35 of you. On a self-guided trip, you spend an average of 15 days in the Canyon; on a commercial, you get 6. (These six days cost you 2, 3, 4 times as much, but never mind; it is the experience we are trying to quantify.) No surprise, 98% of the boats on self-guided trips use oars or paddles, and while commercial boats are about 50% motor-free, the motored rafts carry 75% of the passengers. Again, no surprise, rowed boats are smaller, carrying 2-3 people on average, compared to the 20 on a motor-driven raft. Smaller means that you get to ride more intimately with the Canyon, coupled into the river's serenity and its roaring. Just as safe, too, don't forget. Oh, and if you take that comm op trip, you have a 50% chance of being taken out by helicopter, two-thirds of the way through the Canyon, shorted of 90 miles.

So taken all in all, there seems little problem in appreciating the difference in attitudes. How easy it is to be on your and your friends' self-guided trip and be appalled and saddened as the politically privileged motor rafts pass by, and pass by, and pass by. And, reciprocally, it is easy, I guess, as you power on down the river, to be puzzled about those slow little boats cluttering up your highway. Little chance for mutual mind-changing here. Particularly since commercial motor trip operators are hardly about to spend any of the few hours on their trips introducing their passengers to people who are having a superior time.

CHAPTER 7

1974: NPS Dancing: With Many Partners, Many Tunes

Motor Music

With pro-wilderness, pro-Park forces distracted, and self-guided efforts not yet above the threshold of effectiveness, the comm ops and the Park Service continued their tense dance in 1974. The comm ops, in order to secure their 1973 success in preventing any immediate action against them, reacted jealously to any Park Service move, pressing what they claimed as their strong point: no action without research results. Meanwhile, the Park Service, the 1972 policy still their over-arching mandate, bounced back and forth between 1972's strengths and 1973's weakening. It might help if we envision the NPS foot shifting as dance steps attached to individuals with different views and different political weight, although it is as hard now as it was then to ascertain who was hearing what music.

On the ground, there was the Regional Director, the Superintendent, his Deputy, and the River Manager. Did each truly favor one or the other policy emphasis on motors and use, or were they only trying to sniff the variable winds? To what degree did they work in concert or at cross-purposes? Certainly, to take one example, those who were involved in research worked under one set of assumptions, those who handled Park concessions a quite different set. We had an expression of personal opinion from the Superintendent's Deputy.[1] Did he come out with it because of or in spite of his bosses' opinions? Within the various offices—Park, Region, Washington h.q.—we heard of differing allegiances, all the way into the precincts of the Secretarial office. The conundrum of the bureaucracy—with seniority and the superficial ability to make an impact, come caution and a reluctance to make substantive decisions—was in full play throughout the mid-1970s, spiced up by the range of personality differences.

Yes, the Park Service could legitimately grumble about flip-flop at the top. Reed's 1972 decision was an abrupt and radical shift from Lovegren's drift. Morton's 1973 non-decision slued matters toward inaction, an invitation to be patient until the wind shifted again. Nevertheless, NPS staff, though not always the same individuals, ran as hard in one direction as in its opposite. And these changes raise one of the questions, a sad one, underlying this story: What is it about the Park Service that so saps the authority that should attach to it, given its lofty mandate? How has it come about that its decisions and policies are so far from definitive, so often controverted and carried to other power centers—senators, secretaries, judges, etc.? How, we kept asking in exasperation, could an agency with so important a mandate be so weak?

The comm ops' allies, on the other hand, strongly argued their position. This is how Senator Moss put their best points in mid-1973:[2]

Interior acted precipitously and with no factual support;
preserve the status quo until there is solid evidence of environmental damage;
the greatest impact is from the constant fluctuation caused by dam releases;
other rivers handle more visitors;
the only safe trip for the average passenger is on larger boats;
sixty percent of those passengers feel motors are essential to their safety;
the most limiting factor for passengers is the time required for the trip;
if motors are eliminated, the cost will double;
the environmental impact of rowing is quadruple that of motorboating;
oar boats carry sanitation equipment only with difficulty;
family groups and older Americans cannot withstand the physical and psychological rigors of small boat travel.

The comm ops' court papers fattened that list:[3]

customers and profit will be lost due to decisions made without proper notice;
motor elimination is a personal preference of officials and conservation groups;
motor elimination accomplishes no statutory objectives;
the reduction to 55,000 user-days will unnecessarily exclude many from the Canyon;
the new river management plan was improperly developed by conservation groups.

I offer the above as a fair-enough encapsulation of the collection of arguments—based on their experiences, prejudices and grievances—that the motor comm ops waved about as they sought to protect and widen their advantage.

Having appealed their District Court defeat, they negotiated in succeeding months with the feds, trying to get a commitment that any decision on motors would be made based on studies, and not before 1976. In February 1974, alarms sounded, and comm op lawyer Brown informed CROA members that GCNP river manager Yearout had submitted what he himself admitted was a "skimpy" safety study, and also had said there was pressure for an immediate decision to start the mandatory phase-out in 1975.[4] Government lawyers compounded this unsettling news by saying that Interior was objecting to motor studies, and would "certainly" announce a mandatory phase-out. Brown then unilaterally widened the scope of Morton's postulated safety concern, saying that not only was the safety information inadequate, it should not be the sole basis for decision; the comm ops' other points needed to be addressed. Having raised this alarm, he urged them to get their "sources of influence" to work on Interior.

We were hearing the same rumors but with a different slant. Chapman told

McComb in mid-February that he thought the motor phase-out, though suspended only for 1974, would not start right up again. Indeed, there was no internal agency agreement yet, though there might be "soon". Two months later, the double message was still what we were hearing: motors banned in 1976, but no action soon.

One comm op who left a trail of his efforts was Fred Burke, the one who had taken Congressman Rhodes on a river trip in August 1973.[5] After the Brown letter was sent, Burke informed an ally he hoped to see the influential Rhodes at an upcoming Republican dinner. Following that dinner, Burke wrote Rhodes that they were getting information from the Park Service that conflicted with what Steiger had told Burke that Morton had said. The rumor Burke passed on was that the phase-out would come before studies were complete. We and "several others will probably be out of business if they go to rowing", and since the public overwhelmingly wants motors, why change? He was more circumspect writing to Goldwater, just asserting the Park Service would not commit itself to keeping the status quo until research was complete.

At this time, GCNP staff followed Chapman's plea for patience by recommending the continuation of the same allocations through the 1975-6 seasons, since no study data would be received until after summer 1975.[6] Indeed, Shaw wrote, if the research program were to have any integrity or credibility, then we "must" defer any decisions "until the research facts are in", lest we be accused of having our minds already made up. Holding such a level would thus bring the analysis of the research and the comm op contract expiration together, in late 1976, although he said it was not too early to begin considering procedures for the concession prospectus. The document then slid by the motor issue, recommending the mandatory phase-out of motors be such that rowing constitute 33% of the "total (commercial and private)" use in 1975 and 66% in 1976. (However, including private rowing trips meant that 33% would require little commercial change. This hand-waving could only encourage the comm ops to keep pressing against any phase-out at all, having one delay already on their belts.) GCNP staff said their new document on motors, to be available shortly, should satisfy the Secretary's request for a study. These recommendations would also have continued the no-repeat plan for self-guided trips instead of a first-come/first-served rule or a lottery. After all, the no-repeat rule was in place and most people were aware of it, and these practicalities out-weighed re-dressing the inequity since there was no practical way to apply no-repeat to commercial passengers due to the burdens imposed on Park staff and the comm ops.

Something prompted the Park Service to be clearer about the definition of a "commercial trip". The new rule held that commercial meant the trip was conducted for profit or even that any charge was added to the actual costs.[7] A trip run by a comm op would not be commercial if there were expense-sharing and no fees added to expenses. A non-profit organization does not automatically run non-commercial trips; it would have to prove it rakes in no profits from a trip. Was this policy connected to the exchange between McComb and the Superintendent of Dinosaur a few months before?[8] Our resistance to paranoia was not helped by such stuff, nor by the comm op who lobbied to have the River excluded from the enlarged Park, leaving it as a "use corridor" for motorboats?[9]

During the spring of 1974, River Manager Yearout had been working on the "oars and/or motors" document.[10] A draft is extant, but its eventual fate can be surmised from the events recounted below. Policy was re-stated: River use should be at the highest standard. "Basically, motors are antithetical to the quality of a wilderness experience." NPS administrative policies for wilderness parks precluded motors. Cited was the lop-sided public opinion as expressed on the 1971 draft master plan against motors (though no tabulation was given of mail after the Reed decision). The draft discussed Wilderness, but since it was in the framework of a soon-to-be-superseded Park boundary, the most it could say was that the river was potential wilderness until motors were removed, as was planned for 1977. Based on a new initiative by NPS, the point was made that interpretation of the natural scene was enhanced on smaller, quieter, rowing craft. Motor noise was noted as a distraction and interference with enjoyment, and even a potential health hazard for motor operators. A weak wave was given to the idea that the question of motors "may well be the kind which data can never decide—a question of what ought to be". (A position being sadly eroded by the public NPS statement that studies were being done.) The draft worked hard at being even-handed about safety, but could only reach as far as it being of "debatable" significance, since insurance rates were the same for both motor and oar powered trips. Energy use and pollution were briefly noted as never having been measured. Time and cost spent on trips were considered, but only from the perspective of the visitor, not the question of whether the only real reason for motors was the greater profit. Also left out was the fact that such a miniscule percentage of the population could go anyway, demand was very likely high enough that it could not matter about the few days and dollars difference between various trips—whatever was offered would be taken. Close to the only unequivocal statement came at the end: Large rafts were not essential to handle human waste.

The document made no big splash, since the alarms caused by Yearout's comments had pushed the Park Service even farther from the Reed decision. The comm op complaints about this "retreat" from what they thought was the Interior attitude were being heard. An April NPS letter to Steiger assured him that Yearout's talk did not mean there would be an immediate decision on motors; the phase-out was being reviewed.[11] There was no pressure to decide immediately, because "the motors decision has already been made", and the Park's accident study was to help re-examine that one aspect. Furthermore, GCNP staff has been working on a statement about the motor ban issues. And when we did meet with Steiger he showed us that his "bottom line" had to do with his friend Burke's allocation.[12] He pushed NPS to begin deciding about redistributing user-days by eliminating some comm ops. This was the same suggestion that Congressman Rhodes had made after his trip with Burke, who as usual was trying to take a lead while paddling his own canoe...so to speak. A letter lobbying a Utah congressman indicated that those who did like to clump together had changed their organization's name from CROA to PROA—Professional River Outfitters Association. And two other Grand Canyon comm ops had become members.[13]

In May, the Washington NPS office leaned on the Region hard.[14] "We feel", said five of the upper echelon, including Marks, that not enough data exist on whether total phase-out is desirable. Then, "Opposition to motors is largely sociological and we do not possess at this time enough data on the ecological impact and safety concern to make a positive decision on whether total phase out is desirable." (This is bad. If by "sociological" they meant something connected to survey data, then that was part of the research. However, it seemed that what they meant was that motor use was a matter of values and opinion that they did not share, since they went on to doubt whether a phase-out was desirable. That it *was* desirable was exactly the Reed policy as enunciated and so far not contravened. Rowing, he had announced, was the Park way to go. But now the NPS in Washington was asserting that the Park System and wilderness values underlying the Reed decision could be ignored, and only ecology and safety data were relevant. Aside from telling their boss to go fishing, this would have been that comfortable bureaucratic posture of not having to stand for anything; it all depends on science.)

Then Marks and company drop the veil: There will be no mandatory phase-out for 1975 either, with 1976 to be at 50% rowing use, which "mandatory" level "will be maintained until the effects of the decision can be evaluated". (Of course, since they have just dimmed further the likelihood of any decrease in motor use, there will not be any effects to evaluate, so the research will never be definitive, and so motors can continue right on into 1977 and beyond. Oh, and we will give the comm ops a one-year notice about any future changes. Well, I suppose if you are going to kiss ass, you need to let them know so they can get in position.)

The friendliness of this memo toward the comm ops—on "motor use" according to its subject line—is then reinforced by its discussion of the "commercial v. private motor [sic] ratio". The current ratio is "most defensible", and should be continued until there is a definite indication that it is "totally unrealistic to the total demand for use". (There was no research or any other effort to find out what was "unrealistic".) The longest discussion is on the no-repeat rule, which is "obviously an unfair sanction against the (self-guided) user" and "impractical to impose on commercial operators". Therefore, they want the Superintendent to strongly suggest to the comm ops that they voluntarily impose a no-repeat rule on their clientele. (That is, since the comm ops were not voluntarily shifting to oars, now they are also to be asked to voluntarily bar repeat users, so they can also not do that, and make the Park Service look even more ineffectual. But wait, here comes the reason.) There is "strong indication that before too terribly long" NPS will be sued by "private operators" to establish equity. (So they think that a Park Service rule imposed on one user group—a rule that is understood to be "unfair" and "impractical"—can be defended in court as a voluntary request to another user group.)

Showing its iota of sense, the memo concludes that it should be reviewed by Park and Region staff, and should remain "in-house" until approved, since "we are not going to dictate" river use policy. One value of this bizarre production is that we have a substantive view of NPS "in-house" policy differences. Projected onto any effort to make a decision, such internal differences could only make it more difficult for the agency to follow its mandates.

In-house at the Park, degradation of the 1972 Reed policy also continued. The Deputy Superintendent at the Park, Bruce Shaw—who had expressed his pro-motor opinion so forcefully in 1972—was now in charge, Superintendent Stitt having suffered a heart attack. In June, Shaw pushed forward to the Regional Director the views of two comm ops, that NPS's indecision on use limits and motors was making it really, really hard for the comm ops to plan, since there was a year's lead time for obtaining new rafts.[15](How can I avoid remarking again that the indecision the comm ops complained about was caused by their own actions?) Thus the matter of a mandatory phase-out affects them. He then referred to the attempt by a Utah boating official to press for pro-motor regulations at Canyonlands National Park. So GCNP needed definitive guidance for a June meeting of NPS officials that he, Shaw, had requested to discuss river policy. (Again, it is hard not to see actions like Shaw's as being precisely aimed at creating or exacerbating a crisis that only existed because of the actions and opinions the comm ops and their allies took.)

The two comm op contributions emphasized their strong point, complaining about the Park Service claiming it would do studies while at the same time re-stating its determination to ban motors and cut use. They pled for keeping the status quo on use with no motor phase-out through 1976 or until the studies are completed.[16] Shaw's concern for the comm ops being victimized is matched by the comm ops' concern for NPS policy victimizing them, as indicated by a Western River Expeditions letter to its mailing list.[17] It groaned about the "intense pressure" from "well-organized environmentalist groups" that might "dictate river policy" "<u>regardless</u> of what the studies may show". No longer was Currey satisfied with his 1973 victory; he wanted all the other items the comm ops had fed to Moss to be considered. He enclosed an article that is stupefying in its distortions.

On June 13, Shaw was given approval to draft the Park's current position, to be used by NPS up to the Director.[18] That day, NPS officials from GCNP, Canyonlands National Park, and the two appropriate regions, met in Denver to review motor use, since "Shaw felt under considerable pressure" for definitive information on the motor ban. The meeting made clear that any discussions, such as in the May 23 memo from D.C., were strictly in-house. After discussion of Canyonlands' need to allow motors on its long stretch of slack water, the meeting decided to "freeze type and kind of use" through the end of 1976, while research was going on. Also, existing use levels would be continued until an EIS was developed from the research, public meetings held on the EIS, and a final decision made. This would allow public input as well as research conclusions to be taken into account.

A week later, Shaw wrote to the Region[19]: We agree to further examination of the motor elimination, with a decision to be part of the final environmental assessment, to be done at the conclusion of the research program. This should occur "within a year or 2 following the original 1977 elimination date". (He was not going to propose pressing hard to get a new plan done in order to remove the uncertainty; better to keep the comm ops happy while GCNP dawdles along.) We want to hold the status quo, i.e., any motor reduction would be only voluntary, and went on to urge that comm ops needed to be notified as quickly as possible, to buy equipment, train crew, and book trips. Mandatory changes should be announced two years ahead of time. (Compare this with the acceleration of use under Lovegren; somehow the comm ops were no longer able to react so fast.) We do not see any need for any other changes, such as speed reductions or campsite scheduling. If there is to be any change in self-guided allotment, it should not come by reducing the comm ops use; that would create "severe" economic problems and could invite lawsuits. (Although not all of the commercial allocations were being used each year.) No-repeat seems to be the "fairest" way to deal with the problem of growing self-guided demand, and we will write to the comm ops suggesting a voluntary rule for their customers.

The new position was sent on to Washington, dropping the phased reduction of motors in favor of a freeze on type and level of use.[20] (Apparently the pro-Reed forces were also frozen "in-house".) This static level would be continued during the research. By the end of 1976, we would prepare an EIS. (Yes, this differs from Shaw's 1978-9 projection; in the event, he was more accurate, and a lot of pain would have been avoided had NPS been honest about its schedule.) We suggest doing the EIS for all NPS units on the Colorado. This will take us into 1977 and beyond, but we believe it is defensible based on NEPA. Shaw's concern for comm op planning was repeated. We must be firm and not yield to pressure from self-guided users. That also can be part of the management plan. And we will write a letter to "our river concessionaires" asking for a voluntary no-repeat rule.

So why not yield to self-guided pressure? Just imagine if they had dared to announce that while the effects of the Reed policy were being researched, they would be introducing adjustments in self-guided use levels in order that the research could more fully deal with all the issues. And after all, they had yielded to pressure from comm ops. Which is of course exactly the point. NPS did not have to yield to self-guided pressures because the latter did not, could not, exert the necessary political force. NPS was engaged in political calculus, determining step-by-step their policy by reckoning which pressures were strong enough to yield to.

Equal Time

Yes, I do think the actions, and words, and therefore quite possibly the beliefs of people like these NPS officials, distort and weaken the basic laws and tenets of the National Park System. What if we suppose they are not wicked? How might they feel justified in the view that it is the legitimate mandate of the Park Service to promote use, and develop for use, and protect commercial domination of providing use? I have stressed that the founding law's language for our National Park System clearly makes conserving Parks dominant over providing enjoyment. What I must now do is acknowledge that the *founders* were convinced otherwise; that providing access for enjoyment was of consuming interest to them. Whether speaking of Stephen Mather, the wealthy businessman who led the Park System into being and initial operation in the 1910s and '20s, or of the early GCNP Superintendents, including the dominant figure of Minor Tillotson, an engineer, what NPS stressed and planned for at first was making Parks easier to visit. Mather, until overruled by the Secretary of the Interior, even supported the idea of a tramway into the Grand Canyon. A century ago, in an American West with a "primitive" infrastructure, roads, trails, bridges, etc., were foremost in the minds of these men.

The impacts of the Great Depression and World War II were little different. Federal works programs throughout the 1930s promoted construction for use in Parks. And after World War II, the 1950s were a time when friends of the Parks were so concerned about dilapidation and the onslaught of post-war visitation that it seemed the proper and necessary thing to launch a building program, called Mission 66 for its ending year, and for the Park Service to be headed by a promoter of such a program. Given this history, is it any wonder, that amid the vigorous calls starting in the 1960s for preservation, non-development, and wilderness, those who were in charge in the 1970s were mostly still attuned to affording the largest possible access? Given the times of their up-bringing and early careers, why would they not be skeptical of wilderness management as a proper tool when it conflicted with the chance to increase visitation? As deeply as I disagree with the course these men followed, I do comprehend that they certainly felt justified in pursuing it in the name of that tradition of providing mass motorized enjoyment and explaining away any impairment that resulted. Even further, I understand that that tradition, although shaken from its unquestioned pre-eminence in NPS thinking by the "new tradition" based on Park and Wilderness law, remains the choice of all too many NPS personnel and administrators. And of course, that choice is so much the easier because of the backing it receives from commercial interests and their political allies.

With a Tin Ear

Moving with unaccustomed speed, NPS announced this new Colorado River Management policy in July in a paper asserting that we have reviewed data, and we do not have enough to decide about motors.[21] So any motor phase-out will be voluntary until there is "conclusive evidence" to show whether or not to remove motors. We will not allow motor use to increase. Also, the use ceiling will be held at the 1973 level. Research will be essentially complete by 1976, leading to an environmental assessment (weaker than an EIS) and an effective management plan. The July notice to the comm ops of this change was friendlier: We concluded that in spite of the considerable opposition to motor use, there is insufficient information for a permanent decision.[22] GCNP was also reassuring, saying there would be no changes for two years and, even once the decision was made, there will be a period for adjustment.

At the Washington level, NPS justified this shift to what they hoped would be more stable ground in a nine-page internal memo to the Director, of which Marks, again, was one of the authors.[23] Responding to a July 3 memo from Reed, NPS asserted that the escalation in use was too sudden for them to measure the ecological pressures. They claimed they could not have predicted the boom. (Actually, GCNP had, back in 1966. And, anyway, as under Lovegren, the point was that NPS did nothing to control the "boom".) What is really hard, NPS whimpered, is determining the river capacity from the social standpoint; the "primitive experience" may be less important than we once thought. (This has to be a lovely example of personal opinion masquerading as an agency "we".) If the ecological capacity is larger than the social, then it will be difficult to defend the latter. (Only if the writer approved of this move away from Park and Wilderness principles to the cop-out of waiting for research.)

On motors, NPS continued, it is the conservation groups like the Sierra Club who oppose them because of their adverse esthetic and pollution impacts. (Again, the writer is showing that he does not understand the principles underlying National Parks, which is why groups like the Club end up having to defend the Parks, often without NPS help.) "Neither side has yet been able to prove or disprove arguments about the relative safety of motors vs. oars." (This, simply, was not true. To repeat: The data show these are safe adventures. The data show trips with motors and trips using oars are equally safe. No datum exists to show that there is any ambiguity about safety. Period.) Motors are "basically an emotional issue". Wilderness status may be the next most important criterion. (Next after safety? That is not what the Wilderness is about. Wilderness users are to craft their safety without diminishing the wilderness, not vice versa.) Using motors to speed greater numbers of people is a questionable management practice. (Then why not say so; Reed already had, and Morton had not really changed that aspect of the Reed policy.)

NPS defended holding down the self-guided allotment because that use was increasing more slowly, and the self-guided are a "small, rather affluent special interest group". Furthermore, keeping the overall ceiling in place implied cutting the commercial allotment, which would be politically, legally, and morally tough. (This is the opposite of the truth; commercial passengers are the affluent ones and the "tough" choice was a false one. What this statement really means is that NPS would change only if the self-guided could politically and/or legally force it to change, just as the comm ops had.)

The authors admitted that NPS had given the comm ops a great deal of latitude, perhaps more than was appropriate; on the other hand, they probably did not receive adequate notice on limits. We have heard a great deal of criticism from two or three comm ops, while most have said little. Any changes may bring out the others. A dozen congressmen show continuing interest; some understand the conflicts among their constituents. Anyway, opposition does tend to die out, so let's make no critical decision until the research is done. (This passage is an amazing exercise in slipperiness: Whatever evil we have done, let's lie low; this too shall pass. Please remember this was the summer of a Presidential resignation for covering up and other high misdemeanors.)

The document concluded with recommendations to the Director: No mandatory phase-out, and encourage a voluntary shift to rowing. (Fair question. If the policy was truly to "encourage" such a shift, how come there were no efforts to do so, no incentives, no keeping track in a public way of who was rowing and who was shifting from motors to rowing?) Keep the self-guided allotment as it is, and enforce the no-repeat rule. (I find it so hard to see this compilation of error and personal opinion as anything other than the response of a motor-friendly official to political pressure he is willing to "bend" to, even as he undercuts the stated and justifiable policy of his agency and his superiors.)

In spite of this news, the comm op's attorney urged his clients to keep up their efforts, "I am relatively certain that the responses to your mailouts as well as the contacts you have made ... have resulted in whatever advantage we may have gained and ... even greater effort will be required in the future".[24] So far he was upbeat about the Park Service's new policy, even passing on a rumor from a Washington NPS source that the NPS has backed down and will never take motors off. He was also pleased that he had help lobbying Morton from lawyers from outboard motor manufacturers.

In August, the Washington NPS office released a strange clutch of documents, claiming to be a general "river running policy statement". Obviously based on the problems in Grand Canyon, they tried to set deadlines for river management plans based on research. Their unreality can be seen in the statement that while the research would not be complete until 1977, there should be approved river management plans for each area in mid-1976, with appropriate environmental assessment.[25] This sort of fantasy document could hardly have made anyone feel easy. When sent out in September, it asserted that the opponents of motor trips object to water pollution and to the intrusion of noise in a primitive setting. Then, asserting that the issue "is largely social", a decision was deferred until more factual information was at hand.[26]

October's batch of form replies to citizens' letters reflected the slippery slope the NPS Directorate now wanted to send Reed's decision down.[27] There are, NPS ventured, arguments both for and against motors. There can be no definite timetable for action until the research is done. The Park Service has not committed itself to phasing out motors, since there is no evidence of adverse impact on the habitat. The safety of rowing is questioned by the comm ops. There is not enough information to ban motors, and, anyway, some believe that motors are a traditional use precluding wilderness designation. With no research to support limits, most feel the status quo is best. (Just when you think NPS can sink no lower ...)

There was a minor chance to let off some steam at a September meeting in Phoenix of a group called the Western Regional Advisory Committee (WRAC).[28] The advice was for the Park Service, and it gave an opportunity for GCNP staff to offer an interesting version of recent events. There were a few of us in the audience offering comments, and some bizarre anti-Park reactions from some WRAC members, including some pro-motor types, such as "the Park Service should not dictate what it is the people should be enjoying"; "I'd hate to see it limited to the point where people could not go and see this river". Others understood what a National Park was about, making the point that a Canyon trip should be more than a thrill ride, and that motors were not really essential. One member pointed out that regulations had already resulted in cleaner beaches. Based on a river trip the group had taken in May, there were some specific complaints, such as the "cotton-pickin races by boatmen to campsites". All in all, the discussants asserted, no real damage seemed done to basic policy as we understand it. Chapman offered the comfort of saying NEPA forced them to a procedurally cautious stance. We were more comforted when a Tucson newspaperman wrote up a whole page on river issues, preaching to our choir.[29]

Yet we deserved no comfort. According to my journal, we had been so absorbed for the previous six months with Park legislation, that we made no effort at all to keep abreast of events, including hearing of the changes described above. Spending our time in another venue altogether, working on Park legislation, we had done little to prevent the Park Service from getting further and further out of tune. The Reed decision had moved in the direction we had been advocating. His statements in favor of a motor-free wilderness river experience were as good as any could be. For that pro-Park view to erode through 1973-4 and then be set aside by out-of-date bureaucrats was sad. The policy that was shuffled into place in 1973-4 could have been celebrated as sound, if it had been the original policy. We would have cheered in 1972 had Reed announced a freeze while research was done and a river management plan developed with its EIS based on the research. Cheered and fought on for a motor ban and use cuts. However, the freeze-and-study policy that would have been acceptable in 1972 was a knock on the head two years later. Ironic justice maybe; first the comm ops were riding high, then they got dumped. For a bit, we were on top, only to be dumped in turn.

Was it then a defeat, a failure? We and our allies were not able to prevail with a policy in tune with what the Park System is all about. So yes, of course, what happened in 1973-4 was a failure. And because it was fought for by the comm ops, it was a defeat. Even tougher, they had been proving their mettle, just at the time we were losing the fight over Park boundaries.

CHAPTER 8

1972-1975: Research 101

Up to this point, I have been telling a story, a triangular tale. Friends of the Canyon, comm ops, and the feds; the first two vying to be in closest with the third while elbowing each other aside; the romancing as much with braggadocio and threats as sweet talk. As 1974 ended, a momentary stasis had been brought into being, by force and exhaustion. In 1975, the personnel of the story were being added to, the triangle expanding to a pentagon. Shifting metaphors, we now have to deal with a more complex choreography, danced to more than one score.

First, this chapter gathers together that research effort everyone claimed they were waiting for and would rely on. A disclaimer: there is an immense amount of Grand Canyon research about areas, especially geology, which is not part of this story. I also did not have access to much material about the internal workings of how the researchers did their job. Then Chapter 9 more fully explores another major claimant, those people who wished to run the river on their own, who organized and took self-guided, or private, trips. With their efforts presented, Chapter 10 switches away from river management policy *per se* to examine how we and the Park Service dealt with the various Wilderness studies, particularly the one mandated by Congress in the 1975 Grand Canyon National Park Enlargement Act. Chapters 11 and 12 will try to weave some coherent pattern for 1976 including our two newer partners, researchers and self-guided users, which will bring us into the pivotal year of 1977.

A quick overview: Research was code in 1972 for "You can't do that!", first for those worried about escalating use, then by the comm ops as pressures grew on them. The comm ops had put up $3000 to get a proposal started.[1] Scientists, particularly Roy Johnson—who moved from Prescott College to GCNP to become the overall program director as of November 25, 1973—were involved in the Eiseman October 1972 meeting, following which GCNP prepared a draft research guideline in November, made final the following spring. From 1973 through 1976, research was being contracted for and done. This led to a draft summary report released in October 1976, although it was not published until a year later. This time span heightened the impatience we felt, in such contrast to the bureaucratic clock the Park Service worked to. We ignored any lesson we might have gained from Reed's decision and its aftermath, of how good an example it was of haste making waste. On the other hand, suppose the previous chapter's scenario of a more measured decision had played out, would the comm ops have accepted it, or would it just have provided them a slightly different target? In any case, no set of decisions could have avoided a research program; the scientists were the necessary guides to get there from here.

1973

Some relevant research was being done before the big program started in 1973, and by some of those who were to be involved. For instance, Steve Carothers, biologist at the Museum of Northern Arizona (MNA), was conducting biological field studies from 1970. Chemical and biological studies of the water in the river had been occupying Lorne Everett and others from the University of Arizona. There was that political football by Boster surveying commercial passengers before 1972. Another University of Arizona researcher, Stan Brickler, was also working that area, usually called the "sociological" impact of river use. Brickler, a member of the short-lived river advisory committee, was particularly active in the meetings and other agitation of 1972-3. Sadly, he felt his data had to be guarded from public view as a work-in-progress, and much of whatever impact he might have had was never realized, even as he continued his work.

A snapshot of what was interesting the scientists, before the river research program was fully underway, was provided at a symposium held at MNA on September 1, 1973.[2] There was a review of recent archeological work, including some sites along the river. Up on the plateaus, forest fire and prescribed burning were a hot topic, as were the studies of Grand Canyon's air quality. Brickler spoke, but without substance. E. Bowman's consideration of wilderness experience suggested that personal factors—ideas of remoteness and how much area was needed—were so dominant that a history of how those ideas have changed indicated an amenability to NPS action, whether toward enhancement or degradation of wilderness experience. There was one report on portable toilets with recommendations on the best procedures. Some preliminary work on beach erosion was a bit vague, noting that with the dams in place upstream, the beaches would last more than ten years, but probably less than 1,000. What is striking about the overall list of projects is how scattershot they were, and how unoriented most were to the crises of the day. Clearly, a centrally organized research program was needed if answers for administrators were to be more than fragmentary.

Clearly, too, such a program's most delicate and contentious area would have to do with surveying passengers to find out who they were and what they thought of their experiences in the Canyon. These studies were called variously the study of river contacts, the social use capacity study, the study of human behavior in the Canyon, the study of the impact of motorized river-running. The Boster study had left a residual feeling among the comm ops that it justified their belief that more people could be taken on trips, since most passengers did not feel crowded. New work, whoever did it, would be under strong scrutiny.

Committed, Brickler was anxious to continue his work and submitted a proposal to NPS in July 1973, competing for approval with a group from the University of Denver. A month later, the proposals had been critiqued by five reviewers and NPS wrote Brickler that it was hiring a consultant to meet with him and the Denver group to strengthen their proposals.[3] Given Brickler's experience on river matters, what was the problem? One reviewer was astonished that the preliminary results were not available, but was even more withering about the inadequacy of the technical strategy. The Denver proposal, while general and showing a lack of familiarity with the subject, seemed professional enough to merit support. The second reviewer thought Brickler was strong on his field procedures, but lacked any theory, and would be unable to make any future projections. The Denver proposal, strong on theory, led to the suggestion that the two would be better combined. The third reviewer flat-out stated that neither effort would stand a chance of being funded by major agencies. The criticism then switched to the uselessness of most such surveys for administrative decision-making. Neither study seemed aware of the need to design a study with NPS participation. Worse, the questions NPS wanted answered were not survey research matters, and the reviewer would have been "very sad" to see management based on the proposed surveys. What was needed was a three-year study that involved the evaluation of alternative management strategies through experimental situations. This was the theme of the fourth reviewer as well, urging that more could be learned through experiments studying how visitors are influenced by the visitation environment, of which agency regulations are only a part. The fifth reviewer echoed this concern for the social organization that brings visitors to the river. The Brickler proposal too narrowly relied on user and crew attitudes about the trip. Again, the Denver group had the theoretical foundation to provide useful data, even though Brickler had the concrete knowledge of the actual situation.

What these comments are good for is highlighting the concern that the connection between research and management was not being made, neither by the agency in framing the request for proposals, nor by the researchers, who did not show how, in the one case, their experience and techniques, and in the other, their theory, related to useful management information. The drumbeat of "research, research" heard over the previous year would only be a prelude to a useless, ignored study if strengthening steps were not taken within the Park Service and by the would-be researchers. This concern must have acted as a tonic to NPS because its disappointed tone of August was altered when an open call for proposals went out in December, asking academics and others for help in finding "the best possible investigators" since "the highest quality social research is demanded".[4]

One of the pleasant aspects of writing this narrative has been talking with others active at the time, and hearing their stories. Here is the tale Tom Heberlein told me.[5] Heberlein, with a Ph.D. from Wisconsin, went to teach at the University of Colorado in Boulder in 1971-2; he shared an office with Joyce Nielsen; Bo Shelby was a student. In the summer of 1972, Heberlein went on a two-week private trip down the Grand Canyon run by Shelby. In the 1972-3 academic year, Heberlein returned to Madison (where he has stayed) with Shelby in tow as a graduate student. Shelby received his Masters degree, and preferring the West, returned in 1973 to

Boulder to work on his doctorate. That fall, Heberlein was brought out to GCNP to meet with Superintendent Stitt and Western Region research chief Bruce Kilgore. They wanted him to evaluate the two proposals discussed above. Heberlein thought them both bad. So he was asked, in general, what could be done in research into human interaction in the Canyon? Heberlein made clear the need for a broad-based request for proposals, reviewed by a slate of independent reviewers, not including him. Kilgore and Stitt insisted that motors were to be phased out, but Heberlein convinced them that the subject was one that could, and should, be studied, along with other factors that might affect people's satisfaction with the trip. How much would it all cost? Heberlein communed, and came up with an estimate of $125,000. (Later on, he mentioned this number to a Colorado professor (Haas) who ran a consulting firm called Human Ecology Research Services (HERS) out of his home.) Thus was selection of the user survey research set in motion.

Discouraged in December with not getting any money to continue, and by the major change the NPS was making in its study plan to meet criticisms, Brickler told us he was feeling "radicalized". He still was not releasing any of his data, however, and his relations with NPS were troubled. Nevertheless, he responded to the new call for proposals in February 1974, this time adding three professorial-level colleagues with experience in outdoor recreation and the study thereof, one of whom had long experience in self-guided trips as well as in arguing for them. The critiques seem to have been absorbed, and the new proposal expanded to meet the deficiencies of the earlier work.

This time, however, there was even more competition due to the Park Service working harder to attract interest. In response to the NPS letter, there were six proposals considered seriously. One in particular Heberlein remembered as being innovative, but far more expensive than his estimate. Meanwhile, shrewd enough to make his research proposal fit the Heberlein estimate, Haas had hired Nielsen and Shelby to do the study (he then seemed to disappear). The award, made in April 1974, did go to Human Ecology Research Services, with Joyce Nielsen in charge and Bo Shelby in the field. Shelby made a Ph.D. and a career out of his contribution. Heberlein's opinion was that the HERS idea of using observers and the 9-point crowding scale were innovative. During the research, Shelby talked with Heberlein a lot by phone, and the latter came up with the "experiment" of studying motor-oar differences by running combined trips, in which some on the trip switched from oars to motors halfway, and the rest switched from motors to oars.

To jump ahead, Heberlein did become disillusioned about policy-oriented research by events of this Colorado River war; he felt there had been an opportunity for decision-makers to be helped by research to acquire a broader, more stable base. As we shall see, NPS took up the challenge, but the opportunity was rubbished by the comm ops. He believes that the work on motors and visitor contact was sound and remains valid. And despite his reservations, he and Shelby did make another effort in the 1980s to influence river management; more on that later.

By summer's end, 1974, the preliminary field work, overseen by Shelby, included eleven trips. HERS made these preliminary findings available before the 1975 season to allow for feedback from NPS and comm ops on what HERS said about the relevant issues and explanations of behavior.[6] This was done, recognizing the disadvantage that river crews might subsequently change their behavior. Data collection had been by participant-observers on the trips, who handled getting the questionnaires filled out, and could record actual contacts and other day-to-day information about the social qualities of the trip. The issue wrestled with most in the February 1975 analysis was contacts, how many there were and what they were related to. This was a subject we worried about because of the possibility that motors might be found to be valuable in lessening contacts because they could speed up and move on downstream to lessen crowding at camping or attraction sites. The report emphasized the role contact between boat crews could have in sorting out who was going to which place.

The statistical picture of the motor passenger, as compared to the rowing passenger, showed one used to and more accepting of motors, used to and more accepting of more people around, and seeing the Canyon as less crowded and less developed. That picture is exactly of the kind of customers that keep motor comm ops convinced that there is no user-based reason not to have more, bigger, faster trips. Going the other way, rowing passengers hoping for fewer contacts were bothered more by noise and evidences of development. That is, getting their way, there would be fewer of everything, including them. The conclusion would seem inescapable: if the goal were to maximize the number of *enjoyment-days* in the Canyon, the solution would be a continuous stream of large, crowded, noisy, fast motor trips. Preliminary as this first season's work was, it was further evidence of the pit we all had accepted falling into: research is wonderful; it will tell us the answers, and we can skip having to make decisions based on laws or values. But what if research showed us that the fundamentals we valued most intensely were of little interest to a larger set of people with transient desires? What if research showed that a motorized river was just what visitors wanted? We always fear having National Parks turned into Disneylands. We might have feared that the research could justify an exchange of wilderness for mass entertainment, a Gresham's law for the river. Or rather, a Grisham's law. As matters turned out, it was the comm ops whose faith in research was most tried.

As the 1975 research season got underway, I heard rumors of experiments that were to be conducted creating very crowded conditions at launch in order to see the effects on visitor perceptions of crowding. Bothered by these rumors, and by the failure to heed the rising complaints from self-guided users, I talked about these matters with HERS and the Superintendent. The former's answer was that it was better to have the greater crowding situation available for study during the research, and thus perhaps find the negative effects before the overall limit on use was raised. And if there were no negative effects?—that is what we were afraid of, adhering to the picture we had of the ideal experience being a float trip moving in grand solitude down through the great natural riverscape. As for studying self-guided users, HERS told me it would only do that if the Park Service added it to their mandate and dollars to their budget. Which the Park Service did do, so that the one full research season, 1975, divided the user population into three: commercial motor (80%), commercial oar (13%), self-guided (7%).

Throughout I was concerned that the research would be tainted by seeming bias or arbitrariness, that the research might justify increasing river use whatever the demand. I expressed that concern by keeping in touch, sifting through rumors and hints, and by providing in 1975, at HERS's request, materials on the history of the controversy so far. We tried to maintain contact with several researchers, an easier task in the winter months, and also easier because a number were at or working with the Museum of Northern Arizona in Flagstaff. MNA was the center for the natural science side, engaged in the studies of campable beaches, beach sand loss, and the impact of visitors on the flora and fauna of the river shore.

A non-NPS study, including an employee of one of the large comm ops, showed up first though. Conducted in 1973, its goal was to find out what the river shore looked like and how it had altered in the ten years of upstream dam operation.[7] It was an early indication of the low likelihood that the natural science studies would give definitive answers on environmental impact. After describing the change from a flood zone with little permanent vegetation to a more stable, but eroding, zone with plant invasion, the researchers tried to find river-trip impact, but "were unable to detect any significant degradation of the beaches and adjacent areas because of littering and waste disposal." What was significant were the results of walking on the beaches: surface erosion of a foot or two, with roughening that contributed to sediment loss during the daily rise and fall of the dam-controlled river. Overall, however, there was nothing to conclude other than that "new data and new investigations were required."

1974

The research program, under the leadership of Roy Johnson, covered four years and cost around $700,000, including the people surveys at $125,000.[8] First fruits, and a contrast with a year before, showed up at the research symposium held at MNA in August 1974.[9] A main contract underway for a year was with Carothers and the MNA Research Center investigating "the effects of man [sic] on the riverside ecology". As might be expected, a fuller picture of species numbers and distribution was reported. However, although human impact had been analyzed along with alternatives for management, these were not discussed, and a more exciting finding for the researchers was a high correlation between a sizable feral burro population and low vegetation and small mammal densities. Oh dear, along with the dam, another excuse not to blame river-runners for environmental impact. The role of plants in making beaches more stable was mixed, since they also affected how much of a beach was available for camping. In a connected study, the vegetation change was being charted by comparing photographs taken over the century of river-running.

A campsite evaluation, also an MNA project, was more substantive, indicating litter was being packed out and that people moved rocks around in various purposive ways. Significantly, management of the 20 tons of human waste was focussed on. The current portable-toilet method involved digging a hole above the high-water line as part of breaking camp, into which the chemically treated waste was dumped. This digging was certainly a disturbance, and some beaches showed the impact of these "blue-hole stains". The possibility was raised that the chemicals used were actually inhibiting bacterial action on the waste.

This first public exposure of the HERS people study indicated a strong emphasis on users' perception of crowding and how this related to satisfaction. As a measure, this item disturbed us, since no one doubted that river trippers ended up hugely satisfied almost no matter what. After all, they had just spent 5-15 days in the Grand Canyon; what kind of dolt would be dissatisfied? Presenter Shelby made a major point of including wilderness values as one of the factors affecting satisfaction, but the problem for us was that we saw National Parks as places where people's wilderness values were to be strengthened if they existed, and shaped positively if vague. That is, HERS was seeing wilderness awareness as an independent variable affecting satisfaction whereas we believed river trips should form or strengthen pro-wilderness values and that should be the measure of a good trip, satisfaction being very high anyway.[10] We were not all that comforted by hearing of a Utah State University study that did seem to be saying that although user perceptions of crowding were important, most critical for visitor perception was the congressional mandate that determines what happens on the land.[11]

1975

Many of the above concerns continued through 1975. There was wrangling about HERS's idea of having a high-use period to measure crowding impact. Word was that the physical carrying capacity of the river was way beyond anything anybody had contemplated. Also, the biologists were pressing the idea that the burros were more trouble for the environment than the people were.[12] Was this good news (lots of people could use the river without damage) or bad news (lots of people would be using the river)? This ambivalence on our part was certainly partly personal—what kind of pleasure is it to hike up the big mountain to discover at the top that there is a crowd that has driven up the road on the other side?

There was also the worry that our intuition about congestion could be wrong; an intuition fed after all by history, experience, and anecdote. Since that "intuition" was exactly what the research was intended to supplant with observations that were repeatable and repeated, and therefore verifiable, the research years should also have been years of education, particularly for the combatants from the pre-research period. Our fussing, and the comm ops and their crews were going through the same process, was a way of getting used to these new claimants, these researchers, who had something to offer that we other participants must accept if our arguments were to retain legitimacy. In return, we were all looking eagle-eyed for bias and skewing of results. One report back to the Superintendent claimed a comm op had said that the survey work was terribly slanted, and would almost certainly result in a conclusion detrimental to the comm ops.[13]

Then there was the Park Service: they were in charge; their solidified position was that the research was to give them a foundation, a data base modulated by conclusions and recommendations, on which to build a management plan. The last thing they wanted was flaky research open to criticism. However, if the research was above reproach, then NPS had to use it, no matter what the political environment. Perhaps these considerations were behind the appearance, the first time ever, at the October 1975 research symposium of an NPS spokesperson from the Western

Regional Office, who reported Chapman as "extremely interested" in each project.[14] He recognized the role of scientific data in providing a sound basis for sound decisions and effective management. He spoke about the exchange of information, and the special emphasis on the river research. It may be significant too that the symposium was held at the Park (a sign of blessing?) instead of Flagstaff, even though it was less convenient for many attendees. That would not explain why it was rare to see a comm op at these get-togethers. I am not totally sure that is meaningful; perhaps they were getting information another way, or perhaps my assumption was correct that they just did not care that much about being bored sitting around listening to a lot of fancy talk about what they, the comm ops, knew best anyway.

Roy Johnson, as the program leader, summarized its evolved form. The three major phases dealing with riparian ecology, sociological aspects, and aquatic ecology, were being carried out through 20 subprojects investigating "the interactions between the park visitor and his environment along the Colorado River, interaction among park visitors themselves and natural processes within the riverine ecosystem". Final results were not available; aims and methods would be discussed. So as this meeting opened, balanced between the time of data gathering and that of report writing, we heard the slow beat of bureaucratic caution, the dance of Salome in reverse. Johnson reported on the money so far spent or committed. A new area was to be explored with an economic and financial study of the comm ops. He then reviewed the work of several people who were not at the meeting, and brought on those who were to give detailed reports.

Nielsen opened for the HERS effort by admitting that the "traditional" model they had started with—relating use and satisfaction—was not supported, and "that the Grand Canyon system is more complex than previously thought."[15] She offered other possibilities to explain high satisfaction:

that user density was too low—which is why they wanted an experimental
    high-density week;
that wilderness purists, more sensitive to crowds (oh, sigh, how delicate
    we are) go elsewhere (and exactly where would *that* have been);
that "the resource itself" (her phrase for the Canyon) is a major determinant
    of user satisfaction (I would be more sarcastic about this over-obvious
    point except for the thought that we had contended just the opposite,
    that there were too many people for visitors to enjoy a quality
    wilderness experience. Unless "satisfaction" and having a quality
    wilderness experience are not the same thing?);
that what she called the "last settler syndrome" may have operated on all
    these first-timers (80-90% of users); they were having a fresh,
    new experience unbothered by, even unaware there was, the congestion
    so apparent to those who had come many times before;
that visitors were perverse enough to enjoy themselves in spite of the
    congestion, a kind of cognitive dissonance (ignoring the other
    possibility that people come on such trips knowing there will be
    other people next to them, a cognitive consonance that starts
    with wanting to be bunched together for mutual reinforcement;

see the brochure pictures for big motor trips with bunches both
on and off the rafts).

One item that Nielsen did not discuss was bias. Not bias in the way the sample
was drawn, but bias in how the population of river-runners was constituted by the
comm ops' ways of soliciting business, which resulted in users being overwhelmingly
motor passengers, with little river-running or wilderness experience. Even if the
sampling were flawless, the sheer number of motor passengers liking their trip (of
course) would swamp answers to every research question that aimed at finding
dissatisfaction. To escape that numbers trap, it would have been necessary to break
down that huge motor population using important discriminators.

The question was only partially whether people were happy with the trip or
unhappy because it was too crowded. The important question for NPS
administrators was what difference it would make among similar visitor groups if
Park and Wilderness ideals were adhered to or not. A division was showing up
between motor and oar passengers on certain pro-wilderness measures. So then how
did you find out whether there would be more dividing out among the motor
passengers, if they had different experiences based on Park and Wilderness values,
insofar as they could be approximated on a motor trip? Suppose of two similar trips,
a Park Service interpreter went along? Or the boat crews were sorted to give ranges
of such items as knowledge of the Canyon, support of Park values, and adherence to
environmental safeguards? Or the passengers were sorted and clumped along the
same lines? Or, given these discriminators, what about the effect of different trip
lengths, if as some motor operators claimed, the 8-day motor trip provided the same
high wilderness quality as the 12-day rowing trip? Or, would differences show up
depending on what kind and how many stops were made at "special places"?

The only way to tell whether *any* kind of motor trip could best inculcate
Park/Wilderness values would have been to control for how the values were
presented. And the absence of such controlled experiments, being beyond the
research's resources, meant that any pro-motor congressman could cite the much
greater number of satisfied users on motor trips and claim such users represented the
American people, even though what they really represented was only the way the
comm ops structured their client population.

The notion of doing research to "answer" the question of whether motors were
appropriate in a Wilderness Park setting was, as Reed stated and we (Eiseman
particularly) argued, irrelevant anyway. To then survey a comm-op-selected,
undifferentiated mass of motor users to find out whether they were happy about
their trips, was playing right into the hands of those who wanted to keep motors.
No matter what their opinion of the contacts they had, they were not going to say
their trip was spoiled.

Which brings us right back to face ourselves: the Goldwater-Eiseman-
conservationist pressure on the Park Service to cut back the number of trips because
the river was "congested". We were now trapped by our own rhetoric that
congestion meant lower quality, and by the motor comm ops being able to pile on
satisfied motor users because they had the numbers. Unless basic Park Wilderness
values, not just satisfaction, were the basis of research evaluation, we would lose
since we were the former "last settlers", long since put off by the newcomers. The

newcomers were the masses attracted by the comm ops' offerings, producing the double effect of keeping the proportion of first-timers high, while preparing them for an experience that assumed motors. In retrospect, did we make a mistake in 1968-72 by focussing on numbers and the quality of the trip? Would our stronger position have been to demand that user impacts on the river environment be monitored, and that comm ops switch to rowing because motors were inappropriate (and illegal) in a Park Wilderness? Once again, history's realities whisper, such a change would just have brought a re-focussing on the new target. Nothing was going to pry the weapons from the clammy heavy hand of motorizer dominance. This was a fight they were determined to win.

Back at the symposium, Shelby followed Nielsen to offer their conclusions that use levels were not clearly related to contact numbers, and the latter did not affect satisfaction or even perceived crowding, due to "the complexity of the wilderness system" and "the over-simplified nature of the user-satisfaction variable".[16] He then went on to differences between motors and oars, a presentation he expanded in a December paper.[17] Starting with a historical review, he suggested three questions. What are the observable differences between rowing and motorized trips? Do the differences lead to different perceptions of the Canyon or the river experience? How can we use the differences to better understand the nature of the motor-free experience and the motorized experience?

His data came from the 1974 participant-observer pilot study and a 1975 experiment giving users the chance to try both rowing and motor trips. The pilot selected trips to give maximum variation and therefore was not representative of all river trips. However, within the sample, motor passengers tended to be older, have families, make more money, have less schooling, and be less likely to belong to conservation groups or engage in outdoor activities like camping etc. Exactly the population with the most *potential* for gaining in appreciation and support of Park Wilderness values, yet with the least likely chance of realizing that potential since they end up on the short, fast, big motor trips. On the other hand, rowing trips were longer, they stopped at more attraction sites, and the crew offered more interpretation, due to no motor noise and the smaller separation of rowers from their passengers. Most motor passengers did not mind the noise and preferred encounters with other trips, especially large motor trips.

Did these differences relate to different perceptions of the Canyon? There might already be a differentiation through trip selection, but as I said, that just gives the motor population more potential for learning. However, Shelby reports, motor passengers were more likely to think they did not meet too many people, that the Canyon was not over-used by people, and that more conveniences would be O.K. Rowing passengers reacted negatively to these items. In line with the point about greater potential to move toward pro-Park sensitivity, one out of five motor passengers were ready to switch at the end of the trip. Indeed, for over half the motor boaters, propulsion mode did not matter, while almost all rowing passengers still preferred oars.

In order to get more direct comparisons, HERS worked on a combination trip with ARTA, a big comm op that used motors and oars. Shelby noted that no other comm op offered to help with this experiment. Fifty-six people selected these trips, starting on either motors or oars, then switching halfway through. There was no way to get a representative sample, but Shelby did analyze possible sources of bias. Whatever the methodological weaknesses, the result was very strongly that the great majority preferred rowing. The words they used for the motor part were speedy, loud, crowded, as compared to leisurely, natural, peaceful, friendly, for rowing. Both were fun and exciting. Taken all together, there were 104 reasons offered for liking rowing and 144 advantages, compared to 5 reasons for motors, and 108 advantages. There were 7 negative words applied to rowing, and 69 to motors.

In looking at the management implications, Shelby boiled the different advantages down to convenience for motors, as compared to rowing's more relaxed pace, quiet, greater openness to the surroundings, and more comfortable social relations. He wanted to go further, however, first noting that we "feel" machines are out of place in wilderness, even when they seem necessary or convenient. They change the focus of a trip away from the place and the people you are with. Taking another step, Shelby moved into psychological theory, the right and left brain, a mental action mode and a receptive one. This last dichotomy was attractive, since it contrasted the manipulative aspect of human environmental interaction with its absorptive aspect, each one a different, but equally valid way of formulating goals for dealing with the world. Working over this distinction, with examples from then-current thinking about wilderness, Shelby ended with this blending: the wilderness experience requires an integration of an active, planning mode with time for the receptive mode to have full play. Grand Canyon river trips would ideally be unique for enjoying receptive experiences, whether on a commercial trip where much of the planning was done for the visitor or on the more active self-guided trips.

What Shelby did was open a theoretical gap between more crowded, hurried, noisy, and less surroundings-sensitive, motor trips and rowing trips where the smaller size, more leisurely travel and natural sounds better afford the chance for the receptive wilderness experience to predominate. Perhaps he wanted to counter the charge that research is irrelevant to the question of banning motors. It is not just that machines and wilderness are antithetical by legal definition, but that social research into motors in the wilderness can show this as well. Motors suck the air out of our behavioral space, occupying our basic human efforts to absorb the natural environment, reducing our options as humans, rather than expanding them. If machines are for us to use to achieve goals, then by demonstrating through research that motors interfere with our achieving our wilderness goals, Shelby could conclude that they cease being even useful, i.e., convenient, in the wilderness. Of course, to the motorizers, his strenuous effort to find a theoretical ground for motors being antithetical to human experience in wilderness would only cast a dark shadow on his claim of doing unbiased research.

More directly, the noise of boat motors is an obvious tool to mark their anti-wilderness essence. Boat operators pooh-poohed the effects of motor noise on crew, passengers, and other visitors. (Curiously, they do not dare argue that motor noise enhances the visitor experience, although making noise, revving up, roaring off, is an obvious plus for many users of motors of all kinds.) Rowing partisans lamented the shattering of the natural quiet (and the natural roar) of the Canyon by the non-natural whine and volume of motor noise. Could these opinions be gauged by research on just how loud the noise was and whether it did degrade people's river environment?

For the latter problem, the HERS researchers asked questions and observed behavior. For the former, surely there would be a thorough study to match the salience of the issue. And there was a study report, published in 1974, titled "Sound-level Evaluations of Motor Noise from Pontoon Rafts in the Grand Canyon".[18] In its introduction, the authors noted "virtually no information available on actual sound-pressure levels" in the Canyon. So, "in conjunction with" the beach carrying capacity study, they assessed noise levels as "a secondary objective ... of an initial survey nature", instead of in "any pre-designed, systematic way". Data were from six days in mid-July, at about a dozen points along the river, a total of 24 recordings.

The researchers, on this narrow base, went on to conclude that noise levels are marginally close to exceeding health standards for those running the motor. Aside from safety information, normal and vital communication with and by passengers is degraded, even precluded, as is their sensing of the environmental soundscape. "In summary, outboard motor noise is a deterrent to normal, relaxed conversation that one would expect in such an environment, a safety hazard in raft operation, and a health hazard to the motor boatmen."[19]

This is great stuff. Unsafe! Unhealthy! Prevents hearing the environment and talking about it! Motors must go! And yet. The details above should help the reader understand how it might well be possible for the motor operators to criticize research results, reject them, and even accuse the researchers of anti-motor bias. In turn, people like me who believed that motors were detrimental would have appreciated sound work that supplemented our view. Tougher, the Park Service had gotten itself into the position of saying it depended on the research to help provide direction for its decisions. Like the summary of accidents on the river requiring evacuation, this noise study held out whiffs of support, which could all too easily be blown away in the blast of opponents' scorn. No surprise here; we would have done the same, and this frail one-shot effort had been summarized with something like, "Oh, motors do not conclusively violate any standards." These measurements and conclusions would be used by NPS and by us to argue our position. We would have preferred to have had data from a variety of locations, times, traffic conditions, and river environments. This work could then have been complemented by people-derived data from the HERS study.

Just the facts please. So here is the mid-July 1973 soundscape in the Grand Canyon. When it is quiet, it compares to a whisper. When windy, a bit like light traffic half a block away. A big rapid can range from freeway traffic to a freight train passing near you. It was too difficult and dangerous to record the sound starting into any rapids, where they are most violent and noisy, and where, of course, crew comments might be necessary. The sound sitting next to a motor, depending on horsepower, could range from that made by a heavy truck to a subway coming into a station. The researchers concluded there could be no speech with motormen without visual attention getting. In the front of the boat, the rapid might or might not drown out the motor; otherwise, the noise was like standing near a freeway.

The principal investigation on the trip during which noise data were gathered as a by-product was an inventory of campsites. Let me take a moment to note that the trip leader, F. Yates Borden, was remembered as a person "whose innovative and significant studies, coupled with his enthusiasm, optimism, and dedication, contributed substantially to the Colorado River Research Program" before his untimely death in 1977.[20] This contribution was highly significant in the campsite inventory report, which he summarized at the October 3, 1975 meeting. Significant because a key to the carrying capacity of the river environment was the question: If you break up the river trip into segments, then how many campsites are there in the segment(s) with the fewest campsites? The answer to this would help determine how many trips could be launched in a day, and therefore how much "crowding" there would be. The number of campsites and the length of the segments depended on propulsion. Assuming all rowing—river-paced, wilderness travel—Borden used the 20-mile length that approximated a regular day's trip. He found three limiting segments with a maximum of 6 campsites, one starting at Lees Ferry, the next about 100 miles down, the other 150 miles. The 1975 NPS rules allowed a total of 150 people (crew, passengers, whatever) launching a day. The campsite limit, allowing six trips, suggested an average of 25 per trip. If we look at the 100 prime launch days, then those 15,000 rowing travelers would account for 180,000 user-days. Motor segments were 30 miles long and the fewest campsites in a segment were 12; no limit there if only 150 people launched. Thus campsite capacity—based on such items as ground surface and stability, how much use the site got, how unfriendly the vegetation was, and what the hazards were—was setting an upper limit so high that other factors like humans impacting humans would become most important.

Borden's work also included a photographic comparison of shoreline erosion and vegetative encroachment. Their suspicions of the first year seemed confirmed the second year, as "the rapidity of erosion and vegetation encroachment were verified" on selected sites. As with the noise study, these snapshot evaluations would require further checks.

The research areas so far discussed are those that dealt with the most contentious issues. Yet the underpinning for everyone's concern, ostensibly, was the river and its shores, their flora and fauna. After all, the overall coordinator of the study program, Roy Johnson was a biologist actively working on the status and distribution of birds in the Grand Canyon. He reported five teams were examining the aquatic biota, the physical, chemical, and quality properties of the water. Especially of note was a bacteriologist's just-begun study of what was happening to the human waste buried in holes on the beaches.

Johnson's closest colleague was the very active field leader Steven Carothers, curator of biology at the Museum of Northern Arizona. Whereas much of the work cited above involved people relatively new to the Canyon, and in some cases was done with small amounts of field work, the biology groups thrived on river trips and collecting. Furthermore, they were especially attuned to connecting what they found to its meaning for river visitation, and part of their assignment was to evaluate actual visitor usage on selected beaches. In his report, Carothers stressed work establishing biota baselines and a habitat vegetation map being laid out on a mosaic of 600 aerial photos. Of their more than 1700 person-field-days, over 90% were spent on 9 float trips. Birds, lizards, small mammals, and insects were being observed, trapped, and cataloged. They were impressed by the numbers of species and individuals being recorded, although recognizing that it was probably tied to the increase in vegetation being allowed by elimination of annual river floods.

An MNA study by M. Theroux showed the vegetation situation was perverse: prickly, uncomfortable, often invasive, shrubs would be left alone by people, while more defenseless, and often native, plants would be walked on or otherwise given a smack. He was concerned about long-lasting imprints, and suggested giving some beaches a rest, and finding better trail routing. S. Aitchison's report on visitor usage suggested there were at least nineteen biologically sensitive places. (And, no, NPS did not close them.)

One study, of an only indirect human impact, was of how devastated some areas were because of the activities of burros, descendents of those used by miners and others early in the Canyon's white-man history. Indeed, just as the dam effects were supposed to swamp the boating impacts, so now it appeared that the feral burros making a home in the Canyon might be more of a "threat"—they were an exotic, after all—than the thousands of river travelers. Carothers did note that some comm ops were still leaving wet organic garbage. He recommended that to minimize the effects of human urination, the place to pee was in the river or on sand already wet by it. The river was also the best dump for food juices and wash-water. He urged that fires only be used off-season, to cut down on charcoal debris graying the beaches. He described some places where permanent trails were emplaced by people moving from boats to camp or attraction sites.

Carothers's greatest contribution, however, the one which deserves to carry his name, is that he finally found how to practically implement the recommendation the Sierra Club and others had been urging for over seven years to carry human fecal waste out of the Canyon. He and his team had worked out a simple solution that involved a toilet seat set over a large, watertight, surplus ammo-can lined with heavy plastic bags. Any boat that could carry its food could carry these items; there was no need for any dumping pits or chemicals on the beaches. The boxes were built for security and to prevent leaks in or out. It was a technologically simple solution that would be low cost for any comm op or self-guided river-runner. A triumph of pro-wilderness technology and a shut-your-mouth answer to the sneering question asked by Bruce Shaw in 1972 (Chapter 3). Unfortunately, at the NPS-comm op meeting the day before the research meeting, there was a long discussion about carrying out fecal waste, and the Carothers solution was not presented. The talk instead was of pit toilets again, research on the breakdown of burials from portable toilets (showing that the method was not effective or harmless), how big boats could carry waste out or carry macerators and battery for them, holding tanks at Phantom Ranch, etc. All this was about to be irrelevant, but somehow the connection could not be made in a timely way between research, innovation, and operations.[21] A most unfortunate bellwether.

At this point, we leave the researchers working away through 1976. We have to go back a bit to bring along those fighting for self-guided river-runners, who, because of growing numbers and discriminatory regulation, were getting a wee bit angry.

CHAPTER 9

1973-75: The Self-Guided Public Steps Out

Just Who Is the Public Anyhow?

My overview, from the standpoint of 2003, of self-guided trips in Chapter 6 was not so clear in 1973. A very big difference between now and then was awareness of the difficulty in traversing the social, administrative and political terrain. Everyone had a lot to learn as to just how wearing the trip would be. So it was with lots of hope and determination that people like Fred Eiseman, Joe Munroe, Ron Hayes, and Rod Nash began building the case for the rights of people who wanted to run their own trips. I increasingly appreciated this case, but was not a participant in its making. Consequently, my knowledge and records of self-guided activities are scanty compared to other subjects.[1] A full account is needed of self-guided river-running's political activity from the 1960s on.

To start, here are some numbers for self-guided trips to provide perspective vis-a-vis the comm ops.

Year	1967	1968	1969	1970	1971	1972	1973
Trips	10	11	18	28	35	44	46
People	101	154	185	428	436	548	648
KUD				4.3	5.5	7.6	7.9

The total number of people from all these seven years is 20% of one year's commercial passengers, and is only 20% more than the number of commercial crew in 1972. The user-day total for four years of self-guided trips was 25% of one year's commercial passenger + crew use. This percentage is so high only because self-guided trips took seriously the time needed to fully appreciate the Canyon. In contrast, the number of self-guided trips was not even reaching 10% of the commercial launches each year.

The numbers do not represent at all, therefore, the weight self-guided users brought to the debate because of the intensity of their effort. They were motivated by their belief that the principles and ideal of our National Park System gave those willing to do-it-yourself an ethical advantage for access. As one Coloradan who did not get a self-guided permit one year complained, they were the ones who most vociferously supported river conservation, opposing dams and supporting the motor ban—some payback.[2] In contrast, self-guided advocates argued, the advantage the comm ops had was that they got in early and promoted hard. But that early-worm argument should not convert to an unalterable, eternal right to suck up over 90% of the use each year. Insult was added over the years by comm ops not being able to use their total allocation, leaving a gap of unused days that approximated 1972's self-guided use.

In November 1973, Eiseman gathered a group of self-guided river-runners and rowing comm ops at his house to organize against implementation of Morton's non-decision decision. Some present were enthusiastic and a few promised to make particular contributions on philosophy, safety, conversion economics, mailing lists, insurance concerns, etc. Fred ran his own letter-writing campaign. In December, he had another promise from Goldwater for an appointment, some information on safety, and the assurance that the Grand Canyon Rowing Outfitters' mailing (described in Chapter 4) would go out at the start of the year. Others were concerned enough to turn out in the comm op capital of Salt Lake City to oppose and slow down a state legislative resolution in favor of motors.[3]

Another voice for non-commercial trips, Joe Munroe, had been active at least since 1972, as indicated by the impact his petition on behalf of self-guided rights had on comm op Burke late in that year. Throughout 1973, he spoke out separately, making a large effort in many letters, writing to fellow friends of wild rivers, as well as to the Park Service.[4] He complained about the river being restricted to wealthy commercial passengers, echoing his general message about the squeeze comm ops were putting on river-running opportunities. More explicitly he attacked the new "no-repeat" rule that allowed only one trip every other year. He was not alone. However, complaints about this rule, often along the lines that the experienced person necessary to lead a self-guided trip would be the one excluded, led only to the Park offering assurances that self-guided interests would be involved in future decisions.[5]

As mentioned above, "no-repeat" was not applied to comm op passengers, who could go as often as they chose to pay the fare. This might not have seemed to matter much, since the Boster and HERS studies reported that 85-90% of commercial passengers were first timers. However, 10% of the commercial passengers in a year amounted to 1200 people, twice as many as the *total* self-guided people allowed to run each year, whereas the self-guided repeaters, at about 30%, came to at most 200 people. Indeed the increase required in self-guided use, if the discriminatory rule were dropped, would have been like adding one more of the smallest comm ops. With all the changes in the past 30 years, this imbalance has not changed much, since if the launching slots used up by commercial repeaters went to self-guided trips, the latter's backlog could be eliminated in 2-3 years, instead of increasing on to the current 20 years and beyond.

Even as it set the rule, NPS admitted the discrimination, saying the no-repeat rule "is obviously an unfair sanction against the private operator or private river user. But being realistic, it is hard to monitor and, therefore, impractical to impose on commercial operators."[6] Then NPS turned reality upside-down, claiming they could not discriminate against commercial passengers, just to avoid discriminating against self-guided users. Argument aside, in practice, the no-repeat rule was bound to cause trouble, because the Park Service had to check each self-guided application to find out if the "trip leader(s) and/or a substantial number (in most cases, all) of his/her boatmen [sic]" had run the previous year, and if so, turn down the application.[7] This made the rule more vicious because it discriminated not just between comm op and self-guided, but also between experienced and less experienced. Of course it invited being gotten around, thus tempting comm ops as well as NPS personnel to claim that self-guided river-runners were a low breed, always trying to beat the rules, and stuffing the waiting list.

Even more sadly, this rule was aimed at a problem the Park Service itself created. Self-guided permits had been issued on a first-come, first-served basis through 1973. Then, according to NPS's tendentious accounting, in the fall of 1973, getting ready for the 1974 season, GCNP *asked* everyone who had run or applied recently to indicate whether they were interested in running again.[8] Of course, lots replied whether they really intended to go or not, causing the Park Service to be shocked at the great increase, "several times" the normal—although there was no normal yet. In truth, there were 150 replies, which might have used an estimated 25 KUD, three times the number used in 1972 or 1973. Having created this phony crisis in demand, NPS then asked people to apply for real, and received 80 applications. Supposing these totaled about 13 KUD, the first question is whether this really constituted a crisis. The 13 KUD was only 5 KUD more than the 8 KUD allotted, not "several times", and ought to be compared to the 105 KUD used on comm op trips, of which more than 10 KUD were repeaters. NPS emphasized the need for consistency in not allowing any increases, but was willing to be inconsistent and penalize self-guided users but not comm ops for trying to go two years in a row. Worse, these twists and turns to mitigate a self-made crisis, further entrenched NPS's inequitable stance and negative attitude toward self-guided users.

If consistency were important, as in use limits, then why not continue the first come, first served rule? There can be no satisfactory answer to this question; NPS claims it was trying to be fair, not wanting to exclude some people through luck or poor mail service, while others might repeat every year. This big-brother-will-look-out-for-you answer ignores the fact that the same problems apply to commercial wannabes, yet self-guided river-runners were and are the only users of the Park to suffer this discrimination wrapped up as tenderness. How bizarre is "no-repeat"? In comparison, the first come, first served rule has always applied to a very similar group, the non-river backcountry users—mostly backpackers. The current website for backcountry permits says, "the demand for permits far exceeds the limits established to protect the canyon and the quality of the user's backpacking experience. Advance reservations are strongly recommended."[9] That demand is now about 30,000 a year, with 13,000 granted. Yet "advance" means only 5-6 months in advance of a trip. Now, if GCNP can handle 30,000 requests every year for the backcountry, up to 800 a day, how come it cannot process the measly 8,000 backlogged requests for the miniscule 250 or so self-guided river trips each year?

Twice as many backpackers do not get their desired trip each year as the total on the river waiting list. They just apply again, and if they wish, again and again, making many trips over the years, just like commercial river passengers.

Lest we just tut-tut over 1972's good intentions about fairness gone astray, recall George Orwell once again. NPS treatment of those who wished to run their own trips did try one's patience. And there is a mystery: Where did the animus against self-guided trips originate? Why has it been so virulent as to cloud decision-making? How much was it well-intended, then incorrigible, missteps? How much bad personal relations? How much comm op prejudice infecting others? How much, who knows what? The result, in any case, was the Park's flat statement, "A waiting list has been established." A pebble in the river in 1973, the list has grown into a boulder-laden rapid blocking the kind of comfortable relations the Park cultivates with the comm ops.

Throughout the early months of 1974, Eiseman continued to press his allies. The result was meager. Some who volunteered didn't come through. Instead of a mailing to tens of thousands, GCRO included a couple of articles in newsletters. Goldwater would no longer respond to his pleas. Joe Munroe's effort to find support for self-guided boaters in the Western River Guides Association was thwarted by the comm ops who, with their employees, controlled the organization's business. (Dee Holladay, during this period an officer of the WRGA, remembers it becoming dominated by motor comm ops who were telling guides to stay with motors if they wanted jobs.[10] By and large, Dee notes, the self-guided users were resented by the comm ops.) Indeed, the WRGA ended up urging a cut in the self-guided allocation. By the time Eiseman went on a "last" Canyon trip in mid-May, he was extremely discouraged about any effort to affect Morton's policy.[11]

Yet there were some positive signs, like a protest from Senator Tunney (D-California) that NPS policies discriminated against self-guided users.[12] Another straw in the breeze was a detailed position sent by the American Canoe Association to the GCNP River Manager.[13] Representatives of the group met with Yearout on June 21 to argue for a lottery and a no-repeat rule, both to be applied to all would-be river-runners. This individual permit system would mean that each successful applicant would decide how to travel after receiving a permit. The ACA did agree the no-repeat rule couldn't apply to commercial guides, but then it should not apply to self-guided trip leaders; experience is required in both cases. They pointed out that the Park was concerned about not discriminating against those who cannot go on their own, but seems not to be concerned about the discrimination inherent in the high prices of commercial trips. They turned upside-down the argument about self-guided river-runners being only young and strong and healthy by saying that this condition lasts only a relatively short time, and therefore it is a shame to allow so few to go that many lose their chance (getting old and weak and rotting, I guess), given that paddling is physically demanding and required training. They were "disheartened" that nothing would be changed before 1977, saying to Yearout: You are two years behind in your reasoning; much of the rapid increase in interest is due to more widespread skills. You feel tied down by the 1965 Concessionaire Act. Your rules restrict our more experienced trip leaders while allowing repeaters on commercial trips. You say being fair is too much work, and for the same reason you reject a lottery. You say your policies are a local GCNP matter, but that decisions are made in Washington; we see that going to Court or to Congress are the only ways to bring change. ACA did then appeal to their congressional delegation.[14]

Another voice offered reassurance that the concern for *public* access to limited wilderness and wild rivers was not just a Grand Canyon issue. The Public Wild Rivers Environmental Project in Oregon issued a legal and theoretical paper in November 1974.[15] Its central thesis rested on a doctrine that public lands were held in trust. Therefore, the general, "undefined" public, rather than any commercial organization, always had priority in access to rationed public lands. Denying permits to citizens who wished to run rivers such as the Salmon and the Colorado actually proved that commercial use was too large and should be cut back instead of protected. Use, as such, could be regulated, but private uses—such as commercial businesses running river trips—should not be allowed to usurp use by the general public. The paper attacked the objectives of the Interagency Whitewater Committee—a group chaired by the GCNP River Manager—on the basis that they were all stated so as to imply a second-class position for self-guided trips. Several offending phrases were cited and countered:

a privilege for private trips should be protected. No. It should have priority;

a reasonable percentage should be set for self-guided use. Again, it should have priority;

limiting river use means limiting both groups. This ignores commercial efforts to generate use;

rely on historic use. This often meant continuing commercial domination.

In conclusion, commercial use was not illegal, but should always have second priority after general public, self-guided, use was met.

These arguments could have been balm to the vexed spirit of the hundreds now wanting to run the Grand Canyon on their own. Instead they had to put up with the standard Interior reply: Any judgment that the self-guided allocation is too small is subjective; 1972 was the only guideline available.[16] The only way we (NPS) have to change your use limits would be to increase use overall, which we will not do now, or to cut the comm ops, which would not be fair. After all, the comm ops do serve the public. (Well, some of the public, but NPS would not say that.)

That NPS form reply may have helped Munroe to crystallize his idea that the problem was not just a matter of discrimination, but that the Park Service was at odds with its own fundamental laws; a conclusion parallel to those who were pushing for a motor-free Wilderness designation. Munroe took this fundamental view to the meeting with Reed he was finally able to obtain on November 22, 1974. The Munroe contingent included his attorney, David Dominick, and Richard Saltonstall, a Reed friend, who had arranged the meeting; both had run the Dolores River on a 1974 Munroe trip. Instead of the friendlier Reed aides of two years previous, NPS was represented by Richard Marks and the NPS concessions supervisor.

According to the account Saltonstall sent to Reed, the latter allowed as how he was concerned, "We've found that we're not running them (the comm ops); they seem to be running us, and I'm not happy about it".[17] However, the Arizona delegation would not stand for changes to the comm ops' allocation "just as these hornets rose up on motors". And he thought they would again, whatever Goldwater and the Western River Guides Association might favor. Anyway, Reed had never seen litmus paper that worked faster than the Canyon. He agreed the no-repeat rule was unfair, but thought it was only symbolic because there were so few commercial repeaters. In any case, Reed fell back on the Secretarial decision as meaning nothing could be done before 1977. Seeming to give in, Saltonstall wrote that after all, comm ops do provide a service "as I joked with Dick Marks after". The lawyer summed up by saying they were asking for reversal of the August 28 river policy, and Reed had said he would talk it over with the new NPS Director, Gary Everhardt.

Dominick followed up with a "formal petition" to Reed on January 13, 1975, on behalf of Munroe aimed at securing "an equitable allocation of permits to the *general public* on restricted-use wilderness rivers" (my italics).[18] The emphasis indicates Dominick's representation that, beyond Munroe's individual interests, what was needed was a fundamental revision in NPS policies, now skewed toward commercial interests. His targets were the lopsided allocation for the comm ops and the no-repeat rule. First, though, he gave us a view of the NPS/Interior thinking at this time of "waiting for the research", by summing up and offering counters to five arguments advanced at the meeting by Interior. Some said political and congressional factors were paramount, so Dominick argued that these were solely administrative, not legislative, matters. One official worried that the comm ops would sue (the irony being that they already had, and had been told by the judge NPS had administrative discretion), which Dominick said was no problem, since the laws governing NPS, including its Concessions Act, gave the comm ops no grounds for a challenge. Reed's assistant wanted to wait until the comm ops' contracts expired at the end of 1976. That worried Dominick, who wanted action now, and because Reed might be gone in 1976. Another official was not sure of NPS regulatory authority over Park waterways, which Dominick countered by saying that there was no question about authority over the part of the Colorado that flowed through the Park (and, I would have added, no question for the Colorado through the entire Canyon, since the legislation putting the river in the Park had been signed the week before). Another thought such changes would require following NEPA procedures, which Dominick thought did not apply since Marks and others at the meeting "were unanimous in denying" any greater impact from self-guided trips. The freeze of the division of river use was arbitrary, and given the increased demand, is now capricious and inequitable, violating Interior's duty to administer the Parks for the *general public's* benefit. Denying self-guided permits because of existing comm op allocations turns the law upside-down. And Marks' suggestion that unused comm ops user-days could go to self-guided trips reinforces this illegally reversed priority. Dominick concluded by asking for the interim step of assigning trips in 1975 on a 50-50 basis, commercial and self-guided. However, he and his allies did not accept that division as a permanent solution. Principle and the laws demanded that "public, non-commercial activity" have a priority of right. Furthermore, according to the law, the comm ops must justify their operations as essential.

The Canyon generated news on its own in February 1975, when some sandstone slabs fell into the river 27 miles downriver from Lees Ferry. One of the researchers got quite excited, saying that at low winter levels, motorized traffic would be blocked. The Park was more blasé, suggesting that at normal river-running levels, no one would even notice the rocks.

Certainly, few self-guided trips would get the chance, blocked by the Park Service policies castigated above. The 1975 rejection letter to Fred Eiseman rubbed it in.[19] First, GCNP staff only looked at letters postmarked January 6, and only up until noon, since that was enough to fill the allotment. They went through each application, screening out those who had gone as participants or commercial crew in 1974. A few were dropped for not meeting NPS qualifications, the rest either being given permits or put on a waiting list. Munroe gave numbers to this discriminatory, labyrinthine process: of 166 trip applications, 41 resulted in permits, 100 in rejections, and 25 were possible substitutes. Estimating 15 people per trip; only 25% were successful, leaving about 1800 people stranded, compared with some 1200 the year before.

This process, "as fair, honest, and as impartial as we could make it" must have been somewhat disturbing to NPS staff, because the letter to Eiseman announced that in 1976-7, a lottery would be used. The Park Service had apparently come to believe that self-guided river-runners preferred it.[20]

Fred and I exchanged letters in February 1975.[21] I emphasized the need to push for a good GCNP Wilderness recommendation, and made a tentative gesture toward the plight of those who wanted to take their own trips. Fred's reply, reflecting the gap of two years, emphasized the cost of the Park legislative fight during which he felt he had been used for his Goldwater connection and then dropped. He had been discouraged in any case by the success of the motor comm ops and the failure of rowing groups. However, he detected some renewed interest in the self-guided cause, and was contacting an environmental legal group to see about challenging the discriminatory allocations. He described Munroe's effort to get action out of the Western River Guides Association through a Private Permit Action Committee, but was pessimistic because too many WRGA members were comm op people. He believed it was time to form a group of self-guided river-runners only, with the aim of challenging the allocation. He had heard of Senator Tunney's sympathetic view; maybe there were others. He seemed to be correct, based on a letter from Colorado Representative Tim Wirth.[22]

Using the materials Munroe and Dominick had produced, Eiseman wrote a number of people, getting encouraging replies from several. The new NPS Director sounded even personally friendly, wanting to deal with the Grand Canyon in person. Goldwater said he, too, was going to get involved. And although the case did not appear to be an environmental one, Fred was hearing only positive news about the chances of a suit. He also was circularizing businesses connected with boat outfitting.[23] He was trying to set up a meeting with Stitt and his river staff to personally make his arguments.

The Park Service was now sensitized, but still not balanced.[24] Their form letters of reply emphasized that people on both commercial and self-guided trips were from the public, still pretended the no-repeat rule would be applied to comm op passengers, and said that motor trips were safe. Self-guided trips could not serve the total public need, even though there was dynamic growth. Anyway, true demand cannot be measured, since both sectors try to influence demand.

As if on cue, the comm ops too became sensitized to the self-guided campaign and counterattacked, generating letters complaining that professionals and comm ops might be excluded from the river if the self-guided river-runners had their way.[25] Some letters said that motors might be banned, a bad idea since they were useful for taking some of the public, too. In particular, they attacked a new group, the Wilderness Public Rights Fund (WPRF).

In pursuit of his idea of organizing, Fred had asked GCNP for self-guided names and addresses. The Park sent a list of the 175 applicants in 1975. Eiseman then announced the formation of the Wilderness Public Rights Fund, with the goal of asserting the public, self-guided, "priority to access to rationed public lands and waters". Meanwhile, his encounter with the Superintendent was deeply unsatisfactory, Fred evaluating the "combined IQ of the NPS side thus scarcely top[ping] the genius level".[26] What Stitt kept repeating, out of hope one supposes, was that the self-guided allotment would be increased under the new plan, but that nothing could be changed until the research was done—no comfort to Eiseman, since his concerns about legal priorities were not researchable; a point Stitt didn't grasp. When Fred worried about whether the NPS would keep its word, Stitt said maybe his job would be easier if the court settled the point. Fred again complained about the no-repeat rule being discriminatory, and when told again that it was too difficult to apply to comm ops, he did not press the point that it should not, therefore, be applied to self-guided either.

The conflict evident in that conversation was quite fundamental. Advocates for Wilderness and self-guided trips believed they were arguing on the basis of Park System and other American principles of public land administration. The administrators, kicked around pretty hard for a few years, were in pie-in-the-sky mode, wishing to think that they could find some "realistic", research-based foundation for practical decisions that would bring incremental change and diminish contention. Yet what was the sense in that wish, since without the power base or connections, wouldn't NPS decisions just be challenged and overturned?

That weakness was highlighted when in June 1975 several representatives, led by Harkin (D-Iowa) and Wirth (D-Colorado), introduced a Resolution explicitly aimed at having Interior review its GCNP user allocation policy, which was "blatantly unfair" and "inconsistent with the intent of the Congress".[27] Using 1972 as the base year for a self-guided limit was capricious, so the Secretary should begin "a comprehensive revision of regulations governing the allocation of use between commercial and qualified noncommercial users of the Colorado River through the Grand Canyon National Park". The thirteen sponsors did not include any from Arizona or Utah, though Colorado, Texas and the northeast were represented. Although this may have helped with the comfort level, and been good for publicity, the lack of priority may be indicated by the three months it took for the Committee just to ask for Interior comment on the resolution. Still, the shot had been fired, and maybe it helped get NPS attention. Later, I heard that Representative Rhodes had passed on the information that Wirth was trying to get his resolution out of the Interior Committee and into Maritime Affairs, where action might be more likely.

It was also that summer that GCNP, in response to the building self-guided pressure, told HERS to add to their research a study of self-guided river-runners.[28] At the same time, McComb took a look, running a self-guided trip down the upper part of the Canyon. He commented on trampling and trail scarring, congestion at attractions, and the long time motor noise could be heard before the boats even appeared.[29] He also found the beaches cleaner than five years before. His letter was certainly only one of many such comments, not necessarily hostile, that hinted to GCNP that the tabby cat it was casually twirling by the tail in 1972 was growing and growling ominously.

A more or less immediate response came on October 20, when the no-repeat rule was dropped.[30] Anyone could apply through November 21 whether they had run in 1975 or not, GCNP explicitly acknowledging the rule was only imposed on one group of river travelers. A lottery would be held on November 25 to select 1976 permittees and a waiting list in case of cancellations. The lottery did not help Eiseman, who was barred in 1975 since he went in 1974, and did not win the lottery in 1976. He busied himself in other ways. In 1976, he, Munroe, and Saltonstall began the WPRF's fundamental court challenge arguing the priority of self-guided trips over commercial trips. A San Francisco attorney, Donald Nemir, had agreed to proceed even without payment. To raise funds for costs, WPRF ran an ad in *Not Man Apart*, an environmental publication. There, WPRF made its case that self-guided users ought to be the priority public served. Eiseman reported Munroe was still trying to get support in the WRGA and influence other agencies.

Eiseman was triumphant at getting the Arizona revenue department interested in why comm ops paid no taxes. He went on to alert a whole bunch of other state agencies as to probable violations (more detail on this effort in Chapter 11). He explicitly directed attention at Martin Litton and his dory operation (too bad he could not have included some of the large out-of-state motorizers). I thought he was a bit off the mark in his effort to use Arizona's ownership of the Colorado riverbed to assert that the state should regulate the river surface, exactly contrary to what we had achieved by putting the entire river surface under GCNP as part of the Park boundary revision. Fred also mounted an offensive against the research program, claiming NPS had already made up its mind, and all the research was just a front for it to hide behind. I thought the real problem was the reverse, to produce research that the comm ops could not accuse of bias. People working toward similar goals do find themselves drifting apart, though Fred and I never quarreled.

The Park Service Has No Answers

If the gap did not grow wider, it may perhaps have been because our perspectives on the Park Service were both negative, more than tinged with scorn and exasperation. In one instance, Superintendent Stitt and I had an exchange over my relations to HERS's work.[31] Stitt complained to McComb about my interfering, which when it got back to me, led to my writing Stitt about all we had done to keep him informed about the boundary legislation and of other rumors, while GCNP never gave us adequate notice about anything. Stitt replied that we needed to talk. This incident reminded us, as Eiseman found, that it was not the particular issues, but the NPS mindset that kept sabotaging efforts to maintain good relations.

The planning schedule was infected with this self-sabotage. Stitt's Deputy, Shaw, had estimated 1979 or so as the date for a new plan. However, in March 1975, Stitt was optimistic to me about making decisions in late 1976.[32] By that time, he hoped, there would be some research results, and the Park could work on allotments, etc. Their planning effort was underway, informally, trying to develop alternatives, though no changes would be made while research was on going. 1977 remained the earliest year for the new program.

The Superintendent forwarded this latest estimate for a river plan schedule to the Region in July.[33] Research was to be done by July 1976, so he thought it would be very tight to get a CRMP+EIS ready so that the Park could make decisions for 1977 on self-guided trips (another indication that NPS hoped an increased allocation would quiet the noise WPRF et al. were making.) Decisions on comm ops would take a year or two more, Stitt thought. (This was different from the picture he had given me.) He called this schedule idealistic, since the Park would need to hold and analyze meetings with Region, researchers, comm ops, and the public, this last in five cities. We could do some advance work on the EIS, he offered, but the job is bigger, since the lower gorge is now in the Park. We would like to have a Region-GCNP coordinating committee meet at the same time as the October comm op and research meetings. The comm ops have told us they want to attend the research symposium, and we intend to run public workshops that month as well. Our schedule, Stitt concluded, foresees preparing certain portions of the EIS even before the research is done, and a final by May 1977.

In September, through a mix-up, I was taken free down the river by the largest rowing comm op, ARTA. The only advantage of this mistake was that I was able to report on what I realized was a superficial look at conditions I found "not detrimental".[34] This was quite different from my visit nine years before, when what people were doing and leaving behind was all too evident. I did see the impacts of thousands visiting attraction sites like Elves Chasm. I was even more convinced that human waste could and should be carried out, not buried. Sadly, the great increase in hiking use appeared to be causing more damage due to a lack of self-policing. Since we were not on an inspection tour, we didn't stop at problem beaches, and as far as little litter went, I saw only scattered instances—except for cigarette butts, of course.

Down river, I had a moment of satisfaction at the mouth of Kanab Creek, standing in a flowing stream joining a flowing river, instead of being stuck in the muck at the start of a reservoir. Lava Falls (two-thirds through the Canyon) marked the ending for many trips, where passengers were helicoptered out. This left the western Canyon much less well-known—except by burros, which some researchers opined showed far less concern about environmental diversity than river-runners did. Farther on, there was the roar of little motorboats coming up from Lake Mead. Attuned as I was to looking for problems, the trip, through the Grand Canyon though it was, could hardly be full of delight. Also, it came during the worst year of my life, though the great currents of history are not, of course, troubled by petty personal eddies. Overall, my sense increased of affairs in flux and full of ambiguity, so unlike the strong sense of direction three years earlier as we celebrated Reed's

1972 decision setting a new course for NPS policy on the river.

This sense of having to wait was reinforced by attending the river concessionaires meeting at the Park on October 2.[35] The Park Service presented a schedule for producing the CRMP, calling for public workshops in several cities in early 1976, the deadline for research reports in June, and analysis leading to alternatives, more public meetings, and a draft EIS by the end of the year.[36] This document was titled "tentative", and 1977 was described as "subject to slippage". It was clear to me that there would not be a new river plan to coincide with the end of the contracts in 1976; indeed, were there to be new contracts, a prospectus would have to be prepared sometime like mid-1976. That had to wait until there was a plan that would offer, for public comment, alternatives on levels of use and a motor ban, among other items. NPS was now saying that the plan options were not going to be in presentable form until the research team completed its work in the fall of 1976. Therefore, I was told by the river manager, the contracts would have to be extended by 1 or 2 years. Uneasy at the plan schedule's conclusion that some parts of a final plan might be implemented immediately, while others might take a couple of years, I speculated on a process "without any end even imaginable".

At the river meeting, the Hualapai, even without giving up on their formal commitment to a dam, spoke of a younger generation in control that wanted to use the Grand Canyon for the tribe's benefit. Monroe Beecher, for the tribe, announced they wanted to expand their weekend trips in the lower end of the Canyon to a full concession starting at Lees Ferry. They were also thinking of charging for camping on their side of the river. These questions remain open to this day, with a mix of land-ownership dispute, heavy helicopter use, ways the Hualapai might benefit from river travel, and insuring that the environment does not degrade no matter which side of the river is involved—a matter that is not simple given that the two sides could be managed well, even if differently.

The river meeting featured comm op complaints about self-guided trips: shocking nakedness and other discourtesies, illegal camping, and lack of toilets. Most spectacularly, Canyon-hero/comm op Martin Litton attacked Munroe, Eiseman, and the WPRF full-bore for "fraudulently" claiming they were the real public users. He declared he wanted some of the self-guided allocation, reducing it to 2% from 8%. Whether this was in retaliation for the *Not Man Apart* ad mentioned above, or had its roots in earlier disputes, the display was a sad straw in the wind: even the most vigorous Canyon defender could be re-educated by profit making. After Litton opened the allocation can of worms, several other comm ops poked their heads out, crying: it was time to boost the little comm ops; how about keeping commitments; I got screwed; some comm ops are too big for quality. A different perspective was offered when GCNP staff noted that the comm ops were the worst among 500 concessionaires at getting their financial reports in.

The Superintendent mused about some of the self-guided issues, puzzled as NPS was by how to find out what self-guided demand really was. One self-guided advocate noted the value of motors in being able to choose campsites. This was part of some rowing advocates' new line that motors were good because they can keep trips away from each other. They seemed to think there was some virtue in having different trips "passing by" during the day as compared to "bumping into" the trips that launched near each other: Ah, to be passed by several motor trips—what joy! To see once again the same rowing trip—how distressing! Thus the erudite speculations of river metaphysicians.

I decided to try again to check the eroded support of rowing comm ops for a motor ban, and went to visit ARTA's Elliott.[37] He pushed the "pearls on a string" view, offering his vision of dozens of rowing rafts bumping into each other all day going down the river at the same speed. More importantly, he was quite open about how competition for his type of rowing trips would be kept low if the big companies were not forced by a motor ban to start rowing.

In November, the Park Service was trying to satisfy itself that it was right to oppose the resolutions calling for a self-guided *public* priority. Senator Hart (D-Colorado) had also introduced it, reinforcing the likelihood that this was an effort from a vigorous Colorado-based self-guided group. So why was the effort not broader-based? So far as I knew or my records show, this congressional move was not joined in by Eiseman, Munroe and friends, and vice versa. For that matter, there are certainly other organizations for which access to public rivers is a fighting matter. How come the vigor shown by one group or individual did not coalesce into a larger effort? Were chances to change policy lost because energy was scattered? Or possibly, just because there were different centers, were there more approaches tried intensively, while one larger effort might have been dragged down by the need for agreement among disparate interests?

That does bring up one element of self-guided activity I have not mentioned. A little side story: Back in 1963, when I was getting involved in fighting to keep dams out of the Grand Canyon, I had a seminal conversation. New to the West, and to all the chances for being out in it, I was talking about the dams one day with a kayaker. A physicist, he was probably not a dolt. Still, when I inquired as to his interest in doing something about the dams, he said that was not something he had time for. But, I pressed, he had time to run an impressive number of rivers. That was the point, he said; if he spent his time fighting to save rivers, he wouldn't have time to run them before they were dammed or otherwise ruined. This split is not unusual. Users are not necessarily conservers of, or fighters for conserving, what they use. Those individuals that do both are special, as well as necessary, e.g. Eiseman. Too often when housed within the same organization, however, these two stances of user and activist can result in fierce debates as to how an organization is to carry on its business. I saw the effects of this difference in attitude in the Sierra Club when I worked there in the 1960s, and later in the Southern Arizona Hiking Club. I would guess that some such difference was important in the 1970s in limiting the amount of action I saw from groups promoting the interests of self-guided users. In our specific case, the difference certainly colored the response to user interests from people like McComb, as Sierra Club Representative. Reciprocally, it may have limited those groups from reaching out to us. Perhaps that was just as well. Given the amount of time wilderness advocates spent trying to keep together or just getting something done, an even broader coalition might just have sucked even more time into maintaining relations, and away from bashing the bad guys. Ah yes, the bad guys.

A Washington NPS functionary reported, on the pro-self-guided Congressional

Resolutions, that they were working on the matter.[38] Any immediate change would be just as arbitrary as the current situation. It could only be at the expense of comm ops, with "severe" economic impact. Worse, the fluctuating self-guided demand would unsettle commercial planning. This would lead to action by the comm ops (they were already complaining). The memo writer then settled into slander and anecdotage, saying some self-guided people made six trips in a year, and that the trips cost more than self-guided advocates said. Demand is really not what it appeared, since there were multiple applications and some were semi-commercial (these were all claims I had heard peddled by comm ops in river meetings). Comm op use does not interfere with free access (a blatant untruth; the river was a rationed resource), and is necessary and appropriate. The 1972 level was not arbitrary, but based on history. (This ignores the history of growth based on arbitrary comm op wishes. This entire problem existed in all its parts because the Park Service had not, until forced to, thought it necessary to study river use and formulate a non-arbitrary plan based on full public input.) The final indication of the writer's bias was the statement that commercial demand was not stimulated.

This view was made even more pointed in a later D.C. letter to Eiseman, "If we had absolute trust in private applicants, we would not be seeking a suitable means of identifying applicants and passengers. Unfortunately, there is enough evidence of irregularity to prevent us from accepting all applications at face value."[39] (What was unfortunate is that the rules that they were applying were ones they made up themselves, and did not apply to commercial passengers, so that what the latter could do regularly was irregular if a self-guided applicant tried it. And when NPS said that checking repeaters on commercial trips was impractical, wasn't that just a euphemism for the truth that they could not have "absolute trust" in the comm ops?) It must have been NPS exasperation with Fred's claims about the huge, unfilled self-guided demand that led to the letter being concluded by the outburst that "to not extend commercial contracts would be an injustice to thousands of innocent visitors". But then, exasperation was a common feeling among all parties as 1976 bumped along. After the intense period of the Reed decision and reaction to it, resolution seemed to be receding as surely as problems were intensifying.

The river situation was highlighted by the speed and attention displayed in the Wilderness study being conducted simultaneously by the NPS Denver Service Center, which, with GCNP staff, was pushing the study process ahead to meet the January 1977 deadline set by the 1975 GCNP Act. Although a number of issues raised by Wilderness status needed to be settled, the grizzly-in-the-berries was, of course, the river and whether it, motor-free, was to be included in the Wilderness recommendation. The river plan and the comm ops' new contracts were dependent on how that matter was settled. Therefore, although the non-river Wilderness issues may seem a distraction, the next chapter reviews action on the wilderness study for the "old" Park, and then takes up the 1975 study process and how it played out in 1976. Chapter 11 will then come back to 1976, the self-guided effort and the research, then tie these into the inconsistent NPS moves on river planning.

CHAPTER 10

1970-76: Wilderness, The Heart of The Matter

This history of the progress of wilderness recommendations complements, with some repetition, what is told in the other chapters. What I wish to do here is give a fuller picture by summarizing the various changes in acreage and in some of the items not related to the river. I use the convention that upper-case Wilderness refers to the legal entities that require congressional designation, and lower-case wilderness is the place and concept itself. GCWilderness refers to the plans, recommendations, etc., that might have led to congressional action on a Grand Canyon Wilderness, even though they never have.

We are dealing with two Grand Canyon National Parks, pre-1975 and the "enlarged" one with boundaries drawn by Public Law 93-620. So there were two periods of work by NPS leading up to Wilderness recommendations. I have already written about the 1968-72 period covering GCWilderness I, so I will only recapitulate events and proposals of that time to bring together in one place how positions changed. That episode's completion in March 1975, nicely dovetails with the origins of its big brother and successor, GCWilderness II. Starting off in December 1974, the later story has a stumble as I recorded at the end of Chapter 5, then gets fully underway in June 1975, running full-tilt to meet the January 1977 deadline set by Congress.

Growing Pains: Grand Canyon Wilderness I

The story begins in hope. The 1968 proposal, though hampered by some weird NPS inhibitions, did include the river. In mid-1970, GCNP staff were working on a preliminary draft study which was printed up in August. This is the one that contemplated the phase-out of motors leading to a recommendation to place the Colorado River in the GCWilderness.[1] That right-minded direction was derailed by Superintendent Lovegren (see Chapter 2), and the released January 1971 preliminary study excluded the river from Wilderness due to Lovegren's prejudice for motor use.

GCWilderness I dealt with a "Grand Canyon Complex" consisting of the Park and two National Monuments, Grand Canyon and Marble Canyon (see Reader's Guide Part D for maps). (Historical notes: this GCNM had nothing to do with the first GCNM out of which the Park was carved in 1919, nor with the third Monument bearing the name, the Grand Canyon–Parashant NM. Marble Canyon is a misnomer; it refers to an inner gorge that is an integral part of the Grand Canyon.) The total acreage of these three entities was 898 KAC. (KAC = thousand acres rounded off). The standard procedure is to identify all roadless areas and then, within that maximum, decide which acres meet the more stringent criteria of the Wilderness Act. (Editorial: By using roads for the first cut, the argument starts right away. What is the definition of "road"? This hurdle passed, we fall right into the thicket of thrashing through those "criteria", and deciding how stringently they are to be applied.) In August 1970, Park staff found roadless areas totaling 838 KAC. By January, they had found a bunch more roads, since the six roadless areas added up to 825 KAC. Worse, Wilderness-worthy lands shrank from 569 KAC to 505 KAC, in part because the river was excluded.

Aside from the river, the major conceptual problem with NPS thinking was that it eliminated almost all lands on the plateaus above the canyon rims. The dirt roads cutting across these lands, about which NPS was so protective, were largely associated with grazing, as in GCNM, or with anti-fire activity, as on the Kaibab Plateau. The latter exclusion was supposed to permit a "carefully planned ... program" to reduce the fire hazard. Grazing was even more baseless as an exclusion reason, since much of it was to end in a decade or two, and the Wilderness Act allows grazing within its criteria. Another item that was to be long in contention was the width of the developed trail and pipeline corridor across the Canyon.

Both plans included a standard NPS silliness of the time, the idea that next to a Wilderness unit, there had to be a 1/8-mile strip for future management needs. Thus in the very narrow corridor of Marble Canyon NM, a cross-section from east to west showed a 1/8-mile buffer, then a strip of Wilderness, then the non-Wilderness River, then a strip of Wilderness, then another buffer, either 1/8-mile or 500 feet (apparently, Bureau of Land Management lands were safe enough so as not to require the extra 180 feet). At this time, it was standard NPS ideology that since Parks were already highly protected, Wilderness was not really needed, and interfered with NPS-style proper management. Conceptual sabotage was therefore the order of the day. Of course, our rejoinder was that we wanted Wilderness to help protect wilderness in Parks from the Park Service.

One of the features of the Wilderness Act procedure for bringing a Wilderness recommendation to Congress was the provision for public hearings on an agency's proposals. This was a radical step forward toward public participation in public land decision-making. Wilderness advocates now had the chance to present their views to the agency itself, theoretically before its final decision was made. In May 1971, we responded in a numerically overwhelming way. We found more roadless area than the Park staff had, and within that area, we were more stringent in favor of wilderness. We then stirred up hundreds of letters in support of our changes. Our recommendation claimed 850.5 KAC for Wilderness in two areas (split by the trail-pipeline corridor), instead of the 505 KAC in the seven NPS units. Not purists, we noted that grazing and pre-existing motorboat use were allowed under the

Wilderness Act, asked that most dirt roads on plateaus be closed, eliminated the buffer zones, and squeezed the trail-pipeline corridor down to a width of fifty feet away from any development.[2]

As recounted in Chapter 2, NPS ignored us as the Park and Southwest Region smoothed the recommendation's edges. A December 1971 draft letter of transmittal from the Secretary of the Interior bumped up the Wilderness to 508.5 KAC. However, NPS could not ignore a June 1972 memo from Assistant Secretary Reed setting forth guidelines for Wilderness proposals. Thus there were a few changes in the September 1972 final recommendation signed by the NPS Director, transmitted on the 14th by the Secretary of the Interior to the President, and sent on to Congress on the 21st.[3] First, much of the buffer was shifted into Wilderness, along with two pieces of the trail-pipeline corridor; the acreage addition was still small, giving a total of 513 KAC. Second, some of the above-rim grazing and fire control areas were placed in a brand-new category, first called a Wilderness Reserve, then Potential Wilderness (so new that labels were pasted in the final documents). The concept, aside from face-saving, was that the areas had an impediment which, when corrected, would allow the areas to be proclaimed Wilderness by the Secretary without further congressional action. Since the areas were, under explicit NPS policy, to be managed as Wilderness anyway, this category could always only be an irritating Pecksniffian assertion of bureaucratic virtue. Worse, it said that Wilderness-worthiness was subordinate to, and blocked by, the impediments. The right-side-up view is that Wilderness is the primary value, and any impediments should give way or be constrained by it until removed. Anyway, NPS found 86 KAC on the plateaus for their new category, which still brought them up to only 599 KAC, a long way from our 850.5. NPS made one deletion: Any lands contested by the Navajo to the east of the Colorado would be restudied later, but pending resolution of Navajo rights, would be dropped in the recommendation.

The Colorado River remained excluded "because of the use of motors".[4]

Our comments on this "final" NPS effort emphasized the detrimental effects of motor noise (planes and boats) magnified because the Canyon is a kind of enclosure.[5] We also repeated our (and Reed's) view that grazed lands could be included, specifically advocating areas excluded by NPS because of Havasupai grazing. We kept pressing on the fire control exclusion and the over-wide corridor. We now wanted coordination with Lake Mead National Recreation Area (LMNRA), as well as the Navajo and Hualapai tribes, to protect wild lands.

Regardless of what we thought, and of the new boundaries being proposed, the NPS recommendation was included in the Grand Canyon National Park bill Senator Goldwater introduced in March 1973.[6] Meanwhile, the Reed October 1972 decision on river matters caused NPS to change its position on the river, so that by April 1973, it was in the Potential Wilderness class, with the intention of moving it to Wilderness status in 1977.[7] In this internal position paper, NPS did recognize the overwhelming opposition to its exclusion of the river. However, NPS had found another bogeyman: the river and associated lands were still encumbered by the Park legislation's (dead-letter) provision for reclamation works. NPS wanted that encumbrance removed within the old Park boundary, but was willing to continue it on any lands added from Lake Mead NRA. This view made no sense from any standpoint, pro-dam, anti-dam, or pro-wilderness.

The NPS position was sent to the Senate Interior Committee in June, with the Potential Wilderness category adjusted up to 91 KAC to accommodate the river. Strangely enough, there was no call either for studying the lands that would be added from Lake Mead NRA or from the Kaibab National Forest.[8] The changed ideas did lead to re-transmittals of the EIS.[9] On August 22, the NPS response to a pro-motor view was back to the desirability of the slow float trip without motor noise and emission. However, the actual EIS, as it passed back and forth between the Park and the Region, kept its total of 513 KAC, saying only that the river was "eligible" for Potential Wilderness pending motor phase-out.

All this became irrelevant when Goldwater dropped Wilderness designation from his bill, and final resolution of the boundary legislation struggle produced an enlarged Park and mandated a Wilderness study for the larger area. The old crock gave a last gasp in March 1975, when, on request of the Interior Department, GC Wilderness I was introduced as S. 1080 by Senators Haskell, Jackson, and Fannin purely as a formality. Strangely, the river seemed to be left out, with the figures the same as in September 1972: a 513 KAC Wilderness, with 86 KAC in Potential Wilderness. The kindest epitaph for this first effort is that, as work on GCWilderness II got underway, a fair amount of time was saved since much of the EIS preparation had been done.

Near Perfect: Grand Canyon Wilderness II

The Park enlargement battle included Wilderness study being in, then out, then in, then out, then finally in. As Udall worked with us on a pro-Park version, a study provision for all the lands within the changed boundary was added, with the Secretary ordered to report a recommendation to the President within two years, a date that turned out to be January 3, 1977. The conference report specifically included for study the entire river from the Paria to the headwaters of Lake Mead, and that part of the National Park labeled as Havasupai Use Lands, as distinguished from the Havasupai Reservation.[10] This language was important to us since we hoped it would quell some NPS nit picking. Silly us. Then the Wilderness study provision disappeared from the enrolled bill through that clerical error (see Chapter 5). A separate piece of legislation reinserted it as section 11. That legislation was signed on June 10, 1975 without extending the January 3, 1977 deadline, having the effect of taking five months away from the two-year period to produce a recommendation.

On June 20, 1975, the NPS Legislation office in Washington sent an activation memo to the Western Regional Director, noting the requirement of a report by January 3, 1977.[11] The study was to supersede the report already submitted to Congress, although the earlier study would serve to expedite the new one. A final report was due from the Region by October 1, 1976. The Lake Mead NRA recommendation would have to be revised, too.

This last was good news for us. LMNRA had published a Wilderness study in November 1973; at the time, much of the western Grand Canyon north of the river was in the Recreation Area.[12] Reflecting NPS views, it was unsatisfactory to us, although it is true that as a Recreation Area, LMNRA was governed by different mandates. The Colorado was excluded of course; motorboats were in use, the lower section was part of the reservoir, and there were dam-building claims on the rest (one of the reasons we wanted it in the Park). However, even on the wild lands north of the river, LMNRA kept its proposal confined to the edge of the lower gorge, excluding an extensive area used part of the year for grazing (a use that, with the area part of the Park, would be ended in 1985). So far from looking on its wild lands as suitable for Wilderness access and recreation, LMNRA wrote about providing some limited development.[13] However, once the out-of-date NPS anti-Wilderness verbiage was culled out, there was again the EIS groundwork that would help speed along the newly mandated re-study.

Public hearings were held on that first LMNRA proposal in late March 1974. Seven pro-wilderness groups called for a doubling of the Wilderness, as the best use and protection for these fragile lands, largely high- and mountain-desert.[14] The major Grand Canyon section should be expanded from 180 KAC to 436 KAC by including the entire Canyon right up to corridors for a few dirt roads. Current GCNP issues were recognized in the call for Wilderness designation to be compatible with Park standards.

In my own statement, and for the Tucson-based Southern Arizona Hiking Club, I emphasized the importance of gathering all the Canyon within federal lands inside the National Park (this was at the moment in the legislative fight when our hopes were at their highest).[15] We wanted, as well, a single-named Grand Canyon Wilderness, with identical and coordinated management policies no matter what the administration. I spoke for wilderness river policy down to the Lake Mead backwater, well-defined as the high-water contour behind the dam. I went further, arguing that the Lake Mead water surface in the Canyon should be managed as wilderness, even if it was not designated as Wilderness, asserting that motors were not really required. (A position to make any Park ranger with experience in the area cringe at the thought of trying to keep motor traffic west of the Grand Wash Cliffs.) Finally, I agreed with the other conservation groups that a few of the dirt roads should be left open for educational and viewing purposes, but otherwise there were no legitimate reasons for not including the western Canyon in a Grand Canyon Wilderness.

The Park Service met us a little more than halfway in its July 1974 revision to the preliminary plan. It now included most of the western Canyon up to the upper rim, increasing the recommendation from 180 KAC to 340 KAC. Still, they had uncovered a reason not to go on top of the Shivwits Plateau. There were century-old railroad mineral rights, reserved when the Santa Fe Railroad traded the lands for others; the Plateau was not a mineralized area.

So in mid-1975, there were two inadequate NPS proposals, with their Environmental Impact Statements, and two go-to-the-limit proposals from Wilderness advocates. Into this area of staked claims stepped Terry Carlstrom and Larry May from the NPS Denver Service Center.[16] They were to prepare the report due in Washington by March 1, 1976, incorporating public input and alternatives, including an NPS-preferred one. (They were busy boys, since they were also involved in the other studies resulting from the Park legislation.) The Park would actually run the public workshops. The overall goal was a final report to Washington by November 1, 1976, and Chapman told Washington that the schedule was tight with little slack, but workable.[17]

As noted above, Assistant Secretary Reed had been pushing the Park Service for being finicky on Wilderness, pressing such matters as the 1/8-mile buffer and whether grazing could be continued in Park Wilderness. For the Grand Canyon, the big issue remained motor use. There could be no doubt that the goal of pro-Wilderness and pro-visitor-experience groups was to have a motor-free Wilderness since only rowing trips provide a trip commensurate with Park and Wilderness standards. Those groups would fight for an administrative and a congressional termination of motor use. As well, Reed and the Park Service were on record, if not in practice, for a policy of terminating motor use. Indeed, the general Reed-NPS policy was that motorboat use was not allowed in National Park Wilderness.

There remained the problem of what to say if motor use already existed in an area of a Park being considered for Wilderness. There was a non-GCNP example in the motorboat use to put-put people around in Crater Lake NP. The Wilderness Act did allow existing motorboat use to continue in Forest Service areas covered at the time of the Act, but did not mandate it, leaving it up to the discretion of the Secretary of Agriculture. By a logical and expected extension, this discretion also applied to NPS Wilderness. Each congressional designation of NPS Wilderness therefore included the discretionary authority for the Secretary of the Interior. Even further reinforcement came via a Solicitor's opinion that Congress intended that motorboats "may" be allowed in a Park Wilderness if already in use.[18]

You might think therefore, that there was no problem. The Colorado is wilderness, so include it in Wilderness. Since there is existing motor use, Congress may explicitly terminate it. Or if Congress says nothing, then all existing law indicates that the Secretary of the Interior "may" continue or "may" terminate the use. This decision might be subject to existing river-rafting contracts, but since they are re-done periodically, that would only be a temporary impediment. The contracts also allowed NPS to change the rules. The new GCNP boundary included the entire water surface in the Park, so there was no question of jurisdiction, or of power and discretion to allow or end motor use. Yet, in spite of all this clear direction, the Park Service repeatedly got its knickers in a twist when it contemplated making a Wilderness recommendation where motors were currently in use. So would NPS now do the right thing, and recommend Wilderness status for the Colorado?

The public got first chance to speak out. Seven public workshops were immediately decided upon and announced to the public in late August 1975.[19] This road show ran from September 22 to October 2, playing Phoenix, Kingman, Las Vegas, St. George, Kanab, Flagstaff, and Grand Canyon Village. The Canyon was surrounded by public participation, with the public getting first shot, for the announcement made clear that *after* the hearings, a proposal and draft EIS would be prepared; the earlier recommendations were no longer valid. The format was to be discussion in small, informal groups. We were ready, sending out an alert on August 26.[20] We claimed we had no specific boundary recommendations, but wanted people to emphasize that the river along with all lands below the rim should be Wilderness. The only exclusion would be the trail-pipeline corridor. Above the rims, we advocated that the "wild portions of the plateau lands" be designated, excluding only corridors for "major access roads".

My notes for these events indicate that about fifty people showed up at Phoenix. There were a handful at Kingman, where points were made about little zodiac boats with motors zooming upriver from Lake Mead. Eight were at Las Vegas. In Kanab, six, mostly local ranchers, showed up. At Flagstaff, the major argument occupying the nineteen there was from Havasupai expressing the view that Wilderness in the Havasupai Use Area (part of the Park, and specifically to be included in the Wilderness study) was taking their land away again. One Havasupai asserted their land extended to wherever they wanted to set their feet. The white-people advocates for the Havasupai then took over and made specific claims for the tribe's traditional uses (all allowed in Wilderness), and suggested the tribe wanted to license Wilderness users. Although I did not attend all seven meetings, I am not sure any were more exciting—or less relevant. Sixty-nine people, the record, were at the Grand Canyon meeting.

GCNP sent out a summary of the meetings that counted 154 attendees.[21] At the end of a meeting, each participant wrote down five issues of importance. By far, motors on the river interested more people, with 86 in favor of a motor-free Wilderness and 19 wanting to keep motors. Grazing in Wilderness was all right with 30 people, but opposed by 9. Twenty-three wanted the Use Area with Havasupai exercising traditional uses in the Wilderness, and 5 did not. The other area of disagreement was controlled fires on the Kaibab Plateau, with 13 people in favor of including such area within Wilderness and 3 not. For some reason, 7 people wanted more corridors across the Wilderness, though 23 did not. There was some unanimity: nobody thought aircraft did not impair Wilderness values, nobody wanted dams, and nobody thought the burros should stay. Interestingly, the former Superintendent who had first dealt with increasing river use, Howard Stricklin, wrote in to say that he thought motors should be banned.[22] Further, he accepted much of the conservationist stand in favor of plateau lands being Wilderness, having reversed his ideas about using vehicles on some dirt roads.

Following the meetings, in September and October, NPS staff at DSC and GCNP worked through the issues.[23] DSC planner Carlstrom and others took a mid-October field trip, and he used his report to offer tentative conclusions. The upside-down view prevailed; encumbrances over Wilderness. The claim of Wilderness came last. So, in September, the Denver Service Center fretted about what the Bureau of Reclamation might want (though the latter could no longer get anything), and what the Havasupai might want (although all their legally valid traditional wants were allowed in Wilderness), and how to clear up NPS administrative jurisdiction over the Colorado (which Congress had already done).

Carlstrom visited and flew over much of the area north of the river following the public meetings.[24] He was careful to note grazing and its de-provements, and the fire-management-sensitive areas on the Kaibab, as well as the mining disturbances near Andrus Canyon. Since the grazing permits were to expire in a few years, Carlstrom agreed with the latest Lake Mead NRA proposal for including the western lands below the upper rim in Wilderness, while excluding the mine-affected area. On the Kaibab, most of the so-called fire-control roads were to be closed, leaving only two dirt roads; thus Wilderness would no longer be "precluded". The Kanab Plateau lands, not recommended in 1972 due to grazing, were now to be Wilderness, though a few access tracks to points and trailheads would be left open. The river and the GCNP-Havasupai Use Area were waved off, deserving no better than Potential Wilderness. What is it that God would have to do to create a wilderness if these lands do not qualify?

Astonishing me, GCNP's reply to Carlstrom's analysis was pro-Wilderness.[25] There was no need to worry, the Superintendent said, about Reclamation claims, and there was no conflict with Havasupai needs on Park lands and Wilderness. As far as the Kanab Plateau lands went, they should be recommended for Wilderness, though the status of the roads needs study. An almost-clean statement was made on the river: Though Potential Wilderness was still thought best pending completion of the CRMP, the Park wanted to stress that the river "is now, and will continue to be, managed as wilderness". "We see one primary issue that affects our recommendations for wilderness on suitable lands and that is the issues of motors vs. no motors on the Colorado River." In conclusion, "It is our contention that what should now be done is to prepare 'optimum' wilderness proposals based upon the recent workshops and public testimony at previous wilderness hearings." As I say, astonishing. A draft Wilderness document reinforced the above opinions by recognizing that the public response was "strongly for maximum wilderness" this year as it had been in 1972 and on Lake Mead in 1974.[26] This time, instead of almost ignoring public support for more wilderness, the document emphasized it.

At the end of the year, when I inquired of DSC staff how matters stood, I was told that the river remained as Potential Wilderness, but otherwise the proposal appeared to be optimal. Approval was due in January 1976. Carlstrom presented his work to the Park and Region that month, and only a few technical matters came up.[27] I was told that Stitt and Chapman had approved DSC's work and presented it to Director Everhardt at the end of January. At this presentation, the constraints of the CRMP and Havasupai needs were chewed over. There was some discussion and a decision to add much of Toroweap Valley and the south rim area west of Hermits Rest. The Director and Assistant Secretary's office cleared the proposal.[28]

Talking to me about this D.C. excursion, Carlstrom related meeting with some congressional staff who were questioning wilderness in general, wanting access maintained. He also encountered some Interior staffers in nit-picking mode, still worried about Reclamation, Havasupai uses, wider dirt road corridors, etc. However, a contrary straw was the reiteration from NPS in Washington to the Region that any areas being studied for Wilderness must be managed as wilderness so as not to undercut wilderness values pending congressional action.[29] ("Reiterate" is the word, since the NPS in D.C. again and again felt it had to make this point formally to the field.) And again, the nits were scrubbed at, with the lawyers assuring Chapman that mineral leasing, grazing, and reclamation were transient concerns on lands formerly in Lake Mead NRA; their transfer to GCNP enhances their suitability for Wilderness.[30]

By March, the writing had been done, and hearings looked set for summer. McComb got a chance to see the plan and was pleased, though he noticed the river boundary was wrong. Carlstrom had no problem with that fix, and a draft EIS was ready in April 1976 to support the preliminary proposal for GCWilderness II.[31] Sadly, the 17 KAC of the Colorado was not recommended, "until such time [as motor use is discontinued, the river] must be considered as a basic deletion from the proposed wilderness". This, in spite of the draft citing our arguments five years before that the river could be Wilderness even if motors were allowed there. Once again, the motor cart was put before the wilderness horse; the Colorado was not wilderness, it was just a body of water to carry motorboats. A few days later came the cavalry (a little one), changing the language to say that motors were a "convenient" use inconsistent with wilderness criteria.[32] So the recommendation seemed to settle for making the river Potential Wilderness pending the CRMP and Secretarial decision, which might ban motors. The acreage figures for the 1,211 KAC Park worked out to roadless areas totaling 1,132 KAC, of which 992 KAC were Wilderness and 121 KAC were Potential Wilderness (mostly the Havasupai Use Area and the river).

When the proposal was actually published in July, however, further word skirmishes had taken place. Any reference to the CRMP and Secretarial discretion were eliminated, leaving only the statement that the river's "wilderness potential ... will be recognized pending a management decision on motorized use".[33] The offensiveness of this statement was high, especially given the number of drafting attempts. In May it went from the NPS Director to the Assistant Secretary for review.[34]

We had our target, which we would take aim at during the public hearings announced in late July for August 24-27 in St. George, Flagstaff, Phoenix, and the Park.[35] The size of the target was measured by the gap between Reed's clarion 1972-3 pronouncements that motors are antithetical to Wilderness and the press release's fuzziness, "If it were decided as a result of on-going research projects that motorized boat use on the river was to be phased-out, the Secretary ... could designate the river corridor as wilderness."

I am too harsh. Except for its back-tracking on the river, the Park Service in this 1976 wilderness proposal and its draft EIS had accepted the 1971 conservation organization principle, supported by public comment, for maximal wilderness. Throughout both wilderness studies, NPS recognized that about 93% of the Park was roadless. In the first study, they could only find Wilderness-worthy land on about two-thirds of the Park. The second study boosted that to over 90% of the Park. So NPS quibbles (aside from the river) faded in comparison to what we now hoped would be an irrevocable stand soon to be ratified by congressional action. The Sierra Club mailing in early August said, "the NPS plan is a good one, worthy of praise and support".[36] As for the "real or imagined conflicts" in Potential Wilderness areas, we dismissed them, along with the potential category itself. The mailing asked for the lands' "immediate" inclusion in the GCWilderness. We were pleased; it seemed that the Denver NPS people, led by Terry Carlstrom, almost understood what we thought clear.

Almost. Our general philosophy I stated above: Wilderness is primary; any conflicts should therefore be seen as items to be cleaned up, an activity highlighted and hastened by Wilderness qualification, not an activity that had to precede or could block Wilderness designation. So I continued to argue, saying that if NPS thought the river was wilderness, it should recommend Wilderness, then clean out the motors.[37] And, since Congress told NPS to allow Havasupai uses in the GCWilderness covering the Use Area, then NPS should not be telling Congress that Wilderness was dependent on what the uses were. And similarly for mineral rights, Navajo, and other non-federal land claims, reclamation pipe dreams, etc. We did not understand why NPS saw these "conflicts" as encumbering Wilderness lands, instead of Wilderness rendering these "conflicts" as settled in Wilderness's favor; an exercise in bureaucratic metaphysics, another instance of Orwell's lament.

We spent some time personally encouraging people to attend and speak at the hearings or send statements. The former numbers were small, ranging from 4 at St. George to about 20 in Phoenix.[38] NPS reported 44 speakers. Overall, individually expressed opinions totaled 787, with 680 pro-Wilderness, 21 opposed, and 15 wanting the river not included. The NPS proposal without change received 40 mentions. We trumped that with about 450 people wanting the Potential Wilderness, including the river, added to Wilderness. This meant they wanted the motors off and the river, and *now*. Of the comm ops, 12 opposed adding the river, and 7 were in favor of including it. Four comm ops came to the hearings, split evenly on including the river. One called the Colorado a wastewater stream, and offered several of the standard pro-motor fabrications.[39] In complete reverse from his 1972 view, the Goldwater friend, Ben Avery, spoke in support of keeping motors. The Bureau of Reclamation and the Hualapai Tribe went overboard in their claims for an acute interest in damming the river.[40] The operators of aircraft doing overflights were greatly desirous of having nothing get in the way of encouraging international tourism. In his report, the hearing officer cited my "rather long presentation", and when I showed up at the third venue, he commented "once again".[41] In my journal's summary, I gloated that "opposition was small and included the motor-raft industry, dam builders, miners, livestock operators, flying industry. Nice group." Most comments came by letter; some, not tabulated, made pro-motor comments.[42]

The Region worked on the proposal through the autumn, forwarding its report to Washington saying that although 60% of the individual comments were in favor of Wilderness for the river, we must retain the Potential Wilderness status until the CRMP is done, "to have credibility for our planning process".[43] Also, they had found some mineral rights that would require more Potential Wilderness. The Region's report went to Director Everhardt on November 18, with the legislative office recommending approval.

As the Region was preparing its report, we kept watch, gathering information and getting it out to our supporters.[44] My contact list for McComb and me for December 1-2 shows seven calls. Given how close the NPS proposal was to our views, we were steadily optimistic about legislation happening, though we knew there would be a fight over motors and the dam-builders would offer distractions. What we wanted above all was to try to reach Reed, at the end of his tenure, appealing to his 1972 principled stand for eliminating motors, hoping his position would override NPS scruples.

Once the proposal reached Washington, we had our chance, and on December 2, ten organizations collaborated on a four-page mailgram to Reed saying that after

8 years, this was the proper time to permit only rowing trips, thus clearing the way for Wilderness designation.[45] We recalled Reed's statements. We cited anti-motor research results. We offered congressional history. We trumpeted the three different sets of public meetings that supported a rowing-only decision. Your original 1972 decision was sound, we said, and we urge you to embrace it in 1976.

A couple of days later, Eiseman told me Goldwater had asked him for a statement, since he was worried about a motor ban leading to pressure for more visitors. Fred hand-delivered it to his home. In a conversation on December 10, McComb learned that Everhardt had talked with Chapman, and pushed him to approve adding the river. The former had also conferred with a Goldwater aide who said Goldwater would go along. Reed would approve, though he was worried about support for the decision. (The old problem: you have to have a decision to support in order to demonstrate support for the decision.) We were checking with Udall, who was pleased about his new chairmanship of the House Interior Committee. We reached newly elected Arizona Senator DeConcini, who had indicated his sympathies enough that we had helped on his campaign.

A few days later, we picked up rumors that Chapman had been back in Washington, and that the proposal from the Region was withdrawn in order to include the river. Chapman reported this to a meeting of the Western Parks Regional Advisory Committee, saying he had been told to take another look at the river (by Everhardt on December 3, we heard). WPRAC members then gave Chapman a hard time, according to reports I received. Ben Avery disgraced himself, raving about mechanized monitoring. As before, he was joined by two other anti-wilderness voices. Fortunately, there were wilderness advocates as well. The WPRAC consensus remained for keeping the river in Potential Wilderness. However, Everhardt's request had greater sway, and the Region re-worked its proposal as he had asked. We waited. Even on December 27, we were not sure what the Park Service would say, though we knew Everhardt had checked with both Goldwater and Udall. Relying on similar reassurances from Goldwater and Udall, we hoped we might obtain wide Arizona congressional support for our position.

Then it happened. In Washington, moving to meet the January 3 deadline, NPS Director Everhardt signed a Wilderness recommendation including the river on December 29, 1976, completing the NPS step by passing it on to Interior's Legislative Counsel and thus to the President's Office of Management and Budget. As in 1972, this was a Washington decision, and Everhardt's action was unambiguous:

> The Colorado River totaling about 17,009 acres is now recommended as wilderness so as to perpetuate the primitive qualities of the canyon with increased opportunities for solitude and enjoyment of the beauty and natural significance of the Grand Canyon. To achieve this, all visitor use of the river will be without motors, and more nearly like the experience of earlier explorers. A three year study of the river with public participation has shown that visitor appreciation, understanding, and enjoyment of the Grand Canyon will be enhanced by this type of use. The objective

for visitor use is to provide the opportunity for an intimate
association with the river environment with good opportunities to
see and gain understanding of the natural and historic features of
the inner canyon.[46]

Six years further on, the NPS Director had reaffirmed the vision of those unknown planners at GCNP who in 1970 proposed the river for Wilderness. Everhardt did so, backed up by the research results, with overwhelming public support from individual citizens and organizations, including seven of the commercial river-running companies. His decision followed and furthered the policy enunciated by Assistant Secretary Reed in 1972-3, just as Reed himself was leaving following the election of Jimmy Carter. Moreover, and a fact to inspire awe at what can happen when there is leadership and will, Everhardt and the Park Service got the job done on time.

We celebrated, calling for letters expressing thanks and approval and support for legislation soon. Surely, though the battle was hardly over, we could reasonably envision this recommendation going from the new pro-environment President to and through the House with momentum. It was good that we celebrated in the moment, however, for actual events turned out so unreasonably as to stand as a permanent lesson in comm op intransigence and bureaucratic inscrutability.

CHAPTER 11

1976: No Harmony, No Lead

After that excitement, we turn back to river matters. I want to chew over for the moment the artificiality of what I am doing. In the earlier years, through 1973, one story line seemed a valid mode of presentation. Then along came the Park boundary legislation, in parallel with the river story, and a diversion. The Wilderness study, with great bearing on the fate of river running, still ran its own course. Likewise with the research, even though there was much contact between researchers and lay people, like me and the comm ops. The efforts of advocates for the self-guided also run along their separate track, with hoots and toots at the rest of us.

However, although these tales can be told separately, the several strands were more or less present all the time in the minds, mouths and motions of all the various actors. Yet even if I knew now all the strands, the full story would be impossible to tell. Was this comm op, angered by that self-guided advocate, moved to break relations with Wilderness advocates? Was that NPS official, openly neutral, secretly pro-comm op, moved to mischief (or away from it) by the arguments of this researcher, who was, perhaps, in contact with several people of contending opinions? Did the introduction of lawsuits intimidate or stiffen resistance, and/or alienate those with different agendas? Such ruminations and speculations give me a chance to re-capture the frame of mind we actors were in as we tried to figure out what to do, what others were doing and how to get them to do something else, whom to work with and whom to attack. The more I can see this history as an observer looking back and as a participant, the closer I may come to offering the reader the joys and sorrows of fighting the good (or the scurrilous) fight.

Given how active the self-guided proponents had become, this chapter starts with their 1976 efforts. Pieces of their story are also in Chapters 6, 9, and will appear again in 13. Next, the Park Service is the focus, as it tried to move river management planning along in 1976; a tough task given their promises, the now-impossible old deadlines, the ending of the comm op contracts in December, and our anger at what we saw as NPS's inconsistent actions. These left us feeling betrayed. We saw NPS undercutting all its assurances of action, and right in the face of the research findings we were all so dependent on.

Self-Guided: Missiles in All Directions

Eiseman's efforts to get at the comm ops by stirring up state agencies brought publicity, for sure. There was a long article on the second section's front page of the Sunday (January 11, 1976) *Arizona Republic.*[1] The sixteen non-Arizona-based comm ops were being investigated as to their liability for state taxes. The idea was that though they were based elsewhere, their business was carried out in Arizona. The idea was shocking to the comm ops, one of whom said that the Grand Canyon is not part of Arizona anyway, and all of whom noted that they paid state taxes where they were based. The article described Eiseman and his "feud" with the Park Service. Fred had also gotten the Game and Fish Department to check on boat registrations, which the comm ops should have had and NPS should have checked at launching time. This fueled Eiseman's charge of double standards, since he thought self-guided trips were hassled by detailed examinations.

An inevitable by-product of the way self-guided boaters were handled was that as the number of applicants, and therefore disappointees, grew, so did the number of complainers. What might have seemed the grousing of a few long-time river-runners became cries of pain by a whole new set of users, potential new allies for Eiseman, Munroe, and others. Changes like the lottery and dropping the no-repeat rule did not really matter if you saw the probability of receiving a permit steadily dropping. Further injury was inflicted by the unused comm op allocation. NPS insistence on a rigid limit, always over-subscribed, for self-guided trips, and another, always underused, for comm ops, helped solidify the sense of discrimination.

That resentment also settled on the comm ops and their "virtual monopoly", as one petitioner for access put it.[2] He went on to describe several ways he saw the comm ops using this monopoly to soak up self-guided demand: applying for part of the self-guided allocation, selling their own user-days, adding non-employees onto crew "training" trips. Eiseman expressed the same ideas to NPS as part of his campaign, particularly attacking the training trips as "long, free vacations".[3] He complained more bitterly about NPS asking for social security numbers for all participants, even prospective ones, on self-guided permit applications. Supposedly to enable cross-checking to catch duplicates, Eiseman called it further discrimination, and questioned its legality. He also wrote the NAACP, charging racial discrimination. The Park Service replied by citing 14 minority comm op employees and federal non-discrimination policy.[4]

The resentment was two-way; comm ops for years had been sniping at self-guided boat trips. Sad evidence of this showed up in the May 1976 issue of *Not Man Apart*, put out by Friends of the Earth. (Although names like this are now commonly used by business and other exploitative, development-minded front groups, FOE was a genuine environmental group. Founded by David Brower, it let me use its name in my Grand Canyon efforts.) As the centerfold, there were two full-page advertisements. On the left, comm op Martin Litton of Grand Canyon Dories asked, "What are 'Wilderness Public Rights'?" Facing that was the question, "What Do You Say, John Muir? Would you have wanted to pay a commercial guide in order to walk the high Sierra?" offered by Richard Saltonstall, WPRF President. Paraphrasing them at length may give a hint of reciprocated feelings, and why each group did consider the other to be a threat and an impediment.

Litton was typically colorful. WPRF's campaign was "suspect in its motives and masquerading" as a defender of public access. "It raises bogeymen" in the form of concessioners, but it was really just trying to get a "radical revision" of Grand Canyon river use. (Although he did not mention it, Litton had been a special target of Eiseman's campaign to get state agencies interested in checking on the comm ops.) He went so far as to fib about David Brower having only been on commercial trips, even though Brower's first time was on a Litton trip in Litton's pre-commercial days. (I know; I was on that trip.) Self-guided trips were "elite" and "closed"; "once launched, are under virtually no restraints at all". He extolled the virtues of the comm ops. To run the Canyon, the public "depends heavily on the presence and availability of the skilled professional concessioner". "Our people are a step ahead in enjoyment and appreciation" and "the Canyon will be none the worse for their having been there". Comm ops kept "tidy campsites". He turned reality upside down, claiming it was "next to impossible to penalize private users" while "it is easy … to determine how an outfitter is treating the Canyon". Disappointed wannabes for commercial trips outnumber "many times over" disappointed self-guided applicants. He pretended commercial visitors went unheard, and said he knew of one WPRF member who charged fees for self-guided trips. Falling into the thicket of "warped statistics", he dismissed 2000 people as insignificant. "*[E]ach* [his italics] of the half-dozen or dozen or so persons who wish to engage in a trip together will submit an application for the same permit." (His reasoning would have produced over four times the actual number of applications.) "[U]sing the names of relatives or friends", self-guided permittees are able to engage in "two or more trips" in the same season. Most comm op trips are filled six months to a year in advance. (Yet the allocation was going unfilled, and when we tried the experiment of calling some comm ops close to the last minute, we could always find an open commercial space.) Comm op customers were "highly dedicated, in a working way, to the protection of wilderness", but self-guided visitors are "more interested in proving they can make it".

Saltonstall, after invoking a threat from "packaged and programmed guide services" in several areas, did focus on Grand Canyon river running. Most important was that "*only 8 percent*"(his emphases throughout) of use was reserved for persons who wanted to go "**independent of guided-tour commercial organizations**". A major point was the great increase in knowledge and equipment for all kinds of outdoor activities. He claimed twice as many people were disappointed as the number Litton scorned. He continued: Since the 92/8 split is against the law, we have filed a suit against the Park Service to protect "a public right", namely that "**the qualified non-commercial category must be given priority**". Legally, comm ops must prove their services are "unique or essential", "*necessary and appropriate*". How much of the demand they claim to serve is "artificially created by widespread, colorful advertising and intensive promotion?" Since comm ops are not necessary for that portion of the allocation that could be used by qualified self-guided users, the government is forcing some of us to pay fees and profits to a private business for using public lands, which "**is simply and patently against the law**". We have support from the American Canoe Association, the American Whitewater

Affiliation, the Colorado White Water Association, and others. We accept ceilings and limits to prevent overuse, and "*seek only an equitable use-allocation*". He ended with an appeal for funds, something Litton did not do.

The congressional approach, using resolutions to ask for administrative relief, remained low-key. Representative Wirth sent a mailer in February to "paddlers", noting that some of his constituents had interested him in their plight, and suggested that they do the same with their legislators.[5] The issue of *Not Man Apart* with the Litton-WPRF debate had also reported attacks by two congressional committees on overall NPS pro-concessionaire administration.

Late in the year, Eiseman tried Goldwater again, meeting on December 7 at the latter's home. It must have been a dismaying meeting, since Fred's follow-up letter was mostly spent arguing against a Goldwater flight-of-fancy, the idea that the entire Park be declared a Wilderness.[6] Fred had wanted Goldwater to introduce the NPS Wilderness with a motor-free river. Goldwater did say he favored banning motors and a Wilderness river, and told Fred about "the NPS man who called him from D.C." with the same message. On the other hand, comm op Burke had brought eight people to Goldwater's office, and Barry was "scared" of them. Nothing came either of Eiseman's hope to enlist Goldwater in the fight to end discrimination against self-guided river runners. The protest to state agencies having sputtered out, Fred publicized a plan to launch an unauthorized protest trip at Lees Ferry in July 1977.[7] Fred tried and failed to make his case to a correspondent for *The New York Times*, who saw only "personal dissatisfaction", though a law suit would be newsworthy.[8] There must have been some satisfaction to him that each effort now was accompanied by some of the new people stirred up by the NPS freeze on access.

Donald Nemir, handling WPRF's legal attack, filed suit in 1976 in the Federal District Court for Northern California (where WPRF was registered as a non-profit corporation) against the Secretary and NPS officials.[9] The basic claim was that the eight-fold rise in self-guided demand from 1972 to 1975 resulted in denying free public access to the river, a limited resource, due to the NPS fixed allocation. The suit asked three things:

1) that the comm op contracts not be extended until the need for commercial services was found to be necessary and appropriate, as called for by laws governing NPS actions;
2) that "noncommercial" (self-guided) trips have priority access to the river;
3) that NPS regulations be revised to provide maximum utilization by self-guided applicants, with comm ops getting what was left.

The government reply was its standard position during this period; NPS was pedaling as hard as it could, but changes had to wait for the completion of the research and a final CRMP. A more forthright view came from Assistant Secretary Reed, when he advised a friend to postpone joining up with the WPRF because of the suit.[10] The WPRF, he wrote, thinks self-guided groups should have first priority under a fixed ceiling. We do not agree with this unrestrained approach, since we think the "largest segment of the public would be ill-served".

On December 16, the judge issued his order in the WPRF suit.[11] He focussed on the extension of the contracts, about which he noted that though they were for three years, the permits could be canceled or altered at any time, should the research results show the need for such a change. (The draft of the research results had been available for over two months.) Therefore, the judge said, no serious harm had been done, and an injunction was denied. Further, the government's motion for summary judgement was granted because NPS actions were clearly within its statutory limits, not arbitrary nor an abuse of discretion. (However, the judge's language was sloppy, at one point saying the NPS fundamental purpose is to "conserve park resources, providing for the enjoyment of parks". Odd that a judge would be so careless with a crucial 'and'.) He also accepted the NPS position that it needed to finish its river plan. He offered the view that WPRF, as individuals, were a limited, not a general, public, and their mode of access was not "free" being as costly as that for a commercial passenger. (In thigh-slapping irony, he cited the Utah judge in the 1973 comm ops case that NPS had acted rationally and within its statutes.) A few days later, the judge ordered that WPRF pay the feds' court costs. On December 30, Nemir responded with a motion to reconsider the summary judgment, arguing there were issues of fact and law that were not resolved, and could not be, given the insufficient evidence before the judge.

NPS prepared for the new year by announcing that self-guided applications had to be postmarked before February 1977 to be considered.[12] Again there would be a lottery, or drawing, on February 15, with 15 trips above the 7600 user-day allocation being put on a waiting list. Then, in NPS mode of creating problems for itself, Stitt concluded the release with "a major change in the 1977 use allocation system - a person may not take more than one recreation trip during the 1977 season whether they go on a private, group or commercial trip."

Of course, there was still no way comm op passengers could or would be checked, so this modified no-repeat rule would still be discriminatory. And how it could be called a change to the allocation system, whether major or not, might best be answered, again, by a recourse to Orwell. And if it really was a "major" change, why was there no EIS, and why were they not waiting for all the planning to be complete before imposing this one, inequitable rule? How inequitable was it? Survey results were reporting about 10% of commercial passengers self-describing themselves as repeaters—somewhat over 1000 people a year.[13] The average yearly number of self-guided users, repeaters or not, was 500. So had the Park really wanted, as Stitt said in the press release, "to allow more people to have the opportunity of experiencing a Colorado River trip through the Grand Canyon National Park", they would have gone to town on the commercial repeaters.

At the beginning of Chapter 9, there is a table showing the numbers for self-guided trips. Here is an update, adding applications starting in 1973, the first time not all were granted. These are NPS numbers from two documents; even the people who kept the records were not always consistent.[14]

CHAPTER ELEVEN

Year	1971	1972	1973	1974	1975	1976	1977	1978	1979
Use:									
Trips	35	47	49	41	42	36	40	37	43
People	436	548	648	462	474	N/A	N/A	395	473
KUD	5.5	7.6	7.9	7.7	7.7	7.7	7.8	7.5	7.6
Length*	13	14	12	17	16			19	16

*(Average days per trip)

	1971	1972	1973	1974	1975	1976	1977	1978	1979
Applications:									
Trips			74	84	173	425	507	370	441
KUD			14.2	17.1	33.6	89.1	86.9	73.8	86.3

Here are the major rule changes for permit selection for each river-running season.
1972 and before: all valid applications granted; on a first-come, first-served (1-1) basis
1973: 1-1 continued
1974: 1-1 continued; no-repeat started (= not two years in a row)
1975: no change
1976: lottery begun, with small waiting list for current season only. No-repeat ended
1977: lottery + seasonal waiting list. No-repeat re-instituted for within current season, supposedly for all users
1978-80: no change.

The application numbers were challenged both ways by all parties, of course. The jump with the start of the lottery especially aroused suspicion. Yet, the number did not keep increasing in a wild way after 1976, and certainly does not validate the charge that lots of people from every trip were applying. On average, one or two duplicates are indicated. I find it odd that the length of trip jumped from 12 to 17 days per trip, 50% from 1973 to 1974. Perhaps the NPS rules, like no-repeat and limiting the trip to 21 days, encouraged people to ask for longer trips. If so, of course it resulted in reducing the number of people who actually went, another count against the user-day concept. This squeeze could have led to some increase in applications.

Some perspective is gained by noting that even assuming no applications overlapped, and given the average of 11 people per actual trip, there was a maximum of some 5000 people in the self-guided pool of desire, about one-third of the total on commercial trips each year. But the user-day figure would be 80-90 KUD, an amount equal to that of the yearly commercial allocation. As well, the number of applications is not that far below the number of commercial launches. On an apparent or naive basis then, self-guided demand may be seen as close to comm ops use, a real threat if self-guided users were given first priority to the river. Given this competition potential, anger and bitterness was bound to increase on both sides. It could only be exacerbated by the perception self-guided applicants had that they were treated as kicked-around second-class citizens, if not cheaters, while the comm ops were cozied up to as friends of the Park Service.

Grinding On, With Bumps

Public action to deal with the river planning squeeze came in February 1976 when the Park announced six workshops, March 15-29, to gather public input.[15] (As a marker, these were midway between the two sets of public meetings on Wilderness.) The meeting sites were in Phoenix, Los Angeles, San Francisco, Salt Lake City, Denver, and the Park. The purpose was for participants, not NPS staff, to informally offer issues and propose responses. Everybody would be able to offer what they thought most important within a group where there could be discussion and even solutions offered. All the input would be collected, summarized, and, with research data, used in preparing the CRMP. The proposed plan and EIS would be available for public comment in early 1977. This suggests that public input and research were in some sense of equal importance, and also suggests they outweighed Park and Wilderness principles. The timetable, "subject to slippage", suggested there could be alternatives and an EIS draft by the end of the year, with a final plan by November 1977; it was almost like a commitment.

The Sierra Club's mailing emphasized its opposition to an increase in use and to motors, called for minimizing visitor impacts, and mentioned that self-guided boaters were attacking the allocation.[16] I attended two meetings. The first, in Phoenix, had the lowest attendance with 29, and the last, at the Canyon, had the highest with 90. Although a variety of issues came up, there were no efforts at resolution; the time constraint worked against that, as did people's attitudes. I made a comment in my notes, "Why be ameliorative?"

Overall, the Park Service counted 365 attendees, almost two-thirds under 35, but only 286 turned in written votes on the five most important issues. GCNP sent out a summary of the fifteen top issue clusters, with perhaps the most interesting item being that it was signed by a new river manager; after four years, Bob Yearout had moved on, replaced in May by Marvin Jensen. What is nice to say about Bob is that he played the role of the bureaucrat doing his job to the hilt, and thus came in for a sizeable amount of shelling by our forces. Our hopes rose when he left. In this case, those hopes may have been realized. Given the role Jensen played in doing the hard work of putting the CRMP together (more about this and Jensen's background in Chapter 15), he gets, from me anyway, a large share of the credit for the quality of the plan. The greatest testimony to that is the blasting he got later from the more rabid of the comm ops.

Reduced from almost 2,000 items collected at the meetings, the fifteen top issues give a picture, after four years of wrangling, of what was on people's minds about the river.[17] Achieving a fair allocation was number one, with each side pushing its definition of fair. Allocation, of course, was related to how people got permits, which was item four. Fortunately for the public's reputation, protecting the river environment was listed second. And although motors vs. oars was third and wilderness fifth, the summary presented the pros and cons as a standoff. How to get the human waste out of the Canyon was important enough to get its own mention. Some emphasized the limit on use, perhaps spreading it out over more of the year, and others worried about the impact of advertising in creating demand. Differences in rules for comm ops and self-guided boaters were heavily mentioned, tied into the question of whether what was needed was more or less regulation, enforcement of regulations, and/or more training. Toward the end of the list came opposition to dams and burros, and in favor of an ongoing monitoring program.

Self-guided boaters showed up as a major presence; discrimination against them over the past few seasons had created a passionate, aggrieved force. Munroe and Eiseman and a few others may have been stirring the pot the hardest. These meetings made clear there was a legitimate, determined, if loosely organized, constituency. That NPS did not completely recognize this force was shown in a standardized response of April, in which complainers were told that while only 1537 people (almost the number of commercial repeaters) were denied the privilege of floating the river on their own trips in 1975, the comm ops turned away 5,000.[18] Aside from the unreliability of these figures, they imply that 75% of comm op passengers got to go, but only 25% of self-guided users. Discrimination? Case made! Oh but, says NPS, the comm ops provide "the sole means of access to the rivers for the vast bulk of the populace". Of course, with a limited resource, that was neither known nor relevant, the main point being that they were "the sole means" because NPS policy made them "the sole means".

No-comment event: On June 18, the NPS Director formally conformed river regulation to the boundaries of the enlarged Park, one-and-a-half years after their enactment.[19]

In early June, McComb and I visited with Jensen at the Park. We found him well informed and ready to discuss matters—a sign either of his river experience elsewhere or else naivete at what I assured him was one of the thorniest tangles around. According to my notes, he opined that there would be a compromise on motors, and that while their bias was for Wilderness, it would be a political decision. He had been told by Steve Carothers, one of the principal researchers, that the river could handle more users or longer trips if rules to protect the beaches and keep them clean were obeyed. So there would be pressure for more use. He had also heard from Shelby that the effect of crowding showed up during peak use.

Jensen went further, in a letter to a river runner, saying he knew about the "extensive research" on human fecal waste disposal and the possibility of hauling it out in holding tanks. He wrote, "we feel the canyon is looking better in terms of litter and human waste disposal" though, perhaps unguardedly, he agreed "there is a long way to go".[20] He suggested the solution was to keep people informed on what is needed to take care of the Canyon. Taken all together, Jensen's comments at this time tell us that, as the researchers were writing up their conclusions during the summer, GCNP administrative staff knew of the results.

Right Hand: A Shake for the Comm Ops; the Back of It to the Environment

On August 2, Stitt had sent to the Region a memo titled an "Environmental Assessment" of renewing concession permits.[21] His recommended action was to "extend permits for 1 to 3 years" since "three years allows sufficient time to complete" research, the plan, and its EIS. He claimed an "absence of data to assess environmental impact" (what was that stuff Jensen had been telling us two months previously?). So, sticking out the GCNP's right hand and ignoring the research information held in its left, he swore that "a three year extension ... is not a major Federal action having a significant impact on the environment." Further, he (or whomever oversaw the writing of the memo; it may well have been Jensen or Shaw) wrote that "all users would be notified of proposed management decisions and given an opportunity to participate". (But just wait.) He emphasized NPS's fear of litigation. He said workshops had "just finished" (four months before, and it was two months since the summary had been sent out). Sanitation and refuse disposal were current problems, but Stitt was not insisting on mitigation measures, even those already known. The alternatives offered were phony and made with phony arguments—ending commercial use or just allowing it to continue, for instance. And as mentioned, the three-year extension was misleadingly titled "1 to 3 years", though the rest of the document made quite clear that "1 to 3" equals 3. The recommendation was approved by Chapman on the 17th.

Let's pause just a moment, and contemplate this, the lowest point to which the Park Service slunk in this river history. The research results were known to relevant administrators. They were engaged in seeking public involvement in multiple, highly obvious ways. The problems were pressing from all sides. The best NPS defense was surely an offense of focussed speed on the plan to deal with those problems. Yet they chose to deal only with "timely arrangements for next year's visitation".[22] Except it was not just next year's, but the next three years'. And it was in the face of known research data that flatly put the lie to the declaration of "no significant impact on the environment". What was this? Stupid malignity or doing anything to keep the comm ops off NPS backs? What?

One ingredient in our reaction was certainly that, in spite of our attempts to maintain good relations with the Park (see Chapter 9), GCNP staff had not made any effort to keep us informed about this decision that justified and foresaw a three-year extension. There were hints. Back in August 1975, the Regional Office was already thinking of extending the contracts for two years in response to the July memo from Stitt cited in Chapter 9, even though Reed's office had just written a Congressman that there would be a new solution by 1977.[23] I also knew from the river meeting in October 1975 that a contract extension was almost certainly necessary for one or two years. The last we had heard though was of a March 1976 schedule, "subject to slippage", for a draft CRMP in mid-1977. So we might have been prepared. We were not. Worse, we were surprised and angered when we heard in August that the comm op contracts were to be extended **for three years**. All of a sudden, we were being told 1980 was the first year the river plan would, might, be in effect, when we had been hoping for 1978 at the latest.

How many months had the Park been working on this environmental assessment? According to the document, the comm ops had already been queried about their willingness to put up with an extension. So clearly there had been time for a little talk with us. And since we had met with Jensen in June, why did he not discuss it with us, or did that imply that the extension decision was done in some other office, that he was ignored and ignorant?

What was really disturbing, however, was the unreasonable length of the extension. As McComb put it in a mailgram to Reed on August 13 (the day we learned of it), a one-year extension with review the next summer would be appropriate since this will keep NPS and all parties on their toes, and a longer extension would simply delay resolution of the problems.[24] We felt even more justified in this position since we also knew the research synthesis of conclusions and recommendations was being written up during the summer. In fact we were urging that there be an integrated presentation at the October research symposium, which again, for maximum impact, was to be held at the same time as the next comm op meeting at the Park. Moreover, we heard that alternative scenarios for CRMP items were being drafted for a workbook that would be out to the public later in the year.

So I went on the road, summarizing my gleanings in mid-September.[25] I was reassured that the research symposium on October 1 was organized for the greatest possible impact. This was good news, since we had heard that the studies showed strongly that motors were not necessary and were detrimental. In a conversation with Chapman, he said he had sent the three-year recommendation to Washington on September 7, but it would have a 30-day comment period starting shortly. I pointed out that our case for a one-year extension was strengthened by the pace now being set; we thought one year would be enough for plan formulation. A conversation with environmental staffers heightened my sense that this was a good time—we could start off a new administration in the right spirit by having the old one do good things at its end.

I did believe that NPS could follow a schedule to produce a draft plan in February 1977 and a final in the summer so contracts could be made in the fall. Also, I had seen the comm ops use the previous four years to shorten trips, increase helicopter use, and exceed quotas; a three-year extension would only aggravate those bad tendencies. So when the *Federal Register* carried the extension notice on September 16, I urged a quiet campaign, just enough to make it clear this was a major matter.[26] As I wrote Reed, we have been waiting four years since his original decision, and all the groundwork is laid.[27] It is time for leadership to bring about a plan within the next year. After all, that will help the comm ops, since stability for them will only come with the new plan. Whether this effort had an effect is hard to gauge; however, the Interior position started emphasizing that the extension was for a period not to exceed three years and may be terminated at an earlier date.[28] I did not understand how this squared with the part of the justification that comm op allotments were "frequently filled many months prior to the year of use".

Any sense of quiet ended at the September 29 comm op meeting.[29] At the Park I saw a pile of neatly typed letters, signed by Bruce Shaw, one for each comm op, assuring them that "we have received official notification that we may extend" the contracts for up to three years.[30] At the meeting itself—with three weeks left for so-called public comment—Park staff told the comm ops the letters, which worriedly asked the comm ops if they wished to continue, would be sent later that week (I learned later they went the next day). As the extension approval letter was being read, I overheard a couple of comm ops comments, "This is good news; now I can cut my losses" and "I could hug Bruce for this".

As I sat in the comm op meeting, watching and taking notes, I grew even more appalled at the thought that these guys, so brazen in their bullying, were being rewarded with three more years' free ride. The theme of the regulated industry taking over the regulators was emphasized in a discussion about audits. The comm ops were supposed to have an independent audit done every year; the Park Service had waived that requirement for the past three years. A regional staffer tried to explain why NPS was now asking the comm ops to follow the rules. He was bombarded: Why don't you just look at our books? We have our own CPA; why do we need an outside auditor? That would be too costly. We can't separate out the Grand Canyon operation. There ought to be special regulations for river operations. Let us offer you ideas for an alternate to an independent audit. Some of us are pretty small for an audit. This is just a form of harassment. This is just a blanket attack. The NPS response was firm at first—you have an obligation to do this so we can be sure you are viable operations—but finally dissolved into "we are really open to suggestions for change".

When he spoke, the Superintendent was optimistic that the self-guided suit filed by the WPRF would be dismissed, though he expected a suit seeking an injunction against the extensions. (Oh, that we had heeded him; and why was he "optimistic" about maintaining discrimination against self-guided users?)

The river ranger reported on problems, primarily caused by crewmembers not knowing the rules; only half had even read them. (So much for their bosses doing a good job of training their employees, and so much for the NPS feeling that better informing people was the answer; the crew, above all, were the ones who were supposed to know.)

Problems were: soap in the side streams; incorrect disposal of kitchen garbage, wastewater, and grease; charcoal dumped on beaches; too-low firepans scorched sand; trees still being broken up for fires; stoves not being used for cooking; six human-started fires; toilet paper should be bagged and carried out, not burned. Also, lifejackets were not being worn at all times. A couple of comm ops tried to defend the practice in certain cases. On the other hand, the essentially safe nature of the trips was indicated by there only being five persons evacuated by helicopter. (No comm op tried to say that should be the end of the safety argument, then.) The helicopters taking people out at Lava Falls were not only noisy, but were buzzing people. This charge caused an argument. The county health officials assured the comm ops they only wanted to help; they were not doing inspections. When Jensen suggested bringing the horsepower limit from 55 to 40, since that was what the comm ops were using, the latter objected, and Jensen backed off. (It is still 55; now the current comm ops talk about quiet motors and electric motors and probably motorless motors—anything, so long as they can move big groups fast.)

At the research meeting on October 1, attended by half the comm ops, one paper after another showed the problems of the status quo, with many practices by river runners shown to have continuing negative impacts. I was told that none of the researchers had been consulted about the Environmental Assessment (EA) on the extension, and contrary to the EA's finding of no impact, the researchers said that if there was no modification in current practices, there would continue, every year, to be irreversible physical, biological, and personal damage to the Park and its users. (I will cover the research conclusions and meeting in the next chapter.)

Astounded and angry at the research showing of ongoing damage, the comm ops' obduracy, and Park Service supineness, I wrote up a report and circulated it, hoping to upset allies as much as I was.[31] A week earlier, I had written a nicey-nicey letter to Reed; now I wrote one detailing the outrages and calling for, in view of the research, changes in river practices before any contracts were extended even for a year. It all got worse on October 6 when I called Chapman to insist that in light of the research, there should be a change of river practices and a one-year extension, and even more adherence to NEPA. Chapman assured me that the letter was only a commitment to negotiate on the extensions. I wrote to him and to Stitt (they had already talked) reiterating what Chapman had assured me of, urging Stitt to get the research synthesis into public circulation, and asking for the relevant papers on the supposed negotiation.[32] McComb did a follow-up to Chapman; there were also letters to Washington.[33] There were optimistic reports about Reed being distressed at the Park Service. However, this bubble quickly burst as McComb uncovered the fact that the "negotiation" had nothing to do with the environmental and planning concerns we were raising, and that Reed had already approved the extensions in mid-October, with the extension letters being sent out on November 4.[34] Asking, "Would the Grand Canyon be Better Administered by Idiots?" I strongly suggested that we consider whether the action was a violation of NEPA and Park concessions law procedures, and that we find a way to hold up the contracts "until NEPA and common honesty are satisfied".[35]

My disgust was compounded by the new line Interior took, asserting that the three years included "implementation" as well as preparation, and taking no account of the research results.[36] "Implementation" was a silly dodge, since a five-year motor phase-out was being talked about. This same letter said the plan was scheduled for approval by late 1977, repeating the same inconsistencies as before: Comm ops need a long lead-time but we can terminate earlier.

We argued that the one-year period was correct, first, because there were problems that needed to be corrected right away, carrying feces out of the Canyon being at the top of the list. Second, it would be a signal that the process was coming to an end, a notice to the comm ops that changes were about to be made, that they should be careful about making commitments too far in the future, particularly if motors were to be eliminated. Instead of this principled stand, Reed and his associates whimpered away. He complained to McComb that he had taken a bath on this issue before and it hurt too much, so the contracts were extended to avoid trouble from the comm ops.[37] Whatever, then, might be the damage to the river environment or the river running experience, whatever the public might be saying on Wilderness, whatever past statements had been made by NPS and Interior (and even the comm ops) about the resource coming first, in fact what came first was security for the comm ops' businesses.[38] Not that we shut up. Consulting an ally on the Western Parks Regional Advisory Board, I summarized the situation at length, suggesting a WPRAC resolution calling for a save-the-river-environment amendment to the contract extensions.[39]

Personal relations deteriorated further, as Chapman insisted to me that NPS commitments and credibility were at stake. There was no talk of impact on the river or of public support of Wilderness or of NPS credibility with us, just his worry about being reversed again. He seemed puzzled as to how to get the job done under any deadline I thought reasonable. The conversation was so unsatisfactory that I felt a long letter was necessary, arguing that the true commitment was to meet the congressional deadline on Wilderness.[40] As far as his sensitivity to commitments, I cited his assurances to me about the contract extension, which he and his subordinates had ignored. I concluded by saying that talk about commitments and credibility carries little weight when it is so selective.

Whether it had anything to do with the storm or not, the Interior lawyers took a strong hand in the response, so that the actual contract language spoke of the extension being subject to cancellation, termination, and revocation before December 31, 1979.[41] The Director reserved the right to change use, allocations, and limits without any recourse for any losses of profit or gain from sale. NPS could modify the permit as well. The original contract incorporated by reference all the rules to protect the Park or for visitor health and safety in the Commercial Operating Requirements. They could be changed from year to year, so it might seem that we could have uttered a small cheer.

Earlier we had learned from talking with Park staff that a draft workbook on river issues would be out at the beginning of December. Then, in mid-December, the workbook approach was junked, to our relief, with the Park promising to go right to a draft CRMP+EIS in April 1977, with public meetings the following month.[42] Could we try a small smile at the thought that the hullabaloo sped things up? Unfortunately, NPS and Interior handling of this matter left us even more convinced that the Park and its bosses were pro-concessionaire, and that the comm ops had a stranglehold on river management. We could not even claim to have gotten anybody's attention, since the Washington people at Interior were already packing their bags. And we were left, at the very moment we could have been celebrating the NPS principled stand on Wilderness, angry, betrayed, distrustful, disgusted, and moving into the embrace of the lawyers.

They initially supported us. Tony Ruckel, the star of the Sierra Club Legal Defense Fund Denver office, reviewed the matter in mid-December, and concluded that the law had not been followed.[43] He used quotes on seven items of degradation from the draft research synthesis to support his opinion that an EIS was needed, and that the Park Service was not doing its job to protect the Park, since "the present degradation has occurred in the fact [sic] of numerous Park Service conditions, rules, and regulations". So with violations occurring under current Park management, his opinion was that even one year's extension, "adding to the impacts described above, quite likely require(s) an impact statement and raise(s) statutory and trust obligation questions". Perhaps coincidentally, in an article on changes being sought for Glen Canyon Dam, the *Denver Post* wrote about a "new" and "confidential" study by the Park Service showing irreversible changes were occurring in the Canyon, and that the Sierra Club and other conservation groups wanted an environmental review of the contract extensions.[44]

Then silence. The Club did not take up the challenge. And in March 1977, after a visit to Washington, I had to write Tony that we had blown any advantage we had in January.[45] The Park Service had never heard formally of our NEPA objections to the extensions. The congressional committees, who could have blocked them, let the contract extensions through without any review. Worse, the comm ops had even managed to convince Congressman Udall, on our side in December, that environmental organizations approved of motors. What if, I wondered, the Sierra

Club had authorized a suit or even just a letter, might we have made a difference? We had not, and did not, and I had to admit, I had never felt so helpless.

So how was it that we missed this opportunity? Were we in a daze in August? Even given that it took us from August to October to wake up and realize the full extent of the perfidy and the damage, why was strong action not considered in October or most of November? Not until December is a first legal opinion offered. Looking back from now, we blew it.

Here is a calmer look. We had known that a three-year research program with conclusions presented in 1976, meant a river plan could not be ready until sometime in 1977, given the need for an EIS and its requirements for public review. So even if the proposal for new contracts was prepared and the concessionaires chosen over the winter of 1977-8, we surely were aware that contract status quo would likely continue through 1977 at least. Furthermore, we knew from bitter experience that it was hard for NPS to hold to deadlines. The pleasant surprise of the quick-moving Wilderness planning was only the exception proving the rule. Additionally, surely the past few years showed that actions that stirred up the comm ops or other interested parties were as likely as not to cause a slow-down in NPS decision-making. Since we wanted a plan, a favorable plan, very soon, surely our better course was to keep our eyes on the main chance and avoid doing anything to that slowed the process.

So, you get to choose. More activism or less? Was there any way we could have achieved amendments to the extension mandating the recommendations of the research? Would we have been better protectors of the Canyon if we had filed suit, if we had stopped the contract extension?

CHAPTER 12

1976: Research, The Final Exam
(Or: The Left Hand, Research Conclusions But No Resolution)

First, some general thoughts about research in so contested a situation. Demanded by all sides though it was, the research program lived in a political atmosphere tight and closed compared to the great outdoors in which it was investigating. The ever-present question was whether researchers were biased toward one position or another, or just in favor of some objective not shared by the contending parties.

They were closed in also by "the greater forces" outside the scope of their mandate, forces that some contestants had already concluded made their work irrelevant. The most obvious and longest-lived of these was the cliché that so much change and damage is due to the existence and operation of Glen Canyon Dam that river-running impacts are trivial by comparison. This was a favorite because it seemed to imply that the dam had already made such a mess of the natural world that the river was not natural, was not wilderness, and could not be made any worse. Then, some took comfort because they heard that the burro damage was so severe that it outweighed any impact by river travelers; the burros actually fouled springs, trampled vegetation, cut trails all across the slopes, and made areas barren. There were the aircraft, so noisy that boat motor whine was not even noticeable. More weighty was the belief that the motors question was legal and congressional, not scientific.

The river researchers had to carve out a sphere of legitimacy inside such "external" influences. Their mandate required them to act and think as if there were a river world which river traffic could affect for good or ill. Unfortunately, their scrupulousness in this regard did not govern those waiting for the research results. So as we go through the details of that river-research world, keep in mind its political environment, infested by charges of bias corrupting it from the inside, while the "more important" factors were pressed down from the outside, a constant threat.

Let me give away the nut of this story: Most of the research projects were wound up in the 1976 season, and through the summer, Project Director Roy Johnson oversaw a first draft of the "Synthesis and Management Implications".[1] The near-complete draft of September was looked over by researchers at symposium-time. We obtained a copy dated October 3. The final document was issued in September 1977, with the conclusions and recommendations largely intact and even word-for-word the same. Thus a year passed with the distillation of the research available to the Park Service—and everybody else; a year when NPS could have acted vigorously on the most pressing of the recommendations, and did not. The previous NPS line—we have to wait for the research results before we can act—was reversed, with action on the research results having to await the plan. And this, in spite of what we shall see are results that should have had the Park loudly celebrating.

Perhaps our upset at this reversal resulted from the great difference between our impatient concern and the bureaucratic temperament, willing to find excuses for not doing its job rather than risk being chastised for timely action. To us, it seemed no different from an active coddling of comm op sensibilities at the expense of the river environment. If a Wilderness proposal could be done to a congressional deadline, why could not the Park Service meet its own promises on the river plan, we fumed.

Life was more pleasant at the beginning of 1976. Shelby was writing up the results of the HERS research on motors and oars. I had the pleasure of helping with information from my files on the history of the controversy. The Region approved the Park's program for continued monitoring, with an expenditure of $67,000 through 1979, $30,000 in 1980-1, with the work then being carried on by GCNP staff.[2] We kept in touch informally, as we had throughout, with people involved in the research, particularly in Flagstaff and at the Canyon.

Most of the research was completed and written up by July 1976; a major exception was the economic analysis of the comm ops, started only late in the process and due October 15. In one of my talks with Johnson and Carothers, in August, I urged that the October symposium feature a summary of the work that would be coherent and carry weight, an integrated presentation at the time of the comm op get-together with NPS at the Park. Roy told me that Chapman had called him and seemed enthusiastic about the idea. Carothers even offered to go to Washington to bring the material to Interior officials. These two principals thought the findings had urgency and importance.

In mid-September, Johnson released a summary listing of the 29 projects, showing the researchers, the cost, status, and a short description. To me, the projects grouped into three clusters:

Physical, chemical:
the river's water and its constituents; periphytes; the way the water moved sediment; erosion and deposition on the beaches;

Biological:
vegetation; smaller vertebrates, the burros, insects and birds, and the fish;

Human:
people's impact on the physical and biological environment, especially waste disposal; campsite carrying capacity; human experience i.e., impact of noise and of travelers on each other; economics of each of the comm ops.

The researchers held their fall harvest at the October 1 Research Symposium in the Park. There were ten presentations, ending with Johnson's summary. I attended, reaping my own rich crop of notes. While the researchers were gathered, they looked over Johnson's first draft of the synthesis, and made comments, leading quickly to that second draft after the symposium, the one I was given.[3] In an anonymous collection of documents, prepared over a year later, there is a handwritten note that a research board of Dolan, Carothers, Borden, Nielsen and Johnson reviewed the synthesis for accuracy in October, presenting a "working draft" in November.[4]

What you will be reading here is the result of the iterations as I coped with the mass of information in the research results; first as I listened at the research symposium making notes of what was said, then as I winnowed that material for reporting to friends and allies, and then as I culled the Synthesis. Though I tried to track all the work in a general way, I paid most attention to the details of three studies: the carrying capacity for river travel, river contacts—including motors/oars, use and crowding, self-guided/commercial—and concession economics. These contained the material most pertinent to the two questions we had been agitating over the past several years: a motor-free wilderness including the river, and the appropriate level of use. After the conversations I had had with the researchers over the previous few years, I felt comfortable relying on them for the correct implications on the overriding environmental question, which did save my having to digest the 25 physical and biological studies. What appears here is my understanding of those implications. This chapter, then, provides a snapshot of the material I absorbed and used to argue our positions.

First a list of who spoke on what:[5]

> Robert Dolan: Increased river use and irreversible degradation
> Gerald Cole: Limnologic study of the river in the Canyon
> Kim Johnson and Bob Phillips: Human waste disposal
> Steve Carothers: Ecological impact
> Milton Sommerfeld: Water quality of the river
> Stewart Aitchison: Impact of types of campsite activities on beach areas
> Joyce Nielsen: Sociological study of river-running
> Yates Borden: Physical carrying capacity of campsites
> Michael Parent: Economic characteristics of concessions
> Roy Johnson: Overall project summary.

Dolan focussed on the relic beaches, those areas once flooded in the spring, but well above the dam-released high water. Absent replenishment by the river, the dominant natural processor was the wind. The human processes were incorporation of litter, burial of chemically treated waste, and stress from foot traffic. Overall, since the wind cannot bring enough material to replenish the beaches, there needs to be "careful management" of the people to avoid ending up with "sand-box" beaches.

He offered some numbers: to mile 176, about two-thirds of the shoreline was silt-sand, the rest being rock or alluvial fans; there was erosion along one-third, stability along half, and the rest showed deposition of material from terrace sand and movement down-slope from footprints. He stated that the beaches did have soils, a surface of salts and organic matter that was easily broken down and lost. As people walked, for instance, the crust and fines would be broken and peeled away, moving 1 to 1.5 meters/year, leaving the coarse stuff that did not move much, although there was a general downgrade movement. The sand ended up in the river's holes and channel. On the more stable terraces above the pre-dam flood line, the impact was concentrated and long lasting. Farther away, the damage was from trails. He cited Nankoweap and Granite as the worst examples of impact, based on their measurements that showed that heavy-use beaches had six times the impact as light-use. He described the charcoal as an indicator and a contributor to the sand-box condition even when it was too small to see. The practice of dumping it in the river only meant it blew onto shore or drifted to a beach farther down. Along with other litter, this was leading to an "alarming" rate of "irreversible" degradation. Even with stable use, the degradation will continue, so "one might have to control foot traffic altogether". He urged that a control beach be set aside to test recovery.

Two comm ops offered their version by blaming animals (only the four-legged kind) for breaking up the surface.

Cole, in summarizing the limnology, noted the temperature went from the high forties to 60°F. The high carbon dioxide from the depths of the reservoir behind the dam upset the photosynthetic balance. He characterized major contributions of some side streams. He concluded that none of the river carried potable water, and that water quality could be maintained by high discharges from the dam.

My comment on the report concerning disposal of human sewage was "Really disappointing". This was mainly due to all the bad reports I had previously heard about burial of portable toilet contents, and more important, my long-standing conviction that the sewage should be carried out of the Canyon. Instead, the presentation focussed on whether there could be a public health standard. Phillips took the current situation for granted, trashed earlier research, and noted that the chance for disease was low. His final write-up unfortunately recommended pit privies. He did, however, stress the need for facilities being available at long daytime stops. Phillips' conclusions were not included in the Synthesis draft, but did show up in the 1977 final. By that time, the dispute was a matter of history, because the long-desired technology for packaging and removal, developed in 1976, was starting to be used, and was being pushed, ever so gently, by the Park, as I shall relate.

Carothers' report spent a lot of time on the burros, a very successful human introduction, which in spite of two or three attempts since 1920 at elimination by the Park Service using guns, now numbered several hundred. There seemed to be high reproduction success, and low incidence of intestinal parasites, based on their 17 autopsies, not to mention a palatable meat.

Sommerfeld's conclusions on water quality reinforced the need for chlorine treatment of river water for culinary purposes and hand cleaning, in addition to drinking. The tributaries, once again, were the most variable in their contributions, with some total coliform at heavily used attractions sites (where the potties were not set up) being "off the scale".

Aitchison presented the conclusions with the most salient impact as he summarized the study of on-shore use. In brief, the amount of impact did not directly reflect the amount of use, i.e., the number of users. Rather, certain specific uses had deleterious results that required counter-measures. And no matter what such measures might be—regulations or changes in techniques and/or equipment— **all required continuously educating all users** (my emphasis; we will come back to this point again and again). Aitchison said that 325 out of 350 campsites had been assessed from use cards the project had distributed, including such items as fire, litter, trampling and soil erosion, moving of objects, and impact of toilets. Then plots were made of a "biotic resource rating". This measure was compared to the number of users, and the correlation turned out to be random. Comparison with impact type, however, showed up as a direct linear relation, leading to the conclusion that certain activities should be targeted. Again, monitoring would be essential, especially at sensitive sites; some might even need to be closed.

Aitchison made specific recommendations. Before I get to those, let me re-inspect the timelines. The researchers were, on October 1, 1976, announcing specific results, recommending very specific changes in practice. Chapman and other officials, some of whom were listening to the researchers, were telling me the contract extensions, at that moment supposedly open for public review and comment, allowed NPS to tell the comm ops to make changes to prevent damage along the river by their users and crews. Many comm ops and employees were in the room as this was being said. What could be simpler? The word was out; there were no secrets. Therefore, the Park Service in the next week put together rule changes to act on their long-stated promise to prevent degradation and to heed the research. Right? Dream on.

Speaking for the research project, Aitchison spelled it out: Any dumping at all impaired the resource. Carry it all out. Urinate into the river, or on wet sand the river will cover. Have the toilet out at all stops, use it, and tell other people to use it. Eighteen beaches should be closed to any dumping immediately. Put liquid kitchen waste—wash water, food juice—in the river; no pouring on the beach. Where there were several tracks from the river shore to attraction sites, designate and mark one; again, education of users was the key. Reinforce the rule on no soap in the tributaries; impact on fish was especially bad at the junctions. No more driftwood fires; only make fires with what is brought in, e.g., gas, charcoal. The researchers had now given us all eight simple recommendations. How much good faith the Park Service could have generated had they implemented them right away. The Park booted away this prime opportunity to start building a positive reputation for pro-environment river traffic management, and for living up to its promises about depending on the research. By the way, these practices are an integral part of river-running today.

Aitchison concluded by bringing up the question of how natural the river shore should be; it was, he said, the Park Service's to answer. Dolan offered his view, that the dam had brought about a new, tighter stratification of the river shore, "tidal" near the river, and arid above, where the impacts were concentrated. He argued that this new habitat was not "unnatural". He also suggested that the impacts of the first few visitors were heaviest, then the differences would be less noticeable. At this point, Fred Eiseman attacked the researchers for making recommendations. I never was quite sure why Fred decided that all research was useless in policy-making, but Carothers defended what they were doing.

Nielsen, speaking of the human impact on humans, reiterated the HERS conclusion that satisfaction from a Canyon experience was so high that almost no negative factors, such as crowding or levels of use, mattered. This meant that decisions on having a use level consistent with wilderness were up to NPS and the users, there was no "social" carrying capacity model to fall back on. There was some indication that sensitivity to crowding increased with experience. Again, the decision about how much of the experience was to be of wilderness quality would be up to the policy-makers. Visitors would accept what they were offered. She summarized this as "what you have is what you like". First-timers, HERS assumed, coming without expectations, especially endorsed their experiences. That said, HERS had found that no rowing people wanted to switch to motors, while a significant percentage of motor passengers liked what they saw of rowing trips.

Dolan offered his opinion that if more people were on the river, crews would modify their behavior to keep impacts at a level such that people would still be satisfied. (The problem was how to get that crew behavior to automatically include educating themselves and their passengers, thus avoiding the practices Aitchison highlighted. What a difference real leadership would have made. And by the way, Dolan's opinion turned out to be an accurate prediction.)

Whatever the Aitchison conclusion, there was still the assumption that there was a limiting physical carrying capacity. Determining that was Borden's job, and he started by discussing the distribution and size of campsites in four critical sections— upper Marble (to mile 30), Granite gorge (in the vicinity of Bright Angel Creek), Muav ledges (mile 139 to 171), and the western end of the Canyon. In order to arrive at a capacity, he stressed, it was necessary to make certain assumptions, based in the best case on law and policy. He included an assumption of privacy, which cut the "bed count" on certain beaches by 50%. To agree with Park and Wilderness policy, he assumed that all trips would move at river speed, a little over 4 miles/hour. Taking a day's activities into account, he thought 20-21 miles per day was a reasonable daily progress. So the first 20 miles of campsites set the critical upper limit on launches. Other considerations such as not using every campsite every day reduced the campsite limit. Borden ended up with an overall capacity for each launch day of 148 users on various-sized trips, no trip bigger than 40 persons total. The pace and spacing would cut contacts. He assumed a trip length at river speed of 11 days, the trips on each launch day thus averaging 1628 user-days including crew and passengers. With a season of six months, 180 days, his model gave a capacity of 293,640 user-days for all users on every kind of trip, self-guided, commercial, research, administrative, VIP, training, clean-up, turn-on, etc. These ~300 KUD of rowing trips would launch over 26,000 people. He skipped the question of how many might go in the other six months, when the weather ranges from largely excellent to intermittently cold, cold, cold.)

Borden described day-by-day guideposts for his "ideal high-season" trip of eleven days. It put in everybody's face the contrast between some fuzzy nineteenth-century romance of river-running and what we were all headed toward: the conducted tour. No matter whether trips passed each other or not, and no matter whether there was some variation from trip to trip in campsites selected, overall trips, by comm ops particularly, were not a spontaneous, choose-as-you-go adventure. River trips were a method of transporting people to provide them with the experience of viewing and enjoying the Grand Canyon. Most of them had little or no experience and would have a grand time. And whether Borden's assumptions or some others were used, somebody—comm ops or NPS or self-guided trip leaders—would schedule that transport. Borden was very clear that the problem of scheduling or "repetitious patterning" arising from regulation and the conducted tour syndrome need trouble only the crew; to passengers, mostly first-timers, it was all new, all an adventure, and as long as the crew made no complaints to passengers, the illusion and the truth would be maintained.

Once Borden's characterization of river travel was accepted, then each of us had to decide whether the experience was still to be one of wilderness. If so, how would we enhance that quality, given the dam and its effects, the need for rules and user education, and the conducted, non-spontaneous nature of the trip? Purists or profiteers could claim that with all these impediments—not to mention that some of the trips were quite luxurious adventures—this was about as far as you could get from a wilderness experience without building a highway, rail line, or even reservoirs. We refused to be stampeded by this sophistry, arguing that no one would kill a friend just because he had lost an arm or had psoriasis. Distressed by our exploitation as the Colorado River may be, the correct motion for the Grand Canyon is not to increase the exploitation, but to stem it, even reverse it. Then we can all pitch in to help the place heal. The work of generations, surely, but removing motors from the Grand Canyon is an earnest of our conviction that restoration is worthwhile work. It is just as worthwhile to insure that every person who visits is given the chance to enjoy their generation's best possible effort at protecting and presenting the Canyon wilderness in such manner as to leave the place and the enjoyment unimpaired.

Parent's interim report was next up, on the economic characteristics of the comm ops. (No one studied their ideological characteristics. They could fulminate against environmental silliness or Park regulation or self-guided trips, but they were supposed to be sustainable businesses.) Parent was aiming at an economic profile of each comm op, looking at profitability, how efficient they were and how well they met demand. He was charged with finding out something about impact on the local economy, and making comparisons with similar operations. So far, his analysis showed a range in profit from zero up to 28%, although the latter figure depended on income from treasury bonds. (The dollar figures are for the mid-1970s, and are only offered for comparisons valid at the time.) Broken down, rowing profits went from 7.5% to 17%, while motor comm ops made zero to 19%. River trips in the Tetons, a far different trip, had profits from 12-65%, on gross income of $11,000 - $197,000, and none paid any income tax. The Grand Canyon grosses ranged from $17,000 - $608,000, and 60% paid some taxes. He broke down the range (averages were not feasible) of costs on a per day basis:

trip length (days)	rowing costs ($)	motor costs ($)
5	245 - 295	125 - 410
8	345 - 395	345 - 440
9	360	385 – 395
12	460 – 490	350 – 550

The tougher questions, as to whether conversion to all-rowing was possible, and if

21 separate companies could all survive, were still to be analyzed.

Roy Johnson summed up the integrated presentation by stressing the mass of baseline data. He thought the data and other information would help provide a better selection of management options.

There was one curious episode. Roderick Nash, a historian of wilderness and a long-time self-guided river-runner, announced that he had been asked by Assistant Secretary Reed to work on the allocation between comm ops and self-guided river-runners. He described his concept of allocation based on the percentages of commercial and self-guided people who were disappointed in their attempt to take a trip. Carothers asked who was doing the work, since he thought there were to be recommendations by researchers to the managers. Jensen told me privately he was pissed off by this news and would object. Although Nash spoke of working with everybody, his reactions to comments indicated he had his own mind-set. As events turned out, Nash later told me, the request from Reed was withdrawn.

After the symposium, I went through my copy of the draft Synthesis to pick out the choice bits, confident from what Johnson and others had told me, that what was in the draft was what the researchers themselves agreed to say. Although there would be stylistic changes and additions in the final version, the material I depended on over the next year remained valid.[6] I used it in reports to allies and in a short article in the Friends of the Earth monthly.[7] In the latter, I listed some of the findings, calling them evidence of "irreversible destruction of part of the river shore". I emphasized that the researchers had made strong, specific, feasible suggestions for immediate, ameliorative measures. From the Synthesis, I was able to glean that motors were dangerous to their operators' hearing, interfere with conversation and thus interpretation, are less attractive to passengers than rowing, and do not lessen the impact on the Canyon, even though they move people through faster. I added that the increasing use of helicopters cheated the passenger of a full Canyon trip and added to the noise. And all that was needed was to modify river practices and support legislation for a Grand Canyon Wilderness without motors. In short, I could go on saying what I had been, knowing that not only did the research support my views, but that the troublesome question of how many people should go down the river seemed to have a flexible answer. The Park Service could increase the numbers as long as all users were educated (or regulated) on the spot and throughout the trip to behave with care for the environment.

The striking achievement of this recommendation, that inexperienced people can be educated directly, by example, and by the special Park place they are in, grows out of the Grand Canyon's designation as a National Park, and feeds back, strengthening the justification for that designation. People taking a trip could, if educated properly, come out more sensitized to how lightly and carefully we need to move in the Grand Canyon and in the world generally. (This, remember, was what Litton claimed commercial trips were better at.) Thus instead of talking about limiting people or enjoyment, the researchers had sounded the tocsin for a brighter day by concluding that more people could have a thrilling and wilderness trip that, done properly, would make them better denizens of this Earth. How could anyone resist such a conclusion calling for a better-educated *and* larger population of river-running alumni? The cost of under a million dollars had proved itself; now it was up to the Park Service and the public—groups and in general—to carry through on the promise.

Except. Except there was a fly in the honey. As detailed below, one of the HERS results was that 75-80% of the river travelers thought the Canyon unaffected and undamaged by human activity or overuse. So how, if most people were not seeing the problems specified by the research, could you educate them to prevent the problem? New regulations would seem puzzling or worse. Much of the documented abuse arose from crew ignorance or failure to introduce visitors to the need for care. Which meant, if it were the patterns of use that needed to be changed, it was necessary to take a step back and change crew perceptions of damage and change, calling for a licensing/education program.

The value of the Synthesis, first the 1976 draft, then the 1977 final, was that it contained the baseline findings in a form for public and Park Service comprehension. Much of what was said then is still valid, often confirmed by subsequent actions, and as a baseline is part of our understanding of river history, and even what still needs to be done. First of course, is the fact that the Park Service did base the 1978 draft CRMP on, anchor it in, the research results, interweaving them inextricably, confounding all of us who had despaired of anything but NPS business as usual. So let's go through the Synthesis using the 1977 final as base. I will pick and choose the topics and point out any changes from the 1976 draft that seem significant. Where amplification seems revealing, I will also mix in material from the reports prepared by Shelby and Nielsen on human-human impact, Borden on carrying capacity, and Parent on comm op economics.[8]

The Abstract was right up front: In some situations, degradation was high enough that irreversible changes were occurring. The causes were, first, the dam's operation, and then increasing numbers of river recreationists. The environmental impacts cited were loss of riverbed and beaches, spread of exotic plants and animals, trampling of vegetation, trail proliferation, incorporation of human waste of all kinds into the beaches, wildlife eating human-introduced food. The sociologists found that most users thought the Canyon uncrowded, and defined their trip as wilderness, based on their statements favoring non-motorized travel. The concessions were profitable and capable of converting to all-rowing travel. The Canyon was one of the last refuges for several species of endangered fish.

The Park Service Foreword was a bland, misleading, even inaccurate, reading of history, so it was up to Johnson's Introduction to make the issues clear. He wrote that before the dam and high river-running use, the area was "a true wilderness", but those two agents of change led NPS to conclude in the early 1970s that the river's carrying capacity may have been reached. Irreversible changes were "unacceptable" to NPS because of its Organic Act's primary charge to "conserve" and the goals reiterated in the 1976 Master Plan to perpetuate wilderness river-running and mitigate man's influences in order to preserve the total environment.

The Introduction corrected the Abstract's pointing at "numbers". The former emphasized that the changes were due to "use patterns not visitor use levels." Six measures were necessary, though stated with less specificity than the Aitchison presentation:

stop burying human waste in the beaches;

end use of fires;

control chaotic foot traffic patterns;

reduce congestion at attraction sites;

even out densities at campsites;

set up an education/licensing program for comm op crew and self-guided users.

In addition, investigations on motors showed they were contrary to health and safety standards, and "clearly inconsistent" with Master Plan guidelines. "Therefore, use of motorized craft should be eliminated."

Chapter II dealt with the "primary environmental issues". Primary of all was the operation of Glen Canyon Dam, run to maximize power revenues under the overall guideline of providing a minimum yearly amount of water. The temperature was up to 18°F colder than before the dam. The dam had also produced a more stable water quality. Back in 1972, health officials had decided the river was a safe source of drinking water. The researchers thought differently, noting that while the chemical quality met current standards, there were still "potential bacteriological health hazards". One researcher concluded there were minimal overall effects on river water from toilet dumping; another cautioned about the potential hazard due to seepage, having measured total viable coliform counts in excess of standards in the river and most of the tributaries.

The Colorado is a high alkalinity and conductivity system with a tremendous loss of carbon dioxide going downstream from Lees Ferry, where it exceeded saturation. The Little Colorado, famously alkaline, had a small measurable effect on saltiness even way down river, below Diamond Creek, from which point "natural unpolluted conditions" were found in the river.

As another by-product of the dam, 15 of the 19 fish species found in the river were exotics, exerting pressure on the native fish. And while the only fish humans directly impacted was the endangered humpback chub, caught using hook and line, aquatic habitat restoration, particularly near tributaries, was an "absolute" requirement if the genus *Gila* were to recover. Using soap in and near the tributaries was a really bad idea.

By one measure, the river was rich in plant nutrients; by another it supported a diverse but sparse plankton population, and was judged relatively unproductive, affected by the degree of siltiness.

The colder, unsilted water from the dam, never attaining the old spring flood stage, had resulted in a 10% growth in the rocky alluvial fans at tributaries, and the erosion of about a third of the fine-grained shoreline. Rapids were becoming more severe. Some beaches were increasing where sediment was available, e.g., below the Little Colorado and Separation Canyon.

There was a more rigid stratification between the shore the water could now reach (and might almost every day, as the dam releases went up and down to meet electricity peaks), and the always-dry (precipitation excepted) area, now getting all the camping impact with renewal from wind-blown material, not river silt. This stratification meant the human user impacts would be visible and permanent. The "sandbox effect" was caused by walking, the mixed-in litter, and waste. These impacts were exceeding the renewal capacity at the 20-30 prime campsites, just as surely as the river was eroding that one-third of the shoreline. The only protection was dense vegetation; otherwise the "fragile soil profiles and delicate vegetation" were destroyed. Some paths were trenched 3-4 feet. The initial damage was the worst and was long-since done. From now on, the question was one of showing visitors and employees how to avoid making the situation worse and how to behave so that they would not trample vegetation, make multiple trails, "prune" plants for their bedsites, trash germination "beds" for some plants, start brush fires by burning toilet paper, or drop all those bits of food and other litter that were stirred into the sand. Though no one dared use such a boring metaphor, floating through the Grand Canyon National Park needed to become like attending environmental school—with the rapids for recess.

The exotic tamarisk was the dominant tree and "totally beyond control"; fortunately, it provided wildlife cover, beach stabilization, and shade. The Russian olive, on the other hand, could and should be controlled, like the feral asses, which were rapidly destroying habitat, though the research conclusions did not try to balance which had more impact, burros or river-runners. (Anyway, the latter were educable—yes—while the former should be, ah, removed.) Sparrows and starlings, both exotics, were starting to show up. And scavengers—ringtails, skunks, blow and flesh flies, harvester ants, ravens—increasingly enjoyed socializing where humans did. Lizards and small ground-dwelling vertebrates, on the other hand, were subject to stress and reduction in numbers. The lizards were particularly bothered because they liked to show off, etc. on the now-dwindling driftwood piles.

There were two sets of studies, one from the Park, the other from academia, on the disposal of human feces. The method in use for several years at campsites had been to put out a portable toilet and then bury the chemically doused contents next morning high up on the beach. On hikes or other stops, including lunch, the toilets were not brought out. One comm op used a toilet on a boat, going directly into a large tank.

The Park study said river-runners' health is "potentially endangered" because the coliform bacteria were found to survive almost a year. The university folks concluded the coliform died very rapidly, with a 99.998% reduction in a month. Both found fecal coliform in various parts of the beach, not just the burial sites. They agreed that the chemicals used were useless. They agreed that there was an adequate rule for landings during the day. The Park researchers went on to find solid material erupting to the beach surface, and some smaller beaches having multiple dumps in the same place, while 100-150 dumpsites might be present on the prime beaches. So prime that by the end of the summer, urine and fecal odors were apparent.

The conclusion that the ~5000 fecal dumps contributed to destruction of soil and microbiota tied in with their overall picture of beaches, where disregard of rules was leading to dirty gray sandboxes, crawling with the dramatically increased ant and fly populations.

For some reason, the sociological findings were included in the section on the river environment, even though only one of the thirteen findings in the 1976 version, and none of the ten in the final, belonged there. They were the most noticeably rewritten items, though most of the 1976 findings were incorporated, not dropped, in 1977. The only 1976 finding that linked the visitor to the environment does not appear in the 1977 document, despite its crucial relevance. This is the one referred to above that said that few (10-30%) users feel there is damage by litter, trampling, and overuse. This disturbing indication of visitors' low understanding of their own impact directly affected the major conclusion, that what needed to change were use patterns.

This missing socio-environmental finding may have drifted off to a later section, where, comparing passengers on rowing and motorized trips, the Synthesis says that those on motor trips perceived the Canyon as less affected by over-use. Perhaps the Synthesis writers were so focussed on motor vs. rowing, they edited out the environmental implication. However, in one of the supporting research reports, the finding that "75% felt the Canyon was not being damaged by over-use" is applied to "most river-runners", not singling out motor passengers.[9] Another report cited both figures, the 75% and the 10-30%.[10] The data referred to are found in the appendix, in a table for "Perceived Impact of Use on the Canyon; percent agreeing". Here are those results, where MP means motor passenger, OP commercial rowing passenger, and SG self-guided traveler. All the differences are statistically significant; my verbal interpretation of the items:

	Percent Agreeing			
	all	MP	OP	SG
Canyon UNaffected by humans	78	82	65	46
Canyon NOT damaged by humans	75	80	53	43
That is, users thought, contrary to research view of damage:				
Litter excessive	11	8	21	24
Vegetation trampled	18	14	31	38
Campsites overused	19	15	37	31
Attraction sites overused	27	22	44	48

Thus, for instance, nine out of ten passengers wandered around the beaches, not noticing the litter, the charcoal and ash being incorporated in, the "sandbox" condition that so exercised the researchers. (This table, by the way, is a fine example of the "bias" introduced by the sheer numbers of motor passengers tilting the overall numbers.) These numbers are only a snapshot of visitor sensitivity. But while the average of all users gives a misleading view, it is hard to find much comfort in results that show so few river users, no matter in which category, recognized what the researchers were seeing, and what was so often in front of their noses.

More important, in this chapter on "primary environmental issues", was that the one piece of sociological evidence most relevant to the environment was not only not emphasized, it was deleted. Since the sociological issues that were included in the environmental section all had to do with human-human contact, and did not logically belong in the environment section, maybe this was just bad editing. Or maybe the researchers did not see the problem posed, when their view of a river shore being damaged and their call for users to change practices to avoid that damage was juxtaposed with the users' view of a river shore not being damaged. None of my papers indicate I saw the problem; I just accepted the view that people were educable, and never noticed that, according to HERS's detailed data, most saw nothing to learn.

It is a loss that this finding was not emphasized in the Synthesis in order to indicate the magnitude of the task of implementing the project's central finding that use patterns, not use levels, needed to change. It is also too bad that people, especially the crew and other experienced users, were not quizzed extensively about their perceptions of the river environment. That could have been enlightening about the impact of river management from 1980 to the late 1990s, since some of this research repeated again twenty years later.

Leaving the rest of the sociological findings until further along where they belong, here are the summary and conclusions of the Synthesis' environmental chapter, "Rapid irreversible physical and ecological changes are occurring as a result of the present visitor use patterns." However, the changes can be reduced and even eliminated if use patterns are modified. Since the changes are not due to numbers of people, then no matter what happens to the amount of use, modifications must be made, as follows:

eliminate incorporation in the beaches of all kinds of human wastes;

eliminate fires to keep charcoal and ash out of the beaches and leave driftwood;

control present chaotic patterns of foot traffic;

mitigate congestion at attraction sites;

distribute environmental stresses arising from concentrated high campsite use, where 75% of the use is at 25% of the campsites.

As campsites go, so goes carrying capacity. The full Borden report was submitted in late November 1976, and it was anything but vague. Indeed, its specificity was almost frightening, since it got right down to the trip launches, and how their timing meshed with campsite availability. Availability was affected by the environmental question of whether some portions of the camps were getting too much of the use. However, these two parts of the research were not tied together for specific sites; Borden only asserted the need to monitor critical campsites closely and, if they were damaged, make adjustments in scheduling or even close them. He played the numbers game he was asked to, though one based soundly on his team's observations of the river shore and a conceptual picture of the necessary policy and management. Research was providing information on constraints, e.g., if you want isolated campsites, say a mile apart, how many are there? He was quite clear that he was showing the Park Service a method of arriving at a carrying capacity by starting with a particular policy choice; his approach would be valid even should the policy be altered.

Borden rated the Grand Canyon's river trip on five dimensions. As a wilderness, it was unique. Even the dam effects did not alter its wilderness character; in Borden's view, the environment showed a minimum of recent human impact. As an adventure, it was again unique, especially for its length and whitewater opportunities. Visually, he rated the Canyon outstanding, if not unique, but aurally, he cited problems from boat and plane motor noise. The negative impacts on motor passengers were marked and controllable. Those four dimensions, taken together with social factors, led him to a policy that envisioned small, self-contained, solitary groups propelled by the river, camping at designated sites. Goals included health and safety, absorption of information, maintaining the undeveloped wilderness, and a range of activities.

Borden then reasoned through the resulting trip parameters. A trip maximum (really, a campsite size maximum) of 40 people (always, he included crew), a spacing of about three miles between trips, five hours each day just for travel, the remainder devoted to all the needs for health and well-being. With a river speed of 4-1/2 miles/hour, the minimum trip would be 11 days, or actually 11 nights, since the first and last days were only partially on the river trip. Next he classified campsite capacity and critical river reaches with few campsites, as described above. He projected launch scenarios so trips of various sizes could reach appropriate campsites in each of the critical sections. He factored in the attraction sites, noting that congestion could be handled by general guidelines as to length and overlap of visit. Only if guidelines did not work, would features and critical campsites need to be scheduled, which would reduce carrying capacity severely.

His carrying capacity worked out, his scenario would daily launch three groups of 40 and one each of 20 and 8. These were maxima and included everyone. The overall number of people for the six-month season was 27,000. (This would have meant an increase of about 10,000 people, about twice as many as applied each year to go on self-guided trips.) To show how his model could work, he then went through a scheduling exercise, working out where each of the five groups would camp over the trip. He also made allowance for some trips going for a longer time. He was quite explicit that the intergroup contacts would be controlled by the crew (a point Dolan had made the previous year in the discussion). "The rigidity of an ordered progression downriver at a set minimum spacing is ruled out."[11] He stressed that ideal scheduling, including flexibility, would not even be noticed by passengers, though all would be aware of the need to maintain the long-term environment and enjoyment for every trip. He preferred scheduling patterns that most evenly distributed campsite use and maximum space between groups. Even with all these assumptions (or Park Wilderness constraints if you will), he still found there to be a vast number of scheduling options. He ended up with "a very simple scheduling scheme", and applied it day by day for his five 11-night trips. He also worked out how longer trips would operate and how days of under-capacity launches could go, as well as those where over-capacity was unavoidable. For the latter, he wanted habitual offenders to be firmly discouraged by curtailing their use.

He judged his system to be simple and flexible, about midway between rigidity and *laissez faire*. The rules did not conflict with normal travel or other activities. Passengers, he emphasized again, would not likely recognize restrictions on a pattern-scheduled river section "unless the boatmen made it an issue".[12] Moreover, his particular scheme would allow for a slight boost in carrying capacity, although many research or administrative trips would cut into the recreational capacity. He doubted there would be many trips outside the six months. (Given that the many virtues of travel in the uncrowded season were not so evident in 1976, this is a pardonable misjudgment. Still, even one 15-person trip a day during that season would allow an increase of some 10% in the capacity; 3000 people launched could have helped satisfy self-guided demand. Research on the low use, winter season is scant; we do not know how trip impacts relate to environmental needs.)

Borden's working assumptions pointed toward a motor-free river in order to attain the outstanding aural dimension that the Canyon could provide in a full wilderness setting. However, he recognized that motor use might continue as it was phased out, and that motor trips could fit in his scheduling pattern. He spent some time on the question of allocations, urging that seasonal allocations be abandoned and allotments be tied to the carrying capacity, figured on a weekly basis. When the comm ops submitted their proposals for contracts (now delayed for three years giving them plenty of time) they should include their preferences for trip dates and sizes. These would then be subject to negotiation with the Park Service on an annual basis. (It is not giving too much away to say such negotiation could only work with a surplus of good will and faith.)

Now, given all this—the increased (wilderness) carrying capacity and the central environmental conclusion that damage was controllable by user education—what could be better? The policy-makers had their research and it justified Wilderness management that would keep the comm ops in business *and* satisfy self-guided demand. Bureaucratic heaven!

Not so fast. What if, in spite of Borden's assurances about the Canyon's qualities and his scheduling patterns providing a quality experience, the users did not agree? Indeed, what were their experiences? Chapters III-VI of the Research Synthesis, along with the non-environmental items from the environmental chapter, are concerned with the human use of human beings. Rearranging the items a bit, I will discuss the findings about noise from boats and airplanes first, then segue into other points about motors, from which we can rise to deal with wilderness and Park values, take up other user and perception issues, and end finally with the delights of comm op economics.

In Chapter 8, I dealt with the main study on motorboat noise. The Synthesis pulled from that study the findings on possible harm to the motor operators. It added the disruption by motor noise of normal conversation, interpretive commentary, questions from passengers to operators, and the aural dimension of the Canyon wilderness—wind, water, birds, the natural quiet. That disruption also came from planes, with helicopters being the most distracting, according to a cited study of hikers.[13] The noisiest times were mid-morning and mid-afternoon. Although three of the four conclusions in Chapter IV dealt with noise from the air, no findings on planes were described. The fourth said that unnatural noise could be reduced by eliminating or muffling outboard motors. For such a major bone in the NPS throat, this was thin relief.

Supplementing the noise interference work, HERS concluded that people's preference for rowing boats over motorized rafts came partially from the perception that the former were consistent with the wilderness everyone perceived. Due to the slower speed and the greater possibility of conversation among all people, rowing passengers ended up learning more about the Canyon, including learning more about how to behave in less-damaging ways. Motor trips are different, having more people and more people per boat and, HERS found, meeting more parties each day and making more adjustments to avoid crowding, while spending less time in the Canyon and having fewer and shorter attraction stops. Most motor boaters were not bothered by the noise, illustrating again one of the great difficulties in such research: the likelihood that, in the context of such a wonderful experience, people adjust to or edit out the negatives.

One of the more striking findings in this regard was in trip size. When asked, everybody preferred trips of 30 persons total or less. Nevertheless, one-third of the trips (all motorized save one) sampled by researchers carried over 30 people. Indeed, in spite of this overwhelming preference, comm ops relentlessly ran trips above that preference level. When Shelby and a colleague re-ran part of his research in 1998, the preference for trips remained 30 or fewer, with 60% wanting 20 or fewer.[14] Nevertheless, the *average* size commercial trip at the time was 25 people total. If we remember that one of the phony buzz-words the comm ops use to defend motor use is "choice", then imposing trips larger than people want is best understood as an indicator that passengers could only choose what comm ops gave them, want it or not.

The point is, no surprise, that comm op control of river traffic was not beneficial. Another piece of evidence is that the 1970s research found that about 50% of comm op passengers were in the upper 20% American income bracket. In the 1998 repeat of the research, that 50% was now squeezed out of the upper 12%. Then there is average length of trip, which for both motor and rowing comm op trips has dropped a day, so on motor trips you get an average of 5 instead of 6, and rowing gives you 8, down from 9. Some of that change is certainly due to cutting the trip short at mile 187 (100 miles from the end of the Canyon), where half the passengers are helicoptered out. And furthermore, rowing passengers seem, according to the rerun of the HERS work, to be degrading in their sensitivity to the Canyon.

Back with HERS in the Synthesis, they had checked to make sure that motor-rowing differences were not tied to the few social and demographic factors they obtained. Pretty much the same elite took both trips. Moreover, they were alike in preferring the trip they took, just as you expect from the adjustment phenomenon. Contrary to comm op myth making, passengers did not discern any difference in the safety of the trips. However, those on rowing trips were more alert to the environmental damage found by research.

In an effort to get closer to any differential impact from motoring vs. rowing, the two-trip experiment suggested by Heberlein was set up with one of the comm ops who ran both ways. Two trips, one motor, one rowing, started so they would meet at mile 110 and exchange passengers. The trips were advertised as a chance to experience both travel modes; which meant the groups had to be more motor-tolerant than I care to be. Still, HERS argued that as best they could tell from comparisons, this was not a biased group, and the majority of the passengers said they did want to try both, while a quarter indicated they would have preferred rowing. The researchers then gathered information about reasons for preferences, the advantages of each trip type, and one-word characterizations. The results were presented in Part II of the River Contact Study. Motors had the advantage of being more convenient and faster, and carrying more. Rowing, on the other hand, was more relaxed, with more stops, quieter, slower, and allowing a more Canyon-attuned experience, including the adventure of being able to row. Rowing also featured the social advantages of smaller, more conversational groups who could talk with crew more easily. HERS reported that motors collected 98 positive and 76 negative one-word descriptions, rowing 171 plus words and only 7 minuses.

One distinction HERS did not deal with was that between the "worst" (5-6 days) and the "not so worst" (9-11 days) motor trips. Some comm ops claimed they offered quality, i.e., longer, trips. Did their passengers come away more like rowing passengers? Or did motors, as we contended, overwhelm such factors in their effect of insulating motorboat riders? Is pace, the rate of travel, a more important element in what the traveler takes away from the Canyon trip than motor noise? Is there an element of relaxation time, of stretching out as the days float by, necessary to gain the information and sensitivity a Park and wilderness experience are there to afford? Certainly Shelby had thought so in his earlier theory about the wilderness experience, and since there were some "longer" motor trips, there would have been a chance to test the differential impacts of noise and pace.

Differences distinguishing motor and oar commercial passengers were tested against self-guided river-runners. The second two groups had similar experiences, though self-guided views were somewhat more intense, pro-wilderness, pro-Canyon, pro-river. As between the two allocation groups, the commercial passengers were more affluent and less experienced in wilderness, rivers, and the outdoors generally. The research did, then, verify for us that among the tiny elite (1% of Americans in a century, remember) who would ever go down the Colorado River in the Grand Canyon by any means, there were those two groupings: the money elite and the experience elite. However, unlike Borden and his list of policy elements leading to a structured recommendation, HERS offered a more tentative picture, with many qualifications, of a motor-free river. Why was the year between the two Syntheses not used to synthesize more? Did Borden's death close off the possibility? (But when I really want to ponder what-ifs, I ask why NPS, and we too maybe, failed once again to make a huge celebratory event out of the findings. The research, in and of itself, was never properly presented—and debated for that matter—in a public way. There should have been news conferences and seminars, presentations and rebuttals, locally and in Washington. As I have already indicated, however, NPS squirreled the research away, never providing a chance for a pre-CRMP public venting, and making it all too easy for the comm ops to snipe and sabotage the research impact. *Mea culpa*.)

One of HERS's goals was to study how congestion and crowding—contacts with other groups—affected people. Shelby and Nielsen had been wrestling with the problem of looking for effects using a tool that showed no differences. That is, they imported the idea that differential experiences would be tied to differential satisfaction, but the Canyon overwhelmed any differences. Also, the background differences, what people brought with them, were not particularly strong, given the narrow clientele base. So HERS had to seek other discriminators and tie them back to the questions about motors and self-guided trips that their work was to help resolve. They settled on trying to count congestion and crowding. (Although HERS did not question it, I think it odd that people can go along, adjusting to intimacy with a group of 30 or 40 strangers, but then might be bothered by seeing a trip of 10 or 15 pass by. Maybe this concept of The Contact is supposed to tap into some suspicion of aliens. Like swallow your own saliva is O.K., but it is gross to spit in a glass and then drink it. Anyway, crew members, by and large, know their job is to provide passengers with a good time. Trip leaders can adjust along the way—just as

Borden and Dolan and HERS knew and said they would—depending on what they see at various attractions or potential campsites.)

Once again, maybe the most important conclusion from all the pages churned out on congestion, is that it did not matter. Congestion does bother some river-runners; unsurprisingly, those most likely to want the most isolated wilderness experience. The beauty of the Borden patterned scheduling was that it worked to offer that isolation from other trips if desired. Motorboats of course blow that sense of isolation away as they power on past trip after trip. Why did that not seem to bother passengers much? First, because most passengers motored. Second and more important, humans can take action to avoid undesirable outcomes. In 1975 HERS defined a High use level of people per season; in 1998 this level was substantially exceeded in practice. Yet the data—for daily contacts, for alien-trip people seen in a day, for the total time other such trips were in sight—from the 1998 repeat study are all *below* the numbers for 1975. This would seem to support Borden's assessment of crew capability to deal with greater traffic in a river where the guides know they are on a schedule even if the passengers do not. HERS worried about making "radical" changes like having a motor-free river, and wondered if there could be a testing period. Well, on one item, there has been a thirty-year test: adjustments by crew show up in a motor-oars context leaving no doubt they could handle the patterned scheduling Borden envisioned. River-running may still be an adventure; its character now has more of a conducted than a spontaneous quality.

And another thing about Borden's work; his limits on trip numbers and total size would not have been a radical change, as HERS seemed to imply. Based on the schedules in the HERS report itself, Borden's limits were exceeded at most seven times in the most crowded months.

We have already encountered Shelby's effort to tie the concept of wilderness, beyond its legal standing, to what sort of creatures we are. The impacts of motor noise and motors being non-wilderness propulsion added experiential strength. Shelby and Nielsen sampled people's opinions, and added more reinforcement to the anti-motor stance. Almost everybody thought the Canyon was a wilderness—and wanted to increase their wilderness experience by not camping near other parties—one of Borden's policy guidelines. HERS's numbers showed that rowing trip participants also thought the Canyon would be more of a wilderness if motors were banned; even a third of the motor boaters thought that. Indeed, 15% of motor passengers wanted to use oar boats next time, while motors won no converts. Yet while all this provided information on the margin for those of us arguing that rowing was the best way to go, the Canyon's overwhelming positive presence swamped most efforts to distinguish differences. So the real point remained what it always had been: this was a Park, a wilderness Park, and it should be managed that way. Although HERS was rarely explicit about Park values, their work did offer us an assurance that a "more" wild Park, i.e., without motors, would generate just as much enthusiasm and satisfaction, and educate ever more caring Park visitors.

HERS's part of the 1977 Synthesis reached for a more general level compared to the 1976 draft, e.g., a 1976 page of detailed findings on use levels and contacts was boiled down to the statement that use level affects contact level. The detailed reports did offer numbers on the characteristics of high and low density trips. Yet, how could that matter when people's perception of crowding grew out of their conception of wilderness; instead of being related only to how many people they saw? Again, the Canyon gives too much satisfaction for a great deal of worry about congestion. Yes, when you get to an attraction site, and there are already 100 people there, it is off-putting. But in the context of the Canyon? In the context of an entire Canyon trip? In the context of the Canyon, compared to other experiences?

So both sides of the motor-oar argument could be comforted: See, said the motor boaters, people love our trips. See, said rowing advocates, even if there are more boats, people in an all-rowing Canyon will love their trips. See, said the study, no matter how you boat, you will end up liking how you went. One thing was sure. Though arguments at the edges favored rowing and wilderness, the comm ops would be under-whelmed by such evidence. The research program was a learning experience for those interested in the Canyon and people's experience of it. The comm ops, however, had their political bottom line, research or no: the status quo, with a bit more for each of them, was best.

And what about their financial bottom lines? Parent's report on the economics of the river-running industry worked hard to make sense of the inconsistent and incomplete financial information the comm ops provided him; he had no independent sources. Nor did he have any usable information on demand for river use and services. Nevertheless, he punctured a number of balloons, and left one big mystery.

Bottom line, most of the comm ops were profitable; some earned large profits and paid high salaries. There were no economies of scale, meaning that large comm ops did not provide any more or any less costly trips than small ones. There was a wide range of choice in rates charged, based on revenue per day. He concluded that consumers got their money's worth. Trip quality, as related to profit and loss, was one item he could not analyze. Contrary to motor boater puffery, rowing trips were slightly more economically efficient than motor trips, and only a tiny bit less profitable. In any case, however, there was such a wide variation among the comm ops, that this difference was not meaningful, except to prove false the smear that rowing was a less advantageous business than motoring. (Similar in this to the safety data.) The overall difference in the earning power of motor trips vs. rowing was less than the variation among companies. Indeed, a major finding was that profitability was due to sound business management, not motors or allocation. His detailed comm op analyses were hidden away, but we did learn about some of the most secure and weaker firms, so we knew that among the biggest, there were some with a strong position, and some with extreme variability and losses, and a high negative net worth. The same comments were true of smaller firms; they could run unpredictable operations way below allotment, or show impressive financial viability and strength with favorable profits.

In talking about costs, we were surprised that Parent concluded that advertising was a very low percentage of sales, though we liked his idea that there would be consumer benefit if the advertising standardized the type of information offered. His discussion on equipment investment was good stuff. Investment was relatively low and cash flow high, and many concessions had self-financed new equipment in less than one year. Some could switch from motors to all-rowing in six months; all were financially capable of making the switch with a three-year phase-in. If they could not, it would be due only to the firm's poor business management. He also debunked the argument about much of an impact on local communities, finding it was small, the companies and employees too dispersed, and purchase data not available.

So, the environment can be kept healthy by educating users, use can be increased to make more people happy, everybody is happy in the Canyon anyway, and the comm ops make a profit so long as they run their businesses well. The research had spoken, it brought the good news. Bureaucratic paradise! Pop the champagne! Ah well.

And what about those comm ops we have heard so little from lately? Half of them had been at the research presentation. How could the evidence not sway them? Why was this not comm op paradise, too? Which brings us to the mystery no economic study could solve: If the profit margins, equipment financing, and all the other economic items were dependent only on how good a management the firm had, why did the comm ops care about motors? When they thought of selling out, why did they think it was advantageous to say motors were more profitable, when it was a sound business operation that really mattered? Could it be that economics did not matter either? If not, what did? Did they just want to win the war, no matter how little they needed to from the business point of view? How could it be that a decision that had to do with Parks and wilderness and the environment and visitor enjoyment, ended up being twisted by a bunch of fairy tales about safety and economic base and accessibility and preferences and choice and convenience? What perverse motive drove the comm ops to slander the research they had demanded as biased, inadequate, and irrelevant? When the research showed the way toward accommodation, why did they prefer their make-believe and intransigence?

CHAPTER 13

1977: Everything But The Kitchen Sink

New Year of 1977 found river management staggering. Pushed forward by the heady NPS decision for a comprehensive Grand Canyon Wilderness, there was a hard sideways shove as NPS gave the comm ops three more years of the status quo without having to alleviate the "irreversible environmental degradation" they were causing. The self-guided effort was working in the courts towards a different direction entirely. Helping to keep the CRMP+EIS process moving ahead, the researchers had summarized and synthesized their work in a helpful, hopeful way.

Some 1977 personnel changes may have made a difference. John McComb defected to Washington, leaving no local involved conservation organization official; the new Southwest Representative did not have McComb's interest or experience on Grand Canyon matters. The move could have been a plus in Washington, since McComb as a Tucsonan had cultivated relations with his congressman, Morris Udall, now the chairman of the House Interior and Insular Affairs Committee. In mid-year, I gave up the joys of full-time unpaid work on the Grand Canyon, and took a job to put money in my family's pocket.

A likely minus was that two officials—NPS Director Everhardt and Interior Undersecretary Curtis Bohlen—who had dealt with Grand Canyon's complex affairs in the previous Republican administration, were excused from service in, respectively, May and August 1977. The new Director, William Whalen, had some experience; he had been Deputy Director in the period when the comm ops were getting Reed's 1972 decision put on hold.

Outweighing such considerations, the Carter administration took office on January 20 with a commitment to Alaska as its prime conservation effort, one Udall shared. The 1977-80 effort to reserve and protect significant Alaska lands sucked up huge amounts of all the conservation organizations' attention and resources. The priority was clear and apt, but other issues had to suffer when, for example, the Sierra Club Southwest Representative turned into another Washington lobbyist for saving Alaskan wildlands.

NPS personnel at the Park and Regional level stayed in place, as did the comm op line-up, with Burke and Staveley as the two noisiest, or at least the two leaving the most traces.

The story, unlike the Colorado's canyons, now braids out into distinguishable channels:

handling of the Wilderness recommendation;

GCNP's preparation of a CRMP+EIS draft for the public to consume or rend;

resorts to the courts.

Weaving back and forth in these channels, we and the comm ops kept trying to divert the stream of events in our very separate directions.

Wilderness:

As 1976 flamed out, I made some notes about "Policy" to answer the question: Since the amount of river use (then called the carrying capacity) is set based on values as well as the physical setting, what cluster of values will we encourage? My answer came in part from that legislative fight over the Park boundary. The American people, through Congress, had put all of the Colorado River in the Grand Canyon into the National Park to manage according to National Park values. Obviously then, visitors were best served by those trips more likely to promote the Park values of Grand Canyon, a primary one of which was its freedom from development, its continued existence as a wild place, a wilderness. I saw Wilderness designation as starting up a cycle that would work constructively for Park values; the research strengthened my belief, since it was conclusive that visitors on rowing trips absorbed and retained more about the Canyon and how to behave in it. That cycle would gain momentum as the sluice-em-thru motor trips were phased out, shifting those Park-value-destructive trips to the more Park-friendly rowing trips. Moving at river speed, a fairly steady four miles per hour, rowing is normal Grand Canyon travel; motor trips had all along been a freak, a momentary historical accident resulting from a no-longer-unquestioned worship of motors, hardened in place by profiteering and weak NPS policy-making.

To get the cycle underway, we needed the definitive act of a motor-free Wilderness established by Congress. Moving a Wilderness recommendation into the congressional arena followed a well-marked road, which NPS Director Everhardt had started on when he had sent its recommendation through Interior channels to the President's Executive Office. Once it was approved for the President's program, a process usually automatic, off it would go to Congress. All we had to do was monitor its progress, and prepare our friends for a legislative showdown.

Indeed, when I talked with Reed's staff on January 6, I was told that NPS had sent the recommendation to the Interior Legislative Counsel on December 29, and was talking about "expediting" review by the Office of Management and Budget, where the recommendation would go next.[1] It was now on a two-day wait to ensure there were no objections; they were trying to get it done before the 20th, Inauguration Day. Everhardt was hoping it would move right along since he wanted a public announcement. Reed, even as he exited, was still cautious. In any case, we had reason to be pleased at language that justified inclusion of the river so as to perpetuate wilderness qualities and an enhanced visitor experience, as shown by the research and overwhelming public support. Ever hopeful, I sent off a packet of pro-wilderness materials to a reporter from *The New York Times*; what appeared instead was an article about the Bureau of Reclamation's irrelevant dam objections.[2]

Everhardt's commitment became clearer four weeks into the new administration when he addressed Cecil Andrus, the new Secretary of the Interior.[3] What is noteworthy about this memo is that it focussed on both the main issue and the process, and as such, is just as true 25 years later. The primary issue is motors, the Director wrote; we are working on the CRMP, aiming for completion by the end of the year, but we could begin to remove motors now "if there are negative impacts of sufficient magnitude to warrant such a decision." If the Wilderness recommendation were enacted, motors would be eliminated. Everhardt enclosed a draft press release, saying there was widespread public interest, this would be a generally popular recommendation, and the phase-out would mitigate most negative impacts. The release cited the studies showing motor incompatibility with visitor enjoyment and resource management. The public would have forums in both congressional and CRMP hearings.

At the end of February, the Secretary's office was saying the Wilderness recommendation was still in the hands of Interior's Legislative Counsel, from which it would be sent to the President via the Office of Management and Budget. A briefing for Everhardt on the CRMP in mid-March brought out no worries about moving Wilderness along.[4] The recommendation was to be in the President's environmental message in May. The only problem noted was the uncontrolled traffic up from Lake Mead, but the decision was to leave the entire river in the recommendation.

Impatient as always, I wrote Congressman Udall on February 27 about what I thought was slow action on the motor-free proposal, asserting that it would bring out the wide support it has always enjoyed.[5] (I was not impressed by the uncertainties that can occur during a change in presidential administration.) I asked him to make inquiries or even to introduce a Wilderness bill himself, noting that he had given Everhardt the go-ahead when the latter had talked with him in December. At the same time, I wrote an ally about my concern over the snail-like progress of something that should sail along smoothly.[6] I fussed that it ought to be pushed early before opposition could get heavily organized. Perhaps we needed a mailing, or to get the Washington people to lend a hand, though I had not heard from McComb for over a month. Then I had an early March warning from a House Interior Committee staff person that the comm ops had been around pushing a motorized wilderness. Another early warning came from a report that the comm ops, motor and rowing, had united to get the Western River Guides Association to vote for keeping motors in the Canyon.[7]

I was not impatient enough. When I finally managed to get to Washington in late March, I found disaster. In conversations with Udall, and with the staffs of other members of the Arizona delegation, I heard that only ten days before, a group of fifteen comm ops, motor and rowing, had been around making their case.[8] They could not have been more reasonable, I was told, saying they favored wilderness, but just wanted motors to be continued so that the part of the public that needs them will be able to see the Canyon. The rowing operators confirmed their belief that motors should continue so that visitors would have a choice. (No surprise; if all comm ops went to rowing, the competition would be greater, destroying the comfortable little niche the rowing comm ops had.) They all favored wilderness and *maintaining the status quo*. The aides were impressed, but worse, Udall had been bamboozled. The comm ops had told him that many, if not most, environmental groups supported the idea of keeping motors! When I flat-out told him this was not true, he was surprised. Sadly, the comm ops had been effective enough that he would not promise to introduce any wilderness bill.

So we had lost our little advantage. The comm ops, building on their victory over contract extensions, had now prepared friendly ground for their arguments against a motor-free wilderness bill and CRMP. Washington environmentalists seemed to have no time to follow up on this matter.

While in Washington, I talked with the OMB person, an examiner named Stuart Sessions, who cleared Interior legislation for introduction as conforming to the President's program. Knowledgeable, he listed four areas of concern: motors, the river boundary, Reclamation's interest in a dam, and the Park lands that the Havasupai could use for traditional purposes. It was at this low point that I wrote of rarely having felt so helpless. What we needed was a heavy-duty campaign to counter our opponents' distortions, to create favor for a proposal that seemed stuck in bureaucratic depths. And this, just after urging letters about the unjustified contract extensions. The comm ops seemed to be able to build on their victories. We seemed unable to organize effective responses that used the favorable decisions we had won.

Meanwhile, back at the CRMP:
Perhaps, in that situation, bureaucratic pace and momentum were our ally. A team composed of Jensen, Martin, and Carothers (under contract), was set up in January. This group produced a very rough CRMP draft in February, which then went to the Regional Office for review.[9] As this work began, motors were to go, since the investigations had shown them to be contrary to established health and safety standards, and inconsistent with resource management. Chapman received a briefing on the draft's proposals March 10 and, on March 16, Stitt and Jensen made a presentation to the Director. The plan then contained 21 options on 7 issues and was to be presented to the public in May. The section on the impacts of excluding motors was still being worked on. The Park forecast the plan would be done in 1977 and fully implemented by 1980.

There were straws blowing about. In the March issue of a pro-Park magazine, the researchers summarized their results as strongly anti-motor: they were not safer, not more economical to operate, not preferred by those who experienced both motors and rowing, and were noisy above standards.[10] In a May deposition taken during the WPRF lawsuit (described below), Chapman mentioned various alternatives being considered for the plan and that some decisions had to be matters of judgment.[11] Still, he was not forthcoming about motors' desirability and thought small boats might not be able to carry out waste. He also thought the final EIS would be out by the end of 1978. In June, the Director replied to a congressional inquiry about the discrimination against self-guided trips by suggesting NPS favored a CRMP that would give an equal chance to travel the river to anyone who applied, whether for a commercial or self-guided trip.[12] He hoped the draft plan would be available in 4-6 weeks for public comment. Nevertheless, when Eiseman requested a copy of the draft, given the myriad rumors, he was turned down on the basis that the first draft had been rejected, and being rewritten, did not have to be disclosed since it would preclude uninhibited intra-NPS exchanges.[13]

During the river-running season, the NPS river patrol, using rowing rafts, collected information about conditions, no doubt furnishing it to the CRMP writers.[14] The post-season review made clear that the researchers' worry about conditions remained relevant. The need for a plan featuring boater education was emphasized by finding notable impacts on several beaches (Badger, Granite, Hermit, South Canyon, and lower Bass) and side canyons (Havasu, Tapeats and Deer Creeks, Elves Chasm, Saddle Canyon, and Nankoweap) from littering, trampling, and multiple trails. Again, though incredibly by this time, the point was made that rules were often violated because of ignorance. Self-guided trips were still not getting sufficient orientation. However, for the first time, interpretive rangers were traveling on some comm op trips; only one comm op would not participate. A sour note was sounded when a self-guided trip was cited for using soap in a side stream, but a comm op trip was not.

That summer was also marked because it started out with such low water releases from Glen Canyon Dam that a number of commercial trips were canceled. Eiseman and I, both suspicious, queried the Park Superintendent as to whether he would bend the rules and allow the comm ops to make up the lost trips. His reassurances were less important than our assumption that NPS was not to be trusted.[15] This skepticism might seem odd, a dissonance with our satisfaction with the NPS pro-wilderness proposals. Yet I believe it correctly pointed at our sense of insecurity about even the tiniest NPS action. And looking over the near-forty years of river management decision-making, it does seem that skepticism, distrust, anger, and bitterness are its public characteristics.

In April, the Superintendent sent out a notice that the plan was delayed, hoping it could be made public in mid-summer.[16] His excuse, that considering all the issues followed by NPS-Interior review was a lengthy process, was hardly news, and looked to us more like a cover for less nameable causes. On May 23, the plan's EIS draft was returned to the Park from Region, where Jensen and the regional NEPA overseer, Astrid Schenk, had been writing the first full draft of the EIS. (Chapter 16 reviews the drafts in detail.) That new draft was back in Washington in June. There was another revision at the Park starting in late August, and the publishable draft was back in D.C. on September 22. After last review, printing and other clearance, the EIS was ready for the public in December.

The logical question—Was the very public opposition from the comm ops bringing pressure for revisions?—is unanswerable in part because the record does not contain or describe all the versions or the changes. As far as direct pressure was concerned, Jensen says he was not lobbied by the comm ops. In any case, the May version of the plan seemed almost perversely oriented *against* comm op concerns. Given the absence of documents from early 1977 that might reflect starting positions and basic decisions, the process of draft-and-review remain murky. It may well be that as with the Research Synthesis—which was available in October 1976, used in the plan drafts in early 1977, and yet not officially released until September, when it showed up with little significant change—the CRMP+EIS draft-and-review process was not to produce a more solid document or make important changes, but to collect signatures and assuage egos. Given the lobbying position of the comm ops in March, the Park Service would have saved many months by releasing whatever it had at that time, and letting the inevitable bashing and battle get underway.

Meanwhile, back at the court:
In Chapter 11, we left the self-guided river-runner advocates pondering an appeal of a contrary ruling against the Wilderness Public Rights Fund effort by a District Court judge in San Francisco, who even ordered the WPRF to pay the government's legal costs. On the other hand, WPRF thought there was some victory because the contract extensions were used by the judge to justify ruling against WPRF since the contracts' wording said they could be canceled or changed at any time without recourse by the comm ops.[17] WPRF had asked the judge to reconsider his summary judgment and hold a trial on the issues of fact and law that were at issue. The latter declined the suggestion, and the expensive route of going to the Court of Appeals was next. WPRF reinforced its recourse to law by stressing that concession operations were only authorized *if necessary*.

Its three Directors—Munroe, Saltonstall, and Deane Hall of Colorado—had broadened the organization, enlisting the aid of several big names as an advisory committee, though they did not have to be members (WPRF had 374 in 27 states) or agree with WPRF positions. They also wanted to drop the word "private", since "non-commercial" parties were truly from the "general public". They called on those in the non-commercial sector to avoid trying to tilt the odds through multiple trip applications in order to distance themselves from the distorting image of a few individuals just trying to get river trips and to better ensure that demand would be genuine. They pledged to work for standards of safety, environmental protection, and wilderness education.

Fred Eiseman and his local allies, separate from WPRF, had been casting about for avenues of action after their fruitless meeting with Goldwater in December 1976. They considered staging a protest trip, attracting some national media program, and grabbing Representative Udall's attention. By early February, Eiseman was ready with their position, and wrote to McComb (still in Tucson).[18] The Arizona Center for Law in the Public Interest (ACLPI), a local non-profit firm, had agreed on February 1 to press a lawsuit challenging NPS's right to grant permits under the 1972 division of 92% commercial, and 8% self-guided, since non-commercial trips had a priority. They were thinking of trying to get an injunction against the February 15 lottery.

What Eiseman suggested to McComb was that those interested in the environmental aspect of the CRMP get together to formulate their own set of standards. He was worried because in the past, individuals at public meetings just offered their own pet ideas. So how about working together to decide on the essentials we want the NPS to put in its plan? Perhaps at his house? McComb agreed with the idea, but pointed out that the interested parties were scattered all over, so the mail was probably going to be necessary.[19] Eiseman, as so often, was right, but the idea never came alive. In consequence, the lack of our own alternative left us with nothing to do but promote the NPS offering. This was a strategic mistake you will see I take most blame for.

McComb had also recently learned from a staffer with Congressman Tim Wirth of Colorado that Wirth was considering a lottery system. This may have been the proposal from another group, RRAC, the River Runners Action Committee, in Denver.[20] Although the Sierra Club took no position about allocation of use, McComb personally liked the idea of everybody who wanted to go sending in an application for the season. If they were drawn in the lottery, they could travel with their own gear, contract with an outfitter for the equipment, or sign up as a commercial passenger. This would also end the system of allocating use to each comm op. Such an individual application system would bring the visitor more directly in contact with the Park Service, which could be beneficial.

The RRAC proposal wanted each application, which would include preferred launch dates, to be labeled as for a commercial passenger or otherwise, thereby continuing the allocation system, though on a seasonal basis. Anyone chosen in the lottery, would get one of their launch dates or be given the chance to select another. The RRAC thought this system fairer than fixed allocations, since it would be set based on the applications received for each season, thus reflecting demand. There would be more uncertainty for the comm ops. The commercial passenger would have a more complicated procedure than just calling a comm op and making a reservation; overall the system would be the same for everybody. Those who might be disadvantaged would be single individuals or groups of small size, since they would have to combine with other groups to make up a trip. The problem of cheating through multiple applications was admitted, with no solution being offered.

Fred's lawsuit crystallized on March 4, filed by ACLPI on behalf of the Eisemans, J. R. Hertzler, and M. St.Clair against the usual suspects—the Secretary, the Director, and the Superintendent.[21] Its claims were that dividing the public into commercial passengers and non-commercial applicants unconstitutionally created two classes of users. The laws governing NPS concessions restricted them to those that are necessary and appropriate, but in GCNP, the concessions were guaranteed 92% of the use, even though demand from self-guided users was now larger than commercial use. This guarantee denied equal access, and forced would-be users to pay a fee to concessionaires to gain entry to the Park on a river trip. They asked for an injunction against the current allocation and an order directing immediate implementation of an equal access plan.

An accompanying fund appeal noted the lawyers were free, but other costs had to be paid by the plaintiffs. Since the cause of equal access to public lands was for all who wished to enjoy outdoor recreation without the need to resort to commercial services, Eiseman et al. hoped the suit would have broad appeal.

Meanwhile, back at the Wilderness:
There were other locales of Grand Canyon wilderness activity than Washington, D.C. Wilderness workshops on Lake Mead National Recreation Area brought out a few of us in February, urging that those parts of the Canyon still in LMNRA be protected.[22] Local articles, talks, and letters trickled on; we could maintain the

impression I conveyed to the Sierra Club Grand Canyon chapter chair (when I thanked him for helping cover my expenses) that, doing our part in Arizona, we could overcome the comm op opposition to a motor-free Grand Canyon Wilderness.[23]

The effort to move a Wilderness recommendation should have been buoyed by the news, on May 23, of President Carter's Environmental Message.[24] Alaska featured large, but GCNP's wilderness was listed as one of the areas to be recommended, a proposal that "will include the Colorado River". Curiously, newspaper stories were based on comments by "an aide to" Congressman Udall. Offering information not in the message on the proposal to ban motors, he noted that Udall had no comment and that the recommendation was under study by other departments. That aide told me that as of June 5, Udall was still waiting. Anyway, with lots of Alaska action to come up, there would be no quick introduction for a Grand Canyon Wilderness.

The "other department" was quite specifically OMB examiner Sessions. This part of our tale is among the most mysterious, a puzzle only intensified by an interview I had with Sessions while writing this book.[25] I thought in 1977, which Sessions confirmed, that OMB consideration of a departmental proposal for Wilderness was usually perfunctory and short, with the legislation then being forwarded to Congress for introduction within a week or two. In the GCNP's case, NPS had done the work according to congressional dictates, and the plan was forwarded in proper form; it was included as part of the President's Environmental Message. The mystery arises as to why supposedly *pro forma* OMB review did not lead to it being forwarded to Congress by mid-1977, or in fact, ever.

The contemporary Sessions has no memory of the relevant events. He confirmed my impressions as to OMB's place in the process. He was not lacking in work, handling a range of proposals, including the budget; there were two career chiefs above him, topped by a politically appointed Program Assistant Director, Eliot Cutler. The latter was interested in park and resource issues, and so dealt with Sessions' area more. However, he was not an outdoors user or environmentalist. Sessions's family, on the other hand, was. Early in the 1970s, they had gone on a nine-day *motorized* Grand Canyon river trip, which so excited Sessions that he thought for a while about becoming a boatman. Loving the trip, he also saw it for its business potential. He liked the opportunities to go ashore, and noticed wear on the river shore. He recalled being excited by seeing rowing boats going through a rapid, but was put off when there was trouble and someone got hurt.

Sessions did not deal directly with NPS, generally; Interior's Legislative Counsel was the liaison. Thinking back, in our interview he noted that the Park Service sometimes dealt directly with friendly Representatives. Although he thought Cutler, rather than him, would have been visited by the comm ops, he did think that motors raised "tricky issues", and in our interview mentioned the "loud" noise of motors, as well as the length of the trip (though he was on one of the longer ones, which went all the way through the Canyon). Although he had no memory of the comm ops, he did remember letters being stirred up by the National Parks Conservation Association (NPCA), something unusual for OMB. In the end, he could not accept or remember the issue as being special, was surprised that the proposal sat in OMB for a couple of years, and had no explanation for this unusual outcome, this death by inattention.

But was it? We know the comm ops went to OMB. We know we did. We know, as I will relate, that OMB worked on the proposal into 1978. The latter is clear from the papers I have. What makes the mystery more frustrating is that there are no OMB records on the Grand Canyon preserved in the National Archives. All kinds of other issues get a file, thin or fat; the Grand Canyon gets zip. Yet we know OMB received letters and that Sessions wrote memos. In his interview he suggested that any papers he would have had would have been dumped when he left rather than archived. With no path to a definitive answer, I ponder the question, why was the usual course for Wilderness legislation not followed? Did the opposition, or controversy itself, cause Wilderness to be sidelined? Can we blame someone (NPS, Mo, Interior, Wilderness advocates), who might have suggested that it be held up to avoid a distracting fight?

Were this not the central issue for us, I would have spared you the above details. To get on with the story, let me offer a general summary to point up how different from the usual "week or two" was the Grand Canyon's treatment. The Grand Canyon Wilderness legislation was in OMB in March 1977 and in the presidential message in May. Sessions sent questions about it to NPS in June and got a reply a month later. Sessions sent a memo to Cutler in August. In September, NPS was expecting OMB clearance in October. In December, Sessions said he was trying to move it. January 1978, Cutler said it should go back to Interior to resolve difficult questions and, in that period, Sessions thought a bill might be ready in February. Then silence until August when an NPS official thought something might happen, but that OMB was an obstacle.

My 1977 contacts with Sessions were by phone and on paper. Since his concerns remained those four listed above, I tried to answer them in a long letter on May 27, hoping that it would help lead to as "supportable and coherent" a recommendation as possible.[26] First, I went over the successful effort to have the "entire river surface" included within GCNP, since we believed this inclusion would add to the Park's topographic and ecological integrity, and a more orderly understandable policy could be developed if the water surface were administered by one office within the Park Service.

With that goal achieved, the next step would be to place the entire river within Wilderness without motors, in line with Wilderness and Park policies, research results and public support. In this argument I stressed the need for the western end to be included to keep two-way motor traffic out, destroying the possibility of a two-day wilderness trip on the reach from Diamond Creek to the Grand Wash Cliffs. I noted the damage from casual upstream traffic. An oars-only Wilderness including the entire river would, I argued, "promote uniformity in policy, administrative actions, and public understanding." I took a hard line on the motors, calling for a ban by the end of 1978, with 1979, the last year of the contract extensions, as a possible compromise. The economics of the comm ops were such that this date would be no hardship, particularly if they saw a determined administration stand pushing the legislation along.

I also offered arguments on the Park lands used by the Havasupai for traditional purposes, citing congressional, Superintendent, and Havasupai statements saying such use posed no reason to block Wilderness status for those lands. I thought a potential Wilderness status was therefore "dumb", and that it was unnecessary for the administration to embarrass itself defending the "potential" status.

A personal note: That letter was the last item I did on the loose, for as June started, I had become a 40-hour-a-week salaryman in Pima County government. I celebrated with a long piece to other Friends of the Canyon, bringing them up-to-date after a long period of quiet on the Wilderness recommendation.[27] That may have been my illusion, of course, since if the comm ops were lobbying in D.C. in March, why would they not have been in April and/or May? So I reported that OMB was now conducting a final review of the Interior proposal, which still had "most" of the river in the Wilderness with motors out. Since there might be an administration proposal in Congress in early July, we should prepare by writing to Congressman Udall, and Arizona's other senator, DeConcini. When the proposal was firm, we could do a broader mailing; I had a list of 300 people who had commented in favor of a motor-free wilderness. My proposed call to action started by attacking the comm op proposal as "the contradictory nonsense of a motorized wilderness". I then listed and answered the pro-motor arguments (which never change; see Chapter 1 or any current piece by pro-motor groups).

More pleasing was a letter from David Brower, as President of Friends of the Earth, to Udall, recounting his just-finished rowing trip, and asking Udall to lead the fight now to see every possible acre of GCNP in Wilderness, and motors phased out.[28] Inspiring as always, and quoting Thoreau, he compared that trip with the motor trip he took with John McPhee and Floyd Dominy (see *Encounters with the Arch-Druid*) that "missed the essential drama".

Sessions had replied that he was meeting with Interior officials in mid-June, but the Interior Legislative Counsel canceled this meeting, so Sessions sent over five questions to be cleared up. He wanted to see the wilderness rationale in the CRMP and the research studies. Was the upper four miles in or out? How were the Hualapai arguments about the boundary answered? What about the Havasupai uses? And was anybody serious about reclamation projects of any kind? [29]

Whatever Sessions had heard from me and the motor-boaters, he could legitimately claim to be confused, since the Park Service was continuing to have qualms about including all the river, in particular after Everhardt was discharged in May.[30] NPS was circulating in June a handwritten version of a new position, with the four miles from the Paria junction to Navajo Bridge being dropped, as well as the Lake Mead section, from Separation Canyon down, leaving 235 miles of "free-flowing" river. (Though how Navajo Bridge impaired the flow is a study.) This dropped the acreage of the river in Wilderness from 17,000 to 11,300 acres. The verbiage was even more vexing, since it said that the public was used to motors in the Separation-down section, and they were appropriate for those not physically able to withstand the rigors of floating. These were dangerous words, since they echoed what the comm ops were claiming for the entire river.

The position was firmed internally when the new NPS Director sent to the Legislative Counsel the recommendation that the lower 35 miles of the river should be excluded, due to its different character of being "slack water".[31] The 5700 acres was excised completely, leaving 998,000 acres as Wilderness and 109,000 as potential. A note on the request for maps said "Needed earliest". There is no record of formal action.

July opened with the reappearance of John McComb, calling me from Washington with his news. He had heard that the CRMP was back in Washington, and that the Wilderness recommendation was with OMB. He thought the latter represented "other" interests, and were bastards. NPS now wanted to drop the slack water, and John was unsure about fighting that. In a later call, he reported he had located the person overseeing the CRMP in D.C. He had secured copies of the research project's technical reports, including the economic report, which appeared to be suggesting a three-year phase-out for motors. Chapman had approved the end date, but the D.C. people thought it might cause trouble in Congress. On the lower river exclusion, McComb cited a history of excluding reservoirs and said The Wilderness Society did not care. He confirmed that in February the Park Service had sent a good recommendation, but then had later changed on the lower river through a letter from the Secretary. However, there was to be a meeting with the Assistant Secretary now in charge of Parks to review Wilderness proposals, so what should we say. He also introduced a new name: Elizabeth Carr, an artist who wanted to do something helpful in Washington.

I replied on July 24 with two pages of arguments, starting with the case for getting an end date for motors in the legislative history of a Wilderness bill, so the Park Service will be on the record.[32] My suspicions were high, and I wanted the Park Service to have a deadline that came soon. I then argued the case for the lower river. Given that the entire river is affected by the upstream dam's operation, Lake Mead's intrusion is no argument for exclusion. The type of motor traffic that comes upstream is also detrimental, even more so as it is a show-off place for speedboats. I suggested the upstream users do more damage, and may have set a fire in Rampart Cave, an important paleontologic site. Also, a river trip from Diamond down could be a short wilderness introduction. Barring upstream motors seemed to me to be similar to the arguments for closing dirt tracks that intruded into land wilderness. Strategically, I argued for maintaining the maximum position, since if there were hints we were willing to drop land, no one else would make the argument. Finally, I did not want people in Washington, like him, with their access, and people out in the country, like me, to get awry of each other. Meanwhile, I obtained the support of Dave Foreman, The Wilderness Society's regional representative.

When next I checked with Sessions, he had received Interior's answers to his questions.[33] He thought the position on the Havasupai uses was "nonsensical", and had to be further considered. Interior stuck by its position that the Hualapai boundary was on the south shore, so the entire river surface was in the Park. It also wanted removal of the reclamation provision (don't ask). He had heard about excluding the "flat water", but no letter had arrived yet. He had also received a copy of the research synthesis, though it was still not public. Yes, he said, OMB had been getting calls from the comm ops, naming Burke and Sparks of Fort Lee Company, who were repeating that motors provided people with a choice. I said that according to the research, choice comes from other quality-of-trip factors, and not motors, that is, the choice motors give is only for faster travel, which is an anti-wilderness, anti-Park choice.

I reported all this to McComb, and wondered if it was possible to prevent the letter recommending the exclusion from being sent. McComb said Liz Carr had obtained a complete set of the research program's technical reports, and would be passing them on to the regional representative soon. He also sent a memo to an aide of the Assistant Secretary setting forth the arguments for starting the motor phase-out immediately, as an administrative decision, in order for the comm ops to have time to prepare and so that all can see that this is a done deal, instead of waiting for Congress to act.[34] He noted the debate was really over, since the CRMP was based on the elimination of motors. So it might be best to implement the phase-out upon release of the EIS.

And now, a little light entertainment:

In May, one of my Tucson conservation organization supporters, AWWW (A triple-W to us), had published an article of mine, "Shall motors be continued in a Grand Canyon Wilderness?" This prompted a letter to me from a comm op, Ted Hatch, who had one of the largest allocations. I replied, and we had a lively exchange of four letters over the next two months.[35] He regretted that many of my statements were untrue, and that I should take another look at my moral approach, since sincere, honest statements would help my position. He said that river-runners "do not always exploit" the Grand Canyon; they provide a much needed service, take the utmost care of the Park, and their presence can be very beneficial. It was also unfair to say one river-runner favors a dam when 99% do not; that is really slanting the truth.

I of course challenged him to list any untrue statements. I charged that Burke, the pro-dam comm op (though he had not been the only one to favor dams in the past), was his friend, ally, and responsibility. I claimed my approach was to work with everybody, while the comm ops waged a campaign against Wilderness. I called them anti-Park, anti-Wilderness, anti-Canyon, anti-people exploiters, and said that when they were ready to repudiate helicopters and boat motors, they could talk about morality.

He thanked me, pleased that I asked him to be specific. He noted Burke was not his responsibility, and had every right to speak his mind. The comm ops were not waging a campaign, but supplying a needed service. He tossed in that backpackers do much more harm by leaving garbage and trails. He said the comm ops were not anti-Park and do not wish to destroy it or its Wilderness areas. Helicopters helped get people off the river quickly, which was better than using mules with their feces and stench. Mules have become such a problem, he asserted, NPS is planning to shoot them. And if I wanted to have him elaborate on my other untrue statements, please let him know. P.S. Where was I during their last clean-up trip?

I noted he still pointed out nothing untrue in my article. I then described Burke as a spokesman for comm ops, who visits Congress, and has never been disavowed by any comm op that I knew of. Nor did I know of any statements by comm ops opposing dams in the Grand Canyon. I noted that 15 comm ops visited several congressional offices in their pro-motor campaign. As far as their services being needed, I admitted that a few thousand wealthy people each year were able to afford the luxury of a Canyon trip. He had accused backpackers; I asked for proof, saying that the river research had shown irreversible environmental degradation from river use patterns.

I argued that helicopters are banned from the Park except for emergencies, so evading that rule by landing on Hualapai land was anti-Park. They use motors, so motor-boaters are anti-wilderness. One of the great Canyon attributes is its quiet and serenity, so any motor operator is anti-Canyon and anti-people. Anyway, who said getting people off the river quickly is something to praise? It is just another gimmick to squeeze more dollars out of your allocation. I noted several ways to leave the Canyon aside from mules and helicopters: walking, driving out at Diamond or from Lake Mead. Then I caught him, since it was feral burros the Park wanted to shoot, not the sterile mules. My P.S. was that if comm ops had followed the guidelines we had been urging for ten years, clean-up trips would be unnecessary.

Hatch said Burke is not a spokesman for all the comm ops. Backpackers leave trails, and river-runners do not when they travel on the water. If it were true that landing helicopters on Indian land were evading NPS rules, then NPS would not allow a helicopter to land. (I did not say so, but that possibility was explored, you may remember, and the lawyers said no.) They did not use helicopters to get more days out of their quota, since they did not fill their quota in 1976 and probably would not in 1977. He agreed he had been wrong about calling burros mules. He concluded by saying that when I stop driving a car and start walking to work, I could tell him to stop running motors in his work. He could move 15 persons on his raft while I used my big engine to move 5 or 6. P.S. It will take over an hour or two of work to get the false newspaper statements to me.

So I said, O.K. Burke is not your spokesperson just because he is always mouthing off in public about how you want things. Then how about a public statement by the comm ops opposing any dams? I agreed walking damages the fragile soils, and there was research to show the damage river-runners do. Where is your evidence on hikers? I do not disagree; I just want to see you prove it. I do not understand your stand on helicopters; you seem to agree you evade the NPS rule by landing on Hualapai land. I said I was sorry he had not filled his quota, and maybe he should run rowing trips so conservationists will love him again (he was the comm op dropped by the Sierra Club several years before when the motor controversy got hot). I asked him to agree helicopters were not needed except for emergencies. Finally, I told him he had guessed wrong; I bicycled to work. I gave up my work motor; how about him giving up his?

He said he was quite enjoying himself. He pointed out that he was sure I benefited from motors in travel, eating, etc. He pointed to the damage in Havasu done by hikers, who have really torn that area apart, with cans scattered all through the area. He complained that yes there was damage by all, but comm ops seem to get most of the blame. He still did not understand why landing on Indian land was evading NPS rules. And he was surprised that our approach to preserving the Canyon was through rowing, since the only way, according to extreme conservationists, is to keep people completely out. So what was I really pushing toward?

My reply was short: I understand you and your arguments. Everything boils down to this: Are we going to get motors off the river? If we can work that out, much else will fall into place.

No reply.

Meanwhile, back at the CRMP:
During the summer of 1977, I tried to short-circuit my frustration over the NPS not releasing research information. In particular, knowing something of the economic study results, I wrote the author, C. R. Michael Parent, in order to check out whether I was off-base in my arguments. I had heard and talked with him at the 1976 research symposium, and hoped he might be helpful.[36]

I asked for his comments on four statements. Conversion to oars would not economically disrupt the river industry or any particular comm op (the largest comm op had said just this in 1972). The cost of equivalent-length trips for motors and oars was the same, i.e., for a given amount of money, a rowing trip gives a better time value. If motors are not prohibited, there will be more shorter (including more part-trips), bigger trips by fewer companies (another large comm op, who preferred rowing, chose in 1971 to go where the money is, concentrating on motors), and more helicopter use. Comm ops could convert in two years or less, and even save money by selling their motor equipment.

In his reply, Parent agreed conversion would not be an economic hardship, BUT only assuming an average of three years, due to the different arrangements in each company, along with the influence of banks and tax considerations. He agreed that there was no difference in the overall average cost-per-day between all rowing and motor trips. Moreover, a substantial range existed between the cheapest and dearest motor and rowing trips, leading him to conclude that price and profit both are a function of management, not trip length, boat type, motor/oars, etc. This was healthy, indicating firms were satisfying a variety of consumer needs. He thought perceived trip quality correlated well with profitability, but the data were *very* incomplete. What he thought ridiculous was to have exactly similar trips, whether a big one (there were no economies of scale for river trips) or several small ones. This was nothing to do with the river, but a large economic reality of mediocrity resulting from a lack of variety. He ended by cautioning me that he wanted to stay in a neutral position capable of responding to all sides, so I should not think of his remarks as an endorsement.

I was surprised and displeased at the three-year conversion figure, so I wrote back, arguing that the comm ops had had plenty of notice, and if they had continued spending money on the assumption motors were forever, that was their problem. The answer would be a conversion plan for each comm op that would be as rapid as possible. (This is a good example of how the animus generated in controversy can cloud tactical judgment. The goal of a congressionally designated motor-free Wilderness was not a matter of one or two or even five years; the goal should have been an unchangeable fixed date by which the conversion would be complete.) I restated my understanding about trip quality: good, enjoyable trips are a function of good management. I also tried to transfer some of my frustration by wondering why the "scandalous" NPS behavior in suppressing research results did not upset the researchers.

Parent replied about the three-year average by saying he had found a range of one to seven years. He thought there could be rewards for those who accelerate the conversion. He also implied that the plan could actually reach the Supreme Court with all the potential conflicts between laws governing the Park System and businesses. His informed opinion remained that 95-100% of motors could have been eliminated by 1980 if the decision had been final before the 1977 season. However, he had not recommended going to rowing; the economic data did not justify one trip over another.

He defended the Park Service, suggesting some of the delays were caused by researchers who were asked to review NPS interpretations of the research. And of course, responding to questions from interested individuals slowed things down. "In your haste to get a policy adopted, I would recommend that you exercise caution not to 'snatch defeat from the jaws of victory' by making unreasonable requests." He softened this hard truth with a handwritten note that I and others had heightened his appreciation of the Canyon environment, and that he enjoyed the personalities and shared the concerns of those who have taken up the Canyon's cause. Older, if no more prescient, I can see the excellence of Parent's advice; yet as with the question of whether the Lake-Mead-influenced part of the river should be in Wilderness or not, it was advice I could not, would not, take, and felt compelled to argue down.

In my reply, I did say that I feared I had fallen into hectoring, but in my view the comm ops had had innumerable chances to show good faith, and instead had blocked progress in river management. So I reviewed the history of the six-year effort to have an NPS recommendation for a motor-free Wilderness including the river. I then drew a horrific projection of what an unbridled river industry would have done. Then I threw up a whole bunch of questions about his assumptions that led to the phase-out. I argued that "we are long past the time when an economist could do a calculation while ignoring non-economic factors". I rejected his defense of the Park Service, saying I knew the difference between an agency that drags its feet, and one that does its job on time. Worse, NPS had no trouble rushing through the contract extensions, ignoring the research, and putting out a laughable excuse for an environmental assessment. And how come the researchers were not consulted about that? My tirade against the Park Service continued: It could have done its job on time, and did not. There had been court suits; there would be more. Due to NPS dilatoriness, this would all happen later, and the comm ops will be able to convince economic researchers they need until 1983, or 1988, or ... (I can add now, 2006, or 2010, or ...). "I am as rigid as the comm ops: I cannot see handing the Grand Canyon, its visitors, or any of its many environments, over to people who think only of the large crowd, the quick trip, and the fast buck."

It took a month to write that letter; time does not necessarily weaken intemperance. There was no reply. Justifiably. Or not? How dare I now tut-tut at that younger self, a figure dashing about with lance and sword, ready to duel anyone offering less frenetic counsel, seeking to come to grips with opponents amorphous and slippery, in an arena where clarity and definitive action were watchwords drowned in a miasma of obscurity and frustration? What better course could I suggest, even from this vantage?

In mid-summer, I also expressed my impatience by writing the Secretary of the Interior twice, complaining about the slowness of the Park Service in making public the research summary and the CRMP itself.[37] Given the environmental degradation taking place, I wanted something done.

Meanwhile, back in the court:

Eiseman kept us all well informed about their case.[38] In mid-May, they prepared to depose Chapman to elicit the information that the research and the plan were not set up to answer the Eiseman et al. objections. Eiseman had heard rumors about the plan that strengthened this view. His suit aimed at equal access, not more access; not a matter of numbers but of a single process applied to all. The government had moved for a summary judgment, but the judge said Chapman's deposition had to be taken first.

Fred summarized Chapman's testimony on May 20 as showing there was no need to wait for the plan, since no research addressed the concerns of their suit. So on June 22, the Center filed a motion for summary judgment since the deposition established that there were no disputed facts. The government opposed the injunction because it needed the time to finish up the research and the plan, even though Chapman's testimony had helped show the research was done a year ago and none was aimed at Eiseman's issues. Chapman also admitted that a lottery system where everyone applies for a permit was feasible. He also admitted that the Administrative Procedures Act was violated in 1972 since hearings were not held on the Reed decision.

However, once again, judges were of no help to complainants against the government. As reported by the Center on July 18, the judge held the Administrative Procedure Act did not apply, that the Secretary had broad discretion over Parks and concessions, and that there was no violation of the Fifth Amendment in setting up two classes of river-runners. The lawyers were thinking about an appeal.

During this period, the River Runners Action Committee—which shared personnel with the American Canoe Association and the American Whitewater Affiliation—circulated a newsletter, written out of Denver by Randy Frank of Salt Lake City, Ben Harding, Eric Leaper of Denver, and others.[39] Frank described his experience of applying for a permit, then after not winning a place in the drawing, calling several comm ops, quickly finding space on five different trips, none of which interested him since they involved a chunk of money to sit on a motorized boat being "guided" for six days.

The newsletter, although in rhetoric aimed at the general problem of concessionaire dominance of wild river-running in the U.S., had only the Grand Canyon as its substance. (Although other groups concerned with non-Grand-Canyon aspects of river-running certainly existed, their efforts do not show up in the record yet; nor does it show what cooperation there might have been among the three self-guided efforts I am writing about.) The RRAC did report that the congressional effort in 1976 by Wirth and others had died a quiet death, but that he had reintroduced his resolution as House Concurrent Resolution 181. The newsletter reprinted RRAC's proposal for an equal-access lottery. Although there was a review of the first phase of the WPRF case, nothing was said about the Arizona case, another indication that Eiseman's suggestion about working together had found no takers. Indeed, the news in the newsletter was often months after the event, indicating both a lack of coordination, and quite possibly of time and money, too.

Meanwhile, back at the court:

Well, not quite yet. Since neither time nor a job allayed my frustration at Park Service inaction on the environmental impacts from river use, I wrote Tony Ruckel in mid-June about reviving the matter.[40] There were six arguments for reconsideration of some sort of complaint or suit. The research report was still not released. NPS had announced delay in the CRMP and, anyway, unless forced, NPS would not order the comm ops to change before the contract extensions ran out in 1979. Chapman's deposition in the self-guided case implied trouble as far as small boats and waste disposal were concerned. A newspaper article had leaked information about the intent of the plan. So at one and the same time, NPS was saying disclosure is bad, yet information detrimental to a good plan was appearing. From what I had heard about the plan, changes in the plan are not likely to be for the better. In summary, the Park Service knows there are environmental problems, and its not acting on them is a major negative action adversely affecting the environment. (By the way, looking back, it is still not clear why GCNP staff did not issue regulations to handle at least some of the researchers' findings in the winter of 1976-7. Even today, I can sympathize with my frustration then at what seems like a dereliction of duty.)

I received a call from the local Sierra Club representative raising the question of whether a suit would delay the Wilderness proposal. My answer was clear: The actual damage taking place was the more immediate problem, and as my letters to various officials showed, there seemed to be no interest in taking action.

On August 19, Ruckel sent a letter to the Special Assistant for the Assistant Secretary in charge of Parks.[41] He enclosed the October 1976 draft of the Research Synthesis, and reviewed Sierra Club concerns: putting the river in Wilderness, removing motors, use levels and allocations, and maintaining the riparian environment. The allocation question was the subject of separate litigation with the Park Service position being sustained, so the Club is not raising that issue. What the Club was worried about was that the wilderness review and the CRMP were bogged down. He then listed some of the environmental problems that had been ignored in the contract extension process. Although the Club liked much of what was happening in the new administration, the Grand Canyon has been ignored. So we are going to make a decision about litigation in the next week or two in order to try to affect the 1978 river-running season. The Club, as an enthusiastic supporter of river-running, is not interested in stopping river activity, but to work for a settlement of such issues as would "secure adequate safeguards for the protection of the Grand Canyon during the 1978 and 1979 seasons". Tony looked forward to a meeting with the Assistant Secretary shortly.

Over the next two weeks, Ruckel produced, and I reviewed, a draft of a complaint, while the Club bureaucracy prepared a resolution for an Executive Committee meeting on September 10.[42] I had only a few strengthening comments and was full of praise for his "excellent presentation of the case". I did review events to the effect that GCNP and Regional officials had to have known of the research results. Still troubled, I tried to suggest why the Club, likewise, had not acted when the contract extensions were being considered. I did not convince myself. The resolution called for a lawsuit first because the contract extensions violated NEPA, given the research findings. More important, the Park Service was failing to fulfill its responsibility as trustee for and guardian of the Grand Canyon. Since we were contending that the Canyon within the Park was therefore being damaged, Tony felt it was appropriate to add the Park as a plaintiff. This might seem audacious, but the Supreme Court had recently established that individuals and groups had standing to sue on behalf of the environment. So when the complaint was filed two weeks later in Arizona, Ruckel joined together the Sierra Club and the Grand Canyon National Park to sue the usual suspects, Superintendent to Secretary, as well as the concessionaires.[43] The Club chose Gil Venable of Phoenix to be its local attorney.

What was crucial in the complaint was that the Park Service was not protecting the Grand Canyon National Park in that NPS employees had known about the research findings of environmental degradation, and had ignored them in extending the contracts without also issuing regulations to stem the degradation. The specifics came from the research findings. At the top of the list, disposal of human fecal waste using the method of burying porta-potty contents left residues and possibly posed a health hazard. Driftwood was disappearing, while ash and charcoal remnants from fires were getting into the beaches. Uncontrolled foot traffic was erosive and hurt vegetation and animal habitat.

Concentrated camping was causing degradation of the popular sites. Regulations on litter and waste disposal were not being followed. Motors endangered health and safety, while congestion and motor noise interfered with public enjoyment. That the comm ops were added to the case was a riposte to their claim that they were the good guys, with their clean-up trips. The case aimed at them as part of the problem. Since many of them had heard the research results in 1976, they should have had even more incentive to follow existing regulations and, if they were responsible users interested in protecting the Canyon, to push for stricter standards. Nevertheless, the complaint was largely directed at the government for not doing its duty under the National Park System Act and its own policies, as a trustee of the Park for the public, in its capacity as a contractor with concessions, and as a federal agency subject to NEPA. The relief sought was to declare the contracts unlawful, and to adopt regulations to mitigate the negative impacts in 1978 and 1979. We also wanted a river management plan and an EIS.

Meanwhile, back at the Wilderness:
In late August, several local conservationists met with Senator DeConcini, each having a few minutes to discuss their topic: BLM, Alaska, mining, etc., and of course the Grand Canyon.[44] I started by recalling our previous meetings in December 1976 and March 1977. We like what the administration was doing,

including banning motors, a proposal that has had public support for over ten years. The plan was based on research, and included transition measures. So we were looking for congressional support, first and foremost from the Arizona delegation. He replied that he was still favorable to our views, wanted a list of our points, and would consider introducing a Wilderness bill. At this point, he was friendly toward banning motors, but did not seem completely solid, being more worried about use, numbers, and impacts.

At OMB, the summer doldrums would be replaced by budget matters from September on, according to Sessions.[45] He had sent his memo to Cutler accepting most of the NPS recommendation. However, banning motors was controversial and perhaps should not be accepted. My conclusion from this talk was that there might be even more delay, a month or longer.

The D.C. NPS office dealing with Wilderness still thought OMB was almost done, and would clear the proposal "well before" the due date of November 1.[46] This would get it to Congress by December 15. He had heard that the OMB examiner had to discuss river policy with his supervisors and would do so about September 12. McComb, however, was less generous, saying that OMB's basic position was hostile on environmental matters. In his talks there, he had found trouble from staff held over from Republican years, talking about the free enterprise system, etc. Further, he thought Sessions's boss, Eliot Cutler, was a turkey.

At this point, I could not decide whether the motor controversy was felt by OMB to be real, or whether Sessions was just tuned to the comm ops' wavelength.[47] His report to Cutler had taken six months of mulling. Now he told me what the next steps were, indicating they normally took only several days, although if there were a decision to challenge Interior, then there would be more meetings, and staffers would have to work something out. Sessions kept asking whether OMB should get involved in changing Interior policy, as if it were a philosophical question. In any case, on banning motors, he was making no recommendation, just setting forth the comm op claim that the ban would reduce options, and ours that it would preserve quality. On the Havasupai lands, he saw the case for putting them into the Wilderness immediately. None of the NPS memos of the time, however, indicate that OMB ever formally raised these questions. Nor did NPS seem to press OMB. What could have caused Sessions and his boss(es) to hang on to a proposal when their practice was to move such a thing along?

I also spent a bit of time in Washington. A DeConcini aide told me Goldwater was now on the comm ops' side. He thought that going through faster was a matter of values, and it would be absolutely necessary for there to be pro-Wilderness mail. My visit to Goldwater's office did indeed find a candid staffer who was not convinced by our arguments. He agreed with Congressman Stump who was claiming motors allowed some to go who otherwise would not go because the trip was too long. He rejected the idea that there was a "right kind of trip". My visits to other offices just raised questions; there were no commitments.

Later that month, I talked again with Sessions, and this time he was more forthright about his acceptance of the comm ops position, citing the motor ban's controversial nature, the length and expense of rowing trips, safety issues being unclear, whether older folks got less wet and were more comfortable on motor rafts.[48] He pushed Burke's line of limiting trip size and speed (though I noted Burke's ideas were rejected by most motor comm ops), and admitted he had received letters from passengers of another comm op. The question of the lower river was up in the air; he still had no formal request from Interior for a change.

I even tried a letter to this Cutler fellow, summarizing the ten-year history, noting the lobbying, and urging him to let the Interior proposal go on through.[49] He replied—it was now November—that indeed they had been contacted by both sides, hopefully had a balanced view, and their review would be completed "very" soon.

So am I being unfair? There is no OMB paper record I could find. Sessions's memory today of those events is clean of any bias or foot-dragging on his part; he has no explanation for the "unusual" action of not sending the Grand Canyon Wilderness proposal to Congress in a timely manner. Yet all my notes from the time indicate that OMB sat on the proposal for a year, and that Sessions was likely sympathetic with the motorizers' arguments from the start and ended up embracing them. May we conclude then that the reason the Grand Canyon Wilderness never reached Congress was that an OMB staffer, with no reversal from his supervisors, ignored usual OMB practice and the Park Service/Interior decision, rejected our position, accepted that the comm ops were right, and stifled Grand Canyon Wilderness legislation?

Meanwhile, back at the CRMP:

In September I inquired of Stitt about the agenda for the upcoming comm op meeting. I had heard that some trips were not carrying out all fecal matter using the new method of waterproof ammunition boxes, and asked what his staff thought of the method.[50] (Indeed, Jensen told me later some of the comm ops told their employees they would be fired if they used the method.[51]) In his reply, Stitt called the rocket-box method "highly successful".[52] He had not made it mandatory but was sure that all river users would adopt it because it "is a better, non-polluting, easier to handle, more economical, cleaner, and compact package" than any other tried. (And only nine years since that June 1968 meeting when I provoked laughter for urging the Park and the comm ops to come up with a way to carry it all out.) He was telling everybody about it.

Stitt enclosed an article by Carothers, who had led the team of investigators that, under a Colorado River Research Program contract, had developed the method.[53] The latter claimed that though fecal removal was one of the most significant environmental and esthetic problems for river-runners, it was one of the easiest problems to fix. (Too bad it took a decade and more of in-the-rocks/sand, pit toilets, portable toilets and polluting chemicals.) He noted that out of the 400 campable beaches, fewer than 100 received 75% of the use. There could be up to 150 burials a season on the most heavily used areas, with an average of 40. This might not be so bad if the river still had its natural purging capacity, and floods could wash everything further downstream. (I wonder at this; depending on a flood next spring to wash your leavings down to the next beach or two does not deal with what would have to be put up with all summer and fall.) The burial method was not only unpleasant—previous trips had already made their deposit—it had the potential to spread disease if the burial crew were not very careful about cleanliness.

The new method used surplus ammo cans, "rocket boxes"—waterproof rectangular steel cans—into which heavy-duty plastic bags were put, and onto which a toilet seat was fitted when set up at day stops and camp. A disinfectant was used, and after each stop, the bag was tied off to keep air out. The number of boxes for average sized trips was small, four to six. Even the initial cost was low. At the end of the trip, the bags were taken to a landfill. Carothers stressed how important were the example and instructions given by trip leaders and other experienced river party members; it may have been environmental education at its most basic, but when properly presented as a beach-friendly method, everyone could understand it as both environmentally and personally healthy.

Meanwhile...

1977 was a tough juggling act. So we will pause for an interlude, a little play with dialogue from real life.

CHAPTER 14

1977: October 7, A Play. Farce Or Melodrama?

We are about to have a closer look at a group that is central in this account, but rarely present front and center. On October 7, 1977, the GCNP staff held its annual river industry meeting with the comm ops. The get-together was still an "open" meeting, and I was still attending (the meetings are now secret). Given 1977's tempo and pressure of events, at this one, I decided to more closely record each speaker's comments, writing down at least a paraphrase. The dialogue was only two-sided, for there was a tacit understanding that this was the comm ops' meeting, and my two cents were not welcome (my tongue ended up with many tooth-marks). This "transcript" by a biased observer is tidied up only to read more smoothly, not to change the speaker's meaning—the reality is too delicious. I wanted to get down what the comm ops and NPS people really sounded like. Any comments of mine are inside [ ]. Each speaker is identified the first time he or she appears, with **NPS** in **bold**, afterwards only by initials. There is a space when the topic switches.

Test question: What if I had not been present?

Bruce Shaw [GCNP Deputy Superintendent]:
Meeting open at 8:40 a.m. The CRMP and its EIS are going to the printer shortly; then two more months before public distribution.

Martin Litton [former great conservationist; turned small business man operating a small-allocation rowing company]:
The Sierra Club has no more continuity. [He was talking about the suit described at the end of Chapter 13.] I told Tony Ruckel [Sierra Club lawyer] his charges were not right, and he sheepishly said, "I don't know what to do then." We really need a kitty for a legal defense fund; Western and Tour West [the two comm ops who were defendants in our suit] were picked out of a hat. If they [the Club] win, we would all be impacted.
Marv Jensen [GCNP River Manager]:
Their timing was interesting. Why did they wait until now? Maybe their motive is publicity. I'm suspicious that it is something more than interest in the Canyon.

Tour West [I do not know who; one of the faster motorizers; mid-size.]:
We got picked because NPS made us incorporate in Arizona.
MJ: They picked a random two.
TW: They are suing all 21 outfits. So if we lose, all 21 lose.
MJ: It would not be a big deal to lose. We would have to comply with some changes.
ML: Sierra Club still uses comm ops.
MJ: We will be putting together answers to their charges, so if you have ideas, let me know.
ML: Grand Canyon trips make money.
Vladimir Kovalik [small rowing comm op]:
I want to run more trips. I have received letters from conservationists against the suit. I'm disgusted at it.
BS: I want to stress this is a class action.
MJ: The private suits were decided in favor of NPS, and both have been appealed.

MJ: [On Glen Canyon Dam operation] We have no idea on future operations. Low levels were held longer to allow study of fish. It's your duty to provide input to Bureau of Reclamation studies.
On the CRMP, I noticed your clientele were absent at previous public meetings. It is up to you to let them know, since we do not deal with them directly.
ML: Shall we provide lists?
MJ: You know who the interested ones are. We will use their letters if they say more than that they had a good trip. We will consider them on the pro-oars, anti-oars matter. We will put their names on our list if they ask; maybe suggest it in your brochures.

BS: The Wilderness plan is awaiting transmittal
Fred Burke [Small motor-boater; big motor lobbyist; right-wing Republican; pro-dam]:
Is the CRMP contingent on Wilderness? If there is an exception allowing 20 hp motors, could the CRMP nullify that? [This was *his* lobbying line in Washington; other comm ops did not agree.]
BS: It's a one-way street. If Congress approves Wilderness, then there is no recourse for motors. If the river is out of Wilderness, then we would have an option.
FB: If the legislative intent for motors is stated, then NPS won't go against that. I disagree with the study that says we could convert and make a profit. We keep hanging, and wasting energy fighting the battle. [!]
ML: There is precedent for motors in Wilderness. Legislation could spell out allowing motors. The Western River Guides Association has passed our resolution for options of propulsion.
BS: The choice belongs to Congress. If a phase-out is specified, we could allow it, but if no specific exception, then no motors.
FB: I found considerable sentiment for 20-hp motors being left in. I will tell you whom to contact. [The comm ops opposed any change from the 55-hp maximum; it remains today.]

ML: If the river is not Wilderness, then NPS still could take motors out.

FB: So let's get together and push for 20-hp exception. There are a lot of concessions we could make, which we haven't. OMB is looking with an open mind. I'm already set up to testify, and I will fight to my last dying day. This is a choice for people. [Burke always talked about concessions and compromises, but only as a smoke screen. For instance, he claimed they were going to change to quiet motors. That did not happen until twenty years later—after Fred died, and then only as a political counter to renewed advocacy for Wilderness in the late 1990s.]

Mike Zimmerling [NPS Regional office; in charge of getting decent audits from the comm ops. He had showed up at the October 1976 meeting described in Chapter 11]:

I met with some of you and your CPA's in June, but received no letters with suggestions. I have drafted a policy for river-runners *only* [his emphasis] to make a report on overall operations, instead of having to break out GCNP operations. We also want to change the franchise fee, basing it on user-days, not just gross. I also tried to get the lower limit on gross raised, but Interior said no. So the consolidated report procedure is now in effect retroactive to two months ago for any reports still outstanding. I will get this new form to you today, though I'm sure it's illegal to do it this way. I'm only interested in the franchise fee and overall income. I drafted the letter on franchise fees for the Regional Director, orchestrating agreement. [My notes read: just a lobbyist for the operators.]

ML: We are operating below cost now. A franchise fee will keep the trip cost up.

FB: I have a net of $25,000 and a CPA costs $2,500. I'm not making fantastic profits.

MZ: I need your help in pushing to raise the lower limit. Write me a letter.

[Other than Litton and Burke, no one admitted to being above the limit on gross, but **MZ** said there were five, and four were close.]

John Cross [Mid-size motorizer. One of the first comm ops, but not a very public figure. Absorbed eventually by Arizona River Runners, the company Burke founded]:

We are going to be forced into bankruptcy with all the controls.

MZ: I admit giving out this new policy is at least unethical, but we do try to help. Maybe my reward for hassling the Washington office on the policy will be I can get some of you to take me down the river.

BS: This is *not* a *closed* meeting. So there are people here who are interested public, and we were just joined by a group of students.

Roy Johnson [Biologist. Director of the GCNP Research Program]:

Here are copies of the Synthesis. I just received it. There is also an article in *Downriver* magazine. The monitoring program is underway, and there will be annual reports, though the data are not in for this year. We are looking at total distribution of visitor use, doing surveys pre-, during, and post-season. We are focussing on sand size, making of trails, charcoal and other debris. We want to find out what the ability of the system is to clean itself. [Someone asked about the debris already there.] We have a baseline, and are checking changes against that. We can see, over the past 3-4 years, that some heavily used beaches are being washed away.

ML: The beaches are the result of human activity. Before white man came, there wasn't as much mud. The Colorado used to run clean, but we messed up the country. Since we created the beaches, it doesn't matter what happens to them.

FB: I feel there should be further study on motors vs. oars. HERS didn't get into it with depth. The answer for rowing was pre-determined first. The combination motor-oar trip was too fast and crowded. Why not slow down and cut size of trip and motors? All our people say they are satisfied.

RJ: HERS agrees with that; everybody does; no one argues about that. The question is what are the better ways?

FB: Why motors? Because that's the way we are operating; it's smooth. I feel you and some researchers are biased.

TW: The guy on the noise study was so obviously pre-biased. He didn't use any of the pro-motors study.

ML: Any rowing person would laugh at the idea of harm from noise; it's louder outside.

TW: They could have doctored the data.

RJ: Several of us checked the studies.

[There then followed an argument on bias among FB, TW, and RJ]

MJ: How about if we have a day where the researchers and you all get together to review the research so you can talk about the problems and your opinions?

[7-8 comm ops said they were willing.]

Georgie White [Originator of the commercial motor-raft trip and helicopter exchange below Lava Falls; small allocation. Usually in the background]:
Actually, many prefer smaller boats to increase sociability. I've been doing motors since 1955, and my hearing and health are O.K.

JC: The economic study all goes in one direction. I'm not interested in having this crock dished out. [He continued to rant and rave.] Some private parties caused the severe problems, and sometimes the boatmen. Other people know about the management plan and I don't, so I complained to Johnson.

MJ and RJ: Let's have a day to discuss research at the river management plan meeting. RJ: We did have informed input from boatmen.

[At this point, I did speak up to ask for a similar meeting with public organizations, and MJ said there would be. As detailed in Chapter 12, there had been a day of presentation and discussion on the research in October 1976, at which at least some of the comm ops were present.]

MJ: As Bruce said, the EIS is close to being done; may be sent out in mid-November, with meetings after turn of the year.

[A presentation on the burros was next: They were well fed and healthy. They didn't strip the range, but did terrace the slopes with their trails. ML said they were as unnatural as a jeep, whether they did damage or not.]

MJ: There has been controversy over the transfers of permits and user-days. We have now decided to make decisions on a case-by-case basis. If there is a public benefit, then we will O.K. the transfer. We won't approve splitting an allocation, since that looks like a sale of user-days, which is illegal. We have allowed a change of owners for Harris and ARTA, though that was to the actual operators.

Ken Sleight [Wilderness friend. Small allocation]:
You have to take our need for economic base into account.

MJ: User-days belong to the government.

TW: What makes a user-day valuable is all the people who have worked to make the trip safe and popular. It's the outfitters who have made it valuable. It's not a gift of NPS.

ML: We are at the whim of changes in NPS. We could be wiped out on a trivial basis.

BS: That is the trouble; there is no real stake, but that is true even for rim concessions.

MJ: Subletting of user-days was increasingly a problem this year. We generally discourage it, but companies are getting around it, saying boatmen from one company work for another. So, if you cannot use your days, tell us so we can make use of them. [In response to FB pressing:] You cannot sublet user-days, but people are getting around the regulation. There is one company who, in spite of our writing them, has sold user-days three years in a row.

FB: I know of someone who bought days.

BS: There were some for sale in a store in Salt Lake City.

ML: I heard of another example.

Ted Hatch [Largest motor comm op. Another original river company]:
I had 24 boats on the river. So I wanted to allow Resnick [a would-be comm op] some, but I was told NO.

MJ: The trip has to be in the brochure as a scheduled trip, with Resnick as an employee.

TH: There is a travel agent problem; they sub-contract, but don't run the trip.

Carol Burke [Fred's wife]: The CRMP draft raises the quota.

FB: The information about the CRMP is from rumors in Flagstaff running through the boatpeople.

MJ: On your training trips [where comm op employees get to run the river on their own, supposedly to train new employees], you should pay closer attention; there was one trip organized by boatmen and the comm op didn't know about it. [The chiding was gentle.]
The drowning at Lava Falls was someone thrown out of a boat. Someone combining two bad life jackets as one.

FB: We do that.

MJ: It may seem ok, but there is a liability problem, and it's against the law.

FB: I think it should be allowed; otherwise it is a waste of resources.

MJ: I would work with you on using recycled jackets. The drowning on the Sanderson boat was just one of those things, but the straps were missing from the jackets.

Steve Martin [GCNP river ranger]:
It's impossible for the boatmen to constantly check them.

John Thomas [another GCNP river ranger]:
Because of complaints by Burke and Cross, we flew along the river in the helicopter
to find naked people with no lifejackets.
FB: All the private trips are naked. My passengers object. We checked their camp.
We fished one out of the water nearly drowned. I'm not against private trips, but
they're really loose. And, anyway, private trips are really commercial trips.
JC: I've got lots to say about these commercial private trips. It's a tragedy.
MJ: We keep a file of complaints by one river party against another, and what
follow-up action there is. We have the solicitor working on the problem of multiple
applications and quasi-commercial trips.

MJ: On patrols, we ran them from 4-14 days, including hiking time. The main
problem was boatmen who don't know the regulations. Please try harder.
TH: Some of the inspections are quite critical. Now Coconino Health Department
is going on some trips, too. Maybe you are trying to do too much. The inspections
are demoralizing to good boatmen.
MJ: We want rating sheets of some kind, rather than a 1-5 point system.
FB: Why don't you use motors?
SM: We can make more contacts on oar trips. We did evaluations on 19 companies.
The Hualapai have agreed to allow a helispot to go downstream two miles due to
fly-overs. Most take-outs are in the morning.
We had 100 boatmen doing training, covering first aid, climbing rescue,
interpretation. The Hatch people liked it. We want something similar for private
trips.
Almost half the companies did a complete carryout of fecal matter using the new
method of "rocket box" containment. County Health likes it better than porta-
potties. The reasons for the new way are esthetic, no soil disturbance or
contamination, and because its hard to find places to bury porta-potty contents. So
we have decided to have everyone take it all out. [TW says they do not do it.]
Carryout is mandatory, but lunch stops are not included.

SM: On fires, there is an accumulation of charcoal and a loss of driftwood, as well as
a breakage of live trees, like mesquite. So no fires. You can use charcoal, but you
have to haul out all ash and debris.
KS: Fire is an interpretive tool. It helps get close to people. We could carry enough
wood.
MJ: You can't.
KS: Yes I can.
NPS: Fires aren't needed, and even the most careful boaters leave charcoal. How
about a show of hands? Three are for a fire ban or indifferent, nine want fires
allowed.
MJ: New charcoal is being added to the beaches.
FB: I don't see it. It's being left by 5-6 private trips. A ban would take the heart
right out of the trip.
George Wendt [OARS; at the time a small rowing comm op. Now mid-sized]:
I don't use fires; let's experiment.

SM: Hikers cannot have fires.

TW: What about a gas log?

SM continued to argue about fires with KS and FB.

JC: Why do we have to come here only to be <u>told</u> what to do. [Went off on a real toot, for the third time.] Let's stand up and fight.

[I interrupt this program with a passenger's account of a 1975 trip run by "why-doesn't-the-government-leave-us-alone" Cross, found in Randall 67, pp. 5-6. The trip started 4 hours late. The raft smashed into a wall ripping a large gash in the "1955 vintage raft". The backup engine was used for the rest of the trip. Each day the raft had to be re-inflated. There were no instructions on emergency procedures. The engine was so weak, they had to be pulled out from the Deer Creek stop by another trip. The guide retrieved a derelict gas can, and used the contents. In Lava Falls, the engine failed, and some of the straps that held the platform snapped. Five people, along with food, boxes, toilet, and luggage went into the river. The engine was repaired by passengers; not the two Crosses running the trip.]

FB: It's the private trips that cause the damage.

SM: We stopped at 60 sites. Mesquite *are* being damaged.

JC: What's more important, the esthetic value of a fire for the people who own the Canyon or a lizard?

MJ: Why don't you write us about your views, and we will talk it over more, and consider it again.

KS: The fires you have on the rim show the value for down below; we must have it. [My notes say: fires only thing in controversy, and NPS got ready to yield.]

FB: The campsite at Gateway is really a mess. Trips are too tightly scheduled. Some camps have a beaten-down look. Let them rest a bit and freshen up.

JC: Has high water helped? Lava Falls is really bad.

FB: We have to work together or we are going to be caught.

MJ: [Summing up] I am not getting many incident reports.

People are not aware of the soap and shampoo regulation, even the boatmen. Some know about it, they admit, but soap still going in the side streams.

You need to watch training trips.

The fee to take out at Diamond is going from $5 to $25 per person. Helicopter rates are being studied—2 comm ops say they will quit if the rates are increased.

On the numbers of people turned away; we would like names and addresses to do a survey.

FB: We have been hustling right up to the end of this year for passengers. Only 9,000 went this year; last year it was 12,000.

TW: We could take twice as many. Travel agents could sell that many or more.

CB: How about reducing the horsepower to 20?

ARTA [Large comm op; ran most rowing trips]: That would be quieter.

FB: In Washington, the word is to go for 20.

End of session.

I summarized this meeting for the lawyers, stressing how difficult it was for NPS or us to do something, about the environment for instance, when the comm ops disagreed.[1] "The meeting illustrated once again how a regulated industry comes to determine the regulator's policy." The comm ops "are not people we have ever gained anything from except by pressure". I singled out Litton, "A classic case of economic self-interest destroying convictions a person once used to defend mightily."

Amazed at the brazenness of it all, I sent a third complaint to the Interior Secretary, this time aiming at the cozying-up behavior of the NPS audit person, Zimmerling, noting his own claim of doing things he should not and working hard to get a policy friendly to the comm ops.[2] Instead of just complaining, I wistfully suggested that environmentalists could have someone on their side with the same sort of zeal. The reply ignored my comments. Lastly, I pressed Jensen about a river research meeting, and praised the proposed if beaten-back regulation on fires. Marv replied that they had decided that any such meeting would cause trouble, so there would not be special briefings for anybody.[3]

CHAPTER 15

1977-78: After The Play Is Over, We're Back In The Muddle Again

The display presented in the last chapter did little to focus the effort; court actions and wilderness lobbying continued to demand attention.

Watching the comm ops and the National Park Service groom each other strengthened my feeling that the Sierra Club suit on behalf of the Canyon against the comm ops and NPS was a necessary effort. We had to keep up some pressure to counter that of the comm ops, and the Park staff was not making any gestures toward us. Chapter 14 dramatizes the situation of a regulated industry co-opting, and muting the impact of, the regulators. Having only the law, NPS policies, and Park regulations to rely on, GCNP staffers could hardly be expected to stand firm against the very flesh-and-blood reality of comm op battering, even with our not always consistent backing.

The comm ops scorn for the research also revealed what a political trap the research program was for NPS (just as Eiseman had predicted). First the comm ops had complained because the 1972 Reed decision was not based on research. Five years later, with completed research results putting renewed pressure on their position, they attacked the researchers as being biased. Unlike the Park Service, the comm ops did not have to stick by any of their pro-research words. They seemed unembarrassed by the lack of research supporting their views. Anecdotes and distortions sufficed to push their case. NPS, however, was stuck with crafting a CRMP based on the research the comm ops had demanded and were already attacking. So the now five-year delay in the plan had been for naught as far as coming up with a common, widely accepted database for making a plan. The comm ops would only accept a plan that gave them what they wanted, that is, keeping what they already had.

The intense battle of 1978-81 was thus set up; one metaphor that leaps to my mind is the trench war of stalemate and slaughter of the 1914-18 European conflict. With the political alliances they were cultivating intensively in place, the comm ops had no intention of giving in on the main issues of a motor-free Wilderness and equitably divided, environmentally sound, use levels. They would fight on until they "won". And, stuck with that "victory", even today the comm ops dangle from the hook they impaled themselves on. Because of the way the comm ops prevailed, there was no real accommodation among the parties. Instead, the outcome of the struggle was a political structure imposed by one set of contenders that stifled the pressures for Wilderness and more equitable access to river-running. Though seemingly out-of-sight, out-of-mind, for fifteen years, those wilderness/access pressures built up, to burst out again in the late 1990s so strongly that the controversy (today) is as, if not more, strong and broadly-based as in the 1970s. But not to get ahead of ourselves ...

Meanwhile, back at the court:
The Sierra Club filed its suit in mid-September. It was an item at the comm op meeting, with the River Manager indicating he was drafting answers to the charges and wanted comm op help.

The government did put out its answer two months later. It reads like a set of lawyerly knee-jerk admissions or denials, where the admissions were obvious (they did accept that Stitt was Superintendent) and the denials almost automatic.[1] The most glaring of these was that they denied knowledge of the research findings, but claimed the contract extensions took them into account. They did admit some impacts from river-running, without specifying which, and did admit some regulations were not being followed without specifying the offenders. They made the weird distinction that the plan would rely on the research "partly" but not "heavily", as if the entire justification of the research had not been to support a river plan. Technically they objected because only two of the comm ops had been included as plaintiffs, claiming that the concessionaire class was too small for representatives. By this time, the government was ready to claim the CRMP would be published in the next month.

At the same time, Brown, Western River's attorney, answered, saying we had not asked them for anything and, anyway, we had to include all the comm ops, not just them.[2] The Sierra Club's Phoenix attorney answered the question of who had to be included by complaining that some of the 21 comm ops were not easily available and there were too many practical disadvantages in all 21 being involved.[3] Since the two comm ops' only defense—that they had no constitutional requirement to protect the environment—was a common defense, the defense by two would be as vigorous as if by all. Furthermore, even if some contended they did no harm, they still all had the power in common to do harm, and it was that power we needed to enjoin. The last was a point certainly driven home by the NPS-comm op meeting, where it was clear that the effort to deal with the fire/driftwood/ash problem was being hampered, not by NPS foot-dragging, but by the comm ops. Although the suit did not spell it out this way, the comm ops were on record, or at least in my notes, as involving themselves intimately in making river policy that was contrary to the pro-environmental recommendations of the Research Project. A hearing on who was in the defendant class was set for January 9, 1978.[4] Another significant event would be our taking evidence from GCNP officials. And, of course, we eagerly awaited the release of the CRMP and its EIS.

Meanwhile, back in the (other) court(s):
The information I have on the self-guided suits is sketchy. The WPRF attorney,

Nemir, filed his brief in the Ninth Circuit Court of Appeals on July 7, 1977.[5] The government responded in November, acknowledging formally their position, for the first time, that self-guided boaters have *no* statutory priority over commercial trips. Since this was exactly contrary to WPRF's claim, the issue was joined for the Appeals Court to decide. According to WPRF, Nemir also had been furnishing information to the Sierra Club, and hoped for more tangible coordination in the future, even though the Club thought the WPRF effort was not an environmental issue. (But surely it was. Again, we may have been shortsighted in not cultivating this connection. The research said that how people behaved was most important in lessening environmental impact. A major element in this was better NPS involvement with self-guided orientation and river behavior. Since there was certainly going to be an increase in self-guided use under the new CRMP, we could have seen that encouraging a class of environmentally sensitive self-guided river-runners would enhance protection. This would have been entirely consistent with the activity of the arm of the Sierra Club that provided wilderness trips.)

GCNP hardened its self-guided line with a new rule that forbade any substitutions if a self-guided trip member could not make the trip. So the possibility existed of some of the self-guided allocation going unnecessarily unused. This was all part of the effort to squash the bogey of multiple applications, and an obvious indication of how out-of-joint the situation was. WPRF agreed with others that a lottery for *all* would-be river-runners was the answer.

On another self-guided front, Eiseman and the lawyers at the ACLPI decided in October that the case had a reasonable chance if appealed.[6] The general issue of concessionaires' role and their competition with general public access was too important to let drop, Eiseman reported. He also mentioned the Sierra Club suit. In deciding how to draft the appeal, he was going to be looking at the origins of the NPS and its concession policies. Eiseman's research, however, produced no definitive information.[7] Before the National Park System Act, there was lots of flowery rhetoric, but it never occurred to anyone that there could ever be limits on use. As far as the Concessions Act of 1965 goes, again, there was nothing in the legislative history about what the law means when it says concessions must be necessary or what happens when use is such that they are, in fact, unnecessary.

He also reported that the Park Service in Dinosaur National Monument was issuing a river plan that included alternatives such as a lottery for all comers, or a 50-50 division of use between commercial and self-guided, with a lottery for each. And perhaps here, too, was another missed opportunity. Fixation on the Grand Canyon as the premier river experience unfortunately carried with it blinders as to what was happening in other places. The story of Dinosaur shows almost the reverse image of the Grand Canyon. Strong NPS leadership, cooperative (if sometimes grumbling) users, both commercial and self-guided, and perhaps lower-profile, shorter trips with a shorter season, combined to produce river management founded on pro-wilderness, pro-environmental attitudes. All trips row; use is divided 50-50 between commercial and self-guided with four trips a day; campsites are signed up for in advance. This system, in place for over 20 years, apparently has the support and good will of all, a marked difference from the Grand Canyon, where the comm ops' politically maintained motor-boater status quo system generates as much ill will as the Canyon itself produces satisfaction.

Meanwhile, back at the Wilderness:
An October newsletter of The Wilderness Society aptly described the situation for Wilderness legislation: The proposal was kept paddling in circles in OMB due to the motor controversy.[8] One of its mailings also cited Goldwater as the only southwestern senator to vote against the Endangered American Wilderness Act, a significant 1977 effort, not a pleasant straw to watch tumble, given the current wind.[9]

One of my local cooperating organizations, AWWW, allowed me seven large pages to expound on the range of Grand Canyon concerns in their November 1977 newspaper. I listed 21 "issues", some inter-related, which I grouped into eight stories. I was hard on the comm ops as only willing to innovate in matters like shorter, faster trips or helicopter use. We must expect "stubborn resistance" as they try to prevent changes they dislike. I was hard on the Park Service, whose delays on river matters were "a tragedy and a travesty", and which seemed to be able to urge comm ops to get out their votes, but made no effort to reach out to us. Along with the TWS October newsletter, the AWWW spread was graced with exquisite ink drawings of the Canyon by Lizbeth Carr, the new volunteer in Washington working for Wilderness. Our collaboration extended from these publications into the lobbying of the administration, especially OMB, the necessity for which had increased because of behind-the-scenes fussing in Interior over the Wilderness proposal.

First, there was NPS concern about the lower 35 miles of the river. In November, Director Whalen, who had replaced Everhardt, repeated his insistence that the section be dropped from the proposal.[10] The reason was the "substantially different use". The "general" public can see the lower Canyon going downstream and upstream using motor craft, without resource degradation. About 20,000 people use this low-cost option. This "general" public has a lower income and different social profile, with their recreational interests being active water-based activities, including fishing. Since removing motors from the lower river would reduce use by perhaps 75%, motors are the desirable alternate access in that area, and we still see "wilderness designation of the 235 miles of free-flowing river as reflecting our management goal to provide for running the river without motors".

McComb reported that while the Park Service desired the deletion, NPS so far had not transmitted it to OMB, and might not. Nevertheless, the decision had the result that the May CRMP draft, which included a motor ban all the way to the Grand Wash Cliffs, was changed so that the October version was motor-free only to Separation Canyon.

The second problem area stemmed from a zoning in Grand Canyon National Park of 95,000 acres as Havasupai Use Lands(HU Lands), Park land that Congress had said the Havasupai could use for "grazing and other traditional purposes". However, Congress went on, the Secretary should consider the HU Lands for GCNP Wilderness "notwithstanding allowed tribal uses" (see Chapter 5).[11] Yet when formulating its Wilderness recommendation, the Park Service decided to class the HU Lands as Potential Wilderness, following its curious thinking that wilderness ranked below any encumbrances on it (see Chapter 10). This agency position spit in the face of Congress's direction to ignore Havasupai uses in making a Wilderness recommendation.

NPS had said final determination of the Use Lands status as Wilderness depended on a study. So I wrote Superintendent Stitt asking about this study, and we had a little correspondence.[12] He had assigned Robert Euler, Park Anthropologist, to work with Reed Watahomigie, Havasupai Tribal Chairman, and Wayne Sinyella, Vice-Chairman, to develop a Memorandum of Understanding (MOU). There had been several discussions and reviews. Matters to be covered included identifying the uses, grazing capacities and animals, access routes, overnight visit and hunting guidelines, restrictions on religious sites. Also, a plan was being developed for the new Reservation as well, so the MOU might have to be modified.

Naturally, I then wanted to know how any of those uses conflicted with Wilderness. I asked if hunting, not allowed in the Park, was being considered for the Use Lands. Stitt ignored the first question, and insisted that the potential status had to wait for the plan of the Reservation, otherwise we would "presume the outcome of the planning for the reservation". Hunting was one of the Havasupai traditional uses, he said, and so was authorized by Congress. However, he had asked for a legal opinion. In any case, the Havasupai promised not to hunt desert bighorn.

This pressed my button, and I quoted at him the congressional history, and his own memo of November 18, 1975, in which he had said "we see no conflict between traditional ... uses and wilderness designation ... We do not, however, view the use plan as a prerequisite to preparing wilderness proposals." Further, I pointed out that the NPS wilderness proposal did not mention the reservation when it talked about the study. Not only that, but GCNP had recommended wilderness on Park lands that abutted all sorts of other ownership. I then tartly told him that the Park Service had found the Use Lands suitable for wilderness designation, and "that is all the Congress wanted you to do", so your latest statement is contrary to congressional direction, departmental policy, and your own statements.

Not surprisingly, Stitt ignored my logic, and just informed me there was a delay because the MOU writers could not meet. He added the Havasupai wanted to hunt deer, rabbits, and other small animals. They propose to hunt with rifles, though it is not clear whether this is a traditional use. Several weeks later, he wrote again. He knew that the Use Lands *could* have been recommended for wilderness, but since they did not know what uses there would be, they thought it best that we ask for the potential status. Stitt then defended the potential status, and thought it would soon be wilderness "after the wilderness law for the park has been enacted." "We have found no traditional uses incompatible with requirements of the Wilderness Act ... only recently." Orwell's ghost chuckled.

So why did the Park not forward this "finding" to Washington so the proposal, still moldering away in OMB, could be fixed? Still worse, the copy of the draft MOU I have (showing a crossed-out date of Sep 12 (the date of Stitt's last letter) and Nov 12 typed in), is only one-third about the Havasupai uses of grazing, hunting, and gathering. The rest covers a whole set of limitations on *non-Havasupai* visitors.

Meanwhile, Lizbeth and I were trying to make a difference at OMB. She was doing slide talks, and distributing the AWWW opus.[13] However, The Wilderness Society editor thought my writing lacked objectivity (true enough, but "stupid man!" was Carr's comment). She suggested we work together, even offering to be our art and layout editor. Charmingly, she noted "It's probably hard for Arizonans to believe someone in Arlington, Virginia could love your Grand Canyon as much as you do, but you really will really have to adjust to the idea!" Of course, it was not hard at all; after all, I was a transplant from the East, and to paraphrase J. B. Priestley, we all ought to be proud to be on the staff of the Grand Canyon.

Late in December, she spent three hours with OMB's Sessions and two others, briefing them with her slide show.[14] Sessions said they were trying to move the proposal out *now*. He told her many letters from "older" people "afraid of row trips" had convinced *him* that motors with limited user-days and few people would be best (this was only a version of the line Burke had admitted peddling of "high-quality" motor trips.) She replied that a motorized wilderness was a horrible precedent. She noted he was young, about 28-29, though very well informed "and trying to do his best". He did agree that the Carr slides showed that the *entire* river has wilderness quality.

A week later, I talked with Sessions and learned that Cutler had sent a memo back, calling this a difficult issue on which more information was needed about how strongly Interior feels about banning motors. How real are the limitations on those who say they cannot go on rowing trips for the reasons of being more expensive, less comfortable, and less safe? Sessions said they had received about 50 letters, a spate he admitted was obviously stirred up and had now dried up. Sessions stated the argument as being that since this was the greatest "recreational" trip in the US, it should not be limited to certain people, even if the limit was only in their own mind. (This particular argument shows just how sophisticated Sessions had become in maintaining the comm op position.) His idea was that there would be small motors and a declaration by Congress that the ecology should be protected. (It should be stressed again how unreal this debating by a very junior bureaucrat was. Any proposal that got to Congress would be fought over fiercely by all sides, no matter what he, OMB, the President, NPS, or anyone else said. Sessions' big contribution to river history is that he and his boss sat on the proposal long enough for it to suffocate; but why?) He was now considering whether it should go back to Interior, and I could call him in a week or so about that decision.

Interlude for reflection:

I do not want to pretend that this story, any more than any other, has nice chronological divides, but I think as we pitch into 1978 and the fight over the draft CRMP, that it is worthwhile to reflect on 1977 as the year of promise, a moment when we were deploying many options. Though belated, we were able to marshal the research to try to use the legal system to protect the Canyon's environment against river-running impacts. We had the best Wilderness proposal we could hope for from NPS headed for congressional resolution, in a political situation that superficially could not have been more favorable. Public opinion had been clearly deployed on behalf of wilderness. As 1978 played out, however, these options evaporated. With no clear defeat, the legal and congressional arenas proved irrelevant, and all that was left was the Park Service's process to craft an acceptable Colorado River Management Plan. Since that plan's fate has become the historical focus for what happened in the 1970s, I want to emphasize how different the decision-making landscape would have been had our other options been realized: a court decision ordering the Park Service to protect the river environment based on the research; a congressional act creating a motor-free Grand Canyon Wilderness.

That is what we could not achieve in 1977-8. The impact of these silent losses, leaving only a vulnerable administrative CRMP process, can, it seems to me, be measured by this what-if: Even given the change in political climate brought by the 1980 election, had 1977 led to victories in the courts and Congress, there could have been put into place over the past 20 years a CRMP firmly based on environmental protection and wilderness management. The sort of beast it might have been is the subject of Chapter 16, where the NPS's 1977 versions of the CRMP and the EIS are presented and compared. The battering of that beast in public, the subject of Chapter 17, opened the New Year, with the NPS announcement on January 5, 1978. To keep that main story clear, this chapter will carry on a bit further about Wilderness and the courts, increasingly just sideshows.

Meanwhile, back at the Wilderness:
The new Assistant Secretary for Indian Affairs, who had been a staffer on the Senate Interior Committee at the time of the Grand Canyon/Havasupai legislation, decided he needed to be heard, writing to the Interior Legislative Counsel that he had not been around when the Wilderness proposal was sent to OMB. The Havasupai and Hualapai have concerns that must be addressed, so please halt any action until we present our objections.[15] One-and-a-half months later, he wrote that the proposal was objectionable because of the Hualapai boundary claims, and that the Havasupai did not like ambiguous language, saying wilderness would be an infringement.[16] His ignorant claim about the boundary was seconded by his Solicitor.[17]

The NPS Director's reply to all this was to note that the Interior Solicitor is now looking at the Hualapai boundary question.[18] The Havasupai have had the fourth draft of the MOU since November. We see no conflict with wilderness; for instance they are contracting to camouflage their stock improvements using horse and helicopter. Following this rebuff, the record goes silent.

Lizbeth Carr was not. She continued her efforts, reporting in early January that Sessions "expects" the bill to go to the White House in three weeks with some changes.[19] I reported to her and to McComb and Calkin on a January 5, 1978, meeting eight of us had in Tucson with Congressman Udall to talk over various matters including our support for him (and also told them that I had received the draft CRMP on the 7th).[20] My pitch to Udall on the Canyon was that OMB had had the Wilderness proposal for a year and some sort of lever was needed, so I gave him a draft bill and map of our proposal, asking him to introduce it. Mo said he would consider it, and also the idea of including it in an omnibus bill, which he seemed to prefer. (As I ponder this period, I have to admit this thought: In the 1960s Morris Udall got burned as he worked against us to get dams authorized. In the mid-1970s he got burned again as he worked with us to expand the Park. Now we were back, asking him to once again get involved in the super-heated politics of the Grand Canyon. Maybe he was worried about his fire insurance.)

In mid-January, Lizbeth reported she had just been told by Sessions that he had received an Interior Department memo saying they wanted to exclude the last 35 miles of the river from the Wilderness proposal.[21] Clay Peters, of the House Interior minority staff, assured her there was "NO WAY" there could be a motorized wilderness. She added that Calkin said the Hualapai wanted motor rafts as part of their bighorn hunt expeditions. She was going to show her Grand Canyon slide show (with contrasting photos of motorized and rowing rigs) to a staffer at the President's Domestic Policy Council. McComb, she wrote, "continues to be totally disinterested in my venture". She was ready to resign from the Sierra Club over McComb's "snub", but nobody would give a damn anyway.

The next day, she wrote again about her determination to fight for Wilderness designation for the Lake Mead section, apparently under the impression that I did not want wilderness there.[22] (I had included all the 277-mile river in the bill I handed Udall.) She reminded me of how useful her drawings could be for illustration and battle posters. She was not cheered up by the Sierra Club's recent vote to put 25% of Club staff effort on the Alaska legislation, though she could never have hoped for Club help anyway. Her second letter that day told me that there would be House committee action on January 18 to mark up an omnibus Wilderness bill. It included the Grand Canyon with the entire river.[23] However, her January 22 letter has no mention of any action. Sadly, that was the end of her intense assistance. Meanwhile, I had been in touch with Clay Peters, who said action on the omnibus bill was close, but there was no "absolute" decision on the Canyon.

The details of the next few months are murky; at least my records are.[24] From the often-undated slips of paper with notes I kept from phone calls, I can offer certain sketches. First, the priority of Alaska is mentioned. Second, the negative reaction to the CRMP (see Chapter 17) was so heavy as to cast doubt on support for a motor-free Wilderness. Third, there was a scattering of reports, hints really:

that the NPS Director worried about wilderness excluding old people, and other NPS officials thought motors and wilderness involved only value judgments;

that there was a risk of being so "badly hammered" that decisions would be overturned;

that the House Interior Committee staff had prepared an anti-concessionaire memo;

that the Regional Director needed strong numbers to balance the anti-plan comments, and was getting the Director on the river in June;

that the Director thought it the best damn trip he ever took, and his eyes were opened; there was no comparison between rowing and motorized, and his talks with people on the river gave him views about building up a constituency to get motors off over a number of years; it would be the method of removal that would be important;

that comm ops ran things until Stitt came, and the new NPS men have rapport with river-runners;

that the Sierra Club was doing little;

that Udall was relying on McComb, and the two shared the idea of doing nothing so as to avoid a battle, since wilderness would lose;

that Udall took GCWilderness out of omnibus bill, due to noise made by pro-motor congressmen;

that Udall was cross-pressured; his kids wanted the motors out and motors should not be in a Wilderness, versus his many friends who did not think they could do a rowing trip;

that the comm ops made wilder and wilder arguments (NPS tends to communism, only the rich can take rowing trips, etc.), and some of it stuck;

that after all the clamor, Chapman still wanted motors banned, but how soon was the question because of the lack of public support for banning them, and wondering if larger allocations could be a carrot to get comm ops to switch;

that this all added up to a several-month effort in 1978 pushing to get some action, with the reaction being mostly non-supportive.

In August, an NPS "briefing statement" on the Wilderness summed up how little the past several months had accomplished.[25] It claimed that OMB had been "alerted to possible deletion" of the last 35 river miles, though the Park Service had not yet sent a recommendation to be dealt with by the Assistant Secretary. The OMB examiner, however, "favors leaving out entire river and continuance of all motorized use on river". This briefing statement was written by someone knowledgeable, who wanted to get the change made and the documents revised. Once the Assistant Secretary cleared the revision, then the Legislative Counsel would prepare a letter to OMB expressing concern that it had not acted on the proposal (after 1-1/2 years! Why had NPS done nothing in between?).

Eight months later, institutional amnesia had struck. A memo from the Director to the Solicitor suggested that once the CRMP was approved, NPS would send a report on wilderness recommendations "required" by the 1975 GCNP Act.[26] It refers to the Director-approved 1977 document as a "draft", and said it had been held in abeyance in Interior—OMB not even being mentioned—pending completion of the CRMP. (Was this just a change in personnel? It sounds like ignorance. But did this memo hint at some NPS officials tacitly approving OMB's hold-up? Was there really a "report", as Carr said Sessions had received over fifteen months before?) True, the memo was not really about the proposal overall; it just wanted to clear up the tribal legal concerns raised in 1977-8. The Solicitor was asked whether any of the Hualapai and Havasupai issues needed to be resolved before there was further action on the recommendation. The legal reply was direct. Existing law protects any (property) interests involved, and the proposal may continue without the necessity of further resolution of legal issues.[27] And again silence.

These 1979 memos, the only items in the record, suggest to me a death by institutional Alzheimer's. It was as if earlier decisions by a long-gone Director had evaporated as those involved with them moved on. No doubt, the storm stirred up by the CRMP absorbed attention. Whatever, when Wilderness next briefly appears, it is an object being revised, a comatose artifact being tidied up in case anybody ever came looking for the body. So again I have to ask how we could have been so derelict, so weak, as to have let this opportunity sputter and seep away?

Meanwhile, back at the courts:

In their self-guided suit, the WPRF had filed an appeal, answered by government rebuttals. The Arizona Center for Law in the Public Interest did the same for the Eiseman suit in March 1978 in the Ninth Circuit Court of Appeals in San Francisco.[28] Eiseman thought it possible that two years might elapse before a decision, though he offered the opinion that delay was good, since the final CRMP would be done by then, and the government would have lost its argument that the plan would answer the self-guided complaints.

The Sierra Club suit, aiming at the environmental problems, was more active, entangled as it was with GCNP's simultaneous publication of the draft river plan and new regulations on waste disposal and fires.[29] As Ruckel understated in a January 1978 report, "A great deal has happened." He reported that Stitt, in a deposition a week before (see Chapter 17), testified that all waste would be removed, from camps and day stops. This was tighter than expected, and the fire regulations were similarly tight. The issues that remained were chaotic foot traffic, motor use, and concentration on a few campsites. The draft plan has provisions for the first two. This has led government lawyers to press us to declare that the suit can be settled or dismissed. Perhaps we should press for more protection, but we do need to reply.

Shortly thereafter, the court, on the government's motion, said the Club had to add all the other comm ops to the suit, a considerable amount of extra paperwork; there was no class or token representation. (Given the trouble caused by suing the comm ops, it is worth asking if this was a sound move, since all our real effort was aimed at the Park Service; we did not have, of course, anything like evidence of comm op transgression of the regulations.)

The good news was dampened when copies of the new regulations were furnished, and it turned out that, although the provisions represented "very significant gains", the Park Service had "retreated" from Stitt's sworn statement about wastes being taken out from all stop sites.[30] In fact, Stitt had "corrected" his testimony, replacing "all of the Park" with "all campsites". Ruckel now argued that, particularly before a judge "not ... favorably disposed to our point of view", we should move to get an agreement that will build on the achievements so far, trying to include our other demands. He excepted the question of campsite concentration, since the expert testimony turned out to be too weak, leaving the issue murky. His major point was that the government was now in a "favorable judicial posture".

The draft stipulation required that wastes be taken out from all sites in the 1979 season, trail work be done to offset foot damage, and the CRMP finished as soon as "reasonably" possible.[31] I suggested adding a provision not to extend the contracts and for a regular and consistent program of monitoring. The matter of insisting on the motor phase-out was argued, and Tony decided it would just stir up the comm ops, and we might lose what we had gained.[32] The proposal was submitted in April, complimenting the Park Service for its "substantial progress" on the plan and implementing some research findings.[33] So, expecting NPS to continue "in good faith promptly to adopt and implement" a river plan, we are not seeking many of the protections that could have been pursued. (This will gain a flavor of irony in Chapter 17's recounting of the public reaction to the CRMP.) Ruckel cited the many years the Club had been waiting, and the offensive extending of the permits after research showed damage. He listed eleven items no longer pursued by the suit, e.g., no reduction in use, closing of damaged beaches, dispersal of use, no fire ban, no motor ban.

Negotiations on an agreement went on for months. In August, Gil Venable, the local attorney working with Ruckel reported that even though NPS had announced a schedule for the CRMP, the government would not include a deadline in the settlement.[34] The steps to protect the environment were being worked out. The discussions were hung up over what to do if the NPS CRMP schedule was not kept to, and the comm op permit extensions ran out. The government would not accept any of the offered provisions that would prevent contract extension without an EIS. At this point it was very clear what we had lost by not filing suit before the extensions had been granted, since that might have made it possible to tie the comm ops into the CRMP, whereas now they could stall, expecting NPS to grant them another extension.

There was a sideshow with the comm op lawyers in the summer of 1978 as they offered their denials that they were involved. For laughs, Burke's lawyer filed a counterclaim in July against the Sierra Club for damages, which was dismissed by the judge on legal grounds in September. In reporting this, Ruckel repeated his view that the Judge was hostile to the Club's point of view.[35] He was also hoping for some definite action on a settlement—a failed hope, since as 1978 wore on into mid-1979, the revised CRMP did not show up, and the expiration of the contract extension loomed. That pinch must wait its turn, as we grapple with the gorilla itself.

CHAPTER 16

1977: Building A River Plan From The Ground Up

Even if 1977's sad story reads now as one of options closing, vastly overshadowed by the subsequent war over the CRMP, that was not the view at the time. The CRMP, with the research results, the Wilderness proposal, and the suit on behalf of the river environment, looked like it would be another linked step forward. It would be, with its EIS, a document that would bring the elements of environmental protection, wilderness, and more equitable access together for a bold re-start to river management in the Canyon and elsewhere. So we must go back a year or so to look at the documents, leaving the story hanging a while.

The Man of the Plan

First, let's get personal.[1] The change with Marv Jensen's appointment as River Manager was startling, given Jensen's experience, and love of, river-running. When the Park had set up a river management unit in 1972, Bob Yearout was named River Manager. His training and interests were in the field of concessions management, and, not an outdoorsman, he worked to carry out this strange assignment, in particular to gain the respect of the comm ops. Perhaps in the early 1970s this background was not too strange; it is likely that there were few NPS personnel knowledgeable and experienced in river-running as such.

Jensen had started as a real field man, with the Bureau of Land Management in Utah in more traditional land work. Stationed in Moab in 1969, he was introduced to the river and "traded his horse for a boat, an 18' Havasu 2". In 1973-4, Jensen did the river plans for such BLM reaches of the Colorado as Westwater Canyon and the San Juan. As a member of the Interagency Whitewater Committee, he exchanged ideas with Yearout, and told him he wanted his job if it ever opened up. When Yearout went to the Grand Teton, Jensen with his experience, including a dedication to rowing, was a natural choice, and took over in May 1976, just as the research phase was ending and river planning was finally ready to take formal shape.

Jensen's dedication to being on the river as much as possible, always rowing, was a very big change. With the addition of Steve Martin as his assistant and Kim

Crumbo as a rowing ranger, NPS River staff could now build their own basis for judgment of concessionaire operations and of the impacts described in the research, surely making them better participants in drafting the CRMP+EIS. Together, Jensen and Martin worked up the original draft with Steve Carothers, under still another contract. In general, Jensen relied on and believed the research results, such as the Parent economic study, but particularly the HERS work on the people impacts. Jensen and Martin's institutional frame of mind did temper this reliance on the research; both men have had solid NPS careers since leaving the Grand Canyon in 1981. While Jensen did not then shirk the burdens of controversy, the view he expresses today is that taking the long view can often be more productive; getting people to talk and work together on problems is essential. Of course, these were exactly the conditions that never obtained in the river controversy; it already seemed to have dragged on and on, with increasing anger, animosity and self-righteousness. And the freshness brought by Jensen could not have prevailed among the comm ops; for them, he had too much river expertise, was too dedicated to rowing, and gave too much credence to the research results. As far as the second of these goes, Jensen never took a commercial motor trip, and replaced GCNP's motorized boats with rowing craft. He took NPS Directors, first Everhardt, then Whalen, down the river, and said the latter loved dories.

As summarized in Chapter 13, the CRMP-drafting threesome came up with a variety of alternatives early in 1976. Jensen does not recall any strong direction from his superiors; the effort was to generate alternatives. At this point, March 1976, the plan (no documents on this appear in the files), was reviewed in San Francisco and Washington, and then substantially rewritten by Jensen and the Region's environmental specialist, Astrid Schenk. That draft EIS then went to the Park for review in late May.[2] Jensen calls Schenk a "major contributor" in getting through the "umpteen" changes involved in putting this document together, a time when word processing meant lots of hand-written notes and the blessing of having a Selectric II Correctible typewriter.

The Washington office insisted on shifting the original emphasis from the river's social carrying capacity (i.e., what a wilderness experience was for the participants) to the environmental impact. This was difficult for those writing the plan, according to Jensen, since they had concluded the important factor in planning river trips was trying to prevent congestion that would make the experience one of non-wilderness crowding. Jensen said that even Yates Borden told him he thought the big factor was social, not the physical carrying capacity he had worked out for river traffic conducted on wilderness principles. This self-justifying memory of Jensen's is a tad odd, since Borden recognized that congestion was mitigated by behavior, not numbers; indeed, Borden's river management scenario built congestion reduction right into its foundation. Washington officials waved all this aside, Jensen says, tilting toward writing a plan that rested on the dangers posed to the physical environment by motors. This meant relying on arguments about motor effects that were not the most sensitive elements of the situation. Furthermore, Jensen knew the comm ops were finding motors' physical impacts easy to scoff at. Of course, they scoffed at any of the research they disagreed with. Had Eiseman been privy to these debates, he could certainly claim that he had told us all so: motors should go because they were against the Park Wilderness principles that governed GCNP; research was an unnecessary side excursion on the way to the decision for a motor-free river.

EIS: Power Behind the Throne

The Environmental Impact Statement (EIS) is a premier token of openness in American governance. A few years after NEPA started mandating EISs for significant federal actions, they stood astride the scene, forcing agencies to lay before the public (and to listen to the public laying into them) work they wanted to do, damage the action might cause, and alternatives nobody would take seriously—they hoped. In theory, the EIS unwraps the process, while wrapping up the content in one place. In practice ... well, let's just look at this one EIS and how it grew. One caution: This chapter goes through each part of the first draft, then through the draft as published to point out changes. Finally it goes through the CRMP itself in the same detailed way. This analysis is important because of the seminal quality of this CRMP+EIS. However, it makes neither the most exciting writing nor reading.

The CRMP's EIS followed the standard form, with special details for river traffic's peculiarities.[3] Section I was a recapitulation of the draft Plan itself. Section II, by far the longest, described the environment, including river recreation, its social and economic factors. Section III connected I to II by analyzing how the Plan would impact the environment, again including visitors and economics. IV listed measures to mitigate impact, while V admitted to adverse unavoidable impacts. Sections VI and VII, on short-term uses and long-term productivity, and on irreversible commitments of resources, were perfunctory for the CRMP. Section VIII, presenting alternatives to various plan proposals, might have been meaty. Section IX tried to detail the agency-public interface, summarizing meetings, hearings, and submitted comments from the proposal's "publics"—other agencies, non-governmental organizations, and individuals.

The May EIS draft opened with a pointed summary. In 1967-72, Canyon resources "were deteriorating" due to the "dramatic" increase in river-running. Trash, human waste, charcoal in the beaches, trail and artifact erosion, crowding, shorter trips due to motor use, were all mentioned (I:1). Research projects, 29 of them, had studied physical and biological resources, and human impacts on these and on each other. Public meetings on Wilderness had provided a top ten of concerns: motors, total use, amount of self-guided use, comm op allocations, three sorts of environmental damage, congestion, need for interpretation, and monitoring. Later on, at the 1976 river planning workshops, fifteen top issues had been generated (see Chapter 11). Not surprisingly, the order based on a count of responses was different from the Wilderness workshops, though there was extensive overlap. The number one issue was the amount of self-guided use. Then followed a catchall environmental concern: motors, obtaining permits, wilderness, waste disposal, total use, excessive commercial use, excessive trip size, regulation enforcement, dams, self-guided rules, interpretation, wildlife, and monitoring. The draft supported itself first by citing the National Park Act, "most significant". Of detailed relevance were the 1975 GCNP Enlargement Act for the application of "administrative policies affording the highest protection ... uniformly throughout the river corridor" and the Park Management Plan for resource preservation and perpetuating the wilderness experience (I:2).

All the above resulted in the specific river management objectives of no-motors, use limits, equitable allocation for self-guided users, commercial "quality wilderness" trips, equitable and efficient permitting, environmental protection, congestion reduction, water quality preservation, health and safety, more interpretation and education, monitoring (I:4).

Before looking at the detail, contemplate that list with a comm op's eye. There is no good news. This is particularly true given their claim that all things good in river-running—trip quality, care for the resource, health and safety, interpretation—came from them. Everything positive the plan aimed at—wilderness pacing and spacing, rowing trips, more self-guided trips made possible in a friendlier administrative environment, reversing negative river-runner impacts on the beaches and on each other—implied that, given the huge preponderance of commercial use, river-running was being done wrong, the comm ops would have to change their way of doing things, and were perhaps to blame in their resistance to change. The details would only make this general news worse.

Motors were to be phased out over a three-year period, 1980 being motor-free (I:5).

Use-level figures were complicated by the user-day concept, the shift to the river-paced rowing trips, and the increase in self-guided use, but the end result was a cut in commercial passengers each year, from about 11,000 to 9700. Rubbing salt in, self-guided users would increase from 500 to 3100. So from the comm op viewpoint, 2600 people each year who might have been persuaded to go on a commercial trip, plus 1300 for-sure customers, were being taken away. The plan's cost to the comm ops: 4000 potential paying customers. (Shock. Outrage.) This cut of maybe one-third in potential clients was accompanied by limits on launches per day aimed at cutting June-July-August use and moving it to April-May and September. Still more potential clients would be lost from among those for whom only the traditional summer vacation would do.

Another twist was taken in the motor-boaters' tail because the draft used the existing user-day allocations to get percentages of total use, which they applied to their new, and lower, passenger total. That meant that a rowing comm op would keep the same number of people, but the motor-boaters would have a decrease. Example: Two large comm ops have 12,000 user-days, each of which is 13% of the total allocation. The motor-boater runs 6-day trips, and so has 2000 passengers; the rower, at 12 days, has 1000 passengers. The plan would reduce the total number of passengers to approximately 10,000. When it calculates the allocation using the user-day percentage, each of the two companies ends up with 1300 customers. BUT this is a decrease of 700 for the bad guy and an increase of 300 for the good guy who had already switched to rowing.

A pause, because this use thing is vexed from environmental, wilderness, and political points-of-view. Environmentally, the research had said it was not the numbers of people, but how they behaved that mattered. With environmentally correct behavior in place, followed and enforced—taught by word and example to eager passengers by concerned trip leaders—the impacts from river-running would be mitigated. Borden's study sought a capacity number for river-paced (wilderness) trips (see Chapter 12); he came up with 148 persons, 5 trips, launched each day over the six-month summer season. The comparable draft CRMP numbers were 75 persons, 3 trips—1 self-guided at 15 persons, 2 commercial at 25 passengers + 5 crew. When I queried Marv Jensen about this difference, this halving, he said he had seen congestion reduction, particularly at attraction sites, as the prime target for the CRMP, both for congestion's environmental impact and its dilution of a wilderness experience. Yet, as I recounted in Chapter 12, both HERS and Borden thought that crowding could and would be alleviated by trip leader action.

Political and institutional considerations seem to me to have been paramount. The 1972-4 decisions set up a hold-the-line mentality. Still strong, that perspective would influence the CRMP numbers to keep any increase modest; the visitor increase for commercial passengers and self-guided together was proposed to be 12%, not large compared to the Borden capacity of almost triple the 1970s use. Moreover, the commercial passenger-day total for the draft (which assumed river-paced rowing) was what the comm ops claimed they had been promised for 1973 and, indeed, is the number in use in today's motor-dominated regime. The modesty of the change certainly helped protect NPS against a hullabaloo from those, like me, who had campaigned against big use increases in the early 1970s. Moreover, with commercial numbers headed down, the increase was to go to self-guided opportunities, aimed at diminishing that group's anguish. Of course, it would hardly satisfy those who sought a principled basis; the self-guided increase to about a third of the use was not a 50-50 split, or based on demand, or grounded in the belief that commercial use should only come after all self-guided use was taken care of. Still, from a bureaucratic view of the controversy, the new numbers must have appeared as a defensible NPS position.

Nevertheless, in the spirit of hindsight, let's just go back to the Borden numbers and borrow a few. Suppose we add one more trip a day in the six-month prime season to the draft plan's launches, and apportion those trips so that an equal number of self-guided and commercial people get to go. The result adds four months of trips for self-guided, and two months for commercial, each group getting 1800 more people for totals of about 5000 self-guided, and 11,200 commercial passengers with 2300 crew (still nothing like an equal split). These 18,500 launched seats a year would still only be 2/3 of Borden's wilderness-based carrying capacity. Now suppose another 8500 self-guided were added to reach a 50-50 split. The commercial passenger count would not be reduced, and the Borden capacity would still not have been exceeded. Numbers like these would have been received with shock and horror, and further on in the draft, the EIS bashed away at the very idea of such an increase. (The treatment of alternatives was also a matter of some vexation; they seemed to have been offered only to be knocked down; straw men instead of robust goals that might be worked toward. Overall, the draft was a fixed target; flexibility and openness to change and growth were not built in. On the other hand, clearly NPS first had to assert and gain control.)

By the way, 18,500 is about the number of "seats" launched now, except that the launches are not spread out, the overwhelming majority of visitors take, not river-paced wilderness trips, but only partial, speed-along motorboat trips, and instead of 5000 self-guided travelers, there are 3000. And also by the way—central for my theme of how we came to have an arbitrary, politically imposed, status quo river traffic system with no basis in environmental, legal, or human elements—the commercial visitor user-day numbers are what the comm ops said they were promised for 1973. Using speedier trips and helicopter shuttles, they have been able to get more people on shorter trips, exactly the decrease in quality that all those who appreciate the benefits of wilderness feared. So would the comm ops have been satisfied with a plan that maintained their passenger levels, while greatly increasing self-guided visitors and ending motor use? A speculation I leave as an exercise for the reader. We do know that keeping motors AND their use levels have become the twin icons of the imposed political system the comm ops depend upon; to give up either would, shall we say, disarm them.

To return to the draft CRMP, it discussed the division between comm op and self-guided trips by presenting it as a 2/3 - 1/3 split (I:7). But that was in user-days—116 KUD commercial to 55 KUD self-guided—which the CRMP dropped. In terms of the new counting basis, people launched at Lees Ferry, the split was not 1 self-guided out of 3 total, but 1 out of 4, and if commercial crew is included, then self-guided were to get only 1 out of 5 seats launched every year. And if you count, not seats launched, but how many different people occupy that seat as it goes downriver (where there could be two or three different occupants on different stretches), the comm ops get to rub in their advantage even more. Their style emphasizes fast, partial trips that increase the number of people who get to touch down on the river for a night or two. Counted this way, the split today gives self-guided about 1 out of 6 people who "get to go". These are only numbers, but they may help in understanding why this issue, covered up and nailed down for 15 years, blew up starting in the mid-1990s.

Today, Marv Jensen says his big regret is that the draft CRMP kept this uneven split. Since there is no way to derive a split based on "true" demand, he favors dividing the use 50-50, something he did on other rivers. But again, 50-50 of what? User-days, trips, numbers of people launched? If 50-50 is supposed to provide a semblance of fairness, then it only works if everybody gets into the arena through the same gate, that is if each person or party has to secure a ticket—a permit—from NPS without respect to how they will make their trip. Control over their clientele, however, is again something the comm ops clutch tightly.

Putting on a bold face, the draft claimed it would redistribute commercial allocations under new contracts granted through a prospectus based on how well a bidder would provide "quality wilderness" trips, stressing trip length, hiking and other interpretive stops, and crew to passenger ratio (I:9). Once their five-year contract was awarded, the comm op could go about getting passengers any old way, though the draft plan kept the unenforceable no-repeat rule that no one—except crew, of course—could take more than one trip every two years, a change from being allowed to take only one trip each year. Moreover, allocations would now be on the basis of launches rather than user-days, and launch dates would be NPS-assigned.

Anyone who wanted to take a trip on their own would get a permit, based on a lottery drawing for the week applied for (I:10). The draft contains the statement that most of the "legitimate" demand could be satisfied within two years, which implies that 418 trips would be enough. Since the trip applications at that time were running 400 - 500, that must have seemed a sane enough projection to make.

The section on protecting the environment has to remain a puzzle, since it sets forth the ways in which impacts will be handled, thus leaving unanswered the question of why negative impacts, so recognized, were not being dealt with right then (I:10-19). This cavil aside, the draft "proposed" to handle "overuse of 1/3 of the campable beaches" and congestion by: containerizing and carrying out all human waste; a ban on summer wood fires; use of fire pans for any winter or charcoal fires; carrying out all ash; again banning soap in side streams; building several short trails where there was too much wandering; increased efforts to educate crew and trip leaders on environmental practices; continuing the research program in all areas through monitoring projects; and increasing river patrols from 3 to 38 per year. These measures, along with all other changes except the full motor ban, were to be implemented in 1978, strange for a draft that was still circulating within the Park Service in May 1977.

Later on in the draft EIS, a sketchy history of river-running in the Canyon claimed that already in 1969 park managers were "astonished" by the increases (II:40-3). "Incredibly", there were 21 companies by 1973, with an "alarming" visitor increase that forced NPS to a ceiling on use. After the lid was put on, the increases in ungranted self-guided requests indicated a "greater disappointment factor" than for commercial passengers. Although some comm ops used their allotments, the self-guided use requested and granted compared to the unused commercial days "speak for themselves". The files were "replete" with complaints from disappointed self-guided applicants, with not a peep from commercial passengers. Even as some commercial user-days went unclaimed, 76 KUD in self-guided demand went unsatisfied. There were other mal-distributions, too, with launches clumping in a few days of each week and only during the summer.

The research results were heavily relied upon in describing current impacts. The condition of the more popular camping beaches showed "considerable damage" to vegetation and soils due to pedestrian traffic, leading to areas devoid of vegetation (II:45). This condition seemed somewhat self-limiting, decreasing exponentially with distance from the boats. Human use brought erosion and incorporation of litter, including leavings from fires. The high visitor densities at attraction sites were singled out as "detrimental" to physical and biological preservation and user satisfaction, and tied to trip characteristics such as length and speed (II:46). Chaotic traffic patterns and multiple trails were noted. Fire and waste disposal were attacked at length, building the case for the new regulations (II:47-9). The social benefits of campfires were out-weighed by ash incorporation and the overuse of driftwood and even standing trees. Two pages were given to the horrors of waste burial from porta-potties: limited space and multiple burials; inadequate drainage and covering; some possibility of bacterial contamination and spread; improper disposal of paper products; the offensive esthetics.

The "social" section stated right away that the commercial passengers were not representative of the American public, citing the high income and education levels

(II:50). The charge made in the *Congressional Record* (cited without a reference) that rowing "would eliminate a particular socioeconomic/demographic group" from river-running "is not true". The rest of the section contrasts, with fervor, rowing and motorized trips, making it clear, using the HERS reports, that rowing is the appropriate Park and Wilderness trip. The section on crowding sounds balanced, in contrast (II:53). Once again, the near-empty accident record showed if anything that motorized trips had more on-river accidents than rowing, but "the difference is not significant", and visitors perceive equally the trips as safe (II:55).

The *Congressional Record* statement was rebutted again for its "not true" claim that rowing trips cost the comm op twice as much as motorized trips (II:58). And as long as you compare comparable trips, the price ranges are similar. Significantly, there was greater demand for the pricier trips. The draft repeated the mantra: It is not the river-running trip characteristics but the managerial expertise of the company that matters. The motor phase-out was supported since the investment was not sizable and the cash flow was excellent, therefore most comm ops self-finance new equipment within a year, and most are already half depreciated. The regional economics of river-running was put into perspective by the research statement that the disappearance of all commercial trips "would not have a major economic impact on most communities in which these companies are based" (II:57).

Since the plan aimed at reversing degradation and other imbalances, Section III on the environmental impact was necessarily positive; this was not proposed work to disturb nature further, but to protect and restore soils, vegetation, and wildlife. The first proposals, to carry out human waste and to restrict fires, were easy to justify. The next, making a few trails at attraction sites, promised less. Interestingly, and contrary to the defenders of the status quo, the plan claimed that the more uniform rate of launches and travel under wilderness rules would counter overuse by spreading camps and lessening crowding. There would simply be fewer people at one time, thus reducing congestion, and impact. The trips being smaller would mean fewer people on any beach. They would use more beaches since they would spend more nights in the Canyon, but hit each less hard. The plan eschewed NPS post-launch scheduling and other measures unless conditions got even worse.

The drafters took note of the criticism that self-guided visitors may cause greater impact, due to not following the rules and inadequate orientation of and by the trip leaders. NPS proposed added requirements for education before trips. Comm op impacts should be lessened if the new contracts were issued to "companies with the proper background and knowledge protection". Still, the possibility would continue to exist that users could disregard the rules. Water and air quality were minimally affected by river-running, but eliminating motors and summer fires could only be an improvement.

The sections on the plan's environmental impacts were far outnumbered by the space given to impacts on humans, visitors and comm ops (III:10ff). The change in demographics would be small. No current group would be excluded, though no positive measures were proposed to change the elite composition of the visitor population. Changes in trip types would have minor impact on visitor characteristics. Of course, this analysis, though grounded in the HERS surveys, skips over the point important to the comm ops; the changes would decrease their client pool, both actually and potentially.

The cry of the comm ops was that the current system offered "choice". Although only a euphemism for maintaining the predominance of short, fast, expensive, motorized trips, the plan had to take this head on. It chose to do so, first, by citing the survey result that a minority of all passengers (about 30%) preferred motors; the rest preferred rowing or were indifferent. Second, it relied on the results of the "experiment" of having two combination motor-rowing trips, where the result was overwhelmingly in favor of rowing. The real problem of determining the desire for a choice between motor-driven rafts and rowing is that the choice is largely determined by what the comm ops offer. Because their presentations are tilted so heavily toward running mostly motor trips, and because they do not release information on client inquiries, anymore than they do on how many of their clients are repeaters, they are free to claim that what they offer, motor trips, is what their clients want.

Certainly, there is a real difference between the speed at which motorized rafts go and the river pacing of rowing trips—the former cover about twice as many miles in a day. Practically, this ability to speed through more Canyon miles in a day does not translate into much greater choice of trip length, since the comm ops set up partial trips, with the result that less than a quarter of commercial passengers get to travel even to Diamond Creek much less to the Grand Wash Cliffs where the Canyon ends. The comm ops try to flip this concessionaire-determined situation into an argument for motors by claiming that most people do not want to take the time for a rowing trip. However, rowing comm ops also run partial trips, so that the range and number of their trip lengths turn out to both cover and extend the motorized offerings. The draft took up the motorizers' anti-Park and contra-factual argument about trip length by claiming that there were rowing options for partial trips ranging from one day on up. Although true, some entry and exit points were difficult enough to provide another target for ridicule by the comm ops. Still, the plan concluded that eliminating motor trips would "not significantly alter the range of options presently available"; some opportunities would increase. What would be gone would be motors' "rushed miles"; the river would set the pace for people to enjoy the Canyon.

Sadly, instead of staying with Park and Wilderness principles as the justification for rowing, the plan writers felt it necessary to pretend that the point of the plan was to provide visitor enjoyment, which had to be justified on convenience (which really meant motorized comm op) terms, not those of Park and Wilderness values. It has always been my contention that the comm ops, knowing that the Canyon will always provide the satisfaction, undervalue their clients by limiting their options so that they end up paying big fees for a depreciated Park experience. The comm ops then add insult to injury by claiming that these clients actually prefer a part-Canyon rushed motorized situation. Yet no one knows what fraction of the public really might want and would choose, in an open market with full information, a rushed motorized trip of two to five days. If such a trip is a devalued Park experience, why not encourage those clients to seek a greater Park value for their time? How sad that the motorizers do not spend their user-day allocation in ways to maximize their customers' exposure to the Grand Canyon.

In its longest impact section, the drafters examined the river-running experience (III:13-20). The "two major factors" in that "hard to define" quality were the amount of use encountered and trip characteristics. Thus the goal of a wilderness river-paced ideal was not touted as good in itself, but embraced because it promoted the number one goal of reduced contacts, crowding, congestion. And while it might have promoted that goal, the comm ops could argue back that the goal could also be achieved by motorboat operators using their power to get out of other trips' range, while rowing trips would keep bumping into each other. That argument would be countered were trip leaders to maintain the spacing by traveling at river speed; however, placing the experience within the context of avoiding other trips was a weaker argument than championing wilderness travel. The entire argument of contacts and crowding is a bit bizarre, as I have said; what is it about humans that makes traveling with twenty other people, often strangers initially, on one trip more of an acceptable experience than being on a ten-person trip that meets another ten-person trip as you spend a couple of hours at an attraction spot? Perhaps congestion should have been discussed in an Impacts on Human Tolerance section of the EIS, which sadly was not called for.

The plan, of course, did reduce contact numbers, largely by decreasing and spreading launches and cutting trip size, but also by eliminating the more frequent passing that characterized a motorized regime. There was a concern that self-guided trips, longer than commercial trips, would be the source of increased contacts. However, these were just the participants who wanted fewer contacts, so they would also make greater efforts to minimize contact. Another oddity in the plan is that although it cited the majority preference for limiting trip size to 20 persons and for meeting smaller parties, the limit in the plan was only lowered from 40+ including crew to 30. Was the draft's configuration—two trips of 30 and one of 15—really preferable to four trips of 20 people?

Under the plan, trip characteristics were summed up as more, smaller boats each carrying fewer people and more crew, that would spend more time in the Canyon, including off the river, with no motor noise to interfere with conversation (III:15). Lost would be the large, fast motorized craft with many passengers and few crew noisily going quickly down the river in a "convenient" way. The advantages found in the HERS studies for rowing trips were repeated here, reinforced in this case because the writers all understood the benefits of rowing from personal experience and preference, not an advantage that endeared them to the comm ops. After listing such qualities as the relaxing pace, awareness of natural sounds and sights, easy communication with the crew, smaller, more comfortable groups, more off-river exploration, and greater awareness of the canyon and its environment, the draft concludes that there were no significant adverse effects on the visitor experience of an all-rowing plan. Indeed, from the standpoint of a major Park purpose, namely interpretation and increased awareness, the plan would have significant positive impact on the visitors.

Ironically, the draft fussed a bit about those who, because they had only a week, might feel pressured to take only a half trip. Ironically, because as I mentioned, today only about one-fourth of the commercial passengers take anything like a full trip. Presciently, the advantages of spring and fall travel, and even winter trips, were set forth. This was necessary since the lowered ceiling for summer launches would mean that about 3000 persons would have to choose times outside the June-August peak.

Beach esthetics and safety would show improvement, though trail construction might be considered intrusions.

The economic impact section started off with a thumb in the comm op eye. The changes "will have positive economic effects" (III:20ff). Since there were no economies of scale, or advantages in one trip type over another, or any profitability correlation except with managerial expertise, conversion to rowing would not force any motorized firms out of business. Another dig: the only firms operating at a loss currently ran motors, and significant losses were tied to investments outside the Grand Canyon. Smaller firms, by obtaining an increased allotment (one of Jensen's goals was to boost the little firms by giving them some of the larger companies' allocations), could be more profitable. Running through the equipment, labor, and operational changes needed to go to rowing showed short-term costs that could be absorbed without affecting profitability. Overall, all comm ops would have the opportunity to realize a reasonable profit.

The plan insisted that the CRMP-based prospectus for new contracts would improve competitive opportunity. The river industry would thus be more stable; the larger firms that would end up with fewer trips could still be profitable if they were managed well. The plan would result in "no significant adverse economic impact on the river-running industry" (III:23). The visitor should benefit as well (III:23). The range of prices should be about the same; there was "little difference" between the average cost of motor and rowing trips. The new allocation among the comm ops would provide a variety of prices. River guides could also benefit from a longer season with fewer launches per week, and more would be needed. The Hualapai might well earn more due to more trips exiting on their toll road at Diamond Creek (III:24).

The impacts sections concluded, in its discussion of "outside" influences, with an opaque crystal ball (III:25). There was trouble from aircraft noise, but the EIS did not specifically point at helicopter transport of river-runners. At the time of the CRMP writing, the Park had granted a 3-year permit to continue the use of mules at Whitmore Wash to take people out up the short trail there, where they could be transported by machines.[4] (That relatively amiable situation worsened radically in the 1980s when helicopter service became an industry at Whitmore Wash. Currently, over 10,000 people each summer season use helicopters that land on the south bank of the Colorado, avoiding NPS regulations on helicopters by flying over the Park and Monument. The other terminus is a private inholding with an airstrip that can handle flights to Las Vegas. In 1987, the comm ops codified this defiance of the Park idea and rules by their standard technique of appealing, successfully in this case, to their congressional allies for specific legislation protecting their helicopter use.)

There was a discussion of how unusual flows from Glen Canyon Dam affected river recreation, but no inkling of the major controversies that were to erupt in a few years and continue; in 1977, the Bureau of Reclamation still ruled (III:25-6).

Under mitigating measures, there was a reminder that the research showed "irreparable damage ... being inflicted" along the river (IV:1). The plan itself was aimed at alleviating that damage, but a monitoring program must be designed to detect deterioration (IV:4-6). "Of highest priority" is an annual assessment of campsites' environmental health, aiming at an integrated, "multidisciplinary investigations of fishes, terrestrial vertebrates, water quality, algae, vascular plants, beach erosion, etc." There should be aerial photography as well as field surveying. Some heavily impacted beaches should be off-limits; however, there was no mention of how such monitoring could feed back to an on-going determination of the riverine carrying capacity. Water quality and fish also needed further study. Measures "must" be taken to protect the endangered humpback chub (IV:6).

There were unavoidable adverse impacts (V:1-2). There would be 1000 more people each year, and they would spend more time in the Canyon. Accommodating these visitors will result in some, even though controlled, resource loss. A considerable controversy had developed over the relative values of motorized vs. rowing craft; those supporting motors will be disappointed. There would be some disappointments, as well, to those who want summer fires and quickie trips. And although the plan could not return the river to its pristine condition, it could protect and perpetuate the new (post-dam) "naturalness" within the river corridor.

The potential long-term economic productivity, under the increased quality brought by the plan, far outweighs any short-term loss (VI:1-2). The encouragement of responsible behavior through training, orientation, and regulations will provide long-term benefits for the environment. And for the visitors, I wish they had written, as they follow the improved practices of trip leaders and crew.

The file copy of this May 1977 draft shows Section VIII on alternatives most worked over. The following eight were offered:

no action = the status quo;
increase use to the maximum carrying capacity;
reduce use by 50% (to the 55 KUD of the 1972 Reed decision);
provide an exclusive non-motorized period;
keep the status quo for the headwater of Lake Mead;
a comprehensive lottery;
equal allocation for each company;
allocation for educational purposes.

The horrors of the status quo option largely arose from not acting on the environmental damage (VIII:1-7, actually 8 pp.). Fortunately, the Park did not wait for CRMP adoption before altering the status quo by implementing the two most important environmental measures: human waste carryout, and curtailing fires and their litter. As with the other alternatives, the draft's presentation was aimed only at discrediting it, under the rubric that there could be only one correct path. It therefore repeated the negative impacts of motors and the positive aspects of rowing trips. Most (80%) visitors would continue to have "a significantly reduced opportunity for interpretive and educational experiences" from being on motor trips. Since Jensen hoped to help out the smaller comm ops by redistributing allocations, the no-action alternative was cited for its adverse impact on the smaller comm ops. If this were a ploy to win support from that group, it would not work; bloody-mindedness is thicker than the river.

Pushing visitor use to the Borden-derived carrying capacity was likewise scorned (VIII:8-12). However, Borden's presentation is misrepresented by over-the-top insistence that this option would demand an NPS-led "very tight scheduling system". Moreover, the draft rules out trips longer than twelve days, whereas Borden allows for some. Of course, were an alternative of increased use adopted, it would be introduced gradually, just as motors were not immediately banned. But the rules for writing alternatives seemed to include one limiting options to an appearance of unreality. The repeated insistence on the need for rigid scheduling, given that most trips do their own scheduling and also work out interaction with other trips, is so puzzling as to suggest personal distaste or the thought that it felt like a good stick to beat an increase with, even though the draft itself envisioned launch dates set by NPS. If Jensen's recollection is true that the plan drafters were most concerned with reducing contacts and congestion, it is still hard to see why they would base the change on numbers alone, since once again, the research said on-trip behavior was more important. Was it that institutional reluctance to confront the likely criticism from environmentalists that led NPS to settle on numbers close to the status quo? Jensen also mused, in our 2002 conversation, that the plan was "real rigid". Perhaps in this matter, there might have been some sense in more breathing room to try how different numbers would work out.

Some of these observations apply to the next alternative, reducing use (VIII:13-17). However, the main objection here is that about 7000 people a year would be denied the trip. This seems too high a cost, given that "at present use levels, 91% of the river-runners define their trip as a wilderness experience". The discussion also suggests that half of the comm ops would have to quit the river, another too-high cost. But if cutting use would "simply serve to improve" a "generally satisfying" situation, then why, I am allowed to ask, were they worried about congestion at all? The strength of the Borden approach based on wilderness and other principles, along with campsite analysis, is reinforced by the arbitrariness of this "50% cut"; it is not tied to any model at all. Again, one can envision a plan based on a cautious approach of increasing launch numbers as monitoring shows damage being controlled. Otherwise, the options just seem arbitrary or, as I suggested above, based on institutional considerations.

The idea of having part of the year when motors would be banned was often thrown up as a compromise, as if there could be a temporal wilderness, switched off and on depending on whether the motors were running (VIII:18-9). This could not have satisfied us, except as one element in the transition to a motor-free wilderness river. Since the good will to make such a hybrid healthy was certainly lacking, little space was spent on it. Reasons seemed offered almost as jokes—that when motors were allowed, "the lower quality esthetic potential (status quo) would be maintained", and the added investment would decrease profits and increase prices.

I have not spent much space here on that part of the river affected by the back-up of Lake Mead (VIII:20-2). The use by powerboaters coming up from the reservoir is barely part of this story. To some degree, our success in getting the entire river included in the Park came back to bite us. The debate over whether the reservoir-affected stretch, called the lower gorge, should be included in the Grand Canyon Wilderness was vexed by the practical considerations of how to control non-wilderness use. The plan drafts were written as if motors were banned, and this alternative supposed they were not, thus allowing upriver motor use to continue unmolested. Continuing, then, would be the deteriorated esthetics, sanitation, and safety, since the "lake recreationists" were "at the opposite end of the scale" from river-runners. Conditions could be improved with stricter enforcement of regulations, but the benefits would only be for recreation and a speedier Canyon exit using motors, not the environment.

The alternative of having everyone desiring to take a river trip obtain a permit from the Park is one of the favorite suggestions by those, usually self-guided advocates, seeking to give a more prominent place to "real" user demand (VIII:23-26). However, the draft presented only a version that also eliminated allocations. Consequently, the pool of application from which permittees would be selected would be strongly affected by the ability of large comm ops to do mass advertising, thus working to the disadvantage of smaller comm ops and self-guided river-runners. The draft worried that unused launch seats would increase because there would be many applicants merely speculating. It did not discuss such matters as fees and the individual information that would be required to avoid duplication; how much could advertising do if every application had to supply a $100 fee/person, personal identification, and a commitment to take the trip? The draft insisted prices would go up to cover higher costs, thus excluding more visitors. Variety of trips would decrease as smaller comm ops were forced out of business. NPS administration would be more complex. (At that time, of course, the idea of contracting such a system out to the later-developed central reservation systems did not occur; computers and the Internet lay in the river's future as well.) There is no sense arguing about these points; it was not offered as a workable plan, only a hare-brained scheme to be knocked down. The drafters may have been hoping that the increased allotment for self-guided river-runners would end these debates over equity in river access. Once again, an opaque crystal ball.

Since Jensen did desire to help boost the allocations for the smallest comm ops, the alternative to make all commercial allocations equal can be seen as the extreme of this idea (VIII:27-28). Equality could be achieved by redistributing 50% of only the six largest comm ops (the ones who had, and still have, about two-thirds of the use), giving everybody a bit over 4000 user-days, or 15-20 trips each. The first point against this was that not all small comm ops wanted to be even this big. Not mentioned is that the big comm ops did not want to be that small, though the remark is made that if Grand Canyon profits were subsidizing unstable operations elsewhere, a comm op could go out of business under this option. Given that some comm ops admitted they kept motors to maintain salability when they wanted to get out, the even more Park-irrelevant notion that the Grand Canyon was kept motorized to subsidize failing business elsewhere is grim humor, indeed.

The last alternative was 1972's final straw, namely, reserving some user-days for (lower-cost) trips by educational institutions (VIII:29-30). The drafters were hard on this idea: the trip is already educational and there is no indication that it would be more educational if run by colleges or corrective institutions or whomever. Further, there has been a political outcry by semi-commercial groups wanting to create business for themselves, but there is no indication of a real need outside the current commercial/self-guided system, and certainly no reason to provide "special rights" to the Park's resources. Something pushed somebody's button.

The main part of the draft ended with a summary of public input (IX). The wilderness study process showed strong support for a motor-free river in the Grand Canyon Wilderness, as well as noise control and ecosystem preservation. The workshop process was described, and the 15 items of most concern to attendees way back in March 1976 were summarized. Specific acknowledgment for consultation was given to researchers Carothers, Dolan, Parent, Nielsen and Shelby. This was followed by a list of over 100 interested organizations that, presumably, would be involved in public comment.

The appendices started with the computation of launches and passenger-days, and blandly stated (no alternative was presented on this) that the "repeat rule will change from one trip every year to one trip every 2 years" (Appendix A).

The lottery system to be used for granting self-guided permits was like that used for other backcountry uses: people would apply with three date choices; there would be a random drawing for the dates with confirmation 90 days ahead of launch; those who were not drawn would go on a waiting list (Appendix B). Here it was stated that the no-repeat period could increase if applications did. There was no indication how commercial passengers would be checked for repeat visits.

Boating safety and commercial guide requirements were covered, and the final appendix provided a preview of the prospectus for new commercial contracts (Appendices D,E,F). Most of it was oriented toward business operations, but the draft did urge applicants to offer a variety of trip and partial-trip lengths. There would be an annual financial report, and the records were only "subject" to audit. Nothing was said about the no-repeat rule.

EISs Compared: Bureaucratic Face Powder

The above draft was dated May 1977. The printed draft of the plan came out in October, with the revised draft EIS being dated as ready for the public on December 8. So what changes had required another half year?

Some of the initial rhetoric changed, dropping references to Hoover and Glen Canyon Dams, to the Park organic law and the GCNP 1975 act (leaving only the Park master plan as underpinning), and to an introductory listing of what was deteriorating in river-running. Permit systems were added as a major public issue (I:1-2).[5]

Under "A. Mode of Travel" the later draft indicated the change in D.C. NPS thinking about including the western end in Wilderness by saying that motors would be phased out in the 240 miles to Separation Canyon, with motorized traffic allowed in the Lake Mead intrusion (I:4). This would necessitate other changes throughout the document.

Various inconsistencies in the calculation of "B. Use Levels" necessitated increasing some numbers so that the total went from 171 KUD to 193 KUD (I:6).

Most noticeable were the increased trip lengths, particularly in the winter, where the few trips were now estimated to average 21-24 days.

The "C. Allocation" between commercial and self-guided stated more straight-forwardly that there would be a decrease in commercial passengers of 1325. Commercial crew went up, from 21 to 27 KUD (I:6). This suggested that NPS anticipated more employees to carry the fewer people. (One can only wonder, given the reaction to the 1972 decision, how NPS officials could come up with those numbers and not see trouble ahead.) The number of NPS patrol trips each year was cut from 36 to 24 (I:8).

"D. Commercial Allocations" became more comm op friendly (I:8). First, it was made clear that experience and financial status would be factors, and that trip length offerings would not be so crucial. Added in were protection of the Canyon and providing the public with a quality wilderness experience.

The "E. Noncommercial permits" section, with its inequitable no-repeat rule, was unchanged, except the new draft deleted the hope that demand could be satisfied within two years (I:9).

In the May draft, mal-distribution of use and unenforced regulations were blamed in "F. Resource Protection" for beach degradation (I:11). This was deleted in the rewrite, as was the thought that while the research had been valuable, there was much still to learn. Otherwise the protections are the same, with the addition of a requirement for newly employed guides to attend a two-week training session (I:20).

In listing endangered and threatened plants, for some reason, it was thought necessary to say that "very little" is known about their distribution, but "it is believed that human interference" is not inimical to any of the plants in question (II:35). How the second statement could be made, given the first, is a puzzle left to the reader. Under archeology, the statement had been made that a particular site in the western Canyon was so important that it should be salvaged (II:37). This was dropped in favor of a claim that all relevant sites would soon be listed in a national register (II:37).

In writing the river history, the new draft acknowledged that the demand for river use had increased in the Canyon due to such factors as increased leisure and wilderness experience, as well as river expertise and equipment (II:38). (This recognition was welcome; unfortunately, it was not shared by most of the comm ops.)

In a step backward, though, the word "inequitable" was deleted from the description of the difference between the commercial and self-guided allocations (II:40). Going further, the new draft drew a confused picture of self-guided demand, while adding the supposition that commercial use would have been at a much higher level had there not been the 1972 limitation, so it is likely that the demand for commercial trips is greater than shown; this statement contradicting one earlier that commercial allocations do not get used up, and a citizen could always find a trip (II:43). (All of this, of course, went into Marv Jensen's conclusion that demand is impossible to determine, so no allocation can be justified and a 50-50 split is probably best. It is, therefore, a shame that more effort was not put into devising a system where all would-be users have to obtain a permit.) The challenge to the *Congressional Record* excerpt was toned down, no longer "not true". In the new draft, the idea of a motor ban eliminating any group is only "unlikely" according to studies (II:54).

For some reason, in comparing motors and rowing, the new draft increased the number of rowing rafts per trip and cut the number of people on motor rafts (II:55). The research finding that overall there was a preference for rowing was changed to say that research found 61% of motor passengers and 1% of rowing passengers preferred motors. Yet the comparable figures for rowing—98% on rowing trips prefer rowing and 15% of motor passengers want rowing (another 25% were indifferent)—were not cited and the earlier draft was correct that the survey did show that a majority of properly sampled passengers preferred rowing. The write-up on preferences for contacts with other trips was re-done using somewhat different data, but the impression of wishing a low contact level remained (II:56).

Two sections on comm op economics were eliminated (II:57-8). Together these sections presented the economic case that there were no economies of scales and no great differences in the economic viability of motor or rowing companies. The statement that management is the crucial factor in profitability was dropped, as was the section on the economic contribution of self-guided trips.

If any of these changes were made because some NPS reviewers were getting antsy about being so anti-comm op, then perhaps it signaled debate over hitting them so hard simultaneously on motors, number of paying seats launched, and spreading their launches away from the summer. Though maybe it was all just editorial, and no alarm bells were ringing.

The picture of a dark future without the plan was expanded in the new draft. The negative environmental impacts were summarized at more length. A new theme was added, that the Park visitor is aware of deteriorating conditions and can become dissatisfied and frustrated by "overuse and unaesthetic conditions" (II:61). The effects of Glen Canyon Dam were introduced; river use would accelerate some of those impacts. Self-guided visitors were still under anecdotal suspicion, even with "no concrete evidence" of their greater impact (III:5). However, the view that motors would continue to degrade the natural qualities of the Canyon was not voiced. The treatment of the Lake Mead environment was changed since motors were not to be banned there (III:6), so the description now projected a place of continued environmental degradation from ignorant, careless, and unregulated use. Throughout the Canyon, the user population would not be affected by the plan (III:11).

Other stylistic changes suggested more sensitivity to motorized opinion (III:11,13). It seems hardly stylistic that the entire three-page discussion of comm ops economics was eliminated from that section and moved to an ephemeral appendix (III:20-3, and see below). Jensen was convinced of Parent's accuracy but some NPS level above the River Office must not have been.

A balanced, yet still positive, discussion of winter travel was added (III:18). Recommendations for restrictions on aircraft were deleted (III:25). The later draft "understood" that Glen Canyon Dam was operated to satisfy water and power needs (III:24), replacing the sly joke of the May draft that "it is conceivable" that growing power demands "will outweigh the desire of the comparatively few river recreationists" as far as dam releases go (III:26 of the May draft). And it would have been a prescient drafter indeed who could have foreseen just how much dam operations would be affected after 1980 by non-power "desire".

In the section on mitigation, NPS no longer would require itself to ensure that every trip leader have a working knowledge of river regulations (IV:3), even though, as researcher comments made clear, many of the guides did not have such knowledge. As with so many of the changes, this one suggests that the additional six months of review and rewrite were mostly bureaucratic process, hand-waving in a sort of Mitigation of Opposition Impact analysis.

The new draft added that monitoring trends in crowding and demand was essential (IV:4). The data in the current research "cannot" accurately predict future patterns. (And did not, due to mitigating action by trip leaders.) The self-guided lawsuits illustrated the need for data to determine relative demand; an interesting thought to compare to Jensen's judgment today that there is no way to get accurate demand data.

Under unavoidable impacts, discussion of the comm ops economics was eliminated again and a few comments were added about self-guided trips having to spend time learning about the regulations (V:2).

Sharp wording about Glen Canyon Dam's effect was toned down, while more explicit statements about beach disturbance were added (VI:1 and VII:1).

In the section on alternatives, there were changes I will detail at some length. In general, these changes sound certainly cosmetic in the sense of powdering language so the text did not shine so brightly into people's—opponents'—eyes; exactly what would be expected by a bureaucratic review process going from the Park, to the Region, up to Washington; and through the levels within levels. Overall, the decisions and ideological placement of the Plan remain the same. So was a six-month delay, itself controversial and upsetting, a proper cost just to dull the glare?

In the no-action alternative, a juicy bit about "dirty" camps with more flesh and blow flies was deleted (VIII:2). The impact on self-guided visitors became just "adverse" since allocations would stay the same, instead of "highly adverse" since the allocations would stay "inequitable"(VIII:3). A paragraph on the general visitor preference for few day contacts and no campsite contacts was deleted (VIII:4). In the new draft, the reference to excess profits apparently earned by some comm ops was dropped, so there were now only "healthy" profits (VIII:5).

Under the second, increased-use, alternative, a discussion of impact on comm op profitability was once again deleted (VIII:7). Under the third, decreased-use, alternative, the suggestion that profitable business situations for many comm ops could be maintained was deleted (VIII:10).

Since the decision had been made in Washington not to recommend Wilderness for the Lake Mead intrusion, the fifth alternative was changed, from keeping motors from Diamond Creek on down, to banning motors in that stretch. So the discussion now seemed more a presentation of why the ban-motors decision was a bad idea: the environment was already so degraded, and the visitation so heavily motorized, that there would be no overall benefit (VIII:12-3); costs would be higher and the Hualapai economy could be hurt.

The new draft gathered the last three alternatives into one group of "allocation options". The first was now titled "individual applications", though the principle of every person and group having to get a permit from NPS was the same (VIII:14-5). The objections of swamping by comm op advertising, the consequent lessened opportunity for self-guided applicants, and great difficulty—especially for the Park Service—in matching successful applicants with the trips they desire, remained the same. The alternative of equal comm op allocations was recast to emphasize that it was doubtful that either small or large comm ops would be pleased (VIII:15). The language against an educational allotment was toned down, but the strength of the objection remained that there was no need for it or any reasonable way to select who should receive it (VIII:15-6). Many applicants would actually be commercial organizations and would need a commercial permit, not just an educational one.

Under individuals consulted, "river running management" now included members of the Sierra Club in Tucson and the Western River Guides Association (IX:4).

The appendices were different. Those on user level computation, self-guided permit procedure, and resource protection were dropped. Lists of the research projects and of breeding birds and mammals were added. The Comm Op fact sheet underpinning the new contract prospectus and the appendices on boating safety and guide requirement went unchanged.

Most interesting was a new "Appendix G, Summary of Economic Analysis, Grand Canyon River Trip Concessioners"—interesting because it collected the deletions from the main text, and because this appendix did not appear in the final EIS. There was a paragraph on self-guided trips; their daily, non-capital costs were "80 percent less than the average commercial rate". The draft still contradicted (in a toned down way) the *Congressional Record* insert that claimed rowing trips cost twice as much as motorized. Heavy, repeated reliance was put on Parent's finding that profitability is largely correlated with managerial competence, not size or type of boat. The two largest firms had the highest and the lowest amount of profit, and a small firm was among those with the highest profit. The larger motorized companies running the short 5-day trip could have their number of trips cut in half, so the amount of their income and profits would also decline. (The CRMP did not say it, but my reaction to this is: Good, just what they deserve for degrading the experience.) The final, overall conclusions remained satisfactory, "Although high profits may decrease for some firms, the opportunity to realize a reasonable profit for all commercial companies operating in Grand Canyon will not be diminished. No significant adverse economic impact on the river-running industry is expected to result from the proposed plan." (G:5)

The Thing Itself

I have discussed the two EIS drafts first; they were of central importance in validating and legitimizing the CRMP. Also there is no draft of the Plan in the files before the October 1977 version. The Plan clearly came at the end of the drafting process to produce a document for public comment. Still, we need to spend some time with this document since it was ostensibly the principal public presentation.[6]

Its introduction referred to the effects of Lake Mead and Glen Canyon Dam, the latter leaving a "clear, cold, tidal flow" to which "environmental responses have been rapid and significant" (1). But it is the dissatisfactions voiced by comm ops, self-guided river-runners, and interest groups that have driven the need for changing the 1972 status quo. The statement of the Problem is the familiar litany of environmental degradation and human impacts on humans. The struggle for a motor-free Wilderness is ignored. The Park System and Grand Canyon Acts are again mentioned, the research is summarized, and the concerns from the 1976 public meetings were summarized. The plan itself is presented in fifteen typewritten pages (17-33).

Each item has a justification that is a distillation and consolidation of the EIS sections. Again, the first item is called "Motors Vs. Oars", instead, say, of the more correct and positive "A Grand Canyon River Wilderness". Indeed, it is not the Wilderness Act and NPS Wilderness policy that rule, but the research and public comment (18). (Perhaps this says something about the "democratic" legitimacy of citizen opinion, but if so, then it is worthwhile remembering that the Park and Wilderness Acts are embodiments of American democratic opinion, enacted in the contention-friendly crucible of national legislation.) Most of the discussion is about the ills of motorized travel, how no one will be excluded, with a fillip at the end about people preferring rowing and its benefits for understanding of the Canyon and the environment.

The section on use first notes that three trips a day would result in other-group contacts within the range that people want (19). (Again, the echoes sound of the arguments, by Eiseman and others, that research cannot justify wilderness; it is a matter of values. And what would the drafters have said if people wanted ten times as many contacts a day?) The Borden study, though it determined a reasonable maximum use level, is again erroneously dismissed as requiring rigid scheduling.

The increase in self-guided users was colored by the greater "potential ... to misuse the river resources". The reduction in commercial launch seats is powdered over by referring to "their broad appeal to age groups" and to partial trips.

Intra-comm-op allocation is to be based on the plan, which may "warrant serious consideration of a company's ability to provide the type of service established by the plan." (23). Smaller companies need more use, and some larger could do with less.

Self-guided applications were to be handled on a first-come-first-served basis (= put on the waiting list) after an initial computer assignment (= lottery?) (23-4). The computer will watch for duplicates (Big Brother, automated). No repeating within two years.

Waste removal, trail building, and limits on fires were the principal environmental actions (24-5). The monitoring program would try to get better numbers on self-guided and commercial demand, as well as effects on campsites and economics (26-7). Data were also required to allow plan modification whenever change became essential. There would be standards on guiding, resource protection, boats, health and safety (27-30).

Sections on relations with Reclamation and the tribes added nothing new (30-32).

The Plan attacked helicopter use head on (29-30). The new permits would have a condition based on strong public objections, the Park Master Plan, and the goal of maintaining the wilderness river-running experience. Trips could be exited only by hiking, livestock use, vehicle up Diamond Creek, or boat to Lake Mead. Whether on Park or adjacent lands, "the debarkation of commercial passengers by helicopter from the river is to be discontinued."

Brave words, and it is fitting to end with them, since whatever my criticisms, this was a brave plan. Founded on a determination to mortar together law, policy, research, and public opinion, its aim was to provide the sound environmental, wilderness, and people-supportive foundation Grand Canyon river-running so desperately needed. Before we go on to the events that destroyed this initiative, let's pause and reflect on it in the spirit of praise and hope. The 1977 CRMP reflected what was best about our open, messy, American methods of governance. It looked toward a future of greater opportunity, flexibility and innovation, one that celebrated the Canyon while enhancing the lives of those who came to work and visit. Had the Plan stood, over the past 25 years Grand Canyon river-running would have become a wilderness activity full of enjoyment and enrichment (and profit) conducted by all in a spirit of good will and optimism.

Time's up. On to the dark side.

CHAPTER 17

1978: Hot War At Last

To set up the proper mood for the CRMP, the Park sent out a notice about applications for 1978 self-guided trips.[1] Applications had to be in by January 31 (you called or wrote to get one) to be included in the February 15 lottery. Half the release dealt with would-be repeaters: one person, one trip; no person could be listed as a passenger on more than one application; no substitution was allowed for someone listed who could not go; if NPS found any information fictitious or incorrect on an application, it would be voided; if a trip could not use its date, NPS would change it if given two weeks' notice, and this should allow most permittees to carry the people listed on their application. Welcome to the Park; have a good time if you can figure out the rules.

Then came a thud as the draft CRMP+EIS hit the mailbox.[2] The cover letters and news release stressed that these were proposals only, based on research, public concerns, and management goals. Deadline for comments was March 27. There would be six February meetings to hear from the public, in Flagstaff, Phoenix, Denver, Salt Lake City, Los Angeles, and San Francisco. The release listed the plan's highlights:

phase out motors over three years;

spread visitor use over the year to provide increased use, longer trips, and less crowding;

increase self-guided use to 30% of the total;

replace the lottery for self-guided applicants by a first-come/first-served permit system;

issue new commercial "permits" based on the "merits of the new proposals";

prohibit summer wood fires;

require all solid human waste to be hauled out;

confine foot traffic in popular spots to trails.

There it was; now what would people say about it? Although there were many variations, the battle positions clustered around the three poles of wilderness and the environment, self-guided users, and the comm ops. Me first.

For Us, Defense

The day after receiving the documents, I wrote out my position.[3] "I am going to urge that we swallow our desire to perfect this plan; it moves so far toward the ideas we have espoused that I think it justified to say: Conservation organizations support implementation of this plan, and without delay. Put it into action, make it work, and then look toward a review when the contracts again expire in five years." Though I thought the 3-year phase-out for motors was "generous, and undeserved", I felt the decision should be taken as is. Thinking it possible that the next few months would be "a crucial period", I said that our key contribution would be a showing of public support; "we do need to start asking people to write". I did this in notices to local allies, saying I was "tending toward endorsing immediate implementation of the plan as written".[4]

Asking "Is Grand Canyon's River Plan Any Good?" in another mailer, I answered that no one could know, since the only good plan is one in action.[5] We have been putting up with the "highly unsatisfactory status quo", and what was needed was immediate action to alleviate present inadequacies. Certainly, the plan had flaws, but it offered a "large-scale move" toward policies more appropriate to the Grand Canyon as a natural place and more sensitive to visitors. Further delay will bring further damage, more shattering of the wilderness experience by motors, and continuing discrimination in favor of the comm ops. "What has been most unnerving ... is the inability to effect any changes for the better until there was a completed plan." In the past year, NPS has fiddled while problems were not attacked; every year will compound the damage. I ended up by suggesting that I might be naive; perhaps the plan was only put out knowing that the inevitable criticism would bring more delay in the need to make upsetting decisions. Yet my reading led me to ask all concerned about the Canyon to urge NPS to put the plan into effect immediately.

What is wrong with this picture? Aside from its hopefulness, my position meant that a clear statement of our goals for wilderness and protecting the environment was muted, subsumed into the Park Service position. Had we worked out and pushed a strong pro-wilderness-environment counter-plan based on our own conclusions about river management, it could have stood out against the arguments of others, exerting pressure on the Park Service to move our way, or at least hold the line. It would have provided Canyon supporters with a more positive position to advocate. Given the eventual outcome, it could have served as a set of principles to judge river management over the years.

So why did I not take the principled stand? I think first because of impatience; waiting five years had built a pressure to advocate action now; my own "institutional" bias at work. The picture I had in my mind was of a road, and I wanted to see matters move down it. An alternative image would have been more static, of a four-sided tug-of-war pulling on river operations, a game that was going to go on for years, and getting movement in your direction meant pulling really hard from your basic position. Instead, to maintain this metaphor, we threw our strength onto the NPS rope. This may have been with some admiration, if grudging. The Park Service, in a gaggle and with stragglers, was following Jensen's lead as he and the other preparers gathered together a plan that tried to remedy the bad decisions and floundering of the past decade, searching out in the murk where the correct path might be and get over closer to it. (Of course, I did not foresee the ground being yanked out from under the plan by the results of a national election, leaving us with no place left to stand.) It is also true that there was no great debate among conservation allies. My position seemed to be quickly accepted; it was, after all, comforting and energy-efficient. Without internal discussion, it was easy to maintain the view that putting this plan into operation was the best course, and the several conservation organizations who offered statements for the record—Sierra Club chapters, Audubon groups, NPCA, The Wilderness Society—supported the plan.

As a four-sided contest, the unreliability of the side we chose to join was revealed when, as described in Chapter 15, Superintendent Stitt was deposed in February by Tony Ruckel, the Sierra Club lawyer, just before the public meetings on the CRMP began.[6] His answers deal with environmental problems covered by the CRMP draft he, supposedly, was offering to the public. And supposedly, they were problems being taken care of in accordance with the research. But, on a question about campsites, he answered that suitability was "subjective in determination according to the research". On litter on the beach, "I don't agree with the litter and sandbox effect which is open to interpretation." (An interpretation he had signed off on.) When asked about wastes and charcoal becoming incorporated into the sand, he replied, it should not be there "if you can prevent that". Anyway, "litter is very minor and I say that from first-hand observation" in August 1977. Furthermore, "We have taken action". "We couldn't get [action] in the Annual Operating Program in time for the year because of when we got this information". (Since the information was available in the summer of 1976, this is nonsense.) Ruckel tried to nail down a decision that all waste and litter removal will be effected in 1978. Stitt: Some has already taken effect; a number have been hauling all human waste out for years. (I knew of only one comm op for whom this was true.) Then, "a good many of the private operators [sic] are not doing it ... It will be mandatory for everybody in 1978." (As I was sitting there watching, was I wondering about the favoritism?) Then Stitt got in trouble, saying "wastes from all of the Park, yes" were to be hauled out, then reiterated "all", and again, and again. This is the passage that he later amended to say just "campsites", but the iterations were not changed. There is a lot to speculate on here. Why was GCNP still so at odds with us on environmental protections? Why did we have to sue at all, and why was there not more action by the Park Service? Why did Stitt have to make it sound better then it was, when the need for improvements was one of the underpinnings of "his" CRMP? Certainly, the foolishness of trying to support the Park Service is brought into relief by this obfuscation. Even on these issues, where researchers, environmental opinion, Park Service, and even some river-runners, were in agreement about what was needed and could be done, we ended up as adversaries. A sad indicator of weakness on the eve of the public meetings.

Self-Guided Fire Bombs

One debater was a voice I was bound to respect. I heard quickly from Fred Eiseman that he did not share my perspective.[7] First, he pointed out that, even though there was more use for the self-guided visitors, their position in the lawsuit was undermined by any fixed allocation. Second, he believed that all visitors should have to go through an NPS lottery, and dismissed objections to it as irrelevant; whatever system NPS uses, some people will try to cheat, and it is up to the Park to enforce its regulations.

His third point was that use was doubled. He did not believe visits would spread out over the year. He equated user-days with user impact, and wanted it decreased, as we had argued six years ago. He also did not like the provisions on fire and waste and scheduling and Park patrolling—"not what I would call a wilderness experience". NPS has solved its problems, but not the Canyon's problems. He thought this was all a reprise of 1972, and we would end up in the same way. Certainly, non-concessionaires would object violently to the "philosophy of catering to the economic viability" of the comm ops, who in turn would fight the motor ban and trip lengthening.

My answer emphasized that I was glad to accept the research because the alternative was gossip and observation through jaundiced eyes. Even if the research were garbage, "it is magic garbage because I can call it research, and that will get me further in arguing" to defeat the Canyon's ills. The present situation only benefits the comm ops, and while your suit is tremendously important, until it wins, NPS will maintain that benefit. I admitted my position was "opportunistic". I disagreed about user-days; to me what was important was the actual impact as measured and monitored.[8] I was willing to accept the view that there could be more people and more user-days if they behaved according to the pro-environmental research recommendations. I worried that the environmentally "best" trip might be the quickie 5-day motor cheat that just touches briefly and concentrates use, "allowing people to go through in large, supine groups that trample a small area to death". I wanted all the good things for visitors that can happen on a rowing trip, and more visitors if the Canyon is not hurt. I went on, revealing something more about my choices, to say that I might be singing a different tune if I had detected any great interest in fighting for the Canyon. Maybe I was only justifying what was already a defeat, caused by the disinterest of those who were supposed to care. So if, I said, I detect a great outpouring of support for making the plan better, I will join in.

Meanwhile, I was hopeful as usual, putting two pieces in the newsletter of the Sierra Club's Grand Canyon Chapter, which also inserted the AWWW opus I had written the previous fall.[9]

Eiseman's statement on the plan itself spends much space on his contention that the plan aims primarily at increasing use, because of "some considerable pressure".[10] His skepticism about the researchers is subtly elaborated, and that about winter trips direct. He celebrated the motor ban, but presciently feared that political pressure would cause its reversal, unless "those in powerful political positions can be properly influenced". His attack on concession policy and the comm ops was severe, for the preferential treatment they received. What is strange to me is that he thought the comm ops were the paramount influence on the plan since it called for an increase in use. (Later he realized how strongly the comm ops opposed the plan, and tried to sound alarms about their false rhetoric, especially the slogan of "choice".) Most vigorously, of course, Fred attacked the idea of allocation, based on no research, and inherently illegal because it created two classes of citizens and actively discriminated against one and for the other. He undertook, as well, a strong defense of a lottery system applied to all users, arguing in detail that the plan's objections to a lottery were ridiculous or irrelevant.

Another self-guided user was preparing a different view for local Sierra Club members.[11] Jim Vaaler argued that the jump in applications in 1975 and 1976 indicated people "stuffing the ballot box", not an increase in demand. He used figures, supplied by the Park in a November 22, 1977 letter, showing that 48 persons who did not receive a permit showed up on trips of the 40 successful permittees, and this suggested a 50% duplication rate. So he wanted the lottery system scrapped. His ideas for restoring balance were to cut user-days to the 1970 level, increase the self-guided share to 40%, and then accept the CRMP two-year no-repeat rule with permits issued on a first-come/first-served basis. He extended the usual range of offered ideas by suggesting a two-beer-per-day limit. In our follow-up correspondence, he agreed that the immediate implementation of the plan was absolutely necessary.

(The first-come/first-served method includes a waiting list; apply once and you get a spot. As I write, there are over 8200 applications, implying a 20-year wait for new applicants. The lottery eliminates the waiting list, demanding that users re-apply for each period offered, with instant gratification for those selected, with the trade-off that an applicant has around a 5% chance on a yearly basis—it would vary were it monthly, say—and no guarantee. For what it's worth, both Eiseman and Vaaler had taken several trips and owned their own boats; they were serious participants.)

A third view came from a Denver group, American Canoe Association, which was upset that the draft plan did not offer a solution, keeping in place a system that makes the commercial passenger privileged, facing no limit, no lottery, no need for a permit, in spite of the congressional mandate that concessions must not "interfere with free access ... by the public".[12] They pointed out that the research did not include any study of ways to implement an equitable and fair access system. The allocation was completely arbitrary, as was shunting self-guided trips into the winter season.

The American Canoe Association/American Whitewater Affiliation fair-access plan included every person needing a permit, each permit issued by whatever method is chosen on an equal opportunity basis. There should be no fixed allocations, each person obtaining a permit deciding whether to "join a noncommercial group, join a nonprofit organization's trip, hire a guide, take a complete package tour, buy or rent various equipment, pay shuttle drivers, etc., etc. The government has no business determining this for the individual."

(The supposed impracticability of this suggestion in 1978 has been removed by the spread of Internet access, and in variations, the idea is being offered today. Like designating wilderness as Wilderness, fairness in access is an issue that does not go away just because of political arrangements. Indeed the pressure seems to increase, so that the comm ops have spent much time in recent years trying to reduce that pressure by enticing self-guided advocates with the hope that if the comm ops are left alone, they will support more self-guided use.)

The Comm Ops First Strike

The public meetings provided us with a sobering view of the comm ops' determination, in contrast with their recent relative quiet.

In an opening shot, the Arizona Office of Tourism wrote about its agreement with the motorized comm ops' "critique".[13] The State would lose tens of thousands of dollars in taxes. (For how ironic this argument is, remember Eiseman's efforts recounted in Chapter 11.) There would be economic hardship on all motor comm ops, and some would be forced out of business, others would have to re-tool and contact a totally different clientele, destroying any benefits from past advertising. Few of the aged or the handicapped can stand the rigors of rowing trips. People who cannot spend the time or afford the cost for the longer trips will be discriminated against, as will people who can only take time in the summer. Winter travel runs counter to marketing experience. (This, from an official in Phoenix!) Most people think the river trip is already a wilderness. Travelers would be deprived "of their freedom of choice, which is an inherent right". The comm ops do a wonderful job of keeping the Canyon clean, and self-guided trips and hikers cause most of the waste and litter problems.

The accompanying anonymous pro-motor "critique" started by fastening on the (admittedly silly) idea of having people hike out on unmaintained trails, then ludicrously exaggerated it to be a major defect. Next it complained about how quickly motor comm ops would have to buy new equipment. The "treadmill" scheduling of trips would not work because of river fluctuation. April was a bad month to take a trip; too cold and too few customers. Overall, commercial passengers would dwindle. NPS administration was ineffectual; it has not even been able to maintain its 150 persons/day limit. Starting the plan in the next year was not enough lead-time. Environmental problems seem to have been resolved and, anyway, NPS used to allow ash to be dumped in the river. There was no water pollution from motors. The noise research was "sketchy" and dubious. Motorboats "can move out of the way of a rowing trip" (= can roar past), and make more adjustments for crowding (necessary because of motors). Unable to let the safety issue go, it stated that "logically" the "potential" for deaths from hypothermia is greater with smaller oar boats that flip more readily. (Of course "logically", the facts that there are 20-30 more people on a motor raft and they do flip, would seem to increase their danger potential; also a ridiculous, untrue point.)

The Parent economic study was then attacked. The first claim was that there are so many motor trips because they are what has evolved from demand. "All river operators are aware that there will be not enough demand (for rowing) to keep all 21 companies in business." (How is that for a fear-based policy to keep the gang together?) The comparability of price is denied. The EIS did not mention the impact on Page, and the figures on Kane County are wrong, as are the figures on taxes paid to Arizona. These errors "prove how unreliable Parent's study is". And he did not contact any comm ops or state agencies.

As the attack on the HERS study opened, I was given some play for having helped Shelby, "Ingram has been an outspoken and inflammatory advocate of rowing since the beginning of any discussion regarding motors and oars. River operators must suspect the bias of the study from this contribution alone." (Did my chest swell with pride?) There is a fuss about discrepancies in trip length averages, resulting in misleading figures. The figure is repeated that 91% perceived the trip as a wilderness experience, and most do not see it as crowded. (But how come these HERS figures, favorable to the comm ops, are not also unreliable?) The main attack is on the combination motor-rowing experiments. People had pre-formed preferences. The motor portion was run by a company (Relco) that leases equipment but is not a licensed comm op. Nielsen admitted that the results may not generalize to other comm ops (none of whom, remember, would cooperate). Data we have seen indicates the trips violated NPS rules and were inaccurately reported. One of the researchers expressed her preference for rowing and asked a rowing comm op for a job. The motor boatmen were upset at having to travel in only 7 days to Diamond Creek. "Rumor has it" that one boatman hiked out. Rowing companies "frequently" hike their passengers around dangerous rapids, and the studies "have totally neglected the handicapped who cannot scramble through rocks". (The point and purpose of all this seems to be to discredit the plan and contributors with any and all weapons more than it is aimed at presenting a coherent positive statement for motors. It is, of course, a document more for motorizer allies than anyone else, carrying their old messages about how they served choice and the old, young, handicapped, and busy.)

A lighter mortar round came from the rowing/motor comm op ARTA's statement, noting the company "has historically supported the oar power mode of travel ... as more compatible with the natural rhythms of the river and the wilderness experience many people are seeking", said it was ready to comply with the plan, but believed it did not serve the best interests of the Canyon or the public.[14] There would be some increase in environmental degradation. Rigid scheduling of trips would destroy diversity and flexibility of trips. Their suggestions were to increase rowing trips to 40%, require a minimum of 8 days to run the entire river, disallow helicopter use, reduce motor horsepower, institute lower limits on people per boat and trip. Non-commercial river-runners could also have more use. More candidly, the owner told me that they had planned a fuller conversion to rowing, but ran into "the market" that said rowing was unsafe and preferred motors, so he held up, and, based on market considerations, was no longer in favor of a motor ban.

The motor comm op Hatch broke no new ground—choice, and rowing takes too long.[15] He did make clear that his main concern was making the large comm ops give up user-days to the smaller ones. It does not matter, he groaned, if a company has been around for two generations; we would have to give quota to Johnny-come-lately types. "This quota reduction would sound like an approach to communism." We want to preserve the free enterprise system. Unnecessary bureaucracy may be costing every family $2000/year. This headlong curtailment of freedom and personal choice has to stop.

Perhaps the weightiest pro-motors statement came from the Professional River Outfitters Association (PROA), CROA's successor for some of the motorized comm ops.[16] Its summary started by saying the CRMP draft violates the intent of the NPS Organic Act. The Park Service re-ordered the public's priorities. A research sample was insufficient. Hiking would be "mandatory". Research did not sample physical condition or impairments, or outdoor experience. There was a huge increase for self-guided users who impact the Canyon more and are harder to monitor. Comm op river use would be "confiscated". River seasons would be imposed instead of being the result of demand. (The tortured wording must have made the document puzzling to any but the initiated; as if distortions of the draft plan might slip by if tarted up in odd rhetorical clothing.)

Following the summary, the PROA document hawked the mis-statement that the National Park Act had two "co-operant values": preservation and use. The CRMP intends "to drastically restructure" the river trip "industry". It is obsessed with eliminating motors and "dictating" trip lengths, and takes "unconscionable liberties" with data and events. In stretching to demonstrate this obsession, the PROA statement cited the HERS finding that 90% of visitors thought the Canyon was a wilderness (and did not mention that even one-third of motor passengers thought it would be more of a wilderness if motors were banned), and let itself be confused by there being two sets of public meetings, on wilderness and on the river. Three pages are spent in discrediting the motor-rowing "experiment", with a prime accusation being that the results were alleged by NPS to apply to all trips, in spite of the HERS cautions. Beyond that, the NPS documents "are replete with prejudiced references to motorized river boats". By page 6, even the author was aware he appeared "obsessed with the anti-motors obsession".

Moving on to trip length, PROA presented data it had collected showing a broad spectrum of trips in response to the "indicated preferences of the public", although it says nothing about how people get sorted or sort themselves into this spectrum. (Since people reading the brochures can only choose what is offered, overwhelmingly motorized, there was not, and still is not, any way to gauge what demand would be if not channeled, or how the "industry" would structure itself if it had to respond to independently expressed demand, if such a thing is even possible.) And if demand dropped off due to people not wanting to go on Park-required trips, NPS would be "derelict in its responsibility for providing the maximum enjoyment" (a policy of National Parks as amusement parks, in short). PROA insisted that the Plan "required" people to take hikes they were unprepared for, and gives a smack at those "more damaging" self-guided river-runners.

Crocodile tears streaming, the document says the plan is "intimidating", constituting a "hunting license on ... concessionaires". NPS is accused of subtle manipulation of "will" and "may". It then makes the odd criticism that the plan was not a prospectus for concessions. More reasonably, it asked that the plan offer more detail about NPS's desires for the shape of the industry, and challenged NPS to do a competent marketing study or accept the current use as "demonstrated" demand. It then pretends that allocations are not bought and sold, and suggests NPS could facilitate an "equitable restructuring" of the comm ops, using "Due Process, and natural market methods, entirely within the present Permit and Allocation systems, without resorting to controversial, confiscatory" procedures. Foaming, PROA "strenuously" objected to the "atrocity" of assigned departure days, citing the troubles that arose in the merger of two railroads. "The present system is the best way." Interestingly, PROA says the present system is for a comm op to request a date, and receive it *if available*. (And what screams would have been heard if a request were turned down?) PROA refuses to entertain any attempt to spread use.

Having promised to be constructive, the document then offers several items growing out of the above complaints, each item accompanied by the tag "to be the decision of each commercial operator". "We are suspicious" of summer fires for esthetic reasons. There should be no trail-building, but just marked routes; with blocks to prevent wandering. The document winds up with a few more slams at the "amateur" sector, though it generously suggests a gradual increase each year for self-guided use.

Not all commercial opinions were obsessed with motors. A river guide wrote about fires, first making the usual point that they (he mentioned ARTA, Wonderland, Fort Lee, OARS, and Canyoneers) were improving their procedures on fire and fecal waste, not because they were told to, but because "we cared about our Canyon".[17] Give us a chance; let us keep the fires. Anyway, self-guided river-runners, who do not know or care how fragile the Canyon is, cause the continuing problems and they will keep on violating the new rules. (Please keep in mind that for every self-guided trip of up to 15 persons, there were 15 commercial trips of up to 45; so 45/46 of the travelers were as clean as clean could be, we are told; and 1/46 real dirtbags.) And, anyway, the river environment is not a wilderness, but a "tameness", due to Glen Canyon Dam. Impose a clean fires rule requiring a fire permit to be given only to those demonstrating proper knowledge and supplies. Use high-walled fire pans burning wood from outside, with all solid fire products taken out. (These last, with the exception that driftwood could be used in winter, were the procedures already in force for the 1978 season, and continue today; there is no permit or fine.) Impose a fine on violators.

Another comm op was direct about the research, "some people decided they wanted to ban motors ... talked to researchers and told them what they wanted and came out with this end result. The plan—God, this burns me so much ..."[18] "I'm not talking about kids from the ghetto coming out and getting to experience the Grand Canyon. But, amongst those people who do have the time and the money to make a trip with us, I think that there are a number of them who honestly are best served by a motorized trip". The combination trip was "loaded against the motorized outfitters". "Hatch sent me down the canyon with 120 people on one trip ... that was not the kind of trip that should be there." "At least 11 outfitters by the end of (the 1977) season were carrying out all of their waste."

Another got personal.[19] "I know an oarsman's involvement in rowing can be based on personal gratification and the drama of the experience, rather than any concern for public preference or public service. There is a fad now of jumping out of a boat into a rapid; some kind of manhood ritual". It will continue "until it ends tragically". "We used to be ashamed if a boat capsized. Now it's considered by some to be an expedient, a part of the technique", as is "kicking the boats loose above a rapid and having everyone make their way along shore". These slurs against rowing guides continue: They "aren't really the top notch oarsmen", so perhaps if all companies can be made to row, "they will have a better chance for rowing jobs". The record on safety is not relevant; what matters is the potential for drowning, and "there are many more small rowing boats capsized than there are larger motorized pontoons".

Such toxic comments indicate to me a person so determined to have his way that he scorned the idea of compromise; since no offers came my way, I was probably viewed the same way. One indicator was from a Phoenix newspaper column by Ben Avery, in which my malign influence was spotted: HERS "admits" Ingram was one of its advisers, "a Sierra Clubber whose main occupation in the past couple of years seems to me to have been monitoring everything that went on at Grand Canyon in his efforts to get motorized rafts off the river, and to close the park to the general public by making the entire area a part of the National Wilderness System. Personally I like Jeff, but no one citizen with such bias against the general public should be allowed to influence such a public agency." [20] This was part of a column in which Ben reconfirmed his move from pro-rowing to pro-motors, and also attacked ARTA for its biasing of the researchers' combination experiment. "Naturally, I like oar travel best", but the question is whether NPS is going to manage the river for the enjoyment of "all the people" (which is his definition of the 0.005% of Americans who get to go). He notes with approval that motor trips visited fewer spots and for a shorter time, so their environmental impact would leave the Canyon more unimpaired.

Ben was wrong about my being a Sierra Clubber and my occupation. But to accuse me of trying to keep the public out of the Park was such a libel that even now it deserves a loud Bronx cheer. Still, I answered mildly: The river is deserving of Wilderness protection, and the result is that, with rowing trips, the Park Service decision will "finally allow the river to be used by all people in such a manner as to protect the Canyon while providing the maximum enjoyment for the visitor; that's what the law asks for, and that is what will be allowed and encouraged under the new plan." All the pro-motor, anti-rowing arguments "are untrue, used to blind us to the fact that the only thing motors are good for is to rush people through the canyon".

Not content with battering the Park Service, PROA wrote to the Sierra Club Executive Director complaining about the behavior at the San Francisco meeting of three Club representatives. PROA whined that they had supported the plan although they had not read it, and then left. [21] These "blind snipers" are the reason the Sierra Club is in the trouble it's in. Many of us saw your "impulsive" lawsuit as a public relations move. At four of the meetings, the *only* people who have advocated the plan as written also stated they had not read it. "With one exception: Jeff Ingram, who speaks for the Sierra Club in southern Arizona, said in the Phoenix meeting that the plan is admittedly flawed, but we should go ahead with it because he's wanted it for five years. This plan is Ingram's Holy Grail; he would like to hand it to the Club saying 'here it is - its shaped kinda funny and it leaks a lot, but by God, I got it for you!'" (Aw, shucks. Holy Grail is a bit modest.) Your members and staff are placing the Club in the realm of "blind opposition". (I love this; WE support the Park Service plan; HE wants to scrap it and exalt motors over

Wilderness, but the Club is in opposition.) I do not know whether McCloskey reacted to this solicitous concern for his situation where those "who should appropriately articulate organizational positions are pre-empted from doing so by others in the general membership or in staff positions who presume to speak for them." Well, the atmosphere was heated; in a letter to a local paper, I called motors "recreational pornography ... utterly without socially redeeming features."

From the Front: War Correspondents

Newspaper coverage of this period was the most extensive of the controversy to date. Pete Cowgill had written in a Tucson paper that NPS had "come through with flying colors" with its motor ban.[22] There will "probably be some" protest by comm ops. He quoted pro-rowing elements from the draft plan, adding that a visitor will no longer feel "like a steer aboard a cattle truck bound for the slaughterhouse". Safety is not a factor. What comm ops like about motors is that they are faster and push bigger boats.

Avery's paper countered with an article in mid-January on the PROA statement's assault on the plan.[23] Straightforward, the article described such items as the threats to choice, the need for difficult hiking, and the public's preference for motor trips.

An AP report from San Francisco featured the motor ban and "quick reaction" from two comm ops.[24] "I'm dead set against it" from Burke, with ARTA saying, "We favor it." The NPS proposals were a "sharp departure" from current policy. The change in self-guided allocation was mentioned.

An editorial in Cowgill's paper in Tucson called the motor ban "a sensible move".[25] Motors only cater to Americans' urge to speed through everything. The increased allocation to self-guided trips also makes sense. A big spread followed, featuring interviews with three of the motorized comm ops puffing up their smokescreen of horrors that will follow a motor ban.[26] For instance, although rowing trips do not sell and passengers cannot hike, all the hiking and camping permits would be taken for the next five years, with trail congestion and fatalities.

The AP reported on two of the public meetings.[27] In Flagstaff, only 2 of 21 speakers favored the Park's plan during the 3-1/2-hour session, attended by 250 persons. In Los Angeles, the 36 speakers (out of 85 attendees) were "pretty evenly divided" on the plan, according to an NPS source.

The Denver meeting received a lay review from an attendee.[28] He was scornful of the many speakers over the three hours who appeared not to have read the document, or who chose to ignore parts that would interfere with their criticism of the plan. Many of the comments were based on the "long-standing commercial vs. non-commercial antagonism", and several on both sides were offensive. Comm ops Litton and Hatch appeared, each complaining about a specific thing that bothered them. "Your sole, non-arguing supporter" was the Sierra Club's Southwest Representative.

The Salt Lake meeting received a much more thorough report from a local paper, *Deseret News*.[29] The first paragraph was a collage, "undemocratic and harmful to business" from the comm ops; "good protection of wilderness values", we said;

"not sweeping enough", self-guided boaters objected. The plan was more extensively summarized than usual. The motor ban was most controversial among the 170 attendees at the meeting, which "dragged on for hours", with "weary" NPS officials "holding their heads". Children fell asleep; reporters got bored and left. "There were angry mutterings from the crowd about filibusters as professional outfitters talked on and on", with 40 speakers still to come. NPS promised to hear everyone if it took until 3 a.m., but some who signed up left; others shortened their statements. The bulk of the article summarized sixteen statements, e.g., rowing is hazardous, the comm ops truly represent the public by offering a choice, self-guided trips are not qualified, a 70-year-old has a "right" to a safe comfortable trip. One motorized comm op preferred rowing, but he was in business to serve the public. One boatman, having taken 44 trips, said rowing trips run out of food and into trouble. Self-guided spokesmen insisted that everyone should have to get a permit, and condemned allocations directly to "private firms". Pro-wilderness comments stressed the noise of motors.

The *News*'s environmental writer followed up with a column saying NPS solutions "are aimed mostly in the right direction".[30] Few comm ops agree; banning motors "hits them in the wallet". After summarizing the history, he listed the "most telling" arguments against a motor ban: the longer trips would give more chance for environmental destruction; it is hard to get out if danger arises; many folks do not want to spend 12-14 days and feel more secure in motorboats. There are, however, two good reasons for a motor-free wilderness designation: the dam threat would be ended, and as a real wilderness, it should be protected as such. He realized that there are more motor trips because they are what is offered, since they use up fewer user-days for each person. But thousands save their money for years, fly in from the East, and then have their serenity marred by the roar and fumes. People should be willing to spend an entire vacation on this once-only thrill.

Another columnist, reflecting on the Phoenix meeting, which "dragged on past midnight", called the meeting "dominated by boating interests", illustrating the long-standing accusation that NPS has "abrogated" its responsibilities to concessionaires.[31] NPS "took it on the chin" from comm ops, environmentalists, citizens, and "the small coterie of canyon fans who love the river". No one thought NPS was doing a good job on the river. The comm ops were "well organized" and had a group of like-minded friends to push for motors. Speaker after speaker talked about choice, but the dispute over motors overshadowed protection of the environment. So it was a breath of fresh air when a rowing boatman, Wally Rist, got up to defend resource protection by criticizing NPS for increasing, not decreasing, use. Rist noted there was not one time when his group was alone and uncrowded at an attraction spot. He objected to the fire ban; there is more driftwood than there used to be. We boatmen were not consulted on the plan, and we are over-burdened with ridiculous rules. Motors and rowing craft can co-exist on the river. Each person should have to get a permit, and then choose how to travel.

A Utah paper reported on a set of questions sent to Interior by pro-motor congressmen (more on this below).[32] It quoted Congressman McKay, and more interestingly, the newish-senator, Orrin Hatch, who said NPS is being "dictated to by a bunch of radical environmentalists who want to stop river-running for everyone except a small group of athletic youngsters". Hatch's view was echoed in an editorial from Phoenix's second newspaper; the title says it all, "Elitist Lobbying". More subtle was a *Salt Lake Tribune* piece that noted The Wilderness Society's stand against motors in the Grand Canyon and in favor of a new Wilderness just east of the city, saying, "It's a puzzle" that the sights, sounds and smells of an intensely urbanized area are an acceptable invasion of one wilderness, but not fondly embraced in another.

An unfortunate summing up appeared in *Newsweek* in April.[33] Color photos, one of at least six motor rafts swarming with people at Lees Ferry and another of a "tourist-season" fire on or near the rim, set the tone for a piece about crowding and damage. "Purists" were pitted against those who want the Canyon to be "easy to enjoy". Outfitters have started to clean up their act, but draw the line on motors. There are quotes from the Sierra Club and Wilderness Society. Comm ops say people want motor trips, sneering at "the elitists with the time and money to enjoy it in the manner of their liking". The article said a majority of the 3000 letters were pro-motor, and concluded that Interior still seems convinced that the Canyon can best be appreciated by "the silent majority".

I attended the Flagstaff meeting, impressed by the many comm ops and their employees who spoke—Grand Canyon Expeditions, Canyoneers, Del Webb, Harris, Hatch, ARTA, Sanderson—along with Page town boosters, making the points summarized above. One rowing comm op, Kovalik of Wilderness World, challenged the motorized arguments. I sang my tune, that the plan moves forcefully to arrest drift, and while not flawless, its goal is to protect the Canyon and the experience for all visitors. I emphasized the need for increased orientation and monitoring, and hoped for a dynamic process where we could all work together to make the situation even better over the next five years.

Body Counts

On March 9, the Park sent out a notice about the meetings, saying there had been 1000 attendees, and 205 oral statements.[34] Many written statements and hundreds of letters had been received; this was later upgraded to 267 statements and 2300 letters. Therefore, NPS decided to have another meeting, in Washington on March 23, and the comment period was extended to May 1. That was the public face; behind the scenes, the Park Service was shell-shocked by the reaction the comm ops had generated.

I used a bunch of phone calls to assess the situation. When I talked with Howard Chapman on February 27th about the hearings, he described a "disastrous start", but later believed there was lots more from the non-commercial side, and so things were not looking nearly as bleak as after the first two meetings in Phoenix and Flagstaff.[35] Flexibility was needed, and we have to look at the plan again. There was not a strong NPS position set on values, and it was under review. There had to be a better recognition that the Canyon was only one place to go. Eiseman would not stand still for a fixed percentage of use or for increasing use only in the winter season. We can ill afford to fix the plan. Both comm ops and self-guided were attacking the idea of increased NPS patrols.

Marv Jensen was more direct. He was "somewhat" let down by conservation groups as a whole; they had not shown up as knowledgeable supporters. He had depended on his contacts with NPCA, but that group failed in the clutch. There was continued contact with politicians by comm ops. But the latter's opposition was running its course, and getting more irrational. It would be difficult to complete the final EIS, but he would do it, not Washington. He also knew that the OMB guy was still sitting on the Wilderness recommendation. I had also heard from another person that the D.C. groups were saying they wanted to wait on the Wilderness.

Stewart Brandborg, former Director of The Wilderness Society and now an assistant to NPS Director Whalen, said he felt strongly and was saying so. From another NPS official, I learned that the final decisions would be at the Departmental level, but that the Director, who was planning to go to the Park in June to take his first river trip, part-motor and part-rowing, had said there would be no slippage. It would be August when they set the direction they wanted to go. He was bothered most by the arguments about the relation of the raft size and environmental and safety requirements; were motors needed for evacuation? And what about the time factor in rowing? There was a need to look at not just the Canyon, but a total system.

McComb provided a summary of the Washington scene, where about 125 people attended, and 43 spoke.[36] The comm ops got their troops out. Two staffers for congressmen from Arizona (Rhodes and Stump) cited the letters against a motor ban. And while ten environmental Washington-based organizations offered statements, this was matched by the comm op allies, with four comm ops themselves showing up, including the PROA representative, who produced an even more elaborated critique.[37] The comm ops had twice as many citizen supporters as did the plan. No congressional voices were heard supporting either the self-guided or the environmental positions. Overall, the showing was definitely one to increase the pressure on the Park Service to look hard at what it had done.

A senator from Utah attacked the plan as damaging that state's tourism industry; the motor ban was most unfortunate and without justification; all rowing would make a river trip "impossible for any but a very few".[38] The proposal to allocate more use to self-guided trips was arbitrary and lacking empirical justification. "The quicker, shorter commercial trips permit more people." Comm ops have been an important influence in cleaning up and are generally less destructive. NPS "has not made a case for any" of its changes. Senior Arizona Congressman Rhodes was "appalled" at the motor ban, based on his own "enjoyable and worthwhile trip" (he had gone with Burke) and the 60 letters he had received.[39] This is a case where "a very vocal minority has captured the attention of the Park Service"; this plan "will work to the detriment of the vast majority of the citizens of this country". He was seconded by Representative Stump from northern Arizona, who parroted the PROA line.

The odds the Park Service faced were indicated also by a March 3 Washington meeting at which representatives of Interior and the Park Service faced congressional staff, mostly but not wholly anti-plan, and full of what they hoped were tough, embarrassing questions. These, they shortly thereafter wrote up and sent to NPS for formal answers, as reported above.[40] The only other person at the meeting was comm op Burke.

Another voice could not have been entirely comforting, either. Bo Shelby, who had put in the major effort on the HERS study so heavily relied on in the plan, and who then moved on to the faculty of Oregon State, offered the opinion that there was "little basis for arguing that motors ... are ecologically harmful"; the major difference is in the type of experience provided.[41] "The difficulty lies in deciding which kind of experience to provide." Then, just before the meetings, Shelby wrote Stitt praising the plan and its presenters. He said it was exciting to see study results interpreted into proposed policy. He personally agreed with the proposals, and was pleased with how the general goal was defined in workable objectives, and supported by research data. However, perhaps the meetings shook him, too, since a month later Shelby wrote that if the goal is to provide a wilderness experience, then he saw little room for argument over a motor ban. However, if your goal is to provide maximum convenience, then motors are clearly appropriate, and "our research clearly supports this". Such a goal might call for shorter, faster trips. "It may not be possible to maximize convenience and still provide wilderness." (But convenience— did that equal fast and big for Shelby—under what assumptions? Surely there is maximum convenience as well as inconvenience in wilderness settings?)

Shelby was brought back by the Park in researcher mode, distributing and analyzing questionnaires at the seven hearings.[42] Of the somewhat more than 1100 people who attended, 61% turned in name/address cards, and 39% (434 people) completed questionnaires. (NPS reported there were 267 statements.) This contribution might have helped restore NPS spirits, since his report concluded that the data "support wilderness as a goal for river trips" as well as "attempts to reduce interactions among parties". However, wilderness norms of commercial motor passengers differ from those of others, and that group, along with "boatmen", place a lower premium on wilderness. The questionnaire itself is a dense two pages, asking each person to imagine in turn the Canyon as wilderness (generally unaffected by human presence), semi-wilderness (complete solitude not expected), and undeveloped recreation area (meeting people is expected). For each scenario, he asked several questions about the number of encounters on river and off that fit the experience. This was followed by evaluative questions.

Of course, the people who answered were not in any sense representative of the river-running population or even of the hearing attendees, though they may be indicative of the opinionated publics. There were 82 motor passengers and 10 from rowing trips, 163 self-guided boaters, while another 143 made their primary identification as conservationists. The relatively high number of "boatmen" (63) makes sense given that together the Flagstaff and Salt Lake meetings brought out 44% of all attendees. And why, given that this was a continuing issue, did over a third of all attendees fail to turn in name/address cards?

One response strengthened stereotypes: Motor passengers stood out from all the other groups as assigning higher numbers for encounters, and being less willing than any of the others to obtain a wilderness experience by paying more or waiting longer or going in the off-season. And more than twice as many would choose a semi-wilderness experience rather than pay any of those three costs to be in wilderness. The strength of the support for the comm ops "no change" policy among motor passengers and "boatmen" is shown by the close agreement in their evaluation of the river as it is and as it should be. In contrast, the other groups match those two on the statement that it is semi-wilderness, while showing their dissatisfaction by 60% wanting it to change to be wilderness. Three-fourths of self-guided boaters wanted wilderness. However, no matter what gloss is put on the figures, they should not have provided any comfort; they only show this was a political fight with well-defined differences. And even though the numbers of respondents would appear to indicate a two-to-one tilt in favor of change from the existing situation, the comm ops had used their troops to score heavily, as evidenced in the initial impact on NPS and Interior officials.

Re-Grouping

The first shot back from the Park Service came in response to the set of questions sent from the congressional offices represented at the March 3 meeting.[43] It did not come quickly; there was a prodding letter in April, and Congressman Stump noted that NPS's reply arrived right at the deadline for comment.[44] The questions aimed at uncovering the inadequate basis for some of the CRMP's provisions. And NPS had to admit there was no research on people's desire or capability to run the river, their interest in going during the winter, or on the comparative demand for commercial and self-guided trips. They did not know exactly how many duplicate self-guided applications there were, and how many were from commercial crew. Many of the answers sought to be exact, even non-argumentative. Still, there was an effort to re-offer mitigating data, such as the HERS finding that all passengers had much the same socio-economic profile (including having high income). Its comparison of trip cost insisted on the value of competition to keep costs down. There is an admission that the boatman conducting the motor part of the motor-rowing experiment stated he had to rush. We still think that the motor-oar experiment had a representative group of river visitors. Actual operations do show rowing trips are suitable for the old and families, and rowing craft can haul out their waste. We know self-guided trips do not do as good a job of environmental protection, but in any case, we are not able now to run adequate patrols. (The letter, as it could have, did not point out that there was no real point in doing more research, since the comm ops had demonstrated that unless the results supported their views, they would trash them.)

Optimistic or foolish, I offered some thoughts about strategy after assessing the February meetings.[45] The foes were determined; comm op Burke had said he would fight a rowing-only policy until hell freezes over. The comm ops put money and diligence into successfully organizing their faction at the first two hearings (which I had attended) to maintain their control over river policy. The Park Service took a psychological battering at the first two meetings; though Chapman thinks the other four were more balanced. He thought the motor phase-out was O.K., and was glad that Assistant Secretary Herbst had given McComb the same answer. Our lawsuit, given the comm ops' intransigence on the plan, is now a useful tool to pressure the Park to take pro-environment steps anyway (Stitt testified he had the power to do that) and to remind the comm ops that their extensions run out next year. I also wondered how the largest concession could be sold—lock, stock and allotment—to a non-river business without a peep from the Park Service, when there were self-guided and smaller comm ops clamoring for more river time.

McComb had expressed hope, I reported, that there might be some congressional action, the key being Udall (though in the previous month he had already determined it was too controversial; see Chapter 15). So we in Udall's district have a prime responsibility if he is to be willing to move a motor-free Wilderness. The behind-the-scenes Hualapai actions are aimed at hampering action on Wilderness, in part because of a continuing affection for a dam. So we must (I still thought at the time) keep all three of the balls we are juggling in the air. Our Wilderness message has become accepted—by the Park Service, anyway. The comm ops are determined, but sound desperate. We need to persist in keeping this a public struggle.

Friends of the Earth ran an article by a rowing guide that was knowledgeable and correct on the issues, and the newsletter, as well as its Colorado Plateau representative, supported the "timely adoption of the plan".[46] The Wilderness Society sent out a mailer supporting the plan as proposed, with particular emphasis on the motor ban. Later, its newsletter summarized the plan, and urged people to write the Assistant Secretary, particularly opposing motors, a task suggested as well by another of the groups I worked with. Also locally, the Sierra Club asked its members to write the Park Service and Congressman Udall in support of the Plan, though the best we could produce was his tepid comment that "I am pleased with the progress made thus far by the Park Service in attempting to produce a workable management plan for the river to accommodate the greatest number of people while at the same time preserving the resource."[47] Still, he was "firmly opposed" to any more dams and in favor of "the fullest possible protection" for the river.[48] He was willing to meet the challenge of accommodating use while preserving ecological integrity—in the next Congress.

It was a measure of my desperation that I circulated a flyer of my own in Tucson pointing out that while the comm ops had generated 2-3000 letters attacking the plan, conservationists had yet to mount a national appeal.[49] I suggested phoning a select list of people, like Herbst and Udall, and also key conservationist staff. I offered to pay for long distance calls. For Herbst and Udall, our message was support for the plan and Wilderness; for the others, that a national appeal was needed. What good, I asked, will new parks in Alaska be, if park protection for the Canyon is rendered meaningless by the comm ops' campaign?

Prior to NPS Director Whalen's motor/oar trip, I heard second-hand that the Club's Southwest Representative had met with him in Washington and come away "distraught to learn that Whalen seems to have no commitment to save the parks whatsoever".[50] Moreover, Whalen denied a decision had been made on motors. Mail was reported to be three-to-one in favor of keeping motors, and internal NPS lobbying in D.C. was even more dangerous, so Jensen's best hope for keeping the plan on track would be Whalen's trip. The Club Rep offered the opinion that local people should bolster Jensen, and set aside any effort on Wilderness legislation since "the river management portion of the plan is sufficiently detached from the wilderness issue" that dealing with them simultaneously would damage our position. He was aware Arizonans thought the Club had given too little attention to the issue. Writing Whalen several weeks later, the Club Rep told him he could be the leader that the Park Service needed by resisting congressional pressure in Canyonlands National Park.[51] He continued with an elegy on a motor-free Grand Canyon, asking Whalen to reaffirm the 1972 decision to ban motors, the correctness of which was now confirmed by the research.

It will come as no surprise to the reader that I was disappointed, perhaps a normal reaction of frustration at Canyon issues being downgraded. Also, it may be that various environmental organizations' discussion about Grand Canyon strategy was just as riven with internal lobbying as was NPS's. Decisions about effort to be deployed on the Canyon were being taken far from Tucson, emphasizing as with Jensen within NPS, our physical remoteness. Could it be that being in favor of the plan was not as energizing as opposing it? Or in view of the great effort being spent in favor of Alaskan land protection, were there just too few resources? Of course, the time for maximum effectiveness on the Wilderness issue had passed—a determined lobbying effort to get the legislation should have come in March to June 1977.

In July, GCNP offered a schedule. We are now incorporating comments, and expect the final plan early in 1979, with a 30-day comment period, and implementation in 1980.[52] We are already putting some "non-controversial" resource protections in place.

My concern about this pace, along with my distance from starry-eyed preaching, was clear in my own memo to the Director, written on behalf of the four groups (including the Club's local chapter) who had asked me to represent them.[53] Following up on a conversation with Whalen after his eye-opening river trip (Dave Foreman of The Wilderness Society told me Whalen had a great trip, including in the dories), I reiterated that for us, "the foundation issue" is protection of the Canyon in a motor-free legislated Wilderness. Failing to secure such protection would only encourage those dedicated to exploitation and abuse. I cited Arizona Congressman Stump, a dam proponent, who was leading the assault on the wilderness aspects of the plan.

Being positive, I wrote that motorless recreation within a Wilderness coincides with park policy, the research, and the views of many heavy users of the Canyon— how often guides say they prefer rowing themselves, but the public needs motor trips. Public support for Wilderness has been expressed over the past ten years, even if it might be muted by the current Alaska effort. And suppose that all 2500 letters to you about the CRMP were pro-motor—and they are not—that would still only be about 5% of the people on the comm ops' mailing lists; a 5% that coincides with what research and the draft plan say is the number that might be inconvenienced by a motor ban. I know you cannot disregard anti-Park elements in Congress; but given ten years of public support for a motor-free Wilderness, please put the comm ops' "springtime blitz" in perspective as a desperate attempt. After all, the plan will actually help the comm ops, since it will result in certainty and thus sounder long-range planning. I fear needless delay as you try to counter every hypothetical hurt, such as the idea that people do not have time to run the river. Given that river visitors are mostly affluent middle-class, their vacation time is obviously more than the time needed for a river-powered trip. And given the once-in-a-lifetime quality of that trip, that two- or even three-week time is appropriate. So why has inconvenience been puffed up as an issue? Because the plan is not in operation. Only when it is, will these "fevered nightmares of the concessionaire's imagination" go away.

Another reason for high priority of plan completion is its linkage to wilderness legislation; if that were introduced in January, an approved final plan would answer questions about their linkage. Finally, speedy plan issuance is needed for proper contract proposals to be written. We can see then how the comm ops react to a principled plan that has incentives for them. If you aim for early October this year, the plan can be presented to the fall comm op meeting at the Park, allowing for discussion and plan implementation. "I know" that if you make and stand by the decisions, the comm ops will move quickly to take advantage of the opportunity, "beginning a new era of cooperation on the Colorado". (A prophet I was not.)

The formal Park Service reply referred to the "nearly three months" needed so far to analyze response to the draft plan; therefore October was an unlikely date for a final plan, though we are making every effort to expedite it.[54] Less formally, using the phone, I learned that adding to the Director's good feelings, he had been briefed on August 1 that the response had ended up 60% against motors; with a 10-to-1 anti-motor outpouring for the plan since May 1.[55] That was in 500 letters; in the 2500 responses before May, the motor ban was favored by 55%. Even one of the pro-motor congressional staff was "surprised" at the number of pro-wilderness letters. (Oh, had this only have been the battle over a Wilderness bill, when such a preponderance might have led to a more definitive end to the controversy.)

Not all was so rosy. The Club lawyers heard from their government counterparts about an idea for a summer motor season. Another idea floating around was to extend conversion to rowing over several years, with motorless periods; there might be rewards when a comm op had finished converting. The other Arizona senator, DeConcini, although he had had environmental backing in his election, did not see the arguments against motors as clear-cut, and his staff indicated he would wait a while before taking a position. We fussed about media coverage, in particular a reporter who seemed to be making a brief for the motorized comm ops, and did not interview anyone from our side.

At the end of August, my assessment was we were moving, painfully slowly, forward in our "strategy of the four prongs": quick adoption of a pro-wilderness and pro-environment CRMP; convincing NPS to tie new contracts to comm op acceptance of that CRMP; settling the lawsuit with that tie as a provision; and getting an administration-approved Wilderness bill introduced in early 1979.[56] We sorely need Udall's support to counter the anti-park legislators like Garn, Hatch, and Stump, which means that NPS has to be "locked into a pro-wilderness" plan so Udall will know he will not be undercut. We know that after reviewing the responses, NPS is keeping the environmental and monitoring provisions, and a motor phase-out that will possibly be extended over the contracts, even to 1984. Then comes "pre-approval" by Department officials in the next two months, followed by writing, EIS final approval, and the contracts. So I agreed with Venable to tie suit dismissal to NPS following that schedule. I was going to be spending September 11-15 in Washington, to see Whalen, find out where the wilderness proposal was, and check in with some of the pro- and anti-plan congressional offices. Our goal is approval up through the Secretary and President by the first of the year of all four of the above "wind anchors, tied together, so that opponents have to confront all" of them at once.

My appraisal of that trip listed "important" discussions with Udall and his staff, DeConcini, Whalen, staff members of the House and Senate Interior Committees, and pro-wilderness groups.[57] Buoyed by his trip, Whalen had met with Udall and told him he would support the plan. I also talked with other staff in Congress, Interior and OMB. In summary, "our patience and support will be rewarded with proposals that are in accord with our goals". This will be achieved by making the plan economically more acceptable to the comm ops. (Not yet fully appreciating how inextricably rooted were motors in the comm op political psyche, I thought that a worthwhile change.) The schedule I was offered was that the Regional proposals were due September 15, with a review on the 18-19 by the Assistant Secretary, followed by a press conference. In October, the final EIS draft would be reviewed, and come for NEPA approval by early February, with final decisions on March 23, 1979. I could also report that following my visit, NPS presented its idea for the final CRMP+EIS to Assistant Secretary Herbst, who recommended it proceed. There was scuttlebutt about intra-agency disagreements; I was seen as unwilling to compromise; the comm ops had to be heard; a non-ally wanted to know were we going to fight this forever. Ah well, there was nothing new about tendentious gossip in Washington.

On the trip, I had tried to do groundwork for advancing the Wilderness bill, but Alaska remained the priority. Also, the OMB staffer Sessions was now saying that the Park Service "informally" wanted the Wilderness bill held during CRMP process, so it was just sitting there, and movement would depend on who pushed it.[58] (Please recall my 2003 interview with Sessions in which he did not recall any such events, and thought they would have been greatly out of the ordinary.) Nevertheless, I was still full of hope that the 1979 battle would center on the Wilderness legislation, along with approval of a CRMP. This would require intensive lobbying, locally and by telephone, and perhaps a mailing and another Washington trip.

Cease-Fire (mostly); No Truce

Almost a year passed between the above events, and the appearance of the final document in early August 1979, over eighteen months since public release of the draft, almost three years since the writing team gathered in December 1976. That year was the quietest in some time, though probably not for the plan writers; sadly, the record does not detail their agonies. This quiet might have been due to a willingness to wait, or exhaustion after the uproar following the draft's release. My records may just be less complete. So there are only a few events to mark from that year of plan re-writing; the next chapter examines what was wrought by the re-re-drafters.

A distraction was offered by the appearance of a Wilderness proposal for Lake Mead NRA that included some of the Grand Canyon lands in the Parashant and Whitmore Canyons area.[59] Five years had passed since their initial proposal. We responded in favor of those lands, and asked for the Shivwits plateau to be added, letting the road revert. (This is such an incredibly difficult drive that I am not sure what we were worried about, except that it leads to extraordinary viewing of the western Canyon.)

In the new year, the Sierra Club Southwest Rep reported his own efforts to get the CRMP out before the season started. He asked us to send a few letters, since Udall had received another round from the comm ops. A sample was from Ron Smith, of Grand Canyon Expeditions, claiming that "a personal friend (and Park Service employee) informed us that one of the people instrumental in formulating the ... plan holds a personal grudge against" the comm ops.[60] A few people, with a boatman's viewpoint, are molding the plan, instead of resource managers weighing public needs. Many years ago, we offered rowing trips, but, Smith mis-remembered, they were too strenuous for many. Anyway, most people do not have long enough vacations. (I am not quite sure why they kept peddling this, or why anyone accepted it. Even today, they push this line, when the average vacation for all American workers is 15 or 17 days depending on how you juggle weekends, and the average for the well-off people who can afford commercial river trips runs up to more like 4 weeks including weekends. Too bad, also, that vacation length was not one of the questions answered definitively in the HERS study.) We, Smith went on, asked our clients to write the Secretary last summer; nevertheless, people who use the Grand Canyon are not being heard. (So, on the one hand, comm ops savage self-guided boaters as repeat users as if commercial clients were all one-timers; yet they stimulate letters from customers who have already gone and apparently want to go again on comm op trips.) NPS thinking is "inbred" and abused research.

I, too, wrote to Udall, but about the Park Service bending over backward to placate comm ops who were so totally trapped into their corner of opposition that they could not see a real compromise when it was thrust in their faces.[61] They have already had six years of warning about motors, and now have another six. We have tried to deal with the comm ops, and they have used the time to inflame the issue with nonsense about Americans having time for nine-, but not twelve-, day trips. I was also trying to help allies understand our change from a 1972 cut-use stand to our accepting a plan that increased use to accommodate rowing and self-guided.[62]

We heard that work on the draft of the final EIS was proceeding, and it was thought the document might be out in April 1979.[63] Work on preparing for a contract prospectus was underway; NPS wanted it to be concurrent with the CRMP. In March, spurred by hearing from Chapman that there would almost certainly have to be a further contract extension, we considered what could be done legally.[64] The failure of settlement talks in 1978 had left us with little leverage except the passage of time with no action, but perhaps NPS would now be willing to fix a date for plan approval. Nothing came from this discussion, and later on, the news was that Regional review was done and passed on to D.C. for NPS review in mid-May, and a month later to Interior officials.[65] So the attorneys began thinking about sending some formal questions about plan deadlines, which they did in early June.[66] The lawyers considered this an important moment; if we let it pass without getting NPS commitment to plan issuance, we would lose this advantage. The local Sierra Club approved this course.[67] Our position had some viability; another three-year extension seemed unlikely, and NPS rumors indicated a two-year extension then five-year contracts with "no effect" on motor use.

Meanwhile, Ruckel was asking where the plan was and when it would be issued and implemented.[68] We wanted to know about the contract negotiation and whether an EIS would accompany the contracts. The government replied within the requested 30 days.[69] The EIS would be out by the end of July with a 30-day comment period, with the plan to follow and be effective in September. The plan had been waiting on the EIS and would await its final form until after the comment period. Negotiations would begin on the contracts only after the plan was set, using the plan's EIS, since "concession operations on the River are an integral part of the River Plan and Environmental Statement and thus covered by both documents". The Regional Director will make decisions about contracts. I learned from Jensen that the extension might be for 3-6 months and be subject to the CRMP. Udall and DeConcini had been briefed on the Plan. He also said there was an airplane noise study brought on by the overflight activity below Lava Falls, and by the Director who had told them a few months before he wanted GCNP to get rid of the helicopters.

As the rumors firmed up about the imminent release of the EIS, we started thinking about doing a better job of countering comm op reaction by praising the plan to Udall and DeConcini.[70]

CHAPTER 18

1979: The Flag, Tattered, Still Waves

The final EIS, signed by Director Whalen and dated July 31, 1979, was released for a 30-day comment period beginning August 3.[1] The news release said it analyzed a "proposal for the gradual elimination of motorized river-running craft" over five years beginning in 1980. The plan itself would be adopted after the review period. The Park Service issued its own gloss on changes it had thought necessary, but let me first do the exercise of parsing in detail what nineteen months of reaction and re-writing had produced.

These Changes Took a Year?

If the motorized forces had been looking for victory, their repulse was indicated by what happened to the management objectives (I:2-3). Where the draft had first listed "allow only non-motorized watercraft", there was now a stronger three-part statement for a motor-free wilderness, leading off with perpetuating "a wilderness river-running experience" including the natural sounds and silence, relaxed conversation, taking the river on its own terms. That objective was reinforced by a new objective: recommend inclusion of the river for Wilderness designation. In between appeared the "phase out" of motorized use upstream of the Lake Mead backwater.

Reducing congestion was moved up the list, while the phrase "consistent with a quality wilderness river-running experience" was dropped from the goal of providing commercial trips. A revision of the Federal Code dealing with Colorado River whitewater trips was tacked on.

The text of the first Plan "element" became "phase out motorized boats", replacing "mode of travel", and stressed the importance of Park policy, wilderness, public input, and the research (I:3,7). The change was accomplished by an outright ban on motors during the winter season, October through March. The phase-out was then in temporal steps, April would be motor-free starting in 1980, September in 1981, August in 1982, with a two-year pause until May through July were cleared of the clatter-and-rush brigade in the sixth year, 1985. The period of phasing out motors would therefore coincide with the new five-year, 1980-4, contracts, to be negotiated as the extensions expired at the end of 1979. Had they wanted comfort under NPS leadership, the comm ops could have found some in this offer to continue motors for an additional four years, with the first motorless year being 1985 instead of the draft's 1981. Had theirs been an effort to squeeze out a compromise, this gain of four years, an extra ten years past the Reed deadline, might have seemed an important victory to the comm ops. A slower death for motors was not, of course, the comm op goal.

Moving on to "annual use", the draft had dealt with mechanics: how many launches when; various limits on group sizes; calculations of user-days by season. The final dwelt more on justification (I:7-11). Use would increase outside the heavy summer months, but since research showed that contacts between trips determines congestion and therefore negative impacts on environment and experience, "it is essential to limit the number of groups allowed to launch." "To reduce crowding", summer use would be redistributed outside the three main hot months. To enhance the wilderness experience, group size would be reduced. (Though not stated, the assumption appeared to be that use limits would not be phased in, but installed at the plan's start.) Trip length remained important, but the plan now specified a minimum and maximum, not actual lengths. User-days are not the key limiting factor; launches are. "In order to reduce crowding" and "provide a quality river-running experience", daily summer (Apr-Sep) launches would be two commercial with up to 25 passengers each and one self-guided with 15 people. Employees were still not counted in the commercial allocation, although the EIS listed 4-5 crew for each 25-passenger trip. The commercial limit could be pushed to make up for cancellations, "to no more than three" trips each week or an additional 5 passengers on a trip. Self-guided trips would not get this "makeup" privilege until the Park's education program improved self-guided observance of environmental regulations.

A pause here to point out that the latter goal was a *non sequitur*. Though eminently laudable, environmental education has nothing to do with whether someone has to cancel a trip on one date and asks for another. The connection reflects more the unaccountable reasoning we have seen characteristic of NPS attitudes toward self-guided users. Bureaucrats often turn out to be regular sorts of human beings when you get to know them, but the long-standing negative GCNP stance toward those who wish to run the river on their own needs some sort of explanation. NPS and the comm ops seemed to see the self-guided users as a scheming, unruly bunch who cheated, connived, and dirtied the Canyon. As if only the gimlet-eyed Park staff kept such scruffies from over-running the resource by swooping down on the miscreants as they multiplied on the 20-year waiting list, and later as they sashayed down the river mooning delicate commercial sightseers and unloading years' worth of trash on the beaches kept pristine by the oh-so-green comm ops. Was this negative attitude due to the confrontational approach of Eiseman, Munroe, and others, though it was hardly comparable with the motorized comm ops intransigence? Is some sort of abyssal depth psychology called for? Or could there have been an "attitudinal alliance", a meeting of souls, between comm ops, their crew, and NPS, that determined their joint distaste for self-guided users? If the last, then the comm ops are showing cleverness in their more recent efforts to seduce self-guided spokespersons, as if to say that if you former river-trashers support motors and the commercial use level, then we saints will not object to more of you on the river.

Another pause for reflection: The elements of the EIS described a transition plan, not Wilderness management but a continuation of mixed motor/rowing. The average number of miles/day, for instance, is set at 30, whereas river-paced rowing trips were estimated to move at 20 miles/day or less. No diminution in May-July motor use was presented. Throughout the life of the contracts to be covered by the plan, no year-round rowing management was required. The plan's transitional nature, along with the long-demonstrated resistance by the motorized comm ops to conversion, helps explain the over-rigidity that Jensen thinks might have been a flaw in the plan. Had the comm ops been willing cooperators, the plan might have been structured as a flexible object revised every year or two. Experience, however, surely indicated that only a straitjacket would work. Perhaps GCNP hoped that the May-July motor period would make it chafe less. However, motor use as the comm ops' choice was the irreconcilable ground for this war. No matter how specious their arguments or odious their sentiments, the comm ops understood the political reality that if they could keep motor use unfettered, they would demonstrate their control of river-running policy. If the Park Service, basing its decisions on Wilderness and Park principles, and backed by pro-Wilderness public sentiment, succeeded in the major transformation of converting river-running to an all-rowing, river-paced activity, control would obviously have passed out of the comm ops' hands.

So, back to the EIS. The three-trip/week use limit from October through March was now called low enough "to allow the natural cleansing of beaches to continue" and to launch trips so there would be only a remote chance of meeting other trips. The research had "well documented ... that heavily used beaches are significantly cleaner" in the spring than in the fall, although "little is known about the details of this cleansing process". Until the cleansing is investigated, winter use will be kept low. (Of course, this is contrary to the research "finding" that what mattered was not the number of people, but how they behaved. At least there was no misguided remark about how difficult winter travel is.)

The document challenged the criticism of increased use (I:10). The limits are maxima, and will not be allowed to happen. So while projected total (absolutely everything) use would be 209 KUD, the not-to-be-reached maximum total use was 304 KUD. Acceptable use would not be that maximum, but an average—a calculation based on 12 days/trip, not 18 days/trip, and assuming full trips every day. If recreational use escalates beyond the average levels—110 KUD for commercial summer, 12 KUD for commercial winter; 44 KUD for self-guided summer, 10.5 KUD for self-guided winter—new limits will be set. Monitoring was supposed to provide data. (Again, these numerical specifics are contrary to that central finding which, if taken seriously, would have forced the plan-writers to de-emphasize numbers in favor of education and orientation, as well as close patrolling and monitoring.)

Slyly, the EIS takes on the scorn heaped on the draft over partial trips; comm ops "are encouraged to provide partial canyon trips as they have done in the past" (I:10). Figures were cited to show that interest in partial trips was already "high";

almost 8,000 people each year went partway, 3500 of whom hiked in or out. On the other hand, half used helicopters, which the plan was now accepting, but only on lands outside the Park (I:24).

Summing up, the user-days consumed by commercial crew, NPS trips, and research groups were acknowledged (though without any negative characterizations, despite a number of comments made through the years about crew often not knowing the regulations) (I:11). Overall, the discussion of use swelled from a half-page to three pages.

Where the draft spoke only of "a better balance" when presenting the allocation between commercial and self-guided trips, the final went on again for three pages (I:11-13). It noted that commercial services were provided for a fee, and the services provided included operating the boats; therefore a rowing trip "is no more strenuous" for passengers than a motorized one. (I approved the opportunistic swipe at the comm ops' fabrications, but this again is a *non-sequitur*.) Self-guided trips are participatory and cost sharing.

The split was now justified as "based on the best available information" about demand. Potential commercial applicants may be counted more than once, and the number turned down by comm ops is not known. Duplication, faking, and discouragement cause problems in counting self-guided demand. Comm ops report they turn away as many people as they take; while unsatisfied self-guided applicants amount to 40% of comm op use. These figures "are not entirely reliable", but using them, the plan arrived at a figure of 75% for commercial use desire and 25% for self-guided. The ratio would be adjusted as the Park piled up more reliable information. (But one pile would stay anemic, since commercial numbers belonged to the comm ops, while NPS sees the self-guided applications directly. This is one reason why advocates for an equitable split argue that all would-be users should have to get their permit from the Park Service.)

By the numbers, commercial trips went down from a pre-CRMP of 490 to 405, though up from the draft's 387. For self-guided, the pre-plan 37 trips were boosted to 209 in the draft and 222 in the final. Similarly, the actual commercial seats launched ended up at 10,125 (a real decrease of 11%), self-guided at 3,330, a 743% increase (a percentage swollen by the small base). Batting at self-guided use again, the EIS noted that "verbal and written reports" indicate self-guided river-runners were more likely to break the rules. NPS patrol trips recorded incidents of noncompliance. Therefore, self-guided increases will be phased in (as suggested by the comm ops)—the bad news—in order to implement the information program to orient these users—the good news. Half of the allocation will go into effect in 1980-1, and the rest in 1982 if monitoring indicates "resource impacts" are within acceptable limits.

The draft had tried to describe the basis for the new contracts, to be advertised on the basis of awarding concessions on performance, not just historical use. The final eschewed this scary scenario, starting off with the warmer statement that commercial trips were "essential" (I:14-16). The contracts would run from 1980 through 1984 (giving the parties less than six months to negotiate, though not reaching to the first all-rowing year). The contracts would be awarded with preference for those who had provided "satisfactory" service, and while there would not be more contracts than currently, NPS thought 15-18 was a better number of companies, maintaining variety while aiding the economics of smaller companies; nevertheless any decrease would be by "natural attrition". (Today there are 15 companies, and although the top 6 have two-thirds of the use, the smallest allocation is larger than that of 11 of the 1979 comm ops.) Allocations would be based on the current allocations, but using trips and passengers, not user-days. The comm ops scored by being given back their control over launch dates, which would be scheduled according to what each wanted, first-come, first-served. As always, the hollow claim was made that NPS controlled allocations. (In the many changes in ownership and consolidation over the years; there is no evidence of NPS influence in the resulting allocations.)

No warm words welcomed self-guided users (I:16-17). The initial bunch of applications would still be sorted out by a drawing, followed by a waiting list. Instead of listing several dates when applying, an effort would be made to find a date of the applicant's choice when the permit was awarded. The Park would periodically send out cards to applicants; they would return them if they still wanted to go. In place of a rule saying a person could be on only one trip in any two years, the new proposal was that any person who was a participant on a trip and who was also on the waiting list of applicants would be struck off the latter, but could re-apply at the end of the line. (This twist no longer made a rule that applied to commercial passengers, so the question of being equitable was finessed.) Perhaps NPS foretold there would be so many applications that anyone who was at the bottom of the waiting list could not go for some years, though there was no apparent bar to their being a participant again.

Another pause. These repeaters were the people who had gained experience on the river, learning about the Canyon and environmental and safety matters, and thus would be desirable participants on trips where others were first-timers. This is one of the real difficulties with barring repeaters from self-guided trips; whether trip leaders or not, they serve the function of providing experience—by regulation, unpaid. Whereas, of course, commercial repeaters serve no function of this kind. So the latter group should be focussed on if anyone is, and since many outspoken commercial passengers boast of their having gone on many—4, 6, 9—trips, the NPS rules are not only discriminatory and contradictory, but also undermine the comm ops assertion that curtailing their operations would cut public use. In fact, curtailing their operations by allowing them to carry only first-timers would increase the number of individuals who could go. This is not an insignificant consideration; the latest estimate is that about 3000 commercial passengers each year are repeaters. Not only is this 20% of the commercial pool; it is very close to the total number of self-guided people who launch yearly.[2]

The consideration is made more significant if we take the NPS stratification of participants, and elaborate it into three commercial classes—necessary experienced repeater(= crew), repeating passenger, first-timer—and two self-guided classes— necessary experienced repeater, first-timer. The commercial crew class is highly privileged; they may even go on self-guided trips too. Repeating passengers are likewise highly privileged, and their going usurps the places of thousands in the third class, the first-timer public the comm ops love to claim they serve. There are only two self-guided classes, and it would be a delicate exercise to determine which of the two has been more discriminated against by GCNP rules on no-repeat and access. Either way, their low status is one of the prime reasons comm-op-controlled river management is a failed and broken experiment.

Back at the EIS: A permit would be needed to launch from Diamond Creek (I:17); the draft's multi-page table of changes was deleted.

"Resource Protection" became "Environmental Management" (I:17-20). Fires were moved to first place, and the comm ops won their point for "esthetic and warming" summer fires, but only using wood brought in. Since hauling out human waste was now required, it was noted as a necessary, inexpensive, and not inconvenient procedure. Soap restrictions and trail building were retained, while restricted areas were now shown only on the maps. Mention of off-river travel was dropped.

The contribution already made by monitoring research was acknowledged, while noting the need for much more (I:20-21). The environment must have been deemed O.K., since the first monitoring item was a "further refinement of information regarding relative demand". Analysis of self-guided applications was needed to get a more "responsive" allocation. Crowding needed more study. Then came ecological changes (no mention of endangered species now) and campsite health. Economic impact research would still be useful.

A new section on general guidelines started off by promising plan review, annually or at longer intervals as appropriate (I:22-24). Public review would be considered.

The provision for self-guided trip leader education was upgraded to a one-day session at Lees Ferry. To underscore the catch-22 nature of various restrictions on "repeating", it was mandatory that someone on the trip had to have been down the Canyon before (App. D:5). A slide show was still good enough for passengers. (Given that a National Park is about interpretation and awareness, and even being wise in wilderness, this lack of interest in dealing intensively with self-guided trips— a day session for all trip participants, for instance—is perhaps just another indicator of attitude. Just imagine if whoever was in charge of relations with self-guided river-runners actually cared enough about the quality of their experience, on the trip and before, to set up a positive out-reach program. Another item telling us it is the National Parkpolice Service now.)

The safety section allowed life jackets to be taken off on flat water. Emergency communications equipment was required.

The paragraph on helicopters made clear the Park felt there was nothing it could do to restrict this anti-wilderness nuisance since the landing pad was not on Park land (I:24). No comfort was likely, then, from a study of aircraft overflights then in progress (I:25). Mule concessions for passenger transport in and out would continue, at Phantom Ranch of course, and at Whitmore Wash (but not for long, since it was fated to gain the notoriety of becoming the new helicopter take-out point).

Section II, describing the environment, stirred anti-dam paranoids like me, as the Bureau of Reclamation asserted its authority and jurisdiction over "riverfront land" within the Park for future dams (II:3). (This was horn-blowing in a vacuum.)

The ill effects on the Park from dam releases were summarized; the Bureau would be told about them in the future.

The final pointed to the dormant controversy over the boundary on the left side of the riverbank down to the Little Colorado, between the Park and the Navajo Reservation. The distinction was correctly made between the Park's regulation of public use on the Havasupai Use Lands (in the Park, outside the Reservation) and the joint agreement covering Havasupai use.

Modest concern was voiced as to the possibility that larger releases could accelerate erosion (II:9), while flows of less than 3000 cubic feet/second were thought too low for whitewater boating (II:11).

The final admitted that while total coliforms had been measured, there was no data on fecal coliforms in the river or its tributaries, so it was not known whether the waters were within state standards (II:14).

In minor defiance of the ridicule by motorboat operators, the final declared that motor emissions "cause at least short-term" lower water quality (II:17): a change from their being "considered to cause" degradation. The language on motor noise was unchanged (II:22).

The "very noxious exotic" Russian thistle and camelthorn were now just "exotic"; perhaps the lobbyist for exotics had been heard from (II:23). Ecologically sensitive areas were still "unique", but no longer needed to be "afforded special management consideration" (II:27).

There had now been 44 more bird species identified, a total of 284 (II:30). Five more exotic fish species were listed (II:31). A new section was added on insects, including some comments on post-dam effects (II:32-3). However, the final dropped cautionary language about the humpback chub being "doomed to extinction" unless measures restrict visitor activities at the mouth of the Little Colorado River (II:34). Also removed was the speculation that the spinedace might be gone, although a comment was added that the river otter had not been sighted in many years.

Archeological surveys of the river corridor had been finished during the writing of the final (II:36), and three historic sites were added to the list (most tied to mining) for evaluation (II:37).

In recounting river use history, a little bureaucratic smoothing changed the Park's lack of awareness or concern about the river traffic in the early 1960s to a lack of need to be concerned (II:38). NPS "concern" about post-dam increases replaced its "astonishment" (and certainly no mention was made of paralysis or submissiveness). The comment is added that the Hualapai Tribe is "authorized" to run the river from Diamond Creek; apparently a permit had been granted and accepted (II:38).

The final asserted that the allocations of user-days were for the river above Diamond Creek, with no counting against an allocation for continuing beyond that point (II:39). (Whether or not the additional day or two had ever been counted is no longer clear; quite possibly not, since otherwise this clarification would amount to an increase for only some comm ops. Of course, at the time allocations and multi-year contracts were instituted by the Park, its administration did not extend to the last 100 miles of the Canyon, nor include the first few miles below Lees Ferry. I do not know if, before 1975, river traffic administration had been formally ceded to GCNP, or whether the Park just assumed jurisdiction based on its undoubted authority to regulate trips passing through the Park.)

Discussion of the vexed matter of demand deleted the suggestion that data showed that no citizen would have been denied a commercial trip if all comm ops had been contacted (II:42). (Of course, if there were people daunted by the notion of contacting 21 or 16 or even 10 comm ops—no Internet, remember—this would be another argument for a universal permit system contracted out to one of the central reservation firms.) The table on self-guided applications was extended to 1979 (see my Chapter 11). Although it was still noteworthy that 72% of the use was in June, July and August, the final did suggest that winter use was now above the zero level.

The rapid irreversible changes were now "occurring" instead of "being inflicted" upon the riparian resources (II:44).

A new half-page section on partial trips further challenged the comm ops' scorn of the idea that such trips would have appeal (II:50). Of course, leaving or starting at Phantom Ranch was a partial trip, but the text suggested comm op distortion by saying taking out at Lava Falls was a partial trip (two-thirds of the Canyon), even though it "is generally advertised as a full-canyon trip". (A more extensive analysis was not done that would have indicated how partial rowing trips would fit in the same time frame as a motor trip that only covered more distance—not the plan's idea of a "quality wilderness experience". Perhaps the writers worried because the Lava Falls take-out was by helicopter, the finishing insult in degrading trip quality.)

The section on the impact of human waste was kept, making clear how damaging the previous method had been, but it was noted that carrying all waste out, universal since 1978, had resulted in "significant improvement" in beach cleanliness (II:53).

Moving on to the visitors, the final omitted the truth that commercial passengers were "not representative of the American public", describing them only as "select" (II:54).

The final's discussion of motors held NPS ground on the superior quality of rowing, relying heavily on the HERS research (II:55-6). On the phony safety debate, the table on injuries requiring helicopter evacuation was extended, adding ten motorized and two rowing accidents, for eight-year totals of 46 and 9, a period when the percentage of motorized passengers was 80%, not too far off the 84% of evacuations. (However, if the number of user-days is used, which would seem to be a better comparison base, the percentage of motorized use drops about 10-20 points, which would seem to indicate a greater risk on motor trips. Still, these are safe adventures, with off-boat injuries more prevalent.)

Taking up the challenge by pro-motor forces over taxes and economic impact, the final repeated its figures, adding that the data were taken from comm op reports (II:59). A few comm ops asserted they paid more than the Parent study said, but the final replied that even so, they were not a significant proportion of their states' economies, and repeated that if all comm ops disappeared, there would not be major impact. Comparing trip costs, instead of asserting that comparable length trips cost about the same, the text showed that the marginal cost for the greater number of days on a rowing trip was low, in line with the argument that rowing trips were better value (II:60).

Summing up the impact if there were no proposal, the Park Service changed its stance by discussing what it had done on waste removal, fires, and foot traffic, instead of repeating the damage that had been occurring (II:60-1). The final declined to offer future scenarios of unsanitary conditions, use reduction, and visitor dissatisfaction.

Nevertheless, the discussion of the Plan's impact opened with a grim description of the past as a scenario averted: severe damage from digging 5000 waste disposal holes each year to bury 20 tons of waste, with accompanying destruction of soil, micro- and macrobiology (III:1). Day stops were still not included in the waste removal method; that impact was said to be fairly minimal, with experimentation continuing. Natural beach restoration will take many years. (Reflecting back on that 1968 meeting, with its NPS/comm op laughter at the idea of waste removal, it is fair to say that the ten years was required to change attitudes, not develop technology. Additionally, the EIS discussion of items—waste, fire, excess trails—on which work had been started, only underlined our point almost three years earlier that there did not need to be an approved CRMP in order to take measures protecting the environment.)

Again, NPS held the line on the benefits of all-rowing; a more uniform travel rate, along with spreading launches, will indirectly serve to lessen shore impact (III:5).

Moving on to impacts on visitors, the final noted that the Hualapai had been rowing from Diamond Creek to Separation on their trips recently (III:11 and 22). More to the point, it added the assertion that although replication of the combination rowing/motor experiment might be statistically desirable, the results obtained were "sufficiently reliable" to show visitor preference for rowing, other factors being equal (III:12). It then butted away the complaints of pro-motor opinion: for first-timers, the information they have to make a choice of trip is limited to what the comm ops supply. It is natural that comm ops will promote their type of watercraft and that those people with time or money constraints will choose shorter, less expensive trips. "Some public input" asked that short, cheaper "full-length" motor trips be kept. Under the plan there will be the impact on these people of not having available the "full-length" trip less than a week long. Such harried vacationers would be able instead to travel the same number of days on the more relaxed rowing trip that covers fewer miles. The final kept the much-ridiculed section on really short (1-3 days) rowing options that required hiking more difficult trails, even though they only applied to half-a-percent of those taking partial trips (III:13, II:50). (This was confusing, since it seemed to say eat your cake—rowing trips are a higher quality experience—and have it too—you do not have to spend a lot of time to get that higher quality, even though time to unwind and absorb is exactly a central part of that experience, as stated on III:14.)

The comm op criticism of NPS-mandated trip length was met by granting flexibility in adjusting trip length "to meet public demand" (III:14). An even larger portion of the public would be satisfied than under the current situation, since NPS would choose "companies offering a variety of trips" (empty threat-making, and many companies do not offer such a variety).

After its discussion of how motors increase contact density, the final countered the "advantage" of motorboats being able to zip past other trips by arguing that since the new launch limits are lower, there will be fewer groups of boats on the river (III:15). Continuing the counter-attack, congestion in the developed trail corridor and Phantom Ranch from an additional 3000 partial-trippers was called not significant given the over quarter-million visitors already using that area (III:16). However, pointed remarks about the interference of motor noise with conversation were dropped (III:17). It remains a puzzle as to why motorized trips were still called "more active" (III:18). (In spite of the several pages of exposition and argument, the plan kept motors during three full months through 1984. It was a transition, not a wilderness, plan; the vision offered in the Borden report, applying wilderness principles fully, was for the future.)

A new paragraph on the advantages of trout fishing (up to 18 pounds) was inserted in the list of advantages for fall and winter travel (III:18). More to the point for most, it was now calculated that spreading launches meant that 2100 persons who might have taken high-summer trips would have to go in other months (III:19). Having softened the fire limits to allow imported wood for summer fires, the final dropped the negative impact of no social fires (III:19).

The Hualapai were warned about raising the fees they charged those taking out at Diamond Creek, since "some concessioners have indicated" they would go on to Lake Mead if the fees "are too high" (III:23). The final hoped that scheduling of the "intrusive activity" of helicopter take-out from Hualapai land at Lava Falls could "minimize" the impact on other users.

Section IV, Mitigating Measures, opened with a most unfortunate change (IV:1). In the draft, the "existing" total of 122,600 user-days was cited for irreversible impacts. This was changed in the final to the 96,600 user-days from commercial and self-guided visitors. Somehow the commercial employees no longer contributed. Given their likely character as human beings, surely crew's 26 KUD had some impact. More important, their responsibility for behavior of the commercial passengers' 89 KUD actually magnified their impact since, for instance, every crew-day on a motor trip was in charge of 20-30 passenger-days. The text then repeats that it is behavior and not numbers that matter, so not including crew impact is an even odder sophistry.

Congestion now produced "impact", not "destruction" (IV:1). It "accelerates" impacts, instead of leading to "unnecessary destruction of vegetation". The threat to impose limits on how many groups could stop at an attraction site at one time was dropped. A new section on river congestion again contested the point that rowing trips, with more boats, would increase the sense of congestion. It argued that people react to other trips, not their own (once again, an argument on people's perceptions stands in for Park and Wilderness principles), and inter-trip contact was going to decrease.

The description of how trail construction would be minimal was filled out, by using existing trails for instance (IV:2).

Either there was an editing mishap or the mis-use of soap and detergents was bad enough that the final used that section to remind commercial crew and self-guided trip leaders that theirs was the responsibility to ensure that guidelines are followed by visitors for resource protection (IV:2-3). Further it was the NPS's responsibility to state the guidelines clearly and communicate them to trip leaders adequately. This responsibility was reinforced by the following section on NPS providing education on how to minimize impacts. Contrariwise, NPS patrols were cut from one/week to two/month in summer, one/month in winter.

Taking up the challenge on trip length again, the final encouraged the comm ops to provide partial trips (a hardly necessary encouragement; it was to their economic benefit), and noted that traffic at Lava Falls and Whitmore Wash would increase (IV:3). (No indication here that the entire helicopter operation would be moved to the latter location and involve, as it does today, half the passengers.) Tenderly, the final said more people starting trips at Phantom would ease the impact of reduced launches at Lees Ferry. (Aside from the increased revenue/day from partial trips, this mitigation would only work if the number entering was substantially greater than that leaving, which has not been so. Today, it is around 2500 people in and out.) A new paragraph was written on other places in the region for shorter whitewater motorized trips. The extended phase-out was noted as a mitigation of economic impact, with "a minimum of 50% of the summer season allocated to both motorized and non-motorized travel" (IV:4). That is, at least three of the six "summer" months would be motor-laden.

In presenting the monitoring program, the final dropped the idea of closing several heavily impacted beaches to study recovery (IV:5-6). Also omitted were references to dam operation restricting the distribution of the humpback chub (IV:7), an abdication of NPS responsibility to conserve the Park's wildlife.

Under unavoidable impacts, the numbers were again altered to exclude crew and trips for research and administration, allowing the claim that the number of "river runners" would go up by 1725, "approximately 2000" persons, instead of the draft's 1000 (V:1). Wildlife was no longer mentioned. The estimate of 600 persons adversely affected by not having motorboats was dropped, but summer fire lovers would no longer have to suffer. There would still be 3000 persons who would have to find non-summer launch dates, and others would have to start mid-week instead of on the weekend. Helicopter noise was mentioned (V:1).

Not having seriously presented any alternatives, there were few changes in section VIII.

Fecal haul-out being implemented (mostly), over a page of that diatribe was eliminated from the no-action option (VIII:1).

The horrors of pushing use to the maximum now included increasing NPS staff "several times over"; there would have to be campsite assignments (VIII:4-5). The strange assertion that there would be no "average negative effect" from cutting use to the level called for in the 1972 Reed decision was omitted (VIII:8). (NPS here played the agency game of justifying its course as a workable middle between two unworkable extremes. Of course, in doing so and fixing use levels, it avoided the possibilities of intermediate and variable levels, or a plan built around Park Wilderness principles, monitoring impact, and determining "real" demand.)

Keeping motors during part of the year (which is just what this plan was doing) was no longer characterized as allowing a lesser quality experience due to the effect on interpretation (VIII:9).

Discussion about coordination with others now included a section on consultation with the comm ops (IX:3). As river policies were developed, comm ops were "active" and "contacted through several different avenues". Park staff went to the semi-annual Western River Guides Association meetings. There were annual commercial guide training sessions, where ideas were solicited. That meeting and the annual comm op meeting at the Park have discussed the plan; indeed, in 1976 and 1977, the comm ops "were encouraged to provide input". (None of this particularly contradicts Jensen's assertion that he was not lobbied by the comm ops. It is also noteworthy that my attendance at the comm op/Park get-togethers showed us just how pressure was put on the "regulators" by the supposedly regulated. Those meetings are now closed, so the comm ops are free to pressure Park staff without public knowledge.)

The appendices were altered, with the "concessioner fact sheet" and economic analysis summary dropped. The 1980 operational requirements and the health/sanitation guidelines were included, along with an affidavit for self-guided users that emphasized that they understood there were penalties if they disobeyed the rules.

What They Said We Said: The Public Comments; GCNP Responds

From the above comparison, detailed to the point of tedium, I read that the Park Service had concluded that no great change—concessions of the political kind—was necessary. Self-guided river-runners had gained no major points; comm ops, led by the pro-motor clique, had been tossed a few bones; we, asking for nothing, had that nothing eroded, yet still saw the plan as the best, the only, route toward wilderness. The environment, now being somewhat less degraded under the new rules, still had to be considered as up for grabs. If the plan were implemented and monitored properly, what would the impacts turn out to be?

The final EIS's Section IX summarized the comments received and then took 168 pages to joust with a number of particular contributors. Insofar as these mini-debates represent the pressures for changing the draft, they tell us what the Park Service thought its vulnerabilities were.

Though decisions "would not be made on a vote count", the final tallied the responses, claiming high interest and widespread publicity, especially by recreational, environmental, and commercial groups (IX:7). Those who stepped forward were 215 speakers at the meetings, 2501 written comments, and 17 petitions with 739 signatures (which category seems not to be discussed further). The tallied issues were motors, total use, allocation between commercial and self-guided use, and resource protection (IX:8-11). As the discussion goes on, it emerges that 1110 of the responses were those in "general support of the proposal", a category broken down for the last three issues, but not on motors, and it is not clear how many of those 1110 said only they favored the plan, and how many may also have made explicit comments in favor of a motor ban.

Of the 2657 responses countable on motors, 1476 wanted them out and 1181 wanted them kept. Of those in favor of a motor ban, most were not specific on why, just supporting the plan; 426 did mention wilderness, and some 300 of the comments saw it improving the environment, 119 by eliminating fumes. The success of comm op distortions and falsehoods was evident in the reasons people wanted motors kept: rowing trips were too long (693 mentions); too expensive (371); less safe (360); and eliminated the old and "infirm"(497). Hiking was called too strenuous (191), while sunnier personalities claimed motors provided a wilderness experience (221), and their noise was no problem (88). What leaps out here is that these are largely opinions of the supposed drawbacks of rowing trips, not in favor of motors. Was that negativity in how people responded or in how the plan writers framed their comments?

One obvious asymmetry is that there was no similar body of opinions for the rowing trip or on the drawbacks of motors, which makes sense since almost 80% of commercial passengers were motor boaters, and few of the commercial rowing passengers would have been urged to write in by the comm ops. The 300 or so comments explicitly for the self-guided interests were swamped by pro-motor opinion, even had they said anything about rowing.

Another unknown factor was whether or not the pro-motor letters came from those who wanted another motor trip. The numbers are something like this: perhaps 120,000 (give or take ten thousand) passengers had been taken on commercial trips. If 20% were rowing, then 96,000 were pushed through by motors; call it 100,000. HERS found that 90% were first-timers, which means that about 10,000, being repeaters, would think about protesting for their own interests by lobbying against rowing trips as too long, expensive, unsafe, and restrictive. There was a total of 1200 pro-motor statements. Now if the passengers in that group are from the repeaters, their ~10% outpouring is impressive. If on the other hand, the comm ops mailings stirred up 1000 letters, say, from people the overwhelming majority of whom had been given a bad impression of rowing trips but would never take a Grand Canyon trip again anyway, then it is no wonder plan writers felt able to disregard their parroting of the comm-op line. It may also be that the comm op mailing lists included people who had not been through the Grand Canyon, but had made contact for some other trip. In short, just like the demand argument, the public process had not produced, could not produce, a reliable indicator of opinion, informed and otherwise, for rowing and for motor-powered trips.

So what? These public processes are about getting the troops out and trying to push things your way. So another telling number is that 127 of the people who spoke at the public meetings wanted motors, while 88 wanted them banned. This is as much a sign of good organization by the comm ops (and the reverse by us) as was the evidence of their effectiveness in getting out to customer lists their message of explicit reasons to oppose rowing. The fact that the overall response in letters received (1388 for a motor ban; 1054 to keep motors) came out in our favor is little comfort, given pro-rowing lack of detail. The plan writers could claim they had support, but given that environmental organizations surely had memberships far larger than the 100,000 motor clients estimated above, the fact that we had squeezed out 300 more letters than they had is pathetic on the one hand, and, on the other, an indicator of the greater determination or passion on the part of the pro-motor crowd. It could be argued that we were fighting on their ground; had the arena been congressional action on a Grand Canyon wilderness, surely we would have made more of a show. Surely.

Looking at the other matters tallied, it is clear that passion quickly faded. Aside from the 1110 in "general support", there were about 200 comments on total use, 400 on the commercial/self-guided split, and somewhat over 300 on resource protection. The numbers on specifics were usually small, and often split. Thus 20 were for winter use, 28 against; 44 approved of more use, 57 were against; 171 liked the new allocation, 64 wanted a 50/50 division, 65 wanted no change; 111 wanted a lottery. Some specific comments were mentioned: only four people opposed wilderness; there were several "elaborate allocation schemes"; burros should be eliminated; outhouses should be constructed. The Shelby study of the attendees was cited as indicating that they generally endorsed wilderness, but defined it differently. Pro-real-wilderness folks were willing to pay more for it; while the commercial passengers (especially motoring) and crew were not. As throughout this controversy, the largest user group remained the most isolated and extreme against Park and Wilderness values, i.e., the group that would benefit the most from pro-park-wilderness river trips and is least likely to get them.

The first interesting comment—other federal agencies were first, then Arizona and Utah, some counties and towns, then us and the comm ops, and finally a few jus' plain folks—came from the Council on Environmental Quality (the writer was a former Wilderness Society staffer). He lauded the removal of motors and lamented the loss of a primitive experience due to "debris and noise" (IX:19-20). CEQ recommended a decrease in use, and the NPS reply was that it had moderated the increase (though it was just a calculation change based on fiddling with average days/trip; the summer numbers of people were the same, and for winter went up).

The Hualapai justly thought they were being slighted, pointing out the many spots used by river-runners on their side of the river, and charging NPS with condoning trespass (IX:25-28). They complained they could not deal with the way river-runners use Hualapai land and NPS would not help. (This complaint was justified; the Park expansion legislation of 1975 had authorized cooperation, but not much had happened.) They made the logical point that NPS talked a lot about Diamond Creek, so certainly it should be able to deal with other lands along the river. The Park yielded little here, accepting no criticism and stating the Hualapai operated on the river with a NPS permit. Then, unaccountably, in answer to the standard complaint about the boundary, the Park ignorantly stated the boundary question was yet to be resolved. The Bureau of Indian Affairs official writing the letter defended the helicopter operation. Further on, the Tribal Council speaks, repeating its claim to the middle of the river (IX:74-6). GCNP has contributed to the desecration of Hualapai lands by river-running users. River-runners must be excluded until arrangements are made for licensing their use. (NPS replied it could not do patrols for the Hualapai, a disingenuous answer at best.) The Park Service has no right to make river use conditional on no helicopter use if it is not on Park land. (NPS replied it did have that authority, but was not pursuing that goal anyway.)

The Bureau of Reclamation blustered along, as if it still controlled the river, talking about its authority to investigate the Canyon for dams, and its jurisdiction for water storage projects, and it wanted to use motorboats (IX:31-3). NPS accepted the empty talk, but noted motors were not really necessary. The Bureau brought the obsolete viceroy (a butterfly, not the Commissioner of Reclamation, though the description fit) to NPS attention.

As might be expected, Arizona state agencies distinguished themselves through their slavish acceptance of the motorized comm op line (IX:45-64). The Office of Economic Planning and Development, the Tourism Office, and the Northern Arizona Council of Governments repeated the usual complaints about impacts on current vested interests, making no attempt to determine if the new plan would, in fact, lead to greater economic opportunities. (However, the NPS reply that Page was going to benefit from increased numbers of partial trip users or self-guided trips seems suspect to me. The geographic facts are that Flagstaff would be the more likely beneficiary; so where was its statement of support?) The Department of Transportation championed the helicopter operators on Hualapai land—"should helicopter river pickups be eliminated, the indirect impact on commercial flight operators in some cases could be fatal" (that would be just, but the fatalities are usually passengers) (IX:56). Even Game and Fish and the Mineral Resources directors danced to the tune.

Not surprisingly, the most virulent state reaction came from the Utah Boating Advisory Council (IX:66-71). It claimed it had circulated questionnaires among a very large number of interested people and could not understand why NPS had not done the same. And on and on. These strong pro-motor folks liked rhetoric and emphasis, "the architects of this proposal have responded more to the strong and very vocal desires of small but influential interests who represent very few of the Grand Canyon River users" (as written, IX:67). In the tirade, the point is made, an inescapable one, that more user-days would appear to mean more impact. But then, when did this group ever attack GCNP for failing to carry out its responsibilities to protect the Park? And its true colors came out when it argues that use, if motorized, could be doubled.

A choice spread of comm op distortions were selected and repeated by county and city governments (Coconino and Kane; Page, Fredonia and Cottonwood) and their chambers of commerce: safety, the aged, tourist revenues, and the rest of the motor boater firecrackers (IX:78-90). What comes through is just how successful the comm ops had been in getting themselves accepted as the protectors of groups they discriminated against or were indifferent to in their relentless pursuit of upscale clients. Yes, the Park Service answered the points, but the damage done over years was not to be corrected by comments in the back of an EIS. Had we done any better? So far as my records show, we did not make any effort to counter this local opinion, or rather to build counter-opinion based on the idea that rowing would succeed, and be safer and productive of tourist satisfaction. Admittedly, this is where organizations centered on comm ops dedicated to rowing instead of worried about competition, and self-guided river-runners could have helped—had they existed.

Because of repetition and overlap, only a sampling of comm op, self-guided, and conservation statements were printed and commented on by NPS. I too am dragging at this point, so I will just give the short course. Overall, the common front put on by the comm ops had been indicated by their responses as of May 1978, which the Park tallied as eleven for motors, six preferring rowing but wanting motors to be allowed, one against motors, and three not commenting (IX:133).

Vladimir Kovalik of Wilderness World, a small rowing concessionaire, was the only comm op to publicly support the plan and was also for Wilderness designation (IX:140). He noted the plan would increase his competition, but motors do not have a place in the Canyon with their negative effect on the trip experience. Another outfitter, Dee Holladay, was also positive about a motor ban and wilderness; sadly he did not have a Canyon permit (IX:103-4). He did express concern about inflexibilities in the plan that would make it difficult for comm ops to use up their allocations. He also made the case against the "commercial private outfitter", and for campfires. No doubt, these responses were the kind the Park Service would have loved to see in great numbers.

Martin Litton distinguished his statement with an attack on the idea of requiring every river-runner to obtain an NPS permit, expressing great faith in himself and other comm ops to serve "as an arm of the NPS" in handling public demand (IX:101-2). He also made the case for fires, including "tamarisk control" techniques. The words "wilderness" and "motors" did not appear.

Which brings us to the motor boaters' statements that NPS chose to debate: the Burkes of Arizona River Runners (Carol made their statement, while he spoke for the corrupted Western River Guides Association), Staveley of Canyoneers presenting for PROA, and the largest motor comm op, Western River Expeditions (IX:94-134 in part). The seriousness with which the comm ops took the HERS research is indicated by the *ad hominem* hatchet-job done by the Burkes, who tried to paint the selection of HERS to do the research as biased, in conflict of interest, illegal, or worse. They did know of the tie of Heberlein to Shelby; and suspected the former had tilted the award to Haas, the founder of HERS and who had later been found guilty of misusing Federal funds on another matter. They claimed a HERS interviewer was biased in favor of rowing, and they "felt" this was true of many others. Carol Burke hoist herself on her own petard by complaining about use of the phrase "through the entire Canyon" to refer to 5-day trips. NPS responded that comm ops advertise their partial trips this way all the time. The same happened to her complaint about boatman bias on the combination experiment trip. She did raise an excellent point as to why passengers were not asked about how much time they wanted to spend (her wording was prejudicial to rowing, of course). NPS avoided a direct answer, hoisting her up again by pointing out that comm ops already offer partial trips, so it did not really matter whether visitors had one or two or more weeks; they could find a trip to meet their needs. The riposte ended with an NPS endorsement of Park policy: Motors are "inconsistent with the management objective of providing a quality wilderness river-running experience to the visitor".

Of course, the real problem the motorized promoters had was not that researchers were biased, but that rowing is a superior way to travel the river. None of the comm op arguments ever said that motors provide the best park and river experience. They always relied on peripheral issues and untruths involving the aged, the poor, the young, the infirm, overturned rowboats, rushed Americans with no vacation, ... well, you know the drill. Nevertheless, by marshalling these falsehoods and phony comparisons, they made a case, and made it successfully in some quarters.

The PROA statement has already been summarized. The NPS responses, as throughout section IX, tried to appear flat, re-stating policy and decisions non-argumentatively, and not correcting PROA errors and misstatements so much as making its own points using what it saw as the correct numbers and other information. For instance, PROA claimed motor rafts had been in on the start of recreational river-running in the Canyon, that is, for 40 years, and the "prevalent" choice for 25. NPS reply: The first commercial trip, in rowboats, was in 1938 (Staveley should have known that; he had operated that rowing operation later on, before sinking it for motors). The first commercial motor trip was in 1953 (four years after the first motorboat of any kind ran the river). The comm ops' primary offering since 1967 had been using motors, so that was the prevailing "choice". Hash was made of the greater safety margin claim for motorboats, noting that the primary factors had to do with signaling and getting the helicopter in, a matter of 3-4 hours being normal. Cooking fires were banned because even when boaters brought in wood, they "often" ran out and used driftwood. Although motor trips might provide more time for off-river activities, data collected showed they actually provide less.

Some of the Park Service replies indicated its attempts to appease critics. The increase in self-guided use was now to be done in two steps, monitoring the impact of greater education on self-guided behavior. Minimum trip length was reduced to 8 days while motors were still used, and trip length was otherwise up to the comm op, up to 18 days. NPS assignment of launch dates had been dropped in favor of continuing to have comm op ask for dates.

No doubt satisfied that it was making a solid case, comm op Western submitted figures showing great love for short motor trips based on a survey it had taken of its 1977 clientele. NPS commented that the pro-motor sentiments tallied with HERS results, and should be expected given that what Western clientele preferred was what Western offered. This was followed by another offering from comm op Burke, charging that the majority of the plan's reduction in summer passengers would hurt families. (This was dubious; HERS data showed that even if all families only brought one child, it was at most half of the passengers.) He then went through a tortured interpretation of the plan to prove that it was unworkable and would force companies out of business. He also asserted that all comm ops were now in favor of keeping choice on the river.

There were three statements printed from self-guided organizations (IX:92-137 in part). The WPRF repeated the overall argument of its still-ongoing litigation, insisting that any allocation was arbitrary and not based on sound demand data. NPS, saying it had tried to assess a percentage of disappointment as a basis for the new allocation of 25% of users (which meant 35% of trips and 31% of user-days), declined to change the system further. The American Canoe Association representative, too, thought there ought to be a true-demand system, a lottery. Wilderness designation was good, as was resource protection, though kayak-canoe trips would have trouble with waste removal. NPS repeated its belief that a lottery would not work or be fair, and thought the new ammo-can system would work with any size craft. A local Washington canoe club thought motors were a bad idea.

Seven conservation organizations were chosen as representative, though since overall their only contribution was to support the plan, particularly the motor ban, the sense was of duty done, without much sweat or strain. The Flagstaff group of the Sierra Club did want use cut more and an educational allotment added, but otherwise the strategy of straightforward support of the plan was evident.

The public comment section ended with eleven statements from individuals that NPS thought were representative of "the two extreme viewpoints and various middle-ground positions" (IX:141-185). Many of these statements were detailed and were a credit to their authors. I only skim them here. One person was worried about rock falls and flash floods from side canyons. Another, who had been down on a Litton trip, said all self-guided trips he had met were insensitive and unappreciative. He was not the only one to praise the crew on his trip. (This is a common phenomenon, where passengers transfer some of their strong positive feelings about the Canyon onto their guides. A crew perquisite—or burden.) Another put into words the subversive idea that the Grand Canyon is not a wilderness. Due to Glen Canyon, it is trammeled, and solitude is certainly impossible. NPS asserted to another that 12,000 people tried to take commercial trips but were turned away, not a number comm op critics found credible. One of the extreme views was that the "author" of the plan was just advancing "his own philosophy" in trying to discredit motors, but motors had the advantage since they could be turned off and thus give people the best of both worlds.

That view was countered by the last five letters, which not only supported the plan, but critiqued it in various ways that show how useful it might have been to have developed a public-participation process that was not so one-shot, adversarial, and full of long stretches where the Park Service was wrestling with the issues out of sight and sound of the public. These comments, not aimed at undermining the plan, are quite different in their analytical approach. While they may not have affected the plan as much as the need to respond to the comm ops' pummeling, they strongly indicate the value of including the public in all stages of agency deliberation. A straw in the wind was offered when one self-guided boater worried about the availability of ammo cans for fecal carry-out, and suggested that the Park Service rent them (IX:158-9). The NPS reply was that several comm ops were willing to rent units, and NPS encouraged that. Since NPS rules at that time forbade commercial outfitting of self-guided trips, maybe this was the beginning of reversing that, a change that at the present-day makes these kind of trips far more widely available than they were 30 years ago—all you have to do now is sit on the waiting list for 20 years. The Lord giveth and the Lord taketh away.

Done. The original set of alternatives was considered in March 1977, followed by the draft EIS of May, coming out in its public form in January 1978, to be eventually succeeded by this final of July 1979 and the plan formally in December 1979. So were the changes made such that justified this lengthy a process? What if the process instead had been to institute incrementally over those three seasons a set of new regulations based on the research and Park values?

CHAPTER 19

1979-80: The Noisy War

Cannonades! Bombs Away! Other Loud Noises! Yawn, Nothing New ...

The months of August and September 1979 were occupied in stirring up as many comment letters as possible. A 30-day extension ended the public review period on October 2.[1] GCNP staff did summarize what it thought were its accommodations of—mostly comm op—criticism: lengthen motoring's life; reduce total use; phase in self-guided use; keep the current allocation base among comm ops; allow comm op make-up trips; drop specified trip lengths in favor of a minimum and maximum; continue comm op selection of launch days; replace any trace of lottery or no-repeat rule with a waiting list; permit non-cooking summer fires.[2]

The kind of reaction the Park must have hoped for was summed up by two members of Interior's National Parks Advisory Board, who called the plan "workable, comprehensive, and ecologically sound" after taking an 11-day river trip in June.[3] Starting with "open minds", they traveled first with motors, then by rowing. They found that no one can genuinely enjoy the Canyon "while encased in motor sounds", and ended up believing motors "should be phased off the river as expeditiously as possible".

From our base in Tucson, we wrote and stirred others to write to the Park Service, Interior officials, and the congressional delegation. Our August 8 news release was sent out by the Sierra Club chapter, AWWW, The Wilderness Society, and a local wild river group.[4] The plan was supported, and its "vigorous, swift implementation" called for. We applauded the benefits from an increase in self-guided trips, noting that they were the source of virtually all innovations in craft, environmental protection, and enjoyment. We urged allies to back the Park Service, quoting Director Whalen, "As the steward of America's park lands, I've got to call it as I see it. I'm an advocate of taking motors out of the river. The bottom line is that we are making a declaration of value. This should be the epitome of a wilderness experience on a river in America." We warned that NPS could not stand against congressional opposition unless we did our part once again, as we had many times over the past ten years. NPS had responded to our pleas, and it was our turn to respond now. We listed the methods: telephone call, postcard, mailgram, letter, personal visit to legislators home during the summer recess. Another small splash might have come from my being in a PBS documentary (on science and the Parks) titled "The Grand Canyon: Who Needs It?", though it did not get shown until October-November.[5]

We heard that the comm op onslaught of misinformation was as vigorous and well organized as in 1978, and was becoming overwhelming.[6] One indicator was a September 10 letter to Senator Goldwater opposing the plan from all top state officials—except Governor Bruce Babbitt.[7] In turn, we attacked the river industry for its "continuous resistance" based on its "fearing new competition to its entrenched domination". In another piece, we quoted one comm op's flyer to its 49,000 customers saying "the plan sounds like an approach to communism". We had heard that the motor-boaters had prevailed upon Arizona Senator DeConcini (whom we, as environmentalists, had supported in his 1978 election) to demand an extension of the comment period. One comm op was quoted as sending out mailings crying out "goodbye to the family river trip vacation" and asking customers to tell officials that river trips "belong to everyone, not just athletes, idle rich, and park rangers and their friends". Others fumed at the degradation that the self-guided increases would bring, since the latter did not have the comm ops' commitment to the Canyon. We heard about the comm ops' lobbyist and their political contribution of $1000 to Arizona Representative Bob Stump, successor to Sam Steiger; one motorizer stalwart replaced by another just as determined. A comm op wrote about the loss of the American public's choice; the government has "taken away the freedom to choose between rowing or motorized". (Right up there with the freedom of religion and to bear arms, no doubt.) Perhaps the more rabid of the motorized comm ops were carried away by a form of road rage. Or maybe they just did not care about what they said so long as letters piled up in congressional offices that would only be counting pros and cons. Or maybe mutual sympathy saved their ravings from alienating supporters.

Goldwater's archives provide a curious sidelight, on the great man or his staffwork.[8] He replied in early September to anti-motor letters, "I too regret the commotion and noise made by the motorized vehicles on the Colorado River in the Grand Canyon, and will work for the plan to discontinue their use"; motorized use is "incompatible and unnecessary". But shortly after, he wrote to a comm op that he hoped for a meeting of minds to keep both modes. And not long after, he wrote that a "phaseout ... will deprive a great many people of the opportunity" to run the river. There is no environmental impact and "I'm not convinced of the need to ban."

From our "friendly" officials, we got Babbitt's "As a long time student of the Grand Canyon, I see the need for a good management plan to protect the environmental and wilderness characteristics of the Canyon".[9] This, while what seemed like the rest of Arizona state government, administrative and legislative, was hell-bent to keep motors. Or how about Senator DeConcini (just see where electoral support got us): I "hope that the Park Service's final decision in this matter will reflect a balance between environmental and recreational considerations."[10] And Udall's lack of action on Wilderness designation was eloquent enough. Where were the principled endorsements for wilderness and the Park?

The lawyers splashed around. For WPRF, Don Nemir protested the allocation and advocated that every visitor obtain a permit.[11] His clients also wanted more of their use to be in the summer months. Ruckel reported that with the imminent adoption of the CRMP, our suit would likely be dismissed.[12] He indicated that only if the plan were not adopted would there be further action on the contracts. These two letters reinforce the gap between the efforts of wilderness and self-guided advocates, reflecting the larger-scale difference in stance between those who use and those who protect. Among individuals there can be tremendous overlap, but this does not automatically translate into strong organizational (or even intra-organizational) alliances. "I'd rather be on the river rowing, than at Congress fighting" vs. "If we don't fight for it, we won't have it."

Yet the grapevine rustled encouragingly. Calkin reported things were looking up for the plan with the mail turning sharply in its favor.[13] This might almost be a pattern—perhaps their printers and addressing machines were more efficient than ours. Anyway, it did seem too often that we were behind them puffing to catch up. We apparently had one friend, for Senator Bumpers (remember this name) of Arkansas had agreed to discourage any attempt by DeConcini to introduce a sneak pro-motors amendment in an appropriations bill, though the latter had not done anything yet.

The mail count in mid-October divided about the same as after the draft plan.[14] According to one count we received, there were 756 for the plan and 714 against. Letters came from almost all states, with Arizona and California contributing about 40%. Oddly, the tally records 23 pro letters from Utah, but does not show the con number. Only eight comm ops were recorded in this count, all against; but this figure too is certainly incomplete. Another part of the report lists pro/con letters received by congressional offices. Whether the numbers are complete or not, what this list shows is that many offices received at least one letter against the plan and none for, a sign of the comm ops' reach. The numbers were highest to western offices. There was a fairly even split in Arizona; we are talking about maybe 20 letters. In Utah, they were lop-sided against (8 or so letters), and a surprise, letters to California senators were mostly negative. There are anomalies: 8 anti letters from Illinois and 6 from Nebraska, apparently hotbeds of motorboating. Frankly, there is nothing in these incomplete, puzzling figures, supposing them approximately correct, to give comfort to the idea that the Park Service plan had America's endorsement. And certainly they did nothing but encourage efforts by comm ops and their allies to halt the CRMP.

Their major response was the lumbering October 44-page updated version of PROA's "critical analysis" of the CRMP, EISs, and "related matters".[15] Their proposed alternatives (pp. 34-42) were warmed-up 1973. Each comm op would decide on motor use and trip length. The current 89 KUD comm op yearly passenger use would stay as is, and 21 KUD would be added. The addition would, however, only go to rowing trips and that educational institution allotment, which could be used for commercial or self-guided trips. One trip for each comm op in the other seven months—that scorned "winter" season—would be outside the allotments. (These changes had the neat result that the big motor companies would not be cut or face increased competition.) Rowing was offered another bone with three 10-day no-motor spans in June, July, and August. The catch was that trips would have to start on Thursdays, the least popular day, i.e., the motorheads were giving up one weekend a month, and would otherwise not have to change; there were no incentives suggested for converting any motor trip to rowing. (And by the way, PROA's suggestions would have involved lots of regulation, just not for them.)

PROA wanted NPS to act as a clearinghouse to "facilitate concessioner viability" by encouraging mergers and acquisitions, and in general to act more quickly and with more foresight on comm op matters. It wanted to gradually spread launches/day in the "natural" season of May-September, by reducing the maximum people/day from 150 to 100 in two steps. There could be further reductions, but no more than 10 in any one year, and only after a year of evaluation. They wanted commitments for launches two years in advance, allowing for additional applications to fill holes. Thus, the schedule would be fixed by January 1980 for the 1981 season. (Since they had not yet learned how to fill their overall allocation, this suggestion would allow them to advertise longer, including for cut-rate seats.)

They wanted to have motor trips of more than 30 people and to maintain their 40 miles/day speed, double that of river pacing, theoretically allowing two-night trips to Phantom Ranch, four-night trips to Lava Falls (and the helicopters) or Whitmore Wash, five-nighters to Diamond and, with no regulation in the lower gorge, only another day to Lake Mead. These provisions wiped out the fig leaf of motors as necessary for safety and control; what mattered were speed and passenger count. Three pages were spent bashing at "partial trips", one more time taking advantage of the NPS silly idea of including trails outside the Kaibab/Bright Angel corridor. Since the document attacked NPS ideas on partial trips, it had to ignore current comm op practice, though they had no intention of abandoning them.

They wanted self-guided use to only double for a couple of years. Self-guided trips should be strictly monitored (nothing said about checking comm op operations), being less responsible users. In a fit of benevolence, PROA informed the Park Service of a wilderness simulation model that would allow NPS to see what would happen if its drastic changes were put into place, no doubt to the horror of all.

The document is often a nit-picking exercise. Criticism was launched at the use of "perpetuate", "must further define", "river's own terms", "will", "summer", "trip length", "minor", "full trip". During its discussion of this last, the document insisted that going to Phantom Ranch was just an exchange while going to Lava Falls (179 of 277 miles) or Whitmore Wash (188 miles) was a "full trip" avoiding the "dead water of Lake Mead (starts at mile 240). (Now, they sell thousands of one- and two-day trips starting with a helicopter drop-off at Whitmore.) Therefore, by comm op re-definition, there were no "true" partial trips (p.10). As virulently as usual, they went after the competition they saw posed by increases in self-guided use: repeat users, unqualified applicants, over-blown demand.

PROA severely attacked the decrease in use, insisting it would in fact be much larger than suggested in the plan, and suggested that NPS intended to reduce some use while giving windfalls to others. (You can see our problem; all we could offer our supporters was a request to support the plan; the comm ops could do all this juicy rending and tearing that really gets people to write in, to protect their "rights".

If we had been as savage as they, beating up on the plan for its pro-comm-op bias and foot-dragging, would we have gotten more attention? Or would we have been told we were uncompromising and abrasive?) The document was very testy about the idea that NPS could reallocate the user-days of a comm op that quit; existing concessionaires should get those days. They still wanted cooking fires over wood. And PROA still feared the conclusions of the "prejudicial and worthless" economic study, trying to quibble it away (p.14).

They next went after public involvement (pp. 16ff). First they pointed out that 1976 workshop attendees were younger than the river-running population (a comm op mistake that they did not allow to recur in the 1978 meetings). They sneered at the Sierra Club presenter who supported the plan without reading it, and noted that environmental organizations "entered the room [in Washington] together with television cameramen [sic], were called to speak in succession, and then departed", not staying to hear the comm ops go on as they had at the previous hearings, which they had dominated. The NPS count of who supported various parts of the plan was objected to. The document added up all the mentions of pro-rowing and pro-motors, and found that there were almost three times as many of the latter. (Again a problem for our side which only wanted to support the plan, as against the comm ops which wanted to gnash at its pieces before it did the whole thing in. I should mention that the author(s) of the PROA documents reveled in numbers, performing all kinds of calculations, crazy or not, as long as the "result" would help them make a point. Ah, the joys of opposition.) There were charges that the NPS cited petitions from pro-plan people, and ignored those from motor boaters, as well as the comm op passenger surveys. Letters of professional and personal comment were supposedly not included. And finally, the meetings were "manipulated"; a most interesting charge given how the comm ops frightened NPS officials by storming the earlier meetings and, overall, dominating them.

Still number-drunk, there were five pages of detail about quantitative errors, omissions, distortions and misrepresentations, which of course, continued the attack style of quoting out of context and other distortion. "The plan's concealed reducers" were exposed. The motor/oar combination experiment was again attacked because the trips were unusually fast, one boatman was so upset he left the trip, passengers objected to the experimental conditions and, anyway, they only chose it because it was short. Even when the document's arguments may have been correct, this accumulation of rhetorical overkill (yes, not just their problem) made them suspect. The thick smoke obscured even the glints of accuracy. Like the PROA alternatives and, for that matter, like the NPS plan, which this was a fun-house mirror of, everything was aimed at protecting that main goal, control over river management.

Calling the EIS safety data "stale", PROA asserted, once again without data, that smaller boats capsize more easily, so "inevitably" there would be more people in the hypothermia-producing water. Moreover, since people perceived rowing as less safe, fewer would go, one of the plan's "concealed reducers". Indeed, PROA charged, the overall reduction could actually result in the drastic cut in use rejected in one of the EIS's alternatives. Having swelled their once-6 million dollar industry to "perhaps" $95 million, this impact no doubt impressed PROA more than those who desired a lower use level.

The PROA analysis and its alternatives deserved to be taken seriously, for it did expose a large flaw the EIS process made almost inescapable. NEPA, the EIS's parent, got much of its legitimacy as a shield, or at least a speed-reducer, against projects that damaged the environment even though they seemed to serve an economic purpose; highways and dams are good examples. Rapidly, the NEPA process of review was generalized into a way to introduce public participation in federal decision-making, a splendid idea. The trouble was, every "action" now had to be fully proposed, and any alternatives had to be skeletonized and shot down. What was left, in the public comment process, was one target and a bunch of stigmatized sketchy options. If nothing else, the CRMP NEPA history is thus a monument to the joys of opposition; a multitude of other cases could show the same when environmentalists go on the attack. A sad part of the CRMP story, however, is that it was a congeries of actions, many not related. In a world not so riven by controversy, GCNP might have been able to introduce many of the changes incrementally and in various sequences. Instead, the storms and delays were intensified by having to gather together everything before doing anything. My point is made by the exception of the environmental protections, like solid waste hauling, where NPS did not wait on the plan. Overall, however, the mind-set of waiting for Godot, the Plan with its Rube Goldbergian contraption of different objects wrapped together, was certainly harmful. The best example of that harm might be on self-guided use with the evils attendant from having the lid kept on it. Of course, the non-plan-guided expansion of commercial use pre-NEPA gives one pause about mindless yielding to "demand".

I am not arguing that the benefits of NEPA are ill founded. However, in the CRMP's case, no one was well served in the end, not even the winners. We all suffered from the lack of a public participation process that could somehow separate out the various elements of river-running that were in common (monitoring, interpretation/education, environmental protection and restoration, etc.), and implement them just as so many of the river regulations had been. The little debate over motor horsepower limit is an example; the comm ops, suspicious and suspiciously, opposed a change even though they did not use motors above 40 hp. This was all discussed in a comm op/NPS meeting, and there were no arguments that it had to wait for the CRMP. Take waste removal (please!, as they say); suppose everybody's thought had moved more swiftly, and the containerized method was developed in 1974. Nobody sane would have objected to its being put into effect right away. Suppose the Park Service had always lived up to its obligation to educate, orient, and increase awareness among all river-runners about the environment and the Canyon, and had introduced one-day pre-trip sessions for self-guided trips in 1974. Wait until a CRMP was complete? Surely not.

Or consider the most fundamental issue. The Wilderness proposal was developed following NEPA mandates. Suppose a Grand Canyon Wilderness had passed in 1977 overwhelmingly with a directive to phase out motor use over ten years from the Act's passage. Would that phase-out have been put on hold until there was an interpretation plan ready? An allocation based on demand figured out for each comm op and for self-guided use? A monitoring program?

So is it possible to conceive of a legitimate CRMP process in which items are divvied up, parsed out, then prepared and implemented as needed? Could such a process be even more legitimate than gathering everything into one ball, which is then kicked around while a few balls of different sizes and colors are tossed into the corners to be ignored as undesirable alternatives? For instance, taking the heart of this fight, there were two desired alternatives, one by those who wanted a legislated, motor-free Wilderness, and another by those who wanted motor trips. I think today that the best procedure—the one that would have served us, the comm ops, the Park Service, and ultimately the larger public—would have worked out at least these two desired alternatives, clothing them as respectably as possible. With the Park Service not yet making a choice, the argument would not have been about Park Service perfidy or saintliness, but over the issues, and various ways to resolve them. Who knows what good might have come out of such a discussion. Since a choice would eventually have to be made, the question remains whether such an alternative-based process would produce any sort of agreement. Frankly, in the case of Wilderness vs. motors, the passions are too deeply rooted for resolution. America must choose.

So maybe it is hopeless. The only course may be to work up some plan or other, pretend it is delivered from on high, trash all other ideas, and hope, oh hope, that the political forces are such that you get (most of) your way. If so, NPS and its supporters were about to be one disappointed group.

Right in the middle of the thrashing and snarling, the Park wrote the comm ops that the Director had decided to maintain the status quo for 1980, since it was so late, and authorized the Park to set up an operating framework on that basis.[16]

All The News, Even When It Isn't Fit

Different from that following the draft plan release, the coverage from August 1979 had few events to report on and depended on interview material. Articles in the *Washington Post* and *The New York Times* suggested a more national interest, centered on the "motor boat ban".[17] The latter had made a more colorful introduction in its magazine of July 22, with special panoramic photographs of churning water and serene views accompanying a science reporter's trip in Litton's dories.[18] In the first sentence, Litton was already "fulminating"—though at Glen Canyon Dam, not any river plan. The plan indeed got short shrift, there being only one paragraph, which noted that allowing only motorless boats would "presumably" reduce the number of river trippers. One paragraph as well, the last, was all the attention the final hundred miles of the Canyon received, and only as a chance for another fulmination, this time against Lake Mead.

The *Post* article was in the form of an interview with NPS Director Whalen, taking his initial strong stand, "I realize this is unpopular, but ... I'm an advocate of taking motors out of the river ... We want to make it a pure wilderness experience ... I just don't buy the argument that the motor ban discriminates against people." A comm op spokeswoman replied that the Director was "kidding himself to call this a wilderness", citing the "motels, noise, helicopters, planes, traffic jams" on the South Rim. Interestingly, the *Post* editorialized on the Park Service side, barely: Given the time and cost even of a motor trip, "it's hard to see how barring motors will make a crucial difference. Most important, on the central esthetic argument, Mr. Whalen is on the right side."[19]

Arizona reports focussed on comm op reaction, particularly their new line that the plan concealed drastic cuts.[20] One told of a mini-debate at a February Las Vegas meeting between comm op Burke and Whalen; Burke said Whalen told them they could get out of the business; after all they had nothing when they started and should have nothing when they quit. (This sounds like a distorted response to Burke's complaint that if motors were banned, he would not be able to sell his company for a good profit when he got out.) Whalen was "amazed" by commercial opposition, since demand would rise under the NPS plan; maybe, he offered, the comm ops "were reluctant to make a change in their life". In another interview, Burke worried about the plan being "the first step to nationalizing river running in the Grand Canyon and eliminating private enterprise".

Ben Avery and Pete Cowgill, outdoor writers who once championed rowing, sang the motor boater line.[21] Avery: Whalen floated the river and reacted like a "Sierra-Club type purist ... a stuffed-shirt type who believes ... the rest of the population is a common herd that must be kept out". Cowgill, "Surveys taken by these commercial operators" show their passengers feel they have been in a wilderness. Since esthetics are personal, NPS might as well decree a ban on yellow and red life-jackets. (These pitiable 180-degree shifts in opinion by independent thinkers make Park Service consistency over the decade even more admirable.)

Whether news or not, one straw in the wind was a report that Senator DeConcini had taken a motorized trip with Staveley.[22] Maybe we ignored that, buoyed by what we hoped was our own breeze indicated by a *Washington Post* report on "the controversy that ... goes to the heart of the nation-wide wilderness battle. It pits commercial outfitters and conservative members of Congress against environmental groups and the Carter administration." [23] Although the reporter had been on a trip, she still was able to write, "Environmentalists boat down the river wearing plastic rain gear carrying chemical toilets, gas stoves, canned food, cameras, and a park service permit". A marginally better picture than the comm ops' image of naked miscreants dirtying up the beaches and burning down the trees. But why "plastic"? She went on to report that the Park Service, to counter the comm ops' claim of carrying the "fat and flabby", had run "a quadriplegic down the river for one study". However, in spite of the contention that a motor ban favored the "idle rich", she ended with two pro-rowing comments, one from a UPS deliveryman.

Thus the publicity war. Good for a few laughs and dropped jaws. The real struggle was elsewhere.

CHAPTER 20

1979-80: In The Thick Of It

The last chapter described the comm op effort to grab the public advantage in fall 1979. This was only the paper war. Similar to our 1977 effort, their offensive would be multiple: legislative maneuvers like the Stump-Rhodes blockbuster; the subtle weaponry of negotiations, sincere or not, with the Park Service; and the inevitable flanking move through the courts.

Before we get into the yearlong scramble that killed public river management, putting it definitively into the hands of private industry, we need to check on some individuals. Whalen was forced out as NPS Director in May 1980, succeeded by Russell Dickenson. Although the Regional Director and River Unit did not change, Superintendent Stitt retired in January 1980, with Bruce Shaw acting in the interim until May when Richard Marks took over, lasting until December 1988. You will remember Marks from Chapters 4 and 7. A new figure on the scene, lawyer Jon Kyl, was the son of John Kyl, congressional liaison for Secretary Morton in the mid-70s period.

The comm ops, by default or plan, ended up with two chief publicist/negotiators. The politically most active—the one who left the most tracks anyway—comm op was Burke, who, possibly only tactically, was not in PROA, though he was linked with its chairman. Now and then Burke would say he represented the WRGA, but that organization, no longer a broadly representative grouping of people interested in river-running was, for the Grand Canyon, just another hat in Burke's same old act. It is difficult to be sweet about Fred, particularly now, when some of his papers are in public archives. To me, he was always the old pol, the smarmy smoothie usually dangling a bauble for us to grab for, even though he never intended to yield. He was actually worse than that, and I have to wonder what his fellows thought. He offered some opinions in a 1990s oral history interview conducted by Sam Steiger's son, and they so confirm my prejudices about his back-stabbing, self-promoting ways that I want to give him his voice here, at least in my paraphrase.[1] He opined that Currey of Western was mercenary, wanted to PUSH people down (the river) to make money. Though, anyway, what harm does rushing through do; if passengers never touched shore, you'd be doing the environment a big favor. Ted (Hatch) was the same way, dying to be a millionaire; I didn't think much of his trips. The mercenary ones did a lot of damage with large trips. Sanderson ran childish trips, while Sparks of Fort Lee was in with monied people; not the hamburger type, the sirloin. There was animosity between rowing and motor concessionaires. We started with motors and everyone happy, then rowing started. NPS pigeonholed our letters and petitions. We went to Washington numerous times and, surprisingly, got access. We spent a lot of money trooping around, up against the Sierra Club and Wilderness Society. I hope it's in the past, but it may crop up. The 20-25,000 people today is too many. I told NPS way back they weren't strict enough about trash. NPS said they would look at quality, and never did. Why jam it all in summer? Why shouldn't you be able to sell your company? Thus spoke Fred Burke, late in life.

PROA, through its chairman Gay Staveley, claimed to represent only some, though the major, motor boaters. Looking at Burke and Staveley together, the latter may have been the straighter of the two; though a name-caller, he does not seem to be on record as two-faced. Once he switched from rowing to large, fast motor trips, he consistently defended them in the company of the other dedicated motorizers. Of course, defense does not imply a dedication to accuracy, as when Staveley talks of "private trippers ... trashing the canyon, and flaunting all-nude groups in the faces of other river trips encountered", and wonders, "Is it accidental they [the Sierra Club] sound neo-Nazi?"[2]

Those two were Arizona-based; it certainly seems likely that the Utah motormen, e.g., Western, Hatch, Tour West, were also doing their part. The Utah congressional delegation going back to Senator Moss in 1972 was a stalwart in comm op defense or, if you prefer, offense. In any case, a full presentation of comm op activism waits on a future historian with better access. My information is at best sketchy; there was so much going on among the comm ops that we had not even a hint of, just as, in spite of trying to keep tabs, we often did not know the players and events inside the government.

The Offensive, Disguised as Negotiations

The opening salvo did not wait for plan approval. In an October 12 letter, two Arizona congressmen, Rhodes of Phoenix and Stump of the district that included the Canyon, announced to fellow House members their bill to counter the CRMP's motor phase-out and "severe" summer use reduction.[3] This bill would have amended the Grand Canyon National Park Act of 1919 so that the Secretary could not reduce the user-days of "commercial motorized water craft travel" in the Park below that permitted in "calendar year 1978". This noisome special-interest piece was sloppily drafted, for its wording would have allowed NPS to restrict all motorized use to the winter months, even though the letter aimed at the summer reductions. The writers hawked the comm op distortions, talking about 20-hp motors, even though the comm ops had refused to reduce the limit from 55 to even 40 hp, and summarizing other deceits in their wish to prevent NPS discrimination by age, income, safety, or a "bureaucratic notion of a wilderness experience".

Sloppy or not, as a big bang to get NPS attention, the Stump-Rhodes assault worked wonderfully well. On October 19, the Director met with "5 or 6" comm ops in Page, self-declared immovability on its turf confronting bureaucratic irresistibility.[4] The NPS meeting report says it was to give the comm ops the "opportunity for their input to the Director on the river management plan." Whalen listened, and replied that NPS would "not negotiate or compromise on elimination of motors", but would dicker over numbers and launches, a negotiation to be conducted by Chapman.

Marv Jensen offered the opinion, in his interview with me, that over the several-month course of discussions in 1979-80, Chapman's stance shifted, and he recalls the latter calling from Washington to get reconfigurations in the plan that would lessen the impact on the motor companies.[5] Jensen's opinion of Chapman's softness on the motor ban contradicts Chapman's assessment of his commitment. In hindsight, given the political hauling-and-tugging, room is certainly created for both to be true. Granted that the record contains evidence that the Park Service was not of one mind about motors in the years following the 1972 Reed decision, all the official motion was toward wilderness and a motor ban. Differential enthusiasm was certainly present; foot-dragging may have been evident; perhaps even sabotage was attempted (the "Morton decision" to put the matter on hold). Yet for eight years, eliminating motors was the NPS goal, and the foundation of its river planning.

Chapman set up the negotiating session for November 21 at Denver's airport, with Staveley for PROA and Burke "representative [sic, and false] of the small concessionaires".[6] In the event, weather intervened (reminiscent of seven years before when a storm forced Eiseman's Flagstaff meeting to move, minus some participants, to Phoenix), and Burke spent the time watching the snow fall in Colorado Springs. Two other comm ops, Ken Sleight and Clair Quist, did join Staveley, Chapman, Stitt and Jensen, which made for somewhat more diverse opinions. According to the NPS account, the comm ops pushed for an increase in the small allocations, but without decreasing the large ones. NPS wanted to keep the plan maximum for any comm op of 1025 passengers launched each year. So, since this was a negotiation, Chapman agreed that the Park Service would look at increasing total passenger numbers back to the recent level, taken to be the 1978-9 average of 11,550. Then, by "adjusting" group size and increasing the number of trips, there could be a gain of 1400 persons in the summer to 10,550, which increase to go to the 15 comm ops with fewer than 400 passengers. This gave almost 100 more to each, an allocation "in response to the need for sufficient base to support a viable economic operation."

Even though the "final" EIS had been published, and the public's comment period extended to early October, there was still time for this behind-the-scenes winter-time negotiation to get incorporated into the published CRMP, which was approved on December 20, 1979. Paranoids will wonder whether the 2-1/2 months pause was solely to allow this non-public alteration, but it had been allowed for when the final EIS came out. In any case, the tables showing how concession allocation would work (6 on p. I:15 in the EIS and 8 on p. 23 in the Plan) had each of the examples at the smaller end increased by 100, with a footnote saying they were added to provide an economic base.[7] Although the total number of summer trips is increased from 366 to 404, the individual numbers were not changed so that it appeared that 4 trips were now to carry 200 people instead of 100, etc. That could not be right, and indeed, a "modifications" sheet was also offered, adding three trips for those added 100 passengers.[8]

You might think that such correction was a bit off-putting. You might even think this is getting a bit arcane and even confusing. Clarity did not arrive with the "fact sheet" that followed that snowy airport meet. It called for reducing the number of trips from 457 total in the EIS (it was really 405), to 443 in the CRMP itself.[9] This was correct in the plan, showing an added 38 summer trips. However, a "modifications" document says there would be a summer maximum of 468, whatever that might mean. The same treatment was given to maximum passengers per trip: 34 in the "fact sheet" and 36 in the CRMP. (There is not in the record any minutes for the November 21 meeting. Would they be any more accurate?) In the EIS, there were two launches a day, 14 a week. The "fact sheet" says "no basic change", but make-up trips may be eliminated. The CRMP shows 2-3 launches each day and 16 per week. And the "modifications" document explains the 486 (not 468) maximum as allowing for 5-10% overbooking which replaces the make-up provisions. Another mystery was that the "fact sheet" left total user-days unchanged at 121,500, while the CRMP dropped the total to 115,500. How could anyone be certain as to what had been decided? What was the definitive document or number? Maybe I was hasty in complaining about the bureaucratic delays in writing and revising the plan, after what this helter-skelter produced.

Clarity was still not achieved after the plan was sent out on January 4, 1981; some comm ops tried to read the 100/company increase as on top of the 10,500 total in which the increases were in fact included. The Park needed to make a "clarification". The strange assertion was also made that though the number of passengers was "approximately the same", the longer trips meant there would be an "offset" of more user-days for fewer passengers for "some of the larger companies". Such a comment implies that NPS thought these longer trips would be priced higher, running to as much as a 20% increase in the yearly take, an altogether too-bland optimism. Taken altogether, it is hard not to see these events as more salt in the comm ops' bleeding stigmata.

We Attack a Weak (?) Spot

While the Park Service was trying to tweak the CRMP numbers to gain some adherents among the comm ops, we too found some information that kept us busy. I have lamented the drawbacks of the passivity in our role as CRMP supporters whose only role was in urging its speedy implementation. Going back a bit, in November 1979, ignorant of the negotiations and waiting for the plan, I got the chance to make a substantive attack on the comm ops' position. They had prepared a spreadsheet for 1978 trip prices, one side for motors, the other for rowing.[10] Each comm op had a separate line, and the price was listed by length of trip (in days). Gathering such information was not easy; it would have been an excellent flyer for the Park Service to have distributed to potential river-runners, particularly if each person/group had had to obtain a permit. Then power of choice would really have been demonstrated. Anyway, for the first time, we could actually calculate and publicize what "choice" meant; how price, length, and value (in $/day) were distributed. Too bad desktop computers were still a gleam in the eye. I did enjoy the work, and out of it came an article, "The Last Blast or Have a Cigar, Sucker or Exploding the Final Myth about Motorboating through the Grand Canyon".[11]

The central pro-motor claim was that they provided, as compared to rowing, trips that fit within Americans' vacation time and budget. The facts were otherwise. They showed that comm ops with rowing trips (including those who offered both) offered more choices than did the motoring comm ops (3, as compared to 2.3). Rowing choices were evenly spread over the price range; motor trips were clumped (55% in the middle). There were more rowing than motor options in the low price category.

(A sidebar on numbers. I have throughout tried to avoid dollar figures, given the complications of trying to compare rotted apples to newly picked apples. But to give you an idea: In 1978, low range prices were $200-390; middle, $400-590; high $600-1000. Applying the cost-of-living index alone would bring these prices up by about 2.76 times, so a middle price of $470 for a "full" motor trip in 1978 would have grown to about $1300 in 2002.[12] The actual price for these trips by the same comm ops was about $1700, $400 above inflation.[13] Perhaps political support is costly.)

As far as the low-cost shorter trips went, there were more rowing options of 8 days or less (the "one-week" vacation) in the low price range. Another implication of there being fewer motorized options was that lots more of their trips were piled onto the same length, given that motorized use was 80%. So again, less choice. Rowing offered a total of 19 options of 8 days or less, none in the high price range; motors 24, of which 3 were high-priced. For trips of 9 days or more, the offerings were the same in the middle prices. Getting even more extreme, allowing 3-6 days, motors had 9 low-priced and oars 10.

So the river-runner could pay more for less on a motor trip, but for short trips at lower prices, rowing had as many options. This led into the discussion of value, as I pointed out that motor shorty trips were priced at $49-75/day, rowing at $44-57. I immediately added that value here was not quality, which is rowing's advantage in pace, quiet, greater exposure to the Canyon, retention of the experience, higher sensitivity to the environment, more camaraderie with guides and fellow riders, more time spent off the river getting close to the Canyon, etc. But by dollar value, 36% of rowing trips cost under $50/day; 6% of motors. Less than $60/day: rowing 72%, motors 38%. High end: 38% of motors were $70/day or more, 8% of rowing. And, I asked, "what do you get for the piratical rates on motor trips: speed, noise, crowds, a lessened chance for almost everything." (This was so much more fun than propping up the NPS's plan; had the Park Service come out in favor of motors, we could really have gone to town.) Rowing trips spread their options evenly across the price categories; motors in their clumping go for the high side. "The real choice for river touring ... is between getting soaked (financially) on quickie motor runs, or getting the bargain of your life on the experience of your life on a river-powered rowing cruise."

I also took a second look at the 1971-8 numbers for accidents requiring helicopter-evacuation. The actual incidents worked out to an expectation of one per

season for rowing. Since motors had four times as much use, an equivalent
expectation would be four per season, or 32 evacuations in that period. There were
actually 46, or 14 excess injuries on motor trips, 44% over expectation. Well, as I
said in the article, we can all lie with statistics; I was just making the strongest
arguments I could.

My conclusion was that the only hope we had of increasing choice and
competition, and keeping a good price structure and a good river economy was to
get motors off. I personally made sure this message went to the Arizona
congressional delegation, foe and otherwise, the Governor, that "friend of the
Canyon", along with Park Service officials.[14] These letters were not all full of
sweetness, given the level of frustration we were experiencing in getting no
politicians to back the Park Service. I wished I had had the information to distribute
for the 1978 hearings on the draft.

The Ground Fought Over

As we primed our salvo, the doomed heroine's appearance was being prepared,
having been heralded by a handout announcing the CRMP on November 1.[15] It
noted three "significant and controversial" proposals: five-year motor phase-out,
reducing daily launches, increasing self-guided use. (Note that these three items are
not integrally linked, and could have been separately and incrementally handled
over the years, which is also true of the environmental protections. Let's suppose a
Wilderness bill with motor ban, a year-by-year effort to smooth out launches,
responding to self-guided use as it increased, fixing environmental problems as they
were documented. With these policies, and an on-going monitoring program, you
are moving toward a well-managed river, where the politics (Wilderness) is in
Congress, while administrators and users deal directly with their impacts. What we
got instead was ten years of politics infesting every level, and bad decisions from one
end to the other.) The last two of these proposals seemed straightforward. Here is
what the document said (its italics):

> "*The proposal was not made lightly. It was not our recommendation to
> remove motors because they physically impact the environment -
> although they are noisy at close range. It was not our recommendation
> to remove motors because of safety - although oar powered craft have a
> slight edge on the safety record. It was not our recommendation to
> remove motors because of energy consumption - although oar-powered
> craft consume only the physical energy of the boatman/guide. Because
> the Colorado River as it courses through the Grand Canyon represents
> the ultimate whitewater experience, and given the fact there are more
> than 30 other stretches of recreational whitewater in the western river
> system open to the full spectrum of visitor use, we are proposing that
> this most sought after stretch of river be dedicated for use by non-
> motorized craft. This action will provide the user with the opportunity
> within that system to experience fully the natural sounds, silence, sights,
> and full beauty of the canyon.*

This NPS trumpet had a full, sweet sound. It sounds right and true 25 years later (and will 25 or any years from now). But ears, deafened by controversy's clamor, were no longer open; nor to the document's answer to some "common" questions. More, not fewer, people could take a full or partial trip. Fewer, however, could go during the summer, cutting out fluctuations and allowing for more uniform use, to reduce congestion. Spring and fall are good times to go. Motor trips cost more per day, but less overall. Rowing trips are longer, but there are trips of 4 to 18 days, and people may hike or ride (animals, no mention of helicopters) on partial trips. The old, young, and handicapped have been enjoying rowing trips for years. Motor trips are slightly less safe.

This strong statement resonated with a report from the Sierra Club that Whalen "intends to stand firm" on the plan, though the report did not inform us that he had already met with comm ops to alter non-motor parts of the plan.[16] That report also suggested that Udall, the Chairman of the House Interior Committee, might allow Stump's bill to get a hearing, but that DeConcini would not sponsor Senate pro-motor legislation.

A sigh from the old order was the annual call for self-guided applications in early December.[17] The lottery would be used for 1980's ninety permits, to be replaced by the new first-come-first-served basis. But during 1980, no one could take more than one recreation trip, "noncommercial or commercial", so that more people can experience a trip, according to the Superintendent.

Release of the CRMP emphasized the motor phase-out, and noted "several" modifications to adjust quotas for smaller comm ops to insure a "mobile economic base" (not a stable base?), although launches and user days were unchanged.[18] And so it appeared, two years after the draft.[19]

The editors had been at work. The introduction was trimmed, history condensed, language made bland (pp. 1-7). The environmental section of river-running was drastically shorter. The commercial crew user-days vanished, and the plan was concerned with 96,600 visitor-days, not 122,600 user-days. Uniform policy for the river was deleted. The Master Plan's perpetuation of wilderness river experiences was moved. The list of issues under public input was just a list, discussion deleted; wildlife did not make it. What was new, of course, was the summary of input since the EIS came out in August (p. 10). This time, there were 1712 comments, with 911 against motors, and 774 for. And while NPS was negotiating with the comm ops after the comment period (not mentioned), another 232 letters were received, 213 for the plan, 19 against. Self-guided issues gathered 129 responses. The comm op concerns were said to be economic: increasing small allocations, increasing trip size to boat capacity, make-up trips.

A summary list of provisions aimed to give quick answers to the usual comm op objections, including the acceptability of helicopters in connection with partial trips. The overall goals of the plan now started with the wilderness experience (p. 11) and an entire new section on that experience was added (pp. 12-4). The Wilderness Act definition was quoted. A discussion of "philosophy" called for a plan that permitted human use without sacrificing the wilderness Canyon. "Rather than representing an elitist choice", the plan makes "available the fullness of the unique experience" to the river-runner. We have here returned to the glory days after the 1972 Reed decision when NPS rhetoric matched its mandate.

Done with the justification, the specifics came from the EIS (pp. 16-7). The summer season was now April-September, instead of mid-April to mid-October. The section on summer use was re-written, dropping the congestion reduction rationale, and emphasizing adjustments to help the comm ops. On commercial trip limits, for instance, miles/day went up from 30 to 40, minimum length down from 8 days to 6, and the average down from 12 to 10. The 50 passengers/day limit was now 100 in summer and 36 in winter. A third daily launch was possible, as were two more weekly launches. Trip limit was up from 25 to 36 people. Overall people, user-days and launches were increased as agreed in the negotiations. Much more effort was put into making partial trips convincing, "Concessionaires are encouraged to provide partial Canyon trips as they have done in the past." The expectation was that this would increase visitors by 3000. Note was taken of the practice of calling the 2/3 trip to Lava Falls a full trip.

The discussion of demand and why it was difficult to determine was cut in half (p. 20). There was some more adjustment in the numbers, due to the above changes. Since these changes had something to do with motor trips, as these decrease, group size might have to go down (p. 21). As noted, comm op allocations were affected by giving the little ones another 100 passengers (p 23). The date for firming up comm op schedules was moved up from July to February. NPS river patrol contacts with trips would no longer be "low key" (p. 24). The rest of the plan's provisions were unchanged from the EIS Description, as was its discussion of adjoining agencies (pp. 33-6). The appendices were now concerned only with operations requirements, limitations, procedures, etc.

The Plan itself was strengthened in its own behalf, and that die was cast. The dice, however, were not out of reach as far as the opponents were concerned. Earlier, I discussed the notion that key NPS people were not whole-hearted in their devotion to the motor-ban. It is the flip side of the hope that the motormen might have been less than whole-hearted in their determination to keep motors. However, I believed at the time, and even more strongly after this review of the maneuvering, that they did not ever abandon their desire to get the motor-ban reversed. They may well have been quite serious in the negotiations of 1979-80, seeking, under the umbrella of a policy they detested, what protection they could. Perhaps they argued to themselves that it was a transition plan, they would go along, and try to defeat it over the next five years.

Artillery Rounds; Another Round of Negotiating

Along with the Plan, the comm ops received, a bit late for Christmas, an "interim authorization" to continue providing visitor services even as the extended permits (now 8 years old) expired with 1979.[20] This authorization was offered pending negotiation of new concession contracts, and ran no longer than one year. Earlier, the Park had been working on its prospectus for the new five-year contract, though there is no indication that the document was sent out.[21] It asked for launch numbers, but only encouraged a variety of lengths, prices, menus, interpretation programs, boats, and "accessibility to special populations and educational groups". It was, even with its financial provisions, a simple document, barely requiring adherence to the CRMP.

Pressing on, the Park sent the plan out to the comm ops on January 4, asking at the same time for the launch dates they desired for 1981. GCNP was to collate these to be discussed by all at a meeting on February 26 at the Park. As it charted the requests, the Park found all-too-foreseeable problems: individual requests totaled more than the allocation, too many Saturday-Monday launches, too few in April, September and October.

A true indicator of how the comm ops' negotiated was a memorial introduced in late January in the Arizona legislature by 37 representatives and 9 senators.[22] They urged the U.S. Congress to "enact legislation to maintain the number of user days of commercial motorized watercraft travel"; the same goal as the Stump-Rhodes bill. The whereas's were a hodge-podge taken from the motorizers. Revealingly, the virtues of motors were flexibility, maneuverability, safety, efficiency, and speed. Revealingly, these were mostly advantages for the comm op; there is no hint of a claim that the visitor has a better time. The memorial complained about the plan's increase in use; a sign perhaps of the comm ops' deep conservatism and desire only to maintain their tidy little status quo? Not only was the false claim of safety made, but so was the now-disproved claim of convenience and cost. The screed ended with a blast at the "inexperienced, unsupervised, and less qualified persons drawn from an unknown sociological group" who go on noncommercial trips. Perhaps it is guilt by association, but a memorial introduced at the same time called for Congress to approve construction of a state dam in the Grand Canyon in conjunction with the Hualapai tribe.[23] The memorial apparently was considered at a hearing and passed both parts of the Arizona legislature by March 25.[24] My lack of records about this exercise may just be a sense of hopelessness about Arizona politics. Or perhaps we wanted to believe that publication of the CRMP opened the door to a new era, whatever squeaks the Arizona legislature made.

The NPS/comm op meeting on 1981 launch dates suggests it was a revolving door, dumping everybody back in the same old room. Held at the Shrine of the Ages, the talk went on most of the day. An NPS summary says there was good progress spreading launches through the week, not much on the months, and still too many requests. Jensen has a more positive take, saying there was no agreement, but progress was being made when Acting Superintendent Shaw intervened, according to Jensen's recollection, ending the meeting. A few weeks later, Shaw wrote to the comm ops that the staff had developed a schedule, based on the "good progress" made on February 26.[25] Charts in Burke's papers present a different view. They purport to show the terrible effect of this scheduling along with the mandatory rowing months.[26]

In his letter, Shaw summarizes the plan as allowing two trips on five days each week, three on the other two, a limit of 100 passengers/day. But he was willing to modify this to allow for a phasing-in of the plan changes. So the enclosed schedule allowed three trips on five days, and two on the remaining two, a limit of 19 trips, in recognition of the 17-20 trips each week during the popular months. Some dates for each comm op were assigned in the period outside June-August, adhering as closely as possible to turn-around requirements. In spite of the rule, companies with two launches on one day kept most of them. The schedule was adjusted for the use each comm op was allocated; as a group, a 5% overbooking is allowed, varying for each comm op depending on group size. We will make "minor" adjustments provided they fit within the limits of 100 passengers and 3 trips per day, and 20 trips each week, and you accept some trips outside June-August. (The EIS limits were 50 passengers and 2 trips per day, 14/week. So the comm ops' tactics had achieved almost a 50% increase.) In 1982 and later, the plan limits will apply. (And what if pressure were applied again?) A copy of the schedule has handwritten notes on adjustment conversations with 6 comm ops, all small.[27] Shaw wrote that the "maximum number of passengers at any one time on a commercial trip is the number that will be counted against a concessioner allocation". I do not know what this meant in practice, but it seems to say that if 20 people could fit on a trip, then 20 would be counted against the allocation, even if the trip only took 10. Maybe this makes sense in avoiding demand for trips to fill out an allocation later in the season, but it sounds harsh.

Later on, I heard in a third-hand way that at the meeting the comm ops wanted to concentrate on the 100/day limit. Then they got angry when Jensen wanted other things, so they made extra demands. In the end, Jensen sent out the schedule with April, September and October dates. The April briefing document says the Park staff was able to eliminate excessive requests and, by "compromising slightly on the launch limits" write up a 1981 schedule, which was "apparently acceptable". However, somebody was not being accepting, as we all shortly learned.

Rip van Wilderness is Put To Sleep

About this same time, with a lurch and splutter, someone remembered the Wilderness proposal. As described in Chapter 15 and earlier, its history from a strong launch in January 1977 was of a long decline in interest and attention, the last flurry being in May 1979. Whatever explained the decline in interest, certainly the decision not to include it in Arizona Wilderness legislation in early 1978 was a strong signal. With new worries stirred up about the tribal lands and interests, and the suitability of the Lake Mead back-up, excitement over the CRMP could easily have furnished an excuse for inaction. Given the centrality of the wilderness issue, it will always have to remain a mystery as to why all the proponents did not press hard in 1977; not that there were not excuses and distractions, but why could we not see that that year was the Wilderness's moment, and as long as it remained unsettled, the CRMP foundation was political dry sand, just waiting for the next big wave of change?

The flurry took place in December 1979 into January. The Park, Region, and Washington offices all stuck an oar in. GCNP found four matters puzzling it.[28] First was that of non-federal encumbrances on various lands, either private ownership or other sorts of rights (none of which could or would ever be exercised; they were historical artifacts). Altogether, GCNP found 131 tracts totaling 8,558.57 acres. Next, the "proposed" CRMP indicates that motor use will be eliminated in 1985, and the river can be designated as wilderness. On another matter, the Park changed its mind and wanted the Kaibab trail deleted since it is heavily used and mechanized tools are sometimes needed for maintenance. Though at first Havasupai and Hualapai issues were mentioned, they do not appear in a slightly rewritten form of this memo dated January 1980.[29]

Washington alerted the Denver Service Center and the Regional Office, wanting a recommendation prepared for submission.[30] It called the 1977 recommendation a "draft", "held up pending completion" of the CRMP, and "obsolete". (All untrue; an agency with an institutional memory shorter than three years would seem an Orwellian partner.) Whether because it did not know about the completed one or did not care, it said an EIS was required. A tight budget requires we move quickly so we are prepared for congressional hearings. GCNP sent in its four important issues, noting a "hardship" in maintaining the Kaibab Trail, and no word from the tribes in two years. There is no record about how the changes were formulated, nor did we even know about this discussion. Whatever "quickly" meant, the changes took until August to be finalized and printed, being sent to the Assistant Secretary on September 11.[31] It did not really matter; the time for Wilderness recommendations had passed. We had simply stopped paying attention. Aside from returning the river to "potential Wilderness" status, the changes are not relevant until later, much later, when it was again taken up by the Park for contemplation.

Trying to Get a Shot; Mopping Up?

In January, our efforts showed some really small fruit. Governor Babbitt offered the notion that we might be closer than "one might think", and Senator DeConcini, admitting he was not convinced of the need for a motor ban, said that "since the plan has been finalized", they would monitor it and look to a "reevaluation after three years".[32] I offered this agenda for our Washington lobbyists: Tell NPS about Udall's support. What about the Stump-Rhodes pro-motor and NPS pro-wilderness bills? What about the contracts?[33]

Meanwhile, I wrote the Park asking for information I hoped would help "protect the public investment in river policy", since I was "anxious that the angry frustrations of a few bitter-enders will jeopardize" the plan.[34] I inquired about the basis for the extension of the permit extension and the timetable for the new contracts, and also about companies that had been sold. I wanted more information on the schedule being negotiated. I requested an update on monitoring of river conditions.

Jensen's reply came in early April, after events had taken another turn toward the courts (next section). He enclosed a note about the delay, "the concessionaires are very busy with the politicians, which has been keeping us busy preparing responses". He was optimistic that the Stump-Rhodes bill would not go anywhere, though a hearing was likely. He then danced through an explanation that the extension was not an extension, just an authorization to continue operations "in accordance with the conditions" of the CRMP. It would not delay the plan, as he anticipated a prospectus being sent out in the summer and awards made by October. There would be public notice (I'd heard that before). He sent me the schedule they had arrived at. However, a report on the monitoring from 1976-80 was not yet available, and work centered on techniques. Five further years had been authorized to look at the resource, visitor attitude, and congestion.

When Jensen wrote, a bit muddily to me, that two companies had been "transferred" with no change in allocation, I asked if this was a sale setting a precedent for an entrenched right to sell allocation; after all, one sale involved the largest allocation, which could have been split up among the smaller companies.[35] Again, Jensen danced very hard, noting that NPS could adjust allocations, as it planned to do in the plan. In the case I cited, however, the lawyers thought that dividing the allocation would be "selling of user days". In a different world, that topsy-turvy conclusion would have been worth following up. We also heard that Richard Marks was to appear in early May as the new Superintendent, so I wrote a welcome, expressing the hope he could meet with a group of us soon.

Ruckel had returned to action.[36] He wanted a review of the plan from the Arizona chapter, and would go through it with the Phoenix lawyer and me at the end of January. Assuming the plan applied to the contracts, and final review showed no problems, we would move to dismiss the suit. The chapter was asked to pass a resolution to intervene in any lawsuit filed by the comm ops, so that we could react quickly if they try. Tony summed up, "I feel very good about this matter and very happy with the results." Venable wrote that the U. S. Attorney wanted to wrap up the matter, partly so he could sometimes be on the right side of environmental cases, but he does not want the dismissal to make Whalen look bad.[37] I suggested we might be able to set up the dismissal to deal with "foreseeable problems from the concessionaires' likely legal challenge". There was some further back-and-forth, resulting in a Motion to Dismiss by the feds on March 24, which said there was an "adequate" EIS and an "appropriate" CRMP.[38] Further, any contracts would be in "full compliance" with the Plan. On March 26, Ruckel reported that the motion "represents complete success in this litigation" and resolved the last outstanding issue, that of the contracts. He recognized the efforts of those of us who helped. However, it is an "intensely political issue", the NPS must be watched, since the plan might be amended to take account of new conditions. The next legal move was up to the comm ops. Sometime before contracts were signed, they would have to determine "what, if any, legal relief they will seek."

The next day, March 27, 1980, they determined.

Onslaught of the Mortars

The motorizers' legal complaint was filed against Director Whalen and Secretary of the Interior Andrus in Phoenix from two directions.[39] First, James Watt shot from Denver for his Mountain States Legal Foundation (MSLF), nine "River Runners" (see below), and 49 Arizona state legislators, most of whom had been listed as sponsors of that just-passed pro-motor memorial to Congress (see under "Artillery Rounds" above). Closer to court, those nine "River Runners" were also represented by Jon Kyl—well-placed then as an attorney with the Phoenix firm, Jennings, Strouss and Salmon, even better-placed today as a comm-op-friendly senator from Arizona; and whose father was the John Kyl of Chapter 4. In describing the parties, the MSLF said its members were adversely affected since they would not be able to experience the "splendor and beauty of the entire Grand Canyon" (keep this in mind when you read later on of Watt's river experience.) The legislators used or "desired" motor trips. (The latter is not a trivial or uncontested point. Up to what point can potential users take legal action to preserve their self-perceived preferred options? This is a basis for Wilderness protection as well as for Parks. Think of the "future generations" environmentalists so often hope they are conserving places for. So to what degree is an administrator obliged to leave undisturbed not just whatever anybody is doing, but also what anybody says they want?)

We can trace the basic motorizer alliance back ten years to the formation of CROA. Hatch, Sanderson, Tour West, Western, and WhiteWater were its core. (These connections are summarized in Reader's Guide Part C.) They led the lawsuit of 1973, and then were founding members of PROA. Canyoneers' Staveley, while not a founder of CROA, was in on the 1973 lawsuit and PROA. Georgie White stayed away from the earlier suit, but was a member of PROA, joining in the 1980 lawsuit—with a puzzling result, as we shall see. (Both CROA and PROA had a couple of non-GC comm ops, for whatever reason.) Cross was part of the original cabal. Burke did not join CROA, PROA or the 1973 lawsuit, always proclaiming his independence, which he surrendered to openly join in the 1980 suit with his natural, and longtime, allies. Fort Lee completed the gang of nine.

Given the intensity of comm op activity against the plan, the suit has to be seen as just one weapon out of many—quite possibly not one they had much faith in, given what had happened in the 1973 suit. They aimed their suit at the Park Service's stand for motor removal; the airport negotiation and work on the schedule could have led them to think NPS was starting to yield, or was not yielding at all. So, NPS policy banning motors was an "arbitrary restriction on an established use", "elitist", "without environmental justification", and deprived the pubic of "its right to use and enjoy this park ... reasonably accessibl[y]". The "time, money and physical stamina required will be greatly increased, thereby rendering such trips inaccessible to all but a privileged few".

The basic purpose of the Park System is invoked. (Yet the motor phase-out/ban is an excellent example of a policy intended to remove an impairment of the conserved objects, e.g., natural quiet and pace, for future generations' enjoyment. The policy, that is, did not fix an impairment immediately, but aimed at the future.) Motor rafts play the major part in providing public access. (But in stating this, they also admitted that they wanted only a particular subset of motor use; they did not argue for those lashed-together rafts that carried 100-150 or for now-banned motorboats that could "do" the Canyon in a couple of days or for upstream travel; these were NPS policies that they had accepted.) NPS first advocated a motor ban in 1971. (What's a one-year error among friends?) There was no scientific data for the ban. The ban was reiterated several times. (No hint that the 1972 decision was a phase-out, which was put on hold, and never implemented at all.) Environmental regulations in 1977 "have greatly alleviated any environmental damage previously caused ... by river travelers". (Once again, Eiseman's scorn for trying to find "data" to justify a motor ban is justified.) Nine statements from the EIS supporting motor trips are listed. Summarized, they are non-polluting, passengers love the trip, safety, and a trip "through the entire Grand Canyon" is half as long if motorized. (The "entire" adjective is used again, without, for some reason, admitting that few motor passengers go through the entire 277 miles.)

Three claims were offered. The first seems to be a grab bag; the second that the decision process was flawed, and the third that the ban "established" a Wilderness, which only Congress can do.

First, motor rafts do no "lasting ecological damage", and are enjoyed by a majority. The ban is a "completely subjective value judgment" "irrationally and improperly" prohibiting a "preferred" means of enjoying the river and requiring "expensive" conversion to rowing.

Second, there should have been accurate and objective studies of competing factors. There should have been a full public comment process. The studies and process contained "clearly erroneous, biased, and misrepresented data". The Complaint cited three quotes from the HERS study on the limitations of its "experiment" and research in general. It repeated the comm op charge that the tax and impact data "errors" invalidated the economic study. (These citations are embarrassingly thin, again perhaps indicating a slap-dash approach or that legal action was more a place-marker or even frivolous, aimed only at the publicity generated.)

The public comment process was criticized for not properly including all comments submitted, "proselytizing" by NPS at the meetings, relying on comment from "an age group and class of the public significantly different" from the average river traveler. NPS structured the meetings to favor ban supporters. (This is all a fair enough partisan review of NPS interpretation of the public comments, given comm op success at dominating the meetings and scaring NPS officials. Had it suited them, they could easily have boasted that they held NPS supporters to a draw and forced NPS to spend over a year revising the plan to suit them. Was, in retrospect, the research/public comment process anti-motor? Given that the Reed 1972 decision was never revoked, and given general NPS policy under the Wilderness Act, of course it was, as it should have been. Law and policy in this matter are against motor use. The motorizers could "congratulate" themselves on keeping law and policy at bay for over a decade, but not that there was "a sham", a breach of duty, or bad faith. That they chose to perpetuate their position illuminates their dedication to overturning law and policy, not NPS failings.)

Third, the Plan aimed at "perpetuating a wilderness river-running experience", even though "creating a wilderness" is not necessary to prevent environmental damage, and does cause harm to public enjoyment and cost to the comm ops. By "banning use of motorized rafts through the Management Plan, the Director and the Secretary are creating a wilderness area without congressional authorization." (The complaint does not mention that motorizer lobbying was preventing congressional action. Of course, the main counter to this third argument is that the Secretary and Director were entirely within their authority in establishing policies to administer wild lands, designated or not. This is the more strongly so, since in part NPS policy is aimed at protecting congressional options on Wilderness. Comm op lobbying, meanwhile, aimed at congressional action that would foreclose administrative action aimed at avoiding foreclosing congressional action. The core of this argument, continuing today but never debated in Congress, is whether existing motor use in a GCNP Wilderness would be continued under section 4(d)1 of the Wilderness Act permitting a non-conforming use that had "already become established". Such tail-chasing is certainly encouraged by the political history of this issue, but it is essentially a vacuous enterprise; the fact remains that Congress, should it ever deal with a Grand Canyon Wilderness, could order the end of motor use, its continuation, or simply not decide by leaving it up to the Secretary of the Interior again, a decision that would quite possibly keep the issue alive for decades, generations even. And without, perhaps, any new thought being added to those put forth in the original debates of the early 1970s.)

The Complaint ended by asking for an order declaring the motor ban null and void.

The *Arizona Republic* reported on this suit and the dismissal of ours on March 28.[40] The local U.S. Attorney's (unimpressive) contribution on the comm op effort was to stress procedural weaknesses: failure to exhaust administrative remedies, lack of standing, etc.[41] The case ended up being sent on to Washington.

Venable reported to Ruckel that the judge who had the suit was "bright and fair", and not likely to be influenced by the "gang of Arizona Representatives who have signed onto the suit as they are a bunch of Republican conservatives".[42] It would be a good idea to try to educate Senator DeConcini, the judge's sponsor. He then offered to help at the same fee level because of the place the Club and Canyon "occupy in my heart". Ruckel reported a couple of weeks later that the chapter had passed a resolution ahead of time to have the Club intervene.[43] So far there have not been the expected motions from lawyers for the "concessionaire die-hards". We think defending the Park Service plan is the best circumstance for us.

The summer was a slow time for legal matters; only in July was the chapter affidavit to support intervention ready. It cited the chapter efforts in the 1970s, calling the CRMP "the fruit of eight years" to protect the experience, but we worried about NPS inconsistency on the motor issue due to its "political sensitivity" to motor comm ops, and were concerned the government might not "vigorously and unwaveringly defend" the motor ban. In July we were seeing good reason to worry about that vigor. Club intervention was argued before the judge (no longer the "bright and fair" one) in September.[44] In addition, he questioned the involvement of the 46 Arizona legislators and even MSLF as plaintiffs. On the 22nd, the Club was allowed to intervene, and could therefore take part in the depositions on October 6 of NPS river staffers Jensen and Martin. That event was delayed. Meanwhile, during the six months of legal snail-walking, the battling elsewhere was more vigorous.

Crucial Engagement; Pyrrhic Defeats

June 1980 was a pivotal moment. Over the previous several months, the Park Service had published its plan and, in its own view, worked cooperatively with the comm ops to overcome their problems. The motorizers, during the same period, had used the media, their lawyers, and state and federal legislators to bring pressure against the plan, trying to undermine its very foundation even while negotiating as if they accepted the CRMP's existence. In a largely defensive position, we had tried to defend and encourage the Park Service while seeking to keep key legislators like Udall and DeConcini from giving aid and comfort to the anti-CRMP forces. Responding to the pressures, the legislators, with DeConcini as the point man, pushed NPS and the comm ops to settle things "diplomatically".

NPS personnel changes again contributed to softening up the NPS. As mentioned, Marks was now GCNP Superintendent. In his 1973-5 time as an NPS official in D.C., he had become knowledgeable about river issues, and had co-authored memos not friendly to the Reed decision. Certainly he was more determined in his administrative style. More immediately significant was the Carter administration's removal of Whalen as NPS Director. According to reports in *The New York Times*, Secretary Andrus dismissed Whalen on April 24 because of "morale and management problems" and "poor health".[45] Whalen, 39, was "stunned" at the dismissal, since he "never felt better in my life". He did agree there might be morale problems in some parts of NPS, but not his staff. Without speculating, he said he knew the business was politics when he took the job, and he left still knowing it. Politically most to the point, Congressman Udall's office admitted that Mo, lobbied by a Glacier National Park concessionaire who was also a friend from Tucson, had written a letter to Andrus on January 29 accusing Whalen of being "arrogant" when talking to concessionaires, and demanding that he be replaced.

A pro-NPS source said it was political pressure from concessionaires; the Secretary denied that. However, Whalen had led reviews of concessionaire performance and tried to institute uniform contracts, bothered by excessive profits and by deteriorating facilities and services. He also hoped to exert more control over development in the Park System. His assault on entrenched concession interests was widespread, and given the money at stake in other areas, did not much involve our own minor combatants. However, the comments from the concessionaires Whalen did try to shape up showed a mentality similar to the river comm ops, e.g., intense environmentalist pressure to allow only young backpackers will put us out of business; we have less and less security; we have to protect our rights; NPS was making it difficult for us to exist, blah, blah, blah. However, the story was, as always, not clean-cut. A pro-wilderness spokesperson said Whalen was blunt and undiplomatic with everybody, and had managed to antagonize all his supporters. One example was chilling: he had decided to ban snowmobiles in Grand Teton National Park, then reversed the decision after talking with politicians. So perhaps the storm was only up top; if so, the question would be, once again, what flavor wilderness policy did the new Director like?

In April and May, the hit-em-high/hit-em-low anti-CRMP strategy seemed to be concentrating again on making it workable. Senator DeConcini took the lead for the comm ops. From what we could determine, DeConcini was very sympathetic to commercial pressures, but not willing to go to the legislative lengths of the Rhodes-Stump bill. So he pushed the Park Service hard to be more accommodating.[46]

Early in May, his effort received a boost as Senator Goldwater complained to Secretary Andrus.[47] He had, Goldwater said, supported the idea of "a balanced mix of oar and motor trips". He then charged the Park Service with being flagrantly inconsistent in implementing the plan, causing undue confusion and hardship. (He should talk. As usual with Goldwater, memory and facts played less of a role than rhetoric. The comm ops had been working on him and his staff for years, but especially since 1977, as indicated by the "some people need motors" stance in his standard reply letters. It was bound to be disappointing that the Grand Old Principled Man would not defend his own 1972 position in favor of a motor-free river.) So either forget all about control of motors and oars, or declare a moratorium until differences are resolved with the comm ops. A reasonable and balanced decision must be reached; otherwise forget trying to control river travel. And remember, we can always resort to legislation. (The presence of this letter in Burke's files indicates at minimum his keeping up his contacts.) It is hard to overestimate the impact of Goldwater's hard line. Both Jensen and Chapman today remember his change of position as crucial erosion of support for the CRMP. It is strongly arguable that had Goldwater maintained his 1972 position against motors, the story of June-November 1980 would have been quite different. Speaking as Mr. Conservative and as Mr. Grand Canyon, however, his ludicrous gripe that the Park Service's attempts to placate the comm ops made the agency "inconsistent" added vital, even necessary, momentum against the CRMP.

What the Park Service thought was happening was summarized in May's briefing documents, one for the Secretary, another to prepare for a meeting with DeConcini and Udall.[48] The 1981 launch schedule has been developed and is apparently acceptable. The comm op lawsuit is answered in the EIS. Several answers to frequently asked questions were provided, painting a strong pro-rowing picture. One nice touch was the rejoinder to the whining that spring and fall trips were too cold: the Canyon then was warmer than popular rivers in the northern Rockies in the summer. The briefings' political evaluation was that DeConcini was pro-motor, as was Stump. Goldwater, Udall and Babbitt, however, "favor the elimination of motors", though they would take "a compromise position on motors and oars". NPS did not seem to know that Rhodes had sponsored the Stump pro-motor bill. The history of recent efforts to work with the comm ops was summarized, noting their dissatisfactions and NPS attempts to make adjustments for them. Controversy was described as "still intensive". Monitoring was to be continued, but the dollar figures suggest a radical scaling back.

My own notes of conversations with legislative offices refer to their hearing from Staveley and Burke; no other comm op names come up. (This lobbying partnership appears so frequently that perhaps it needs its own designation—Burke-Staveley perhaps, or just B-S.) They are complaining about scheduling, that they are being "screwed", that they want hearings on the Park Service, that NPS is taking a hostile tone, and is arbitrary and capricious. The end result of the continuing Burke-Staveley lobbying (given the lack of fidelity to truth of one and the emotional exaggeration of the other, what tendentious garbage must have been shoveled) was a "short" meeting, apparently on May 8, in Washington between Chapman, Staveley and DeConcini, in which NPS agreed to deal with comm op concerns about allocations and scheduling by discussing changes to make the plan more agreeable with Staveley, "representing more than his own interests", and Burke.[49] That meeting was set for June 5 at the Park.

I did speak with DeConcini in early June, a conversation I described to him as a "splash of cold water in the face".[50] Otherwise my record shows no communications from conservation lobbyists; it would appear that Burke-Staveley had a clear field. Even so, one wonders why nobody raised the question of whether they really represented the comm ops and what those who supported the plan would say when they heard about this effort. On the other hand, if the legislative atmosphere was really as oppressive as indicated, then desperate efforts to placate comm ops might well have seemed urgent to Chapman (Whalen and Stitt were both gone). Certainly, my records show no friendly congressional offices. And no wonder. What Burke and Staveley said in public was strong enough; add to that what they could say in private about the Park Service being pig-headed and proceeding without justification from the research or public support. As receptive as the Utah-Arizona congressional members and staffs already were to the comm op message, we and NPS would have had to work very hard to counter such an effort. And we were not.

So, as we talk about the June 5 meeting and its aftermath, we must see it as a crucial test. Comm op pressure had created a feeling that though the CRMP had been launched, it was not moving downstream. Now if the meeting was to be seen as genuinely aimed at grabbing hold and setting the CRMP off on its course, then Burke and Staveley had to comport themselves as if that, and not just derailing the plan, had been their goal too, over the previous nine months of publicizing and lobbying. Their straddle shows up in a background paper they had prepared that claimed that the phase-outs of motors would be as high as 60% in the first year, resulting in a loss of one-third of the industry.[51] They charged the NPS was inconsistent in its trip length figures. The paper was a mish-mash of detail, general arguments and pointed questions, but was not an overall rejection. For the Park Service, under close scrutiny, the task was to prove (we thought they had already) that they could be reasonable. They would have to offer something more to get the comm ops to give the thing a try. That said, we must also speculate that the rot was already there; Burke and Staveley may simply not have been reliable enough negotiators; they had been spreading misinformation for too long and there were too many die-hard motorizers being very quiet. (This begs the question of whether Burke was ever serious, since he had so consistently declared he would never give up motors.) But let me not pre-judge. We have lots of information about this meeting and its aftermath, so let's just try to see it in the context of a genuine effort to move forward with an acceptable, working CRMP.

The meeting convened at the Park with local staffers for Senator DeConcini and Congressman Stump (no other of the congressional delegations), three representatives from the Governor's Office of Economic Planning and Development (why?), Carol and Fred Burke and Joy and Gay Staveley for the comm ops (the women represented their companies, the men comm op organizations), and NPS staff, Chapman, Marks, Shaw, Jensen and Martin.[52]

Marks and Chapman opened by calling the session one for "listening", and would take whatever time was necessary to cover important issues. Chapman referred to the Denver and subsequent meetings trying to deal with allocation and scheduling issues. He said the object of this meeting was to establish agreed-on "basic principles" that could then be considered by others so as to develop a course of action. Burke insisted he represented the WRGA and was not a member of PROA. Staveley hoped for specific direction so as to resolve 1981 scheduling. Chapman offered that the plan was "complete" and what was needed was implementation.

Staveley said the "central" issue was the number of commercial passengers and that the Denver meeting had decided on 12,540 (the CRMP set the number as 1000 less than this for the entire year). There was a discussion of the numbers launched in 1979; Burke had a set copied from the Lees Ferry records showing 12,701, while the official figures showed 11,792. "Later" it was found that the Lees Ferry records were wrong. Burke insisted that the companies keep their 1972-3 level of use, and he wanted to keep his 1979 level. Jensen then went over how the plan had arrived at its figures, including the Denver adjustment to give the small companies a 100-passenger increase. Burke argued back that he needed the level in 1979 or he would go out of business. (I would have thought such special pleading would undercut his role as a "representative".) He claimed he could not sell April and October rowing trips. He talked about his losses from reductions and rowing. There was back and forth between Jensen and Burke, the latter whining for his 1979 take.

Staveley tried to generalize Burke's self-interested lobbying by saying everybody should get 1979 use, with those who had received a 100-passenger increase keeping that too. (Why, oh why, had the CRMP not thrown another 2-3000 passengers at these people, and bought them off? The research was on their side as far as large-scale environmental impact goes. All this unnecessary bickering over a few hundred more people.) He said that could be done under the limit of 404 trips if each company worked to maximize its allocation. There followed a lot of discussion about all the factors involved. Chapman said that if NPS made a mistake in how it allocated the 1500 customers added to provide an economic base, it would "stand the brunt of this commitment" by letting the comm ops involved keep their increase. He did worry about adverse environmental impact, and thought there should be a study of the economic impact as the plan went on.

The final result was stated as the principle that each company would get the larger of their actual 1979 use or their CRMP allocation (keep this principle in mind). This would be for the six months from mid-April to mid-October. Several other factors were settled about how to calculate use so that each company would be allocated a specific number of trips (instead of a number of passengers). The maximum trip size was still 36. Then lunch.

After lunch, the comm ops argued against specific rowing months. They wanted the conversion to rowing to be handled by each company in the way best for it. Chapman agreed in essence, saying he saw no need for a hard and fast phase-out rule (unlike the mid-1970s unimplemented phase-out policy, the CRMP did not call for company phase-outs, only some no-motor months). He mentioned that other comm ops, not at the meeting, were concerned about the conversion, and he insisted that the conversion end-date of January 1985 be preserved. After discussion, "it was determined" that each company would prepare a conversion plan, and that there would be no months specifically set aside for rowing only, until 1985 when all would be rowing. At this point, 3 p.m., the outsiders left NPS and the comm ops to continue.

Discussion settled on a limit of 100 passengers/day and no more than three trips a day. Burke and Staveley wanted the weekly launch limit raised from 16 to 20 and the river unit noted that was the actual figure for 1981. However, there was no final agreement on weekly launches. Monitoring was discussed. There would be an economic study, and an annual review of the data by comm ops. Everybody now thought that 1981 could be scheduled within the agreements. Informing the other comm ops was discussed, and all agreed that a summary would be sent out by July 7 to comm ops, congressional offices, and "others affected by the changes". Burke thought he could get a concurrence from the "people he represented" in July, and Staveley felt "his people ...were already in accord". (And why not? There was no cut in use, and motors would now be phased out at comm op discretion.) As a final shot, Staveley's plea to have his motor raft rated for 20 people instead of 17 was granted.

The next day, Burke and Staveley put out a PROA press release, "River trip scheduling resolved".[53] Staveley said the meeting was candid and productive; use will not exceed 1979 and each comm op will submit a phase-out plan. Goldwater had said if these problems were not resolved, he would favor Stump legislation. The release then said the meeting had been set up by DeConcini, who had taken a trip at his own expense in 1979, and pushed NPS. (Now comes a nice bit.) Attached to the release is a hand-written note from Staveley that DeConcini's press representative had asked for the release so that the senator would get recognition for all his facilitating, and to beat NPS before the news was stale. "I think it's vital we play it down, not make it sound too important, or the ecofreaks will grab it. Jeff Ingram had already called DeConcini's office and asked what's going on! (He may be one that Chapman bounced the program off before agreeing to it?)"

That Sunday, June 8, I was writing a letter to DeConcini as a follow-up to my phone conversation with him on the 6th, when Howard Chapman did call me.[54] I had told the senator that he had awakened me from being lulled into thinking there would be a truce on the river, a few-year span when we would all work together to make the plan work. "I was foolish, I suppose, to think that a bitter, decade-long contest could really result in anything other than more contest." My disillusionment arose because DeConcini brought up the same old motor boater litany: safety, trip length, number of users, cost, no environmental harm, NPS hostility. I claimed that the real issue was the comm ops' fear of change; a fear that could only be allayed by getting the plan into action.

At that point, I switched the letter's tone, having "just finished a long conversation" with Chapman. According to my notes, Chapman said the meeting went farther than he had indicated to me earlier, but there were no political demands. He told me about the use discussion, and that 1400 had been added, saying Burke did not want more. He reviewed the other changes, and assured me the Plan would be assumed in the new permits. Worried about people feeling misled, NPS staff was calling all comm ops this week. If there were no good faith and no conversion plan, then there would be no assurance of a 1985 permit renewal. He reported that Carol Burke said it was the first time she felt the desire to implement the plan. Burke was willing to begin based on what was accomplished.

(Of course, the agreement meant that he could continue motoring with no change for four more years; and then, who knew?) Staveley ended, Chapman said, with a better feeling about the plan. The state person was highly complimentary. Marks is aggressive; the question is whether he is sensitive enough.

Back at the DeConcini letter, I wrote that Chapman's report indicated a bit of hope may be in order. He said there was tentative agreement, and a letter is being circulated to others. He told me of the individual phase-out plan idea; "a most interesting approach. I believe it has the potential of easing tensions, if good faith is shown." I hope you will also deal with this as a sign of hope, consulting with all including us, before "inflating this contest by bringing it into Congress". And, finally, I agree with your idea of an annual get-together of everybody to discuss river issues. Nevertheless, I sent along my article demolishing the claims about trip length, cost and safety, and also a few other points, "the problem is not how many people, but how they treat the Canyon. So I say have as many people go through as will not damage the river shore", which seems to be what NPS is doing. I also suggested that the Park Service was not inconsistent and hostile, just tired of being battered and badgered.

On June 9, Marks sent out a summary of basic principles, asking for responses by June 23.[55] (These dates were not mentioned in the "recap" of the meeting, which only specified a "summary" sent "no later than July 7, 1981[sic]"). Under "total use and allocation", the 1979 use was 11,665, and there was a potential of 1400 for the smaller companies, giving about 14,000 launch seats for the six-month "summer" season. Each comm op would get a number of trips based on its maximum trip size, putting on the pressure to fill each trip, since there would be no make-ups. The Plan maximum of 404 trips would apply in 1982; 1981 scheduling could accommodate the above decisions. The phase-out would be done by each company and be complete as of January 1985. The weekly launch limit will be 18. There would be an economic impact study to see how the small comm ops fared. If this summary is accepted by "all other concessionaires", the details will be developed and sent out by July 7. If "total concurrence on these principles" is not reached, a joint meeting of all parties (including us and congressionals) will be needed. The CRMP and the EIS "will be adjusted according to the decisions that are made in this process".

Meanwhile, I had talked with DeConcini's staff. The meeting attendee said all were very cooperative, particularly in listening. There was no major change in the plan. DeConcini was not interested in reversing it but wanted maximum flexibility without arbitrariness. Staveley had told this staffer that he would survive; he was good and committed and had appeared reasonable, if emotional. Another DeConcini aide, in Washington, stressed the pressure being put on by Stump, as well as from Goldwater's letter. Staveley was again reported to be pleased, wanting to avoid conflict. Chapman was also pleased. So DeConcini should get praise for his conciliation.

As the plan's author, Marv Jensen thought the plan was still O.K., though he was worried about the amount of use because of crowding and congestion. On the other hand, the Park was in a good position to press conversion, though that might then make it tougher to get use reductions. He reported Staveley said 72 people could be on one trip. I checked out rowing comm op Elliott who, predictably, was concerned about the lack of notice of the meeting and his market share. Did the meeting participants hold their breath, hoping against hope? In this interval, Marks replied positively to a June suggestion of mine for a meeting in mid-July.[56]

Staveley was also busy, writing to his fellows (and giving us a rare view of comm op intra-relations) on June 16, "Folks, if the whole thing is down the tube, we didn't lose it, we gave it away by going after borrowed overages, fudging on load factor, trip size, spreading launches within a narrower season than we had been doing, etc etc etc."[57] This lets NPS say there is disagreement. We might get 1979 levels back. I have a couple of cards yet to play and have started. But you have to endorse the June 5 principles "without any disagreement whatsoever", and figure out how to make them work for you and help me by letting Chapman, Marks, and the (congressional) delegation know. We are now smack-dab between June 5 or December 1979 (the management plan). Which one do you want to live with? In the copy of this letter in Burke's files, there is a hand-written plea, "Fred I have heard you say several times you could live with 400 [passengers/year]; once you were saying 375! If you can't say that to them now, then please don't say anything right now." No doubt this period of ten days after the "DeConcini-push" meeting was one of dense telephonic efforts, with NPS, comm ops, politicos, and environmentalists sorting out what to do. Shortly afterward, it was easy to see it as a time of delusion, not hope; still, given my initial reaction to Chapman's call, I would like to think I stood for a moment on the side of those who thought we all could negotiate our way past entrenched interests and hostilities.

We could not. The Park's River Office must have had the assignment of talking with the smaller, rowing comm ops.[58] Litton's was the first dissent; he was concerned about crowding, and in his own inimitable irrelevance, suggests there should be similar gross revenues for all comm ops. His disagreement and concern about crowding was followed by John Vail's. Kovalik wanted the motor allocations reduced as the phase out proceeded, a point George Wendt seconded. Wendt also opposed more visitors. Two who supported rowing, but used motors, also opposed changes that would lead to increased traffic; Moki Mac specifically called for the economic impact study before there were other changes. These reactions must have been discouraging, they were the very operators who would have gotten the additional passengers. For what it's worth, please remember that these calls were handled by the people who wrote the plan, which made it possible to criticize these responses as interpreted as support for the River Office position, encouraged by a possible split among the comm ops. Or you can be really cynical and conclude that these responses were from people who wanted the CRMP, with its increased competition for rowing, dead.

The Sierra Club's Southwest Representative told the River Office of his opposition to any increases or change in the phase-out. I have no record of talking with him, though there were conversations among some of us.

One of the vilest pieces of mail came from Western (one of those PROA members Staveley felt were "in accord"), attacking Jensen and Martin for not caring "one iota" for preservation of the Canyon or anything other than the ego trip of this ridiculous plan.[59] Cicadas make more noise than motors. Any fool can see that more time in the canyon means more impact. It is better to have 30 people at Elves

Chasm for 10 minutes than 15 for 4 hours. (What better summing up could there be of the motorizer view of their big groups as herds to move quickly down the river?) "Economically it is best for companies to move larger amounts of people through the Canyon in fewer days (via motorized rafts), but is by far better for the Canyon's environment." (Such touching concern.) Popular demand for shorter trips far outweighs longer ones.

A more balanced response, despite her PROA membership, came from Georgie White writing that the phase-out of motors will help "me stay in business", since trips will be more days and more money per passenger.[60] It will take time and advertising to convert people to think about rowing trips, but I can remember when it took a lot of doing to get ten people on a motor trip. "When I first pioneered COMMERCIAL River trips in the canyon I did not realize it would become the thing to do and lead to so many problems. I love the river personally and all I ask is that I am able to take enough people with me to make it financially possible."

Self-guided opinion was opposed to the changes: Motors were not needed or desirable, and no one wants more use except Burke, Staveley and "a few other greedy concessionaires".[61] We deeply resent the four-year waiting list. In a statement that still rings true, Joe Munroe asserted, "As long as the commercial passenger gets easier and more preferential treatment than the non-commercial user, you can be absolutely certain that the struggle will never end."

Probably the most important letter, for what it revealed about the basic motorized comm op thinking, came from MSLF on behalf of the suit it had filed. The June meeting results should not imply that the motor phase out was "accepted or acceptable".[62] (Yet Burke and Staveley were both parties to the suit; who was representing whom?)

ARTA (its name changed to Arizona Raft Adventures, ARA) furnished me with their detailed opposition statement, with a note attached, "got your letter today: Great! Here is our input—happy reading ... so goes the war".[63] The Elliotts called for a "joint meeting of those affected"; they were not notified about the June 5 meeting, nor did Burke or Staveley represent their interests. (What does it say, that Chapman did not push this objection at the May 8 DeConcini meeting? Surely he and his advisors were not ignorant of just whom Burke-Staveley could not speak for.)

ARA first charged that the proposed increase to 13,000 visitors, when converted to rowing trip lengths, strongly raised the question of damage to the Canyon. An allocation based on 1979's would decrease ARA market share since, when the motorized trips convert, their user-day total would increase but ARA's would not because they already run the longer trips.

(This appears to be an obfuscating exercise, made to appear anti-ARA by shifting from people to user-days in the middle of the argument. This problem arose for the motor-boaters because the CRMP used the existing user-day allocations to get percentages, which they applied, to their new, and lower, passenger total. So in the CRMP, ARA kept the same number of people, but the motor-boaters took a decrease. There would be further confusion for the smaller companies who might be eligible for the extra 100 visitors: Is that on top of the larger of their 1979 use or CRMP number? The June 5 principles do give the smaller companies more passengers, but not at the expense of ARA or anyone else. The loss in percent of market, based on user-days, is not a real loss in terms of customers. There is the definite question for ARA, not voiced here, of whether they ran a good enough operation to handle more competition. Since ARA also asserts that longer trips generate less revenue than shorter ones, it would appear that the ones who would be hurt would be those yet to convert; ARA's revenues would stay the same, they just might be a lower or higher percentage of an overall larger pie, depending on how much business the other companies were actually able to generate. A lazy ARA would prefer the status quo; they earn their money just by being the largest rowing comm op. An aggressive, innovative ARA would want the new system, since, as experienced rowers, they could look forward to acquiring more user-days from comm ops that gave up or floundered.)

Next, ARA voiced concern that the pressure put on each comm op to completely fill its trips would lead to a subsequent increase in average trip size. They suggested the pressure would be to use bigger or more boats, lessening the choice of smaller trips that passengers overwhelming prefer. ARA did support individualized phase-out; "a superb idea ... why didn't we think of it long ago?" and liberalized scheduling. They deplored the loss of late-season make-up trips.

In the end, when the Park tallied comm op responses, it found that ARA and the smaller companies, mostly rowing, opposed the June 5 proposals, mentioning the environment, congestion, too-large trips, and that comm ops running short trips would be unfairly rewarded. PROA members supported the principles (in spite of Western's spitefulness), stressing the need to keep their current use and a change in the phase-out.[64] Since three did not express a preference, the final score was ten for, and eight against.

The NPCA objected in vigorous if cursory terms, saying there would now be no motor-free periods, and the changes in use would be 15% above the maximum "recommended by the scientific team [sic]".[65] With two weeks more for consultation and reflection, my response for the local groups had become heavily negative.[66] The plan is out, with a commitment to review after there has been experience with it. The changes may seem subtle or technical but using a non-publicized, non-public, unrepresentative meeting to arrive at them is wrong. We urge operating the plan as published and then, this autumn, convene a meeting of all parties to chew over the various ideas, which could be made operable for the 1982 season. We have put up with a lot of delay but do not turn this ten-year pursuit of patient policy-making into a fool's errand. And, remember, the comm ops already have you in court for the plan being arbitrary; let's see what the judge says.

The individual rowing conversion plan idea is a good one, I wrote. Find some way to reward those comm ops who already support rowing instead of penalizing them. Instead of maximizing the load factor, reward those who provide quality, less crowded trips. Based on various calculations, the plan now allows anywhere from 10,500 to 16,000 users; perhaps these can only be reconciled after there is an operating schedule under the plan. In any case, you are using their best year to set allotments up; doesn't this discriminate against self-guided trips again? Economic concern for small operators is O.K., but what about taking it from the big boys? The motor phase-out should be kept until the individual plans are approved.

I also wrote Senator DeConcini, suggesting he had gotten the Park Service's attention and urging him to help set up regular meetings to consider changes.[67] I urged the same on Governor Babbitt and Senator Goldwater, noting that the latter was considering a "moratorium" on the plan. The better course would be to let it operate, monitor it closely, and make changes in a way that will allow smooth operation. Such stability is the only way to allow the comm ops to plan.

Internally, the Park Service received a chiding from the Solicitor.[68] He noted the long public process. The current motorizers' suit was cited, since "we are defending this lawsuit on the basis of the extensive public process" in producing the plan. Moreover, the Supreme Court earlier this year declined to review the Eiseman case challenging our authority to allow comm op use, and we feel it was the public process defense that was important. Moreover, NEPA dictates that you would need an assessment of the impact, and if you decided an EIS was not needed, then we might be sued again. Departmental policy insures the "fullest practicable provision of timely public information" on program change, surely applicable in this controversial area. So you need an open NEPA process and lots of public involvement. (And of course that is correct, and of course, we all stayed in the trenches we had dug for our interests, but what if this really had been a possible opening to a compromise with the motorizers? It is worthwhile remembering that war may be hell, but negotiation is truly difficult.)

Playing out the string, Chapman's office put together a what-we-have-done in mid-July as promised.[69] It was widely distributed, though one puzzling item is that only Arizona politicians are on the mailing list—where were the Utahans? The meetings in October, November, May, and June were summarized. The June 5 principles were set forth again. The divide among the concessionaires was described along with the opposition of the conservationists. We must move along to implementation, but will remain open to changes that do not alter the basic elements of conversion to oars, river protection, and ensuring a quality experience. The final dirt was shoveled over the coffin when Chapman wrote to Staveley in August that at least one-third of the comm ops had disagreed, and the Solicitor says the changes would violate NEPA.[70] Therefore, the Director has said the changes will not be implemented.

Battle-Crazed; Assaults Repeated

Two larger struggles were so determinative of how our immediate conflict was turning out, I must briefly mention them. The House of Representatives had passed an Alaska bill. The Senate took up a weaker bill in July and, amidst strident debate, strengthened it, though not to the House level, sending it on to conference, a guarantee that organizational attention would remain focussed on this grand struggle. The summer also brought the presidential nominations of Carter and Reagan, shaping a race with unusually wide policy gaps. The impact of the election on the CRMP could not be known, but my phone notes suggest that even if Reagan were to win, the Park would continue to try to implement its plan, though I "was told" that Marks was pro-comm-op.[71]

Curiously, new NPS Director Dickenson felt it necessary in July to express his regret to Burke at the "misunderstanding" over the purpose of the June 5 meeting.[72] It is not clear whether he means that the meeting was based on a misunderstanding, which it certainly did not seem to be, or whether the ensuing ruckus indicated misunderstandings and, if so, about what. In any case, he wished to meet on August 30 with Marks, Chapman and Staveley. (Another new Director; more lessons at the NPS school of masochism). He suggested Burke come. Burke said he was concerned about inequities in allocation (as usual), and his wife would come. There is no record of the meeting, at which Dickenson, Chapman and Marks again talked with Burke and Staveley. NPS said it would consult the Solicitor about the June 5 principles and NEPA, with further discussion at the November meeting between NPS and comm ops.[73]

Meanwhile, Staveley had dug the corpse up and waved it around, using it to excite cries of horror at NPS perfidy. In letters, he documented his zeal.[74] (Or was it just a state of crazed exasperation that his efforts had come to naught? After all, he had delivered PROA members, more or less, so he quite possibly believed he had lived up to his part of the bargain. I am trying to see it from a point-of-view as close as I can get. Nevertheless, if he were really serious about accepting the plan, he needed to deal with the opposing comm ops, our fears, and the impact on the self-guided users whom he had hurt by getting NPS to implement their allocation in two steps. Still, rather than assume he was just playing games with the Park Service while pushing the congressional effort, perhaps he did believe that the Plan was likely to stay in effect, and his goal was to make it more bearable. Another dark part of this activity is why Staveley, and Burke in a lesser way, seemed to be the only ones making noise. All the action for almost a year seemed to involve only Arizonans— comm op, political, pro-plan. Is this just a bias due to the records that are available? Were the long-time PROA members playing a quiet game to see what Staveley could get and, if that failed to suit their needs, counting on the law suit and their own congressional allies?)

To Congressman Stump, Staveley recounted the several contacts about changes, but he thought NPS was just being told what to say. Others were just "flat lying" by claiming that using 1979 passenger counts led to an increase, that plan carrying capacity was exceeded, that longer trips would be penalized, that "all" launches would have 36 passengers, that self-guided use was threatened. (Again, though exaggerating, he is articulating the worries of those of us who had not been involved.) Comments by "ecopeople" are untrue and unreal, and generated deliberately by NPS. (Then who was telling NPS what to say?) He went back to the public hearings on the plan, claiming that only the Denver meeting was overall in favor of the plan, and the Colorado self-guided groups were used by NPS; he blamed the "old Nash-Munroe-Fred Eiseman troika". (Oooh, that slur was sly.) We have tried to get a reasonable implementation, but NPS says it has to be their way. (Was that his experience on June 5?) Anyway, the CRMP cannot be fair to us, and NPS is not capable of carrying it out. (This all only makes sense if he is trying to fire Stump up to action.) So the plan must be discarded or supplanted by legislation that will protect us against administrative malice, bias, and zeal. (The reference is most likely aimed at the River Office, Jensen and Martin, given the Western attack, and comments by Burke about a "personal vendetta that Marv and Steve have".[75] Did the comm ops really fear those two for their expertise, unwillingness to be hoodwinked, and desire to have meaningful changes through the CRMP? Or were their dislikes personal?)

To Chapman, Staveley went after those in "ecobizness for spreading nearly total misrepresentations" of NPS/comm op negotiations. (Given the meagerness of our response, this blast is truly a measure of Staveley's hyper state-of-mind.) Who knows what Jarvis-Tipton-McComb (NPCA and Sierra Club lobbyists) said to the Director during their privileged meetings. (All right, at this point you should be laughing too. I mean even Staveley should blush a bit complaining about "privileged meetings".) Some of the comm ops did not understand because you sent out a memo of understanding that was deliberately distorting, and you did not verify it with us as you promised. (Was this an NPS error, a misunderstanding, or is Staveley protesting too much about his and Burke's failures to line up the comm ops?) I just do not believe that the Director or the Secretary understand that the changes are within the parameters of the plan; there really is no use increase, and the phase-out is not affected. To Marks, he wrote attacking the document on monitoring as "lazy". This was also the period when he labeled the Sierra Club as sounding "neo-Nazi".

Although we did not have direct evidence of Staveley's activities, what we heard in July was sinister enough, and we objected.[76] What seemed to be most upsetting was hearing of Goldwater's determination to introduce legislation.[77] His purpose would be to get hearings. He was blaming self-guided users for all the trouble, and thought NPS had welshed on the number of trips, so he no longer supported the agency. Both the Goldwater and Stump staffs had been very busy on behalf of the comm ops.

In trying to counter this thrust, we pushed the idea of river management oversight meetings in November. We also decided to see if we could stir up the self-guided applicants. I therefore asked Marks for the address list, at the same time that I complained about Burke and Staveley, with DeConcini's help, trying to "bulldoze" the plan into oblivion. I urged him to announce soon that there would be "one or more post-season meetings for the various groups of interested parties", and asked for the breakdown of who was for and against the June 5 principles.

To Udall, I charged that "one" concessionaire faction has provoked the current upset, peddling the "nonsense" that the Park Service was trying "a double cross". Please bring these activities into the light by announcing hearings on the CRMP in Arizona this fall involving all of the Arizona congressional delegation.

As I read these letters now, it seems clear Staveley was not the only one getting increasingly, ah, upset. Certainly, to DeConcini, I was direct that "secret, undercover pressure plays" on the Canyon do not work. I was sorry he and his staff had aligned themselves with one comm op faction. You "could have helped". Now, the Burke-Staveley faction, having obtained your support, will not meet with any other parties. The past history of Grand Canyon controversies suggests that we must all keep discussion going; there is room for negotiation.

For Goldwater, I went up a notch more, being "shocked" to learn he had "gone back on your principles of support for a real Grand Canyon river running experience." Your support in 1972 was crucial, and it is not a happy moment when you abandon that path as the Park Service tries to follow the direction you set. In joining one comm op faction, you leave the other comm ops, friends of the Canyon like yourself, and self-guided river-runners out of consideration. I can only hope there will be a public forum to expose the shoddy maneuvers of a few comm ops. "It is a tragedy that you, who know so well what a Canyon trip can be, are joining in a move to bilk the public of a chance at what you enjoyed."

The Sierra Club mulled this over. Curtiss, of the legal staff, writing to Calkin following up on a phone call, that what Chapman's July 14 summary suggests "does not bode well for administration of the Park".[78] The June 5 meeting with one side is a bad precedent that gave "bad proposals artificial momentum". This process of inviting suggestions to resolve disliked parts of the plan is bound to lead to "political ill-will and frustration which NPS is not equipped to resist" if the proposals are rejected. If this is to become a real process, then the arrangement for objecting is not viable. If changed now, there will be no baseline, and parties will not be able to rely on the plan. If the rules are all up for renegotiation, any comm op who tries to follow the plan may be in trouble. Please take this up with Dickenson. NPS is putting its neck on the chopping block, and either the comm ops or we may swing the axe, so Dickenson should tell Chapman and Marks—and Curtiss notes that they are not defendants in the suit—to implement the plan as written and forget about "improving" it. (In this hard-nosed reply, this truth stands out: in an arena filled with angry, suspicious contestants, changes of any sort will just exacerbate tensions. And, if you consider the entire process from publication of the draft EIS, in December 1977, simply as offering a plan banning motors and limiting use and then trying to mollify its unmollifiable (hysterical, paranoid, power-mad) opponents, it was all hopeless. So a bit of fantasy: Suppose, mixed in with the Burke-Staveley June 5 presentation, there had been a wilderness advocate who had managed to add to the principles that the comm ops would make a written commitment to supporting motor-free Wilderness legislation. Then suppose the contacts with other parties were handled, not as a GCNP poll, but as team diplomacy. Would it have broken down just as swiftly, just as bitterly?)

Marks replied, in sending me the list of self-guided applicants, that he was considering a meeting with all parties in late fall or early winter. In any case, our doors are always open for informal meetings.[79]

Goldwater replied with the standard line his staff had been using for three years, "I would like to see no motors on the Colorado River because I think it's a special place and a place which I don't think God made for everyone to see [sic]." However, the motor ban will deprive a great many people of being able to run the river. What "really bothers me" is the fact the NPS comes up with conflicting data and cannot abide by its own Plan. If they are asking "river runners" to stick to the CRMP, then NPS ought to do so. So, "I have asked various Congressional Delegations to think about putting some legislation together so we can come up with our own management plan". I am not convinced such legislation will pass but it will force NPS to sit down at hearings and stick to "one set of facts and figures". The comm ops can also present their side. (Talk about NPS being hoist on its own petard: Damned if you do negotiate and damned if you don't. That turkey put its neck on the block, and WHACK!)

I did not hear from anyone else.

In August-September, the bureaucratic gears also finished grinding on the revision of the Wilderness recommendation.[80] The river was of course back in its potential status, with the stretch from Separation down eliminated from the recommendation. Some lands on the North Rim were dropped. The total recommendation was 980,000 acres of land for Wilderness, 132,000 for potential status. The Director sent this on to his boss on September 11, in effect to oblivion.

In another mid-September non-event, the Park sent Staveley a comparison of the draft EIS, final EIS, approved CRMP, and the June 5 Principles, asking him to review and comment, and saying they would not finalize it until he replies. (It is not clear whom else this document went to, and why, over two months too late, they were trying to answer the complaints he had been making. And it must remain a puzzle why NPS bothered, with the evidence so crystal-clear of how misconceived was the entire effort from November 1979 on to placate the motorizers.) The comparisons dealt with total use, number and size of trips, launch numbers, and the phase-out. By including all three NPS efforts, the overall effort to appease the motorizers could be seen. Summer use went from 9150 passengers in the EISs to 10,550 in the CRMP, to about 13,000 at the June 5 meeting (winter numbers went up too). NPS noted the last jump of 23% would increase user-days by 25,000 and change the ratio to self-guided use even more in the commercial direction. The increase to a maximum of 36 passengers per trip would increase impacts and crowding, though it was called "consistent with plan". Total trips had been boosted from 366 in the EISs to 404 in the CRMP, and stayed there. Same for passengers launched, from 50 to 100. Launches per day went from 2 to "no more than 3", thus reducing the redistribution goal of the plan, as would the total weekly launches, set at 18, increasing crowding. The phase-out went from 3 years, to 5 years with no-motor months, to 5 years with no no-motor months and individual company plans.

Whether such changes in the final CRMP+EIS a year before would have bought off the comm ops, it was now much too late. The flawed process of post-CRMP negotiating had produced poisonous results, and the Park Service would be forced to drink the deadly brew.

Still Another Offensive; Reinforcements

Developments in September and October show up little in the record; only later would we know the results of this undoubtedly busy time. Of course, the presidential election was careening on full-tilt, with Republicans—Republicans of the right wing such as populated the ranks of the comm ops and their political supporters—increasingly excited about Reagan's prospects. The Rhodes-Stump legislative initiative seemed sidetracked. DeConcini had made his effort, a flare of optimism followed by greater confusion and anger, quite possibly on his and his staff's part, too. Recently, Goldwater had made explicit threats, but no obvious concrete action had followed. One Arizona congressman called the comm op effort "stalled", but it will be carried on.[81]

On October 24, the Park wrote the comm ops that the annual meeting was scheduled for November 12-13 in Flagstaff.[82] The Director will be there, along with

Chapman and Park staff, and the agenda will include discussions on the CRMP. Other topics were contract renewals, monitoring, evaluations, training, rates and financial reporting, and "any" other topic of interest to you. "[C]ome with your comments, speak for your own operation and be prepared to enter into what I think will be a benchmark meeting."

In preparation for that meeting, NPS received a set of questions from Representative Stump.[83]They are a curious hodge-podge of ignorance and slyness. In one, NPS inconsistency is shown, by its having authorized a motor trip in the no-motor month of April 1980. The convoluted answer mostly shows NPS bending over backward to accommodate the comm op involved. We authorized this, someone called in asking for that, we said O.K., but they didn't remember the other thing, so we waived the rule since it was late, etc. A big thing was made about the difference between the plan, not approved until late 1979, and a September 1979 authorization by the Director to continue the status quo for 1980 since the plan was coming so late in the year. Ignorant, Stump said the plan did not include administrative or research trips, which it did. Again, he got the maximum trip numbers wrong. Overall, the questions seem more like bee-bee-gun shots than attempts to make any real case.

The situation was not clarified, though it did not seem out-of-hand, either, in a letter from the Arizona congressional delegation on October 24, saying that implementation was presenting "some" problems.[84] We hope NPS will not have a closed mind so that at the November 12 meeting it can hear suggested modifications to insure economic viability of the comm ops and local communities, and a fair and equitable distribution of passengers. It would be wrong for NPS to refuse to take steps to make needed changes, even if a consensus does not exist. (Given that Goldwater et al. were at that moment planning, by a legislative back-door, to abort the CRMP without any public process, this letter reads as if it were a bit of bullying or a smoke screen.)

On October 21, I heard about what has come to be called the "Hatch rider". It was to be introduced by Senator Hatch (R-Utah) in the lame-duck congressional session to be held after the election. The rider would be an amendment to the Interior Appropriations bill, and it would preserve motorized user-days at the 1978 level. As a rider to a yearly appropriation to the Interior Department, such a legislative action, an order that no money be spent on the CRMP unless motor use was maintained, might seem like just another setback, a temporary one until the next year, a way of really getting NPS attention. Some even thought that as a substantive amendment to an appropriations bill, it would fail, just serving as another warning flag.

Not sanguine, I wrote Goldwater, and also the senator who headed the relevant committee, that this was an "anti-public end run" aimed at cutting off the need for the hearings that Goldwater said he was planning.[85] The futility of this was shortly shown when it turned out that Goldwater was a co-sponsor (with the other Utah senator, Garn) of the rider. It almost seemed like a taunt when the Goldwater reply noted that we have been promised hearings "next year", and hoped that would "ease your concerns".[86]

The Sierra Club had a National Park Subcommittee, and I suggested that the chairwoman prompt Chapman to put out a paper detailing all the meetings and other attempts NPS has made to meet the comm ops' objections.[87] NPS has to counter the argument that it has been unresponsive. I was sure the plan would still be a hot issue over the next year or so, especially if there were a negative change in the Interior Secretary, so we are going to have to push those who use the Canyon to argue for their style of trip, to match what the motorizers do with their passengers. I also wrote Marks asking for recent accident data since, in spite of our, and your, efforts, the safety issue was still being used.[88]

Just before the election, I tried again with DeConcini, reciting the negative actions by the comm ops leading up to the rider that would "negate all public opinion on the motors issue except that of one river running group".[89] The rider would make a mockery of all the non-congressional effort; "we would all know that every Park Service problem might as well be brought to Congress right away for solution—a very sad situation." (And one prediction that has since been proven again and again.)

CHAPTER 21

1980: November, The Pincers Close; The Flag Falls

Altogether Now

On November 4, Reagan was elected President, and Burke sent a mailgram to Senator Hatch supporting the Rider that mandated motorized use.[1]

A week later, in preparation for the annual NPS/comm op meeting in, unusually, Flagstaff, the comm ops met (Colorado Rivers and Trails and Wilderness World stayed away) and considered a statement of position.[2] As typed, eleven signed it on the 11th, eight more the next day. It began by telling the Park Service that it could accept all of the statement or none of it. The undersigned advocated (their word) "continued freedom to choose between oars and motors" for both comm ops and the public. The reasons were the lack of environmental damage from motors, congestion and insurmountable scheduling problems caused by the CRMP, and no justification for a motor ban in the "sociological carrying capacity study". They advocated no decrease in their "historic" allocations and no retraction of "true" economic base increases for the smaller companies. They advocated a season of April 16 to October 15, the only limit on launches to be the 100/day passenger limit, and each partial trip to be counted as "one third passenger". The statement noted that the CRMP had a summer maximum of 164,700 user-days, but this statement was advocating a 127 KUD maximum (they did not point out this was an artifact of keeping motors).

Courtesy of the Superintendent, I was sent a tape recording of the November 12-13 meeting. Although incomplete and with dim sound in parts, the tapes offer the tempting prospect of hearing some of the principals as they confronted each other, a contemporaneous record as the balance was tipped. There is the interpretive problem as to the degree each speaker is play-acting a discussion, when minds had been made up and actions elsewhere were belying this supposed effort to work together to solve problems. The temptation remains to hear significance in what is said and how the speakers sound, and for the latter reason, my paraphrase tries some to capture the styles.

Superintendent Marks started by acknowledging his mistake in writing that the

Director would be present. He recounted his meetings on very short notice with some of the comm ops recently in Salt Lake City and Sacramento. The attendees, mostly comm ops, then introduced themselves. Lawyer Kyl was present, along with staff from Stump's and DeConcini's offices. The chairman of the Parks advisory committee and a new staffer from the National Parks Conservation Association (NPCA) introduced themselves. In addition to Marks, Chapman and Lars Hansen, an Interior attorney, would be the principal NPS speakers, though Jensen and Martin were present in a muted way. Marks noted they had here all the people involved with River issues. (All?! So yes, why did I miss this one? Marks had discouraged me from attending; the tapes were in exchange for my absence. Although the event had moments of high drama, today, I am pleased to have the tapes.)

Chapman's opening remarks indicated no dent in the line they had been taking for over a year. He had met recently with Director Dickenson in Phoenix and talked with him the day before. NPS has a plan as approved last December, written under NEPA. It has been challenged in court. Changes have been a major reason for comm op consternation. Position is that we have to go back through NEPA to make changes. The motor ban is not negotiable. (He makes no reference to the Rider.) However, we have been discussing numbers and scheduling through June 5, but no success on getting agreement. Rowing remains the basic tenet. I repeat, that will stand. (This is impressive; delivered in Chapman's firm baritone, it is hard to think of it as shaken or defensive. It sounds like he is trying to make sure everybody understands NPS ground rules.) Numbers and scheduling are causing the difficulties. We did intend to look at this in 3-5 years, as the plan was in operation. We are open to changes in conversion scheduling, to give flexibility to operators, but 1985 date for no motors stands. To make changes, we will have to go through an assessment or even an EIS. We don't want a plan that will be economically disastrous. We, including the Director, recognize the importance of economic impact, so we need to hear from you. Changes, including in motor-free months, will require a public process. Plan *has* to be implemented until that process is gone through, which might take 6-12 months. And we have brought Lars here from the Solicitor's office to offer advice. The "value judgment" of oars is "not negotiable". In all other areas, we can work with your input. (Even to me, this comes across as a tough-it-out stand. Although I think his stand correct, especially since Chapman was no better at foretelling than the rest of us, it had to confirm the comm ops in their position.) Marks tries for a lighter touch, with no obvious effect. He says he will call on comm ops Staveley and then Litton.

Staveley goes over his version of the "negotiations", stating first his qualms about the tight agenda and the "confrontive" room arrangement. (Throughout, he is measured and calm, appearing even-handed.) At previous meetings, we did not push motors, but wanted historic use and economic base. When we met with GCNP on February 26 to discuss the 1981 schedule, it was apparent the problem was that it would not allow 1979 level of use (now translated into "historic" use, even though historically, the comm ops overall, though only some individually, had not used up the commercial allotment). So I got a May 8 meeting with DeConcini at which he said the GCNP had to make attitudinal adjustments; he wanted measured, a more even, fair, way of implementing the plan. On June 5, we pinned down the principles first stated at the Denver meeting; we had them on a flip chart. The Park Service was to write these up and submit them to those present at the meeting for comment. (The NPS summary did not refer to this step.) Instead a memo went out with very broad dissemination. And that account was not, in my estimation, what happened or what was understood as far as the principles or what was added or omitted. (Since Chapman was talking to me a couple of days after the meeting, and Burke-Staveley were putting out a press release just as fast, there had to have been an underlying uneasiness about what was happening, in spite of the seeming good feeling that June 5 generated.)

Staveley continues that the immediate problem then was that if anybody disagreed about anything, then there was no accord. I have looked at (the NPS) telephone call documents; what the outfitters said was misrepresented. Some called about something else and had no time to get informed; one person who said he didn't know, was recorded as opposed. On two occasions, the NPS person who signed the call record was not the one who received the call. (Feeding off the distaste for Jensen and Martin.) It was all "very far removed from what happened". Then there were environmental comments from Colorado and in Washington that were totally specious. When June 5 came apart, we asked Dickenson, the new Director, why, and he said that Chapman did not have the authority to negotiate. That puzzled us. Then I asked an NPS person a couple of weeks ago at the Parks concessionaires meeting, and he said Chapman did have the authority. So where does that all leave us? Are you all empowered to do anything? (At this point, the comm ops' statement of position was still a secret from the Park Service. So to NPS listeners, Staveley's account would have been standard stuff; he was sounding reasonable, just troubled about whether they could really accomplish anything.)

Chapman then introduced Lars Hansen from the Solicitor's office. In a definitive-sounding way, Hansen said that there could be no "substantial modification" without a public process. Nobody here can make changes without the process of going public. A back-and-forth ensued, as follows:

Burke starts asking how one party can change a contract but not the other, and what about the questions raised by Congressman Stump?

Marks interprets this as a specific question about the April trip by Fort Lee. He asks, in a kind of ironic, near sarcastic, tone, if that was "substantial". It wasn't an overt or covert attempt to change plan. Maybe our fault.

Burke (using his specialty of slightly off-center off-topic questions) claims they used user-days to count 1980 use, and that was a change in plan. Why didn't you go public? (Again, the point he so often tries to make is that the Park Service can be caught in inconsistencies, which of course just raises the question of whether he ever seriously negotiated, or was just trying to muddy the waters enough so he could run back to his congressional allies with more "proof" of NPS inconsistencies.)

Marks, with some sarcasm, replies that his predecessor had written you that it would be status quo for 1980.

Burke keeps niggling: You make changes, you say you can't make changes.

Hansen reminds them about their lawsuit, and that the discussion so far does not seem consistent with the suit.

Jensen offers that the changes pre-1980 were in answer to comm op requests. (Which is true of this entire negotiation period; but if the comm ops admitted this, they would have to admit that NPS was trying to help them, which would undermine their whole stance to their congressional allies, of being victims of callous, inconsistent bureaucrats.)

Burke does an aha! so you didn't operate by plan in 1980. At which point, Marks and Staveley wrangle over the room arrangement in a mingled tough/conciliatory way. So a break is called (remember that Litton had already been called on to speak next) to change the arrangement. Meanwhile the comm ops were to caucus with everybody else out of room.

When the tape resumes, Litton is speaking, in a voice rather more subdued than usual, and which seems to dim even more at the end. He starts off by noting his credentials in the Sierra Club and being on its Board, but "times have changed". Chapman said this morning that motor elimination cannot be changed. But it is apparent that the other items in discussion mean that the entire plan would have to be re-done and re-considered by the public. He is disturbed that NPS and others think we are only concerned about economics. At our meeting yesterday, it was apparent it is more than economics. A statement of position was discussed. Several of us could not sign it. But after statements today, I am ready to sign. (I take his statements as proof that the 19 were present at the November 11 discussion on the Statement of Position, even though several signed the next day. This is one of Martin's flights of drama, not an instant conversion, even if he did wait to sign. And when someone writes this history from the comm ops' side, maybe we will learn the who and when of the Statement's drafting and signing. I was told later that Elliott, the largest rowing comm op, was the one who had circulated the statement of principles, getting almost everybody to sign it. But then, I also heard that the owner of Western was the prime mover behind the June 5 meeting.)

Litton continues that the main question is how many go through and how long they stay. The amount of use imposed on the Canyon over five years means the experience as "wilderness" cannot be sustained. There is no way to convert, given the campsite situation. But we know that motors can skip two out of three campsites. "I don't believe in motors anywhere", but "I have to support this compromise." (For Martin, this was no compromise; he got "historic" use, plus another 100 passengers. Even better, since motors would be kept, a big potential for competition was removed, and he would still be able to pop off about them as they roared past. Sweet deal.) He concluded by offering his great respect for the generations of NPS staff that have been working on the plan. The public wants to use the Canyon, but not with impact, so the only thing is to maintain motors. (Applause.)

A comm op (I do not know who; one of the motorizer ringleaders) then asserted that NPS had started ten years ago with the idea that motors are evil. Our experience has been ignored in the public hearings. He then reads their statement of position, signed by 19 of the 21. (The order of signatures is given in the footnote for the document. It is possible that the final signatures were added in that break. However, Litton had long before accepted motor use. He had had numerous opportunities to stand up for the consequences of his oft-expressed opinions about motors and "baloney boats", but never had, saying nothing in support of motor phase-out in the previous 3-1/2 years. He had, however, been willing to attack self-guided use and defend comm op dominance. How telling, at this critical point when NPS was still standing up for Wilderness, for him to publicly support something he claimed he did not believe in "anywhere". Well, we all have feet of clay, I suppose; sometimes, it goes much farther up.)

Chapman replied. (In his voice and floundering effort to put phrases together, I read in that the Statement, signed by almost all the comm ops, came as a shock and a setback, an indication that he had not seen anything previously happening as a threat to the heart of the plan. Had he and the other NPS folks been led on by Burke and Staveley claiming they just wanted to deal with numbers and scheduling, even though both had again and again made clear their determination to keep motors?)

Caught off-balance, Chapman seems to be thinking out loud. You all recognize the concern and frustration that has brought you to this. Your experience, it seems, was cast aside in making the plan. He defends the process, but "you're obviously in disagreement." Rowing was a value judgment; the decision was not just due to environmental impact of motors. (Of course, it was not a value judgment if that means a personal preference; and I think Chapman did mean it was a necessary decision based on law and policy. It was Lovegren, ten years before, who had made a personal judgment in favor of motors. Years of effort were then necessary to correct that error and get a motor-free Wilderness decision in accord with the value judgments of the American people.) I don't quibble that we are not proceeding on scientific evidence. The Canyon is one among many places, and there are others for motors. As far as the impact Martin mentions, if it occurred, we would have to look at the numbers. We have thought that from what has been pushed from over a year ago, that economics was the issue. If there is other impact, we will have to consider that. Now you are saying that the motors/oars question has to be open. Others, like conservationists, are equally concerned. And I have to say to them, we have to proceed. The things like scheduling, we can go through the public process, but on motors, the Park Service has made a statement.

Two comm ops jumped on the "value judgment" phrasing, the first asking why rowing is the pinnacle of river-running? Maybe it should be one person, one boat. You made the judgment even before the plan was designed. Then Elliott: I have talked with other rowing comm ops, and today we have a sense of solidarity, in spite of our differences, derived from our 3-1/2 hour meeting yesterday. We are going to pull together. (You might want to go back to Chapter 20 and review ARA comments on the June 5 principles to get an idea of why my opinion of Elliott is so low.) Our experience says that the plan will result in a conveyor belt of boats with a tremendous increase in contacts. This means you will reduce numbers, and how does that serve the public? None of us are afraid to re-start the public process, and because of your pre-bias, a new process is needed. (Applause.)

The Stump staffer weighed in, reminding everyone of Stump's dedication to keeping motors. When, he said, I talked with Director Whalen at Wahweap a year ago, he said he would negotiate on all but motors. Now solicitor says nothing is negotiable. Therefore we want you to make everything negotiable. Your bias against motors goes back years, and it seems NPS just decides what it wants. So negotiation is down the drain.

Chapman replies that part of the public was not in favor of the June 5 changes, so we could not make those changes without being sued. When we discussed with them in Washington, they had no give on the motor-free months. So that meant we had to go through public process. I understand your point about us opening some issues and not others, and we are willing to look at the non-conversion issues in your statement of position.

Another back-and-forth takes place.

Stump's staffer insists that if we haven't had negotiation, then it should all be open.

Burke chimes in that this was a general attack on NPS doing the planning and evaluating, since we don't know how we get a fair decision if they do it.

Marks noodles around fantasizing about a third party, a mediator, an arbitrator, as a way of not going back through the public process.

The DeConcini staffer says you have the position of 19 comm ops, so what about discussion with others before you make a decision about a public process?

Marks then admits (a little weirdly, given the presence of the NPCA employee) that he had excluded other groups purposefully; we told them not to come.

DeConcini's man says the Senator wants something to happen, to which Chapman replies that they were gathering input today, and everybody here has made their position very clear.

Another comm op complains that "thousands" of letters sent to Congress were not included in the record, though we asked for that. People, unsophisticated though they are, thought writing Congress was writing for the record.

Still another complains about inaccurate numbers, due to conservation people. He boasts he would like to see some of them at a meeting, so we can tell them what's what. (And I can fantasize about being there, refuting their "what's what" with the truth.)

Marks answers saying he did not send documents about June 5 to conservationists. (He sounds more defensive than placatory. Did he genuinely think the comm ops were being excessive, or was it just a style? There is little in his behavior at this meeting to support the notion that he was the comm ops' ally in overturning the plan; he sounds much more the bureaucrat defending his agency than someone caring about the substance.) You have to give us timely information. There is a need for a meeting of all "factions". There is nothing to hide, and we are not trying to shut things off. (Then why did he tell me to stay home?) We came here to hear your concerns; there are important things to come, and we can work on them here.

Staveley complains about the "environmental ayatollahs" meeting with the Director, when we can't get those meetings. (In view of the record, this is just typical Staveley whining.) Whenever we have a meeting, the results are referred back to "them" and they get to pass on it.

Marks points out the past six months of talking with you, and now we have four hours with the 21 of you here.

Staveley ripostes that comm op conversations go to "them". (Of course, if "they" had known about all the meetings with comm ops in complete detail, the furor would have arisen much earlier. Why, oh why, did NPS get themselves in the pit of just dealing with squeaking wheeler-dealers Burke-Staveley? Why not use the need to consult everybody as an excuse to get broader meetings or none? This may have been due to Chapman, given the lack of leadership at the Park until Marks came in June, and may have been what Jensen remembers as the former's being soft.)

Marks is emphatic; your conversations do not go to "them"; they don't go anywhere but to Chapman. Others I don't know about, but I don't pass it on.

Staveley then whines about how the comm ops don't get a fair shake. (This paranoid inferiority has to run pretty deep, given the amount of reality it has to ignore.)

Chapman suggests that discussions with others are part of the process just like this meeting; it's all necessary, and none get any special weight. (Well, that's nonsense too, but it does re-emphasize what a mistake we made in not putting forth our own more radical plan. Never, never, NEVER, back an agency.) The Director's meetings with conservationists are balanced by comm op meetings; we don't play one off against another.

Litton, from way out-of-bounds, says we can't go to Washington every two weeks. (For some reason, Burke-Staveley do not correct him by pointing out that they have been going plenty often and, anyway, they are awash with congressional support.)

Another comm op commits the howler of saying we are just getting organized. We weren't 6-10 years ago. (Maybe these guys do not know their own history, or they may be congenitally disposed to gripe and whimper?)

Someone (speaking as from an environmental point of view; maybe the chair of the Advisory Board) speaks of two meetings since May 31. Staveley had invited me to the Wahweap meeting (a year ago). We don't meet with the Director twice a month; we had to lean hard to get him to our Hawaii meeting recently. He only sees us if we push and there are issues.

Burke and Marks have a cute little interchange about getting a dialogue, and things happening over people's dead bodies, and Marks objects, and Fred admits he has had eight years of discussions with Chapman.

Someone from Goldwater's office, admitting he is a novice, says that Goldwater is with DeConcini and Stump. He (the staffer) had gone down with Staveley in 1969, and still has not recovered.

Butcher from NPCA, another novice, then boasts that his group has been the most concerned over 50 years, though he is a newcomer as the Southwest Representative. I have an open mind today, wanting to learn all points of view, he avers. Litton is an old friend; he was on the NPCA board. So I sit up and listen when he speaks. NPCA has been supportive of plan. I will go back to Washington and talk to them, conveying your ideas and problems, including the serious problems Litton has raised. Our organization will have to look at these with an open mind. (Never send a boy .... Better he had paid attention to what his "most concerned" organization supposedly stood for. But never let your principles stand in the way of expedient behavior; THAT lesson from Litton he absorbed right away.)

A comm op offers a pre-lunch conciliatory thought that Dickenson does make himself available compared to previous Directors (both of whom were more ardent for a motor-free Wilderness). It would help to have regular meetings with him and NPCA so we could all discuss things. All we want is fairness in discussion before we are given a mandate.

Big Bertha had been fired; the comm ops shells had made their impact. Exhaustion had set in. Nothing like the drama of the morning was repeated. After lunch, there was a presentation of the study to increase the capacity for generating peaking power at Glen Canyon Dam. A good diversion, with the usual fussing over details.

Hansen, from the Solicitor's office, led an excited discussion about the recent attempt by Interior's Inspector General to get the Park Service to formalize its policy on concession transfers.

At one point, Chapman said yes, when asked if the contracts would be under the plan. So Burke wondered if that meant they could not complain about conversion. Chapman said you only have to comply with plan. A discussion on rate increases also excited them, with lots of their usual examples and counter-examples; anything to stir confusion.

The discussion now turned back to what provisions of the position statement could be discussed. Hansen brought up the question of how the self-guided users would be affected, and the need for public process if they were. Staveley referred to an August meeting, insisting if one is protected, then we should be too. Burke went on one of his rants about how they have done so much to protect the Canyon and should get credit. And as often is the case this led to arguing back and forth with little point. (So that one might have been fooled in thinking that this was now business as usual.)

In an exchange about how changing motor-free months affected the plan, Burke asked about what had happened to the 1973 phase-out, and Chapman said the change was made due to public comment. (Well, the truth was maimed enough that it would have been difficult for it to show up at this point.)

Burke tries to heat things up again by claiming NPS was bad and inconsistent on partial trip counting. Chapman wants to correct, and other comm ops weigh in with their marginal quibbles. Still another worries about aggravating the Phantom Ranch hiking situation.

The Interior attorney gets confused, and is told by Burke he is making value judgments. This is all an exercise in futility, he says, you will just say everything has to have a public review.

Hansen doubts the changes can be defended. Marks tries to protect him; he is not here to be cross-examined. (Yet he was clearly brought to provide cover for the administrators.) After more back and forth about what can be changed, Hansen suggests that there is an "undue fear" of public comment; it could be done in a matter of weeks. (Oh, sure.) But how can we do things piecemeal, since statement of position says all the parts have to be taken or none?

Marks and Staveley get into 1982 scheduling, with the latter wanting to do it as if their position was approved, and Marks unwilling.

Burke sounds off about having to go in April. At the February scheduling meeting, he says Jensen said there would have to be trips in April and October, and that caused the meeting to break up. Why do I have to run in April; where in the plan is that?

Another comm op pipes up about the scheduling meeting, noting three letters about it, and then we worked on it all day long, and it was a good meeting. Then I get home, and there is a big change and I was upset about dates in March and April.

Marks tries to defend the plan, and Burke claims it is the limit of 404 trips that is the trouble; it is just too few. You are cutting us again. We cannot run in October; I have encountered snow flurries. (October, like April, is one of the great months to be in the Canyon. That is, if you love being there.)

They then work over the problem of 2-3 trips trying to fill up to the 100/day launch limit. If two trips of 16 each, then a whole bunch of use is gone. Marks concludes that they have made their point; apparently we cannot do a schedule. So is there any sense in having another meeting about doing that within plan—"and I know you have other plans for that" (which may or may not be a reference to congressional efforts to derail plan). We want to move some use out to shoulder periods.

Staveley says he thought the previous February meeting went a long way. When someone points out that some did not come to that meeting, Cross defends his non-attendance by attacking use of a plan that had not been approved by those who know about river running. The whole idea of NPS doing a plan is wrong; we have to do it our way, and you will have to prove to me I'm wrong. (This from a guy who could not use all his allocation, had complaints from passengers, and was apparently in some disarray.)

Marks is tough. I hear your unanimity that the plan is not good, but where is the economic data to prove that? Otherwise, it is just what you say. How do we get information? If you don't advertise an April trip hard enough, that is not economics. To which a voice insists that no one is interested in those trips. So Marks replies: That's what you say. But I need real information. (He is pulling punches about not believing them.)

Another comm op stands up with a graph to show people requesting motor trips, saying, "We cannot find those who want to go rowing." He asserts motors are cheaper at $79/day, and rowing is $120/day. (This discussion reveals their dissatisfaction at not being consulted; their data was not included, and their experience was slighted.) Again there is the round and round, with different people chiming in with their peeves.

Hansen the attorney speaks up about the inconsistencies in the comm op approach. You have a meeting and that is O.K., but then you say if there is public input, you don't want any changes from that. You say you don't want any changes without all the changes. Why? We could amend to give you more scheduling flexibility, but you don't want that if it involves the public. I would amend to get maximum flexibility, but I don't understand your all or nothing approach. Why not let NPS make changes if they can.

This provokes several comments, and Burke tries to get the advantage back by asking if anyone objects to striking the all or nothing part of the Statement of

Position. We've made our point in favor of motors, so we can take the rest of points and see if they are workable.

Chapman tries to build on this by saying that if we had your information, we could do something and take it to the public, but it wouldn't be a long process. He then says that he had just talked with the Director who reiterated the position that conversion stays (no more awareness in Washington than out here of the Rider?), and we will try to correct wherever there is economic impact. Marks then adjourned until the next morning.

Had NPS recovered from its shock somewhat, thinking what was at stake were only changes to support the comm ops economically? On the 13th, Marks picks up by saying that public involvement could be as little as publication in the *Federal Register*.

The discussion then moved to the monitoring program. Staveley challenged Jensen on the latter's characterization of the responses as "favorable", since his was not.

On comes Burke, first vaguely, about the caliber of the researchers. Many, many complaints. There was no question in anybody's mind that many of their opinions were pre-determined.

Jensen blocks by saying they have been sensitized by his previous complaints, but another comm op complains, mentioning Shelby in particular.

Jensen defends by saying they used the bid process for the latest go-round (which ended with Shelby having the monitoring contract). He is cheaper than a new person, and we are comfortable about working with Bo, as far as control of bias. We're not doing another motor-oar combination experiment. Another adverse comment, and again Jensen says that contacts are being studied. If it were motor-oar, that would be different. Bo is competent and qualified.

Litton now goes after the guy who ran HERS (who had nothing to do with the Canyon study). And another comm op says that when he met Bo on a test trip in May the year before the study, he was definitely anti-motor and said "you may get hurt before this is over".

Burke gets avuncular, someone should chat with Bo; the thread ran all through his operation. He had been a student of the Colorado HERS guy. We researched this in Colorado; also there was a connection with Roy Johnson. Maybe Bo has matured in the meantime.

Jensen offers to consider someone else, if they know of anybody. Shelby's work now is drawing up a form to record contacts. This leads to an angels-on-a-pin discussion of what makes up a contact.

Staveley says "we KNOW" rowing has more contacts, so what is point of research? Must be obvious to everybody. Jensen tries to justify it by saying that the non-motor months would let them prepare. (The motor-free periods were the lower-use months.)

Litton points out that some contacts can be useful. With Burke, he then goes after kayaks. Someday a kayak playing at the bottom of a rapid will be run over. (No doubt by a motor raft racing through to meet its quickie-trip helicopter deadline. Again, the comm ops' conservatism and lack of vision is brought out. In a rapidly changing recreational world, these guys were dinosaurs. Unfortunately, they were able to fend off the asteroid, and instead of being succeeded by the mammals, they still lumber around, their backward-looking retrograde operations sucking up the living space. As they talk about doing things their way, they make clear it is not a river-oriented, people-oriented way.)

After more blather about contacts, in which Litton and Burke actually natter at each other over motors vs. oars, Marks gets on with it.

Elliott's opinion that the River Unit develops, administers, and evaluates the plan oozes out.

Marks defends NPS for planning, evaluation, research, admitting he has not yet looked at Shelby's monitoring work.

Burke suggests that the River Unit have comm op representatives working with it. When Staveley opines that environmentalists should have responded on monitoring if they were really interested, Martin of the River Unit says they did not get the document.

More chatter as they talk about evaluations of comm op trips by rangers (the meeting is running down; the talk is all in ruts). Litton and Burke want self-guided trips evaluated. Martin of River Unit then says that for self-guided, it is different than for comm ops, since rangers are looking for violations of rules. Wrote three citations based on comm op crew tattling. Cross was one of the fingerers, and he describes how it took a long time to get his employees to squeal, but now they see it is to their benefit. The complaints about self-guided trips then go on and on: quasi-commercial, renting equipment, repeaters.

Chapman leaves, appreciating openness and candor. There was a frustration level yesterday, where I had to deliver an unwelcome message. You have given us considerable material for re-working plan. Your message is loud and clear. I took the heat and lessons have been learned. (Applause. Dead man walking.)

After some more operational details, Marks floats the idea of new concessions to run winter trips. This allows Litton the chance to pooh-pooh such trips: short days, cold river. Not fair to encourage winter use. (Doin' the dinosaur roar.) You get people who are not too well qualified.

One comm op thinks it might be worth a shot. Others think there is no need. All agree that no more concessions should be allowed, Staveley concluding: They might get a leg up on us, and demand an economic base. This dog-in-the-manger patted, the big-bang meeting slides off into whimpering.

Wielding the Hatch-et, Goldwater Axes the Colorado—and Himself

That day of playing in-your-face by the motorized comm ops saw another terrific smack to National Park System supporters. Representative Udall, leader of the House forces that had passed a strong Alaska lands bill, faced up to the election of a President pledged against any Alaska bill. Disheartened by that, Udall went onto the House floor and accepted the weaker Senate version, saying that neither he nor his allies could consider this a great victory. However, he knew that the bill's opponents could use stalling tactics in a conference committee and on the Senate floor to kill any bill in this lame-duck Congress. Then, with the newly Republican Senate and an anti-Alaska President, that would be enough to doom any Alaska legislation. The House followed Udall's lead; the bill was passed, and President-defeated Carter signed it on December 2, 1980. To the end, the great struggle to preserve and protect Alaska against mindless exploitation over-shadowed, as it drained resources and energy from, the effort to secure a Grand Canyon Wilderness.

As originally drafted, the Hatch-Goldwater-Garn rider, Amendment 67 to H.R. 7724, making appropriations for the Interior Department through September 1981, made the same sloppy mistake as the Stump-Rhodes bill, namely, it said any river plan had to make available motorized user-days "not fewer" than during 1978.[3] Someone caught the mess, and in its final form the Rider reads:

> (a) None of the funds appropriated in this Act shall be used for the implementation of any management plan for the Colorado River within the Grand Canyon National Park which reduces the number of user days or passenger-launches for commercial motorized watercraft excursions, for the preferred use period, from all current launch points below that which was available for the same period of use in the calendar year 1978.
>
> (b) For the purposes of this section "preferred use period" denotes the period May 1 through September 30, inclusive.

It is no comfort, but noteworthy, that another rider was being considered that exempted local airport operations from the noise abatement plan for Grand Teton National Park. Much of the history of our National Park System is tangled up by local efforts to promote short-term resource exploitation at the expense of the continuing, long-term and widespread benefits of the Park System. These two attacks by westerners, however, arise out of the Park System's success, unfortunately perverted by commercial, mass-tourism exploitation—which, unguided by ideas of long-term protection, is just another activity aimed at maximizing immediate revenue simultaneously with future salability. This was a goal dinned into me by comm op Burke—an older man protecting his retirement—just as the "pro-rowing" comm op Elliott taught me that rowers were pro-motor in order to keep their competition limited. I really did pay attention.

On November 14, after the comm ops had done blitzing NPS, Senator Hatch called up the Rider for floor consideration. Providing "for the prudent and equitable management" of the Colorado River in GCNP, it was unprinted—a mark of how this climactic assault was carried out without public consideration. There was no timely introduction, no reports from the administration, no chance for public hearings, and little enough public notice and input of any kind; a hole-in-the-corner action. How come, to protect what the motorizers claimed was the public's choice, it was necessary to use the most anti-public, un-public legislative means? If 80% of the public really wanted, supported, and chose motors, then why did motor supporters so fear a full public congressional debate that they had fought to keep the substantive issue out of Congress for almost four years, and now were only acting in the haste and dimness of a last-minute narrow-interest amendment to a bill dealing with money—a procedure that only the Senate allows.

Let us be kind. The position presented to and by the motorizers' friends was that most people were well satisfied with trips of "relatively modest cost" that fit within a week. "This is what people want! It's just common sense." I can hear them expostulate exasperatedly. To the hawkers of this line all our arguments and corrections must have sounded like quibbles. Armored in their conviction that they represented the People, would it be unnatural if they believed that we, not they, were the elitists? Of course, then they spoil their reasonableness with their fictions about rowing-motor differences.

Senator Hatch started out noting that 80% go by motors. The Plan would make it almost impossible to go in less than 10 or 12 days at a cost of 60-70% more, and "I might add, under more dangerous circumstances". NPS was "imposing" its personal idea on an "unwilling and often unknowing public". All but the "hardy, young, wealthy elite" will be deprived of sharing the grandeur. (Well, I am having to read this swill; why not you?) Yet now, 80% of "trips ... are motorized" with no "measurable" motorized environmental impact, with 91% of visitors saying it's wilderness and 85% calling the trip excellent. Banning motors is a subjective value judgment with no justification in law. The "public" has the right to a choice if there is no "overwhelming negative consequence". He claimed Whalen had said the public would still have a choice: to go down the river or not. The amendment he, Goldwater and Garn were offering would send a message to the Park Service that "Congress does not recognize" Whalen's rationale (Whalen being long gone, and Congress being given no real chance to debate the message). The amendment does not rescind the whole plan; other aspects have merit. "We are simply asking the Senate to concur in curtailing one offensive aspect".

Hatch adds that the amendment also involves the "maximum level of use" the river can sustain, rather than reducing total access below the figure supported by the "management planning effort". He claims, erroneously, that the NPS "analysis" used a May-September (it was April-September) season, as in his amendment. Then, without specifying, he slyly says that in the final plan, NPS had spread the use over an "unrealistically extended" summer season, saying few want to go in April or October, chilly months with unpredictable weather and hazardously low flow. (Of course, those months, the latter of which was not in the NPS summer season, happen to be close to perfect times to go; they have weather quite similar to the popular rivers in the states bordering Hatch's Utah to the north.) He was also willing to claim that demand was exceeding supply now (ignoring that comm ops had rarely used all the commercial allocation in the 1970s). He then offered the notion of a rowing regime of 16 small boats launched a day, "1.2 boats per mile", creating "serious congestion and impossible camping conditions." (Funny, he did not mention that the boats were grouped in 2-3 trips.) "Boats will bunch up in the lower end of the canyon, creating a veritable traffic jam" (Oh, the horror of all those rowboats jammed together, fighting for breath and space, no doubt colliding and sinking; river Titanics. Few row; thousands drown.) Rowboats do not have the "motorized capability" of making adjustments upstream. (Funny he did not mention that capability was the ability of roaring noisily on by.) With motors, there can be 5-7 motorized rafts each day carrying the same numbers.

Concluding, Hatch wanted to preserve "the right of the user-public to determine just what a high-quality, economical experience is by exercising their judgment through free choices rather than its being the prerogative of federal bureaucrats to define those choices and impose these choices upon them against their expressed wishes." (Well, not expressed before Congress; the motorizers and their allies had made sure that would not happen.) He then turned to Goldwater for a supporting speech.

Goldwater now rose to speak. (As he takes the floor, contemplate for a moment a Goldwater speech composed of his 1972 position, when he helped start this whole mess by calling for a motor ban.) He spoke as an "environmentalist". The Grand Canyon was his "mistress". No one alive knows the Canyon as I do, who has been through every trail as often as I have, or "up and down that river so many times". "I want to keep everything beautiful." He cites his version of early river running, noting "a very strange thing", that he was the 70th visitor, a trip for which they had made their own boats. Then came the neoprene rafts. And now we have 16,000 people per year, taking 10 days (oops!) to go "250-odd" miles or 3 days to Phantom Ranch.

During all the years NPS was trying to find a "formula" to allow "all types" of boats that would be safe, "I have leaned toward helping the Grand Canyon." I have stood beside Stitt, attempting to fight his battles (that is, he fulminated to get the 1972 policy change, then funked the subsequent fight to prevent the policy from being put on hold). We were constantly promised by the Park Service that it was studying the problem and would come up with a solution.

"Well, Mr. President, when the final solution came down just a few months ago that motors were going to be disallowed within a few years, this was without any adequate consultation with anybody interested in the river ... I got mad about that. I got mad because a Government agency had been telling me lies." (This makes clear why Chapman and Jensen blame Goldwater, not Hatch. Though perhaps I am giving Goldwater too much credit in thinking that had he stayed with his 1972 position, the Rhodes-Stump-Hatch-Garn legislative effort would have failed. He did not fight, after all, even back in 1973.)

Goldwater wanted to see an amicable agreement so people could go who couldn't afford the oar trip, "as much as $2000", "but could afford the $400, $500 or $800 to be paid for going through on rubber boats". If we restrict travel to rowing, we restrict the numbers. Rowing, "I have to say, is a delightful way to go through, because it is quiet, you do not have the smell of gasoline, you do not have the roar of outboard motors ... I have gone through (the middle fork of the Salmon) on maybe six different trips, without any motors. It was wonderful. It was wonderful before the Government got their hands on it and started this environmental business. If there is a faster way to destroy a beautiful piece of scenery than to make a wildlife preservation out of it or to get an environmentalist group into it, I do not know what it could be ... On this environmental business, Mr. President, I have made it a practice for about the last 12 years, more or less, every year, at a time when I could, to fly a helicopter to the bottom of the canyon, and take a picture where I had taken one back in 1940 ... and, microscopically, try to see what the difference might be ... (Outside of the effects of the dam), there has been no change in the bottom of that river." "I shall continue to examine the bottom of the canyon each year by helicopter." (Well, he was a pilot.)

"Frankly, I would have preferred not to see that Glen Canyon Dam. I voted for it."

Goldwater reminisces about his first trip, burning all the driftwood they could to keep the river clean. He remembers flows of 6000 second-feet (cubic feet per second), "almost impossible to take any boat through any kind of rapid". Now there is a average flow of 24,000 second-feet controlled by the need for electricity, "the ideal amount of water for anybody". There are now about "16" good campsites. Now "that old river is sawing" through rock "so hard that you cannot drill holes in it." (Though the Bureau of Reclamation did pretty well in exploring for those Grand Canyon dams that Goldwater fought for.) You cannot dig cesspools. And although we don't like it, waste is carried out. When I went through, we did not carry anything with us. As to garbage, it has to be carried through the entire trip, although we talked about daily clean-ups using helicopters, but it would be too expensive. "I can say without any hesitancy that there has been no environmental change in the bottom of the Grand Canyon as the result of thousands and thousands of Americans (maybe it is the huge crowd of Latvian river runners doing all that trampling etc.) having gone down that river." We can give the comm ops the "whole credit for this, because they have voluntarily taken on the job of keeping that canyon clean." (Charlie Brown's stomach is not the only one to hurt.)

This amendment is vital; I have been trying my best through years and years to force them into an agreement. "I finally ended my patience with the parks department. As much as I hate to see the Federal Government meddle with this kind of thing, I think it has to be done." There could be a disastrous economic effect on about 50 different groups who operate the boats. NPS has acted as if the temperature is the "delightful temperature of Phoenix ... all year round." (Is this irony; did he smile; did he think 110 degrees was delightful?) But I have seen ice on that river in the middle of the winter, and I have seen a sun temperature of 150 degrees. "So there is no particular time to go down it and find it extremely comfortable." Now I have no more to say at this time, and I know some will say this will dirty up the place, but "as one who probably knows more about that river and the bottom of the canyon than any living person, It just ain't so." (Any living person. Yes indeed.)

And that was it. Two Republican, the minority, senators fill the record with fantasy and distortions and refutable arguments, and get away with it. Here is how they did it, with the backdrop that the week before, the voters had chosen both a Republican President and a Republican-majority Senate for the next Congress, convening in January 1981.

The floor manager of the Interior Appropriations bill, Senator Huddleston, started off by remarking about being again confronted with legislation on this appropriations bill that is more appropriately considered by the authorizing committee. Not unusual here in the Senate, it does complicate conference negotiations with the House, and that is a major consideration of our attitude toward this particular amendment.

Senator Hatfield (Oregon), long-time member of the Appropriations Committee, a Republican though not of the Goldwater-Hatch ilk, rose to oppose the amendment because it could stop implementation of the river plan. Portions of the plan are essential for public health and safety. The motor issue is not connected to these matters. Commercial use is regulated by the Park Service, and I understand that at a meeting in the last few days, nearly all the concessioners objected to the phase-out. But the amendment as proposed, if subjected to a point of order, could result in no funds for any plan implementation. Both commercial and private use is increasing, and we cannot risk having funds denied for all due to controversy over part. I hope the sponsors will consider modification of the amendment so that the essential protections are assured. I suggest the issue be sent to the appropriate committee, and I will do what I can to bring this issue to successful resolution in the next Congress. So I oppose the amendment, though it has merit, and suggest that I, as ranking Republican, and Senator Bumpers (D-Arkansas), as chairman, of the subcommittee on Parks, assure the senators from Utah and Arizona that we will hold hearings on this whole question. The committee has not had the chance to go over these matters, and I feel very strongly that any of these management programs should have our input. So I assure the Senators that there will be a hearing very shortly after the new Senate organizes.

There it was; can you feel our balance trembling as we near the hole; Lean, lean! But Hatfield failed to hold onto the advantage that as a member of the conference on the bill, he could legitimately worry that the amendment could cause delay and trouble. He had to go and add, "if we accept the amendment", it will be a signal to the Park Service that it will be discussed with the House, and "whether it survives that or not", we will hold hearings, and this promise could get us out of this situation so we can move on to other issues.

Hatch replied that he was very grateful for this possible solution because to those of us who love the Colorado, to the "motorized companies who developed the system and opened up the river", and to those who are descendents from pioneer families (as Hatch was—and related to the comm op Hatches—though he was a Pennsylvanian for his first 20-some years) who explored and opened up the river, this is an important issue. To have the Senator's commitment for hearings, whether or not this amendment is held in conference, is a tremendous concession on the Senator's part. (Lean, dammit, lean!)

Hatfield and Hatch then converse to firm up that the latter's concern is the motors and no other management programs are affected. But Hatch adds in his concern about the volume of use. Goldwater agrees that the question of whether the amendment is germane could be raised, but then argues that things have changed in the last two months. GCNP assured us that the use level would be resolved; we are not talking so much about motors. But the park people "doing a complete switch and being dishonest with us", we are forced to have some kind of legislative expression because they are now meeting in Flagstaff to reach some alleviation of the problem. Goldwater gets personal: I have a trip planned for my 10 grandchildren maybe 5 years from now. But the particular comm op cannot tell me now that I can take my 10 grandchildren because he does not know if he will have an allocation then. Hatfield suggests he might have 20 by that time, but Goldwater demurs, saying he has a bunch of "inactive children. I think the fact that they are Republican makes them nonproductive". (He said it, not me; page S14470.) He is grateful to

Hatfield; this is not something we like to do this way. We would prefer NPS reach an agreement with the comm ops in an honest way and say, "Look, boys, we have talked to you, we have talked to both sides, we have talked to the public, we know what is happening on the river, we know how many people it will handle, and this is our answer." (Exactly what NPS had been doing for a year.) But the only answer from NPS is no motorboats after 1985. (Now exactly why would Goldwater want to take his family down on a motorboat, with its noise and smell?) As much as I love to row, I don't want to see the American people denied the opportunity to see the Grand Canyon any more than the Senator from Oregon (Hatfield) wants to see the Rogue River denied to anyone, including my grandchildren who have been down it. So if the Senator's proposition to hold hearings is worded strongly so the people meeting in Arizona get the message that they do it now or next year, that is the best thing to do.

Hatfield replies that, "in accepting this amendment today" (Damn! Over we go!) we do give them the strongest signal. It may not survive in conference because of germaneness, but the message is strong for a hearing. Hatch thanks him.

Senator Bumpers now intervenes, saying the Hatch amendment was not as crystal clear on the point as I would like, about it being aimed only at the motor prohibition and not the plan. Bumpers originally opposed the amendment and was going to ask for a vote, but we will have hearings as soon after the first of the year as we can. We will bring in NPS and let them justify this. (Not to delay the suspense, this was never done, for reasons that will become obvious. And that is true, even though the colloquy here has all the senators accepting the amendment as a mandate for hearings, not for any change in any part of the plan. It is, however, quite possible that this exchange was scripted ahead of time, a not unusual procedure in smoothing bumps for legislation. The question is whether there was any genuineness in the idea that the amendment could have been voted down or withdrawn, and therefore Hatch was genuinely indicating that holding hearings would have been good enough. And after all, they knew that the Senate as well as the Presidency would be in Republican hands.)

Bumpers then recalls two other places where the motorizers pushed, the Buffalo River in Arkansas and Minnesota's Boundary Waters Canoe Area, and we worked out a compromise, where they accommodate each other. As chairman of the Parks committee, I was concerned about this "carte blanche prohibition" of the plan, "with no hearings before my committee, no advance warning of this." This is legislation on an appropriations bill, and I always have some strong reservations about that—"unless it is my amendment. [Laughter.]" So I want the record to be clear that we have a meeting of the minds as to where we are headed.

Hatch replies that they are not approaching any part of the plan other than motors and volume, itself a part of the motors question. Then he adds in the concern about the time of year, too. Bumpers gratuitously offers that an absolute prohibition is not in order since "only the wealthiest and sturdiest of us can row a canoe, particularly down a river that is often very rapid". Many cannot do that, and so some motorized craft will have to be used to accommodate those people. (I do not want to sound too harsh here; it is possible that Bumpers and Hatfield argued as much as they could, and after being briefed by D.C. conservation lobbyists or even

NPS officials. Still, on paper and ignoring the context after the election, there seems a lamentable slimness by which the Rider slipped through.) A senator from Nevada tossed in that he wanted motors kept.

Hatch moved the adoption of his amendment. It was agreed to; the motion to lay reconsideration on the table was then also agreed to. And that, my friends, is the great and only debate in Congress about motor use on the Colorado River in Grand Canyon National Park.

Whimpers

The Associated Press report certainly saw the action as a pro-motor vote.[4]

That debate was on Friday. I had a talk with Chapman after he had gone through the Flagstaff meeting, "not the most cordial".[5] We agreed that the Rider would make the comm ops more inflexible and arrogant; only if it were deleted would they think they had to work within the plan. Chapman thought the comm ops, "speaking almost with one voice", wanted the plan scrapped. Given the composition of the next Senate, the plan may be "doomed". I was still feeling feisty, and wrote attacking an ad taken out by a pro-motor travel agent in the local paper.[6] In opposition to its "terrible distortions", I offered the usual truths. In this period, we thought we might still affect things, though the comm ops were "clearly" trying to kill the plan. The new administration would certainly do more harm than not. Some effort—how belated!—was made toward contacting self-guided users. Nobody was very cheery about environmental matters anyway after the election; both Udall and DeConcini had been put on a liberals-to-get list for 1982 by a right-wing political action committee.[7] I heard from NPCA staff, probably unreliably, that all the NPS people were now saying that motors should stay to avoid congestion, though that could have been due to reporting by the NPCA employee who had been at Flagstaff.

Early in the next week, I contacted Udall, hoping that he would be willing to talk with Congressman Yates, in charge of Interior Appropriations, but he was vague and unresponsive. DeConcini's staff, now more or less pro-motor, defended what had happened. Since he was on the Appropriations Committee in the Senate—as Rhodes was in the House—we truly were left with no leverage to find someone to object to the amendment on germaneness or substantive grounds. And indeed, there was no change in the amendment.

On Thursday, November 20, the Conference Report was submitted by Mr. Yates for the House. Amendment 67 was reported in "technical disagreement" with the House managers (conferees) agreeing to recede and concur in the Senate's amendment "to prohibit use of funds to reduce certain boating activities on the Colorado River" in GCNP. "The managers are in agreement that the implementation of the management plan for the Colorado River should be examined carefully during deliberations on the FY 1982 appropriation bill." At the same time, they protected that airport from Grand Teton's noise abatement plan.

The next day, Representative Yates took the bill to the floor, and along with a bunch of other amendments, moved that the House recede and concur, which it did. The Senate took a bit more time, and on December 1, passed the Interior appropriation including what had been touted as the strong medicine of hearings on the CRMP, but turned out to be its poison pill.

The lawyers made a brief appearance.[8] We were assured that Mountain States Legal Foundation was not ready to dismiss the case just because of the Senate action, since it sounded like a one-year fix that did not resolve the underlying issues. In early December, Jensen gave evidence in the pro-motor suit, and it was "generally helpful"; his reasons for actions were rational and applied even-handedly, although he could produce no written record of his analysis of public comments. No conspiracy was uncovered. Maybe, the lawyer offered, we should do the work of documenting how NPS favored the comm ops during the CRMP process.

When I finally read over the Senate speeches, I became intemperate, writing Goldwater that whoever wrote his statement should be fired; it contained more misstatements than Hance Rapid did rocks. This one, I spluttered, looks like a real slam-bang bitter-ender. I tried to interest a local television station in Goldwater's carrying-on.[9] I complained to the Superintendent about Goldwater's helicopter boasts, though noting that they could have been on tribal lands. His reply said they had no record of any landings, and noted politicians' role in the management, even day-to-day, of the Executive Branch, and affirmed the impact of concessioners in policy-making. "Suffice to say most everybody misread their input and contacts. Be assured it is indeed noted and will be dealt with." Marks came to Tucson to visit with us in November, and we thought it "worthwhile".[10] It was at this meeting that he offered tapes of the Flagstaff confrontation.

The Bad Guys March In

Even before final Senate action, Burke was pushing his interpretation. To Stump he urged that the Rider's impact was that more launches per day were needed to accommodate the additional people.[11]

Insofar as there was any doubt as to how to read the events in Flagstaff and Washington, it was completely dispelled on December 22 (though mentioning had started a week before) when Reagan nominated James Watt, the comm ops' lawyer as head of Mountain States Legal Fund, to be Secretary of the Interior.[12] No other choice could have been so well suited to administer hemlock to the plan. In his regular style of enjoying sticking his thumb in opponents' eyes, he recounted his venturing on a river trip.[13] Addressing the Conference of Park Concessioners, he gloried in bringing "so much controversy and flak. I don't like to walk, and I don't like to paddle ... I went down in September on the Grand Canyon Colorado River .... The first day was spectacular .... The second day started to get a little tedious, but the third day I wanted bigger motors to move that raft out. There is no way you could get me on an oar-powered raft on that river—I'll guarantee you that. On the fourth day we were praying for helicopters, and they came." (Please think about this in the context of the survey finding, so trumpeted by the motorizers, that 95% of visitors love their trip. Here's another joke. As part of his confirmation by the Senate—the vote was 88-12—Watt formally recused himself from, that is, promised not to decide or involve himself in, any dispute in which MSLF had been a participant. Quite a joker, that Watt.)

It is quite possible that the Park Service considered all the recent events, and decided quite on its own that the war was lost, that it had to move quickly to abandon what before it had called non-negotiable and to conform to the new regime. A transitional view was offered on December 18 in a briefing paper for the Secretary-designate.[14] (Done really quickly, since Watt's name had only surfaced 2-3 days before.) It put its best face on a short history and summary. Questions had been raised by comm ops; but only the June 5 meeting is mentioned as dealing with them, and the split reaction was cited. "Considerable effort" was made by comm ops in the "last few months" to convince Arizona and Utah legislators that the plan should be changed to allow motors. That effort was "successful", and "a key part" was played by the Flagstaff statement of position, apparently having considerable influence on the passage of the amendment to Interior Appropriations. The briefing then says that Hatfield agreed to hold hearings soon, while supporters said the "agency downtown had better take this amendment as a strong message". "It is clear that a compromise position will have to be taken on the motor-oar issue." We are now developing an alternative to continue motor use, including changes in use and scheduling. The modification will be reviewed by "a group of well informed and interested people" including comm ops, conservationists, and self-guided users. There will then be public review.

On that same date Chapman was in Washington discussing with Dickenson and staff how to saddle the CRMP for its new Rider. NPS also says it asked the amendment's sponsors for clarification.[15] Several documents were prepared in connection with another Director's meeting, on January 5, with Chapman and Marks in attendance to help move forward on the details of "project completion".

The clarification came as a Christmas present from the Arizona-Utah delegations.[16] The jointly signed letter "would assist your timely and prudent response". The Rider's intent was "not" that the plan "be merely discarded". Its restrictions dealt directly with commercial motorized trips and thus carrying capacities, allocation of recreational access, and scheduling. NPS was to use the "most expeditious", "legally defensible" methods to accommodate the 1978 pattern and level of use while protecting the economic base increases for small comm ops as well as the increased self-guided use. This level of use will be consistent with the plan's projections.

A Final Casualty

The Republican victory in November 1980 was determinative. It was very possible that even if congressional pressure had brought further alterations in the plan, a re-elected Democratic administration and congress would have supported the Park Service in the end. This would be particularly so if the court suit proved, as usual, a dead-end for the complainers. Reagan's election had its effect on the events of November 11-14 and thus after; a signal that the way forwards was no longer toward a motor ban, a shift in the psychological advantage. Without that, the battles would have continued; perhaps those Senate hearings would have been held, and comm op story-telling about motors finally confronted in a public forum. Even with that, we would still be lacking the basic ingredient in getting river management turned away from the status quo of frustration and contention, towards innovation and good will, i.e., passage by Congress of a Grand Canyon Wilderness bill explicitly banning motors as of a date certain.

There was one more casualty of the motorizers' victory, and though a bit out of sequence, coming in late January 1981, the event belongs here as part of the denouement of the 1970s. The next chapters quite properly belong to the implementation of the motor-boaters' uncontested reign through the 1980s and beyond. How the Park Service, operating with bent heads under the basilisk stare of Watt and the motorizers' congressional friends, "ran" the river is a very different story from the one that ends here. That twelve or so years of trying to bring about a Grand Canyon Wilderness had ended in failure would, in more definitive cultures, have naturally resulted in my falling on my sword. That we are more physically forgiving may be an improvement in human affairs, but often hard enough on the individual who has no social guidance to decide whether and when to continue or leave the scene. Defeat might have been quite enough to justify disappearance, and indignation fatigue was certainly also urging me out the door. Yet as I mulled over what had happened, and what might be the issues of coming years, what most strongly occurred to me was that, like the old dog who always barks the same note anytime a bell rings, I was in the way.

This issue, establishing a Grand Canyon Wilderness, was finished, its final punctuation a feeble fart to the great set of issues that were launched in the early 1960s by the nationwide effort that scorned and junked the miserable craziness of building dams in the Grand Canyon. That effort was a total success. Its follow-on, expanding the Park to include all of the Grand Canyon, was a mixture of minor advances and what seemed like major losses; it is only in very recent times that we can reasonably shift our view closer to an all-positive one of this effort and, even now, the incremental advances are crab-wise, back-end foremost, leaving much to the future's imagination.

Perhaps there are causes for celebration about river matters, too. Perhaps we might claim success in our environmental efforts in the 1960s and '70s, insisting on the Canyon being protected against the impacts of river recreation. Perhaps again, the fight of Eiseman and like-minded worriers did prevent an unbridled acceleration in river running use. If so, we were surely part of a larger, growing sense of what was right and proper conduct in that place, and indeed all over America. I certainly do not believe that any set of circumstances could have led to 50,000, or 100,000, people flooding through a filthy, trashed, and degraded river corridor. Perhaps one more time, we can feel good about the Park Service maintaining its position throughout the 1970s, right up to the moment in November 1980, when a national election made it possible for their enemy to become their boss. The Park Service had to change its policy; I still think there should be a motor-free Grand Canyon Wilderness.

And I said so in a position paper for a Sierra Club meeting in Tucson on January 24, 1981.[17] I recounted the past ten years, and summarized the positions of the various parties. I offered three goals, and three recommendations in support of them. The history started with the 1971 pro-motor, anti-wilderness policy of the Park Service. In 1972 came the conservationist-Goldwater success, reversed in part in 1973 by Congressman Steiger. The research supported fixing the damage, on which we filed suit, and rowing. Throughout eight years of hearings and meetings, the issues had never varied. Moving toward our views as it did, the CRMP got our support. But, through those eight years, the comm ops waged "unremitting warfare" on anything that altered their domination of actual river operations. NPS tried to accommodate them, but they turned to the courts and Congress, and succeeded in tossing out the plan's major tenet.

We wanted a wilderness, increased opportunity for people to run their own trips, and no destructive use of the Canyon. The comm ops wanted power over river running operations. Self-guided users want to end the discrimination against them; indeed, most users were being cheated by practices favoring commercial trips. The Park Service has made tremendous strides toward a pro-Canyon pro-public stance; it has been jerked backward by the comm ops' victory.

The three goals I advocated were 1. a comprehensive, protective, motor-free Grand Canyon Wilderness; 2. adequate environmental protection of the river corridor and reliable information on it; 3. a greater share of use for self-guided trips. To achieve these, I recommended building support for a legislated Wilderness designation. I further urged that we abandon support of the Park Service and its planning process. "We have been caught in a snare and delusion of reasonableness, while the concessionaires have succeeded through intransigence and the spreading of falsehoods." We should ask for close scrutiny of the river environment and expansion of self-guided use including pre-trip orientation and in-trip encouragement. The management plan process should be replaced by a yearly review of practice and a yearly issuance of river-running permits in place of concession contracts. We should try to build a common front of conservationists and self-guided users.

Having made my presentation to the group, I announced that I was withdrawing from the battlefield. Marks, a guest at the meeting, was skeptical of my determination; not his only error. And as I think today of that time, I was hopeful that I would leave an open course for others better-attuned to new issues, with minds emptier of knee-jerk responses, and with fresh ideas as to how to celebrate and protect the Grand Canyon.

CHAPTER 22

1981: Victory And Its Casualties

Picking Up the Pieces; Throwing Away the Store

The haste with which the Park Service scrambled to drop the "new" management plan and replace it with an "old" plan was not entirely abject. Some NPS documents coping with the changed scene display a tone and arguments that try to make clear the negative implications of the November 11 Statement of Position, the Rider, and Watt's appointment. Another indication that NPS was not really happy was Chapman's presence at a meeting where the Rider was lamented.[1] On the other hand, he called CRMP implementation "curtailed"; reevaluation and public involvement would have to come quickly. Regardless of any tussle in December and January, the end result was fixed by the February decisions that led to the June 1981 set of alternatives. (Since many of these documents lack clear date and author material, I have grouped them to present the positions taken and my best guess as to their likely date of production.[2] Please do not assume that this order means that writers of a "later" document knew about all "earlier" ones.)

The Rider specifically mentions user days and launches, which shall be at least those "available" in 1978. Those numbers were ambiguous. The comm ops gathered their thoughts in a document warning that any interpretation granting motor-boaters a number of groups or launches too low would be "a defiance of the intent and provisions" of the Rider. Curiously, however, their suggested "conformance" lumped the fourteen companies with any motor trips together, assigning each its 1978 allocation for the May-September period, a total of 75,800 user-days. The seven smaller rowing companies "will have" the "economic base" boost that the CRMP had assigned them, altogether 29,460 u-d. This brought the commercial total to 105,250 for five months, a few less than the CRMP had allocated for six months. The document insisted that the additional trips needed to meet this level for 1981 must be scheduled "at once". It told NPS just which CRMP rules to loosen or scrap, e.g., raising the daily launch maximum from 100 passengers to 150, one company could launch more than one trip a day.

The River Unit's first interpretation of the Statement of Position calculated

101,975 u-d. The CRMP had arrived at 105,500 by taking the 1978 allocation and converting it to passengers using each comm op's average trip length, and then converting back to user-days by multiplying by an average overall length of 10 days. So this early conclusion was that the comm ops had asked for 3525 u-d less than the CRMP. Problems were "inherent" using either number. The plan was being "chopped up" and only the parts benefiting the comm ops were being kept. Modifications in the plan to make the larger numbers workable were ignored, e.g., the comm ops were using May-September instead of a six-month season. There would be more visitor contact and congestion. Putting more people through in a shorter time might cause damage, like pollution at Elves Chasm. Other impacts might be found by the monitoring. The self-guided increases would compound the problems.

Preparing for a January 5 Washington meeting on the plan, the River Unit worked through two "models" for total commercial passenger use, 102,200 and 105,000 u-d. The first figure resulted from the Statement of Position, which NPS interpreted as increasing all fourteen smaller companies—rowing or not—by 100 passengers each season. The 105 KUD total would "more than accommodate" the Statement of Position with an increase of 2.7%. Where the 2.7% came from is not stated, but in these preparatory papers, it was distributed over all 21 comm ops. The Statement of Position had also "advocated" a maximum use of 127 KUD, a number GCNP stated and ignored thereafter. (Compare actual use in 1978-80, ranging from 83,700 to 87,000 u-d; the allocation was 89,000. The percentage of allocation used by most comm ops ranged from 91 to 114. A table of user-day comparisons for each comm op is on the next page.)

This River Unit paper noted that the limit on trips per day would have to be eliminated to handle the increase. The changes of either model would impact the Canyon "differently" from the CRMP or current use. The CRMP proposed 337 launches in May-September; currently there were 463, and the two models would need 530 and 544. The number of people launched, 11,000 currently, would jump to over 13,000, as against 8800 in the CRMP. The increases were then gone over again to make sure that the reader got the point. Then the self-guided use was added in to reinforce the case of "significant" increases, which lead to crowding, which is "directly related" to multiple trailing at attractions and soil and vegetation impacts on campsites. Increased crowding and congestion "are inevitable" with the increased commercial and self-guided use, shorter season and changed launch limits.

The mysterious 2.7% increase was soon altered, perhaps at the January 5 meeting; only the seven largest companies received it (this plus can be set against the early CRMP hope of taking user-days from these companies to strengthen the littler ones). Moreover, the 2.7% had gotten another little boost of 500 u-d, so that the big fellas were to share 3300. The smaller ones kept their economic base increase of the user-day equivalent of 100 passengers. What is satisfyingly curious is that the grand total went up to 105,500 u-d, exactly the number in the CRMP. However, the CRMP used a season of April 16 to October 15, now contracted to May to September, 30 days less. Another spreadsheet showed that the actual 1978 use in the shorter period was 86,300 u-d, so the per-day increase would be almost 140 users, 25% above current use and the CRMP levels.

So the comm ops' eight-year fight was won to regain the "promise" that the Reed October 1972 decision had taken away; their allocation of 105 KUD for 1973 was now restored. The goal of ending use increases was also achieved, though at the inflated 1972 allotment level, rather than 1972 use. And although the bigger companies had received increases, their allocations were still below their dreams of 1972; a re-distribution in allocation wealth had occurred. Oh, and Litton received his reward, a 40% increase.

COMMERCIAL OPERATORS: USER-DAYS

Comm Op	1971 use (rounded)	1972 allotment	1973-80 allotment ~1972 use	Avg. Use 1978-80	1/13/81 allot- ment**
Arizona Raft Adventures	8200	11000	9240	8486	9782
Arizona River Runners	1400	3000	2600	2814	3300
Canyoneers	2300	4000	3360	3333	4060
Colorado River and Trail	500	2000	1800	1904	2500
Cross	3800	8000	6720	4074	7113
Fort Lee	950	2600	2200	2144	2900
Georgie	0	2300	2000	2135	2600
Grand Canyon Dories	2300	3600	3025	2850	4225
GC Expeditions	8350	10000	8400	8029	8892
GC Youth Expeditions	700	1300	1125	1127	2325
Harris —> Diamond	500	2000	1680	5805	*6204
Hatch	11000	12000	10080	9452	10671
Moki Mac	300	2400	2050	2091	3300
OARS	1000	1600	1600	1607	2800
Outdoors Unlimited	70	1200	1200	1200	2300
Sanderson	10400	12000	10080	5847	*6247
Tour West	3550	4500	3780	3739	4480
Western	8000	12000	10080	10189	10671
White Water	2450	4500	3780	3855	4380
Wilderness World	—	3000	2520	2459	3720
Wonderland	500	2000	1680	1630	2980
TOTALS	66000	105000	89000	85665	105500

*Diamond was working with Sanderson when the former bought Harris's permit; they split the Sanderson allocation after 1978. In March 1981, Diamond received another 656 u-d (see below), for the total of 6860 shown in the June 1981 plan.
**The increases in this division of spoils were split at the 4000 level of the 1973-80 allocations. They were calculated using a trip length number for each comm op; the small motorizers receiving 6-700 u-d, rowers 11-1300.

Except for Diamond's increase to 6860, these were the allocations in the June 1981 plan. Going back, the plan's 10 KUD for "winter" use corresponded to the promised 1973 "supplement" of 10 KUD and the summer total corresponded to the allocations for 1972. These company allocations have stayed the same for over 20 years, even as the number of comm ops dropped to 15. The individual allocations have followed through all the buy-outs, splits, absorptions and name changes, just as if they were physical assets owned by the comm ops.

In addition to wrestling with the numbers, the Park Service had been trying to work out the mechanics of plan revision.[3] One recommendation was that since "clearly the plan will have to be substantially or[sic] if not completely rewritten", the task should be assigned to the Denver Service Center. A supplement should be prepared to the existing EIS, and there should probably be a draft and final version, given the public interest. The complexity could be substantially reduced if only the motor issue is discussed. However, the schedule offered has DSC spending all of 1981 preparing a draft of a draft, with final preparation in June 1982. This suggestion apparently was not acceptable.

The January 5 Washington meeting dealt with a list of specific changes with the aim of having public meetings on the alternatives and plan amendment in June 1981, with final approval by November 1. An associated document indicated that the Wilderness Experience sub-heading of the Plan would be eliminated, replaced by a paean to the Rafting Experience. Marv Jensen says that he re-did the Plan under Marks' supervision, though his heart was not in the task (believable if the papers about congestion described above were his). They made the tighter schedule.

All these decisions were announced in letters to the comm ops on January 13, 1981. Each comm op received numbers for use and trips, and a handwritten schedule.[4] The letter cited the Rider, and admitted that "therefore the National Park Service" would be revising the plan, so that the public will have the option of motor or rowing trips "in the future". A copy of the press release on plan revision was enclosed. At least for 1981, the use in the "preferred-use" season would be 105,500 u-d, and there would be "no fewer than 497 launches". The fourteen smaller companies received their 1978 allocation plus the economic base prescribed in the plan. The increase for the seven larger companies was announced; still without any reason. The launch schedule previously developed was enclosed. Please enter any additions or changes and send it in by January 23. We want to work out problems quickly, and could meet at the WRGA meeting on February 12 in Salt Lake.

The press release did kowtow.[5] The public was to have the option of motor or oars, according to congressional direction. Chapman noted that while there were "strong advocates" for rowing only, motor passengers had found their trip "highly satisfying". And NPS had "not been able to show" damage by motors. The use limits will be within the limits of the plan, which NPS was beginning immediately to amend, with a revision expected by early summer.

A decision sheet of January 27 codified the loosening regime for 1981. Outside the May-September season, trips were not to count against the allocation. The launch maximum was kept at 150, with no limits on the number of trips per day or per week. Trips in the now extended "winter" (actually fall and spring) season had filled the total 10 KUD allowed, so there would be no other trips. Motors would be allowed during any and all parts of the year. User days counted only to Diamond Creek, and a full day would be counted for an uneven exchange.

The initial reaction from the comm ops, to what should be re-labeled the CommopRMP, was not all happy. Staveley felt impelled to defend himself against accusations that he was responsible for the new numbers. He blamed the Park Service, saying it was the result of their changing from a base of 133 KUD in the rejected CRMP to the 105 KUD.[6] He also claimed that the economic base calculation used unreal trip lengths. "For almost 10 years there have been discriminatory thrusts against allocations for motorized trips, and shorter trips", he wailed. (Why was he unable to celebrate the great success?) Those thrusts have been supported by several comm ops or by those who failed to oppose them. But we will not fight rowing or longer trips, just so long as increases do not come from other comm ops. (It was good he did not look back at the 1972 allocations; maybe his 20% increase made him more sanguine about the hits the larger companies took.) Still looking for something to unite his bellyachers, he wrote later saying that in Diamond's taking over Harris, and splitting the Sanderson allocation, there was no economic base increase (since the resulting two companies were both over 6 KUD), so we can all get together on that and write to Marks.[7]

Marks came to visit us in Tucson in late January, as the CRMP rewriting was being pressed.[8] He told us that the new allocation total would be 105,500 u-d, and spoke of a meeting on December 19 with the Director where he had told the comm ops about that decision and allowing it to be used within May-September. There was to be a scheduling meeting held on the 29th to deal with both 1981 and 1982. Marks told us that one comm op, Elliott, wanted 8500 u-d more, perhaps as a reward for his role in putting together the November 11 Statement of Position. As recounted earlier, I took the opportunity of this meeting to formally bow out, although the separation turned out to be more of an operation than I figured on. I made some tentative efforts at trying to stir up self-guided and pro-Wilderness opposition to the comm ops' grab, but they petered out.

Sierra Club lawyers gave a wave at all this in February, when the SCLDF wrote the Director with a request for any and all papers concerning changes in the CRMP.[9] There were rumors about a big revision, but no verified information, and "we are disturbed by the prospect of politically-inspired changes". The request had to be repeated in mid-March, even though this was a Freedom of Information request.

Maybe the delay was due to NPS workload.[10] On March 3, Chapman led a regional office CRMP meeting at which the need for flexibility to avoid yearly revision was stressed. There seems to have been a decision that no further "NEPA documentation" was required. The suggestion was made to include yearly allocations in the annual operations plan, not the CRMP. The congressional delegation, as well as the Director, would review the plan before the public got it. The schedule was for the Superintendent to bring the draft for mid-March review by Region, with all issues worked out between Park and Region by mid-April, when Chapman would take the results to Washington.

The Denver Service Center again offered its expertise, an offer not taken according to the above meeting. A wordy, and apparently unapproved, task directive reviews the obvious, arguing for issuing an amendment to the CRMP, even though decisions had already been made. It did recommend a rowing spring-fall shoulder season with lower use to allow monitoring levels proposed in the CRMP; something to show environmental organizations. Public meetings would be skipped, though the schedule, now altered to provide a final document by mid-August, called for public review in June.

Trying to keep its decision-making on track, NPS responded to the latest PROA gripe by stating it intended to keep the 105,500 u-d level in 1982.[11] The question about the economic increase not being given to Diamond, formerly Harris, was tackled by arguing that at the time of the plan, Diamond was clearly a large company, the latter having "purchased" a 4180 u-d "portion of the Sanderson operation". But NPS concedes it was in error in that it had not yet approved the sale, and Harris-being-bought-by-Diamond should have received an economic base increase. After some hand-waving, this was stated to be an addition of 456 u-d. Since this would be over the 105,500, there would be a "size over-run". So we propose to reduce each of the larger comm ops a bit. Further on, the 105,500 number is explained as the average of use over the life of the now-junked CRMP.

There was also a discussion of Georgie White's "situation"; her 1972 allocation of 2300 u-d had ended up as 2000 in 1973-80. We do not see how we can re-adjust her old allocation unless we readjust everybody. (The documents include a copy of the allotment request form Georgie submitted in 1972, showing the actual for 1970 and 1971, the allotment for 1971, and her request for 1972. How easy Lovegren made it; no wonder the allocations ballooned even more than the use. Perhaps eight years of battle did cool their expectations.)

The briefing discussion continues that the small rowing companies were affected because the CRMP's conversion formula gave them an increase that the Rider allocations omitted, and NPS had no intention of using the 133,543 u-d figure from the CRMP. The larger comm ops seem not to have pushed for an increase, wanting only not to be reduced, so the increase they received could be shifted to the smaller comm ops "to ease problems" in the future. Meanwhile, the 105,500 provides everybody with some increase and allows time to monitor this and the self-guided increase. There is no record of whether this teeny tempest went further or not; but Diamond was shut up by getting 656 u-d as an economic increase to the company that he had bought out, while none of the biggies lost the little "keep them quiet" increase. Such a beautiful example of an over-powered agency puffing and huffing, and blowing its house down.

On March 10, the *Federal Register* made the revision official.[12] Phase One rescinded for 1981 the objective of eliminating motors and increased permitted use from 89 KUD to 115,500 u-d annually, with a reduced season of five months. Phase Two will revise the CRMP by November. Since this will be too late for 1982, Phase One decisions will be maintained for that year. No further environmental documentation is required since the changes were covered under the no-action alternative of the CRMP and its final EIS. This does not imply the no-action alternative is adopted and the plan junked. Eleven of fourteen objectives will still be met. There will be no reduction in launches of motorized craft. The Director had approved the notice on February 19.

In a Regional Office memo pointing to needed changes in the CRMP draft, the text on the "Hatch Amendment" was to be deleted, since "It's over with—let's not hang our hat on it since it was for one year (Jarvis/Stavely [sic] agree)."[13] And the major reason why the Rider hat was no longer necessary to cover NPS collapse was displayed a few weeks later as Interior Secretary Watt told a Park concessionaires meeting that "there is no way you could get me on an oar-powered raft".[14] Public testimony like that must have been a great relief to those in the Park Service who accepted as permanent the decision to maintain the so-called choice of motors.

Pro-wilderness opinion was less perspicacious. Watt's view was countered by quotes from an NPCA staffer, who claimed NPS could "easily propose a longer phase-out" or other changes "without being bound by the one-year restriction imposed by Congress". For the NPCA, "the goal is to reverse" the current decision; it had already "devoted more than two years" to fighting motors. (More recently that staffer has been spending his old age as a pro-motor lobbyist.) Set against any long-range optimism was the decision by the Senate Subcommittee not to hold oversight hearings on the plan after all.

Meanwhile, the Director had responded to Curtiss on the SCLDF request for documents.[15] He disputes the charge that CRMP changes "were developed without adequate public participation", noting that the changes are "a direct outgrowth of Congressional action ... a process we do not control". Use levels based on this action were unclear, but after meeting with "these Congressional members", the decision was to set commercial levels at 106,156 u-d (including quieting the Diamond fuss). The details of meetings (no congressional/NPS meeting is listed) and documents furnished are then listed. That provided us with an excellent view of how thoroughly we had been excluded from the NPS effort to placate the comm ops. The Director asserted that GCNP had received no instructions from the Department on changing the plan, "other than those portions affected by the Hatch amendment". (But then, why would Watt or his minions have had to instruct the Park Service in how to salaam before the comm ops? Most NPS documents show a rush to effectuate the November events.)

Curtiss, after also reviewing documents at the Park and discussing the situation with Marv Jensen, was gloomy about any court action.[16] We would have to show compelling proof of environmental damage, when NPS says it will not be significant. "I do not believe that anyone can confidently predict what those environmental effects will be." I cannot find any analysis that would help us, and "we'll need very powerful evidence to win". Curtiss thought that NPS had done a "smart thing" in dragging its feet on changes. (It is actually the speed that is amazing.) Any environmental damage would not be permanent enough to lead a judge to shut down river running. And contrary to what I thought, comm ops have booked trips based on NPS assurances (known to them and us since January), so they can argue that change now will harm the public. Curtiss then subtly pins some blame; given the poor chances in court, he would prefer SCLDF resources "not be gambled without some assurances that the Club intends to make a national political effort (with) a reasonable likelihood of ultimate success". He sees two other options: to de-emphasize the motor/wilderness issue, awaiting a better day, while keeping a close watch on the monitoring results, or mount a "political" effort that might lead to eventual compromise based on the common recognition that flip-flops on these issues will continue unless agreement among the parties is reached. In any case, legal action is really only warranted if we can protect any result in the political arena.

This clear-sighted (it did agree with my January 24 memo, after all) letter, even as it criticized NPS actions, is further evidence that our eight years of "winning" were now history's detritus as a consequence of Reagan's election. To the major what-ifs, such as our failure to push Wilderness legislation into Congress in 1977-8, we could add a what-if the Park Service, back in October-November 1979, had engaged us as well as Burke and Staveley. Could there have been, in that period, a successful effort to reach a long-term settlement that would have avoided "flip-flops"—not to mention out-and-out defeat?

One Sierra Club voice wanted to make a noise if the Park Service did not offer a no-motors option, but the more realistic view was given by a long-time volunteer who condescendingly opined that the Grand Canyon would always be a Club priority; it had just not been an "active" one for many years.[17] Anyway, the Canyon was unlikely to suffer irreversible harm while I recovered from my "bout of burnout" after being the "logical choice for chief Grand Canyon advocate" given my "unique knowledge of the Canyon, experience in dealing with the Park Service and political processes, and understanding of campaign organization". Perhaps this intended comforting was not condescending after all, just agreement with my analysis, using the two-aspirins of "burnout" as a palliative for the bitterness of having to recognize defeat.

The New Order; America Has Spoken, But the Villainy Runs Deep

In June 1981, the "Draft" plan alternatives and the "Draft" operating rules were distributed for public comment during the month of July.[18] The appearance of both these documents at once, and the fact that the latter listed the individual allocations was proof enough of the collapse of the CRMP, which had been written, in part, to provide guidelines for the new contracting process for commercial use. That process, however, was now short-circuited, with the operating decisions important to the comm ops already set forth.

In addition to that major change, the motor-free Wilderness goal was driven from the temple, the moneychangers in full charge. The rhetoric was itself purged of the hateful idea. In its place was the thrilling goal of a "high quality, rewarding river running experience", one that was "consistent with the magnificent setting of the Grand Canyon" (but not with the Wilderness or the National Park Act). Indeed, the motorized CRMP abused the latter. On page 4 of the alternatives, the Organic Act is rewritten "to provide for the enjoyment of the same [and] leave them unimpaired". Only in comm op-ese is "[and]" a synonym for "in such manner and by such means as will" (see Chapter 1 for the full quote). Why NPS staff felt they had to sink to the level of perverting their own Organic Act to placate a bunch of penny-ante businessmen and their right-wing political friends is no mystery given the post-election events. America had spoken; who was the Park Service to object? Who, after all, in the Park Service really did object? How many were, to the contrary, relieved not to have to defend that damned inconvenience, Wilderness?

The CRMP Introduction was now just plain weird. People come with different expectations, "a dream"; "an experience capable of temporarily dismantling their lives"; "a place that offers discomfort and bares hidden fears, marked at times by exhaustion, tension, and sand encrusted sleeping bags"; "underpinnings are removed and people quickly have to face themselves and those in their small, isolated group". My, my. Sounds like a Redwood-hater trying to explain his anti-wilderness neurosis.

The Rider is euphemized as "Congressional input". And the alternatives, similarly, would lead to a decision "to allow a diversity of river running experiences". Moreover, the objective is only to protect the river environment from "unacceptable" change caused by river running. (And who, now, would define "unacceptable"?)

In setting the total May-September recreational use, commercial and self-guided, at 150,076 u-d, the monitoring program was mentioned as possibly providing information for adjustments. NPS still wanted to limit visitors to one trip per year, though no matter how many times commercial crew had the privilege of traveling the river, they might also have one self-guided trip each year. The commercial use number ended up at 106,156 u-d, perhaps as a demonstration of how NPS would "aggressively pursue an active evaluation policy" of the comm ops. A lot of verbiage was tossed in about NPS approval of sales and mergers of companies. Sure, boss.

"Latitude in public choice" was given by the option of motor or oar-powered trips. Some latitude; some choice. The four alternatives being offered, a "reasonable range", started off with no restrictions on motors. The next one, indeed reasonable if we accepted defeat, was a "temporal wilderness": no motors from mid-October to mid-April. Then, as if frightened at this bold move, the next alternative was to have only October-December as rowing-only. One interesting feature is that this period would have no limits on use, it could fluctuate based on demand. Strangest of all was the fourth alternative of having three two-week periods in the summer when only rowing trips would be launched. To make clear just how laughable an idea this was, arguments why this alternative would not work were made—the only alternative so countered—and took up as much space as any of the alternatives. (Surreal? Talk about persistence of memory; twenty years later this limp idea still gets waved about.)

Trash really excited the writers, "Removal of human waste and refuse gives river runners the feeling that they are the first ones on the beach, and therefore is a key NPS aim". Cleanliness may be next to godliness, but is it also next to stupidity? How perceptive and environmentally sensitive is the person on a six-day whiz-bang driven down by a motor, passing trip after trip, who lands on a beach where the footprints make it look like a face ravaged by acne, and thinks he is first?

In the discussion of take-out points, helicopters are not mentioned. Almost three pages of the 17-page document is spent on monitoring. That subject, so important, so boring, and so, as it turned out, ill treated, will be discussed in a later chapter.

The press release, from the Regional office, was only noteworthy in its claim that the number of people allowed to use the river would remain the same as at present.[19] There would be five public meetings from July 6-13, with a comment deadline of August 12.

The "annual" operating requirements did include many of the usual items: watercraft types (text was cut); emergency and first aid; crew qualifications; cleanliness (much the same, though cut in the trash section); fires; restricted areas. The one-trip-only rule now had even its rhetorical teeth removed; also disappeared was the requirement for records on would-be passengers—no need to measure demand anymore. What was added indicated the shape of the new order. Company allocations were listed, and there was a long section on buying and selling of companies, although surely no one ever thought it was more than hand-waving. Perhaps by setting down procedures, NPS was trying to reassure the comm ops— just follow the "rules", and we will always approve. I may be too harsh, but I did not find any records of allocations ever reduced or redistributed, or of sales prohibited. I remember clearly Fred Burke trying to convince me of the centrality of motors by telling me how important it was for a motorized comm op to enhance the salability of the operation by maintaining the value of each user-day. The 1981 CRMP changes would help Burke rest easy.

Reaction: Not Going Gently

There was no gathering of the forces this time, no great effort to pile up the public numbers; no organizational mailings. Records are scant; some preliminary NPS figures showed 58 statements at the meetings, and a trickle of letters, many in favor of the alternative calling for motor-free weeks in the summer, already trashed by the Park Service.[20] There seemed no support for the choice with the longest motor-free period. Perhaps in that long-ago time, people were conditioning their desires on the temperature; another victory for the comm ops' claim they served the public, since even those who embraced "the wilderness experience", seemed willing to support it only when the air was hot and the crowds were big. NPS "analysis" after the hearings starts, "It appears obvious that concessioner influence on river management is paramount." The alternative of motors year-round was best for them. The possibility of motor-free periods in October-April would have little effect on motor trips, though there are a few around Easter. The conclusion was that "anything that disrupts" what the comm ops want "will be strenuously opposed", with possible congressional intervention. Even so, the statement is made that the longer motor-free period was "best".

A Staveley wrote in defending her plan.[21] Dancing on the grave of pro-rowing sentiment, she, with much underlining, hurled accusations at self-guided users, former Directors, wilderness and safety. "There is NO reason other than intolerance" to be against motors. Shelby wrote on the other side, wondering why there had not been a "no motors" alternative. He offered his research finding that trip size limits were "well in excess of visitor preferences". He called the 150 number for passengers launched "arbitrary" and "pre-research". He argued for the limit by number of trips, and that the new regime might result in 7-10 launches a day, "well in excess of social carrying capacity". (But after all, Borden's model had allowed 5 trips and 148 (total) people. It is one of the ironies that the behavioral analysts depended so much on numbers instead of on how people would behave. The congestion research goal of studying passengers may have been mis-directed; what might have been more fruitfully analyzed was how trip leaders and experienced river runners would deal with congestion as they sought to maximize beneficial aspects of the trips. Ah well, hindsight ...) Shelby concluded that the benefits of the past 6-7 years from research, public involvement and careful planning were being lost, he thought, to "a last-minute, short-term congressional action". (I hope I have replaced this myth—that the "Hatch amendment" killed the CRMP effort—by a larger view of how the river fight was lost by our own missteps, comm ops persistence, and overall American political change. The Hatch amendment no more killed the CRMP than the fall of Fort Sumter caused the Civil War. But thank you, Bo; it was good of you to express the passion that is so often necessary to drive research.)

Wilderness advocates' inactivity only strengthened the mournful picture. In San Francisco, one person spoke in favor of banning motors; several for retaining them.[22] I gave my statement at the first meeting, in Flagstaff on July 6. Marks reported that no one spoke for the Club in Phoenix. In Denver, the spokesperson confessed ignorance about the issues.

As I listened in Flagstaff to the offal being dumped before us about plan modifications, I composed this introduction to my statement about a plan "produced thru a bankrupt process of public participation at the same time as the legislated organic mission of the author agency is being distorted, upended, and perverted by an arbitrary administrative tyranny." Then I claimed that "something has at last been settled."[23] We no longer have to pretend there is a process of planning, negotiation, compromise, or long-term goals. The procedure is "whoever has the muscle, use it".

I restated our basic ideas. Since protection of the Canyon is first and fundamental, we have to constantly look for new ways to encourage users to be careful, caring, educated, and minimal in their impacts; a search often successful "in spite of the concessionaires' resistance". We continue to believe in further protection of the Canyon as a congressionally designated Wilderness, obviously without motors—those "distractions, nuisances, and unneeded toys". Under the "current concessionaire regime", use is subject to the desire to exploit visitation economically. I had predicted in 1977 that the largest river problem was not from natural causes, but the comm ops. It is natural for regulated businesses to try to dominate the regulating agency, as proven by the past few years as the Park Service has retreated again and again. I predicted that environmental protections will be heeded only as long as convenient for the comm ops. Innovation will wither. Enforcement will become fearful.

Those who claim motor trips have no environmental impacts ignore that they occur over time, and the initial doublings in use were due solely to trying to run lots of people through, increases that were the direct cause of the initial heavy impacts. Public reaction curbed the worst of these excesses. But now a more subtle threat looms (and here I pointed to the HERS study, calling it the "study cited by Senator Hatch"), since motor passengers are the least sensitive to environmental impacts of all users. Motors "cause" this diminution in education and perception, insulating their passengers. I then brought up Watt's recent experience—what that "poor, blighted man" needed was exactly the chance to confront himself that a three-week rowing trip could bring about. The larger, faster trips of the future will mean even less sensitivity, and greater impact which even the elaborate monitoring cannot help to limit. Information bad for the comm ops will not be acted upon, publicized, perhaps not even collected. Degradation by motor trips has only been held in check by outside pressures.

The comm ops will continue their campaign of slander against self-guided users to curtail their access, since the competition that is truly dangerous comes from these independents who are more environmentally sensitive and responsible for all major innovations in river running. I predicted that "choice" would disappear as economic pressures would lead to fewer, larger companies running faster, shorter, larger, ever more exclusively motorized trips. My peroration began with an uncontested truth: no one tries to prove motors give a better trip; the best way "to spend a day or two, a week, a month, or any time on the river is in a rowed boat". Motor trips give cheaper miles, and they cheapen every one of them. Rowing provides less expensive days, and enriches every single minute.

This swan had sung.

Poking Through the Ashes

Later in July, the motor-boaters dropped their lawsuit.[24] The judge was not favorable to their failure to push their case. As for us, there was no broad Sierra Club consensus or strategy, so the matter would be put on the back burner (in the off position). Had we wanted to stay vigorous, we might have been alerted in September by the Park's having to write twelve of the comm ops about not turning in their trip logs.[25] Monitoring and evaluation, indeed. Newspaper coverage that environmentalists "have been handed a stinging defeat by the Reagan administration" was only a parting kick in the ribs.[26]

That fall, there seemed to be good news in that the Bureau of Reclamation announced it was dropping its proposal for increasing Glen Canyon Dam's power capacity. Opponents were dubious, calling for continuing opposition.[27] PROA, not opposing the Bureau's proposals, had sent out a bulletin using them as a reason to have motors in all but November-February, since the flows from Glen might be too low at preferred times to use all their allocations. Ah, the environmental sensitivity of motorizers.

The CRMP was completed in December.[28] In comparing the final with the draft, it is amusing to see that the reference to 70 KUD of motorized use was dropped. However, we were told that over 500 letters were received with many favoring "some combination of oars and motors while voicing an interest to have a period for oar only use" (p. 4). A rowing-only period was set for September 16 through December 15 (p. 10). Still, all the plan wanted was a "high quality, rewarding river running experience"; pretty low expectations (p. 5).

Then, another reward for comm ops: The contract term was increased to ten years, from five (p. 7). Giving the comm ops a preferential "right" in contract renewal was now listed as the number one item, while ensuring health and safety was changed to "evaluate ... to ensure"; the phrase "aggressively pursue an active evaluation policy" had disappeared in another nod to realism. The operating "requirements" document no longer called for three evaluations each year, and the evaluation goals were now primarily to do with business matters, not river operations (p. 2). Trip leaders were urged to make stops prior to attraction sites to allow people to relieve themselves, thus keeping the sites cleaner (p. 12).

A bit more detail was added to the self-guided permit system, where "a person merely contacts the NPS" to get put on the waiting list (p. 9, Plan). Permits were to be assigned in November, but again if an applicant goes on any trip, the trip they applied for would be dropped.

A Record of Decision and notice were sent out in January, with a news release following on February 9, noting that Chapman was to present it at a WRGA meeting on the 11th.[29]

The "vigorous" monitoring program was emphasized, along with the "30 percent" increase in commercial use. Eleven alternatives, from both CRMP efforts, were listed. This document was a "final resolution of issues". The "foremost" and "longstanding" issue of allocation between motorized and non-motorized craft was "resolved". "Certain" management practices have been adopted, "relatively unchanged from existing conditions", since there was "little opportunity for meaningful alternatives". The provision of the Wilderness Act permitting already established motor uses, "clearly applies to motor use on the Colorado River". No resource damage due to motors has been found. There is "no overriding policy", so the motors issue is "a philosophical one". NPS is committed to "providing freedom of choice". (Chapman signed this cynical slime. After his eight years of effort, what were his thoughts?) The EIS "rigorously analyzed" use levels from 55 to 323 KUD, but the use level chosen, 75% increase over 1973 use including non-commercial, "has not been tested", so NPS cannot say what impacts will result. It claimed to have reduced the ratio of commercial to self-guided use from 12:1 in 1973 to 2:1 in this decision.

One accompanying document said "motorized trips may not launch from September 16 to December 15." The second was softer: the plan "specifies exclusive oar use in the fall and early winter". This plan would "provide the best solution to meeting the interests of both oar and motor users." In the release, Marks emphasized that there would be more NPS involvement in contracts and transfers than in the past. Fools, hold your breath.

EPILOGUE

CHAPTER 23

1980s: Entrenching The Status Quo

Introduction

... and now my story is done. Yet there is another, a continuation without me as witness or participant. One of the reasons to take a dash at it here is the truth of that old political saw—what goes around, comes around. Yes, there was an ending, a CRMP written for the comm ops, and published and administered for years without controversy. However, that ending was an imposed settlement, not one arrived at in our vaunted American way, by compromise. Worse, in a fractious, argumentative environment where all sides were convinced of their own infallibility, the settlement was imposed for the overwhelming benefit of only one of the contending parties. Other claimants were silenced, at least for a time.

Evading blame is not the reason I use the word "imposed" to characterize the ingredients of that settlement: the Reagan election; the common front the comm ops showed NPS for the status quo including motors; the acceptance of the Goldwater-Hatch pro-motor Rider; the appointment of the motor comm ops lawyer, Watt, as the Park Service's boss. By our—pro-wilderness advocates—failure in 1977 to bring a Grand Canyon Wilderness to Congress, we had missed THE opportunity for public debate over the crucial issue and our best chance to make sure that the events of November 1980 could never happen. That the motorizers contributed to the 1977 no-show through their lobbying points up, not excuses, our failure. Surely no one could be happy to concede that the appropriate arena for public debate in our American system is in the offices of lower-level bureaucrats; we were distressed by that OMB budget examiner sitting on the Wilderness proposal for over a year; the comm ops felt the same about the River Office in 1977-80.

The 1980 Reagan-Goldwater-Hatch-Watt dispensation did not set up a different river policy; it only locked in the existing one. So, disheartened and with little or no access, those who had been defeated were left feeling cheated and disenfranchised. Often enough, such defeated parties fade away, and the imposed decision, however autocratically arrived at, becomes the unchallenged order. The story from 1982 on would be of little interest were it simply such a chronicle. However, the pressures driving the excluded claims remained vital, and since the mid-1990s, the settlement has been under sustained attack. Only preliminary, this three-part epilogue sketches how that settlement was implemented as the status quo, and how it has come now under renewed and active challenge.

The "new" order, I repeat, was only the old order, nailed down. The comm ops were conservative not just in the ideological sense, but in how they wanted the river managed. Fearing competition, relatively content (with the usual gum gnashing) with their cozy niches, the one quality they did not want in river management was change. In the face of an America undergoing tremendous change and innovation— including in outdoor activity and participation, and, in particular, river-running— they have been using their external political support to fossilize the status quo they depend upon. Yet suppressing other interests and oppressing bureaucrats has only ensured that the conflicts would re-erupt given the opportunity.

The opportunity took over 15 years to arrive. With the scanty record available, I can only suggest what happened in those years, and how it is that recent years have seen an explosion of controversy as the two primary excluded groups—self-guided river-runners and wilderness advocates—saw the opportunity for change, and clamored for it. The comm ops upped the volume as they scrambled in their closet of old political tools to find the implements that would once again exclude all but themselves from effective participation in decision-making. Irrespective of all these louder noises, we must keep in mind other participants: the tribes, especially the Hualapai, sometimes beneficiaries of the comm ops; the Park Service, with its multiple schizoid impulses; and those concerned about the environment, as its protectors or its students. It is these last who take the stage now for a bit.

Monitoring the Monitoring

In spite of the rattly way it got its start, the 1974-6 research program was ostensibly to produce information about the river environment that would provide a non-anecdotal, public, commonly accepted (even undisputed) foundation for the river plan's EIS, and then exist as a basis for future comparisons to be made through regular, rigorous monitoring. If the first goal was not met, it was surely first because, as Eiseman pointed out at the very beginning, a motor-free Wilderness was a decision deriving from American values already set forth in law and policy. The attempt, by researchers all too easily labeled as wilderness-lovers (if not motor-haters), to find research support for wilderness, even if sound, was bound to confound the clarity of the policy mandate by the muddiness of the actual research activities. Second, and it is easier to see this today than it was 25 years ago, the CRMP's interpretation of the research results as they affected use limits was just wrong. Focussed on the numbers "measuring" congestion and crowding, the plan-writers depended on straight-line projections, while ignoring the research results supporting carrying capacity levels related to the central research finding of "it's not how many; it is how they behave". The CRMP ignored how trip leaders and passengers would behave as they faced and personally defined "unwelcome contacts".

Nevertheless, the data and findings were out there, published and available. Monitoring based on the research had been announced, cheered on, and funded.

With a CRMP settled upon, surely the 1980s would be a time for cementing in research as a management tool, providing the Marks regime with a sound basis for its year-to-year decisions on operating requirements and for an eventual updating of the CRMP. The available records are only for 1980-4.[1] I will summarize them here, repeating the caution that during most of this time and for many years more, I was not involved.

The impact of Glen Canyon Dam became a major issue in this period, as the Bureau chewed over increasing its capacity to generate electricity at times of peak demand. In March 1980, a river patrol ran transects and stream profiles at five locations, data to be used in the evaluation of increased peaking-power operations. A work paper at the time listed the tasks needed to "predict" the impact of increasing the dam's peak daily flow from 32,000 cfs to 40,000.[2] It was remarked about the various topics—plants, endangered species, mammals, amphibians, reptiles, birds, and erosion and sedimentation—that "much" of the information was already available in published reports. No doubt that included such items as the 39-page 1980 annual report on human impact on the beaches, with Carothers, still active, as the principal investigator.[3]

In its introduction, a summary listed quarterly reports for 1977-79, and a 1978 annual report. One challenge was "determining the eventual ecological steady state" due to the dam, and these same biologists were involved in the peaking power study. Interestingly, the 1976 data were called "preliminary" in their showing of vegetation proliferating and human debris accumulating on the beaches, absent the natural river's scouring and purging. Since river use under the CRMP would increase by a third (including self-guided traffic) and with possible dam release changes, it would be essential to monitor long-term. Non-river backcountry campsite areas showed a "state of decay".

The questions concerned incorporation of human debris and the impacts on vegetation and wildlife. There had been many "false starts" in methodology, but four procedures had been settled on that could be carried out by NPS patrols: vegetation transect (100m through plot center); digitizing aerial photography data of vegetation; litter density (by point-center quarter); and sampling 20 meter-square plots/beach for litter, charcoal, and discoloration. The sampling was particularly important because winter use and self-guided use were to increase. Sampling would more heavily analyze off-river impact by backpackers. Some hypotheses were offered as to how increasing use might expand impact areas and encourage tougher plants. There were presentations of the methods, including a choice of trash, harvester ant hills, damaged vegetation, human feces, and charcoal to indicate human use.

The work at Tanner Rapids site was summarized. There were results for sand sampling at 28 sites for 1976, 1979, and 1980 (though not at the same time each season). Beaches got worse, then better, or some beaches got cleaner and some more soiled. More work would be done. Interestingly, the quantitative bias creeps into the conclusions: increasing carrying capacity is expected to increase degradation asymptotically to a new level. (This inability to use one's imagination to project how different behavior will avoid bad effects is a bit surprising in Carothers, given his involvement in solving the fecal carry-out problem.) The section on management implications reinforces the sense that this was a "we are ready to get serious" report.

Even clearer is the fact that there was weak follow-up at best to the 1974-6 research program; otherwise, there would have been four years of solid data for this report. But now they were ready to go.

GCNP, with Resources Management Chief Larry May leading, took up the challenge in February 1981, with some modification of procedures based on a recent river trip.[4] Plots were to be read at the beginning and end of the summer season, and in the winter "to monitor recovery" (though the processes of recovery were not spelled out). Aerial photography would be more heavily used; sampling would be decreased. May noted that once the data were available, then figuring out how they affected NPS ability to reach management goals would be more subjective and "require more thought!" (His exclamation point. Perhaps what required thought was whether there was a connection from data to NPS ability; this could be interpreted to say that data of negative impact would cause NPS to run and hide lest the comm ops give them a bad time.) Still getting ready to get ready, a July report on May-June activity detailed locations at thirteen study sites, noting "a consistent evaluation" is important.[5] In spite of its title, no data were presented; analysis was to be carried out by Carothers' group.

Shelby reported on his efforts, the subject of so much chatter and scorn at the November 1980 comm op meeting.[6] His August 1981 report wrapped up three areas. There had been informal exchanges on use allocation between self-guided and commercial users, to make use of his work in other places. The major task lay in developing techniques for NPS patrols to gather contact data. He thought that an interesting comparison would be with the representative sampling data from the HERS study. And then (as usual), the baseline would be established. (One has to wonder what the research in 1974-6 was for, then.) He had also adapted a Forest Service computer model to simulate river traffic, and referred GCNP to a pretty recent book on how to use the system. (This was disingenuous at best. Having spent 20 years in computer work, including programming, I know that "adapting" other people's programs is at best vexing and at worst a catastrophe. There should have been a performance clause in this contract.) Shelby alleged the model could be used to "predict" the impacts of changes in use, launches, etc. It could interface with biological impacts. He suggested a model could be set up for backpacking, too; the current NPS system was just clerical.

Shelby claimed that the delay in this report was agreed to by Jensen, since it was due to the NPS shift caused by the Rider. "I see no reason why this should jeopardize any future contracts", and submitted a continuing proposal. An anonymous "assessment" was not so sure. The first goal had led to "satisfactorily" incorporating social data collection with other patrol duties. However, the computer model had not been tested, and NPS did not have the hardware or software to do so. So Shelby should help them get the model up and running and tested, making sure we can modify it. Shelby's interpretation of his work on allocations left us with no documentation, so the result was "nil". As far as another goal, ensuring data validity, the writer appeared confused: we must rely on Shelby's professionalism.

May's budget memo makes clear the condition of monitoring as of late 1981.[7] The decision had just been made to assign the task to Resources Management. Over the past years, the program has been evolving, and investigations lacked continuity.

The utility of results has been compromised by inadequate contracting, and there has been no attempt to assess impact so we can meet our mandates and objectives. Due to past unfortunate contracting procedures, we have a credibility problem. So I would prefer to slow down and give more thought to what we are doing. I recommend we set up a research committee, working with the Region. He then points out various funding problems that if not rectified would have "a significant detrimental effect on river monitoring". These mundane problems would continue to absorb the attention of Mays and Marks.[8]

A December 1981 trip report brought to May's attention an intriguing problem of a different kind.[9] In addition to those who boated down and hiked in, some of the researchers arrived by helicopter. Another "point of note" was the impact of the monitors. One transect runs up a "steep, unstable slope covered by mesquite, tortula, and moss", and reading the transect causes "substantial disturbance", encouraging other people to follow. "I can see future vegetation analysis examining the impacts of researchers not river parties." Furthermore, at Deer Creek, the research sites enter the Phragmites forest. The author recommends ways of eliminating or minimizing such impacts, also taken up in a meeting of river staff, who brought up the persisting problem that "methods of data collection for both vegetation and human impact data have been inconsistent, depending on personnel". A procedure manual was needed.

The January 1982 summary once again spent much space describing the methods and the problems.[10] To researcher impacts and inconsistent procedures was added the lack of information on use; only 25% of river trips were turning in the logs that were necessary to link use to impact. Further, there was no way to distinguish between trips, commercial or otherwise. Also, control beaches were needed to distinguish between impact and succession. The process of digitizing the map data was in limbo, and consistent support from USGS was not assured. Aerial photography is expensive and dangerous. Finally, though a report from Shelby has been received using the 1980 "sociological logs", there is nothing on the computer model.

In mid-1982 the Superintendent got involved in how well the Museum of Northern Arizona was doing the digitization.[11] He also heard about potential problems in the funding.[12] Everything was brought together in an 11-page "report on the state" of monitoring by Resources Management staffer, J. Thomas.[13] Even a cursory reading reveals that all the stuff about methods and "accomplishments" includes virtually no information made available for river management. After "a major discrepancy" in expected and actual contacts using the computer model, that project "is currently with" a University of Arizona researcher. Another UofA scientist, Stan Brickler—encountered almost ten years before doing user surveys—was analyzing the water quality. Pride was evident in the new research site at the self-guided campsite at Lees Ferry. It had been unused, and was the only site with visitation records.

All 1981 campsite data was still in raw form, and many questions had been raised about methods. Nevertheless, once 1981-2 data were analyzed, there would be recommendations as to the level of acceptable change, leading to policy for mitigating impacts. Doubt about this goal was raised by the report's conclusions;

speaking only in terms of if, could, and might. Even distinguishing between dam and river-runner impacts was an "issue [that] needs to be pursued". Reports of meetings with MNA staff tell of report due dates being changed and procedural alterations.[14] The overall tone is almost defensive about original ideas being modified later by implementation.

Laudatory comments about the UofA computer work were in order because the model "appears to reflect situations on the river".[15] As a side note, the anticipated 30-40% increase in river use had not materialized; commercial and self-guided use was not much over 90% of allocation. The big problem was how to anticipate the variability in use, since yes, 100 people at Deer Creek or Elves Chasm were too many, but then, two hours later, there would be nobody. The model could not handle such variation.

The August 1983 account of the "state of the project" was finally able to cite a report, produced by MNA with data analysis.[16] However, the summer of 1983 had seen tremendous flows due to precipitation in the upper Colorado River Basin (over 90,000 cfs), which modified the river corridor and invalidated the established baselines; the full effect is yet to be determined.

MNA results showed that litter, charcoal, and anthills were more dense on heavy use beaches and in heavy use zones. No trend showed for feces. Nine out of sixteen transects showed significant change related to the small sample size, not beach use. Some of the work would require a span longer than one year. Aerial photography comparisons, 1973 with 1982, showed no spread of tamarisk, but considerable expansion of arrow weed and coyote willow. There were more heavy use trails, and open sandy areas decreased. In conclusion, MNA says the time is too short, and monitoring must continue to insure a balance between camping space and stabilizing vegetation. "Potential" human impacts to be checked included sand loss from traffic, tree "pruning", trailing, wildfire, and heavy springtime use during growth. River-runners had dealt with the floods by camping in desert areas rather than beaches, doubling up and otherwise grouping together, specifically in the upper Granite Gorge, spending more time at attraction sites, and even canceling trips. (An unmonitored, uncontrolled experiment in crowding?)

A new factor would be the large Cooperative Glen Canyon Dam Impact study of the next two years. Our program does not address several significant areas, so we want to "expand" our objectives. First, we are dropping transects since they cost too much and tell us too little. Second, we are dropping our method of measuring litter, etc., and taking up another method worked out by Carothers. (That is, all on-the-ground procedures were now scrapped; the baselines anyway "wiped out" by the floods.) Aerial photography is good for campsites, not attraction sites, so we are dropping the latter in favor of stereo ground photography. We have not been monitoring erosion of the sand substrate at campsites, now changed by the summer's floods. This will be an important research area.

The water quality work reported on for 1978-81 shows acceptable quality for full-body contact, but not for drinking water. Brickler states that watershed "flushing" determines the lowering of water quality. (As in 2002, when there were diarrhea attacks from a source outside the Canyon.) Monitoring stations should be set up on the Paria and Little Colorado.

The section on "congestion reduction" showed no advance in NPS mentality about the topic. First the authors fussed about minimizing contacts, concluding that the only ways to do that would be to cut use and strictly schedule launches, camps and stops. Then they noted without comment that congestion is dependent on trip length and that it varies greatly (indicators of the behavioral, rather than the quantitative, nature of congestion). Moreover, they cited the HERS finding that congestion and satisfaction are not correlated. (So exactly who was still worried that "minimizing contacts ... is basic to maintaining" the experience, however defined?) Use of the computer simulation model was touted. (Although it too will fail to predict that increased use leads to decreased contacts, since this result, as shown by a 1996 Shelby-led study, is due to "how they behave" rather than "how many there are". And of course, congestion is a by-product, i.e., a cost, of the bulk of people being run through in June-August. So in truth, the real solution to the congestion problem is to note that it is handled by trip leaders maximizing trip enjoyment and, anyway, it is not a problem measured by people's satisfaction, and even if it is, it is acceptable as a variable cost of going in the most popular times. This whole subject is another example of how the conservative clampdown on river-running management prevented new or even re-thinking, possibly resulting in the exclusion of thousands of people who might have taken river trips.) And the Park now had its own computer to store data such as trip logs. Hope was expressed that work being done at the Canyon by Robert Manning, a researcher in outdoor recreation, might produce a research synthesis that would affect the "future course of river corridor monitoring and management". Even with a real report analyzing real data, the result remained a washout. Monitoring remained a prospect, not an accomplishment.

When GCNP staff did get out on the river, they found that the number of campsites had increased from 336 in 1975 to 449 in 1983.[17] However, a more detailed survey reported in July 1984, found the increases were in areas of low river gradient and wide channels: lower Marble Gorge, Furnace Flats, Conquistador Aisle, Tuckup to Granite Park. In the narrower, faster parts, upper Granite Gorge and Kanab to Havasu, there were fewer campsites.[18] Although some sites in the upper reaches added sediment, overall, there was a downstream movement.

The July 1984 summary is the last research item the record contains. There was a new player, Glen Canyon Environmental Studies (GCES), authorized in December 1982. It included a "Contingent Valuation Study of River Recreation" to be completed in 1986. As usual, most was prospect, e.g., vegetation trends will be digitized from aerial photography. There was a GCES sediment hydrologist to analyze sediment transport and beach erosion. The Carothers method of checking beach litter would now be used, the work to be carried out by students. The computer simulator was used to show that average contacts might be cut by 1 per day, from an average of 3.6 to 2.7, by "manipulating launch schedules". For the first time, the report mentioned that no work had been done on demand for different trips or on comm op economics. As always, monitoring "will" provide. Godot will come.

Ends and Odds

Marv Jensen, the NPS sparkplug for the 1977 plan, was still in place in 1981, and had to write up the new old-CRMP, although his heart was not in the job.[19] His idea of giving an allocation boost to the smaller comm ops was kept, providing the bulk of the commercial allocation increase. Not too long after, Marks made it clear that Jensen's choices were to be a powerless "go-fer" at the Park or to move on, with Marks encouraging him to do the latter. Fortunately, Jensen had sponsors, and landed on his feet, as did Steve Martin, the other River Unit staffer detested by the motor-boaters. Should we wonder whether Shelby, also anathematized by the comm ops, was made similarly unwelcome during the Marks years? Chapman remained as Regional Director for several years.

The comm ops did finally figure out by the late 1980s how to use their full (1973, remember) allocation, although there is a little documentation, e.g., from Burke and Elliott, about minor dissatisfactions.[20] The former, in particular, always pushed his limit, going over and getting penalized, even with his "enemies" in the River Unit gone. A large outside company, Del Webb, made a grab for 20% of the market, but Marks was steady on the status quo course, and tempered the effort by a new "rule" that no company could get larger than either of the biggest, Western and Hatch. So my prediction of a gradual consolidation was thwarted. Over 20 years of constant allotments, the number of comm ops shrank only from 21 to 15, as allocations have been sold and bought, always, of course, with NPS "permission". In the 1983 floods, a motor raft did flip, with one person drowned, but of course motorizers still tout their greater sense of security.[21]

That same year, with the self-guided waiting list at 2900 applicants (for 220 permits/year), the Park found a way for people to determine whether any cancellations (there were about 25% each year) had opened up dates.[22] The waiting list (even in 1983 at 13 years, after being started in 1980) was now to be open only in February. From now on, every applicant would have to notify the Park of continued interest—preferably by certified mail each year—not vice versa. Other tougher petty rules were instituted. "Our goal", said Marks, is "to shorten the length of waiting time" but only for "genuinely interested and qualified" applicants. Good; only the fakes would suffer.

There were oddities in the record on Wilderness.[23] Larry May, at GCNP, thought in 1982 that the 1980 recommendation for the river being in potential status would have to be revised since the CRMP allows motors. But a letter from the Region in 1983 to Congressman Stump enclosed a copy of the 1976 "preliminary" Wilderness proposal and said that final recommendations were undergoing review in the Department. A modest Backcountry Management Plan was published in August 1983 to deal with hiking and backpacking; there was no stir, and in 1987, Marks was interested in convening a workshop of "experts" on its revision, a course he repeated in the CRMP revision. In 1985, the Superintendent agreed that the wilderness status was a 1980 proposal resting in Washington, and he reaffirmed that status in 1987, prodded by the NPS effort to stir up, "Servicewide", awareness of wilderness management responsibilities. These responsibilities included "ensuring that *designated, potential, and proposed* wilderness areas ... are managed according to the principles of the Wilderness Act" (my emphasis, though the report's text as well).[24] Every Park was now to have a Wilderness Coordinator, who at GCNP was soon to be, for the next decade and more, Kim Crumbo, who had joined the River Unit as a rowing ranger under Jensen in the 1970s, and was (is) both a true believer in wilderness/Wilderness and river travel without motors (of any kind).

The next step in fuzzing up the matter was Marks' assertion that the "current" (1980) draft recommendation for potential Wilderness for the river was based on the 5-year motor phase-out, which "is no longer the case" (meaning the phase-out, not the river's wilderness character).[25] Both the Act and NPS policy allow motors as a "pre-existing use", though we know of no designated NPS Wilderness river allowing motors. This would be precedent setting, and policy guidance is important as we are revising the CRMP next year.

The draft revision of the Backcountry plan the next year ignored the Servicewide policy.[26] Wilderness designation would change little, since the only motor use "below the rim" (finessing the problems of proposed lands with dirt roads on the plateaus), aside from river traffic, was for "emergency, safety, research, and/or maintenance situations" that "cannot be resolved by other means" (the seed of continuing conflict). This plan was just to control visitors, not NPS personnel. What it did do was loosen up the rules for commercial outfitters (there was one) so they could make reservations whether they had any clients or not, a proposal that generated three-fourths of the comments, not surprisingly given the history of comm op behavior on the river; for some reason the backcountry-using public did not trust the Park Service to protect its interests.

Concern for wilderness resumed its place in the far back row as Marks began closely stage-managing the CRMP revision in 1988. Based on the record, or rather its bareness, Marks' tenure, begun in the warfare of 1980, was one of administering that imposed settlement installing the status quo—maintaining peace and quiet for the comm ops. Since the overall political situation did not change, other courses were of no interest. He kept his head in the Park and down, and made sure that river policy stayed down there, out of sight, along with him. And as CRMP revision became a contested ground in December 1988, he slipped away, his task completed. The story of that revision was not going to entirely support the old maxim, however; there were lots of people for whom river management was very much not "out of mind".

CHAPTER 24

1986-89: Marksing Time, A Tidy CRMP Operation

This may all seem rushed, skimpy. And so it is. What I am discovering in summarizing the post-1981 record—only documents, no personal memories—is that my sense of people and events is radically different from the 1970s. I have no personal context to set the documents into; they are objects in a row into which I am trying to pump a little life. From the perspective of 2003, the period 1981-1997 bridges from one intense controversy to another. I hope I am making enough of a bridge to get the reader across, so that the parallels are clear between the actions and positions of the 1970s and those of the present.

If silence is golden, then the mid-1980s were a golden age for the comm ops, for the NPS record is spare. I offer here only a few tidbits. A 1982 meeting on traffic below Diamond Creek noted that trips were being offered that began at Lava Falls and Whitmore Wash.[1] Customers liked them for their lower cost and 3-4 day length. Comm ops benefited by filling empty seats already launched. The self-guided permit system settled down a bit in 1983 with 2760 applications.[2] The comm ops obtained their ten-year contracts in December.

In 1983, a set of management objectives to deal with dam impacts was formulated as an amendment to the CRMP. They mostly sounded tentative. The Park "seeks to maintain" native fish, alluvial deposits, riparian vegetation, etc.[3] Number 8 said that "specific aspects of the post-dam riverine system enrich the river running experience", and the Park would try to maintain them. The Park "seeks to perpetuate" the "trophy trout fishery ... in the absence of further impact by trout to existing native aquatic ecosystems".

The jump to October-November 1986 lands at the beginning of the CRMP revision. The comm ops gather their wish list—mostly details—and Marks addresses them.[4] He assures them that GCNP does not want to start all over; this will be just a revision. We want to rewrite without making great changes. Still, the door is not closed on any changes. "Past CRMP decisions were made from a solid rational and reasonable basis." (Six years of being told how to toe the line had apparently made an impression.) NPS will listen to environmental and self-guided groups separately. The Park "will not let the general public in on the whole plan, just particular issues". A comm op offered that they be considered as more than experts and interested companies, since they also were representatives of their public. NPS staff admitted that the past six years of monitoring had just been "refining techniques"; in general, the Canyon is in good shape. (For something that, in general, is collapsing.)

The comm op priorities were to:

re-define the user-day to include a half-user-day;

have a pool of unused and penalty days that would be easily and quickly available;

be able to run either rowing or motor trips;

allow user-day increases if conditions warrant;

use wholesalers/booking agents.

They all wanted to increase the maximum trip size from 36 to 40. Nobody wanted to change the overall allocations, commercial/self-guided or summer/winter. There was lots of talk about how to handle sales of user-days. They wanted winter launches increased to two/day, but that was only to handle the demand in April.

By February 1987, the Park was seeking Regional approval for the process and, in June, there was public notice with a "planning guide" being sent out.[5] There were to be public workshops in the fall, with a draft plan by the end of the year, and a final plan in March 1988 after another round of meetings and comments. Internally, the Park had a "cookbook" to help direct its efforts at involving the public, and, perhaps more important after its experience with the first CRMP, to shore up its own image as professionals, "We must gain confidence in the process for all users so as to avoid conflicts prior to the process", or "possibly sacrifice our ability to implement the final plan due to controversy". The plan had to have enough support to be implemented, although a cost of getting that support would be "giving up ABSOLUTE control".

A new wrinkle, or maybe a substitute for not having done any research or meaningful monitoring, was a "professional" workshop held July 1987.[6] (There had been a similar effort for the Backcountry Plan, using mostly NPS personnel.[7]) Carothers and Heberlein were invited; Shelby was not (the last two were again collaborating, now on a book dealing with recreational carrying capacity). The two-day session was informal. After discussing the past, they went on to "brainstorm" alternatives and public involvement. The first statement on several pages of NPS notes was, "The term 'Wilderness' is not to be used".

In August, Marks asked the comm ops to set up a liaison committee for the plan review, which had broadened and would take more time.[8] He wanted to "ensure the fullest representation of concessioner interests" and hoped the group would provide focussed input. There has been substantial response from the public. We also want to meet with your trip leaders.

This was a very timely gesture, since the comm ops had just employed their now-habitual tool of getting Congress to remind NPS who was boss. Not that Marks needed a reminder, but it never hurts. The nut of the matter was that a helicopter landing spot had been established near Whitmore Wash, but on the southern, Hualapai shore. Passengers were moved between the helispot and an airstrip north of the Park and Lake Mead NRA, and from there by plane to Las

Vegas. There was also a ranch on private land for eats and an overnight. About 10,000 people are now carried on this route, more than half of all commercial passengers. For some time in the 1980s, there had been agitation about overflights of national parks, including GCNP. The result was a law aimed at restoring the Park's "natural quiet", passed also in August 1987.[9] Now, although the law's major concern was the general deterioration of the Canyon's soundscape, the helicopter ferrying is a localized and noisome degradation, a prime target of campaigners for natural quiet. On the other hand, the allocation structure of user-days makes partial trips very attractive to the comm ops, including the short, short trip from Whitmore downstream. So you can guess what happened. The law explicitly exempted from its other provisions flights that carry individuals from "boat trips". So maybe the comm ops do innovate; here they had forged a new, rich alliance with helicopter companies and a ranch owner, and managed to stick it to NPS and the Canyon one more time.

In early October 1987, Park staff led by the Superintendent went to the Telluride "River Rendezvous ... a gathering of private and commercial boatmen".[10] Attendees raised the issues of permit system difficulty, limits on trip size and frequency, and even motors. The rule of deleting a trip application just because the trip leader went on another trip was labeled unfair. When he opened the comm op meeting at the end of October, Marks described the Telluride meeting as comprised of self-guided river-runners who wanted to cooperate, and "were not as antagonistic (toward NPS and comm ops) as was expected".[11] (What a revealing comment about the fears, just under the surface, of the Silent Years. But how could he have known, with no self-guided connections to speak of in comparison with the NPS/comm op relationship?)

Turning to business, the Superintendent told the comm ops he was "generally happy" about current operations, though concerned about crowding at Havasu, beaches in Marble, and sales (Grand Canyon Expeditions, Wilderness World, and Grand Canyon Dories had been sold in the past 18 months). There was a long discussion of what to do about unused user-days, spurred by the always-failing Cross company, up for sale and its allocation the subject of suit by smaller comm ops. (Up until the year before, there had been no issue, since neither commercial nor self-guided allocations were fully used. This situation was now to disappear, so the comm ops who filled their quotas wanted to be able to get hold of any unused days as early as possible. Self-guided trips were using all the launches, but not all the user-days; another indicator of that measure's disadvantages.) The comm ops pressed their new idea to count a half user-day for people leaving or joining trips at Phantom and Whitmore. NPS presented information on aircraft regulation (or lack thereof) and the five-year-old study of dam impacts; no comments were recorded. The comm op work groups presented their views on the CRMP revision. (This was the second major discussion, while most of the public had only received mailings.)

By January 1988, 150 written responses had been received. In March 1988, Tom Heberlein delivered a major indictment of the Marks Golden Silence regime in letters to "Dear Dick", and a bunch of other researchers.[12] His "grave concerns" were that the CRMP process would ignore research on crowding and carrying capacity. There now existed a "substantial body" of knowledge "directly applicable" to river-running in GCNP. It would be "a failure of professional management" for this research not to be used for the plan. He spoke of the frontier work done 15 years before, and the hopes of scientists and managers alike at that time that the data would be "effectively" used in the first CRMP. Although 70% of public comments relate to carrying capacity, the planning is not paying attention to the data and expertise available. Only commercial interests are on your advisory committee. The researchers you consulted last year have been left out. NPS staff most attuned to this research are "no longer at the Park". He offered two examples of research "subverted by the political process or ignored by the Park Service". First, research shows "there are too many visitors on the river." Second, "excellent quasi experimental data published in refereed scientific journals clearly demonstrate" the adverse effect of motorized travel; it is kept by the "persistent efforts of those who stand to gain financially". "A new generation of visitors will be given a demonstrable inferior recreational experience". Heberlein recommended a team of top researchers to bring forward the "investment in scientific knowledge" so that planning would not be "simply an arbitration between varieties of political special interests".

If NPS continues to ignore research in its planning, "the Nation is poorly served indeed". In his letter to researchers, Heberlein summarized the past, arguing that the Grand Canyon offered an excellent opportunity to use carrying capacity research. The public comments mirror the concerns of such research, but the public "has no official mechanism through which it can state its case", as compared to the comm ops. He stated his concerns about excessive use, motor trips, inequitable allocation forcing self-guided users to wait over four years, unclear plan goals. He asked for people to contact him, since "if data are to have any influence on management, we must speak out vigorously".

The record does not contain any reply from the Park; the obvious explanation is that it was just swallowed up in the "public comments" on the revision. However, and particularly because we are nearing the end of Marks's tenure, Heberlein's salvo scored direct hits conceptually if not in effect, for he points at the pillars of Marks's regime (I speak of action, not words): NPS and the comm ops were a working team; no research or monitoring was being done. The political victory scored for the comm ops by the Reagan-Watt/Goldwater-Hatch anti-public coup was turned into a political system dedicated to protecting and projecting the status quo in river-running management. Even on the items pushed by the comm ops, they wanted little more than marginal advantage, and no effort whatsoever to further advance their position in substantial, large-scale or radical ways. A conservative system being run by conservative businessmen who all at bottom suspect anything that might stir up competition. Such a system has no use for research or monitoring. After all, if the status quo is found to be sound, then money was wasted, and if trouble is found, then who wants to know? So how simple it is for the head of an always budget-strapped Park not to argue and push and lobby and squeeze to obtain the resources and staff for monitoring, when he knows that the best situation to preserve the status quo (him and his staff included) is ignorance. Even if monitoring showed no problems, that possibility would hardly be worth the risk that some results might show impacts that would have to be dealt with in ways that would disturb the system. So, if Marks ever read Heberlein's letter, it is easy to imagine him agreeing: exactly right, Tom; that is just the danger research poses, and the political system you finger is just the one I have spent seven years maintaining. So thanks for the vote of confidence; you may not like what I've done, but you sure got it down pat. Or maybe Marks did reply; when I talked to Tom in 2002, he was disgusted with the entire field of using research to assist Park administration.

The status quo had other markers. "Winter" use for everybody remained almost entirely in October and April. One motor comm op applied to run a rowing trip, and was told "No" since his contract was for motors only, an internal NPS comment being that "we would open ourselves up to significant administrative problems".[13] On the other hand, from 20% of passengers in 1984, helicopter take-outs, primarily at Whitmore Wash, had doubled in 1985 (they are now above 50%).

By the spring of 1988, NPS had gotten to the stage of distributing CRMP "issue workbooks" to about 550 people—the mailing list was about twice that— asking for comments on winter use, equity of commercial/noncommercial allocation, commercial fishing trips, crowding and congestion, and effects of the dam.[14] Scoping workshop sessions then followed into May. There was also an "experiment"; since self-guided launches were all used, but user-days were not, the Park scheduled 30 double-launch days outside the summer high-use period.[15] The comments from the guinea pigs who returned questionnaires could have been taken as warnings of dissatisfaction with motors, numbers, and commercial use—or not, depending on the interpreter's predilection. Notes from public meetings and the workbooks strengthen this feeling. With no organized positions or opposition, the individual comments, though no doubt having some clustering, are widely enough spread to protect administrative discretion in assessing them.[16] Differing points-of-view from "paddlers", educators, comm ops, and boat crew insured a range of comments, as well as a fair amount of special pleading. Though there was no apparent wilderness advocacy, motors were criticized. The problems of self-guided boaters, the most salient excludees from the status quo, predominated. Heberlein and Shelby appeared at Denver pushing for a larger view, beyond just "tinkering".

Once the meetings were done, the revised schedule hoped to see alternatives prepared by the end of June, followed by a meeting with the comm ops; this was held in July to discuss the "proposed preferred alternatives".[17] A new word appears: there would also be a meeting with "constituents" in July. After the alternatives were vetted by the public, the draft would be started in September, with the final by the end of the year. Issues for self-guided included increased fees, a pool of user-days to maximize utilization, dropping the penalty for an applicant being a passenger on a trip, encouraging winter trips. Congestion reduction was a large goal attacked by small tactics: better education, cutting layovers, beach sharing, no helicopters. There should be monitoring and better defined objectives.

Kim Crumbo, a GCNP voice for wilderness that would be increasingly heard, charged the July draft with being for "increased use and decreased quality of experience".[18] He attacked the "tenuous nature" of the plan's goals, since the allocations were arbitrary and set up as use ceilings, not targets. Working for full utilization could lead to damage, particularly if visitor perception of crowding would be lessened by lowering their expectations. Since, Crumbo contended, we abandoned the wilderness concept quantified in the 1979 plan, we have no basis to judge any changes like increasing group size from 36 to 40 passengers. There were clearer goals a year ago, when we were concerned with monitoring resource impacts and protection against special interests. Resource protection is not even identified as an issue now, while "enhance utilization" has taken on major importance.

Crumbo's new boss reported his impressions to Marks of the first "constituent advisory meeting" at the end of July 1988.[19] Throughout the memo, he sets up Heberlein as his opponent, while talking smooth to the Superintendent. He notes that the plan is user-, not resource-, oriented, though that is "not a criticism". He expresses his view that resource impacts are incremental, and urges monitoring, though not much of the meeting was devoted to that topic. He was emphatic in disagreeing that impacts are a function of perception; we need a consensus on a "metric of change". People talked a lot about crowding, with the notion that it should be relieved, but not with restrictive rules. My professional opinion is that any resource impacts can only be reduced by reducing users and the time they use the resource. I am not completely convinced about the LAC (Limits of Acceptable Change) concept, and in any case there would need to be a commitment to monitoring. Heberlein seems to deride "biocentrism" and boost the place of scientific data. But we should understand that we respond to laws like protection of endangered species and our Organic Act.

Almost 900 were on the mailing list for the "draft preferred alternatives".[20] The claim was made that the choices derived from public input. There were lots of rules for self-guided users, including a $100 fee and restrictions on secondary—no longer "winter"—season use to prevent them getting an increase. The waiting list did not show real demand. The user now had the responsibility to know about crowding and be prepared with lowered expectations; though some popular stops do need action. Comm ops use 91% of their user-days; self-guided use 94% of their launches, and 75% of their use-days. A staff summary shows heavy opposition to the $100 fee, scheduling two years ahead, and to the current allocation.[21]

The comm ops offered their views in another meeting with Marks and his ranger.[22] Their wishes included increased use in April and May (the months they said would not be able to fill), time limits at attraction sites (from the people who detested scheduling), clearing campsites to get more space (out of their concern for the Canyon's environment, of course), and large sites reserved for large groups (they wouldn't have to use their motors to race for them). They wanted the pool of "unused" use to be more available. There was also another October jaunt to Telluride to talk with self-guided users. And Crumbo again weighed in (to his boss) about the vague objectives and lack of wilderness foundation for the plan, pointed up by the non-conforming uses of crowding, helicopters, and increasing motor use.[23] Particularly noteworthy was the jump in helicopter use from 1985 to 1988, 2300 to 8500, almost 50% of all commercial passengers. He did not like the doubled self-guided launch days.

The draft CRMP and its Environmental Assessment were released in late November with a very short comment period of less than three weeks, later extended to the end of January 1989.[24] The plan would be reviewed in ten years after a comprehensive review. Objectives included the usual about monitoring, some mumbo-jumbo about crowding and natural quiet, and little else of note. A table was included to show when NPS would act if a LAC were exceeded. Most of the changes since 1981 dealt with self-guided trips. Only small numbers came to the public meetings and wrote in. Note was not taken of the pre-meeting meetings with the comm ops in 1986-7. The "modern" passenger removal operation at Whitmore was described; the comm ops had developed a market for 2-3 day trips, since user-days were not counted below Diamond. The developments by the Hualapai for quickie excursions from Las Vegas also received space; the potential wilderness did not. The good word in the Marks years was "whitewater". Interestingly, the increases in the 1981 plan were described as "across the board", which they were not. Perhaps Marks was a fisherman; the plan dealt with fishing disproportionately. There were no real alternatives offered, and an evaluation said there would be little or no impact, just as the now-departed Marks planned.

The public was not listening. The largest single comment was, Eliminate motors.[25] (What are those puffs of smoke from that dead volcano?) Next came the demand for more self-guided launches. Third was to reduce aircraft impact. A general concern for the environment was fourth. (Simmer, simmer.) Wilderness advocates and self-guided users were still scorned by the alliance of the comm ops and NPS, who felt only a need to offer a bow to monitoring. One Interior official was not fooled, and asked Marks why a ten-year revision needed no EIS.[26] But Marks was no longer there to answer; he left in December 1988, having successfully managed the institutionalization of the November 1980 "settlement".

The comm ops did get their knickers in a twist over winter/secondary (meaning April mainly) allocations, with littler ones wanting an equal allocation for each, and some biggies wanting "historical" use. One small old-timer even went so far as to say that NPS made a "gigantic" mistake with fixed summer allocations; even Lovegren had admitted they were unfair. In this same period, NPS again made something very clear about "status quo" to a motor comm op asking permission to take rowing trips. GCNP replied that it is not the purpose of the contracts to respond to demand; they authorize "precisely" what we think necessary.[27] This weirdness was repeated in July 1990.

In July 1989, there was a finding by the Park Service of no significant impact.[28] There would be surveying and monitoring of visitor use, though other work would wait upon the EIS on Glen Canyon Dam. A new feature was to be a river management constituency panel to review the monitoring and "represent" the needs of self-guided users, comm ops and their employees, fishermen, research, the Bureau of Reclamation, and NPS. (There were no environmental or wilderness members as such.) Final publication was in January 1990, celebrating three years (a year or so more than NPS hoped when they started their no-revision revision) of tap dancing away from the real issues. Whatever the warning signs might seem in retrospect, another decade had to pass and confusion come to reign before it was clear that the Reagan-Goldwater-Hatch-Watt-Marks settlement had not made the comm ops' control permanent and uncontested.

CHAPTER 25

1990-2003: False Peace; War Resumes

The post-Marks period, 1990 into the present, so much more full of event than the Ice Age of the 1980s, awaits a historian of some dedication, a participant-chronicler of nerve, or both. This meager summary, once again, is written from incomplete NPS records by someone who was not there.[1] As with the narrative in the preceding two chapters, what I do not have is a feel for the time and the players, that narrative sense that is still so strong in my recollections of the 1970s. You know my biases, and the summaries of these later years do not have the backup that personal judgments need to have. These are thoughts of a 1970s participant looking at events so current that there are many activists who can make legitimate claims for their own interpretations. I hope they do, for my conclusion is that while the last twelve years have not been a re-play of the 1970s, the issues, the arguments, the arenas, and even a few of the players appear to me like elaborating variations on themes first composed 30 years ago.

Several major threads wind through the NPS record. The comm ops' contract renewal took from 1991 through 1995, with seven-year contracts running from 1996 through 2002. Between 1992 and 1996, GCNP staff worked on a revised and more sophisticated Backcountry Management Plan. In the same period, there was Service-wide and Park activity on Wilderness and its management. At the same time, the Park was working on a General Management Plan, which though strongly focussed on the most populous destination, Grand Canyon Village, did deal with river and wilderness issues. A new Superintendent—who wanted to be a strong long-termer—turned an updating of the Backcountry Management Plan into development of a Wilderness Management Plan. In 1998, the published WMP draft ran into a thunder-hail-flashflood storm of misunderstanding, opposition, and support. A CRMP revision, mumbled about from 1995, did start in 1997, and ran into another entangling blizzard. So in a daring, or blundering, or cuckoo, or cowardly, set of decisions, the Superintendent first set into motion in 1998-9 a process to combine work on the WMP and CRMP, and then a year later, in February 2000, shut down planning altogether, before skedaddling off to Alaska, thus, I cannot help but remark, escaping the heat. Self-guided river-runners filed two lawsuits, and one, joined in by wilderness advocates, was settled with a 2002 agreement to re-start just the CRMP, including a look at a motor-free wilderness river alternative.

The period started with the revolving door superintendents, four (2 acting) in 5-1/2 years, until in 1994 Robert Arnberger moved to his throne for six years. From 1990 through 1996, the Colorado River Constituency Panel met and talked. Secretary of the Interior Babbitt, intimately familiar with the Canyon, was a potentially important, but finally disappointing, figure from 1993 to 1999. Throughout the period, Kim Crumbo, wilderness advocate and GCNP Wilderness Coordinator (they do not have to be the same), functioned as conscience, belaborer, and gadfly before leaving with his health and determination intact to fight for wilderness from the outside. In 1996, a truly important step was taken when self-guided river-runners formed the Grand Canyon Private Boaters Association (GCPBA), which promised and tried to be the most effective such organization working for equitable use of the river. The GCPBA filed the suit in 2000 that led to the re-start of CRMP revision. Finally, I will list the active and influential environmental groups that the record shows fighting for the Canyon through the period, raising the banner high for a Grand Canyon Wilderness.

Early Nineties

And what were the big issues people got all tangled up trying to do something about? No surprises: wilderness and inequitable treatment of users. Wilderness at GCNP ought to have been an NPS concern in the 1990s, except that the details were diddled by the devils. The Region passed on the word in 1990 that wilderness lands were to be protected as if they were congressionally designated Wilderness.[2] But down below, the Superintendent said motors could be used to administer the river. Such use was contrary to wilderness mandates of using the "minimum tool" or "minimum requirement"—minimal in anti-wilderness impact—to get a job done. For the river, that meant rangers rowing as in the 1970s under Jensen. Crumbo, in his job as Wilderness Coordinator, upheld the wilderness. In 1991, he compiled a list of wilderness-degrading activities along the river: use increase; helicopter exchanges; three cable cars; crowding; no minimum tool policy; impact on hikers; no protection on east side of Marble Gorge; train whistle; dam impact; campsite problems; over-flying aircraft. He reported that half the comm op passengers used helicopters—a thousand flights each season.

In 1991, firm thoughts were voiced, internally, about the upcoming renewal of river contracts. There should be tighter control over user-days, no helicopters, flexibility to use motors or oars, five-year permits.[3] The comm ops were taking advantage, using over-booking and other devices. Then the process was paused in 1993 due to the new Secretary of the Interior launching a Concession Initiative.

Although one staffer thought wilderness "is not an issue likely to be very popular with the Superintendent ... right now", Crumbo kept pressing to "just go with stated policy".[4] He insisted motors were a "temporary incompatible condition", so we should seek to eliminate them from the river in spite of the staff's erroneous view that rowing has more impact. He spent some time trying to tie down just what the current GCNP Wilderness recommendation was; one participant told him the 1980 offering was a "cut-and-paste" of the 1977 plan, with the river dropped since there was considerable NPS opposition based on continuing motor use. He favored integrating the river and backcountry management plans in a Wilderness Management Plan. Occasionally the pro-wilderness view would find rhetorical support by those who would then wonder whether NPS should "actively manage" to remove or "passively accept" non-conforming use. The answer was that the Marks-Watt-Reagan-Goldwater-Hatch political settlement was still in force, regardless of seeming shifts in NPS attitudes. There was a bit of cheer when the next superintendent formally recognized the 1980 plan (in which most of the river was only potentially wild) in December 1992, giving some legitimacy to Crumbo's continuing to detail the major and minor outrages committed against wilderness.

In August 1993, the Superintendent strengthened this tendency on paper, writing to his bosses that it would be "fitting" to enact a 1,139,077-acre Wilderness in 1994. By this time, the lands that might be used by the Havasupai no longer exercised anyone, so they were included in Wilderness; not so the river, still only "potential". This superintendent, who was gone two months later, thought that the plan could be sold with considerable staff work, a task "we are up to". We want to elicit support from wilderness advocates for the whole package and to reassure the comm ops that we are dealing fairly. He forwarded a 1993 "update" of the "final" Wilderness Recommendation.

The answer came via the comm ops' favored messenger. Utah Representative Hansen reminded the next Superintendent of the 1970s' "overwhelming public and congressional disapproval" of the motor ban. (No one says that our representatives have to know history or respect it, do they?) The "purist approach is not supported by policy or law". There is "no need to revisit this question now". (Or, what don't you understand about threats?) The next superintendent, acting and short-term, was either more expansive or more reserved, calling for integrating wilderness preservation and management, picking up the idea of combining the backcountry and river management plans. He wondered if GCNP was still constrained by the 1980 rider since it "contradicts" the Wilderness Act and the 1975 GCNP Act. However, he also drafted a letter for the Secretary so the latter could tell the former to hold off on the Wilderness until the Secretary's pet, the General Management Plan (which, generally, mostly dealt with the south rim crowds), was completed in 1995; the two were not to mix.

Strong, But Not Steady

By September 1994, the new superintendent, Robert Arnberger, had arrived.[5] All was to be clarified. He made some decisions: Motors will remain, and we will update the backcountry plan. In November, the Director said NPS should lead on wilderness. Previous recommendations had not been acted on. We must embed wilderness stewardship within the fabric of NPS. The new man immediately leaped to the fore, saying that there would not be any GCNP Wilderness legislation; nobody—NPS, environmentalists, Congress—will support it. He then added some more organization, including assigning Crumbo to chair a "wilderness resource management team", although, organizationally, Crumbo worked best as a gadfly and conscience.

The Western Regional Office was handling the revived contract renewal process, telling the Superintendent that his concerns—noise, emissions, launches, allocations—could delay the process, already delayed two years by Babbitt's legislative initiative. So put into the prospectus that NPS "may need" to change some provisions.[6] Washington was told that fees would be raised, and there would be a river fund for "improvements". But beware of the comm ops' armory, "The river-runners have been an effective political force in the past and as recently as the discussions last year about a new concession policy act. Our standards in this prospectus are high. Look for objection from the current river-runners." One small indicator came at the 1994 NPS/comm op meeting at which Arnberger, the new guy, listed NPS interest in allocations, wilderness, quiet (changing motors from 2 to 4 stroke), pollution, crowding. The computer-based software to simulate river traffic provoked the most opposition; it was a threat to the scheduling status quo. The June 1995 prospectus called for seven-year river contracts to run through 2002 and allowed for revisions by the Secretary that would be effective "when made"; therefore, "responsive" offers "must reflect willingness" to abide by modifications. Motor operators were to explain how they would minimize noise and emissions.

From the standpoint granted by this inadequate NPS-based record, one might wonder how matters could look better for wilderness than at the beginning of 1995. A new, take-charge, can-do superintendent was determined to get things moving and completed. Wilderness and wilderness management had a recently renewed NPS-wide priority. New contracts were being negotiated, in which resource-based concerns could be written in. A dedicated and knowledgeable wilderness advocate had been appointed within the Park to advance wilderness concepts in management.

Contrariwise, the next five years were a delight of bureaucratic delay and obfuscation, political obduracy and persistency, and public uproar as suppressed concerns were given public forums and voice.[7] The 1995 effort at a wilderness management team foundered on the deep NPS staff divide as to how seriously operations staff took its duty to follow the minimum requirement, analyzing how to do their work using tools with minimum impact on wilderness qualities. Persistent issues were motorboats on the river and keeping dirt roads open for fire fighting. Work on a Backcountry Management Plan was going on in 1995-6, but its staffing needs were contested.

In July 1996, Arnberger once again set things straight with "an initiative to have a Final Wilderness Plan for this park in place by September 1997".[8] He thought there was a chance for legislation, and a Wilderness plan was essential for a CRMP revision as well as proper implementation of wilderness management. There was another re-organization with a wilderness steering committee guiding a planning team with different leadership. The BMP effort was to become a Wilderness Management Plan process; the river would not be included. He wanted GCNP to be "leading the way in implementing Wilderness policy and developing creative and effective Wilderness plans. We have expectations that GCNP's first Wilderness Management Plan (WMP) will serve as an example of effective and creative Wilderness planning."

The expectations were recognized by staff participants as aggressive and exciting, very ambitious, particularly in view of the plan to revise the CRMP starting in late 1997. The WMP was to be drafted by March 1997. A strategy was offered on how to get Wilderness legislation. As work continued on the WMP, it generated skepticism about the fast-track schedule for the CRMP; for one thing, there was no recent research, and the 20-year-old data would weaken GCNP's position under the certain legal and political scrutiny. CRMP objectives included restoring altered ecosystems, protecting natural quiet, wilderness management without making decisions on motors. (Definition of fast track: one track, two 100-mph trains, one headed east from Flagstaff, the other west from Albuquerque.)

Meetings were held with the Hualapai, Havasupai, and Navajo; problems persisted and even were aggravated. There were meetings with self-guided boaters, particularly about fees and their being imposed with little notice. River rangers pushed their arguments that they needed motorboats; they wanted to "surprise" malefactors, and were frustrated when they thought the Wilderness Act meant no "common sense" approach in day-to-day operations. The comm ops assured the Superintendent they were working on a self-management plan and quiet motors; he applauded. (The tone differs noticeably in these NPS documents when they deal with the aggrieved self-guided boaters and with the self-congratulating comm ops; still one of the themes of river life.) Public workshops on the CRMP were set for September 1997, and by the next May, GCNP had released a summary of 300 comments.

As the WMP was being drafted, a ranger objected to listing law enforcement as adversely affecting visitor experience. Researchers joined in the call for looser restrictions. In early 1998, NPS in Washington reaffirmed its wilderness priorities agency-wide, calling for integrating management and protection into a park plan. Arnberger felt trapped, with resolution of issues farther away and staff more strident. The minimum tool never seems to grow and change. (His ignorance. For instance, technology and expertise keep enhancing rowing and paddling. Motors, on the other hand, were stuck in the mud; it took twenty years after Burke's telling me they were going to quieter motors for this to happen, and then it was under political duress.) His exasperation with Crumbo's wilderness advocacy was expressed through emails in a way that would have been unlikely using old-fashioned print memos. In any case, those protecting road access did not give in.

Then, in June 1998, all the intramural wrangling faded into inconsequence. On June 1, the draft Wilderness Management Plan was released for comment. By the 5th, Arnberger was defending himself to Washington for what he called the "misleading and unfortunate" newspaper headlines, which had created the idea we were pushing Wilderness legislation. We, he claimed, do know how to coordinate with Arizona delegation on plans and press releases, and I have talked with Congressman Hansen, who was "cordial and sympathetic", saying he had learned not to make decisions from headlines. (Republican Hansen was now chairman of a relevant subcommittee in a Republican House). However that may have been, the comm ops were not happy; they told NPS they worked hard to adjust to their market and if GCNP changed things, there could be considerable disruption. And in mid-June, a Hansen staffer was on the phone, expressing "strong concern" based on reports from more than one comm op that GCNP wanted to reduce short trips and force the public to go on long trips they did not want. Unimpressed by the NPS view that longer trips allowed visitors to have a significant experience, Hansen, Arnberger was warned, would be watching closely. And a month later, the Grand Canyon River Outfitters Trade Association (GCROA) stated its belief that the WMP showed GCNP wanted to eliminate motors, reducing public access. The GCROA, descending from CROA and PROA, lobbied for predictably status quo views, but did innovate by including every comm op and being all tricked out with paid staff. It wanted the river's potential wilderness status "upgraded" to a non-wilderness corridor. Meanwhile, the rangers did a job on minimum tool by unnecessarily bringing in a jet ski to free a motorboat stranded in a rapid.

The Park tried to contain the increasing disquiet. Crumbo noted that Marks had told him to use the word "backcountry", not "wilderness", but he, Crumbo, still thought the latter word was correct. Public comments kept "confusing" river management with what the Wilderness Management Plan was to do. Congressional staff planned a visit, and the Superintendent was to go to Congress. GCNP planning staff met with the comm ops for the sixth time on CRMP work. The latter said they did not want a battle, but the "rather strong" pro-Wilderness response meant they had to gear up for a fight. The Superintendent wanted to avoid a train wreck while being consistent with the NPS pursuit of Wilderness. Other steps would be taken to tone down the conflict. Arnberger responded, "It appears we have all underestimated the power of the issue and I take full responsibility for that."[9]

And, though he did not say so, he had the responsibility of having cultivated the comm ops while keeping self-guided boaters at arm's length and ignoring pro-wilderness feeling. As if to compensate for almost two decades of attending to other matters, wilderness advocacy groups rode the power of the issue, calling for Wilderness status for the river, even as they worried about "premature" (as compared to "inevitable") congressional action.

There was no worry in the minds of the five Representatives (including that old friend of the comm ops, Stump) when Hansen brought Arnberger before them on September 24, 1998. First the Superintendent was grilled because of the attempts to regulate aircraft and their noise. Then he was roasted because of excessive friendliness to wilderness ideas, including a searing over the idea of a motor ban. One congressman noted there had been no wilderness hearings for 20 years. Arnberger asserted that the CRMP "has not gone through a meaningful public review since 1980" (a thumb in the Marks eye). Hansen said it was the most controversial wilderness proposal he had ever seen. Arnberger responded that they were not pursuing motor removal, and asserted that he was neither the enemy nor the problem (though he had taken full responsibility). There followed attacks by helicopter companies and the river comm ops, the latter proclaiming that the river corridor is not wilderness. Public testimony was meager.

The session was a classic example of the congressional hearing as bullying weapon; the questioners were uniformly hostile to NPS and wilderness ideas; no friends of these values provided balance. In my 2002 interview with Marv Jensen, one of his conclusions after 25 years with NPS was that it was doing better on congressional relations now than in the 1970s; this hearing is not great evidence. It is, instead, an excellent example of the strength of the November 1980 status quo political system and how it worked, exercising as needed its Utah-Arizona delegation weapon. The comm ops wielded it to counter the threat they detected, not just from the NPS work, but from the support that work aroused among wilderness advocates. The record does have enough pro-wilderness comments to allow me to argue that the support for a motor-free wilderness had been unheard for a decade because of the lack of opportunity. A fuller history would also take account of overall American political changes and the condition of wilderness advocacy groups. What the strength of wilderness support really was, as compared to that of the pro-motor lobby, remains unknown since the story moves away from Congress. What does remain is a strong sense that the status quo's protectors got a scare.

Safely back within the compound, GCNP staff mulled over the beating Arnberger took. Crumbo thought Park staff did not support wilderness. His immediate boss opined that wilderness support was widespread and consistent, though motors were accepted by "many elements of the public". Wilderness was correct NPS policy, he remembered, and the past twenty years of river management were inconsistent with the Wilderness Act, NPS law, and public desires. The excessively large, motorized trips may have contributed to increased damage to resources (and now wasn't it nice for the status quo that there had not been consistent monitoring to verify that view). So the segment of public attracted to short, highly catered trips requiring no effort is well served, but not NPS need to maintain wilderness suitability.

Burned, Arnberger turned to his superiors trying to get a decision on how to square motors and wilderness policy, given there seemed no intent or method to remove the former. At this point, in the fall of 1998, the comm ops were daring him to make any administrative anti-motor moves. His staff also reminded him that the comm ops had nothing to gain from the CRMP process. In a letter to the nominal chief of the status quo, Senator Hatch, Arnberger wrote that GCNP's initial stance on motors in the CRMP was challenged by wilderness advocates, and so precipitated comm op concern. He promised there would be alternatives based on public involvement while protecting wilderness suitability until Congress acted.

Several pro-wilderness groups, impressed by continued favorable mail, asked the Secretary to end administrative motor use and to support a motor-free Wilderness. They were glad to hear he would not support a "flawed" wilderness, though comforting words were all they received. Not to be left out, those who wanted the dirt roads left open for recreational use launched their own mail campaign.

The Washington response to Arnberger's cries for help was flabby compared to earlier ringing NPS calls for wilderness. The NPS "wilderness leader" cited several examples of motors being allowed to continue in National Park Wildernesses, namely Crater Lake, Glacier Bay, the Everglades.[10] (All "flat" water, none of these involved river-running.) Therefore GCNP could recommend wilderness for the river that included motors. He blundered in asserting that no one disputed the idea that motors are an established use. You can permit them to continue, as long as there is no degradation of wilderness (ignoring Crumbo's list). In any case, it is up to Congress how to handle continuing their use. (Oddly, there is no suggestion in this anti-wilderness discourse that Congress might ban motors.)

As 1999 began, CRMP and WMP planning and public involvement were stopped as Arnberger went to Washington to get direction by talking with lawyers, the Secretary, Congress, and wilderness groups. He wanted to explore the idea of having the public input managed by an outside contractor (insulating NPS staff from having to experience, much less participate, in the passion and debate) and to find out what the full cost of the planning effort would be. (The can-do, decisive administrator morphed into the bureaucrat seeking layers of protection.) He defended administrative use of motors, since using the minimally disruptive tool in wilderness did not mean using the most "primitive" tool. (Again, that ignorance of where innovation had really taken place.) He muddied this view in a March letter to Hansen, claiming that NPS and the Secretary had authority over motors. However, nothing required their removal, although a motorless river would not necessarily reduce the number of visitors. In spite of this bold equivocation, all seemed to recognize there was no middle ground on motors.

Perhaps; but after 35 years, I cannot help wondering about a middle ground, an alternative to an immediate motor ban, of a motor-free wilderness, happening far enough in the future so that, though we have failed to provide wilderness for ourselves, we could pass one on to our grandchildren and beyond. Or an alternative of a temporally expanding wilderness, starting with the six months of winter use and growing. Or an alternative of a "bought" wilderness, where motorizing decreases due to NPS and public incentives. Discussion of this sort was what we lost by never having had a congressional debate; a point made all the more forceful by the clueless debate within NPS that took place in 1998-9. Discussion of this sort was what we lost by its being squashed by the dead weight of the status quo settlement.

Wilderness groups, disappointed in their hopes for Secretarial initiative, took up the idea (Crumbo's originally) of combining wilderness and river planning, while maintaining their anti-motor stance. In April 1999, Park staff was seeing virtues in the combination of the Colorado River and the Wilderness Management Plans, and in May, this goal became a "comprehensive" plan to provide guidance on the ecosystem, resources, and visitor management, integrating the CRMP and WMP. Resolution of the motors issue, however, was still premature.

Driving that point home was a June 1999 GCROA statement, "The commercial outfitters will not support a policy at GCNP that would result in a reallocation of commercial use to any other group. We will not support any plan that eliminates motorized access to the river corridor, either."[11] There will not be a wilderness bill anytime soon, and it will not be up to NPS, since we maintain our relationship with Congress by hard work and daily interaction. The November 1980 settlement remains firmly in place. However, we "might" be willing to see changes in other aspects of river management that would benefit self-guided use and wilderness values, such as changes in helicopter use. Arnberger thought the comm ops were being very reasonable.

An ecumenical event took place on a July river trip focussed on the social science.[12] Representatives of comm ops, self-guided boaters, commercial employees, and wilderness advocates traveled and talked together. Research on trip simulation software, a re-do of the HERS 1970s' survey, and work on user attitudes and preferences were discussed. Interesting tidbits were chewed over. For instance, the comm ops relied on Congress. The passengers had an average income of over $100,000, and time was most important for them. Motors were not included on anybody's list of ideal trip characteristics. Routinely, a researcher had heard commercial crew badmouthing self-guided trips to their passengers. There was intriguing gossip. The comm op trip participants stayed together on the trip, contributing to a view of them by others, including researchers, as elitist and defensive. It helped that the self-guided people on this trip were not from the regular Flagstaff gang. NPS wanted to help on self-guided issues, but mainly wanted compromises that would avoid anyone going to Congress.

A report of that trip, if conveyed to the Superintendent, could only have strengthened the view that the comm ops saw nothing to gain from CRMP/WMP changes. Maintaining the status quo was the price of avoiding congressional backlash (and Arnberger knew what that lash felt like). And how could the status quo be maintained, if there were a genuine comprehensive CRMP/WMP, now to be called the Comprehensive Plan for Proposed Wilderness, CPPW?

In August 1999, Arnberger's tilt toward a CPPW was evident in the hiring of additional staff. There were several meetings among staff to determine budget and personnel needs. There were talks about how to have a full public involvement process. So far in the CRMP process, public involvement, often tempestuously, had been through the usual meetings, on-line forums, and discussion groups. The overall impression was one of passionately held views from people long-frustrated by the policies of the status quo. Like the congressional trial by fire Arnberger underwent, these experiences could either engender a renewed dedication to the immense, intense effort needed to arrive at a new more widely based public/political settlement, or a retreat into defensiveness. Yet Congress had its own fears. A biased roasting of the Superintendent was one thing. There would be no attempt toward legislation that might bring the issues before Congress in an open way. That might, given the vagaries of the legislative process, end up in a new political settlement disadvantageous to the winners in November 1980.

As the summer ended, Park staffers were assuring themselves that they were not starting over, that they already had a solid planning framework. The estimate called for over half a million dollars over the next four years, later upped to $800,000 over three years. An EIS was certainly needed; there were many associated matters, such as Hualapai interests and forest restoration. Planning continued throughout the fall on a merged river-wilderness effort; the Superintendent wanted to make a final decision in December. In what might have seemed to normal NPS staff like an easing of the road, Crumbo left to take a position with a wilderness advocacy organization.

To show their reasonableness, the comm ops discussed among themselves and with Arnberger, whether there could be changes in the heavy helicopter traffic at the Whitmore take-out point. They did not wish to hurt the Bar-10, part of the operation that fed, sometimes housed, and flew out the near-10,000 visitors who used Whitmore. The Hualapai might want a change, too. Nothing came of the initiative. In this period, another batch, the fourth, of similar emails went to the Secretary urging "balance" by banning motors and other actions to de-mechanize Grand Canyon visits. Environmental groups were maintaining their attention. In contrast to the warm relations with the comm ops, an NPS meeting with self-guided boaters was stiff.

A decision meeting was held, and must have gone well, for in January 2000, a draft notice of intent was prepared to announce an EIS on a combined plan. This would follow overall NPS directives and meet GCNP's general plan. All the public input would be included. The issues to be dealt with were visitor use and experience, the ecosystem, tribal concerns, motors, primitive roads, the spectrum of available uses and the allocation among them, administrative uses, helicopter use, wilderness designation including alternatives on motors, aircraft traffic, dam operations, designation as a wild river, amount and type of commercial operations. The Park's worker bees met, trying to chart a course into what now was obviously a very large undertaking. GCROA and GCPBA representatives were also getting together, trying to see whether there could be an improvement in relations. In early February, NPS was assuring environmental groups that planning was moving ahead.

However, one player was re-assessing the worth of the game. There were indications even in December that Superintendent Arnberger was plotting, all by himself, the future course of river and wilderness planning.

Bathwater, Bath, Baby and All

The narrative of Arnberger's unilateral decision to abort the river/wilderness planning process, is the narrative of the documents he authored along the way. If only for entertainment, let's tell the story by putting his papers into the hot seat, presenting them in a read-and-response fashion; my corrections are as always in parentheses.

In mid-February, the record contains the first documentation of this latest example of the Arnberger, I-am-in-charge, go-ahead, take-the-lead style.[13] He sought the counsel of his Regional Director, while informing Washington about his new position; earlier he had discussed the situation with the Deputy Regional Director, who had a sophisticated understanding of Arnberger's difficulties.

First off, he presents a fair summary of the history until he claims the WMP draft was "seriously confusing to the public, media, and congressional delegation", who all mixed it up with the 1980/1993 Wilderness proposal. (Given the NPS emphasis on Wilderness, this would be natural, but the record does not reflect confusion so much as people seeing the draft WMP as an opportunity to advocate their views and what Arnberger calls 'confusion' is that people took his ball and ran with it, after dumping him in the mud.) He then contends that all parties to CRMP revision in 1997 agreed to avoid the inflammatory issues of motors and Wilderness, and this agreement unraveled immediately. (Neither the record nor common sense contain any such agreement; indeed there is no record of much consultation.) He then produces a summary (highly tendentious) of "highly contentious" activity with negative press, public confusion, and delegation contacts that were anti-wilderness and polarizing. (His tactic here is to confound the reaction to the draft WMP with the CRMP, which was not accurate.) User groups all pursued their individual agendas. (The disingenuousness of this statement is breath taking. This is what user groups do, of course.) This led to further polarizing. (Aha! It is the fault of those pesky user groups; they start out confused, then they pursue their agendas, and then they are polarized. First, one wants to ask: Well, Super, what did you think would happen? Most importantly, there is the major charge to level here: It is exactly the job of a person in his position to grapple with such groups, agendas, confusion, and polarization, not use them as excuses to avoid his responsibilities. This is the more true if as the record hints, though does not prove, there were jerks and twitches away from fixed positions toward discussion. And of course, if there were, then Arnberger's throttling of the process was even more pernicious, since it not only ended pressures toward working on a plan, but did it in such a way as to destroy NPS credibility—who would trust a Superintendent's word again—and force user groups into the even more confrontational arenas of court and Congress, which it has.) He then posited that the Wilderness proposal was not "clear in several areas" and also that the Hatch rider had "negated" part of it. (Those of course are just falsehoods. The main proposal was absolutely clear; those vexing areas in potential status had shrunk; and whatever else it did, the November 1980 settlement did not negate the Wilderness proposal, it just ignored it.) Polarization continued, with neither able to land a knockout punch. (The only way to interpret this statement is that the public, in voicing its views, was making it really, really hard for NPS to do its job.)

Having blamed the public for NPS failures, he then says that the funding and personnel were not available; NPS cannot hope to complete planning with the severity of unsolvable issues and the lack of human and fiscal resources. (Let's start with the 1994, the 1996, the 1998 Arnberger, the go-ahead man, the man of decisive decisions. Where did he go, this take-charge, GCNP-will-be-the-leader man? The problem with discovering in 2000 that the resources were not there is that he kept insisting on plunging ahead on these matters on accelerated schedules and apparently with ignorance aforethought. Then there is the record, in no part of which is there any expression of problems about the funding. Possibly, staff was writing one thing, and saying another, but the available record shows NPS moving ahead with planning for the comprehensive planning process, with no crying out about inadequate resources.) He reiterates that an EIS effort is something "that we are unable to mount in any capacity". (Again, a conclusion with no support. His summary of costs is also not documented, and indeed what he says will be needed was more or less what the record shows about work being done on the BMP, WMP, and CRMP.)

The next line of reasoning is pathetic, "There are other projects of higher importance we must accomplish." (This, of course, contradicts what he had said in his August 12 1999 memo.) These other projects were:

the Noise Management Plan (it would be helped by a completed CRMP);

"Intense" negotiations with Hualapai on a management agreement (again, this was a matter where the CRMP would be deeply involved and, anyway, the record shows occasional, not "intense" negotiations);

joint planning with the Bureau of Land Management on a new Monument at the western end of the Canyon (this one is personally offensive; I have been trying for 30 years to get GCNP to pay attention to this area, and have been rebuffed again and again. Moreover, Lake Mead NRA was the NPS entity involved in the Monument);

federal water rights (balderdash; water rights are a continuing, but never over-riding, matter from time immemorial and into time immemorial);

working with Reclamation on an EIS for unallocated Central Arizona Project water. (Never mind the details. His bosses would have had to be total dopes if they thought GCNP had anything to contribute on this matter. Notice that he does not mention working with Bureau of Reclamation on the effects of Glen Canyon Dam; now there would have been a priority);

finally, we need to complete parts of the GMP (again, he had taken this into account in his August 12 memo).

Then comes his decision. Planning is halted on the CRMP, WMP, and CMMP until Congress formally acts on Wilderness designation. (Having blamed the public, he is now telling Congress what it must do. Even after my scanty presentation of six years of this Superintendent, surely there is a case that he and Lovegren in 1969-72 make a sobering pair enclosing Grand Canyon river history in a vise of anti-Park decisions.)

He continues. I have conducted internal staff discussions, which find merit in this decision. (A sort of weasel-worded statement, and of course, there is no record of such discussions.) "I have conducted confidential discussions with the polarized constituency groups who all believe the process we are now involved in is so adversarial and contentious, that it limits their own abilities to find more productive areas of issue resolution". (Again, there is no record of any such contacts. Given what I will recount below about the GCPBA and given how wilderness advocacy groups reacted, it seems quite unlikely that he consulted them. This does not rule out his having talked to various lap dogs, nor does it rule out his having made comments and hints to people and calling it consultation. The one group he may very well have talked to, and the one group that benefited from this action and stood to lose from a wide-ranging WMMP, is the comm ops. Nevertheless, as a blanket statement, it is one that a good lawyer would have had a lot of fun with had Arnberger ever been deposed.)

All groups seem to agree that without congressional action, any comprehensive plan will be negatively influenced and easily mired down with highly suspect outcomes. (Nice rhetoric. O.K, what I have to say, before you remind me, is that I agree with him, and had since 1981. Congressional action leading to a definitive ban on motors is the only certain way to break up the November 1980 settlement. The problem for a Superintendent is what do you do, given that Congress has not acted, may well not act, and even if it does act, may just toss the problem back into Interior's lap? It is that question that Arnberger ran away from.) But, he himself adds, the Arizona delegation is not ready to embark on such a contentious course. Then he says, and this is my emphasis, "The status quo may be best for all." (Not so. The only interest his decision served was that of the comm ops. I suggest he looked around, and decided that in the world as he saw it, change required strength, stamina, and imagination he could not muster.)

Now here is some more editorial comment; all part of the wind-up. I should be happy that Arnberger came to this conclusion. After all, it is exactly what I think the river's political history tells us. The imposed settlement of November 1980, solidified by the Marks regime, was proving its durability right into the 21st century. But after I have patted myself on the back, I still have to ask, does it have to be so? We change the status quo in other endeavors all the time. Americans are famous for changing it; we even use it as a swear word. So why does it have to be preserved on the Colorado River in Grand Canyon National Park? Why did Arnberger show his political astuteness about the need for congressional action and the existence of a very durable status quo, and then fail at doing his job, an operational one after all, not one of political theorizing? For six years, he had been puffing himself out there about taking the lead in the renewed NPS wilderness initiative, and then when push came to shove (really hard, I admit), he deflated. Instead of being the man of the new century at Grand Canyon (when he arrived in 1994, he talked of spending the rest of his career there), why did he choose to be a supporter of 1980?

But Arnberger was not done. He trashed the self-guided boaters as likely to be unreasonable and unsupportive, unless there could be some "administrative mitigation of the inequities within the present plan". (At this inconsistency, the mind reels.) He then says that maybe we should change the WMP back to the BMP, so as not to continue to confuse the public. (Still reeling.) "We will continue to allow motorized rafts on the Colorado River, as has been the case for decades." (Still reeling. Why was he working so hard to look like the cats-paw of the comm ops?)

A few days later, he sent off a formal memo to the congressional delegation, Interior, and the Director. This was merely summary, including a statement that a decision on Wilderness was needed first. He spoke of the core issues of motors and allocation, although the latter is not necessarily a congressional matter.

The next day, February 23, was the big one. What really turned him and his staff on was that the GCPBA had scheduled an afternoon meeting with him and he set up the release to the press of his decision at exactly the time of the meeting. Indeed, when the meeting started, he announced he wanted to take up the CRMP last. Then he took a hard line, saying there would be no regular meetings, no liaison with GCPBA, and he had no awareness that GCPBA wanted to meet with him (so much for consultations with user groups). The NPS note-taker then writes that the moment "we were waiting for" came when GCPBA again asked about the CRMP status. Arnberger got his desired effect as he handed out his press release, which blamed polarization of interested groups and lack of resources. He then suggested GCPBA work with the GCROA. There would be no changes in allocation of river use until the CRMP was revised (catch-22), although they might look at it when contracts are renewed in three years. An agreement with the Hualapai would provide guidance for river management.

That same day, he had circulated an "invitation" to staff to talk about the planning effort. At that meeting, he continued his little game by springing his surprise on those still unaware. He distributed his document, and gave people some time to read it. Additional points were emphasized. Not everything was lost, and he intended to make progress, although he would be criticized by the environmental community and others. (But he said he had consulted and found agreement on this reasonable course.) He wanted to get to work on implementing this decision, and appointed the Chief Ranger to head a renewed Wilderness Steering Committee.

Another document, dated only as of February, was grandly called a "decision document", "an internal thought piece and decision matrix", that would record his "personal deliberations" in halting the comprehensive plan. It speaks again of his confidential survey of a number of parties. He slurs his staff by saying "this organization doesn't have the capacity to staff the planning in a reasonable time". The WMP will be put out as a BMP, and the 1989 CRMP will continue in force. LMNRA will do the work for the lower gorge. (Why? It's not their Park.) And that, with the Hualapai negotiations, will take care of a "tremendous" planning segment. (Please remember that the congressional purpose in having the 1975 Park legislation assign the river surface to GCNP was so that the river in its entirety could have a unified administration.) We could do something about the dirt roads. We could do something about helicopters in the comm op contracts (ruled out time and time again). We will allow motorized rafts to continue, since some feel they allow faster, safer trips that facilitate the visitor experience, allowing more people to travel the river. (This is not so either; it is likely that the motorized status quo has deprived thousands of the chance to travel the river.) The comm ops have made "spectacular voluntary gains for quiet and clean air". (The comm op bias continues.) Since demand exceeds supply, all schemes to deal with allocation inequities are problem-ridden. So let's delay CRMP until we have resources to revise the CRMP consistent with a formal congressional wilderness designation. (Funny thing. He did not include in this to-do list an order to his staff to make sure the 1993 wilderness document was updated so he could send it off to Congress ASAP. Oh yes, and tell me again how allocation depends on Congress.) He repeats his thought that the self-guided allocation might be considered at comm op contract time. (This would seem to imply that the self-guided users would then have an NPS-sanctioned interest in the contract process. Sure, they would.) Administrative motors are O.K. in order to promote staff safety and lower cost. (Well, neither is true, but he does not have any staff who will argue to the contrary.) And he ends with the silly assertion that NPS has taken the time to listen to all concerns, but the Park was not successful in its strategy to proceed with planning so as to avoid a costly and unproductive public debate.

Of course, this decision could do nothing to avoid public debate; it only served to delay the effort to revise the CRMP, while incurring attorney costs when the government was sued. The question of why Arnberger's superiors let him do it has no answer in the record; that will be for a future historian with more stamina than I have; the very idea of trying to penetrate any further into the murk of this retrograde decision is wearying. This epilogue could end here, again on an exhausted note, with Lovegren and Arnberger as matching bookends. That, however, would under-value the spirit and energy of those who rallied against Arnberger's single-handed attempt to duplicate November 1980.

The (political) River Goes Roiling On

Arnberger was certainly right about reaction.[14] Wilderness advocate groups and self-guided river-runners, along with individuals, attacked the decision. Nine individuals filed a federal suit (the Randall suit) in New Mexico on March 7, followed on July 7 in Arizona by the GCPBA, American Whitewater, American Canoe Association, the NPCA, and four individuals. The latter effort was preceded by correspondence with the Park suggesting a course of action to get work back on track, though if this did not happen, there would be a suit. What is interesting about Arnberger's refusal to deal was that his staff was in fact following his orders to start working on the issues. Yet the Superintendent, instead of offering this effort as evidence of good will, stiffed the GCPBA, saying only that everything was within his discretion, and he was not reversing.   As might be expected, the opposition just allowed Arnberger to get his back up in righteous indignation.[15] One really burned response went to the GCPBA, claiming his record at GCNP demonstrates just the opposite of abdicating his responsibilities. "Your agreement is not the litmus test of my record." (Well, given the way he treated GCPBA before and on February 23, that is certainly true, but it can be argued that his not working hard at securing that agreement, and he did not, was an abdication and is a litmus test of just what river interests he thought worth working with.) He even charges that some groups wanted to use the plan rather than legislation to achieve wilderness. (Was any group that stupid? Was he, too, even to pretend that anyone thought that would work? It was one of the phonier charges leveled by comm ops at the 1977 CRMP.) Having got off his shots, he then sniffs that since he is being sued, he can no longer discuss this issue with the plaintiffs.

Meanwhile, the staff Arnberger had undercut and criticized was trying to retrieve something from the savaged planning process. (Note for future historian. It will be important, one hopes soon, to talk with various parties involved in the CRMP to determine whether the fractiousness that Arnberger called "polarization"—including one supposes in the sense that it froze the process—had brought public participation to the point of counter-production, or whether it was the venting necessary after 20 years of suppression before there could be serious discussion and accommodation.) Suggestions were circulating as to what could be done without a CRMP, for instance, to keep the waiting list for self-guided trips from growing uncontrollably, and to relax the rules and provide more service.[16] A lottery would help reduce the list, and cut the wait to less than five years. There could be other changes dealing with repeat trips, scheduling, seasons. The comm op contracts could be used to work toward launch-based allocations, moving more launches out of most crowded months, deadhead elimination, group size reduction, encouraging voluntary elimination of motors. With a CRMP, there could be a move to equalize launches between both groups in both seasons.

The new Wilderness Steering Committee met in late March, with an agenda of considering what could be accomplished through the comm op contracts: helicopters at Whitmore; quiet and clean motors; more rowing; improving permit process. The perennials appeared of the minimum requirement and dirt road closure. However, the end result was the chair apologizing for "confusion" and lack of clarity as to what they were supposed to do. A couple of months later, confusion was less and a program set up for the coming year, with the first priority to work on minimum requirement. Arnberger went off to Washington to defend himself, stressing that motors can be continued, and wilderness will not be harmed. He blamed the public for being confused. By October, he was gone, off to his new post in Alaska.

The GCPBA lawsuit could not have seemed like a defensible position to the government lawyers. Clearly, there were problems in river management, and clearly the Park was on record that a CRMP revision was the route to work on those problems. If the Superintendent had made errors through the years by raising expectations about Wilderness, in conflating the river and land planning, and in taking a lop-sided view of who his friend and foes were, that was no excuse for not carrying out NPS responsibilities. Arnberger's departure, though disappointing in that it would have been delicious to get him on the witness stand, removed an obstacle to getting back to work after his tantrum of February 23, 2000.

Discussions led to a settlement two years later, January 17, 2002.[17] The principal effect was to re-start the CRMP-EIS planning with a deadline of December 31, 2004, and a contract extension to the end of 2005. Issues to be taken up were the number of visitors, allocations between the comm ops and self-guided users (and alternatives to this division) and between commercial trip types (e.g., motors), helicopter use at Whitmore, motor impacts and alternative motor-rowing ratios including motor-free, and the range of services provided to the public. In some vague future, the Backcountry Management Plan would also be reviewed, including proposed Wilderness. The government, without admitting its position was unjustified, paid legal costs to the plaintiffs.

The CRMP process got underway in 2002 with meetings and other media to receive comments and suggestions. In a marked change from the innocent days of the 1970s, private companies were hired to channel public participation, write the EIS, and other chores. This reduces NPS exposure, indeed for part of the process relegating them to the status of observers. Some of the arguments, positions and suggested resolutions resonate with ideas of years past. Of course, that is certainly because some are sound ideas that scare preservationists of the status quo. Although many of the participants are relative newcomers, my sense of here-we-are-again is reinforced by seeing two principals of the 1970s' research and initial CRMP drafting, Steve Carothers and Bo Shelby, involved in the EIS. The comm op past as well haunts the current attempt. Off in Washington, the names of Kyl and Hatch are not yet history, though Goldwater, Stump and other champions are. Keeping their weapons sharp, the comm ops repeatedly make stabs at keeping their status quo in place by enlisting their congressional allies in schemes to short-circuit the planning process. This has the benefit or drawback of keeping the pro-wilderness, pro-self-guided, pro-river, pro-public forces in practice for the time, whenever it may come, of the larger, more decisive battle. Meanwhile, we are all assured of the delights of controversy.

Of course, particular individuals are irrelevant if we understand the years from November 1980 to be the institutionalization of a political settlement that imposed a comm-op-based status quo regime. The question of whether that regime is shakable in any but marginal ways remains. The use of for-profit companies to assess the working of a status quo system run for the benefit of for-profit companies may be too-subtle a criticism, but the fact remains that the process could too easily end up packaging products which GCNP can meld into a set of alternatives containing the status quo plus a collection of easily dismissable straw men. A hardheaded judgment would note that the process is designed to control, not encourage and accommodate, the marshalling of publicly held interests. Certainly, its aim is to prevent the return of what many consider the chaos of the Arnberger years, ironic in that he himself appeared to be a take-charge sort. Perhaps then we are witnessing the change from such individual top-down control to control by near-anonymous hired guns, with the hope that an appearance of automatism will encourage acceptance of the final product. Or at least its being impervious to challenge in courts or Congress.

What can certainly be asserted is that whatever control is exerted by whatever means, the passions expressed in the 1970s and now in the 21st century, by comm ops, wilderness advocates, and self-guided river runners, are passions that must be allowed to be fully expressed, if there are ever to be discussions and negotiations that would lead to the replacement of the imposed status quo by a management system based on the political accommodation of all interests. And if not? Then the struggle will go on, no doubt with varying intensity, as each combatant seeks allies, tests the ground, probes for advantage, and primes their weapons.

Epilogue as Prologue

How can we leave the story there? That would be too hard, too bad, too Orwellian. America is more than imposed political arrangements in support of commercial interests, more than repetitious and fruitless scrambles to get a place at the table. Too often, and these years seem to be one of those times, we may be less than our most profound and our most elevated principles. And yes, the struggle these principles have to survive and remain influential often appears daunting and does breed smart-ass cynicism. It should not breed despair.

The National Park idea. The Wilderness Preservation idea. American ideas, home-bred and given life in and through our social and political arrangements. I am not going to re-elaborate them here. I am going to assert them. They exist; we created them, and the vision we have of them and from them exists and animates the best of our discourse about this amazing continent we have over-spread. Insofar as we are guided by those ideas, our decisions about the American landscape truly rise above our individual immediate interests, and provide for the future, of our children and succeeding generations, and of this land, this place in which we live and on the health and well-being of which our health and well-being depend.

The Grand Canyon, seemingly indifferent, seemingly vast, seemingly harsh, can serve as a measure of our decisions. The key words continue to be "conserve", "unimpaired", "untrammeled", "primeval". Taken together, they commend us to care for (in all senses) that Park, that Wilderness, that place the Grand Canyon, and for us, the people of whose home it is a part. And they say outboard motors don't belong in the house. And, they add, treat every visitor the same.

There is more. Principles remind us that there are choices, that we have imagination in order to envision alternatives. In a rut, we can try a new path. We do damage; we can work at restoration. We pursue outmoded or dangerous economic notions; we can transform them. We do not, and do not have to, continue broken, failed, destructive ways of treating the land and ourselves. A Park, a Wilderness, is a reminder of our ground, a signifier of our potential to make amends, a treasure rewarding us all for taking care of our home.

Ideas. Principles. Guides. Interests. Decisions. Arrangements. Procedures. People. The very stuff of our politics and government: the stuff we accumulate power to affect. So far, we have effected over thirty years of conflict, even when quieted beneath the oppression of an imposed status quo. Our principles, the Grand Canyon too, tell us it need not be so. We can envision an alternative; we can transform our ways of conducting the business; we can try new paths; we can repair and restore. We can work for a time of good will, equal access for all, and river travel in accord with the wild character of the Canyon. All we need do is accept, be guided by, and support these most American of ideas, and start running the Grand Canyon National Park and its Colorado River on Park and Wilderness principles.

READER'S GUIDE

Part A. Identifications and Abbreviations

ACLPI, Arizona Center for Law in the Public Interest: Non-profit legal firm that sued on behalf of Eiseman and other self-guided river runners, 1977

ARTA or ARA: American River Touring Association, comm op (Elliott) running motor and oar trips, later renamed Arizona Raft Adventures

Assistant Secretary: Refers to the Interior Department political appointee who oversees the National Park Service; full title: the Assistant Secretary for Fish and Wildlife and Parks

Avery, Ben: *Arizona Republic* (Phoenix) newspaperman; hunting/outdoors news and column into 1970s

AWWW: also AQE; Arizonans for Water Without Waste (Arizonans for a Quality Environment), a Tucson group that had fought the Grand Canyon dams and the Central Arizona Project, and was one of my "alliance" organizations

Babbitt, Bruce: Long-time user of the Grand Canyon; Democrat; Arizona governor, 1978-87; Secretary of the Interior, 1993-2001

Bible, Alan: Senator (D-Nevada). Chairman of Senate subcommittee dealing with Parks, 1973-4

BMP: Backcountry Management Plan

Borden, F. Yates: Did research on carrying capacity; influential on Synthesis

Boster, Mark: Wrote master's thesis that did survey of river trips, 1971-2

Brickler, Stan: Sociology/Natural Resources; Univ. of Ariz. Dept. of Watershed Management; surveying river trip people early 1970s

Brower, David: If you have to ask ...

Brown, Richard: Salt Lake City attorney for CROA and Currey

Burke, Fred: owner/founder: Arizona River Runners; Republican politician; a prime lobbyist for the comm ops; pro-dam; wife: **Carol**

Calkin, Brant: Southwest Representative, Sierra Club, 1977 to 1980s

Carlstrom, Terry: Planner, Denver Service Center, NPS, for 1975-6 Wilderness and other GC park studies

Carothers, Steven: Biologist, Museum of Northern Arizona Research Center, one of the lead scientists in the mid-'70s research program. Returned to lead a private team working on EIS for CRMP in 2000s

Carr, Lizbeth: designer/illustrator; late 1977 into 1978, lobbying in D.C. on GC Wilderness

cfs: Cubic feet per second, the common measure of river flow; sometimes called second-feet

Chapman, Howard: NPS Western Regional Director, 1971-1987

comm ops: Short for owners/operators on the river in the Grand Canyon, called variously concessionaires, river companies, commercial river-runners, river industry or commercial operators. They run trips with paying customers. Before 1972, had NPS seasonal permits. Starting in 1972 they were under multi-year contracts or extensions thereof

conservationists: Later: environmentalists, tree-huggers, green pinkos, primitivists. Help make up "friends of the Grand Canyon", as opposed to exploiters or bureaucrats. Wilderness advocates also an appropriate term

Cowgill, Pete: Outdoor writer for Tucson newspaper *Arizona Daily Star*, experienced and avid backpacker

CPPW: Comprehensive Plan for Proposed Wilderness, 1999-2000

CRBP: Colorado River Basin Project; mid-1960s legislation that initially contained authorization for two dams in the Grand Canyon. Enacted in 1968 without dams

CRMP: Colorado River Management Plan, 1976 on. In early 1970s the phrase did not designate so formal and comprehensive a document. Use was sometimes just RMP

CRMP+EIS: the plan and its EIS, used for the 1977-80 products

CROA: Colorado River Outfitters Association; main founders, in 1970, motor comm ops Western, Hatch, Cross, Tour West, Sanderson, Canyoneers, White Water

Crumbo, Kim: Pro-wilderness advocate, 1970s-2000s. Guide for comm ops, GCNP river ranger under Jensen, GCNP Wilderness Coordinator; left GCNP to work on and for wilderness

Currey, Jack: founder, Western River Expeditions, Salt Lake, largest allotment in GCNP in 1970s; sold in late 1970s

Curry, Richard: Interior Dept official; NPS legislation director in mid-1970s

Curtiss, William: Sierra Club Legal Defense Fund lawyer, active in 1980-1 on motors

DeConcini, Dennis: Senator (D-Arizona), 1977-95

DSC: Denver Service Center, National Park Service; centralized office for staff, expertise and other resources for various studies and projects, in liaison with the GCNP staff

EA: Environmental Assessment; used by agencies trying to avoid doing an EIS

EIS: Environmental Impact Statement, required by NEPA, National Environmental Policy Act, to analyze impact of significant federal actions

Eiseman, Fred: self-guided river runner and activist on behalf of wilderness and use limits; 1956 until around 1978

Elliott, Robert: Largest non-motor comm op, ARTA/ARA

Emerson, Terry: Goldwater's legislative aide during 1972-5 Park/Havasupai legislation

Everhardt, Gary: NPS Director, 1975-77. A good influence on GC matters

Foreman, Dave: The Wilderness Society's Southwestern Representative in the 1970s

Friends of the Earth (FOE): Organization, with an Arizona chapter, founded by David Brower; one of my "alliance" groups due to the support of Kevin Dahl

Garn, Jake: Senator (R-Utah) in late 1970s

GCNHA: Grand Canyon Natural History Association; N H dropped later on

GCNP: Grand Canyon National Park, can refer to place or NPS administration thereof

GCPBA, organization and records. Grand Canyon Private Boaters Association; founded in mid-1990s as self-guided advocacy group; very active. Filed 2000 suit that resulted in compilation of 30 volumes of NPS records

GCRO: Grand Canyon Rowing Outfitters: ARTA, GC Dories, OARS, Inc, Outdoors Unlimited, Wilderness World; started fall 1972; short-lived

GCROA: Grand Canyon River Outfitters Trade Association, latest and current incarnation of comm ops lobbying group, includes all comm ops and paid staff

Goldwater, Barry: Senator (R-Arizona), ran river in 1940, and after. Key figure on Grand Canyon matters due to interest and prestige

Grisham, Mark: Paid lobbyist for comm ops' GCROA starting in 1990s

Hansen, James: Representative (R-Utah) in the 1990s; comm op defender; chairman of subcommittee on Parks

Hartzog, George: NPS Director 1964-1972. Then lobbyist

Hatch: Motor comm op; largest allotment in GCNP in 1970s

Hatch, Orrin: Senator (R-Utah), 1977-. Sponsor of, with Goldwater and Garn, and spokesman for, 1980 legislation that maintained motor use level

Heberlein, Thomas: Outdoor recreation research (esp. carrying capacity); Professor, U. of Wisconsin, 1970s-; involved in genesis of social survey work on river, mid-70s

HERS: see Shelby, Bo

Holladay, Dee: Owner of Holiday Expeditions, founded in 1966. Before that, worked for Jack Currey of Western River Expeditions. Pro-rowing, operates in Dinosaur N.M. et al

Ingram, Jeff: Unpaid activist against Grand Canyon dams, 1964-5. Sierra Club Southwest Representative (the first), 1966-9. Out of town 1969-72. Citizen activist on many Grand Canyon issues 1972-81, still unpaid, but got expenses sometimes. In this period, worked with and/or represented Sierra Club (Grand Canyon-Arizona chapter), Southern Arizona Hiking Club, AWWW, FOE. Inactive 1981-98

Jensen, Marvin: GCNP Inner Canyon Unit (river) Manager, 1976-81

Johnson, R. Roy: Biologist doing research in Canyon, first at Prescott College, then from 1973 at GCNP as leader of the research program

KAC: K = thousands, ac = acres; where used the figures are rounded, e.g., 534,834 acres becomes 535 KAC, though 5,522 acres will be 5.5 KAC

Kovalik, Vladimir: Small rowing comm op; pro-wilderness

KUD: K = thousands, UD = user-days = one person on the river all or part of a day. Usually refers to just passengers/visitors, but sometimes to passengers + crew. The latter case can be labeled "total". For self-guided and other non-commercial trips, KUD includes all people on trip. The ambiguities in usage of the term user-day do make tracing the changes and claims difficult

Kyl, John/Jon: Father/son; Republican legislators. Pro-comm-op

LAC: Limit of Acceptable Change. Bureaucratic wish-word for a quantitative standard that would tell administrators when to act
Lewis, Linda: Activist on Canyon matters and conservation chair, Grand Canyon Chapter, Sierra Club; 1977-81
Litton, Martin: longtime lover of and fighter for the land; travel editor of *Sunset* magazine, 1960s; Self-guided boater, then comm op (Grand Canyon Dories), river runner using dories (wooden rowboats)
LMNRA: Lake Mead National Recreation Area. Due to reclamation history, now irrelevant, parts of the northwestern Grand Canyon, though distinct in administrative and natural science terms, is part of LMNRA
Lovegren, Robert: GCNP Superintendent, 1969-72, then NPS Arizona State Director

Marks, Richard: NPS Asst. Director, Visitor Services, 1973-5; GCNP Superintendent, 1980-8
Martin, Steve: GCNP, Inner Canyon Unit, River Ranger, 1976?-1981
May, Larry: Denver Service Center, NPS, staff for 1975-6 Wilderness study; on GCNP research staff in 1980s
McComb, John: Southwest Representative, Sierra Club, 1969-1977, Tucson. Then Washington lobbyist for Club
MNA: Museum of Northern Arizona and its Research Center, Flagstaff
Morton, Rogers C.B.: Congressman (R-Maryland), on Interior Committee until 1971, then Secretary of the Interior under Nixon, Jan 1971 - Apr 1975
Moss, Frank: Senator (D-Utah), 1959-77; comm op defender, esp. 1972-3
Mountain States Legal Foundation, MSLF: See Watt
Munroe, Joe: Photographer, self-guided river-runner, founded WPRF

NAU: Northern Arizona University Special Collections, Flagstaff
Nemir, Donald: Attorney for Wilderness Public Rights Fund, self-guided river runners group
Nielsen, Joyce: HERS principal; see Shelby
NPCA: National Parks Conservation Association, a long-time defender of the National Park System against threats, but often hobbled by its concern for not being too controversialist
NPS: National Park Service

OMB: Office of Management and Budget, part of President's Executive Office, in charge of clearing administration and agency-proposed legislation in conformance with President's program

Parent, C.R. Michael: Did research on comm op economics
Peters, Clay: Minority (Republican) staffer, House Interior Committee, late 1970s
Pontius, Dale: Legislative aide (as committee staff) for Rep Morris Udall; of major assistance to pro-Park position during Park/Havasupai legislation, 1973-5

PROA: Professional River Outfitters Association, 1978 form of some of the motorized comm ops; members: Canyoneers, Georgie's, Hatch, Sanderson, Tour West, Western, WhiteWater, and a couple of non-Grand Canyon companies

Randall files: Record generated by suit in 2000 by self-guided river runners filed in New Mexico
Reagan, Ronald: Appointed Watt (see)
Reed, Nathaniel: Florida conservationist, Assistant Secretary of Fish and Wildlife and Parks, 1971-77
Rhodes, John: Representative (R-Arizona) from Phoenix, 1953-1982
Rider, the: An amendment, passed in late 1980, to the 1981 Interior Appropriations bill calling for the continuation of motors on the river in Grand Canyon; usually referred to with the adjective (pejorative) "Hatch", referring to a then-Senator from Utah. I eschew this usage to underscore the more important role played by other actors and events
Ruch, James: Reed aide, active on river matters, 1972-3
Ruckel, H. Anthony: Chief attorney, SCLDF in Denver, in 1960s and 1970s

SAHC: Southern Arizona Hiking Club, of Tucson, one of my alliance organizations
SCLDF: Sierra Club Legal Defense Fund, Inc., q.v.
self-guided, private, non-commercial: refers to trips and the people who take them who, if they live long enough or lived long enough ago, run their own trips sharing costs, mostly using oars. NPS permit required for each trip
Sessions, Stuart: budget examiner in OMB (1975-9) who looked over, then held up, Grand Canyon Wilderness recommendation
Shaw, Bruce: GCNP Deputy Superintendent in 1970s; often acting superintendent
Shelby, Bo: Principal investigator, reporting to Nielsen, for Human Ecology Research Services (**HERS**) on the River Contact Study, 1974-7. Continued on monitoring contract into early 1980s. In mid-1990s, principal for repeat of the Contact Study
Sierra Club, as standing for it and allies: Conservation organization, San Francisco; term often used generically by exploiters. Sometimes, the Club
Sierra Club Legal Defense Fund: organization of staff attorneys to pursue legal opportunities for environmental action. Denver branch was involved with Grand Canyon
Sleight, Ken: Comm op (small); conservation instincts
Smith, Ron (and Sheila): one of the larger comm ops; active for wilderness, rowing-only in early '70s
Sparks, Joe: Arizona lawyer who in 1974 was chief lobbyist for the Havasupai during the GCNP legislation fight. A good example of the difference competence, contacts, and determination make
Staveley, Gaylord: motor comm op; still active in 2002; had started rowing wooden boats; switched to large rafts that carried containerized human waste. One of public leaders as head of PROA in opposition to controls on use and, more particularly, to ban of motors
Steiger, Sam: U. S. Representative (R-Arizona), 1967-77, representing the district

containing the Grand Canyon. A stalwart opponent of ours and friend of the comm ops. His son, Lew, was a motor river guide and chronicler of river runners
Stitt, Merle: GCNP Superintendent, 1972-80
Stricklin, Howard: GCNP Superintendent, 1964-1969
Stump, Bob: Representative (D, then R) for northern Arizona, 1977-2003; succeeded Steiger; same views on comm ops
Synthesis: The document produced in 1966 and published in 1967 that summarized the Colorado River Research Project's findings, conclusions, and management implications

Taylor, Roy: U.S. Representative, Chairman, Parks Subcommittee during GCNP legislation fight, 1973-5
Taylor, Vernon: Prescott College faculty; self-guided river runner

Udall, Morris: longtime U.S. Representative (D-Arizona), southern Arizona, 1961-1991; active member and later chairman of House Interior and Insular Affairs Committee. As powerful a friend of the environment as we were likely to get.
Udall, Stewart: Representative (D-Arizona) (for non-Phoenix) before his brother; Secretary of the Interior, 1961-69
User-day: See KUD

Venable, Gilbert: Phoenix lawyer working on SCLDF legal action for Canyon in 1977-80
Verkler, Jerry: Lead staff person for the majority, Senator Interior Committee during Park expansion legislation fight

Watt, James: head of Denver-based Mountain States Legal Foundation, lawyer for comm ops in late 1970s, then Reagan's Secretary of the Interior, 1981-3. It better not get worse than this
Whalen, William: NPS Director, 1977-1980; became strong pro-rowing after river trip
White, Georgie: First large scale motor raft comm op
WMP: Wilderness Management Plan
WPRF: Wilderness Public Rights Fund; advocacy group for self-guided river runners
WRGA: Western River Guides Association. A river runners' organization active from the 1960s in many parts of the West. It started in an ecumenical way including all sorts of river runners, but eventually was dominated by commercial interests. Early on in the Grand Canyon controversies, the Park staff used it as a sounding board, but it played little role as the 1970s went on

Yearout, Robert: GCNP River Manager, 1972-76

Part B. Dates and Time Spans

This part is a collection of some of the date spans and events relevant to this history. Gaps are of officials who do not appear in the book.

Federal Administration
Democratic 1961-1969
Republican 1969-1977
Democratic 1977-1981
Republican 1981-1993
Democratic 1993-2001
Republican 2001-

Congress was Democratic until 1981, when the Republicans became the Senate majority.

Secretary of the Interior
Udall	1961-1969
Hickel	1969-1971
Morton	1972-1975
...	
Andrus	1977-1981
Watt	1981-1983
...	
Babbitt	1993-2001
Norton	2001-

Assistant Secretary of the Interior for Fish and Wildlife and Parks
Reed	1971-1977
Herbst	1977-1981

National Park Service

Director
Hartzog	1964-1972
Walker	1973-1975
Everhardt	1975-1977
Whalen	1977-1980
Dickenson	1980-1985

Director, Western Region
Chapman	1971-1987

GCNP Superintendent
Stricklin	1964-1969
Lovegren	1969-1972
Stitt	1972-1980
Shaw	1980 acting
Marks	1980-1988
Reed	1988-1989 acting
Davis	1989-1991
Chandler	1991-1993
Evison	1994 acting
Arnberger	1994-2000
Alston	2000-

Some important events

1964	Passage of the Wilderness Act
1965	Start of river environmental and running impacts by Glen Canyon dam
1965-1968	Grand Canyon dams fight; CRBP legislation
1970	CROA founded
1970-1971	GCNP decision not to recommend river for Wilderness
1971	NEPA in force
1971-1972	Multi-year contracts introduced for river comm ops
1972	October decision by Reed to ban motors and reduce use
	NPS Wilderness recommendation without river
1973	CROA suit against Reed decision
	September "decision" by Morton to hold up motor ban
	Beginning of restrictions on self-guided users, incl. no-repeat rule
1972-1975	Winter 1972-73 to June 1975; legislative fight over GCNP enlargement
1973-1977	GCNP river research program; Synthesis published late 1977
1975-1976	GC Wilderness study; Dec. 1976 recommendation includes river
	Pro-self-guided resolution in Congress
1976	Research results available in summer; Synthesis in October
	Comm op contracts extended for three years
	WPRF suit filed
	River workshops held in March
1976-1980	CRMP+EIS drafted, discussed, debated and doomed
1977	Small team begins CRMP+EIS draft; mid-year revision
	WPRF suit dismissed; Eiseman suit filed and dismissed. Both appealed, Eiseman's in 1978
1977-1979	Struggle over GC Wilderness recommendation held in OMB
1977-1980	SCLDF + GCNP sue on GC river environmental impact
1978	Public comment on CRMP+EIS; re-drafting
1979	EIS out in summer for comment; Final CRMP+EIS published
1979-1980	Nov 1979-June 1980:
	NPS, esp. Chapman, negotiates with comm ops, esp. Burke and Staveley
1980	Comm op suit against CRMP, esp. motor ban
	NPS revises GC Wilderness proposal's corpse to drop river
	November: Election brings Republican Presidency and Senate
	Comm ops united for motors
	The Rider passes Senate
	December: Watt appointed Secretary of the Interior
1981	Status quo embedded in CRMP on use and for motors
1986-1989	Marks-led revision of CRMP
1996	GCPBA founded
1997	CRMP revision process started
1998	Arnberger before House subcommittee on Wilderness planning
1999	CRMP and WMP development combined
2000	Arnberger decides to end CRMP planning
	Suits by self-guided river runners to restore CRMP planning
2002	Settlement of GCPBA suit; CRMP planning re-started
2003-2004	Debate over CRMP provisions

Part C. Information on River Concessionaires

1970s companies	1981 User-days
ARTA (American River Touring Association) renamed Arizona Raft Adventures	9782
Arizona River Runners	3300
Canyoneers	4060
Colorado River Expeditions later Colorado River and Trail Expeditions	2500
Cross Tours and Explorations	7113
Fort Lee Company	2900
Georgie's Royal River Rats	2600
Grand Canyon Dories	4225
Grand Canyon Expeditions	8892
Grand Canyon Youth Expeditions	2325
Harris Boat Trips (owned by Diamond)	6204
Hatch River Expeditions	10671
Moki Mac River Expeditions	3300
OARS	2800
Outdoors, Unlimited	2300
Sanderson River Expeditions (split w/ Diamond)	6247
Tour West	4480
Western River Expeditions	10671
White Water Expeditions	4380
Wilderness World	3720
Wonderland Expeditions	2980

The total of somewhat over 105,000 user-days equaled the 1972 passenger allotment; it did not therefore include the 10,000 late-season supplement proposed in the summer of 1972 for 1973.

2003 companies	2001 user-days	non-summer
Aramark-Wilderness River Adventures	9132	414
Arizona Raft Adventures	9782	586
Arizona River Runners	10413	686
Canyoneers	4060	343
Canyon Expeditions/Canyon Explorations	6045	978
Colorado River and Trail Expeditions	2500	348
Diamond River Adventures	6860	343
Grand Canyon Expeditions	13257	710
Hatch River Expeditions	10656	371
High Desert Adventures	2980	343
Moki Mac River Expeditions	3350	343
OARS	4912	343 + 2100
Outdoors Unlimited	4478	343
Tour West	4480	343
Western River Expeditions	13251	750

The total is about 106,000 for the left column, and a bit under 10,000 for non-summer. According to owner George Wendt, OARS's non-summer allocation is due to the success and desirability of its (and GC Dories, absorbed by OARS) April and October trips over the years.

From 21 companies to 15. What happened? There have been new owners from outside the original 1970s group, but not many. Depending on how you define your terms, at least two-thirds of the 15 today are with the same person or in the family. About 13 of the comm op principals in the 1970s are gone. Nevertheless, the allocation numbers show the Grand Canyon river business has been kept tightly within the status quo arrangement, only shifting as some have been absorbed by others. I do not have a record of some changes that took place between the 1970s and today, so only the starting and ending comm ops are shown.

Seven with no significant change (most with owners same or same family)
Arizona Raft Adventures
Canyoneers
Colorado River and Trail Expeditions ("Trail" was added)
Hatch River Expeditions
High Desert Adventures (name change from Wonderland)
Moki Mac River Expeditions
Tour West

Seven increased	by absorbing
Aramark	Fort Lee, plus part of Sanderson
Arizona River Runners	Cross
Diamond	Harris, plus part of Sanderson
Grand Canyon Expeditions	White Water
OARS	part of Grand Canyon Dories
	plus a non-summer increase from other allocations
Outdoors Unlimited	part of Grand Canyon Dories
Western	Georgie's

As of November 2003, Arizona Raft Adventures was working on absorbing High Desert Adventures. The more things change, …

Somewhat more complicated
Grand Canyon Youth Expeditions and Wilderness World have ended up as the combined Canyon Explorations/Canyon Expeditions.

Motor-oriented associations
Colorado River Outfitters Association (CROA), founded 1970
Cross, Hatch, Sanderson (w/ Diamond), Tour West, Western, White Water + 2 non-GC

1973 lawsuit plaintiffs:
CROA + Canyoneers

Professional River Outfitters Association (PROA), date unknown
CROA minus Cross + Canyoneers and Georgie's + 1 non-GC

1980 lawsuit plaintiffs:
PROA + Arizona River Runners and Fort Lee

Part D. Maps

Boundaries are not intended to be exact

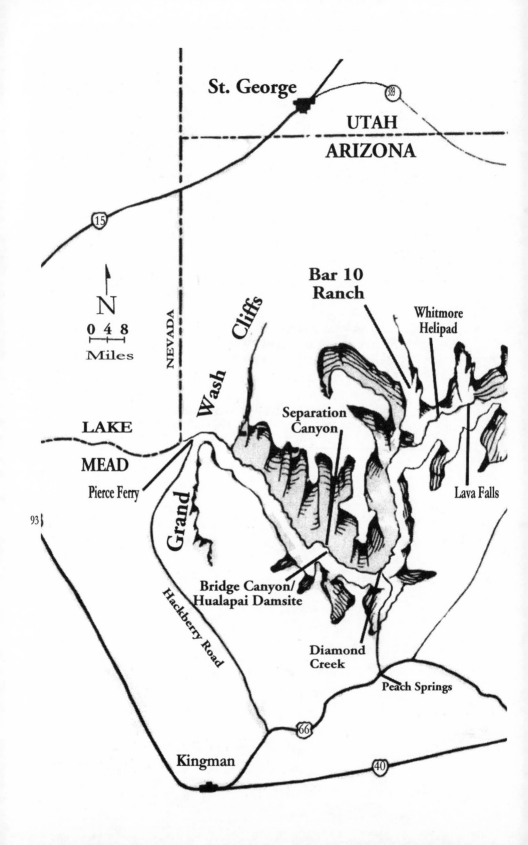

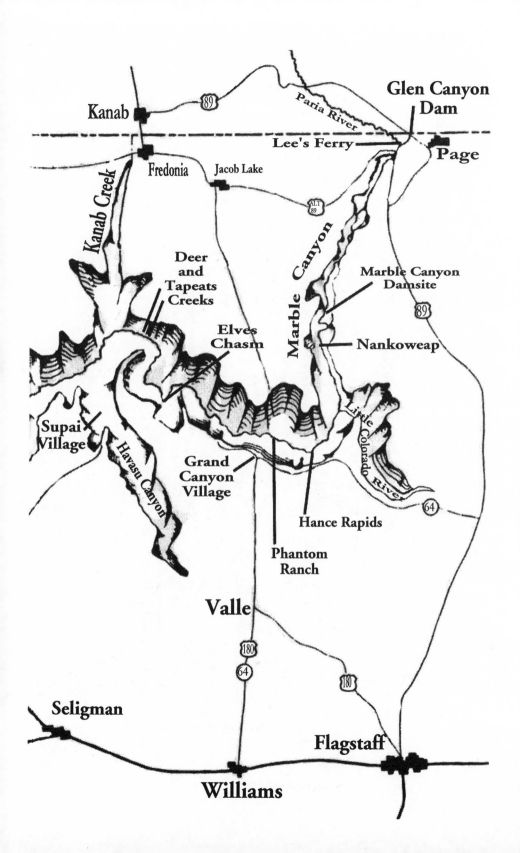

Map A: Boundaries as of 1970

Before the enlargement legislation of 1972-5, GCNP administered the Park itself, the Grand Canyon National Monument proclaimed in 1932, and the Marble Canyon National Monument proclaimed in 1969. Then as now, the Kaibab National Forest bordered the Park (and included parts of the Canyon) on the north and south. Glen Canyon NRA abuts the Canyon upstream of Navajo Bridge, and contains Lees Ferry, river trip launch point. In the far west, Lake Mead NRA included most of the Canyon north of the Colorado and east of the Grand Wash Cliffs.

The Navajo lands had been extended toward the left bank of the Colorado, but remained "undefined" due to water-power and reclamation withdrawals. The Havasupai Reservation itself consisted only of two tiny pieces, one surrounding Supai, the other farther upstream in the usually dry Cataract Canyon. The Hualapai Reservation boundary was set in 1883, starting on the east side as running north "to the Colorado river, thence along said river" to its western boundary.

River running, regardless of other jurisdictions, had come under the authority of the Park because of NPS's undisputed power to regulate traffic through GCNP, and with the cooperation of Glen Canyon and Lake Mead NRA's. Grand Canyon Wilderness I included lands under GCNP administration. The river, at first excluded, ended up as an encumbered Potential Wilderness.

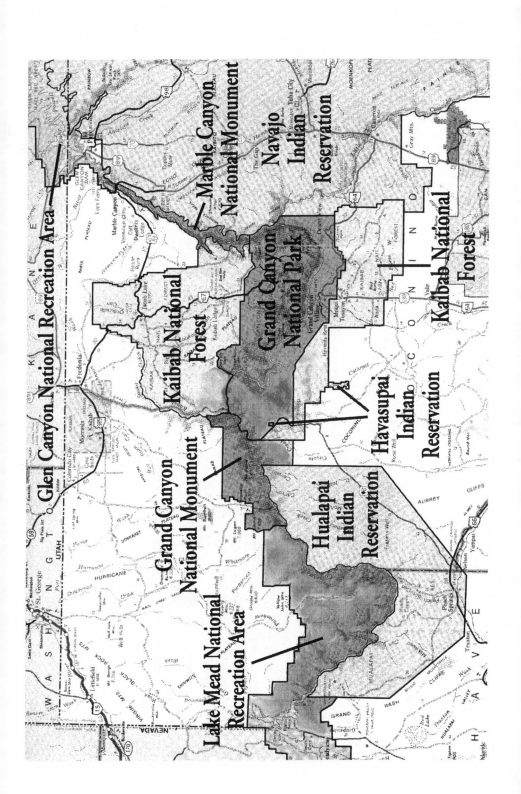

Map B: Boundaries as of 1975

This map shows the boundaries resulting from the passage of Public Law 93-620. Highlighted are the Navajo, the (expanded) Havasupai, and the Hualapai Reservations, GCNP, and that part of Lake Mead National Recreation Area north of GCNP. Public Law 93-620 included within the National Park boundary, without any qualifications, the entire river surface from the Paria junction to the Grand Wash Cliffs. As well as expanding the Havasupai Reservation, P.L. 93-620 zoned 95,000 acres of GNCP as Havasupai Use Lands for traditional uses, indicated by x's on Map C. The boundary between GCNP and Navajo lands in the upper Canyon sits between the rim and the left bank of the Colorado, and has never had to be exactly determined. The river boundary of the Park with Hualapai lands is the left bank such that the entire river surface is within the National Park.

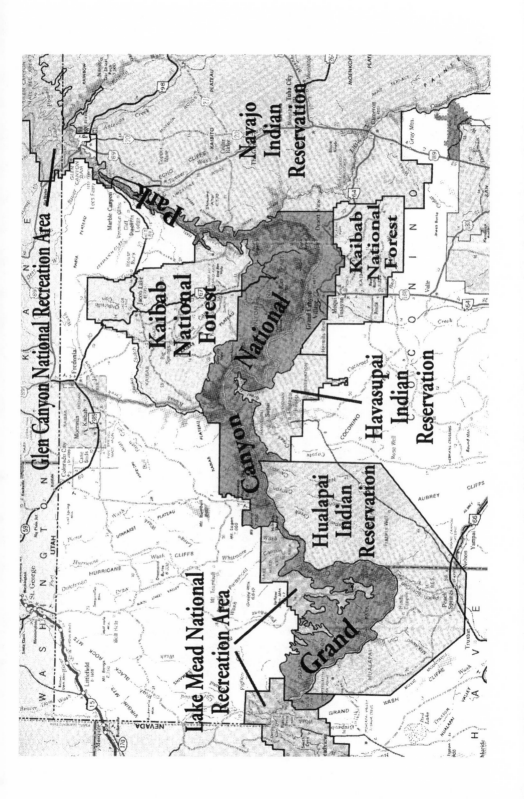

MAP C: 1972 to present: contested areas

This map points out certain areas of dispute and resolution. During the Park "enlargement" fight, there were proposals to delete certain lands from the then-existing GCNM (crosses). The lands were retained after a study.

We proposed that some lands be added to the Park from other federal agencies; these were Kanab, Whitmore, Parashant and Andrus Canyons, and the southern ends of the Shivwits Plateau — all indicated by dashed horizontal lines. The proposal passed the House, but was refused by the Senate. The result was a study which found the lands Park-worthy but better off if left with their current administrators.

Kanab Canyon is now a Wilderness under Forest Service and BLM administration (dashes). The other areas in our proposal plus Toroweap Valley, along with a great swath of land not in the Grand Canyon, were proclaimed in 2000 as the Grand Canyon – Parashant National Monument (bold outline); its administration was left with Lake Mead NRA and the BLM Arizona Strip District.

The Grand Canyon Wilderness II recommendation in 1977 included the Colorado River. Later NPS decisions removed the river downstream from Separation Canyon, bounded by the Lake Mead high-water mark; this was the so-called Lower Gorge. The Havasupai Use Lands (shown by x's) were in Potential Wilderness status. The Grand Canyon portion of Lake Mead National Recreation Area recommended for Wilderness (half as Potential Wilderness) was in our proposed addition to the Park shown by dashes.

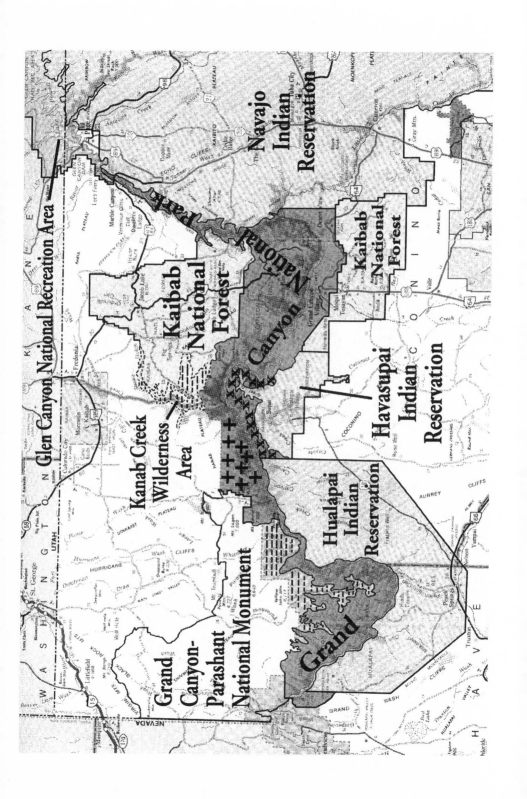

Part E. Sources

Burke papers: in Northern Arizona University Special Collections, collection 30. There are three boxes, containing numbered folders. Items are referred to as Burke (folder) #.

GCPBA: Copies of documents, letters, etc., compiled by GCNP from its files in response to suit by GCPBA; overlap with Randall after 1990. Both of these sets of papers are in the Special Collections of Northern Arizona University library.

Goldwater: Goldwater archives are at Arizona State University, Hayden library, at the Arizona Historical Foundation, fourth floor. The relevant materials are in the 96th Congress, Colorado River 1978-9, and are identified as Goldwater, box number and folder number, e.g. 37, 14. As best I could tell, there is no 1979-80 material.

Ingram files and journal: Currently still in my possession. Documents and letters from various sources collected during active years 1963-81. Specific items without other source identification are from this archive. Also a handwritten journal, 1972-75, and a summary of papers in the Randall and GCPBA records.

NPS archives, Laguna Niguel: Some GCNP files in late '60s-75 were sent to this National Archives and Records Administration (NARA) depository.

Northern Arizona University: Special Collections is located in the Cline Library, Flagstaff.

Randall: Copies of documents, letters, etc., compiled by GCNP from its files in response to a suit filed in 2000 by self-guided river runners; titled "GCNP CRMP Administrative Record - 1996-2000"; good for pre-1990. Documents not overlapping with GCPBA are in NAU Special Collections.

Steiger: NAU, special collection 196. Divided into sections, then files, then items. Referred to as Steiger, section #, file #, item #.

Interviews with:

Marvin Jensen	August 5, 2002
Howard Chapman	June 8, 2002
Tom Heberlein	April 28, 2002
Dee Holladay	June 18, 2003
Stuart Sessions	April 8, 2003

Part F. Acknowledgements

And now, looking back, it is time to give thanks that I am done and that I have had such excellent help along the way. With Tom Martin and Hazel Clark, there has been true collaboration in bringing this book to life. Prodding and supportive over two years, they made the work feel justified; editing and giving it form, they made it real. Through their Vishnu Temple Press, it has reached your hands. That their views about the Canyon align with mine only gives energy to our working together. The same is true as well for Jo Johnson, whose dedication to the issues is only matched by her acuity in understanding.

Though starting from my own records, the book has a greater reach due to the records compiled by NPS for the court cases filed in 2000. I thank the GCPBA and Bob Lippman for providing access to their set of papers, and especially to Linda Jalbert of GCNP for her assistance in gathering together those files from the Randall case that were not in the GCPBA record. The time I spent in NAU's Special Collections and in NARA's Laguna Niguel center was fruitful because of the efforts of their professionals.

Indebted as I am to Fred for his efforts in the 1970s, it is to Maggie Eiseman that my thanks go here, for her willingness to share with us her ideas and her photographs. The cover is a beauty, blending title and photo to go right to the heart of the story. For that, all my gratitude to Ron Short for his contribution of understanding and design sense.

In addition to Tom, Hazel, and Jo, I was blessed by the willingness of several people to read this book, and then offer their suggestions and corrections: Ken Agnew, Kim Crumbo, Jim Hasbargen, Maia Ingram, James Sanders, Geri Stiers and John Weisheit. I hope the final product is good enough to entice them to enjoy it again. A former GCNP official who wishes to remain anonymous offered a critique of the book's tone that I took to heart, softening my intemperance—some, anyway.

I have listed the people I interviewed elsewhere; I know how much I appreciate their willingness to talk by the freshness their material gave the narrative; I wish time, circumstance, and willingness had made it possible for me to add to their number.

Lastly, and ambiguously, I wish to acknowledge—and salute in many cases—the great crowd of people who participated in the adventure this book tries to chronicle. I have not treated them all with kid gloves; and certainly some in my eyes are heroes and some are not. Nevertheless, if they appear here it is because in one way or another they took a place in American public life; they acted as citizens; they contributed to that great clanking, clunky contraption we call American governance. We were all, for better or worse, on the staff of the Grand Canyon.

NOTES

INTRODUCTION
[1]Priestley, J. B., *Midnight on the Desert*, Harper and Brothers, New York and London, 1937

CHAPTER ONE
[1]Document, Aug 8 1966, Director, NPS, "Wilderness Planning Procedures Statement", GCPBA 2
[2]National Park System Organic Act of 1916
[3]Memorandum, Nov 21, 1966, Grand Canyon National Park Chief Park Ranger Theodore R. Thompson to Superintendent; "Colorado River Boating", Randall 1
[4]The narrative for 1967-69 is supported by my notes based on NPS files in the National Archives, Laguna Niguel, CA, center, in GCNP, 75-967, 78826, A90 River Trips. Other material can be found in Randall 2-4
[5]Memo, Nov 9 1967, Southwest Regional Director to NPS Director, Randall 2, p 22
[6]As reported on by himself in Udall, Stewart L., "Shooting the Wild Colorado", *Venture* Magazine, February 1968, pp 62-71.
[7]Interview, Jun 18 2003, Ingram with Dee Holladay
[8]Memo, Jun 6 1967, Chief Park Ranger Von der Lippe to Supt, "Colorado River Sanitation Survey, April 10-12, 1967". Items not otherwise designated are in my files, saved from the period when I was Southwest Representative, or later. Some materials went to my successor as SW Rep; his successor reportedly destroyed all the files when he left the position.
[9]Letter, Apr 23 1968, Ingram to Supt
[10]Memo, Dec 2 1968, Regional Director to Supt.
[11]Report, Jun 10 1968, Ingram, "Development Activities in the Grand Canyon N.P."
[12]Memo, Mar 15 1968, Supt to Regional Director, "Proposed Wilderness Boundaries, GCNP", GCPBA 3
[13]Minutes, Sep 23 1968, B. Barnett, Conservation Chairman, Grand Canyon, Sierra Club, "Special meeting on Grand Canyon Master Plan Proposal"
[14]Document, Oct 29 1968, Grand Canyon Chapter, "Meeting of River and Rim Subcommittee"
[15]Memo, May 27 1969, Ingram to Barnett, "Grand Canyon Master Plan"
also, Document, n. d. (probably mid-1969), "Sierra Club Master Plan Proposal for Grand Canyon National Park"

CHAPTER TWO
[1]Udall, op.cit.
[2]Website address: www.gcex.com/grandcanyon. This is a page that discusses motors as a current issue.
[3]The narrative for 1969-72 is supported by notes I took on NPS files stored in the National Archives center at Laguna Niguel, CA, in Grand Canyon National Park record files L3413 and C3823, River trips, general correspondence.
[4]Almost all of the numbers I have used are from GCNP records in my files; however, the detail of these counts covers their lack of exactness. Worse, NPS changed what they counted over the years.
[5]Letter, Sep 30 1970, Ron Smith to John McComb, Sierra Club Southwest Rep
[6]Letter, Mar 16 1970, Chief Park Ranger Von der Lippe to R.R.Smith
[7]op. cit., Smith to McComb

[8]Letter, Aug 19 1970, Senator Barry Goldwater to "Bob", GCNP Superintendent Robert Lovegren

[9]Column, Aug 13 1970, Pete Cowgill, *Arizona Daily Star*

[10]Letter, Jul 16 1970, G. Staveley to Superintendent, GCNP

[11]Memo, Oct 15 1970, Superintendent Lovegren, in NARA, Laguna Niguel, CA, Grand Canyon National Park record files L3413 and C3823.

[12]Letter, Nov 20 1970, GCNP to comm ops, NARA, Laguna Niguel

[13]Letter, Jul 14 1970, A. Kales to Supt.

[14]Letter, Nov. 10 1970, Superintendent, Grand Canyon National Park, Robert R. Lovegren, to E. B. Danson, Director, Museum of Northern Arizona, Flagstaff AZ

[15]Letter, Feb 9 1971, F. Burke to B. M. Goldwater, Burke 8

[16]Letter, Gaylord Staveley, Canyoneers, Inc., to Senator Barry M. Goldwater, Sep 23 1971

[17]Items in NARA Laguna Niguel, CA, in Grand Canyon National Park record files L3413 and C3823, River trips, general correspondence. Also
Letter, Dec 10 1971, Supt. Lovegren to McComb

[18]Document, Aug 1970, Grand Canyon National Park, Wilderness Study, Preliminary GCPBA 4

[19]Document, Jan 1971, Grand Canyon National Park, Wilderness Study, Preliminary

[20]Document, Jan 1971, GCNP and signed by the Superintendent, A Master Plan for Grand Canyon National Park, Preliminary Working Draft

[21]Letter, Feb. 16, 1971, Superintendent, Grand Canyon National Park, Robert Lovegren, to Frank Masland Jr.

[22]Leaflet, Apr 30 1971, The Wilderness Society, Public Hearing Alert for Grand Canyon

[23]Article, Jun 17 1971, Avery, Ben, "Quiet river idea backed", *Arizona Republic*

[24]Document, Jun 1971, GCNP, Summary of Responses on Wilderness Proposal, GCPBA 10

[25]Document, Aug 1971, GCNP, Final Draft Wilderness Recommendation, GCPBA 11
Document, Nov 1971, GCNP, Wilderness Recommendation, GCPBA 12
Memos, Dec 10 and 21 1971, Southwest Regional Director to GCNP, GCPBA 13 and 14
Letter, Dec 23 1971, Secretary of the Interior to the President, transmitting GCNP Wilderness bill
recommendation and environmental statement, Dec. 23, 1971, GCPBA 15

CHAPTER THREE

[1]The narrative for 1972 is supported by notes I took on NPS files stored in the National Archives center at Laguna Niguel, CA, in Grand Canyon National Park record files L3413 and C3823, River trips, general correspondence. I also kept a journal, which furnished material for the narrative from September 1972 on.

[2]Letter, Aug 4 1972, Acting Supt. P.A. Suazo to comm op list

[3]Letter, Feb 9 1972, Superintendent Robert Lovegren to Phoenix NPS Office, Randall 7
Letter, Feb 24 1972, Superintendent to concessionaires, with Feb 11 1972 Salt Lake City meeting summary, Randall 8

[4]Letter, Apr 26 1972, G. Staveley to Superintendent Lovegren

[5]Note, Apr 4 1972, Dana Burden, Steiger 2,28,138

[6]Boster, Mark A., "Colorado River Trips Within the Grand Canyon National Park and Monument: A Socio-Economic Analysis", June 1972, University of Arizona Technical Report on Hydrology and Water Resources No. 10

[7]Document, n.d. (1972), Burke, Burke 1.

[8]The numbers in the following discussion come from various documents put out by Grand Canyon National Park in the early 1970s, and kept in my files, and from Lovegren Feb 11 1972 letter above

[9]Letter, Dec 10 1971, Lovegren to McComb
[10]Letter, Feb 29 1972, Eiseman to McComb; refers to a February letter to Goldwater and reply
[11]Letter, Mar 31 1972, McComb to Superintendent Lovegren
[12]Letter, Aug 4 1972, op. cit., Suazo to comm op list
[13]Letters: Jul 7 1972, Eiseman to E. Danson
Jul 31 1972, Goldwater to Eiseman
Aug 7 1972, Goldwater to Secretary of the Interior
[14]Letter, Aug 16 1972, Eiseman to Secretary of the Interior et al.
[15]Letter, Sep 1 1972, Ingram to Superintendent M. Stitt
[16]Letter, Aug 8 1972, J. L. Currey to "Dear River Runner"
[17]Memo, Sep 5 1972, F. Eiseman
[18]Letter, Sep 11 1972, Superintendent, GCNP, to each concessionaire
[19]Letter, Sep 21 1972, Gaylord Staveley to the Secretary of the Interior
[20]Minutes, Oct 16 1972, Colorado River Outfitters Association, Burke 17
[21]Report Sep 27 1972, K.M.Boyer and M.H.Merson, "Shigella Epidemic, Grand Canyon National Park, Arizona", Center for Disease Control.
[22]Proposal, Sep 1972, "The Cyclic Patterns of Bacteriology and Water Chemistry Fluctuations in the Grand Canyon", Dept. of Hydrology and Water Resources, Univ. of Arizona to GCNHA
[23]Communication, Sep 1972, Eiseman to Stitt, GCNP 3923, NARA-Laguna Niguel
[24]Letter, Sep 29 1972, J.McComb to Superintendent M. Stitt
[25]Document, Sep 1972, NPS, "Wilderness Recommendation, Grand Canyon National Park Complex", signed by the Director, G. B. Hartzog
accompanied by transmittal letter, Sep 14 1972, Secretary of the Interior to the President, draft of "A BILL to designate certain lands...as wilderness", and
"Revised Draft Environmental Statement, Proposed Wilderness Classification Grand Canyon Complex, Arizona". Eiseman, in his Oct 16 1972 background paper says the recommendation was sent to Congress on Sep 21.
[26]Letter, Oct 3 1972, Ingram to Supt.
[27]In Laguna Niguel archives; see above note 1
[28]Minutes, Oct 16 1972, Colorado River Outfitters Association, Burke 17
[29]Letter, Oct 26 1972, CROA to GCNP River Manager R. Yearout
[30]Memo, Oct 9 1972, F Eiseman
Letter, Oct 13 1972, Acting Asst. Sec. of the Interior C. Bohlen to F. Eiseman
Memo, Oct 16 1972, F. Eiseman.
Memo, Oct 22 1972, F. Eiseman, "Proposal for Interim Quota" on Colorado River
[31]Letter, Oct 23 1972, Goldwater to G.H. Driggs, Burke 8
[32]Letter, Oct 19 1972, P.A.Suazo, for the Superintendent, to 21 concessionaires
earlier letter was dated Aug 4 1972.
[33]Article, Oct 10, 1972, L.K.Altman, "Epidemic of Dysentery Affected Excursions on Colorado Rapids", *The New York Times*
[34]Letters, Oct 27 1972, Eiseman: to "Friends of the Colorado River", and to Ruch
Letter, Nov 7 1972, Senator Goldwater to "Nat Reid, Bureau of Outdoor Recreation"
Letter, Nov 10 1972, same, but now "Nat Reed"
Letter, Nov 11 1972, Eiseman to Steiger, Steiger 3, 70, 439
[35]Memo, Nov 2 1972, J. McComb to Grand Canyon Chapter
Document, Nov 6 1972, J. McComb and J. Ingram, "Not Fooled Again?! No!"
[36]Letter, Nov 6 1972, Eiseman to GCNP Superintendent

Document, Nov 1972, Sierra Club Southwest Office, "Comments on Revised Environmental   Statement, Proposed Wilderness Classification, Grand Canyon Complex"
[37]Much of the material for the next several months comes from my personal journal, and from a summary prepared from Superintendent Stitt's phone logs, Randall 4, pp 11-18
[38]Document, Nov 2 1972, GCNP Ecological Studies Lab, "Draft Research Proposal, Colorado River and Its Environs, GCNP"
[39]various documents: Nov 6 1972, D. R. Abbott, Coconino County Sanitarian, "Guidelines for Good Sanitary Practices while on the Colorado River"
Letter and enclosures, Nov 6 1972, GCNP Superintendent to Colorado River Advisory Committee
[40]Documents, Nov 6 1972 and Nov/Dec 1972, "Guidelines on Food Handling, Food Service, and Related Sanitary Practices on the Colorado River"
[41]Letter, Nov 13 1972, Carol Burke to Senator Goldwater, Burke 9
[42]Statement, Dec 4 1972, Grand Canyon Expeditions, Steiger 3, 116, 987
[43]Document, Nov 14 1972, NPS D.C. office, Briefing on Grand Canyon backcountry, Randall 14, pp 3-6
[44]Letter, Nov 24 1972, F. Burke to Steiger, Steiger 3, 116, 987
[45]Letter, Nov 29 1972, ARTA to GCNP River Manager Yearout, Randall 19, pp 58-60
[46]Letter, Nov 21 1972. Ass't. Sec Reed to me et al. Also see Randall 19
[47]Letter, Nov 20 1972, F Burke to Superintendent Stitt, Burke 12
[48]Letter, Nov 27 1972, Senator Goldwater to Regional Director Chapman, in Laguna Niguel branch of National Archives, GCNP, C3823, River Running General
[49]Letter, Nov 28 1972, F Burke to Stitt, Steiger 3, 70, 439
[50]Note, Nov 21 1972, "To Helen and the girls: Here are five more letters on Grand Canyon; please use the correct tape." Randall 19, p. 37

CHAPTER FOUR

[1]Letter, Dec 4 1972, R. G. Brown, of Strong, Poelman and Fox, Salt Lake City, to Secretary Morton
Other comm op statements:
Letters, Martin Litton, Grand Canyon Dories:
Nov 14 1972, to GCNP River Manager, Randall 19, pp 48-51
Nov 17 1972, to Asst. Sec. Reed, Randall 19, pp 43-47
Letter, Nov 21 1972, Grand Canyon Expeditions to Ruch, Randall 19, pp 15-34
Letter, Nov 29 1972, ARTA, to GCNP River Manager, Randall 19, pp 58-60
Statement, Dec 4 1972 Grand Canyon Expeditions, Steiger 3, 116, 987
Statement, Dec 26 1972, Tour West, Steiger 3, 119, 1013
[2]News Release, Dec 6 1972, NPS Western Region, San Francisco, "New Management Plan to Protect Colorado River"
Document, Dec 18 1972 "River Use Plan, Grand Canyon National Park Complex", also "Draft, Back-country Use and Operations Plan, Colorado River Management Zone"
[3]Article, Dec 5 1973, in *Arizona Republic* by Ben Avery, "U.S. will restrict river canyon trips"
[4]As in the previous chapter, I have depended in the narrative on my journal, Superintendent Stitt's phone log, and material archived in NARA previously footnoted.
[5]Document, Dec 11 1972, "1973 Commercial Allotments", provided by GCNP
[6]There are two identical documents, Dec 11 1972, GCNP, one called the "River Use Plan GCNP Complex" GCPBA 24, the other "Draft, Chapter III, Back-country Use and Operations Plan, Colorado River Management Zone"
[7]Letter, Jan 2 1973, Chapman to McComb

[8]Letter, Dec 18 1972, Senator Frank Moss to Secretary Morton, Burke 12

[9]Memo, Dec 20 1972, Ingram/McComb to allies, "The New Year May Really Be a Happy One!"

[10]Letters, Dec 1972 - Jan 1973, Diamond to Goldwater, Steiger 3, 119, 1018

[11]Letter, Jan 5 1973, Goldwater to Eiseman

[12]Journal, Dec 27 1972, Stitt-Ingram

Letter, Jan 5 1973, Ruch to Eiseman

[13]Document, Feb 13 1973, GCNP, Environmental Impact Statement, draft

[14]Document, Feb 13 1973, Grand Canyon National Park, Draft Environmental Impact Statement "Establishment of Visitor Use Limits on the Colorado River", Randall 24.

[15]Letters, Jan-Oct 1973, public to Steiger w/ form replies, approx. 300, Steiger 3, 119, 1013 -1018

Associated Press article, Jan 30 1973, on Goldwater meeting, Steiger 3, 116, 987

Letter, Mar 26 1973, GCNP, form reply, NARA Laguna Niguel, C3823

[16]Letter, Jan 1973, W. Diamond, Sanderson River Expeditions, to Interior et al.

Letter, Jan 15 1973, G. Staveley, Canyoneers, to Supt, GCNP, et al.

[17]Journal, conversation, Jan 19 1973, Ingram-Gum

and conversation, Jan 22 1973, Ingram-Brickler

[18]Journal, conversation, Jan 26 1973, Ingram-T.Bracey

and conversation, Jan 27 1973, Ingram-Eiseman on Ruch-Eiseman call

[19]Communication, Jan 30 1973, J. Currey to J. Ruch, Randall, Supt phone log

[20]Letter, Feb 20 1973, Reed to J. Currey, Burke 12

[21]Letter, Mar 2 1973, Asst. Sec. Reed to R.G. Brown

Document, Mar 1973, "Colorado River-Grand Canyon", NPS, Washington, D.C.

[22]Letter, Apr 4 1973, Burke to Goldwater, Burke 8

[23]Letter, Apr 6 1973, Burke to Juel Rodack, Burke 12

[24]Letter, Apr 11 1973,Steiger to Burke, Burke 8

[25]Letters, Burke to various, Burke 11 and 12

[26]Letter, Feb 20 1973, Eiseman to Reg. Dir. et al., Randall 38, p. 114

Letter, Mar 7 1973, Eiseman to Ingram

[27]Letter, Apr 3 1973, Eiseman to Reed, Randall, 38, p. 101

[28]Letter, Mar 30 1973, Goldwater to Eiseman

[29]Letter, Mar 8 1973, Goldwater to McComb

[30]Joint Resolution, Mar 8 1973, 40th Legislature of Utah

[31]Letters: Mar 26 1973, Hatch to Morton, Randall 39, pp 87-8

Apr 2 1973, Rep. McKay to Interior, Randall 39, p. 73

[32]Letter, Apr 19 1973, Regional Office to Senator Bible, draft, Laguna Niguel, C3823

[33]Stitt phone log for Apr 1973

Memo, Apr 27 1972, Office of Solicitor to Director, "Western River Expeditions et al. V. Secretary of the Interior et al. Randall 29, p. 14.

[34]Complaint, Civil No. C-125-73, in United States District Court for the District of Utah

[35]Memo, May 18 1973, Solicitor's Office, Interior, to the Dept of Justice, Randall 29

[36]Letters in Steiger 3, 119, 1014-7. Hatch and Currey appeals in my files

[37]Order of Dismissal, Civil # C-125-73; signed June 4, filed June 14 1973; also Jun 9 1973 *Arizona Republic*

[38]Articles, Jul 28 1973, *Arizona Daily Star*, "River Flow in Canyon to be Cut"

Aug 2 1973, *Deseret News*, "Court dismisses river case"

Aug 21 1974, *Arizona Republic*, "Firms lose appeal in river flow

[39]Statement, Senator F. Moss (D-Utah), Jul 20 1973 *Congressional Record*, Vol 119.

[40]Letter, Apr 30 1975, K. Sleight to Ingram
[41]Letters, Jul-Aug 1973, Burke 11 -12
[42]Letter, Oct 30 1973, U.S. Representative Rhodes to Morton; "Dear Rog"
[43]Journal, Nov 1 1973, R. Smith to Ingram
[44]Letters, Steiger 3, 119, 1015-1017
[45]Letters, Jun 13, Jun 20, Aug 24, Aug 30 1973, NPS Western Region to list
[46]Journal, Aug 31 1973
Letter, Aug 29 1973, Reed to Burke, Randall 39, p. 5
[47]Memos, Randall 34:
Sep 5 1973, Secretary to NPS Director
Sep 6 1973, R. Curry, Special Assistant, to Reed
Sep 7 1973, Asst. Sec. office to Solicitor
[48]Memo and letter draft, Sep 7 and Sep 10 1973, NPS to Asst. Sec., Randall 35
[49]Oct 1 1973, Asst. Sec. to Chapman, Randall 34, p. 1
[50]Letter, Sep 20 1970, Steiger to Morton
Letters, Sep and Oct 1973, Steiger to inquirers, Box 119, folder 1016
[51]Letter, Oct 30 1973, R. Brown to GCNP River Manager
[52]Letter, Sep 10 1973, Fannin to Morton, Randall 38, pp 29-30
Letter, Oct 12 1973, Tunney to Morton, Randall 39, p. 183
[53]journal, Dec 5 1973
Letters, Sep-Oct 1973, Eiseman-Curry, Randall 39 passim
[54]Letter, Sep 26 1973, Goldwater to Eiseman
Letter, Sep 18 1973, Eiseman to Goldwater
[55]Letter, Sep 12 1973, Supt. to comm op list
[56]Letter, Sep 25 1973, Acting Regional Director, Western Region to list
[57]Document, Oct 18 1973, R. R. Yearout, "River Management Briefing Statement"
[58]News Release, Oct 31 1973, Western Region, NPS, "MANDATORY PHASEOUT OF
MOTOR RAFTS ON COLORADO RIVER TRIPS DEFERRED"
[59]Document, May 1973, GCNP, "Natural Resources Project Statement" for Colorado River
Ecological Studies
[60]Documents, Jul 30 and Sep 18 1973, Chapman-Stitt, Laguna Niguel GCNP C3823
[61]Journal, Dec 1973
Letter, recd. May 25 1973, GCNP to McComb et al.
[62]Letter, Nov (not clear) 1973, J.C.Whitaker, Acting Secretary of the Interior, to Goldwater

CHAPTER FIVE
[1]Memo, Feb 26 1973, Superintendent to Regional Director, "Legal Data on Ownership of
the Colorado River", GCPBA 25

CHAPTER SIX
[1]Letter, Mar 5 1973, Ingram to Rep. Udall
[2]Newspaper article, Mar 17 1973, in *National Observer*, "Should Colorado River Rafting
Boom Be Cooled?"
Magazine article, Jun 18 1973, in *Newsweek*, "Troubled Waters"
[3]Letter, Apr 5 1973, Senator F. "Ted" Moss to J. Viavant ("Dear June")
[4]Letter, Apr 18 1973, Ingram to George Wendt, OARS, Inc.
[5]Documents, Sep 4 1973, ARTA officials for GCRO, "Proposal on Colorado River
Management" and "Toward a New Management Plan for River Adventure in the Grand
Canyon"

[6]See Boster, op. cit., and Hall, T and Shelby, B., 1998 Colorado River Boater Study, prepared for GCNP and Grand Canyon Association
[7]Letter, Oct 10 1973, Dep. Supt. B. W. Shaw to B. Elliott of ARTA
[8]Letter, Sep 12 1973, American River Conservation Council, Comments on GCRO
[9]Letter, Sep 13 1973, G. H. Meral, Staff Scientist, Environmental Defense Fund, to Superintendent
[10]Letters, D. A. Kay to McComb, Sep 20 and Oct 16 1973
[11]Letter, Eiseman to Goldwater, Oct 7 1973
[12]Letter, Sep 9 1973, F. Eiseman to Superintendent
[13]Letters, Oct 2 1973, Kay to Eiseman,
Oct 9 1973, Eiseman to Kay
Oct 20 1973, Eiseman to Kay
[14]Document, n.d. (Sep 1973), n.a. (GCNP), "Report on River Running Matters"
[15]Letter, Oct 9 1973, Eiseman to Yearout
[16]Letter, Oct 15 1973, Ingram to Morton
[17]Letters: Nov 13 1973, Supt., Dinosaur National Monument, to McComb
Dec 3 1973, McComb to Supt., DNM
Memo, Nov 5 1973, Solicitor to NPS Director, Randall 39, p 176
[18]Letters, Dec 8 1973, Eiseman to Rhodes
Dec 18 1973, Rhodes to Morton, enclosing Oct 30 1973 to Morton
Jan 5 1974, Eiseman to McComb
[19]Letters, Dec 8 1973, Eiseman to R. Curry
Dec 17 1973, Stitt to Eiseman
Dec 20 1973, Eiseman to Stitt
[20]Document, Nov 27 1973, GCNP, Injuries: Commercial River Trips; Resulting in Helicopter Evacuation, Randall 40, p. 4
[21]Memos: Nov 16 1973, Asst. Sec. to NPS Director; Dec 4 1973, NPS to Asst. Sec.; Randall 40
[22]Document, Sep 24 1973, GCNP, List of Research Topics, draft, Randall 39, pp 200-1
[23]Email, Jun 23 1999, GCROA to "Richard", GCPBA 625, pp 55-59
[24]Documents, Autumn 1994, GCNP, Colorado River 1994 Use Statistics

CHAPTER SEVEN
[1]Bruce Shaw, in Chapter 3
[2]Insertion, Jul 20 1973, *Congressional Record*, vol. 119, no. 115
[3]Complaint, Apr 18 1973, Western River Expeditions et al. vs. Rogers C. B. Morton et al., C-125-73 in U.S. District Court for Utah
[4]Letter, Feb 13 1974, R.G. Brown to CROA members
[5]Letter, Feb 21 1974, Burke to Staveley, Burke 9
Letter, Mar 7 1974, Burke to Rep. Rhodes, Burke 11
Letter, Mar 8 1974, Burke to Goldwater, Burke 9
[6]Memo, Feb 26 1974, Dep. Supt. Shaw to Regional Director, "River Use Management and Research Programs"
[7]Proposed rule, Apr 1 1974, *Federal Register*, vol. 39, no. 63, NPS, "Proposed Definition of Commercial Trips"
[8]Chapter 6
[9]Letter, Apr 26 1974, Canyoneers Inc to Senator Jackson

[10]Draft document, Mar-May 1974, R. Yearout, GCNP, "Oars and/or motors on the Colorado River in Marble and Grand Canyons" (n. b. The title errs. Not a separate canyon, Marble is part of one of the inner gorges of, the Grand Canyon.)

[11]Letter, Apr 2 1974, NPS Director to Steiger, Randall 45

[12]Memo, May 16 1974, NPS D.C. Meeting w/ Steiger, Randall 47, p. 210

[13]Letter, May 30 1974, PROA atty. to Rep. Owens, Randall 47, p. 10

[14]Memo, May 23 1974, NPS D.C. (meeting of J. Brown, R. Curry, R. Marks, N. Guse, R. Tousley) to Regional Director, "Colorado River - Motor Use"

[15]Memo, Jun 6 1974, B. Shaw to Regional Director, "River Use Management"

[16]Letter, May 28 1974, Burke to Superintendent, Regional Director, NPS Director Newspaper letter, Jun 1 1974, G. Staveley, "River runners object to arbitrary decisions"

[17]Letter, Jun 1974, Western River Expeditions to "Interested River Runner", encl. Article, May 1974, *True*, P. Czura "Running the River: Conflict on the Colorado"

[18]Memo, Jun 24 1974, Regional Director to File, "Colorado River Meeting— Western/Rocky Mountain Regions"

[19]Memo, Jun 19 1974, Shaw to Regional Director, "Colorado River Management, GRCA"

[20]Memo, Jun 21 1974, Regional Director to Assoc. Dir. Park System Management

[21]Statement, Jul 1974, "Colorado River Management"

[22]Letter, July 9 1974, NPS in D.C. to comm ops
Letter, Aug 2 1974, Superintendent to Burke. Both in Burke 12

[23]Memo, Jul 12 1974, Asst. Dir. Marks et al. to Director, "NPS policy on float trips", Randall 46

[24]Letter, Aug 5 1974, R.G. Brown to PROA members, Burke 11

[25]Memo, Aug 28 1974, Director to all Regions, "River Running Policy Management"

[26]Letter, Sep 16 1974, NPS Director to Senator Goldwater

[27]Letters:
Sep 1974, NPS to various, Randall 49
Oct 2 1974, G.C. Expeditions to Senator Moss, Randall 48, p 154
Oct 8 1974, NPS D.C. to Masland, Randall 48, p 168
Oct 16 1974, NPS D.C. to citizen, Randall 48, p 165
Nov 29 1974, NPS to citizen, Randall 49, p 82 (this item is filed out of order p. 2 only)

[28]Minutes, Sep 27 1974, WRAC

[29]Article and Column, Oct 20 1974, Pete Cowgill, p 10-B, *Arizona Daily Star*, "People Problems Beset Colorado River Users"

CHAPTER EIGHT

[1]See Chapter 3.

[2]Schedule and Abstracts, Sep 1 1973, Grand Canyon Research Symposium
Also, Investigators Annual Reports to the Superintendent, GCNP, are referred to throughout the period covered by this chapter.
I have had to limit the references in this chapter, leaving out the names and contributions of many, many people who contributed to the research effort. It deserves a full history, placing the 1970s' program in its context as a scientific and an NPS effort.

[3]Letter and enclosures, Aug 16 1973, B. M. Kilgore, Assoc. Reg. Dir., Professional Services, Western Region, NPS, to S. K. Brickler, Dept. of Watershed Mgt., Univ. of Arizona

[4]Letter, Dec 27 1973, B.M. Kilgore, Assoc. Reg. Dir., Professional Services, Western Region, NPS, to Chm., Sociology Dept, Univ. of Arizona.

[5]Conversation, Apr 28-9 2002, Ingram with Thomas Heberlein, Lodi WI

[6]Report, Feb 1975, Human Ecology Research Services, "Progress Report II, River Contact Study"

[7]Article, Jul-Aug 1974, R. Dolan, A. Howard, A. Gallenson, "Man's Impact on the Colorado River in the Grand Canyon", *American Scientist*, vol. 62, p 392-401

[8]Document, May 1974, GCNP, "Partial List of Current Research Projects on the Colorado River"

[9]Schedule and Abstracts, Aug 29 1974, MNA, "Grand Canyon Research Symposium"

[10]Letter, Apr 4 1975, Ingram to Shelby

[11]Article, Jan 25 1975, Arizona Republic, "Impact of river running to be studied"

[12]Memo, Apr 1 1975, R. Johnson to Supt.

[13]Letter, Aug 8 1975, Lew Eaton, Western Regional Parks Advisory Comm., to Supt GCNP, Laguna Niguel archives, GCNP, L3413

[14]Schedule and Abstracts, Oct 3 1975, Grand Canyon Research Symposium. Some of the material comes from notes I made at the meeting.

[15]Paper, n.d., J. M. Nielsen, B. Shelby, J. E. Haas, "Sociological Carrying Capacity and the Last Settler Syndrome", GCNP Colorado River Research Series # 8

[16]Abstract, op. cit.,item 4

[17]Document, Dec 1975, Shelby, Bo, "Social-Psychological Effects of Motorized Travel in Wild Areas: The Case of River Trips in the Grand Canyon".

[18]Progress Report, 1974, Thompson, D.N., A. J. Rogers Jr., F. Y. Borden, C. R. Technical Report 18, GCNP Colorado River Research Series # 48

[19]idem., pp 29-30

[20]Dedication, September 1977, R. R. Johnson, in "Synthesis and Management Implications of he Colorado River Research Program", CRRP #17, GCNP CRR Series contrib. 47

[21]Ingram notes, Oct 2 1975

CHAPTER NINE

[1]For instance, the personal records of Eiseman and Munroe on their very important activities are no longer extant. One group I knew of only later was the American Canoe Association in Denver.

[2]Letter, Mar 31 1974, American Canoe Association to GCNP, Randall 48, pp 207-8

[3]Article, Jan 24 1974, *Salt Lake Tribune*, "Senate Vote Delays Rivers Resolution"

[4]Letters, Nov and Dec 1973 and Jan 1974, Joe Munroe to GCNP et al., Randall 47, pp186-200

Randall 47 contains several pro-self-guided letters.

[5] NPS document, n.d., n.a., Randall 47, p 61

[6]Memorandum, May 23 1974, Associate Director, Park System Management to Regional Director, Western Region, "Colorado River - Motor Use"

[7]Document, May 1974, GCNP, "Private River Permits"

[8]ibid

[9]Internet address, Mar 13 2002: www.nps.gov/grca/backcountry. Click on "permit procedures", and see esp. item 5 "How to apply".

[10]Interview, Jun 18 2003

[11]Letter, May 13 1974, Eiseman to McComb and Ingram

[12]Letter, May 8 1974, Senator Tunney to NPS Director, Randall 47, p 51

[13]Letter, with enclosures, Aug 13 1974, Amer. Canoe Assoc., Denver Colorado, to River Mgr. R. Yearout, Randall 49, pp 123-5. ACA uses "paddling" and "paddlers" in its documents.

[14]Letters, Aug 14 1974, Amer. Canoe Assoc. to Sen. Dominick and Rep. Brotzman, Randall 49 p 119 and 122

[15]Document, Nov 1974, G. O. Grimm and R. A. Wyman, "Public Rights to Rivers"

[16]Letter, Oct 16 1974, Dept. Interior to citizen, Randall 48, pp 165-6

[17]Letter, Dec 6 1974, R. Saltonstall to Asst. Sec. Reed, Randall 48, pp 142-5

[18]Letter, Jan 13 1975, D.D. Dominick to Asst. Sec. Reed

Document, undated (early 1975), "Petition seeks to resolve National Park Dilemma", offered by J. Munroe, R. Saltonstall Jr, F. Eiseman

[19]Letter, Feb 13 1975, GCNP Supt. to F. Eiseman

[20]Letter, Mar 5 1976, NPS to citizen, Randall 49, p 81

[21]Letters, Feb 13 1975, Ingram to Eiseman

Feb 17 1975, Eiseman to Ingram

[22]Letter Mar 31 1975, Rep. T. Wirth (D-Colorado) to GCNP, Laguna Niguel GCNP archives, L3413

[23]Letters, Mar 20 1975, Eiseman to friends, enclosing Munroe materials

Mar 28 1975, Eiseman to suppliers, manufacturers, and sellers of camping and boating equipment

Mar 18 1975, Goldwater to Eiseman

Mar 18 1975, NPS Director to Eiseman

Mar 25 1975, Environmental Defense Fund to Eiseman

Other Eiseman items in Randall 49, pp 1-36

[24]Letters: Apr 28 1975, NPS Director to F.E. Masland

May 14 1975, Interior to citizen, Randall 48, pp 109-110

Various dates, Randall 48

Jul 16 1975, NPS D.C. to G. Staveley

[25]Letters in Randall 48 and 49

[26]Letter, Apr 10 1975, Eiseman to Ingram

[27]Letter, Jun 3 1975, Rep. Harkin and Wirth to colleagues

H. Con. Res. 319 (Jun 19 1975) and 331 (Jul 8 1975), sponsored by Wirth et al.

Bill Status, Oct 3 1975, on H.Con.Res.331

[28]Letter, Apr 19 1975, Eiseman to Superintendent

[29]Letter, Sep 18 1975, McComb to Superintendent

[30]News Release, Oct 20 1975, GCNP (Yearout), "Controversial no repeat provision dropped..."

[31]Letters, Apr 22 1975, Ingram to Stitt

n.d., Stitt to Ingram

[32]Letter, Mar 4 1975, Stitt to Ingram

[33]Memo, Jul 11 1975, GCNP Superintendent to Regional Director, "River Management Plan Development", Randall 50

[34]Report, Oct 14 1975, Ingram to AWWW, Inc., Friends of the Earth, Southern Arizona Hiking Club, "Colorado River Use, Grand Canyon"

[35]Ingram personal notes, Sep 29 - Oct 2 1975

[36]Document, Oct 2 1975, GCNP, "Tentative River Management Plan Development Schedule"

[37]Letters, Oct 14 1975, Ingram to Elliott

Oct 23 1975, Elliott to Ingram

[38]Memo, Nov 4 1975, NPS D.C.: Resource Mgt. and Visitor Services to Div. of Legislation, "Report on H. Con. Res. 294" (and 319, 331, S. Con. 56), Randall 51

[39]Letter, Feb 11 1977, NPS to Eiseman, Randall 49, p 32

CHAPTER TEN

[1]Preliminary Wilderness Study, Grand Canyon National Park, August 1970

Preliminary Wilderness Study, Grand Canyon National Park, January 1971

[2]Leaflet, Apr 30 1971, The Wilderness Society, Public Hearing Alert for Grand Canyon
[3]Wilderness Recommendation, Sep 1972, NPS
Transmittal Letter and EIS, Sep 14 1972, Secretary of the Interior to the President
[4]Wilderness Recommendation, p. 15
[5] Document, Nov 1972, Sierra Club Southwest Office, "Comments on Revised
Environmental Statement, Proposed Wilderness Classification, Grand Canyon Complex"
[6]*Congressional Record* Statement, Mar 20 1973, Senator Goldwater re S.1296
[7]Memo, May 2 1973, NPS (no author), "Important Issues concerning Wilderness in
GCNP"; GCPBA 26
[8]Letter, Jun 20 1973, Asst. Sec. of the Interior J. W. Kyl to Senator Jackson, Chairman, the
Senate Interior and Insular Affairs Committee
[9]Final EIS, Aug 22 1973, Dec 7 1973, Jan 24 1974, Proposed Wilderness Classification,
GCNP; GCPBA 28, 29, and 31
 also Memo, Feb 25 1974, Superintendent to Assoc. Dir. Legislation, D.C.; "Statement of
Important Issues", GCPBA 32
[10]Conference Report on S. 1296, Dec 17 1974, *Congressional Record*, pp H12135-6
[11]Memo, Jun 20 1975, Assoc. Dir. Legislation to Reg. Dir., "Grand Canyon Wilderness -
Activation Memorandum"; GCPBA 41
[12]Document, Nov 1973, NPS, LMNRA, "Wilderness Study"
[13]Draft EIS, Jan 22 1974, NPS Denver Service Center, "Proposed Wilderness Areas
LMNRA, Nevada and Arizona"
[14]Document, undated, but Feb/Mar 1974, Arizona Audubon Council, Saguaro Ecology
Club, Nevada Open Spaces Council, Friends, of the Earth, Sierra Club Toiyabe Chapter,
Lahontan Audubon Society, Wilderness Society, "Wilderness Hearing Alert, LMNRA"
[15]Statement, Mar 28 1974, Ingram and for S.A.H.C., "LMNRA Wilderness Proposal"
[16]Memorandum, Jul 22 1975, NPS DSC to Western Regional Director, "Roles for
Wilderness Studies"
[17]Memorandum, Aug 27 1975, Chapman to R. Curry, NPS-Legislation
[18]Memorandum, Feb 26 1975, Assoc. Solicitor, Conservation and Wildlife to NPS Director,
"Applicability of Wilderness Act provisions"
[19]Notice of Intent, Aug 1 1975, NPS
Federal Register Notice, Aug 21 1975, p. 36601, "Grand Canyon National Park Wilderness
Study"
News Release, Aug 25 1975, GCNP, "Grand Canyon Announces Wilderness Workshops"
[20]Leaflet, Aug 26 1975, Sierra Club Southwest Office, "Grand Canyon Wilderness
Workshop Alert"
[21]Document, undated, GCNP, reports on workshops
[22]Letter, Sep 4 1975, H.B. Stricklin to Supt GCNP
[23] Memo, Sep 30 1975, NPS Denver Service Center to GCNP Supt., "Studies/Issues which
will affect wilderness proposals for LMNRA and GCNP", GCPBA 51
[24]Memorandum, Oct 30 1975, T. Carlstrom to Asst. Mgr., Pacific NW/Western Team,
DSC, "Trip Report, Grand Canyon Wilderness Agreements, October 18-24"
[25]Memorandum, Nov 18 1975, GCNP Superintendent to Asst. Mgr., Pacific NW/Western
Team, DSC, "Issues Affecting Wilderness Proposals for Grand Canyon"
[26]Documents, n.d., n.a., "Draft Preliminary Proposal, Grand Canyon Wilderness", GCPBA
35 and
Jan 16 1976, Carlstrom DSC, Draft Preliminary Proposal, Grand Canyon Wilderness",
GCPBA 59

[27]Report, Jan 15 1976, T. Carlstrom to DSC, "Trip Report 1/7-9/76 w/ Regional Staff, GCPBA 58

[28]Memorandum, Feb 6 1976, Chief, Wilderness Branch, D.C. NPS to Assoc. Dir. Legislation, "Wilderness briefings for Director and Depy. Asst. Sec. Concerning GCNP", GCPBA 63

[29]Memorandum, Jan 13 1976, D.C. NPS to Western Region, GCPBA 62, pp 3-4

[30]Memorandum, Mar 3 1976, Regional Solicitor to Western Regional Director, "GC Wilderness Study - Lands Formerly within Lake Mead NRA", GCPBA 66

[31]Draft EIS, Apr 14 1976, GCNP, Preliminary Wilderness Proposal, GCPBA 69

[32]Revision to Preliminary Proposal, Apr 19 1976, DSC to Region, GCPBA 70

[33]Preliminary Wilderness Proposal, Jul 1976, GCNP

[34]Memorandum, May 21 1976, Director NPS to Asst. Sec., "Preliminary Wilderness Proposal, GCNP", GCPBA 71

[35]News Release, Jul 23 1976, GCNP, "Grand Canyon National Park Wilderness Hearings Announced"

[36]Leaflet, Aug 6 1976, J. McComb, "Grand Canyon Wilderness Hearing Alert"

[37]Statement, Aug 20 1976, J. Ingram, Hearings on GCNP Wilderness, for AWWW, Inc., Friends of the Earth, Southern Arizona Hiking Club

[38]Transcripts of hearings, Aug 1976, GCPBA 82, p 17 ff.
Document, n.d. (Oct 1976), n.a. (GCNP), "Tabulation of Responses", GCPBA 88
Documents, n.d. (early Oct 1976), Jon Haman, "So-far synopsis of responses to the Wilderness
Proposal and DES for Grand Canyon", GCPBA 82 pp 15-16
Note: There is no way to reconcile all this information to a clean tabulation. I have tried to get to
the essence of the numbers.

[39]From my notes taken at the hearings.

[40]Draft Comments, Aug 1976, Bureau of Reclamation, GCPBA 83; and see GCPBA 82 p 16.

[41]Letter, Aug 28 1976, J. C. Preston to NPS Director, Hearing Officer Summary, GCBPA 82 pp 2-13

[42]Letters, Aug 1976 on, Public Response to Wilderness Proposal, GCPBA 85, 86, 87

[43]Memorandum, Oct 15 1976, Chapman to Everhardt, GCPBA 92
Memorandum, Nov 18 1976, Office of Legislation to Director, GCPBA 94

[44]The narrative through December 1976 is supported by notes and reports in my files

[45]Mailgram, Dec 2 1976, to Asst. Sec. Reed, from: Arizona groups: Arizonans for a Quality Environment, Arizonans for Wild and Scenic Rivers, Arizona Wilderness Study Committee, Southern Arizona Hiking Club, and national groups: Friends of the Earth, National Audubon Society, National Parks Conservation Assn., Sierra Club, Wilderness Society.

[46]Memorandum, Dec 29 1976, NPS Director through Asst. Sec. for Fish and Wildlife and Parks to Legislative Counsel. Includes draft bill and draft Final Wilderness Recommendation, the copy which I have is dated February 1977.

CHAPTER ELEVEN

[1]Article, Jan 11 1976, "State probing river runners on tax liability", R.L. Thomas, in *The Arizona Republic*

[2]Letter, n.d. (approx. Feb-Mar 1976), Fletcher Anderson to Superintendent

[3]Letter, Dec 7 1976, Eiseman to Stitt, Everhardt, Reed

[4]Letters, May 3 1976, Eiseman to National Association for the Advancement of Colored People. Jun 24 1976, Assoc. Dir., NPS, to Rep Steiger. Randall 49, p 54 and 51-2

---

[5]Letter, Feb 20 1976, Rep. T.E. Wirth to "Dear Paddler"
[6]Letter, Dec 7 1976, Eiseman to Goldwater
my notes, Wilderness file
[7]Letter, Nov 19 1976, Eiseman, JRHertzler, MStClair; no addressee
[8]Letter, Nov 16 1976, G. Hill to Eiseman
[9]No definite date, but before May1976. Civil Suit Number C-76-187-CFP, U.S. District Court for Northern District of California, WPRF vs. T.F. Kleppe, Secretary of the Interior, G. Everhardt, NPS Director, H.W. Chapman, NPS Western Regional Director, M. Stitt, GCNP Superintendent
[10]Letter, Nov 11 1976, Reed to L. Thomas Jr. (Lt. Gov. of Alaska)
[11]Memorandum and Order, filed Dec 16 1976, in C-76-187-CFP op. cit. Also Judgment, Dec 22 1976
[12]News release, Dec 15 1976, GCNP (on a Western Regional office form), "Grand Canyon accepting applications for private trips on Colorado River"
[13]Report, June 1976, Shelby, B. and J. M. Nielsen, "Private and Commercial Trips in the Grand Canyon...Part IV", Table A8, p 6 of App. 1
[14]NPS: Mar 1976, "Boating Use on the Colorado River, Grand Canyon"
Final EIS, Jul 31 1979, "Proposed Colorado River Management Plan"
[15]Mailing documents, Feb 1976, GCNP, locations, procedures, timetable, river use summaries, list of research, decision history
[16]Memorandum, Mar 3 1976, McComb to list of 45 groups and individuals
[17]Letter, Jun 1976, Inner Canyon Unit Manager M. O. Jensen to "Friend of the Park"
[18]Letter, Apr 15 1976, NPS to citizens, Randall 49, pp 77-8
[19]Proposed Rule, Jun 18 1976, *Federal Register*, vol 41, no. 119, p 24714; "Whitewater Boat Trips Colorado River"
[20]Letter, Jul 13 1976, Jensen to J. Vaaler
[21]Memorandum, Aug 2 1976, GCNP Superintendent to Western Regional Director, "Environmental Assessment, Concession permits renewal for" list of 21 companies
[22]ibid., p. 3
[23]Memo, Aug 11 1975, Western Region
Letter, Jul 3 1975, C. Bohlen, for Asst. Sec., to Rep. S. Yates
[24]Mailgram, Aug 13 1976, McComb to Reed
[25]Report, Sep 14 1976, Ingram
[26]Report, Sep 23 1976, Ingram, "Grand Canyon Wilderness: The Next Needed Step"
Notice, Sep 16 1976, *Federal Register*, 41 FR 39806
[27]Letter Sep 27 1976, Ingram to Reed
[28]Letter, Sep 20 1976, Dep. Asst. Sec. Interior C. Bohlen to McComb
[29]My notes on the meeting
[30]Letter, Sep 30 1976, Bruce Shaw, for Superintendent, to each comm op
[31]Report, Oct 3 1976, Ingram, "Grand Canyon Wilderness Bulletin (of the type to cause outrage)"
[32]Letters, Oct 6 1976, Ingram to Chapman and to Stitt
[33]Letters, Oct 11 1976, McComb to Chapman
Oct 7 1976, NPCA to NPS Director; Oct 13 1976, TWS Exec. Director to Ingram
[34]River Running Concession Permit, executed Aug 9 1972, Amendment No. 1. The copy I have is signed Nov 8 1976 by the concessionaire.
[35]Report, Oct 27 1976, Ingram, "Would the Grand Canyon be better administered by idiots?"

[36]Letters, Oct 18 1976, Dep. Asst. Sec. Interior C. Bohlen to McComb, and to Dave Foreman, Southwest Representative, The Wilderness Society

[37]Notes, Nov 15 and 16, conversations: McComb-Reed, Ingram-Wheeler

[38]Report, Nov 15 1976, Ingram, "Grand Canyon Wilderness: There is time left for the Ford administration to do the right things"

[39]Letter, Nov 29 1976, Ingram to Sonya

[40]Letters (2), Dec 23 1976, Ingram to Chapman

[41]River Running Concession Permit executed Aug 9 1972; Amendment No. 1 to Concession Permit, signed Nov 8 1976

[42]Letter, Dec 15 1976, Superintendent to "Friend of the Park"

[43]Letter, Dec 16 1976, H.A. Ruckel to McComb, "Re: Grand Canyon (AZ); Renewal of River Concessioners' Contracts by the National Park Service"

[44]Newspaper article, Dec 19 1976, S. Wynkoop, in *Denver Post*, "New Hassle Looms Over Hydropower Dam Proposals"

[45]Letter, Mar 3 1977, Ingram to Ruckel

CHAPTER TWELVE

[1]Document, Oct 3 1976, R.Roy Johnson, Project Director, Second Rough Draft, "Synthesis and Management Implications of the Colorado River Research Project"

[2]As always, some information comes from notes in my files. Memorandum, Feb 27 1976, Regional Director to Superintendent, "Approval of Colorado River Research and Monitoring Program"

[3]Letter, Oct 20 1976, Superintendent to Ingram

[4]Papers, n.d., n.a., Randall 4, p 8ff

[5]Pre-meeting summaries of talks at Oct 3 1976 River Research Symposium

[6]Technical Report, Sep 1977, Number 17, R.Roy Johnson, "Synthesis and Management Implications of the Colorado River Research Project"

[7]Memorandum, n.d., Ingram, "Research and the river" Article, Dec 1976, Ingram, "Eroding the Grand Canyon", in *Not Man Apart*, publication of Friends of the Earth

[8]Research Reports, Grand Canyon: "River Contact", June 1976, HERS Inc., Prepared by B.Shelby and J.M.Nielsen, in 4 parts: Design and Method of the Sociological Research, Motors and Oars, Use Levels and Crowding, Private and Commercial Trips. "User Carrying Capacity for River-Running the Colorado River", Nov 22 1976, Principal Investigator: F.Yates Borden. "Economic Analysis of River Companies Running the Colorado River", Dec 1976, Michael Parent

[9]In "River Contact", Part II, "Motors and Oars", p. 36

[10]In "River Contact", Part III, "Use Levels and Crowding", p. 24 and Appendix 1, p. 4,

[11] Borden, op. cit., p. 42

[12] ibid. p. 66

[13]Unpublished research reports, 1975 and 1976, E.G. Bowman, "Aircraft noise evaluation Grand Canyon, May-Aug 1975" and "Statistical summary aircraft noise evaluation, May-Aug 1975".

[14]Research Report, Jun 15 2000, Hall, T. and Shelby, B., "1998 Colorado River Boater Study; Grand Canyon National Park"

CHAPTER THIRTEEN

[1]As always, many of the references come from notes I made for my files.

Memorandum, Jan 5 1977, NPS Legislative Office to Western Regional Director, "Wilderness Recommendation, Grand Canyon National Park, and Conclusions", GCPBA 96.

[2]News article, Jan 14 1977, *The New York Times*, R. Jones, "Wilderness designation for dam site being fought"

[3]Memorandum, Feb 17 1977, NPS Director to Secretary of the Interior, "Grand Canyon wilderness recommendation", GCPBA 102

[4]Briefing notes, Mar 17 1977, Director's briefing on CRMP and EIS, GCPBA 110, p. 8 ff

[5]Letter, Feb 27 1977, Ingram to Udall

[6]Letter, Feb 27 1977, Ingram to B. McCarthy

[7]Letter, Mar 5 1977, Ingram to L. Hymans

[8]Reports, Mar 27 and Apr 4 1977, Ingram, "Grand Canyon Wilderness Challenges" and "Grand Canyon Challenges—More challenging"

[9]Documents compiled by NPS, Randall 4, p. 8. Also Ingram interview of Jensen, Aug 5 2002, see Chapter 15

[10]Article, Mar 1977, in *National Parks and Conservation Magazine*, cited in letter, May 5 1977, K. Dahl to Congressman Udall

[11]Deposition, May 20 1977, by Regional Director Chapman, handwritten notes in my file

[12]Letter, Jun 20 1977, NPS Director to Representative D. Clark (D-Iowa), GCPBA 107

[13]Letter, Jun 8 1977, NPS D.C. to Eiseman

[14]Report, Oct 13 1977, GCNP River Ranger, Patrol Summary, GCPBA 112

[15]Letters, May 9 1977, Superintendent to Ingram
May 19 1977, Ingram to Superintendent
May 19 1977, Eiseman to Superintendent
Jun 7 1977, Superintendent to Ingram

[16]Letter, Apr 29 1977, GCNP Superintendent to "Friend of the Park"

[17]Letter, Jan 17 1977, D. Nemir, attorney for WPRF, to Eiseman.
WPRF Newsletter, Feb 1 1977

[18]Letter, Jan 3 1977, Eiseman to Ingram
Letter, Jan 3 1977, Eiseman to GCNP Biologist R. Johnson
Essay, Feb 1, 1977, Eiseman, "advocating the priority of private... use of the public lands upon which use limits have been imposed..."
Letter, Feb 2 1977, Eiseman to McComb

[19]Letter, Feb 9 1977, McComb to Eiseman

[20]Document, n.d., RRAC, "A proposal for an equitable permit system on a wild river"

[21]Complaint, Feb 28 1977, filed in U. S. District Court for Arizona, by Bruce Meyerson, Arizona Center for Law in the Public Interest
With press release and fund appeal from Eisemans, Hertzler, St.Clair

[22]Letter, Feb 27 1977, Ingram to B. McCarthy. Also LMNRA material, including Jan 19 1977 press release, "Wilderness Planning Workshops Offered by Recreation Area", and Mar 25 1977 Summary of Statements

[23]Letter, May 19 1977, Ingram to Hawkins; also
Letter, May 5 1977, Friends of the Earth to Udall
Minutes, n.d., Arizona Academy of Science, Resolution endorsing NPS GC Wilderness
Article, May 1977, W. Breed, "Wilderness - Wild and Free or Wild and Noisy?" in *Canyon Echo* of Grand Canyon chapter of Sierra Club
Speech, May 13 1977, F. Norris, "Wilderness and the Grand Canyon" at Governor's Commission on Arizona Environment

[24]Press release, May 23 1977, The White House, President's Environmental Message, and Detailed Fact Sheet

Articles, n.d. (May/June) 1977, Associated Press, "Ban on big rafts in canyon advised"

Jun 3 1977, E. Stiles in *Tucson Citizen*, "President's message; Arivaipa Canyon first new state wild area?"

[25]Interview, Apr 8 2003, Ingram with Stuart Sessions, Bethesda MD.

[26]Letter, May 27 1977, Ingram to Stu Sessions, Interior Branch, OMB

[27]Letter and article, Jun 7 1977, Ingram to list, "Grand Canyon Wilderness: The Final (?) Fight Begins"

[28]Letter, Jun 15 1977, D. Brower to M. Udall

[29]Note, Jun 22 1977, Ingram on conversation with Sessions

[30]Document, Feb 1977 version of Wilderness recommendation with June 1977 handwritten changes, GCPBA 110

[31]Memo, Jun 29 1977, NPS Director to Interior Legislative Counsel, "Wilderness Recommendation, Lake Mead impoundment exclusion"

Memo, Jul 13 1977, NPS D.C. Office of Legislation to Denver Service Center, "Wilderness recommendation include portion above Separation Canyon"

[32]Letter, Jul 24 1977, Ingram to McComb, and

Jul 29 1977, Ingram to Foreman; reply, n.d.

[33]Letter, Jul 29 1977, Ingram to McComb

[34]Memo, Aug 11 1977, McComb to Juanita Alvarez

[35]Article, May 1977, Ingram, in *AWWW Newsletter*

1977 Correspondence, Ted Hatch - Ingram: May 24, Jun 18; Jun 20, Jun 26; Jun 30, Jul 6; Jul 18, Jul 25.

[36]1977 Correspondence, Ingram - C.R.M. Parent: Jun 9, Jun 22; Jul 27, Aug 2; Sep 4

[37]Letters, Jun 26 and Jul 31 1977, Ingram to the Secretary of the Interior

[38]Letters/reports, 1977, Eiseman to list: May 10, May 16, May 23, Jun 22, Jul 11, Jul 18

[39]Newsletter, Summer 1977, River Rights Action Committee, Denver Colorado

[40]Letter, Jun 18 1977, Ingram to H. Anthony Ruckel

[41]Letter, Aug 19 1977, Ruckel to R. Way, Office of Asst. Sec. R. Herbst

[42]Letter, Sep 4 1977, Ingram to Ruckel

Memo, Sep 4 1977, E. Blauner to Sierra Club list, re draft resolution authorizing lawsuit

[43]Complaint, Sep 19 1977, Civil Action 77-722 in District Court for Arizona, GCNP and Sierra Club vs. GCNP Superintendent, Regional Director, NPS Director, Interior Secretary, and Western River Expedition and Tour West individually and as representatives of river concessionaires in Grand Canyon.

[44]Agenda and notes, Aug 26 1977, meeting with Senator DeConcini in Tucson

[45]Phone talk notes, late Aug 1977, Ingram-Sessions

also, Report, Sep 1 1977, Ingram, "Grand Canyon Wilderness Proposal (non-)Progress"

[46]Memo, Sep 2 1977, NPS D.C. Wilderness Chief to Denver Service Center et al., GCPBA 111

[47]phone notes, Sep 7 1977, Ingram-Sessions

[48]phone notes, Sep 26 1977, Ingram-Sessions

Memo Sep 26 1977, Ingram to McComb, Calkin, "Grand Canyon Wilderness and OMB"

[49]Letters, Oct 10 1977, Ingram to Eliot Cutler, Assoc. Dir. Natural Resources, Energy and Science, and Nov 7 1977, Cutler to Ingram

[50]Letter, Sep 4 1977, Ingram to Superintendent

[51]Interview with M. Jensen

[52]Letter, Sep 20 1977, Superintendent to Ingram

[53]Magazine article, n.d., S. W. Carothers, in *Downriver*, "It's Time for Change; Let's Carry It All Out"

CHAPTER FOURTEEN

[1]Letter, Oct 10 1977, Ingram to Ruckel and Venable
[2]Letters, Oct 10 1977, Ingram to Interior Secretary,
reply, Dec 9 1977, D.C. NPS staffer to Ingram
[3]Letters, Oct 10 1977, Ingram to Jensen and reply, Oct 27 1977, Jensen to Ingram

CHAPTER FIFTEEN

[1]Answer, Nov 22 1977, for federal defendants in Civ. Action 77-722, as cited.
[2]Answer, Nov 23 1977, for concessionaire defendants in Civ. Action 77-722, as cited
[3]Motion to certify the defendant class, Nov 23 1977, by plaintiffs attorney in Civ. Action 77-722, as cited
[4]Notice of hearing, Nov 30 1977, op. cit.
[5]Newsletter, Winter 1977-8, WPRF, Orinda CA.
[6]Memo, Oct 7 1977, Eiseman to list, "Progress Report on Eiseman et al. vs. Andrus et al.
[7]Letter, Oct 13 1977, Eiseman to Ingram
[8]Article, Oct 1977, "Motorboat Controversy Delaying Grand Canyon Wilderness Bill", in TWS's *Wilderness Report*
[9]Letter, Nov 8 1977, D. Foreman to list
[10]Memo, Nov 2 1977, NPS Director to Legislative Counsel, "Wilderness Recommendation on Lake Mead Portion; Grand Canyon NP", GCPBA 113
[11]Public Law 93-620, section 10e, and Conference Report, Dec 17 1974, to accompany S.1296, recommendation 4
[12]Correspondence, Ingram-Stitt and Stitt-Ingram, all 1977: Jun 12 and Jun 21, Jun 25 and Jul 1, Jul 7 and Jul 29/Sep 12
[13]Letter, Nov 28 1977, Carr to Ingram
[14]Card, Dec 23 1977, Carr to Ingram
[15]Memo, Dec 2 1977, Asst. Sec. for Indian Affairs (F. Gerard) to Legislative Counsel, "Grand Canyon Wilderness Bill", GCPBA 115
[16]Memo, Jan 18 1978, same as previous, GCPBA 120
[17]Memo, Jan 26 1978, Associate Solicitor, Indian Affairs, to Leg. Counsel, "Designation of GCNP lands as a Wilderness area", GCPBA 121
[18]Memo, Feb 6 1978, NPS Director to Leg. Coun., "Response to comments by Asst. Sec. For Indian Affairs", GCPBA 122
[19]Letter, Jan 3 1978, Carr to Ingram
[20]Letter, Jan 8 1978, Ingram to Carr, McComb, Calkin. Includes draft bill, map, and introductory remarks
[21]Letter, Jan 16 1978, Carr to Ingram. No record of NPS memo
[22]Letter, Jan 17 1978, Carr to Ingram
[23]Letter, Jan 17 1978, noon, Carr to Ingram
[24]Notes, 1978, Ingram with various. These are from phone conversations, and are often mostly suggestive, not rising to the level of documentation in many cases.
[25]Memo, Aug 1978, no author, "Briefing Statement", Wilderness Study, Grand Canyon National Park, GCPBA 123
[26]Memo, Apr 3 1979, Director (names: D. Hales, I. Hutchison) to Solicitor through Assistant Secretary, "Wilderness Recommendations, Grand Canyon National Park", GCPBA 124

[27]Memo, May 16 1979, Associate Solicitor for Conservation and Wildlife to Director, "Wilderness Recommendations, Grand Canyon National Park", GCPBA 125

[28]Document, Mar 21 1978, F. Eiseman, "News concerning Eiseman et al. vs. Andrus et al."

[29]Memo, Jan 23 1978, Ruckel to Sierra Club Leadership, "Grand Canyon River Running Concessioners Litigation"

[30]Memo, Mar 1 1978, Ruckel to Sierra Club Leadership, "Grand Canyon River Running Concessioners Litigation"

[31]Drafts, Mar 1 and 17 1978, Ruckel, "Stipulation and Agreement", in GCNP... v. Stitt ...

[32]Memo, Mar 171978, Ruckel to Sierra Club Leadership, "Grand Canyon River Running Concessioners Litigation"

[33]Letter, Apr 14 1978, Ruckel to J. F. Flynn, Asst. U. S. Attorney, Phoenix

[34]Letter, Aug 15 1978, Gilbert T. Venable to Ruckel

[35]Letter, Sep 27 1978, Ruckel to Sierra Club Leadership, "Grand Canyon River Running Concessioners Litigation". The legal documents dealing with the comm ops, adding no interest to our story, are retained in my file.

CHAPTER SIXTEEN

[1]Interview, Aug 5 2002, Jensen by Ingram, in Fort Collins, Colorado. This conversation, and my rendering of it, provides the non-document-derived material in this section.

[2]Memo, May 23 1977, Reg. Dir. to Supt., "Colorado River Management Plan Draft Environmental Statement" covering the draft; Randall 60, pp 2-21

[3]The draft is in Randall 60. The text discussed is located by the numbers in parentheses, e.g., (I:2), referring to the section, then the page

[4]News release, Nov 14 1977, GCNP, "Concession Permit, Mule Train Tours, Grand Canyon"

[5]These are page references in the EIS draft dated Dec 8 1977, Grand Canyon National Park, "Draft Environmental Statement, Proposed Colorado River Management Plan, DES 77-37", Randall 62

[6]Document, Oct 1977, Grand Canyon National Park, "Draft Colorado River Management Plan". Randall 61. Numbers in parentheses refer to the plan's pages

CHAPTER SEVENTEEN

[1]News release, Jan 4 1978, GCNP (Jensen), "January 31 Deadline for Permits to Run Colorado River"

[2]Letter, Jan 5 1978, Supt to "Friend of the Park", cover for copies of draft Colorado River Management Plan and its draft Environmental Impact Statement
News Release, Jan 6 1978, GCNP(Jensen), "Grand Canyon's Colorado River Management Plan is Available for Public Review"

[3]Letter, Jan 8 1978, Ingram to Carr, McComb, Calkin

[4]Leaflet, Jan 1978, Ingram, "Extra***Grand Canyon/Colorado River Management Plan"

[5]Leaflet, Jan 14 1978, Ingram

[6]Transcript, Feb 9 1978, pp 45-49, Q. is Ruckel, A. is Stitt; in GCNP et al. v. Stitt et al.

[7]Letter, Jan 14 1978, Eiseman to Ingram

[8]Letter, Jan 25 1978, Ingram to Eiseman

[9]Newsletter, Feb 1978, Grand Canyon Chapter, "Canyon Echo"

[10]Letter, Feb 14 and Apr 7 1978, Eiseman to Superintendent; also
Mailgram, Mar 12 1978, Eiseman to Goldwater, and document, Mar 21 1978, "News..."

[11]Article draft, Jan 1978, Jim Vaaler, "Grand Canyon River Running: Eliminating the Lottery", also
Letters, Jan 25 1978, Ingram to Vaaler; Jan 23 1978, Vaaler to Ingram

[12]Newsletter, n.d., R. Frank, E. Leaper, M. Cohen, "River Rights Action Newsletter", "Position Statement: Fair River Access"

[13]Letter, Feb 1 1978, Director, Arizona Office of Tourism, to Supt, GCNP, accompanied by Document, n.d., n.a., n.t.

[14]Document, Feb 10 1978, ARTA Southwest Inc., "Position Statement Regarding the Colorado River Management Plan". Also notes from phone call; Ingram to Elliott

[15]Letter, n.d., Ted Hatch, Hatch River Expeditions to River Running Friends

[16]Document, n.d., G. Staveley (presenter and PROA chairman; no author indicated), Statement prepared for February public meetings. Covered by summary letter, Feb 22 1978, PROA to Congressman Udall

[17]Letter, Jan 26 1978, B. Dimock (Canyoneers employee) to Supt, GCPBA 118, pp 22-25. Item 118 is a few items from the hearings. The full transcripts are in GCNP's special collections.

[18]Transcript, n.d., Mr. Conley (almost certainly of the comm op Fort Lee). Randall 67, pp 18-19

[19]Transcript, n.d., G. Staveley (Canyoneers). Randall 67, p. 20

[20]Newspaper column, Feb 2 1978, Ben Avery, in *The Arizona Republic*, "Motorized Canyon raft trips needed", Randall 67, p. 49

[21]Letter, Feb 24 1978, PROA chairman Staveley to M. McCloskey

[22]Column, Jan 12 1978, Pete Cowgill, "Boat motors face ban from Canyon" in *Arizona Daily Star*

[23]Article, Jan 17 1978, John Schroeder, "Plans to limit Colorado raft trips assailed" in *Arizona Republic*

[24]Article, Jan 28 1978, Associated Press, "Ban on motorized Canyon raft trips proposed" in *Arizona Daily Star*

[25]Editorial, Feb 3 1978, "Use river power" in *Arizona Daily Star*

[26]Article, Feb 5 1978, Pete Cowgill, "Motorized Grand Canyon trips may be ended" in *Arizona Daily Star*

[27]Articles, Feb 15 and 23 1978, Associated Press, "Canyon motorboat ban opposed" and "Opinions split on bid to ban motorboats in Grand Canyon" in *Arizona Daily Star*

[28]Letter, Mar 17 1978, James E. Peterson to Supt., in Final EIS on CRMP, p. IX:160-1

[29]Article, Feb 17 1978, Joe Bauman, "Park Service river plan draws flak" in *Deseret News*

[30]Column, Feb 20 1978, Joe Bauman, "Keep Grand Canyon a quiet Wilderness" in *Deseret News*

[31]Column, Feb 19 1978, Robert Thomas, "Colorado River hassle continues" in *The Arizona Republic*

[32]Article, Mar 17 1978, "Boaters upset over new regulations" in *Salt Lake Times*
Editorial, Mar 27 1978, in *The Phoenix Gazette*
Editorial, May 26 1978, "Hard to Understand", *Salt Lake Tribune*

[33]Article, Apr 17 1978, D.K. Shah and M. Lord, "Cleaning up the Canyon"

[34]Letter, Mar 9 1978, Stitt to Friend of the Park
Letter, Jul 20 1978, Stitt to Friend of the Park

[35]The following paragraphs are from notes I took during telephone conversations, and the Jensen interview

[36]Notes, Mar 23 1978, McComb, "Grand Canyon River Management Plan Meeting, Washington D.C."

[37]Statement, Mar 23 1978, PROA, on CRMP+EIS, presented by G. Staveley

[38]Release, Mar 22 1978, Senator Jake Garn (Rep-Utah), "Garn Attacks Colorado River Plan"

[39]Statement, Mar 23 1978, Representative J.J. Rhodes (R-Arizona), on the draft CRMP;

Statement, Mar 23 1978, Bob Stump (D/R,-Arizona), CRMP and EIS

[40]Sign-up list for Mar 3 1978 meeting, Goldwater papers, Colorado River 1978-9, Box 9, 9

[41]Letter, Jan 1978, Shelby to editor, *Wilderness Report*, The Wilderness Society

Letters, Feb 9 and Mar 17 1978, Shelby to Stitt

[42]Report, May 1978, Shelby to Jensen, "Analysis of Public Involvement Questionnaires for the River Management Plan", Randall 64.1

[43]Letter, May 4 1978, Western Regional Director to Representative G. McKay (R-Utah)

[44]Letters, Apr 19 1978, Stump to Secretary;

Apr 28 1978, Stump to attendees of March 3 1978 meeting

[45]Memo, Mar 1 1978, Ingram to Calkin, McComb, Ruckel, Venable, "Grand Canyon focus—protection of the river's environment"

[46]Article, Mid-March 1978, Liz Hymans (worked for OARS), "The Grand Canyon of the Colorado: The Flow of Wilderness" in *Not Man Apart*

Letter, Apr 16 1978, G. Anderson to Superintendent

Leaflet, Mar 27 1978, The Wilderness Society, "Park Service Needs Support to Eliminate Motors from Grand Canyon"

Article, Apr 1978, Dave Foreman, "NPS Proposes Grand Canyon Motorboat Ban", in *Wilderness Report*

Leaflet, (Apr) 1978, Grand Canyon chapter, Sierra Club, "Letters are Urgently Needed to Protect the Grand Canyon"

Article, May 1978, AWWW (of Tucson), "Grand Canyon" in *AWWW Newsletter*

[47]Letter, May 24 1978, Udall to Secretary of the Interior

[48]Document, Aug 4 1978, Udall to AWWW, Answers to pre-election questionnaire

[49]Leaflet, (Apr) 1978, Ingram, "Using the Telephone as a Magnifying Glass to Amplify Our Support for the Grand Canyon"

[50]Letter, Jun 5 1978, L. Lewis (conservation chair for Club chapter) to Ingram

[51]Letter, Jul 19 1978, Sierra Club Southwest Representative B. Calkin to Whalen

[52]Letter, Jul 20 1978, Stitt to Friend of the Park

[53]Letter, Jul 31 1978, Ingram (for AWWW, Friends of the Earth, Sierra Club Grand Canyon Chapter, Southern Arizona Hiking Club) to Whalen

[54]Letter, Aug 23 1978, NPS-D.C. to Ingram

[55]Much of this information is contained in notes, too often undated, from conversations I had, most by phone, with a variety of allies and officials, not always identified. This is not the first time I regret not maintaining the journal I kept in 1972-5.

[56]Memo, Aug 28 1978, Ingram to allies, "Continuing the strategy of the four prongs"

[57]Memo, n.d., Ingram to Grand Canyon chapter, Southern Arizona Hiking Club, AWWW, "Report on my trip to Washington, September 11-15", with working notes.

[58]An undated note of this conversation says that the NPS contact was Richard Curry, NPS legislative liaison.

[59]Documents, Jan 1979 (published date Mar 16 1979), Lake Mead National Recreation Area, "Preliminary Wilderness Proposal" and "Draft Environmental Statement"

Leaflet, n.d., Sierra Club, Toiyabe Chapter, Notice of May 1979 Wilderness hearings

Statement, May 23 1979, Ingram, "A Grand Canyon item in disguise"

[60]Letter, Feb 3 1979, Smith to "Senator" Udall

[61]Letter, Mar 28 1979, Ingram to Udall

[62]Letters, Feb 4 1979, F. Hoover to Sierra Club,

Feb 13 1979, Sierra Club to Hoover

Mar 28 1979, Ingram to Hoover

[63]Notes, n.d (Feb-Mar 1979)., NPS, Calkin; to me

[64]Letters, Mar 13 1979, Ruckel to Venable

Mar 26 1979, Ingram to Venable and Ruckel
[65]Letter, May 16 1979, Venable to Ruckel
[66]Memo, Jun 5 1979, Ruckel to Sierra Club Leadership, "Grand Canyon Concessioners River-Running Litigation"
Letter, Jun 5 1979, Ruckel to McComb
[67]Letter, Jun 11 1979, Ingram to Ruckel
[68]Interrogatories and Request for Documents, Jun 5 1979, by Ruckel, for GCNP et al. v. Stitt et al.
[69]Answers to Interrogatories, Jul 5 1979, J.F. Flynn, attorney for defendant, Stitt.
[70]Letter, Jul 26 1979, L. Lewis to Ingram

CHAPTER EIGHTEEN

[1]Document, Jul 31 1979, Grand Canyon National Park, "Final Environmental Statement, Proposed Colorado River Management Plan, Grand Canyon National Park, Arizona", (page numbers in parentheses refer to this document);
News Release, Aug 3 1979 and (reference to *Federal Register* notice expected on Aug 3 1979), GCNP, "Final environmental statement on Colorado River Management Plan Available for Review", Randall 71;
Document, Jul 1979, GCNP, "Summary of the Proposed Action of the Final Environmental Statement for the Colorado River Management Plan"
[2]The figures come from GCNP 1996 statistics and the Shelby-Hall survey of river-runners done in the same period.

CHAPTER NINETEEN

[1]News release, Aug 23 1979, GCNP, "Public review period on Colorado River plan extended"
[2]Document, Jul 1979, GCNP, "Summary of the Proposed Action for the Final EIS for the CRMP"
[3]Letter, Jul 10 1979, Douglas Schwartz (archeologist, School of American Research) to Secretary of the Interior, GCPBA 127
[4]News release, Aug 8 1979, Grand Canyon Chapter et al., "Conservation Groups Support Grand Canyon River Plan"
Also, Action alert, Aug 1979, same source, "Grand Canyon"
Article, Sep 1979, same source, "Club Supports Park Service Grand Canyon River Plan" in *Canyon Echo*
Leaflet, Sep 1979, Sierra Club (national office), "The Grand Canyon—A Chance to Praise the Park Service", and Aug 17 1979, same source, in *National News Report*, "New Grand Canyon Plan Resisted by Concessionaires"
My files contain a few copies of letters sent by others.
[5]Letter, Aug 15 1979, Donald Coughlin to Ingram
Article and note, Oct-Nov 1979, D. Crook to L. Lewis
[6]What follows was reported in our mailers listed above.
[7]Letter, Sep 10 1979, Arizona state officials to Goldwater, in Goldwater 9, 9
[8]Correspondence, Sep 2, 8, 14 and Nov 12 1979, citizens to Goldwater and replies; and Sep 19 1979, Goldwater to Staveley; Goldwater 9, 9
[9]Letter, Aug 20 1979, Babbitt to Lewis
[10]Letter, Sep 5 1979, DeConcini to L. Lewis, Sierra Club
[11]Letter, Aug 28 1979, Donald Nemir to Superintendent

[12]Memo, Sep 13 1979, Ruckel to Sierra Club Leadership, "Grand Canyon River-running Concessionaire Litigation"

[13]Letter, Sep 25 1979, L. Lewis to Ingram

[14]Document, about Oct 12 1979, no author or source, though it would seem from the Park Service somewhere

[15]Document, Oct 1 1979, PROA, "A critical analysis of the proposed CRMP's Draft and Final Environmental Statements and related matters"

[16]Letter, Sep 12 1979, NPS (my guess was, Director) to comm op list; referred to in Response to Stump Questions, Nov 12 1980

[17]Articles, Aug 4 1979, "Outboard motor ban likely for Grand Canyon Park" in *Washington Post* and *Tucson Citizen*; Aug 6 "Grand Canyon ban on Engines Faces Boaters on Colorado" in *The New York Times*

[18]Article, Jul 22 1979, J. N. Wilford, "Lure of the White Water", in *The New York Times Magazine*

[19]Editorial, Aug 7 1979, "Echoing Down the Canyon" in *Washington Post*

[20]Articles: Aug 21 1979, "Ferry boat man objects to river trip rules" in *Tucson Citizen*, Aug 20 1979, "River operators say U.S. plan will cut traffic on Colorado" Sep 9 1979, "Cost of banning motors ignored, Colorado River raft firms say" in *Arizona Republic*

[21]Columns, Sep 2 1979, Ben Avery, "Park service ruling on Colorado River caters to purists" in *Arizona Republic*, and Sep 16 1979, Pete Cowgill, "Aesthetics should be a personal thing" in *Arizona Daily Star*,

[22]Article, Sep 6 1979, "River Running" in *Northlander*. This article also has extensive quotes from me and Staveley

[23] Article, Oct 22 1979, "Conflict in the Canyon: An Oar's Splash vs. a Motor's Whine" in *Washington Post*

CHAPTER TWENTY

[1]Interview transcript, 1993, w/ wife Carol, by Lew Steiger, in "River Runners Oral History Project", in NAU Special Collections, item 53-7.

[2]Letter, Sep 17 1980, Staveley to F. Tikalsky

[3]Letter and draft bill, Oct 12 1979, Stump and Rhodes to "Dear Colleague", "No more motorized rafting down the Colorado River through the Grand Canyon after 1986"

[4]Document, Apr 29 1980, n.a., NPS briefing statement for meeting on CRMP with DeConcini and Udall. Randall 79. No indication of author or intended recipient. Chapman c/o Directors Office is at top right, indicating drafter or approver. River Unit is cc'ed. This document is the source for much of the following paragraphs.

[5]Jensen interview w/ Ingram, Aug 5 2002. Ingram interview with Chapman, Jun 8 2002.

[6]op.cit. Apr 29 1980 briefing document

[7]Document, Dec 20 1979, GCNP (signed on that date by Director, Regional Director and Superintendent), "Colorado River Management Plan"

[8]Document, Dec 20 1979, n.a. (with CRMP), "Modifications to CRMP", Randall 75

[9]Document, Dec 7 1979, n.a. to P. Gove, Chief, Office of Legislation, "Fact sheet: Final Decisions on CRMP GCNP", Randall 72.1

[10]n.d., n.a. (captions indicate concessionaire source), "1978 Trip and Fare Spectrum"

[11]Article, Dec 1979-Jan 1980, Ingram, "The Last Blast" in *Canyon Echo*

[12]Cost of living calculator on www.aier.org.

[13]Websites, Sep 2002, Arizona River Runners, Canyoneers, Hatch. (recorded by hand, not printed)

[14]Letters, Dec 10 1979, Ingram to Stump, Rhodes, Goldwater, DeConcini, Udall, Babbitt, Whalen et al.

[15]Document, Nov 1 1980, NPS, "Fact sheet on the proposed CRMP for GCNP"

[16]Letter, Nov 6 1979, L. Lewis to Ingram

[17]News release, Dec 3 1979, GCNP, "Noncommercial river trip applications being accepted by Grand Canyon for Colorado River"

[18]News release, Dec 20 1979, GCNP, "NPS adopts environmental plan for the Colorado River at GCNP"

[19]Document, Dec 20 1979, GCNP, "Colorado River Management Plan"

[20]Letter, Dec 28 1979, Regional Director to each comm op, Certified Mail

[21]Document, n.d. mid-late 1979, n.a., no title. 20 pp;

[22]Document, Jan 28 1980, Concurrent Memorial HCM 2001, "Urging the Congress of the United States to enact legislation to maintain current use of the Colorado River in GCNP by commercial motorized watercraft"

[23]Document, date unknown, Concurrent Memorial HCM 2003, printed in *Congressional Record*, U.S. Senate, S3249, Mar 28 1980

[24]email, May 17 1999, B. Hayes to list, "AZ state", Randall 76.1

[25]Letter, Mar 19 1980, Acting Supt to each comm op

[26]Charts, n.d., on 1981 schedules, Burke 13.

[27]Schedule, n.d., but before Mar 26 1980, hand-made, with each trip entered for each day throughout the year.

[28]Document, Dec 11 1979, n.a., "Important Issues for Wilderness Recommendation for GCNP". Language indicates GCNP staff authorship, GCPBA 133, p. 2

[29]Document, Jan 1980, n.a., "Important Issues..." GCPBA 130

[30]Memo, Jan 13 1980, D.C. Wilderness Coordinator to Denver Service Center, "Wilderness Recommendation, Grand Canyon", GCPBA 131

Memo, Jan 24 1980, NPS Dep. Director Hutchison to Regional Director, "Wilderness Recommendation, Grand Canyon", GCPBA 132

Memo, Jan 29 1980, Acting Supt Shaw to Regional Director, "Important Issues...", GCPBA 133

[31]Memo and Document, Sep 11 1980, NPS Director to Assistant Secretary for Fish and Wildlife and Parks, "Wilderness Recommendation, GCNP", GCPBA 134 and 135, and Aug 1980, GCNP, "Final Wilderness Recommendation". This is a marked-up copy of the Feb 1977 document.

[32]Letter, Jan 4 1980, Babbitt to Ingram

Letter, Jan 14 1980, DeConcini to Ingram

[33]Memo, Jan 3 1980, Ingram, "Where the CRMP for the GCNP may see action"

[34]Letters: Feb 29 1980, Ingram to Acting Supt. GCNP

Apr 7 and 8 1980, Jensen to Ingram

[35]Apr 30 1980, Ingram to Jensen, and Ingram to Superintendent Richard Marks

May 21 1980, Jensen to Ingram

[36]Letter, Jan 9 1980, Ruckel to S.C. Leadership, "Grand Canyon River-running Concessionaire litigation"

Letter, Jan 9 1980, Ruckel to L. Lewis, Grand Canyon chapter

[37]Letters, Jan 10 1980, Venable to Ruckel,

Jan 10, Venable to US Attorney J. Flynn

Mar 17 1980, US Attorney M. Hawkins to Venable

[38]Motion to Dismiss, Mar 24 1980, filed by US Attorney in CIV-77-722-PCT-WEC, GCNP et al. Vs. M. E. Stitt et al.

Letter, Mar 26 1980, Ruckel to S.C. Leadership, "Grand Canyon River-running Concessionaire litigation"

[39]Complaint, Mar 27 1980, Mountain States Legal Foundation et al. v. NPS Director and Secretary of the Interior, Civ. 80-233, U. S. District Court for Arizona,

[40]Article, Mar 28 1980, "Suit opposes motor-raft ban" in *Arizona Republic*

[41]Letter, Apr 4 1980, P. A. Katz, U. S. Attorney Arizona, to Field Solicitor, Interior, San Francisco;

Memo, Apr 9 1980, Field Solicitor to D.C. Associate Solicitor, Conservation and Wildlife, "MSLF v. Whalen", both in Randall 77

[42]Letter, Mar 28 1980, Venable to Ruckel

[43]Memo, Apr 17 1980, Ruckel to S.C. Leadership, "G.C. River-running Concessionaires II; MSLF v NPS"

Letter, May 23 1980, W. S. Curtiss, SCLDF, to Grand Canyon chapter

Letter, Jul 16 1980, Curtiss to L. Lewis

[44]Letter, Sep 19 1980, Curtiss to Ingram et al.

Order, Sep 22 1980, Granting motion to intervene, in CIV 80-233-PHX CLH

Letter, Sep 25 1980, Curtiss to Ingram et al.

[45]Articles, P. Shabecoff, *The New York Times*, Apr 25 1980, "Director Ousted Over 'Problems' in Federal Parks" and May 15 1980, "Park Service Conflict: Concessions vs. Conservation"

[46]Notes I took from several conversations during this period, supplemented by later documents summarizing events.

[47]Letter, May 6 1980, Goldwater to Andrus, Burke 9

[48]Briefing statements: May 1 1980, Jensen for Secretary Andrus; A later version is dated June and July 21 1980

Apr 29 1980 (May 8 1980), "For meeting with Senator DeConcini and Congressman Udall on CRMP for GCNP", Chapman's name appears as if in D.C.

[49]Document, n.d. (mid-July 1980), n.a. (NPS, GCNP), "Chronology and Action on the CRMP Relating to the Proposed Modification of the Plan's Implementation"

[50]Letter, Jun 8 1980, Ingram to DeConcini

[51]Document in Burke 7, under Jun 5 1980

[52]Documents, Jun 5 and Jun 16 1980, GCNP (no author), summary and recap

[53]Document, Jun 6 1980, Staveley and Burke, Burke 12

[54]Letter, Jun 8 1980, Ingram to DeConcini, w/ enc. "Recurrent issues in Grand Canyon river-running" and "The Last Blast..."

[55]Letter, Jun 9 1980, Superintendent Marks to Udall, Ingram, rest of congressional delegation, and others.

[56]Letters, Jun 1 1980, Ingram to Marks; Jun 12 1980 Marks to Ingram

[57]Letter, Jun 16 1980, "G" (Staveley) on PROA letterhead to "Folks", Burke 17

[58]NPS call records, Jun 1980, copies located in Burke 14; Specifically:

Jun 10 Martin Litton, Jun 12 John Vail, Jun 17 Vladimir Kovalik and Sierra Club Southwest Rep, Jun 18 George Wendt, Jun 20 Dick McCallum, Jun 23 Moki Mac. (Interestingly, none of these records or letters of reactions are included in the GCPBA or Randall collections of NPS materials)

[59]Letter, Jun 19 1980, Western River Expeditions to Superintendent, Burke 17

[60]Letter, Jun 18 1980, G.White to Superintendent, Burke 17

[61]Letters, Jul 7 1980, National Organization for River Sports to Superintendent, and Jun 16 1980, J. Munroe to Superintendent, Burke 17.

[62]Letter, Jun 23 1980, Mountain States Legal Foundation to Superintendent, Burke 17

[63]Letter, Jun 28 1980, ARTA to Superintendent

[64]Documents, Jul 16 1980 and n.d., Marks and n.a., tally sheets for support/opposition of June 5 statement of principles

[65]Letter, Jun 20 1980, T. D. Jarvis, NPCA, to NPS Director, Dickenson

[66]Letter, Jun 20 1980, Ingram to Superintendent

[67]Letters, Jun 20 1980, Ingram to DeConcini, Jun 22 1980, to Babbitt, Jun 25, to Goldwater

[68]Memo, Jul 22 1980, Assoc. Solicitor, Conservation and Wildlife, to NPS Director, "Amendments to the CRMP"

[69]Letter, Jul 14 1980, Chapman to Ingram, and list: Congress, comm ops, state, environmentalists, self-guided groups, researchers. With "Chronology and Action" memo

[70]Letter, Aug 13 1980, Chapman to Staveley, Burke folder 7

[71]Note, n.d. July 1980, Ingram-Marks; Ingram-D. Jarvis

[72]Letter, Jul 22 1980, Dickenson to Burke, Burke 9
Mailgram, Aug 6 1980, Burke to Dickenson, Burke 9

[73]Letter, Apr 2 1981, NPS Director to W. S. Curtiss, Sierra Club Legal Defense Fund, item 2(a)2

[74]Letters, Aug 19 1980, Staveley to Congressman Stump, Burke 7;
Aug 21 1980, Staveley to Chapman; Burke 17;
Aug 18 1980, Staveley to Superintendent, Burke 17.

[75]Letter (page 2 only), n.d., Burke to unknown, quite possibly Marks, Burke 9

[76]Letters, July 30 1980, Ingram to Marks, DeConcini, Goldwater, Udall

[77]Notes, Jul 14 1980, Ingram to DeConcini, Udall

[78]Letter, Jul 30 1980, Wm. S. Curtiss, Sierra Club Legal Defense Fund, to Calkin

[79]Letter, Aug 20 1980, Marks to Ingram
Letter, Sep 11 1980, Goldwater to Ingram

[80]Document, Aug 1980, Final Wilderness Recommendation, Grand Canyon National Park;
Memo, Sep 11 1980, Director to Assistant Secretary, "Wilderness Recommendation, GCNP" GCPBA 134-5

[81]Letter, Oct 20 1980, Representative E. Rudd to P. Manning, Burke 12

[82]Letter, Oct 24 1980, Superintendent (by S. Martin, 10/21) to Elliotts (comm op list)

[83]Document, n.d., n.a., "Response to questions submitted by Congressman Bob Stump for the River Concessioner Meeting November 12, 1980"

[84]Letter, Oct 24 1980, Arizona senators and congressmen to NPS Director, Burke 7

[85]Letters, Oct 22 1980, Ingram to Goldwater and Senator H. Jackson

[86]Letter, Nov 20 1980, Goldwater to Ingram

[87]Letter, Oct 25 1980, Ingram to B. Evans

[88]Letter, Oct 25 1980, Ingram to Superintendent

[89]Letter, Oct 31 1980, Ingram to DeConcini

CHAPTER TWENTY-ONE

[1]Mailgram, Nov 4 1980, Burke to Hatch, Burke 7

[2]Document, Nov 11 1980, "Statement of Position", w/ signatures, Randall 81.1.
Signatures w/ date "11-11-80": Fort Lee: Tony Sparks, ARA (ARTA's new name): Rob Elliott, ARR: Fred Burke, Western: Bill George and (?) Keller, Georgie: herself, Tour West: F. Stratton, Sanderson: Jerry, Hatch: Ted, WhiteWater: M. Denoyer for Falany, Canyoneers: G. Staveley, Harris: Wm. Diamond;
date "11-12-80": G. C. Exp.: Marc Smith, G. C. Youth: D. McCallum, Moki Mac: Clair Quist, G. C. Dories, Litton, Sleight Exp.: Mark Sleight, OARS: Pam Wendt, Cross : John, Outdoors Unl.: John Vail

[3]Congressional documents:

n.d., unnumbered amendment to H.R. 7724 by Hatch

Congressional Record for Nov 14 1980, Senate, pp S14466-70

Bill, Nov 17 1980, H.R. 7724 (as passed by Senate), p. 40, amendment 67, sec. 112

Conference Report, Nov 20 1980, by Mr. Yates, "Making appropriations for the Department of the Interior and related agencies", p. 21, amendment 67

Congressional Record for Nov 21 1980, House of Representatives, pp 11138-48; amendment 67 on H11148

Congressional Record for Dec 1 1980, Senate, S15211-18

[4]Articles, Nov 15 1980, A. P. in various, "Motorized river trips preserved", "Senate votes for motorized boats in canyon"

[5]Letter, Nov 19 1980, Chapman to Becky Evans, Sierra Club

[6]Letter, Nov 16 1980, Ingram to *Arizona Daily Star*, "re Ray Manley ad"

and Letter, Nov 16 1980, Ingram to Becky Evans

[7]Material contained in my notes from the period.

Letters, Nov 11 1980, Ingram to Udall, DeConcini, Babbitt

Letter, Nov 12 1980, Becky Evans (Sierra Club staffer) to Ingram

[8]Letters, Nov 24 1980, W. S. Curtiss to Ingram et al. and Dec 10 1980, Curtiss to Ingram

[9]Letters, Nov 25 1980, Ingram to Goldwater, and to KVOA

also, Dec 14 1980, Ingram to Marks; Dec 31 1980, Marks to Ingram

[10]Letter, Nov 21 1980, Ingram to Marks

[11]Letter, Nov 29 1980, Burke to Stump, Burke 12

[12]Articles, Dec 16 and 23 1980, *The New York Times*

[13]Article, Apr 20 1981, A. M. Hyde, "Watt signals he favors keeping motors on Colorado River", in *The Arizona Daily Star*

[14]Document, Dec 18 1980, n.a. "magnafaxed to ... WASO", "Briefing for Secretary of Interior Designate James Watt," CRMP in GCNP

[15] Letter, Apr 2 1981, Director to SCLDF, p. 1

[16]Letter, Dec 23 1980, joint letter from DeConcini, Hatch, Goldwater, Garn, Stump to Director

[17]Memo, Jan 24 1981, Ingram to Sierra Club Southwest Regional Conservation Committee, "A Review and Recommendations; Grand Canyon River Policy"

CHAPTER TWENTY-TWO

[1]Letter, Jan 9 1981, Becky Evans to Ingram

[2]Documents from NPS et al.:

"Conformance of River Trip Scheduling with the Hatch Amendment", n.d., n.a.—sounds like Staveley

"Model for Commercial River Running Use - May 1 to September 30 - Based on 105,500", n.d., n.a., Randall 87 p. 5

"Current Status", NPS

no title, starts out "Status Quo", likely River Unit, GCNP

"Summary and Review of Charts for meeting on CRMP, 1/5/81 WASO"

Tables, NPS, probably GCNP

1978 River Use Statistics

1980 River Use Statistics

various allocations, 1980, 1981

Commercial Use Statistics 1972, 1978, 79, 80

Models for Use, 105,000 u-d and 102,200 u-d (2 versions)

[3]Again, these papers lack date and author information:

"Recommendation for Project Completion" NPS, Randall 86.1 p. 1-2

"1/5/81", NPS, "Steps toward final modification of the CRMP", Randall 86.1 p. 5-8

Jan 27 1981, GCNP, "Commercial River Running Operations, 1981 season"

[4]Letter w/ enclosures, Jan 13 1981, Superintendent to each comm op

[5]Release, Jan 12 1981, GCNP (Jensen), "NPS to permit motor/oar options on the Colorado River in GCNP"

[6]Letter, Jan 13 1981, Staveley, PROA chairman, to comm ops, Burke folder 12

[7]Letter, Feb 3 1981, Staveley, PROA, to comm ops

[8]Notes and drafts in my files support the following.

Also letter, Feb 6 1981, Supt to comm ops

[9]Letters, Feb 24 and Mar 18 1981, W. S. Curtiss, Sierra Club Legal Defense Fund to Director

[10]Minutes, Mar 4 1981, S. Hodapp, CRMP Meeting w/ Chapman, Davis, White, Ward, Hodapp

Task Directive, Feb (5 unclear) 1982, NPS DSC, "Revisions to CRMP"

[11]Briefing, Mar 9 1981, For Director, in response to PROA letter, Feb 4 1981

[12]Notice, Mar 10 1981, NPS in *Federal Register* vol. 46 no. 46 p. 15954-5, "CRMP, GCNP, Arizona, Amendment"

[13]Memo, Apr 8 1981, Chief, Environmental Quality Div., Western Region, to Regional Director, "Summary of major changes to the WRO draft of the CRMP"

[14]See Chapter 21, note 13, for this Apr 20 1981 article, which also furnishes the quotes from D. Jarvis, National Parks Conservation Association

[15]Letter, Apr 2 1981, Director to Curtiss, SCLDF. This reply brought us many of the papers used in this chapter.

[16]Letter, Apr 22 1981, Curtiss to Ingram et al, "Motors on the Colorado River"

[17]Letters, May 12 1981, Becky Evans to Ingram et al,

Jun 29 1981, B. Barnett to Ingram

[18]Documents, Jun 1981, GCNP, "Draft Alternatives for the CRMP" and "Draft Annual Operating Requirements"

[19]Release, Jun 5 1981, Western Regional Office, "Four alternatives for Colorado River Running Proposed by Park Service"

[20]Documents, Jul 1981, n.a., but probably GCNP, "Assessment, July 14" and page on count of letters and meetings. Randall 96

[21]Letters, Jul 31 1981, J. Staveley to Supt

Aug 10 1981, Shelby to Supt. Randall 97, pp 4-5

[22]Letter, Jul 14 1981, Evans to Ingram, w/ two Jul 13 Sierra Club statements

[23]Statement, Jul 6 1981, Ingram, at Flagstaff public meeting, "Statement on River Use and Management thereof, GCNP"

[24]Letter, Jul 22 1981, Curtiss to Ingram et al., "Grand Canyon litigation update"

[25]Letter, Sep 11 1981, Supt to list of 12 comm ops, Randall 98

[26]Article, Oct 15 1981, Associated Press, "Canyon river-traffic limit boosted"

[27]Article, Oct 22 1981, *Arizona Republic*, "U.S. scraps Glen Canyon Dam project"

Documents, Sep 1981 to Apr 1982, Friends of the River, "Grand Canyon threatened..."

Release, Jul 1981, PROA, "Public Information Bulletin, CRMP, July 1981"

[28]Document, Dec 1981, GCNP, "CRMP and Annual Operating Requirements", GCPBA 136

[29]Document, Jan 1982, GCNP, no title;

Record of Decision, Jan 28 1982, Chapman signature, "CRMP Record of Decision, GCNP", GCPBA 138

Release, Feb 9 1982, GCNP, "GCNP Management Plan now available"

CHAPTER TWENTY-THREE
[1]Memo, Apr 11 1980, GCNP River Rangers, "River Patrol, 3/10-24", Randall 86, pp 1-3. Randall 86, about 200 pages long, is a haphazardly arranged compilation of NPS research-related documents for 1980-4. I will cite them, footnotes 1-18, by page numbers
[2]Document, Mar 31 1980, K. Butterfield, "Specific Issues to be Addressed...", Randall 86, pp 4-10
[3]Document, n.d.1980 annual report (which contains a reference to a 1981 winter trip), S. W. Carothers, R. A. Johnson, A. M. Phillips III, "Human Impact on the Beaches of the Colorado River in GCNP", contract CX2100022 in River Resource Monitoring Project, Randall 86, pp 11-49
[4]Briefing, Feb 12 1981, L. May to Supt, "Environmental Impact of River Use", Randall 86, pp 64-72
Memo, Feb 16 1981, M. Jensen to L. May et al., "Monitoring Program for River/Backcountry, Randall 86, p. 63
[5]Report(rough draft), Jul 15 1981, L. Pence, "Resource Monitoring Data from Spring 1981", Randall 86, pp 73-89
[6]Memo, Aug 13 1981, Shelby to Supt, "Final Report, Monitoring Social Impacts of River Management Plan, 7/80-9/81", Randall 86, pp 52-3
Document, n.d., n.a., "Assessment of work done under Contract CX-8210-0-0021; Monitoring Social Impacts of the CRMP", Randall 86, pp 50-1
[7]Draft memo, Sep 18 1981, L. May to Supt, "River Monitoring Program FY 82", Randall 86, pp 92-7
[8]Several items, 110-6, Randall 86, pp 54-61
[9]Memo, Dec 18 1981, D. Sharrow to L. May, "Trip Report - Colorado River from Havasu Creek to Diamond Creek, 12/2-9/81", Randall 86, pp 54-6
Dec 14 1981, Burns to May, "Colorado River Monitoring Trip Debriefing", Randall 86, pp 90-1
[10]Jan 15 1982, n.a., "Briefing Statement for River Monitoring Project Meeting", Randall 86, pp 145-50
[11]Memo, Apr 12 1982, Supt to Regional Director, "Comments on MNA digitization proposal", Randall 86, pp 134-5
[12]Memo, May 4 1982, Region to Supt, "GC Burro Management and River Monitoring Project and Research Needs", Randall 86, p. 127
[13]Document, Jul 12 1982, John Thomas, Resources Management Specialist, "Report on the State of the River Impact Monitoring Project, June 1 1982", Randall 86, pp 116-26
[14]Memo, Aug 24 1982, J. Thomas to Chief, Res. Mgt., "Meeting with MNA staff, 7/29/82, 151,4
Memo, Jan 1983, Chief, Res. Mgt. to Supt., "12/6/82 Meeting with MNA", Randall 86, pp 163-5
[15]Memo, Feb 18 1983, Ranger to Res. Mgt., "Informal Comments on Computer "Contact Simulation" model", 160-1 and Letter, Feb 7 1983, Supt to H. Underhill, Randall 86, p. 159
[16]Document, Aug 30 1983, John Thomas, Resources Management Specialist, "State of River Monitoring Program and Proposed Fiscal Year 1984 Program", Randall 86, pp 169-85
[17]Memo, Dec 13 1983, Thomas to Hodapp, Chief, Res. Mgt, "River Monitoring Trip, 9/17-11/2, 1983", Randall 86, pp 166-8
[18]Document, Jul 6 1984, J. Thomas, "Colorado River Monitoring Program 1980-4", Randall 86, pp 186-204

[19]Interview w/ Marv Jensen
[20]Burke records, folders 11 and 12
Letters, Apr 29 and May 17 1982, Ingram-Marks
[21]Article, Jun 26 1983, *The New York Times*, "High Water in Grand Canyon Kills One Boater and Hurts 15". Also, see Grand Canyon Expeditions website for pro-motor blather
[22]Release, n.d. Jan-Feb 1983, GCNP, "Revisions to Noncommercial River Permit Allocation System"
[23]Call record, Apr 29 1980, L.May/T.White, GCPBA 139
Letter, May 20 1983,Chapman to Stump, GCPBA 143
Document, Aug 1983, GCNP, "Backcountry Management Plan, GCPBA 145
Letter, Apr 22 1987, Supt to list, GCPBA 150
Memo, Apr 5 1985, Supt to DSC, GCPBA 146
Briefing statement, Jan 1987, NPS, "100th Congress Issues", GCPBA 147
Memo, Jun 25 1987, Region to all offices, "Wilderness Policy and Management Coordination", GCPBA 151
[24]Document, Nov 1986, NPS, "Final Report, Servicewide Task Force on Wilderness Policy and Management", GCPBA 151, p. 2ff
[25]Memo, Aug 13 1987, Superintendent GCNP to Western Regional Director, "Wilderness Management Policy", GCPBA 154
[26]Documents, Apr 1988, GCNP, "Backcountry Management Plan, Draft Revision" GCPBA 155, Jul 1988 "Draft Environmental Assessment", GCPBA 162

CHAPTER TWENTY-FOUR

[1]Memo, Nov 29 1982, River Subdistrict to Supt, "Orientation Meeting for Lower Gorge Management Plan", Randall 103
[2]Document, Apr 1984, River Subdistrict, "River Management Chronology, 1869-present", Randall 105.1. (Not always a reliable account)
[3]Memo, Feb 8 1983, Supt to Reg. Dir., "Update of CRMP Objectives" w/ "Management Objectives for Colorado River Resources", Randall 105
[4]Documents,
   n.d., n.a., "Synopsis of G.C. River Concessioners Meetings,10/29/86 and 11/4/86", Randall 108,
   p. 13 ff.
   and "Outfitters Meeting, 11/5-6/86, CRMP Revision" Randall 107
   Feb 25 1987, Supt to Comm op list, "Pertinent Information and Topics discussed at 1986 River Concessioners Meeting" Randall 108, pp 1-12
[5]Memo, Feb 5 1987, Supt. to Reg. Dir., "...CRMP Task Directive...", Randall 111
Documents: Jun 1987, GCNP, "Planning Guide for the Revision of the CRMP", Randall 113
Aug 1987, "GRCA RMP Review and Update—a Cookbook", Randall 114
[6]Documents, Jul 7-8 1987, GCNP, "CRMP Professional Workshop I", agenda, participants, objectives, issues. Randall 115 and 117
[7]Letter, Apr 22 1987, Supt. to list, GCPBA 150
[8]Letter, Aug 25 1987, Supt. to Comm op, Randall 118, pp 27-8
[9]Public Law 100-91, enacted Aug 18 1987; Section 3 is on GCNP, and contains the comm op exception
[10]Documents, Oct 2-4 1987, River Rendezvous V, agenda, suggestions. Randall 117.1-.2, Randall 118

[11]Document, n.d., n.a. (GCNP), "Summary of Discussions and Comments from 1987 Colorado River Concessioners' Meeting, 10/29-30/87"

[12]Letters, Mar 18 1988, Heberlein to Marks, and to list of "recreation researchers" and other "interested parties", Randall 119.2

[13]Letters, Apr 20 1988, Sobek (White Water) Expeditions to Supt, GCPBA 156; reply Jun 16 1988, GCPBA 161. Also, note, May 20 1988

[14]Document, n.d., but apparently Apr 1988, GCNP, "CRMP Review Issue Workbook", Randall 113, p. 11 ff

[15]Documents in Randall 122 and 126; questionnaires and data sheets from 1988

[16]Notes, May 1988, NPS, Flagstaff and Denver meetings, GCPBA 159 and 160; n.d., n.a., workbooks in Randall 127.

[17]Document, n.d., n.a., "Status and Schedule of CRMP review following public workshops/meetings" GCPBA 157

[18]Memo, Jul 8 1988, K. Crumbo, Park Ranger, to Chief, Resource Mgt., "Comments on the CRMP Review: Draft", GCPBA 162.1

[19]Memo, Aug 2 1988, Chief, Resources Management (no name) to Supt, "River Management Meeting of July 30-31, 1988", GCPBA 162.2

[20]Document, n.d.(end of 1988), n.a., poor quality copy in Randall 114 of "CRMP Review Briefing Statement"
Document, Aug 1988, GCNP, "Draft Preferred alternatives for CRMP" GCPBA 164

[21]Document, Sep 27 1988, n.a., "Summary of public comments on CRMP", GCPBA 166

[22]Document, Oct 7 1988, n.a. (GCNP), "Discussion at meeting with river concessionaires committee" GCPBA 167

[23]Memo, Nov 14 1988, Crumbo to Chf., Resources Management (C,RM), GCPBA 168

[24]Notice, Nov 28 1988, *Federal Register*, Draft CRMP available on Nov 21; comment until December 9. GCPBA 170
Notice, Dec 16 1988, Western Region, 54 FR 195 1/4/89, Extension to Jan 30. Randall 144.1
Document, Nov 1988, GCNP, Draft CRMP. GCPBA 171

[25]Notes, n.d (about Dec 1988), n.a. (GCNP), summary of public response w/ tabulation. GCPBA 173

[26]Letter, Dec 7 1988, environmental reviewer in Dept. Interior to Supt, and Feb 23 1989 reply, GCPBA 188

[27]Letter, Jan 12 1989, Acting Supt to Sobek. GCPBA 181
Letter, July 10 1990, Supt (Davis) to Krasnow, GCPBA 208

[28]Letter, May 26 1989, Supt to comm ops GCPBA 190
Document, July 1989, Supt and Regional Director, FONSI GCPBA 191
GCPBA 192 through 200 contain other materials on completion of CRMP process
Item 210 is a 245-page record of the 1990-6 meetings of the Constituency Panel

CHAPTER TWENTY-FIVE

[1]Since most of the participants are still available, you may wonder why I did not interview to get local color. 1. There is no way I could be comprehensive. 2. This 25th chapter is the tip of my dog's tail, even if it is cloning off as a huge new animal of controversy. 3. That is for someone else to do. 4. The NPS record is more or less equally unfair to everybody, and thus a somewhat consistent platform for me to comment, in the way old men love to do, on the activities of the young and vigorous.

[2]Memo, May 31 1990, Western Regional Director to Superintendents, GCPBA 204
Memo, Jul 12 1990, Superintendent Policy Statement, GCPBA 209
and Jul 27 1990, Crumbo to Chief, Resources Management (CRM), GCPBA 209 p. 3

Memo, Oct 22 1991, Crumbo, Wilderness Coordinator, to Superintendent, GCPBA 217
[3]Meeting notes, Apr 24 1991, n.a., on river contracts, GCPBA 213
Memo, Nov 4 1991, GCNP concessions to region, GCPBA 218
Letter, Mar 25 1992, GCNP to comm ops, GCPBA 231
Letter, Sep 10 1992, Region to comm ops, GCPBA 246
[4]Memo, Jul 7 1992, B. West to Crumbo, GCPBA 239
and Jul 8 1992, Crumbo to CRM, GCPBA 240
Documents, Apr 6 1992,n.a., on wilderness recommendation, GCPBA 233 and 234
Call record, Aug 10 1992, Crumbo-L.May, GCPBA 244
Memo, Aug 10 1992, Crumbo to CRM, GCPBA 245
Memo, Oct 30 1992, Crumbo to CRM, GCPBA 412 p. 43
Call record and memo, Nov 3 1992, Denver Service Center and D.C., GCPBA 248
Memo, Dec 15 1992, Crumbo to CRM, GCPBA 258
Memo, Aug 3 1993, Superintendent through Region to Director, GCPBA 272
Document, 1993, n.a., GCNP, "Final Wilderness Recommendation, 1993 Update"
Letter, Oct 20 1993, Rep Hansen to Superintendent, GCNPB 279
Letter, Mar 7 1994, Superintendent to NPS-D.C., GCPBA 287
Memo, May 10 1994, Superintendent to Region, GCPBA 296
[5]Memo, Sep 25 1994, Supt to GCNP division chiefs, GCPBA 320
Memo, Nov 4 1994, Director to all Superintendents, GCPBA 323
Memo, Nov 30 1994, Supt to Deputy Supt, GCPBA 326
[6]Memo, Nov 17 1994, Regional Concessions Chief to Superintendent, GCPBA 325
Memo, Dec 13 1994, Reg. Concessions Chief to Director, GCPBA 329, p. 3-4
Memo, Feb 2 1995, GCNP Concessions Specialist to Supt, "Report on Nov 17 1994
concessionaire meeting", GCPBA 338
[7]For the summary of the years 1995-1999, I have used documents in the GCPBA record
from item 341 to 640, when planning was halted in February 2000. I have often combined
and summarized documents without specifically footnoting each.
[8]GCPBA 404, Jul 12 1996, Supt. to list
[9]GCPBA 520.
[10]Memo, Dec 14 1998, NPS Wilderness Program Leader to Supt, GCPBA 540.
[11]GCPBA 625, pp 55-9, and 576
[12]Material on this trip in GCPBA 579, 1, 582, 590
[13]The documents involved here are GCPBA 644 p. 13ff, 641, 642 p. 6, 643
Memo, Feb 16 2000, Supt to Reg. Dir., GCPBA 644 p. 13ff
Memo, Feb 22 2000, Supt to Arizona Congressional delegation, Asst. Sec. Interior, Dir,
GCPBA 641
Notes, Feb 23 2000, Jalbert to file on GCPBA mtg, GCPBA 642 p. 6
Press Release, Feb 23 2000, GCNP, GCPBA 643
Document, Feb 23 2000, Supt invitation to staff etc., GCPBA 644, incl 19ff and 37ff
[14]My record is not at all complete, for it shows only NPCA, Wilderness Society, GCPBA
reaction, along with limited newspaper coverage. GCPBA 642, 646, 658 and Randall 269
[15]Letter, Mar 15 2000, Supt to GCPBA, GCPBA 642
[16]Documents, Feb 27 and Mar 28 2000, n.a., discussion notes, GCPBA 657
Also, Mar-May 2000, documents in GCPBA 674
[17]Settlement Agreement and associated documents, Jan 17 2002,
in CV-00-1277-PCT-PGR-TSZ, GCPBA et al v. Supt, GCNP, et al., from GCPBA website

See Reader's Guide, Part A, for further description of some individuals and organizations.

River trips, 5, 6, 42, 65, 145, 239;
allocation of, 248-49, 250-51, 252-53;
carrying capacity for, 182-83; choices
in, 310-11; CRMP and, 301-3, 313-
14; demographics of, 7-9, 24-25, 243-
44; economics of, 193-94; Goldwater
and, 322-23; lengths of, 242, 245-47,
276-77, 289-90; logistics of, 10-12,
20; motorized vs. rowing, 19-23, 26-
28, 49, 50, 96-99, 188-89; Park
Service policies and, 55, 56-57, 58-59,
66, 71-72, 99-100, 144, 210, 319-20,
362-63; profit and, 28-29;
questionnaires on, 35-36; research on,
98-99, 124-26, 177, 387-89;
restrictions on, 44-45; self-guided vs.
commercial, 102-7; Sierra Club, 31-
32; size of, 37-38, 190-91, 327-28;
social science, 400-401; user days and,
39-40, 62-63, 70-71, 99, 287, 347.
See also Motorized trips/operators;
Rowing trips/operators
River Unit (GCNP): CRMP and, 361-62;
management by, 387-88; river usage
and, 307, 326, 349, 362-63, 382-83
River Use Plan: commercial operators and,
62-64, 67; responses to, 58-62, 229
Roads: wilderness proposals and, 150-51,
155-56
Rock falls, 141
Rowing-motor combined-trip experiment,
124, 130, 190, 245, 265-66, 268,
274, 289, 296, 303, 320, 348
Rowing trips/operators, 56, 136, 164, 167,
177, 193, 197-98, 223, 311, 343;
CRMP, 264, 267, 293, 302, 325-26,
330, 340; demographics of, 21, 26,
51, 244; economics of, 182, 288-89;
329; Goldwater and, 322-23, 352;
HERS study of, 124-25; vs. motors,
220, 233, 267-68, 308, 313; NPS
river management and, 237-38;
participant observations of, 130, 131;
passenger numbers and, 39, 71, 253;
passenger perceptions of, 186, 246;
profitability of, 29, 100; promoting,
96-98, 100, 117, 196, 275; safety of,
28, 62, 69, 70, 101, 221-22; size of,

190-91; support for, 112, 113; time
for, 35-36; user days and, 97, 99, 245;
wilderness and, 158-59, 203
RRAC. *See* River Runners Action
Committee
Ruch, Jim, 46-48, 50-53; on river use, 61-
62, 64, 67, 69, 85, 95
Ruckel, Tony, 173, 211-12, 217, 234,
318, 321; on CRMP, 234-35, 261,
280, 301

Saddle Canyon, 199
Safety, 11, 20-21, 23, 29, 31-32, 45, 49-
51, 59, 60-65, 68-71, 100-2, 110,
112-13, 117-18, 132, 136, 184, 190,
198, 212-13, 250-51, 264, 268-69,
272, 285-86, 297, 302-3, 315, 319-
20, 326, 337, 370, 406; Morton and,
13, 69; PROA and, 303-4; river-
running, 12, 14, 28, 62, 65, 70, 96-
97, 171, 221-22, 247, 251, 288, 311-
12, *See* Accidents
St.Clair, M., 201
St. George: public meetings in, 154, 157,
158
Salt Lake City, 136; public meetings in,
167, 259, 269-70, 273
Salt Lake Tribune, 271
Saltonstall, Richard, 139-40, 143, 162-63,
200
Sandbox effect, 184-85
Sanderson (comm op), 26, 48, 50, 61, 64,
221, 271, 308, 319, 363, 365-66
San Francisco: public meetings in, 167,
259, 268, 371
Sanitation, 48, 126, 134, 169; river trips
and, 11, 13, 16, 27, 31, 40-42, 46,
49-50, 57, 99-100, 110, 112, 250,
292. *See also* Human waste; Litter;
Water quality
Santa Fe, 3
Santa Fe Railroad, 153
Saylor, John, 4, 80-81
SCDLF. *See* Sierra Club Legal Defense
Fund
Schenk, Astrid, 199, 238
Secretary of Agriculture: wilderness issues,
154, 197